WINDOWS CUSTOM CONTROLS

WILLIAM SMITH
ROBERT WARD

R&D Technical Books
Lawrence, Kansas 66046
USA

R & D Publications, Inc.
1601 West 23rd Street, Suite 200
Lawrence, Kansas 66046-0127
USA

The programs in this book are presented for instructional value. The programs have been carefully tested, but are not guaranteed for any particular purpose. The publisher does not offer any warranties and does not guarantee the accuracy, adequacy, or completeness of any information and is not responsible for any errors or omissions or the results obtained from use of such information.

Trademarks:
Borland Turbo C++, , Borland International.
Microsoft Windows, Microsoft Corporation.

Copyright © 1993 by R & D Publications, Inc. All rights reserved. Printed in the United States of America. No part of this publication may be reproduced or distributed in any form or by any means, or stored in a database or retrieval system, without the prior written permission of the publisher; with the exception that the program listings may be entered, stored, and executed in a computer system, but they may not be reproduced for publication.

Distributed by **Prentice Hall**
ISBN 0-13-034497-4

Table of Contents

Preface   v

Part I — Foundations
  Chapter 1 — Introduction   1
  Chapter 2 — The Style Interface   7
  Chapter 3 — The Data Interface   25
  Chapter 4 — The Function & Message Interfaces   33

Part II — Controls
  Chapter 5 — Static Controls   93
  Chapter 6 — Dynamic Controls   145
  Chapter 7 — Subclassed Controls   225
  Chapter 8 — Virtual Memory Controls   267

Part III — Other Custom Components
  Chapter 9 — Custom ToolBox Class   321
  Chapter 10 — Custom Dialog Class   353

Part IV — Dialog Editor Interface
  Chapter 11 — DLL Requirements   379
  Chapter 12 — Dialog Editor Requirements   399

Part V — Appendices
  Appendix A — Source for Editor Interface Modules   439
  Appendix B — Bibliography   519

Index   523

Preface

This book explains how to write custom controls for Windows. We wrote this book with two goals: to create a powerful and valuable set of finished, ready-to-use custom controls; and to present a coherent design and implementation strategy that will minimize the amount of code necessary to create a new control.

We believe every serious Windows programmer should know how to create a custom control. Custom controls are important vehicles for extending the Windows API. Custom controls encapsulate and integrate specialized functions, making them appear to be a part of Windows, itself. Writing a sizable Windows application without creating the appropriate custom controls is much like writing a large C program without reusing general purpose functions from earlier projects. You can do it, but it's unnecessarily time-consuming.

Who Should Read This Book

This book is for programmers who have already written some nontrivial Windows programs — programmers who are comfortable working directly on the Windows API. We assume you understand how a message loop works, how to respond to a `WM_PAINT` message, and that you've used lots of controls on lots of dialog boxes. If you've mastered the fundamentals and are ready to give your applications a distinctive look — this book is for you.

If you write specialized applications and have been frustrated because the standard Windows components just don't adequately address your needs, this book is for you. By writing your own custom controls, you can extend the Windows API with components that are perfectly suited to your particular needs. In many cases, you'll be able to create the "perfect" control by making some minor modifications to our source code.

If you have already written one or two custom controls, but found they required a daunting amount of code, you will benefit from the implementation techniques presented here. We supply a support library that can significantly reduce the code required for a new control.

Finally, if you simply want some ready-to-use controls, they're here. You don't even have to read the book. In fact, if you have the companion code disk, you don't even have to compile the code — just copy the DLLs to your hard disk and start using them. We've even supplied a Windows help file for the custom controls and the custom control function library. You can access this on-line help through the style dialogs in the dialog chapter.

The Controls

We selected the controls in this book for their utility and their ability to illustrate basic concepts. Each control illustrates a solution to a different fundamental design issue.

The first several controls are visually enhanced replacements for most of the Windows standard controls. Most of these replacement controls are relatively simple, but collectively, they really distinguish even a simple user interface, as the comparison in Figures I and II shows.

In addition to building replacements for the standard controls, we show you how to create controls that can handle huge amounts of text, how to create hybrid controls that subclass several other controls, and (even though they aren't controls in the strict sense), how to create a custom toolbox class, and a custom dialog box class.

Finally, we show you how to interface all the custom controls to the Dialog Editor. This is the step that truly integrates the control to the development environment. Once interfaced to the Dialog Editor, a custom control is truly as easy to use as a standard control.

The book includes all of the code for all of the controls, all of the demonstration programs, and all of the dialog interface modules. The companion disk contains all of the code in the book, along with icons, bitmaps, and precompiled executables and DLLs. All of the code compiles properly under Microsoft C/C++ 7.0, Quick C for Windows 1.0, and Borland C++ 3.1. The code has been tested only under Windows 3.1, but should also work under Windows 3.0. The code disk also includes the Microsoft help file and make files for all three compilers.

Our goal is to build some useful tools. While we've retained copyright to the code, you may freely embed these controls, without change and without fee, in any application you develop. We only ask that you don't

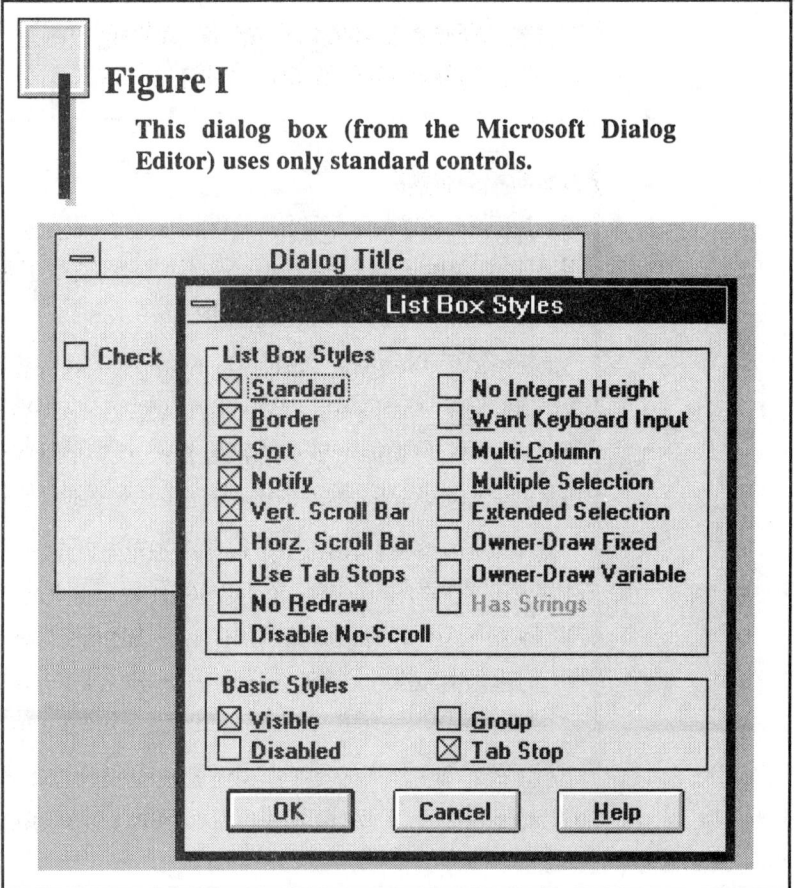

Figure I

This dialog box (from the Microsoft Dialog Editor) uses only standard controls.

sell the controls separately, as a development tool, and that you don't republish the code elsewhere.

We sincerely hope you find this book and the accompanying tools useful and informative. We welcome your comments, just write to us, William Smith and Robert Ward, at:

R & D Publications, Inc.
1601 W. 23rd St., Suite 200
Lawrence, KS 66046

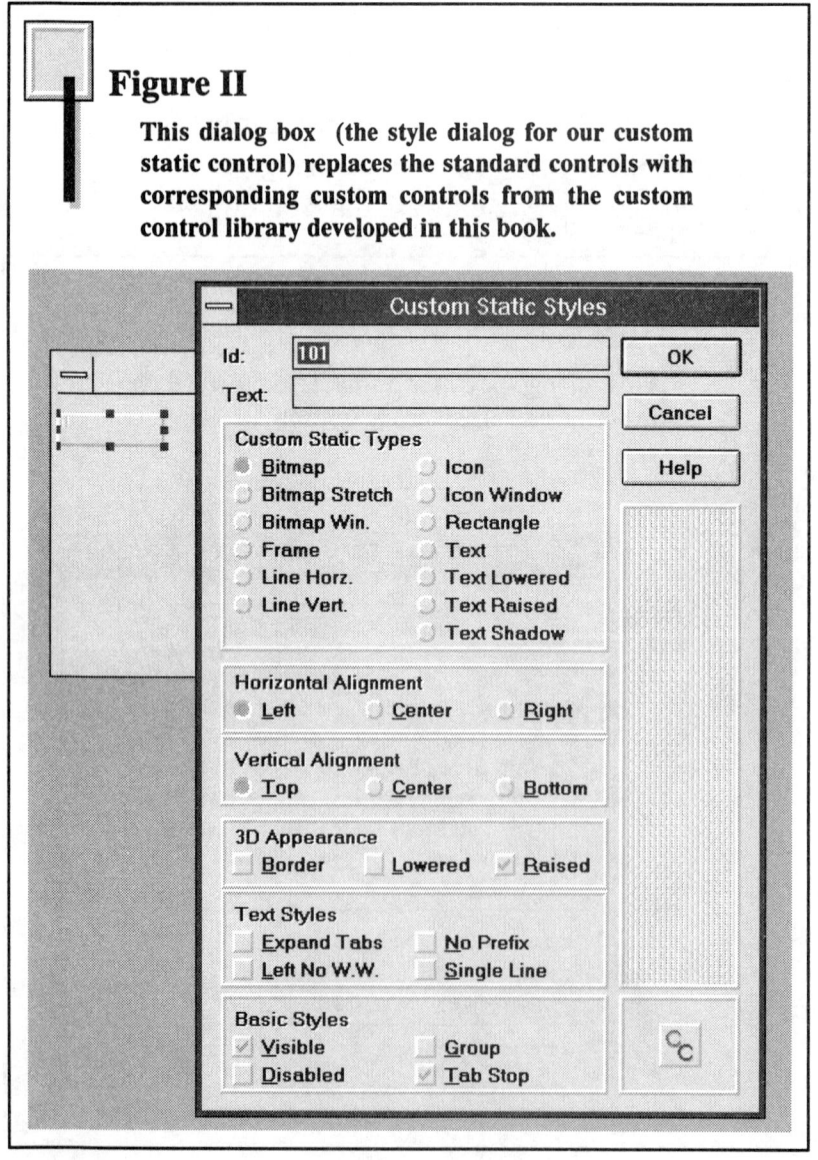

Figure II

This dialog box (the style dialog for our custom static control) replaces the standard controls with corresponding custom controls from the custom control library developed in this book.

Introduction

In Windows parlance, a *control* is a *specialized* window class. Controls are usually single-purpose, self-contained, reentrant, and designed to support parent-child relationships. Each control has its own window procedure, and may have its own set of window messages and window styles. Controls are used most commonly as child windows in dialog boxes. Windows provides the predefined control classes `BUTTON`, `COMBOBOX`, `EDIT`, `LISTBOX`, `SCROLLBAR`, and `STATIC`.

Programmers write custom controls to *extend* Windows or to make it act differently. While Windows' standard, predefined window classes represent a diverse, feature-rich pallet, there are always situations that require something different. Custom controls offer individuality, creativity and imagination, within the context of an organized framework. Because each custom control is a self-contained, extensible class, which supports multiple instances and standard Windows messaging, custom controls can also bring additional structure and modularity to your Windows code.

Besides all that, custom controls are fun; here's your chance to unleash you creativity. Enjoy!

Types of Controls

Windows controls divide into two major categories: static and dynamic. Static controls are output only; dynamic controls produce output and accept input from the user. Additionally, one may classify dynamic controls based on the type of user interface they support. The simplest class of dynamic controls supports action initiation or item selection (e.g., a "yes/no" dialog box or a push button). Alternatively, the control can support a data entry interface (e.g., an edit control in a filename dialog box). The standard *COMBOBOX* control supports both interfaces. Table 1.1 groups the standard Windows controls into these categories.

Design Goals

Custom controls interface with the world on three domains: the user's, the programmer's, and the development environment's. A well-designed control must blend smoothly into the surrounding context in all three domains. We believe a well-designed control should:

- create a consistent, intuitive, and device-independent user interface
- be of manageable size and complexity and be reusable and maintainable.

Table 1.1

The standard Windows controls can be organized according to the types of user input they accept. Static controls do not accept any input.

Static Controls	Dynamic Controls	
	Action Selection	Data Entry
STATIC	BUTTON COMBOBOX LISTBOX SCROLLBAR	COMBOBOX EDIT

- create a consistent, convenient, and robust programming interface
- integrate seamlessly into the Windows development environment.

The User Interface

Of the three interfaces, the user interface is the most important. At a minimum, a well-designed control must be predictable; it must behave like the standard Windows controls. A well-designed control will give a visual indication when it has the input focus. An enabled control will be easily distinguished from a disabled control. Dynamic controls should provide both mouse and keyboard interfaces.

The control should also be device independent; effective presentation shouldn't be dependent upon a certain hardware configuration. When possible, the control should use standard system colors. If the control uses bitmaps, it may need to have access to several different bitmaps to support different display types and resolutions. In general, a good custom control should handle variations in hardware gracefully.

These again, are the minimum requirements. Effective user interface design demands far more than simple consistency — and is not really the topic of this book. This book addresses the control's programming interface and it's integration into the development environment.

Manageable Complexity

A custom control should do one thing and do it well. In other words, "keep it simple." Simple, however, does not mean primitive. The control should be only as complex as necessary to do the job well. It should *not* be so complex that it is difficult to use *or* difficult to develop. Both the end user and the developer must find the control convenient and manageable.

Particularly on the developer's side, the control should hide details, allowing the developer to work with a relatively abstract object. Developers should be able to use a custom control without submerging themselves in details of the custom control code.

Windows code tends to be so repetitive that it is sometimes hard to avoid the temptation to "save time and space" by combining diverse functionality into a single control. Don't do it! Instead, put the common code into a utility library that many different custom controls can share.

The code for a custom control should be small — small, at least for Windows. The code must, *at a minimum*, be small enough that you can wrap your consciousness around it without losing sight of the intended goal. Although we are reluctant to set a length limit, anytime we find ourselves working on a single control of more than one thousand lines, we begin to seriously question whether the control is still "single purpose."

The Programming Interface

A Windows programming interface isn't just a compendium of function calling protocols. A well-designed Windows programming interface will integrate four relatively independent subdesigns: the style interface, the data interface, the function interface, and the message interface. These interfaces are the central topic of this book.

The style interface specifies the range of behaviors and appearances supported by the control and defines a coding scheme for representing these behaviors. The data interface specifies the instance and default data used by the class and defines how this data will be stored and accessed. The message interface specifies what messages will be sent and serviced by the control. The function interface (as in traditional environments) specifies what functions are available to applications that might use the control.

Accessibility

If you follow some basic principles when creating a custom control, your custom control can become a reusable addition to the Windows API — a control that's just as accessible and easy to use as a standard control.

First, the control should be written so that it can be stored in a DLL (Dynamic Link Library). Storing the control in a DLL makes it easier to reuse and makes it possible for several applications to share the same code.

Second, for greatest usability, the control must be supported by an interface library. An interface library allows the control to be used with a resource scripting tool, such as the Microsoft Dialog Editor or the Borland Resource Workshop. This capability is especially important if you plan to include your control in a commercial library.

When successfully interfaced with the Dialog Editor, your control will be a seamless and transparent extension of the Windows API. Any developer can then add your custom control to a dialog box, adjust its style, and exercise it, just as if it were a standard Windows control.

The Book's Structure

Chapters 2, 3 and 4 lay a foundation for the chapters that follow. These chapters discuss the general issues involved in the programming interface, with special emphasis on designing the style and data interface.

Chapters 5 through 8 each introduce at least one new custom control. These controls are each chosen to illustrate a particular technique or implementation problem. Chapter 5 uses a static control to show the basic outline of the design process. Chapter 6 shows how to handle bitmaps, how to process user interaction, and how to handle the state information associated with various kinds of buttons.

Chapter 7 uses a list box with editing capabilities to introduce subclassing and hybrid controls. Chapter 8 uses class specific messages and virtual memory techniques to build a text browsing control that can handle huge files or large amounts of text output.

Chapters 9 and 10 introduce two custom components that aren't technically controls. Chapter 9 combines various techniques to produce an easily configured tool bar. Chapter 10 shows how to get control of a dialog box's appearance by building a custom dialog class.

The final two chapters, Chapters 11 and 12 show how to package the controls in a DLL and how to interface the controls to the dialog editor.

We expect that most readers should read the book from beginning to end. We have tried, however, to structure the material so that those who are already familiar with custom controls can skim the data interface and function interface sections in Chapters 3 and 4, and then jump to whichever control interests them most.

However you read this book, we sincerely hope you find it useful and enjoyable.

2 The Style Interface

Generally windows objects can exhibit a variety of behaviors. Windows refers to these behaviors as "styles." When designing a custom control, the developer must decide what behaviors it should have (the user interface) and how other programmers will select a given behavior (the style interface). Because designing a style interface forces you to enumerate all of a control's possible behaviors and to consider the relationships between these behaviors, you should complete the style interface design early in the development cycle. If you can't answer the questions posed by the style interface, then you don't have a clear enough understanding of the problem to start writing code.

The Parts

Each window is influenced by three different style interfaces: the class styles, the class general window styles, and the class specific window styles. The class style interface is defined by Microsoft; the number of styles available, their coding, and their meaning is fixed. These styles are stored as part of the class information (`WNDCLASS` structure). Generally, class styles control how Windows will draw a window, e.g., `CS_BYTEALIGNCLIENT` or `CS_SAVEBITS` (Table 2.1). Since these styles control Windows internals more than the application code, they have no special impact on custom control design.

8   *Windows Custom Controls*

The class general portion of the window style interface also has limited importance to custom control design. The class general styles are fixed and defined by Microsoft, and are used mostly to direct Windows to supply certain standard window attributes (e.g., scroll bars). Class general style values are stored in the upper half of the window style word. Table 2.2 lists the class general window styles and comments on those that might affect a custom control.

The class specific window styles, by contrast, are extremely important to the custom control design. The developer controls the definition of these styles, and uses them to control the behavior of application specific code, e.g., to direct an object to paint itself in black instead of grey. Class specific window styles are stored in the lower word of the window style double word.   *(The text resumes on page 13.)*

Table 2.1

This table describes how each of the window class styles relates to custom control design.

CS_BYTEALIGNCLIENT

This style will force the client area of a window to be aligned on byte boundaries in the x direction. Byte alignment may or may not be appropriate for a custom control; in some instances the slight shift will cause the control to look slightly misplaced. Byte alignment will speed up drawing of the control.

CS_BYTEALIGNWINDOW

This style will force a window to be aligned on byte boundaries in the x direction. The comments for CS_BYTEALIGNCLIENT also apply to this style.

CS_CLASSDC

This style causes all instances of a control type (window class) to share a single device context. This style is rarely appropriate for a custom control, but would be necessary if a control were to have the same drawing attributes in all instances. The persistent device context forced by this control, causes all changes made by one instance to affect all instances.

Table 2.1

Continued. See page eight for the beginning of this table.

CS_DBLCLKS

Custom controls that need to process double-click messages must use this style. Controls which are interfaced to the Dialog Editor, should use this style, so that the editor's "Styles" dialog box can be invoked with a double click.

CS_GLOBALCLASS

Any control which may be used by more than one application at a time (which includes all controls packaged in a public DLL), must use this style.

CS_HREDRAW

This style forces the entire window to be redrawn if the horizontal size changes. This style is needed if the control can be resized. Since the programmer can resize a window with *MoveWindow()*, this style may be appropriate even if the window class will not support resizing by the user. In some cases, this style may cause unnecessary redrawing.

CS_NOCLOSE

This style disables the close option on the system menu. This style may be appropriate and necessary for controls that support a system menu. A custom control should only be destroyed when the parent window of the control is destroyed. If a control is designed to destroy itself, then it must notify its parent window with a *WM_PARENTNOTIFY* message. The parent should respond appropriately, e.g. by halting use of the control's now invalid window handle.

CS_OWNDC

This style gives each window instance its own device context. With this style the device context will have persistence. Whereas the program must set and reset the drawing attributes of any device context borrowed from the system, with this

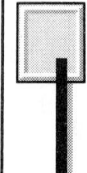 **Table 2.1**

Continued. See page eight for the beginning of this table.

style, the program sets the drawing attributes once, and they will remain in effect each time the program returns to the window. This extra performance may be required by speed-critical controls. This style adds about 200 bytes of resource memory overhead for each instance of the control.

CS_PARENTDC

Controls with this style receive a special device context from the system. The device context has special clipping properties that extend the clipping region beyond the client area of the control to the client area of the parent. Extending the clipping region allows the control to draw outside its own client area, speeds drawing, and prevents unexpected clipping of the control. (When Windows maps the control's dialog coordinates into device coordinates differently for the control than for the parent dialog box, the control will sometimes be clipped.)

Windows' standard controls use this style. Because the device context is not persistent, the control must set and reset the device context's drawing attributes.

A child window may not use the CS_PARENTDC style if it's parent uses the WS_CLIPCHILDREN style.

CS_SAVEBITS

This style causes Windows to save the display area under the control so that it may be restored quickly and without a WM_PAINT message, when the control is removed. Unfortunately saving the display area slows down the original display of the control. This style should be used only with small controls that will be displayed for short periods of time.

CS_VREDRAW

This style forces the entire window to be redrawn if the vertical size changes. The comments about CS_HREDRAW also apply to this style.

# Table 2.2

Several window styles impact custom designs. This table explains how.

WS_OVERLAPPED

This, the default fundamental style, creates an overlapped window. Do not confuse this style with `WS_OVERLAPPEDWINDOW`, which is a shorthand for several combined styles.

WS_POPUP

This fundamental style creates a window that may appear outside the parent window's client area. This style is not compatible with the `WS_CHILD` style. The `WS_POPUP` style is most appropriate for a dialog box or secondary window, but it could be used with a toolbox or floating menu type of custom control.

WS_CHILD

This is the fundamental style most commonly used for custom controls. This is the default style for a control created in a resource script. Windows confines every `WS_CHILD` object to the client area of its parent window.

WS_CLIPSIBLINGS

This style keeps overlapping siblings from drawing over each other. A child window with this style will not draw on any drawing area that belongs to other windows with the same parent. This style slows drawing, but may be required for certain effects. For example, a custom control that displays a bitmap should use this style if the bitmap is to be the background for other controls.

WS_CLIPCHILDREN

This style prevents a parent window from drawing over its children. This style is seldom used for custom controls.

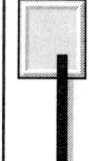

Table 2.2
Continued. See page 11 for the beginning of this table.

WS_VISIBLE

This style, which causes a window to be initially visible, is important for top level and popup windows. It is less important for custom controls, since Windows will manage child windows properly without it.

WS_DISABLED

This style sets the initial state of a window to disabled.

WS_MINIMIZE

This style causes a window to be initially displayed as an icon. This style is not typically used for custom controls.

WS_CAPTION
WS_BORDER
WS_DLGFRAME
WS_VSCROLL
WS_HSCROLL
WS_SYSMENU
WS_THICKFRAME
WS_MINIMIZEBOX
WS_MAXIMIZEBOX

These styles control the nonclient components of a window. Controls with a client area, e.g. the LISTBOX class, might make use of some of these styles. These styles are irrelevant to many custom controls, such as the BUTTON class, because they do not have a nonclient area.

Once a style interface has been defined, the programmer specifies the style of a given window or control by setting the 32-bit style member in the *CREATESTRUCT* before calling *CreateWindow()*. (In a resource file, the style value is a field in a *CONTROL* or *STYLE* statement.) The upper 16 bits of the style value contain the class general portion of the window style; the lower 16 bits contain the class specific portion.

For our purposes, the style interface is just the coding scheme and naming convention which associates each 16-bit (class specific) style value with a specific behavior from our custom control.

Design Conventions

To keep the custom control easy to learn and use, the style interface design should conform to existing Windows practice and naming conventions whenever possible. Windows predefined style values are *#define*'d in *WINDOWS.H* with names of the form *?S_<feature>*, where *?S* is a mnemonic for the type of style. For example, all of the class general window styles begin with *WS_* (for window style); *BUTTON* window styles begin with *BS_*, *EDIT* styles with *ES_*. An edit control that left aligns text has window style *ES_LEFT*; one that centers text has style *ES_CENTER*. All

---

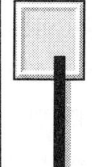

Table 2.2

Continued. See page 11 for the beginning of this table.

WS_MAXIMIZE

This style causes a window to be initially displayed in a maximized state. This style is not typically used for custom controls.

WS_GROUP

Resource scripts use this style to identify members of a control group.

WS_TABSTOP

This style allows tab key to cycle the focus among controls in a dialog box.

of our custom controls will observe a similar naming convention for styles.

Since many style attributes are independent of one another (e.g., whether a window has a minimize box has nothing to do with whether its background is painted black or blue), it's standard practice to specify a particular combination of styles by *OR*ing several styles together. For example,

```
WS_OVERLAPPED | WS_CAPTION | WS_SYSMENU | WS_THICKFRAME
```

specifies a standard (overlapped) window with a caption, system menu and a frame that allows dragging and resizing. Custom controls should support combinable styles whenever possible — and not just for the sake of conformance. The alternative is to create (and memorize) a separate name for every separate combination of traits. If styles couldn't be *OR*d, then instead of learning the four traits above, the programmer would be forced to learn the names of 16 different combinations of traits! (Four things taken zero, one, two, three, and four at a time.)

Analyzing the Structure

A well-designed style interface combines coding techniques in a mapping that reflects the intrinsic relationships among the control's various styles. Thus the style interface design begins with an analysis of how the control's styles relate to one another. Do the styles partition into coherent subsets? How do the members of each subset relate to one another? How do the subsets relate to one another?

Some styles are so intrinsically different that any attempted combination would be nonsense. For example, if a control's shape were controlled by the styles *XS_ROUND* and *XS_SQUARE*, the combination

```
XS_SQUARE | XS_ROUND
```

would have no intuitive meaning. We will refer to such mutually exclusive styles as "fundamental" styles.

On the other hand, many styles combine quite naturally with a variety of fundamental styles. Unlike fundamental styles, these styles merely specify some slight variation in the controlling fundamental behavior. Using the same example, if the shape of the control were always outlined in black, all of these combinations would be perfectly sensible:

```
XS_ROUND    | XS_THICKLINE
XS_ROUND    | XS_THINLINE
XS_SQUARE   | XS_THICKLINE
XS_SQUARE   | XS_THINLINE
```

The *THINLINE* and *THICKLINE* styles are completely independent of the *ROUND* and *SQUARE* styles and merely supply *supplemental* information about how the fundamental shape is to be drawn. We will call these "supplemental" styles.

Note that a control will often have several independent sets of supplemental styles. The members of each set may be mutually exclusive, but they will combine easily with members of the other sets. For example, these two combinations

```
XS_THINLINE | XS_THICKLINE
XS_WHITE    | XS_BLACK
```

are intrinsically contradictory. (One could argue that these combinations *imply* a medium thick line and the color gray, but we think that's contrived.) These combinations, however, are quite natural:

```
XS_SQUARE | XS_THINLINE  | XS_WHITE
XS_ROUND  | XS_THICKLINE | XS_WHITE
```

Finally, some supplemental styles only have meaning when combined with certain of the control's fundamental styles. For example, if we add the shape *XS_RECTANGLE* to the same control, then these combinations

```
XS_RECTANGLE | XS_VERTICAL
XS_RECTANGLE | XS_HORIZONTAL
```

Windows Custom Controls

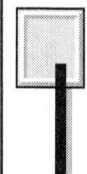

Figure 2.1
This illustration shows the mapping used by a hypothetical style interface. This interface uses only fundamental and supplemental styles.

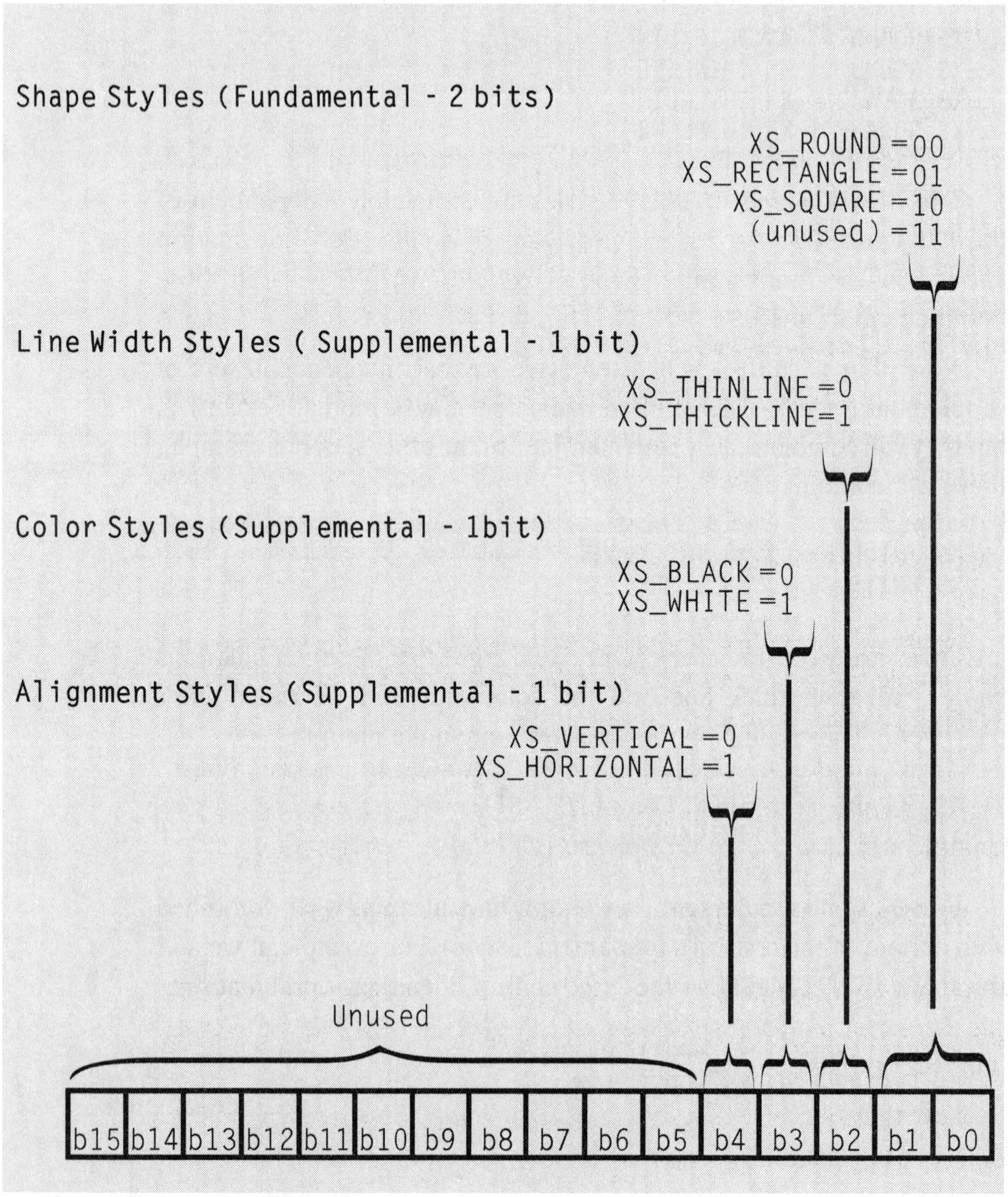

Shape Styles (Fundamental - 2 bits)

```
        XS_ROUND     = 00
        XS_RECTANGLE = 01
        XS_SQUARE    = 10
        (unused)     = 11
```

Line Width Styles (Supplemental - 1 bit)

```
        XS_THINLINE  = 0
        XS_THICKLINE = 1
```

Color Styles (Supplemental - 1bit)

```
        XS_BLACK = 0
        XS_WHITE = 1
```

Alignment Styles (Supplemental - 1 bit)

```
        XS_VERTICAL   = 0
        XS_HORIZONTAL = 1
```

Unused

| b15 | b14 | b13 | b12 | b11 | b10 | b9 | b8 | b7 | b6 | b5 | b4 | b3 | b2 | b1 | b0 |

might mean, draw the rectangle with the long side aligned vertically (first combination) or with the long side aligned horizontally (second combination), but the combination

```
XS_ROUND | XS_VERTICAL
```

would be unnatural. We will refer to these specialized supplemental styles as "modal" styles.

Coding Alternatives

In addition to reflecting the underlying structure of the styles, a well-chosen coding scheme will produce compact results, thus leaving as much room as reasonable for future additions and changes. For that reason we'll fully encode each set of mutually exclusive styles on a minimum size bit-field, and allocate a separate bit-field for each fundamental or supplemental set.

Applying this strategy to the example multi-shape control would yield a mapping like Figure 2.1. The three fundamental styles (round, square, rectangle), require a two bit field, and use three of the four codes available in that field. Each of the supplemental sets (line width, color, alignment) is assigned a one bit field, since each set has only two member styles.

Figure 2.2 shows how to declare this mapping and Figure 2.3 shows how simple bit masks and a bit-wise *AND* can be used to extract specific style information from a 16 bit style word.

When a mutually exclusive set doesn't use all the available binary codes, a simple programming mistake can have disastrous results. For example, a simple editing error might produce the combination

```
XS_ROUND | XS_ SQUARE | XS_BLACK | XS_THICKLINE"
```

which will slip through the *switch* in Figure 2.3. A default case will trap this error, but a prioritized decoding will give the program reasonable "fallback" behavior.

Note that *XS_SQUARE* is the *only* style that ever (properly) sets bit one. So, why not define the cases so that *any* style which sets bit one is interpreted as *XS_SQUARE*? (See Figure 2.4.) With this change, *XS_SQUARE* will always have priority if combined with any other shape style.

Modal Styles

When a control has more than one set of modal styles, the modal styles can sometimes be "overlapped" on a single set of bits, by defining alternate interpretations for the modal bit field.

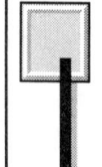

Figure 2.2

This header file defines the style interface of Figure 2.3 and a set of masks that can be used to extract style information from the style word.

```
/* Shape styles */

#define XS_ROUND         x0000L
#define XS_RECTANGLE     x0001L
#define XS_SQUARE        x0002L

/* Line width Styles */

#define XS_THINLINE      x0000L
#define XS_THICKLINE     x0004L

/* Color Styles */

#define XS_BLACK         x0000L
#define XS_WHITE         x0008L

/* Alignment Styles */

#define XS_VERTICAL      x0000L
#define XS_HORIZONTAL    x0010L

/* Decoding Masks */

#define XS_MSK_SHAPE     x0003L
#define XS_MSK_LINE      x0004L
#define XS_MSK_COLOR     x0008L
```

For example, if the *XS_* control fundamental styles included an arrow shape, then it might make sense to have a set of supplemental styles that specified the direction of the arrow's point, say

```
XS_UP
XS_DOWN
XS_LEFT
XS_RIGHT.
```

Like the alignment styles, these styles are modal; they make sense only when used with the triangle style. Figure 2.5 shows how these styles can be overlapped with the alignment styles. When *XS_RECTANGLE* is selected as the fundamental style, bit four is interpreted as an alignment style and bit five is ignored. When *XS_TRIANGLE* is selected, bit four, together with bit five, is interpreted as a direction style.

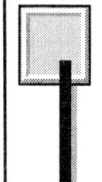

Figure 2.3

This code fragment shows how to use the masks defined in Figure 2.2 to control style-specific code.

```
WORD wStyle;

wStyle = XCTLGETSTYLE( hWnd );

switch(wStyle & XS_MSK_SHAPE){
   case XS_ROUND:
       do_round();
       break;
         case XS_RECTANGLE:
       do_rectangle();
       break;
   case XS_SQUARE:
       do_square();
       break;
}
```

Defaults and Synonyms

Figure 2.2 gives *0x0000L* four different names: *XS_ROUND*, *XS_THINLINE*, *XS_BLACK*, and *XS_VERTICAL*. Technically, these names aren't necessary. The line

```
wStyle() = XS_THICKLINE;
```

will be interpreted as a round, black shape with a thick outline, even though the shape and color styles aren't included in the assignment. Any style that is mapped onto zero is implicitly the default style for that characteristic; you get zero unless you ask for something else.

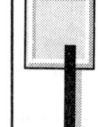

Figure 2.4

This fragment is more robust than the code in Figure 2.3. Here we have added "fallback" options and a default case.

```
/* Add this definition to the style header */

#define XS_SQUARE2        0x0003L

WORD wStyle;

wStyle = XCTLGETSTYLE( hWnd );

switch(wStyle & XS_MSK_SHAPE){
   case XS_ROUND:
      do_round();
      break;
        case XS_RECTANGLE:
      do_rectangle();
      break;
   case XS_SQUARE:
   case XS_SQUARE2:
      do_square();
      break;
   default:
      ReportError("Shape Decoding Error\n");
}
```

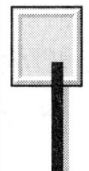

Figure 2.5
This style interface adds four modal styles to the interface of Figure 2.1.

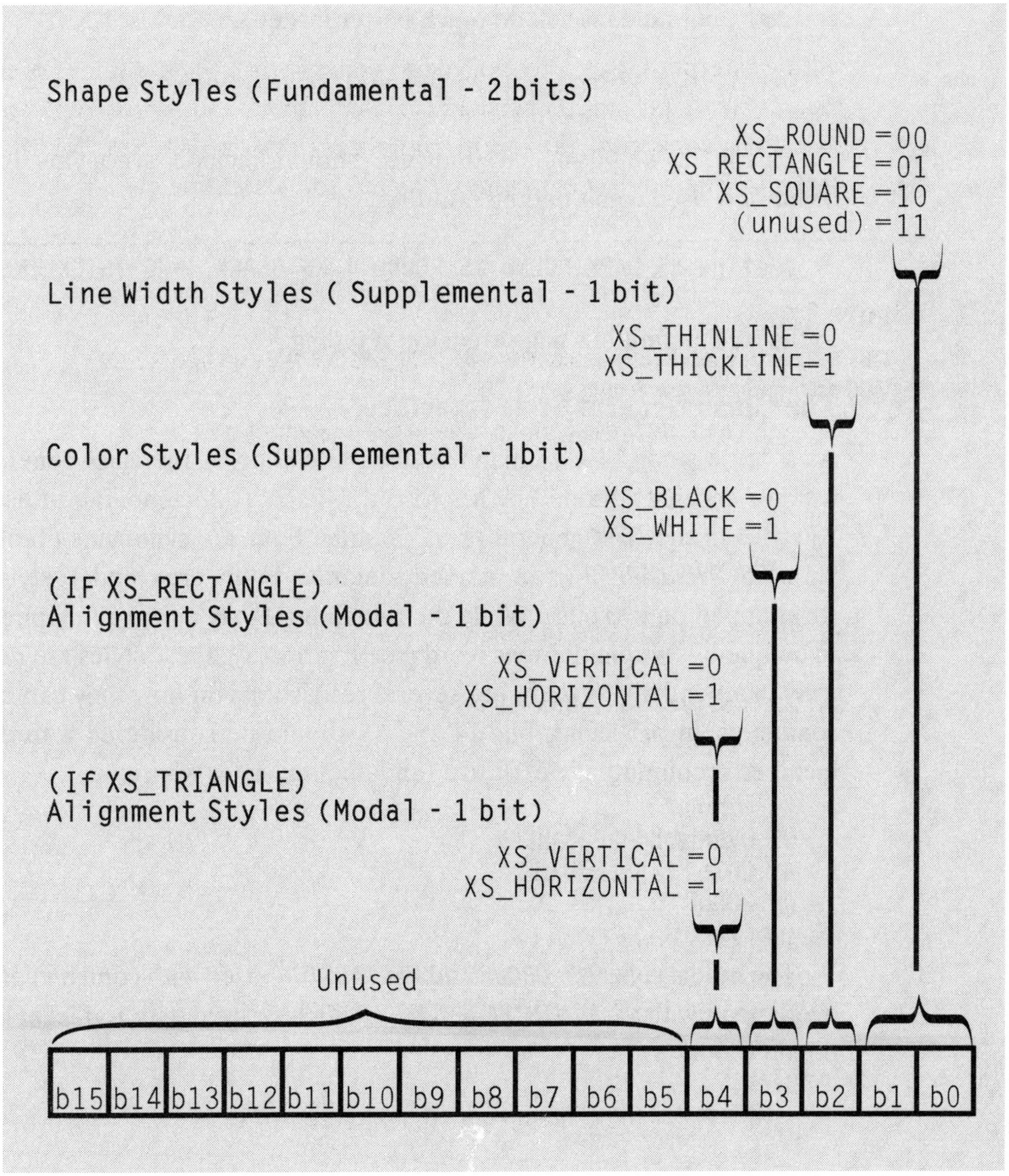

```
Shape Styles (Fundamental - 2 bits)
                              XS_ROUND    =00
                              XS_RECTANGLE=01
                              XS_SQUARE   =10
                              (unused)    =11

Line Width Styles ( Supplemental - 1 bit)
                              XS_THINLINE =0
                              XS_THICKLINE=1

Color Styles (Supplemental - 1bit)
                              XS_BLACK =0
                              XS_WHITE =1

(IF XS_RECTANGLE)
Alignment Styles (Modal - 1 bit)
                              XS_VERTICAL  =0
                              XS_HORIZONTAL=1

(If XS_TRIANGLE)
Alignment Styles (Modal - 1 bit)
                              XS_VERTICAL  =0
                              XS_HORIZONTAL=1
```

Unused

| b15 | b14 | b13 | b12 | b11 | b10 | b9 | b8 | b7 | b6 | b5 | b4 | b3 | b2 | b1 | b0 |

Though not technically necessary, named defaults are an important part of the program's internal documentation. The compiler will always translate

```
wStyle() = XS_THICKLINE;
```

correctly, but humans will do much better if they see

```
wStyle() = XS_ROUND | XS_BLACK | XS_THICKLINE;
```

Finally, a well-designed interface should include synonyms for commonly used combinations. Adding

```
#define XS_DARK_ROUND XS_ROUND | XS_BLACK | XS_THICKLINE
```

to the style definitions will save a lot of typing.

The Class General Style Interface

As a "case study," we've mapped out the coding of the class general window styles, as defined by Microsoft. Microsoft documentation lists 23 styles in the class general or *WS_* family. Four are synonyms (Table 2.3). *WS_OVERLAPPED* is a named default. Four are modal styles (overlapped on two bits). While the remaining 14 styles are all mapped to unique bits within the style word (see Figure 2.6), these styles are not truly independent, as there are several restrictions on how they can be combined. In particular, bits 14 and 15 should be considered a three member set of mutually exclusive fundamental styles where:

```
WS_OVERLAPPED   = 00
WS_CHILD        = 01
WS_POPUP        = 10
(not used)      = 11
```

The modal styles *WS_GROUP* and *WS_TABSTOP* (used with controls) are overlapped with *WS_MINIMIZE* and *WS_MAXIMIZE* (used with top level or popup windows).

The Style Interface 23

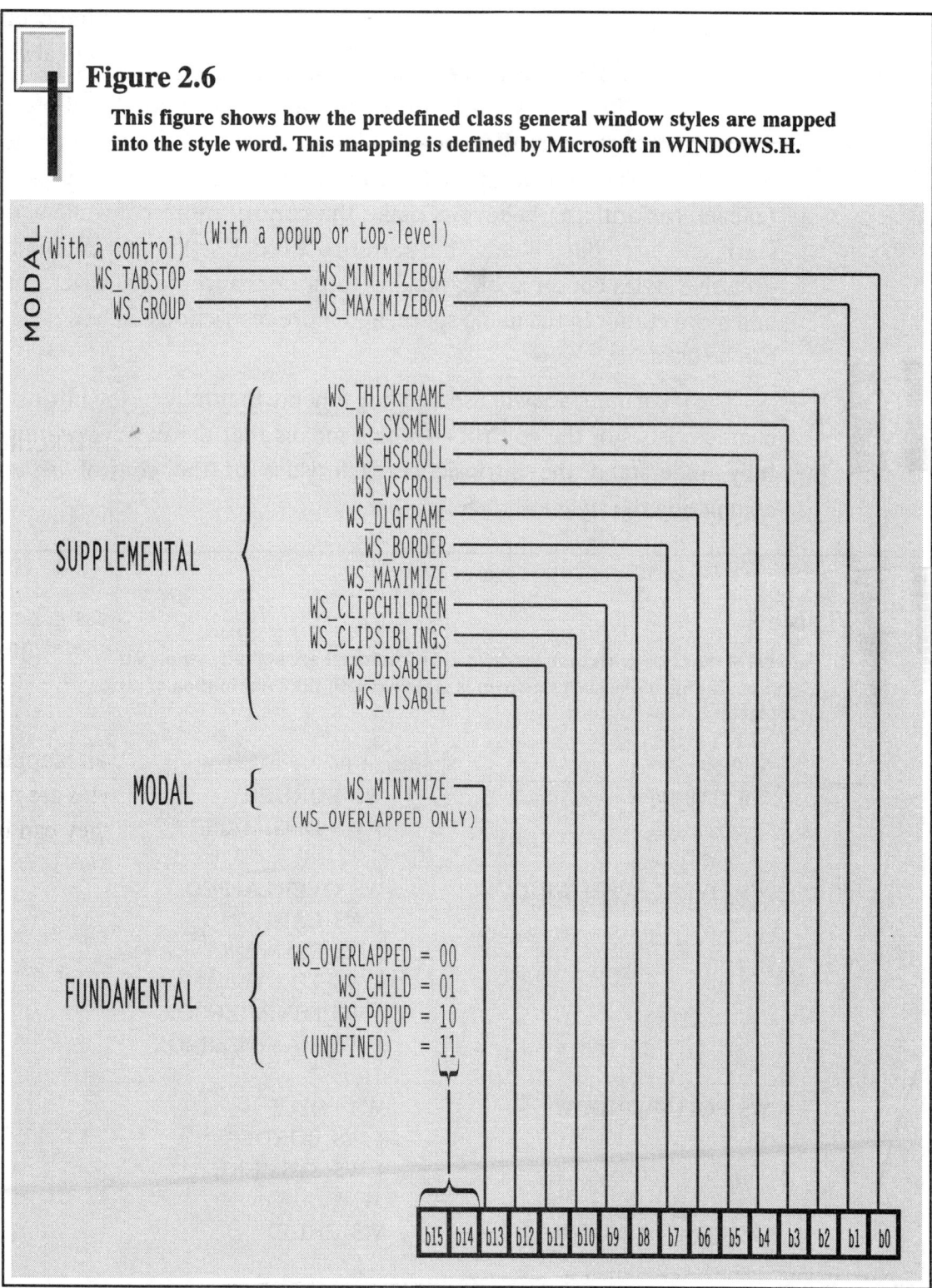

Figure 2.6
This figure shows how the predefined class general window styles are mapped into the style word. This mapping is defined by Microsoft in WINDOWS.H.

Conclusion

While the style interface is "just" a list of *#define*'d constants, its design significantly affects how easily a control can be understood and used. The style interface challenges the designer to find an appropriate tradeoff between bit usage and convenience. Combinable styles and fallback (prioritized) behaviors make the control more convenient to learn and use, but "waste" bit patterns. Modal styles and mutually exclusive styles conserve bits, making future enhancements easier, but add more clutter in the name space, and more restrictions on how styles can be used.

The ideal interface will use a coding scheme that reflects the intrinsic characteristics of the control — which means that the developer must fully understand the intrinsic characteristics of the control *before* completing the style interface.

Table 2.3

Several of the class general styles defined by Microsoft are actually synonyms or defaults. In this table, each synonym is matched with the combination of styles it replaces.

Synonym	Shorthand For
WS_CAPTION	WS_BORDER | WS_DLGFRAME
WS_OVERLAPPEDWINDOW	WS_OVERLAPPED | WS_CAPTION | WS_SYSMENU | WS_THICKFRAME | WS_MINIMIZEBOX | WS_MAXIMIZEBOX
WS_POPUPWINDOW	WS_POPUP | WS_BORDER | WS_SYSMENU
WS_CHILDWINDOW	WS_CHILD

3 The Data Interface

Because Windows is a rich, complex, multitasking environment, designing a data interface involves more than defining variables and structures that reflect the characteristics of the data. The data interface for a custom control must distinguish between window instance and window class data, must provide a mechanism for associating instance data with the appropriate window, and must always conserve certain limited resources (e.g., the local heap).

This chapter begins by explaining the various storage alternatives available under Windows and then introduces a common data structure that we use throughout the balance of the book.

Storage Requirements

Most custom controls have a certain amount of data overhead. Controls may need to keep track of their state, decoded style information, or particulars about drawing the control, to name a few possibilities. Each separate instance of the control must have private storage of this information, and the storage must persist as the thread of program execution jumps in and out of the control's window procedure. Thus, instance data must exhibit the characteristics of instance uniqueness and persistence.

The stack cannot be used for persistent data. Every time the thread of execution enters and exits the control's window procedure, data values in the stack are lost. Static or external data has persistence, but not instance uniqueness; static or external data is shared between all the instances of a control. Since all instances can read and write static or external variables, unique values from one instance can be destroyed by another instance. To get both persistence and instance uniqueness, separate storage must be dynamically allocated for each instance of the control.

There are three storage alternatives that meet these requirements: window extra bytes (as opposed to class extra bytes, which we'll discuss later in this chapter), property lists, and dynamically allocated memory. Windows will manage the dynamic allocation if you use a property list or the window extra bytes, but Windows will allocate the storage from the scarce local heap in the *USER.EXE* module. Alternatively, you can allocate dynamic memory for the data, in which case the storage will be taken from the more abundant global heap. In all three cases, however, the storage will be associated with a particular window and accessed through its *window handle*.

Window Extra Bytes

When the program registers a window class, it can instruct Windows to include a certain number of "extra bytes" in the window structure created for each instance of the class. The *cbWndExtra()* member of the *WNDCLASS* structure tells Windows how many extra bytes to allocate. Windows will tack *cbWndExtra()* bytes to the end of each window structure and allocate space for the enlarged window structure from the local heap.

Microsoft does not make the layout of the window structure public. Thus, instead of directly accessing members through a pointer and offset, programs should use one of the predefined access functions. A call to *GetWindowRect()*, for example, will extract the dimensions of a window's bounding rectangle; *GetClientRect()* does the same for a window's client area.

The "generic" access functions `GetWindowLong()`, `GetWindowWord()`, `SetWindowLong()`, and `SetWindowWord()` manipulate data stored in the window structure, including data stored in the window's extra bytes. These functions take a zero-based offset that specifies the data's position within the window structure. A positive offset addresses data in the extra bytes; a negative offset addresses the private members of the window structure.

Property Lists

Each window may own a list of "properties," where each property is a "named" data handle. The name is a string pointer or an atom that will be used to identify the property whenever it is accessed. The data handle can be any handle (memory, icon, text, device context, etc.) or any other useful 16-bit (`WORD`) value.

Unlike a window's extra bytes, its property list can add and subtract members dynamically. Each window is created with an empty property list. The function `SetProp()` will add a property to the list, and can later be used to change the data handle associated with the property. `RemoveProp()` deletes a property from the list. `GetProp()` retrieves the data handle associated with a given property. `EnumProp()` lists all the properties currently in a particular list.

Windows internally manages which window owns what property, but does *not* deallocate properties when the window is destroyed. Since Windows stores both properties and property names as fixed objects in the local heap of the *USER.EXE* module, the application must consistently and reliably delete all unused properties or risk an overflow of the *USER* heap. Unfortunately, the property name will remain in the *USER* heap even after the property has been destroyed.

Because a program can change the number of properties after a window has been created, properties are more flexible than extra bytes. (A program cannot "allocate" more extra bytes after a window has been created.) Extra bytes, however, are easier to manage; Windows deallocates the window structure *including all extra bytes* when the window is destroyed. Also, storing instance data in extra bytes avoids the overhead of searching a property list, though in most applications the performance difference isn't significant.

Dynamic Memory

Both extra bytes and property lists have the *major* drawback of taking up precious resource space in the *USER.EXE* local heap. You can store instance data without significantly impacting the local heap, however, by storing only a pointer to the instance data in the window extra bytes or property list; the data itself is then stored in dynamic memory taken from the global heap.

Since Windows memory management services support dynamic allocation from both the local and global heaps, you could (and in special cases should) choose to use memory from the local heap, but usually you will want to place instance data in the more plentiful global heap.

An application program requests Windows memory services through the *Global*()* or *Local*()* families of functions. Once allocated, heap memory is accessed like any other structure, thus avoiding the overhead and inconvenience of special access functions. As with property lists, the application is responsible for freeing all unused dynamic memory, but unlike property lists, dynamic memory doesn't leave the heap littered with name strings.

If the *GMEM_SHARE* flag is set, then instance data stored in the global heap can be shared among different applications. Windows requires this flag for custom controls stored in a DLL.

Regardless of what the application requests, *GlobalAlloc()* always allocates a multiple of 32 bytes (the granularity). In the worst case, each global allocation will waste 31 bytes — on average, 16 bytes. Moreover, each global allocation consumes one of the 8192 segment selectors available to Windows. A subsegment manager (like the one built into the Borland compiler) will avoid these limitations.

Defaults

When the program registers a class, it can also request *class* extra bytes (as opposed to *window* extra bytes) by passing a value in the *cbClsExtra* member of the *WNDCLASS* structure. Class extra bytes are allocated only once for each window class, thus they aren't instance unique and can't be used for instance data storage. They are, however, a convenient place to store defaults; the application writes default values into the class extra bytes once, when it creates the first instance of the class, and then copies these values into the instance data storage each time a new window is created.

Again, since class extra bytes also consume *USER* heap, if the amount of data is greater than eight bytes, we recommend using dynamic memory to store the default data and using the class extra bytes to store a handle or pointer to this memory. Windows supplies the *GetClassWord()* family of functions to manipulate class extra bytes. The file *CST_XTRA.C* (see Chapter 4) defines similar functions that are easier to use when a window has been subclassed (see Chapter 7).

Figure 3.1

All the controls in this book store their instance data in a copy of the following structure.

```
/* Custom control instance data */
typedef struct tagCSTCTLDATA
    {
    COLORREF lColor[CC_NUM_COLORS];   /* Array of Colors */
    HBITMAP hBitmap[CC_NUM_BITMAPS]; /* Array of Bitmaps */
    HBRUSH hBrush[CC_NUM_BRUSHS];    /* Array of Brushes */
    HFONT hFont;        /* Font used by control */
    HWND hWnd;          /* Handle of Window (implementation dependant) */
    int iBkMode;        /* Background mode for dsiplaying text */
    int iFrame;         /* Thickness of default frame */
    int iShadow;        /* Thickness of 3D shadow and highlight */
    RECT RectBitmap;    /* Client area that contains bitmap */
    RECT RectText;      /* Client area that contains text */
    WORD wCtlColorMsg;  /* Response flags to WM_CTLCOLOR message */
    WORD wState;        /* State of control (implementation dependant) */
    WORD wStyle;        /* Auxilary style (implementation dependant) */
    LONG lValue;        /* Value of control (implementation dependant) */
    } CSTCTLDATA, FAR *LPCSTCTLDATA;
typedef unsigned int HCSTCTLDATA;
```

A General Purpose Structure For Instance Data

All of the custom controls presented in this book will use a common structure, *CSTCTLDATA*, for their instance data (see Figure 3.1). The code that creates an instance of a control must also allocate dynamic memory for this structure and then install a handle to the structure in the control's extra bytes or property list.

Of course a general purpose structure doesn't optimize the use of memory, but it does simplify the programming environment. With one structure, the programmer has only one set of field names and functionalities to master and remember. Windows is a complex enough environment without the extra variations! Moreover, a common data structure makes it easier to write general purpose support utilities, e.g., functions that paint icons and bitmaps.

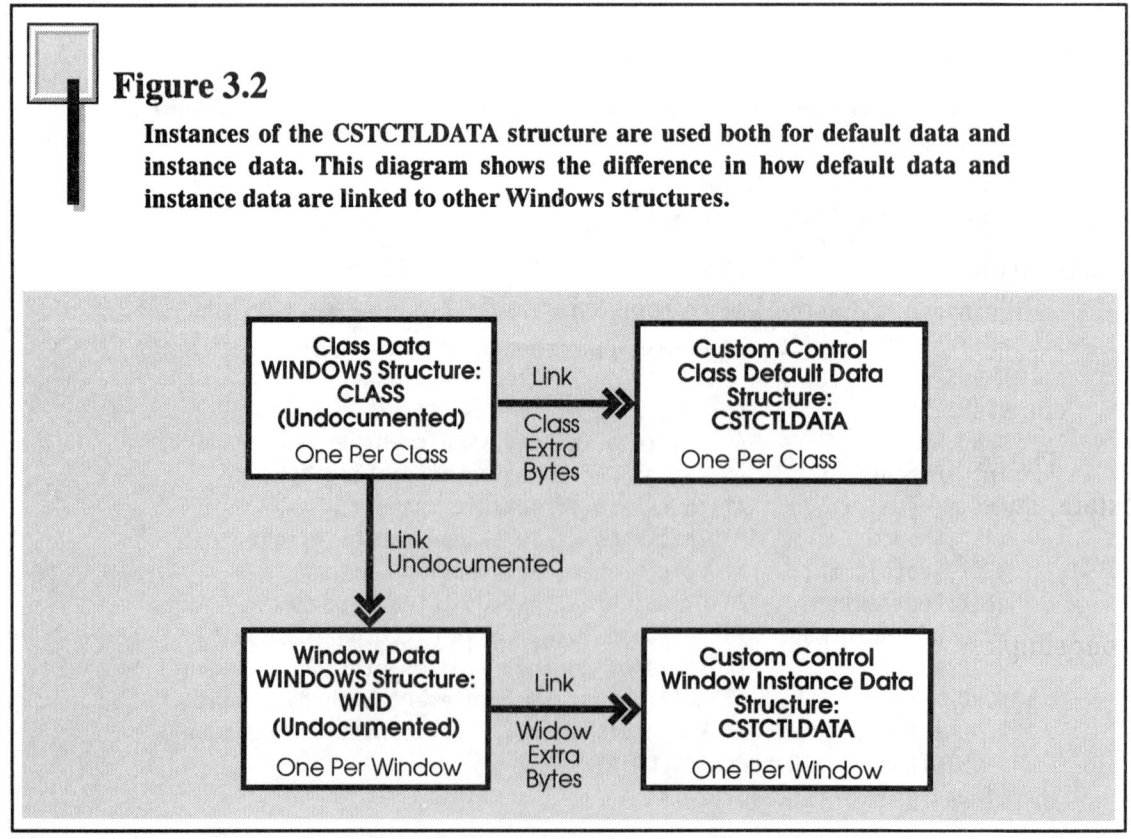

Figure 3.2

Instances of the CSTCTLDATA structure are used both for default data and instance data. This diagram shows the difference in how default data and instance data are linked to other Windows structures.

Figure 3.2 shows how instances of this structure are linked to the *WND* and *CLASS* structures to provide instance data storage and default data storage respectively.

CSTCTLDATA follows standard Windows design and naming conventions. The structure name begins with the prefix *tag*. The body of the structure name is upper case and matches its *typedef* name. We define a *typedef* for both a long pointer to the structure, *LPCSTCTLDATA*, and a handle to the structure, *HCSTCTLDATA*.

The first three members are declared as arrays, since controls often need to keep track of multiple colors, brushes, and bitmaps. The first member of the structure is an array of colors that the control uses. Storing colors in the instance data allows for custom tailoring of colors on an instance by instance basis. The second member is an array of bitmaps. Some controls will need a different bitmap to represent different states. By storing only the handle to the bitmap in the instance data we can change the bitmap even after the control is created. The third member is an array of handles to brushes. Storing the brushes in the instance data (instead of in the window procedure) allows the application to change these values for each individual instance of a control.

Controls that display text can use the *hFont* and *iBkMode* members to select the text font and background display mode. The *iFrame* and *iShadow* members control the width of lines, borders, rectangles, frames, 3D highlights and 3D shadows. *RectBitmap* and *RectText* identify the portions of the client area where bitmaps or text are to be drawn.

The *wCtlColorMsg* is a response flag to the *WM_CTLCOLOR* message.

The last three members, *wState*, *wStyle*, and *lValue*, reflect the state, style and value of a control. Their meaning is unique to each custom control.

CSTCTLDATA is admittedly a large structure, but it's not too large; even our simplest static control uses nearly every field in this structure.

Conclusion

At a minimum the data interface design must address these issues:

- how to associate an instance and its data,
- how to conserve local heap space,
- where to store default values, and
- whether to make the interface single purpose or general purpose.

All the custom components in this book use a pointer stored in the window extra bytes (rather than a property list) to associate the instance and its data, and store as much as practical on the global heap. We use the same method for default values.

Because we wanted to minimize the code required to write a new control, we opted for a general purpose interface. This common data structure makes it easier to write widely usable support functions. By investing more effort in the support code, we've reduced the amount of new code we must write for each new control.

The Function And Message Interfaces

The function and message interfaces of all our controls have several common features. Some of these commonalities are products of certain Windows requirements, some are simply common access support for our shared data interface, and some are indirect consequences of how we have implemented our instance data storage. This chapter explains what requirements Windows imposes on the function and message interface designs, and then explains how we solved certain implementation problems. The chapter closes with a survey of the utility functions our controls rely upon and of the messages that will be of most interest to the typical custom control.

Reentrancy

If more than a single instance of a control (window class) may exist simultaneously, then the code for the control must be reentrant. Since custom controls are usually multiple instance windows, reentrancy will be the norm, rather than the exception.

The one fixed prerequisite for writing reentrant code is: do not use static or global (*extern*) data to store instance data. Our controls meet this requirement, by storing all of their instance data in some form of dynamic memory — either extra bytes that are allocated along with the instance, or global memory that is allocated separately by a window procedure.

33

Avoiding static and external data to store instance data is not a guarantee that the code will be reentrant but it is a prerequisite.

Safe Messaging

Like other windows, a custom control communicates with Windows and with other controls and windows by sending and receiving messages. The control usually sends a message by calling *SendMessage()*, and responds to a message by returning a requested value or performing some task.

Since *SendMessage()* yields control to the destination window, the sending window (instance) could conceivably be destroyed while the message is being processed. Thus, it is good practice to confirm that the sending instance's window handle is still valid after *SendMessage()* returns. The window procedure should exit immediately if the window handle has become invalid. The following code fragment illustrates this test.

```
SendMessage( .... );
if ( !IsWindow( hWnd ) )
    {
    return( 0L );
    }
```

Similarly, it's good practice to verify the window handle of a parent or sibling window before sending it a message.

The Window Procedure

Every custom control must have at least one function — the window procedure for the custom control window class. For consistency and to simplify interfacing with the Dialog Editor, the window procedure name should begin with the name of the custom control and end with *WndFn* — short for Window Function. The window procedure will process messages, both from Windows and from other application windows.

The window procedure is an exported call back function. It resides either in a DLL, or, if the application was statically linked, within the application's executable.

Other Entry Points

Code that will be stored in a DLL must include the entry points *LibMain()* and *WEP()*. Windows calls the *LibMain()* procedure upon initialization of the DLL. Windows calls *WEP()* right before the library is unloaded.

Interfacing to the Dialog Editor requires five functions in addition to *LibMain()* and *WEP()*, namely *Info()*, *Style()*, *Flags()*, *WndFn()*, and *DlgFn()*. To conform with the standard Windows naming convention, the developer should prefix each of these names with the name of the custom control. These functions are discussed in more detail in Chapters 11 and 12.

Creating Default Data

Ideally, one would like to allocate the default data structure and install an appropriate pointer in the class extra bytes as part of the class registration routine. Two quirks in Windows make this ideal solution unworkable for our controls. The Windows access functions for class extra bytes all require a valid handle to a window that is an instance of the class. Unfortunately, one can't have a valid handle to an instance of the class if the class hasn't even been registered yet!

But for the second quirk (described in the next paragraph), one could easily work around this limitation by creating a dummy window at registration time. The registration code could create a dummy window, use its handle to initialize the class extra bytes, and then destroy the dummy window. Unfortunately, the second quirk makes it impossible for a control stored in a DLL to create a window at registration time.

Windows treats a DLL's start up code (*LibMain()*) as an "untasked process," meaning that the message loop is *not* running when *LibMain()* is executed. Consequently, *LibMain()* must not call any functions (such as *CreateWindow()*) that would result in sending a message. Because of this limitation, *LibMain()* cannot create a window. Thus, if the control is packaged in a DLL and the registration performed (as it should be) as part of *LibMain()*, then the control can't even create a dummy window at registration time.

One could move the registration function outside of *LibMain()*, but doing so forces the application to maintain a registration counter, so that it can avoid duplicate registrations in those cases where multiple applications are using the same control class. More importantly to us, though, moving the registration function outside of *LibMain()* sacrifices many of the more convenient features that would cause one to place the control in a DLL in the first place.

In our implementation, we solve this dilemma by performing the registration in the natural place (in *LibMain()* when packaged in a DLL, and in *WinMain()* otherwise). We then delay the allocation and initialization of the default data until the first instance of the class receives its *WM_CREATE* message. To keep each instance of the control from re-creating the default data, we maintain a static window counter in the window procedure for each control class. If a window procedure receives the *WM_CREATE* message while this counter is zero, the procedure allocates and initializes the class default data and increments the counter. Otherwise, the procedure simply increments the counter.

The same counter also controls the cleanup procedures. The control responds to a *WM_DESTROY* message by decrementing the counter and testing the result. If the result is zero, then the current instance is the only instance of this control and it should free the default data storage as part of its cleanup procedure. If the result is nonzero, then other instances of the control still exist and the default data must be left intact. Figure 4.1 gives the general outline.

Other Cleanup Issues

As pointed out earlier, since events can occur asynchronously in the Windows environment, before freeing anything, the *WM_DESTROY* handler should first check that the window class is registered and that the particular instance has actually allocated memory or resources.

A well-behaved window procedure will also notify the parent that the window is about to be destroyed. This gives the parent an opportunity to clean up any related resources that it may have allocated. To notify the parent, send the *WM_PARENTNOTIFY* message with *WM_DESTROY* in *wParam*.

Figure 4.1
The first instance of a control is responsible for creating the default instance data structure. This code shows how a window counter triggers this creation.

```
case WM_CREATE:
    {
    .
    .
    .
    if ( !_WindowCount )
        {
        if ( !CstStaticDefDataCreate( hWnd ) )
            {
            return ( -1 );
            }
        }
    _WindowCount++;
    } /* case WM_CREATE */

case WM_DESTROY:
    {

    HWND hWndParent = GetParent( hWnd );

    /* Notify the parent and then delete the instance data */
    if ( hWndParent )
        {
        SendMessage( hWndParent, WM_PARENTNOTIFY, WM_DESTROY,
            MAKELPARAM( hWnd, GetDlgCtrlID( hWnd ) ) );
        }
    if ( IsWindow( hWnd ) )
        {
        LONG lStyle = GetWindowLong( hWnd, GWL_STYLE );

        /* Window is still valid so free instance data */
        .
        .
        .
        delete other resources as needed
        .
        .
        .
        CstCtlDataDelete( hWnd );
        }   /* if ( IsWindow( hWnd ) ) */
```

If the sending window's handle is still valid after sending the WM_PARENTNOTIFY message it can free any resources and memory that the control created in response to the WM_CREATE message.

Four support functions (defined in CST_DATA.C), simplify the management of instance and default data. CstCtlDataCreate() creates an instance and copies the default data into the newly created instance. CstCtlDataDelete() deletes (frees) an instance of the data structure. Each control has customizing wrappers which call CstCtlDefData-Create() and CstCtlDefDataDelete() to create, initialize, and free the data structure for the class defaults.

Accessing Instance and Default Data

As a matter of good design, the entire application should not be knowledgeable about the specific implementation details of the instance data structure. Instead, most of the application should request instance data through an interface that hides the details of the data storage. In the Windows environment, the designer may hide these details by creating either a message or a function interface.

With a message interface, the application manipulates a control's instance data by sending messages to the control's window procedure. The window procedure responds by setting or retrieving the appropriate value directly from the instance data structure. A function interface

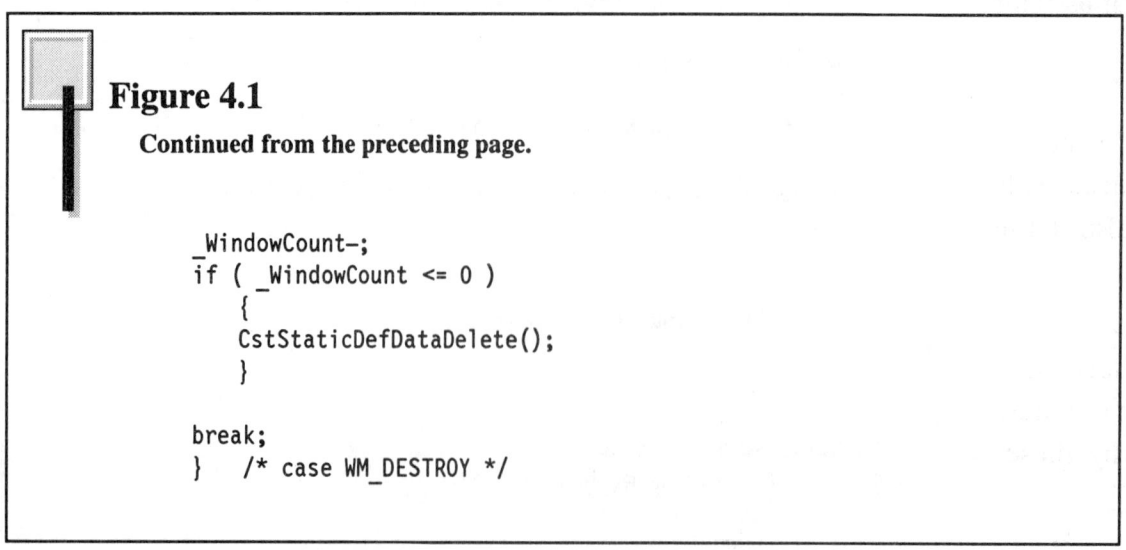

Figure 4.1

Continued from the preceding page.

```
_WindowCount-;
if ( _WindowCount <= 0 )
    {
    CstStaticDefDataDelete();
    }

break;
}   /* case WM_DESTROY */
```

consists of two functions (set and read) for every member in the instance data structure.

Both interfaces separate the developer from the details of the instance data structure members and are compatible with C and other languages. Each approach has its strengths and weaknesses. The less direct message interface adds complexity to the control's window procedure, defines additional window messages, and has high execution overhead. A function interface increases the number of functions that must be exported.

To illustrate the techniques, we've supplied both function and message interfaces for our instance data structure. The file *CST_DATA.C* supplies a complete set of access functions for both instance data and class default data (see Table 4.1).

Code outside our library may request specific instance data either by calling one of the access functions (the function interface) or by sending one of the messages in Table 4.2 (the message interface).

The message interface defines four new class specific messages: WM_CSTCTLGETDATA, WM_CSTCTLGETDEFDATA, WM_CSTCTLSETDATA, and WM_CSTCTLSETDEFDATA. The numbers assigned to these messages must not conflict with numbers we might assign to other class specific messages. We have tried to lessen the likelihood of conflict by graciously avoiding the lower numbers (i.e., WM_USER + 1, et seq.) and beginning our assignments at WM_USER + 100. This assignment allows new controls to use the common message interface, but still declare class specific messages beginning at WM_USER + 1.

The message interface adds very little code to each new control, because all the real work is done by the support function *CstCtlData()* (also defined in *CST_DATA.C*). Table 4.3 gives the calling interface for *CstCtlData()*.

(Please note that, because of some hidden mechanisms that make subclassing easier, you *must* use the functions in *CST_XTRA.C* to manipulate the extra bytes, instance data, and default data. We'll explain why these mechanisms are necessary when we cover subclassing in Chapter 7.)

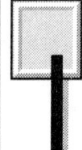

Table 4.1
The function interface to the instance and default data includes the following functions (grouped by function).

```
Functions to retrieve default class data:

    Parameters: hWnd - handle to custom control window
        Return: single data item from CSTCTLDATA structure

    CstCtlDefGetBitmap
    CstCtlDefGetBkMode
    CstCtlDefGetBrush
    CstCtlDefGetColor
    CstCtlDefGetFrame
    CstCtlDefGetFont
    CstCtlDefGetShadow
    CstCtlDefGetState
    CstCtlDefGetStyle
    CstCtlDefGetValue
    CstCtlDefGetWnd

Functions to set the value of class default data:

    Parameters: hWnd - handle to custom control window
                *Id - index id  required for array access of certain data
                * - data value to set
        Return: old data value

    CstCtlDefSetBitmap
    CstCtlDefSetBkMode
    CstCtlDefSetBrush
    CstCtlDefSetColor
    CstCtlDefSetFrame
    CstCtlDefSetFont
    CstCtlDefSetShadow
    CstCtlDefSetState
    CstCtlDefSetStyle
    CstCtlDefSetValue
    CstCtlDefSetWnd
```

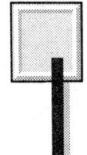

Table 4.1
  Continued from the preceding page.

```
Functions to retrieve instance data:

    Parameters: hWnd - handle to custom control window
        Return: single data item from CSTCTLDATA structure

    CstCtlGetBitmap
    CstCtlGetBkMode
    CstCtlGetBrush
    CstCtlGetColor
    CstCtlGetFrame
    CstCtlGetFont
    CstCtlGetLpRectBitmap
    CstCtlGetLpRectText
    CstCtlGetShadow
    CstCtlGetState
    CstCtlGetStyle
    CstCtlGetValue
    CstCtlGetWnd

Functions to set instance data values:

    Parameters: hWnd - handle to custom control window
                *Id - index id  required for array access of certain data
                * - data value to set
        Return: old data value

    CstCtlSetBitmap
    CstCtlSetBkMode
    CstCtlSetBrush
    CstCtlSetColor
    CstCtlSetFrame
    CstCtlSetFont
    CstCtlSetRects
    CstCtlSetShadow
    CstCtlSetState
    CstCtlSetStyle
    CstCtlSetValue
    CstCtlSetWnd
```

42   Windows Custom Controls

For the sake of efficiency, all of our code manipulates instance data using a macro version of the functions in Table 4.1 (in CST_DATA.H). Corresponding functions and macros are named identically, except that we use all upper case for the macro names.

Of course, the macros are available only when developing in C. Eliminating this macro interface and moving the structure definition from CST_DATA.H to CST_DATA.C would make the instance data structure

Table 4.2

The instance data message interface consists of four user defined messages and constants that index specific members.

```
/* Instance data interface messages */

#define WM_CSTCTLGETDATA     ( WM_USER + 101 )
#define WM_CSTCTLGETDEFDATA  ( WM_USER + 102 )
#define WM_CSTCTLSETDATA     ( WM_USER + 103 )
#define WM_CSTCTLSETDEFDATA  ( WM_USER + 104 )

/* Ids for instance data members */

#define ID_LCOLOR         1
#define ID_HBITMAP        2
#define ID_HBRUSH         3
#define ID_HFONT          4
#define ID_HWND           5
#define ID_IBKMODE        6
#define ID_IFRAME         7
#define ID_ISHADOW        8
#define ID_RECTBITMAP     9
#define ID_RECTTEXT       10
#define ID_WCTLCOLORMSG   11
#define ID_WSTATE         12
#define ID_WSTYLE         13
#define ID_LVALUE         14
```

(These definitions are from cst_data.h)

private to *CST_DATA.C,* preventing developers from directly accessing the instance or default data.

Handling WM_CTLCOLOR

Windows controls send the *WM_CTLCOLOR* message to their parent window procedure just before painting their client area. The parent window's procedure responds by passing a valid brush to the child. This mechanism allows the parent to adjust the presentation (color, etc.) of the child.

If the parent window procedure doesn't trap the *WM_CTLCOLOR* message, then *DefWindowProc()* will supply a brush, based on the system colors (see Table 4.4). Depending upon how the parent window or dialog box is colored, this response may or may not be appropriate.

The most straightforward solution is to have the parent window procedure trap every *WM_CTLCOLOR* message and construct an appropriate brush. This approach adds significant complexity to the parent's window procedure, complexity that must be duplicated in every window procedure using an instance of the control.

Table 4.3

The utility function CstCtlData() performs most of the work necessary to support the instance data message interface. This table summarizes its calling interface.

```
CstCtlData( HWND hWnd, UINT wMsg, WPARAM wParam, LPARAM lParam );

    Parameters: hWnd - handle to custom control window
                wMsg - window message
                wParam - instance data structure member id
                lParam - new value of instance data
        Return: old value of instance data
```

Our solution may seem round-a-bout, but it keeps most of the brush-related complexity in the control, simplifying the parent window procedure.

Normally, our controls ignore the brush created by *DefWndProc()* and instead create their own brush based on the colors stored in the instance data structure. The parent window procedure can still trap the *WM_CTLCOLOR* message if it needs to adjust the brush dynamically, but instead of communicating through the return brush, the two procedures communicate through a set of bit flags (*wCtlColorMsg*) in the control's instance data structure. These flags are simpler to manipulate than a brush, and, as a side effect, enable the control to distinguish between a "real" response to *WM_CTLCOLOR* and a DefWinProc() response.

The support function *CstCtlColorMsg()* (see Table 4.5) both sets and queries these flags. To set the flags, the parent window procedure calls *CstCtlColorMsg()* with a nonzero set of flags. *CstCtlColorMsg()* copies these flags into the instance data and returns the flags' previous values. To read the flags, the control calls the same procedure, but passes

Table 4.4

By trapping the WM_CTLCOLOR message, the custom controls are able to avoid Windows' normal color defaults. This table shows the differences.

DefWinProc() Response To WM_CTLCOLOR	Default Instance Data Values

Background = COLOR_WINDOW
Foreground = COLOR_WINDOWTEXT
Background Brush = COLOR_WINDOW
	Background = COLOR_BTNFACE
	Foreground = COLOR_WINDOWTEXT
	if parent has background brush then
	    Background Brush =
	    parent window's background brush
	else Background Brush = COLOR_WINDOW

Text background mode = OPAQUE	Text background mode = TRANSPARENT
Font = SYSTEM_FONT	Font = parent window's font

an all-zero set of flags. The result will be nonzero *only* if the parent window procedure trapped the most recent *WM_CTLCOLOR* message.

The parent window procedure sets selected flags to indicate what drawing attributes have been changed. The following code illustrates how a parent window may respond to the *WM_CTLCOLOR* message.

```
case WM_CTLCOLOR:
    wCtlType = HIWORD( lParam );
    hCtlWnd = LOWORD( lParam );
    wCtlId = GetWindowWord( hCtlWnd, GWW_ID );
    switch ( wCtlType )
        {
        case CTLCOLOR_CSTSTATIC:
            CstCtlColorMsg( hCtlWnd, CTLCOLORMSG_BRUSH |
                    CTLCOLORMSG_COLORTEXT )
            SetTextColor( wParam, COLOR_GRAYTEXT );
            return ( GetStockObject( WHITE_BRUSH ) ):
        case
```

•
•
•

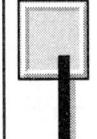

Table 4.5

Applications which use this custom control library should use these bit flags to respond to the WM_CTLCOLOR message.

Flag	Meaning if Set
CTLCOLORMSG_BRUSH	0x01 Background brush has changed
CTLCOLORMSG_COLORTEXT	0x02 Color of Text has changed
CTLCOLORMSG_COLORTEXTBK	0x04 Color of Text Background has changed
CTLCOLORMSG_MODETEXTBK	0x08 Text Background Drawing Mode has changed
CTLCOLORMSG_FONT	0x10 Font has changed

Parsing *lParam* yields the type of the control and the window handle. If needed, the control ID can be obtained via the window handle.

After the control sends the *WM_CTLCOLOR* message, the control's window handle is checked to make sure it is still valid before continuing. Next the response to the *WM_CTLCOLOR* message is retrieved and checked to see if the brush has been set. If the parent has not set the brush the parent's brush is retrieved.

In most cases, however, the parent will be able to place all the necessary color information in the instance data structure as the control is created, and ignore all *WM_CTLCOLOR* messages.

Utility Functions

The library also includes several utility functions that are used by various custom controls. The file *CST_DRAW.C* holds general purpose drawing functions. A few additional miscellaneous functions are in *CST_UTIL.C*. Table 4.6 summarizes the utility functions.

Several of these functions support brush alignment. Brush alignment is important for custom controls when the control's background uses a pattern brush. If the control and the parent window use the same background brush, the brush should be aligned the same for both the parent and the control. The functions in *CST_DRAW.C* do this by calling the function *AlignBrush()* in *CST_UTIL.C*. *AlignBrush()* sets the origin of a brush to the origin of a window's client area. The alignment window is the first parameter to the functions *CstDraw3DFrame()*, *CstDraw3DLine()* and *CstDraw3DRect()*. When drawing custom controls, this window should be the control's parent window.

Specific Message Responses

Table 4.7 contains an alphabetical list of messages that are of particular interest to custom controls. A brief explanation accompanies each entry. Where appropriate, the explanation identifies the sender and receiver of the message.

Conclusion

The common portion of our function interface breaks neatly into three separate function groups: the instance and default data access functions; the utility drawing functions; and the `WM_CTLCOLOR` support function, `CstCtlColorMsg()`. The common portion of the message interface divides into three groups: the default data initialization and cleanup associated with `WM_CREATE` and `WM_DESTROY`; the self-draw response to `WM_CTLCOLOR`; and the standard window maintenance messages. These common interfaces or responses are present in every control in this book.

This chapter completes our examination of the common features of the four programmer interfaces. Beginning with the next chapter, we shift our attention to the implementation of specific controls.

Table 4.6

All of our custom controls draw on these support functions.

Utility Functions (In *CST_UTILS.C*)

AlignBrush:
Sets the origin of a brush to match the origin of a window.

PtInWnd:
Determines if a point lies within a window's client area.

ResetBrushFix:
Allows brush origin to be reset after a window has been moved (a workaround for a Windows 3.1 bug).

SafeDeleteObject:
A version of *DeleteObject()* that always checks to make certain the handle is valid before performing the deletion.

Drawing Functions (In *CST_DRAW.C*)

CstDrawBitmap:
Draws a bitmap at X, Y. If the requested horizontal or vertical sizes are non-zero the bitmap is stretched to fit.

CstDraw3DFrame:
Draws a box or frame with 3-D shading.

CstDraw3DLine:
Draws either a vertical or horizontal line with 3-D shading.

CstDraw3DRect:
Draws a filled rectangle with a 3-D border.

Table 4.7

This table summarizes the impact of window messages on custom controls.

WM_CANCELMODE

Windows sends this message to the control when the application displays a message box. The control can respond by releasing the mouse if it is captured and setting the appropriate state if it changes.

WM_CREATE

Windows sends this message to the control to give the control a chance to initialize instance data and set initial values.

WM_COMMAND

The control sends this message to its parent to pass information to the parent.

WM_CTLCOLOR

The control sends this message to its parent before the control draws itself. This gives the parent a chance to change the colors used by the control. The control also identifies its type by setting the high order word of *lParam()*. Windows predefines the following types:

CTLCOLOR_MSGBOX	*CTLCOLOR_EDIT*
CTLCOLOR_LISTBOX	*CTLCOLOR_BTN*
CTLCOLOR_DLG	*CTLCOLOR_SCROLLBAR*
CTLCOLOR_STATIC	

These types are mutually exclusive values that take up the first three bits of a word (values 0 through 8). A custom control should either set the first three bits to the standard value that most closely matches the custom control, or else define

Table 4.7
Continued from the preceding page.

a new type that does not use the first three bits. For example to define a *CTLCOLOR* value for a custom static control.

#define *CTLCOLOR_CSTSTATIC() (CTLCOLOR_STATIC | 0x010)*

WM_DESTROY

Windows sends this message to the control's window procedure to give the control a chance to clean up and release instance data.

WM_ENABLE

Windows sends this message to the control to specify whether the control is enabled or disabled.

WM_ERASEBKGND

Windows sends this message to the control's window procedure when the control's background needs erasing.

WM_GETDLGCODE

Windows uses this message to ask the control's window procedure what kind of input it plans to process. The control can respond by returning a combination of the following codes (the codes are combinable bit flags).

DLGC_WANTARROWS	*Cursor movement keys*
DLGC_WANTTAB	*Tab key*
DLGC_WANTALLKEYS	*All keyboard input*
DLGC_WANTMESSAGE	*All keyboard input*
DLGC_HASSETSEL	*EM_SETSEL messages*
DLGC_DEFPUSHBUTTON	*Default push button*

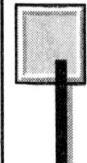

Table 4.7

Continued. This table begins on page 49.

```
DLGC_UNDEFPUSHBUTTON  Pushbutton
DLGC_RADIOBUTTON      Radio button
DLGC_WANTCHARS        WM_CHAR message
DLGC_STATIC           No keyboard input
DLGC_BUTTON           Button control
```

WM_GETFONT

The control can send this message to its parent or another control to make sure the control's font matches the parent.

WM_MOVE

Windows sends this message to the control after the control has been moved.

WM_PAINT

Windows sends this message to the control when all or a portion of the control needs painting.

WM_PARENTNOTIFY

The control sends this message to notify its parent that the control has been created, destroyed, or that the user has clicked a mouse inside the child client area.

WM_NCCREATE

Windows sends this message to the control right before the nonclient area of the control is created, and before sending WM_CREATE. The WM_NCCREATE message represents an alternative opportunity to create and initialize instance data. If a

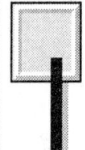

Table 4.7

Continued. This table begins on page 49.

control does not support certain window styles or requires certain special styles, this message is an opportunity to make the adjustment. The following code fragment illustrates how to force a style on or off.

```
lStyle = GetWindowLong( hWnd(), GWL_STYLE );
/* Force a style on */
SetWindowLong( hWnd(), GWL_STYLE, lStyle | WS_forcestyleon );
/* Force a style off */
SetWindowLong( hWnd(), GWL_STYLE, lStyle & ~ WS_forcestyleoff );
```

WM_NCACTIVATE

Keep caption bar activated, even if window doesn't have focus.

WM_NCHITTEST

Reports a mouse event. Controls intercept this message so that it can be passed to other windows.

WM_NCDESTROY

Windows sends this message to the control right after the *WM_DESTROY* message, as an alternative opportunity to free instance data.

WM_KEYDOWN

Windows sends this message to the control when the user has pressed a key and the control has the input focus. If the control accepts input, the control may change state.

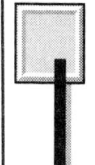 **Table 4.7**

   Continued. This table begins on page 49.

WM_KEYUP

Windows sends this message to the control when the user has released a key and the control has the input focus. If the control accepts input, the control may change state.

WM_KILLFOCUS

Windows sends this message to the control when it is losing the input focus. This message gives the control a chance to change its state to reflect that it no longer has the input focus.

WM_LBUTTONDOWN

Windows sends this message to the control when the user presses the left mouse button while the mouse cursor is within the control's client area. If the control accepts mouse input, the control can capture the mouse in response to this message. The control may also change state in response to this message.

WM_LBUTTONDBLCLK

Windows sends this message to the control when the user has double clicked the left mouse button while the mouse cursor was in the control's client area.

WM_LBUTTONUP

Windows sends this message to the control when the user has released the left mouse button. If the control accepts mouse input and has captured the mouse, this is a chance to release the mouse.

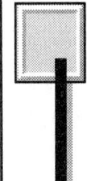 **Table 4.7**
Continued. This table begins on page 49.

WM_MOUSEMOVE

Windows sends this message to the control when the user has moved the mouse while the control has captured the mouse.

WM_SETFOCUS

Windows sends this message to the control when the control has received the input focus. This is an opportunity for the control window procedure to change the state and appearance of the control to indicate focus.

WM_SETFONT

Windows sends this message to the control to set the control's font and possibly redraw the control.

WM_SETTEXT

Windows sends this message to the control to change the text for the control. This is an opportunity for the control to generate a paint message if needed.

WM_SIZE

Windows sends this message to the control after the control size has been changed.

WM_SYSCOLORCHANGE

Windows sends this message to top level windows when the system colors are changed. This will affect the appearance of custom controls that utilize system colors. The application that registered the custom controls and created default brushes based on system colors should respond to this message by deleting those brushes and creating new ones.

Listing 4.1

```
/******************************************************************
         File Name: CST_XTRA.H
     Expanded Name: Custom Extra Bytes
       Description: Include file for CST_XTRA.C
       Portability: Microsoft Windows 3.X
******************************************************************/

#if !defined ( CST_XTRA_DEFINED )
    #define CST_XTRA_DEFINED

    /* Prototypes for functions in CST_XTRA.C */
    LONG FAR PASCAL CstGetClassLong( HWND hWnd, int iOffset );
    WORD FAR PASCAL CstGetClassWord( HWND hWnd, int iOffset );
    LONG FAR PASCAL CstSetClassLong( HWND hWnd, int iOffset, LONG lValue );
    WORD FAR PASCAL CstSetClassWord( HWND hWnd, int iOffset, WORD wValue );
    LONG FAR PASCAL CstGetWindowLong( HWND hWnd, int iOffset );
    WORD FAR PASCAL CstGetWindowWord( HWND hWnd, int iOffset );
    LONG FAR PASCAL CstSetWindowLong( HWND hWnd, int iOffset, LONG lValue );
    WORD FAR PASCAL CstSetWindowWord( HWND hWnd, int iOffset, WORD wValue );

    /* Macros for functions in CST_XTRA.C */
    #define CSTGETCLASSLONG( hWnd, iOffset ) \
            ( GetClassLong( hWnd, (int)GetClassWord( hWnd, GCW_CBCLSEXTRA ) - \
            (int)iOffset - (int)sizeof ( LONG ) ) )

    #define CSTGETCLASSWORD( hWnd, iOffset ) \
            ( GetClassWord( hWnd, (int)GetClassWord( hWnd, GCW_CBCLSEXTRA ) - \
            (int)iOffset - (int)sizeof ( WORD ) ) )

    #define CSTSETCLASSLONG( hWnd, iOffset, lValue ) \
            ( SetClassLong( hWnd, (int)GetClassWord( hWnd, GCW_CBCLSEXTRA ) - \
            (int)iOffset - (int)sizeof ( LONG ), (LONG)lValue ) )

    #define CSTSETCLASSWORD( hWnd, iOffset, wValue ) \
            ( SetClassWord( hWnd, (int)GetClassWord( hWnd, GCW_CBCLSEXTRA ) - \
            (int)iOffset - (int)sizeof ( WORD ), (WORD)wValue ) )

    #define CSTGETWINDOWLONG( hWnd, iOffset ) \
            ( GetWindowLong( hWnd, (int)GetClassWord( hWnd, GCW_CBWNDEXTRA ) - \
            (int)iOffset - (int)sizeof ( LONG ) ) )

    #define CSTGETWINDOWWORD( hWnd, iOffset ) \
            ( GetWindowWord( hWnd, (int)GetClassWord( hWnd, GCW_CBWNDEXTRA ) - \
            (int)iOffset - (int)sizeof ( WORD ) ) )

    #define CSTSETWINDOWLONG( hWnd, iOffset, lValue ) \
            ( SetWindowLong( hWnd, (int)GetClassWord( hWnd, GCW_CBWNDEXTRA ) - \
            (int)iOffset - (int)sizeof ( LONG ), (LONG)lValue ) )

    #define CSTSETWINDOWWORD( hWnd, iOffset, wValue ) \
            ( SetWindowWord( hWnd, (int)GetClassWord( hWnd, GCW_CBWNDEXTRA ) - \
            (int)iOffset - (int)sizeof ( WORD ), (WORD)wValue ) )

#endif

/* End of CST_XTRA.H */
```

Listing 4.2

```
/*****************************************************************************
        File Name: CST_XTRA.C
    Expanded Name: Custom Extra Bytes
      Description: Library of functions for getting and setting class and
                   window extra bytes.  The byte offsets are adjusted to
                   offset from the end of the extra class or window bytes
                   memory area.  This allows for extra bytes to be used
                   with window classes that are subclasses of existing
                   window classes.  The parent class number of extra bytes
                   can only be determined at run time to be considered
                   portable.  The subclass must add the parent class
                   extra bytes to those needed for the subclass.  This
                   forces indexing from the end of the extra bytes.
Global Function List: CstGetClassLong
                   CstGetClassWord
                   CstSetClassLong
                   CstSetClassWord
                   CstGetWindowLong
                   CstGetWindowWord
                   CstSetWindowLong
                   CstSetWindowWord
      Portability: Microsoft Windows 3.X
*****************************************************************************/

/* Microsoft Windows */
#include <windows.h>

/* Own */
#include <cst_xtra.h>

LONG FAR PASCAL CstGetClassLong( HWND hWnd, int iOffset )
    {
    return ( CSTGETCLASSLONG( hWnd, iOffset ) );
    }   /* function CstGetClassWord */

WORD FAR PASCAL CstGetClassWord( HWND hWnd, int iOffset )
    {
    return ( CSTGETCLASSWORD( hWnd, iOffset ) );
    }   /* function CstGetClassWord */

LONG FAR PASCAL CstSetClassLong( HWND hWnd, int iOffset, LONG lValue )
    {
    return ( CSTSETCLASSLONG( hWnd, iOffset, lValue ) );
    }   /* function CstGetClassLong */

WORD FAR PASCAL CstSetClassWord( HWND hWnd, int iOffset, WORD wValue )
    {
    return ( CSTSETCLASSWORD( hWnd, iOffset, wValue ) );
    }   /* function CstGetClassWord */

LONG FAR PASCAL CstGetWindowLong( HWND hWnd, int iOffset )
    {
    return ( CSTGETWINDOWLONG( hWnd, iOffset ) );
    }   /* function CstGetWindowWord */

WORD FAR PASCAL CstGetWindowWord( HWND hWnd, int iOffset )
    {
```

Listing 4.2 continued

```
    return ( CSTGETWINDOWWORD( hWnd, iOffset ) );
    }   /* function CstGetWindowWord */

LONG FAR PASCAL CstSetWindowLong( HWND hWnd, int iOffset, LONG lValue )
    {
    return ( CSTSETWINDOWLONG( hWnd, iOffset, lValue ) );
    }   /* function CstGetWindowLong */

WORD FAR PASCAL CstSetWindowWord( HWND hWnd, int iOffset, WORD wValue )
    {
    return ( CSTSETWINDOWWORD( hWnd, iOffset, wValue ) );
    }   /* function CstGetWindowWord */

/* End of CST_XTRA.C */
```

Listing 4.3

```c
/****************************************************************************
          File Name: CST_DRAW.H
      Expanded Name: Custom Control Draw
        Description: Include file for CST_DRAW.C
        Portability: Microsoft Windows 3.X
****************************************************************************/

#if !defined ( CST_DRAW_DEFINED )
    #define CST_DRAW_DEFINED

    /* Styles for 3D Boxes or Frames */
    #define CST_FRAME_BORDER      0x001
    #define CST_FRAME_FLAT        0x002
    #define CST_FRAME_GROOVE      0x004
    #define CST_FRAME_LOWERED     0x008
    #define CST_FRAME_NOCORNERS   0x010
    #define CST_FRAME_RAISED      0x020
    #define CST_FRAME_RIDGE       0x040

    /* Styles for 3D Lines */
    #define CST_LINE_FLAT         0x002
    #define CST_LINE_GROOVE       0x004
    #define CST_LINE_RIDGE        0x040
    #define CST_LINE_HORZ         0x080
    #define CST_LINE_VERT         0x100

    /* Styles for 3D Rectangles (same as Frames) */
    #define CST_RECT_BORDER       0x001
    #define CST_RECT_FLAT         0x002
    #define CST_RECT_GROOVE       0x004
    #define CST_RECT_LOWERED      0x008
    #define CST_RECT_NOCORNERS    0x010
    #define CST_RECT_RAISED       0x020
    #define CST_RECT_RIDGE        0x040

    /* Prototypes of functions in CST_DRAW.C */
    BOOL PASCAL CstDrawBitmap( HDC hDC, HBITMAP hBitmap, int X, int Y,
            int iWidth, int iHeight );
    BOOL PASCAL CstDraw3DFrame( HWND hWnd, HDC hDC, LPRECT lpRect,
            WORD wStyle, HBRUSH hBrushHighlight, HBRUSH hBrushShadow,
            int iThick );
    BOOL PASCAL CstDraw3DLine( HWND hWnd, HDC hDC, LPRECT lpRect, WORD wStyle,
            HBRUSH hBrushHighlight, HBRUSH hBrushShadow, int iThick );
    BOOL PASCAL CstDraw3DRect( HWND hWnd, HDC hDC, HBRUSH hBrushBackground,
            LPRECT lpRect, WORD wStyle, HBRUSH hBrushHighlight,
            HBRUSH hBrushShadow, int iThick );

#endif

/* End of CST_DRAW.H */
```

Listing 4.4

```c
/*****************************************************************************
           File Name: CST_DRAW.C
       Expanded Name: Custom Control Draw
         Description: Function library for drawing custom controls
Global Function List: CstDrawBitmap
                      CstDraw3DFrame
                      CstDraw3DLine
                      CstDraw3DRect
         Portability: Microsoft Windows 3.X
*****************************************************************************/

/* Microsoft Windows */
#include <windows.h>

/* Types and Prototypes */
#include <cst_data.h>
#include <cst_util.h>

/* Own */
#include <cst_draw.h>

/*****************************************************************************
         Name: CstDrawBitmap
Expanded Name: Draw Bitmap
   Parameters: hDC - handle of device context
               hBitmap - handle of bitmap
               X, Y - Location of bitmap in logical coordinates
               iWidth, iHeight - Size of bitmap in logical coordinates
       Return: Zero if bitmap not drawn, non-zero if drawn
  Description: Draws a bitmap at X, Y.  If iWidth or iHeight are non-zero
               the bitmap is stretched to fit.
*****************************************************************************/
BOOL PASCAL CstDrawBitmap( HDC hDC, HBITMAP hBitmap, int X, int Y, int iWidth,
        int iHeight )
    {

    BITMAP Bitmap;
    BOOL bStatus;
    HDC hDCMem;
    POINT BitmapSize, BitmapOrigin;

    /* Create memory device context */
    hDCMem = CreateCompatibleDC( hDC );
    SelectObject( hDCMem, hBitmap );
    SetMapMode( hDCMem, GetMapMode( hDC ) );

    /* Get dimensions of bitmap */
    GetObject( hBitmap, sizeof ( BITMAP ), (LPSTR)&Bitmap );
    BitmapSize.x = Bitmap.bmWidth;
    BitmapSize.y = Bitmap.bmHeight;
    BitmapOrigin.x = BitmapOrigin.y = 0;

    /* Convert from device to logical coordinates */
    DPtoLP( hDC, &BitmapSize, 1 );
    DPtoLP( hDCMem, &BitmapOrigin, 1 );
```

Listing 4.4 continued

```
    /* Display the bitmap */
    if ( ( iWidth == 0 ) && ( iHeight == 0 ) )
        {
        /* Display the bitmap pixel for pixel */
        bStatus = BitBlt( hDC, X, Y, BitmapSize.x, BitmapSize.y, hDCMem,
                BitmapOrigin.x, BitmapOrigin.y, SRCCOPY );
        }
    else
        {
        /* Size the bitmap to match the desired size */
        int iStretchBltModeOrg;
        iStretchBltModeOrg = SetStretchBltMode( hDC, COLORONCOLOR );
        bStatus = StretchBlt( hDC, X, Y, iWidth, iHeight, hDCMem, BitmapOrigin.x,
                BitmapOrigin.y, BitmapSize.x, BitmapSize.y, SRCCOPY );
        SetStretchBltMode( hDC, iStretchBltModeOrg );
        }

    DeleteDC( hDCMem );

    return ( bStatus );

    }   /* function CstDrawBitmap */


/*******************************************************************************
          Name: CstDraw3DFrame
 Expanded Name: Draw 3-D Box Frame
    Parameters: hWnd - handle of the window to use for brush origin
                hDC - device context for drawing
                lpRect - coordinates of frame
                wStyle - style flags of frame
                hBrushLight - line lighted color
                hBrushShadow - shadow color
                iThick - thickness of frame
        Return: Zero if failure, non-zero if success
   Description: Draw box / frame with 3-D appearance
*******************************************************************************/
BOOL PASCAL CstDraw3DFrame( HWND hWnd, HDC hDC, LPRECT lpRect, WORD wStyle,
        HBRUSH hBrushLight, HBRUSH hBrushShadow, int iThick )
    {

    BOOL bStatus = 0;
    HBRUSH hBrushOrg;
    int i, j, Corner = 0;

    for ( i = 0, j = 1; i < iThick; i++, j += 2 )
        {
        if ( i )
            {
            Corner = 0;
            }
        else if ( wStyle & CST_FRAME_NOCORNERS )
            {
            /* This is used for a rounded corner effect,
            ** mainly for the default frame draw around buttons */
            Corner = 1;
            }
```

Listing 4.4 *continued*

```
/* Set up the brush for left and top lines */
UnrealizeObject( hBrushLight );
AlignBrush( hWnd, hDC, hBrushShadow );
if ( ( ( wStyle & CST_FRAME_RAISED ) ||
        ( ( wStyle & CST_FRAME_RIDGE ) && ( j < iThick ) ) ||
        ( ( wStyle & CST_FRAME_GROOVE ) && ( j > iThick ) ) )
    {
    hBrushOrg = SelectObject( hDC, hBrushLight );
    }
else
    {
    hBrushOrg = SelectObject( hDC, hBrushShadow );
    }

/* Draw the top horizontal line */
PatBlt( hDC, lpRect->left + i + Corner,
        lpRect->top + i,
        lpRect->right - lpRect->left - ( 2 * ( i + Corner ) ),
        1,
        PATCOPY );

/* Draw the left vertical line */
PatBlt( hDC, lpRect->left + i,
        lpRect->top + i + Corner,
        1,
        lpRect->bottom - lpRect->top - ( 2 * i + 1 + Corner ),
        PATCOPY );

/* Set up the brush for bottom and right lines */
SelectObject( hDC, hBrushOrg );
UnrealizeObject( hBrushLight );
AlignBrush( hWnd, hDC, hBrushShadow );
if ( ( ( wStyle & CST_FRAME_RAISED ) || ( wStyle & CST_FRAME_FLAT ) ||
        ( ( wStyle & CST_FRAME_RIDGE ) && ( j < iThick ) ) ||
        ( ( wStyle & CST_FRAME_GROOVE ) && ( j > iThick ) ) )
    {
    hBrushOrg = SelectObject( hDC, hBrushShadow );
    }
else
    {
    hBrushOrg = SelectObject( hDC, hBrushLight );
    }

/* Draw the bottom horizontal line */
bStatus = PatBlt( hDC, lpRect->left + i + Corner,
        lpRect->bottom - ( i + 1 ),
        lpRect->right - lpRect->left - ( 2 * ( i + Corner ) ), 1,
        PATCOPY );

/* Draw the right vertical line */
PatBlt( hDC, lpRect->right - ( i + 1 ),
        lpRect->top + i + Corner,
        1,
        lpRect->bottom - lpRect->top - ( 2 * ( i + Corner ) ),
        PATCOPY );
```

Listing 4.4 *continued*

```
        SelectObject( hDC, hBrushOrg );
            }   /* for i */

    return ( bStatus );

    }   /* function CstDraw3DFrame */


/*****************************************************************************
        Name: CstDraw3DLine
Expanded Name: Draw 3-D Line
   Parameters: hWnd - handle of the window to use for brush origin
               hDC - device context for drawing
               lpRect - coordinates of line to draw
               wStyle - style flags of line
               hBrushLight - lighted color
               hBrushShadow - shadow color
               iThick - thickness of line
       Return: Zero if failure, non-zero if success
  Description: Draws either vertical or horizontal line that has a 3-D
               appearance.
*****************************************************************************/
BOOL PASCAL CstDraw3DLine( HWND hWnd, HDC hDC, LPRECT lpRect, WORD wStyle,
        HBRUSH hBrushLight, HBRUSH hBrushShadow, int iThick )
    {

    BOOL bStatus;
    HBRUSH hBrushOrg;
    int X, Y, Width, Height;

    /* Set and select the brush based on the line style */
    UnrealizeObject( hBrushLight );
    AlignBrush( hWnd, hDC, hBrushShadow );
    hBrushOrg = SelectObject( hDC, ( wStyle & CST_LINE_RIDGE ) ?
            hBrushLight : hBrushShadow );
    X = lpRect->left;
    Y = lpRect->top;
    if ( wStyle & CST_LINE_HORZ )
        {
        Y = ( Y + lpRect->bottom ) / 2;
        Width = lpRect->right - lpRect->left;
        Height = iThick;
        }
    else
        {
        X = ( X + lpRect->right ) / 2;
        Width = iThick;
        Height = lpRect->bottom - lpRect->top;
        }

    /* Draw the first half of the line */
    if ( wStyle & CST_LINE_HORZ )
        {
        /* Draw top half of line */
        PatBlt( hDC, X, Y - iThick, Width, Height, PATCOPY );
        }
```

Listing 4.4 *continued*

```
    else
        {
        /* Draw left half of line */
        PatBlt( hDC, X - iThick, Y, Width, Height, PATCOPY );
        }

    /* Set and select the brush based on the line style */
    SelectObject( hDC, hBrushOrg );
    UnrealizeObject( hBrushLight );
    AlignBrush( hWnd, hDC, hBrushShadow );
    hBrushOrg = SelectObject( hDC, ( wStyle & CST_LINE_GROOVE ) ?
            hBrushLight : hBrushShadow );

    /* Draw the second half of the line
    ** Draw bottom half of horz. line or
    ** Draw right half of vert. line */
    bStatus = PatBlt( hDC, X, Y, Width, Height, PATCOPY );

    /* Reset the original brush */
    SelectObject( hDC, hBrushOrg );

    return ( bStatus );

    }   /* function CstDraw3DLine */


/***************************************************************************
         Name: CstDraw3DRect
Expanded Name: Draw 3-D Filled Rectangle
   Parameters: hWnd - handle of the window to use as brush origin
               hDC - device context for drawing
               hBrushBk - brush to fill rectangle with
               lpRect - coordinates of rectangle to draw
               wStyle - style flags of rectangle
               hBrushLight - lighted color
               hBrushShadow - shadow color
               iThick - thickness of border
       Return: Zero if failure, non-zero if success
  Description: Draws filled rectangle with 3-D border
***************************************************************************/
BOOL PASCAL CstDraw3DRect( HWND hWnd, HDC hDC, HBRUSH hBrushBk, LPRECT lpRect,
        WORD wStyle, HBRUSH hBrushLight, HBRUSH hBrushShadow, int iThick )
    {

    BOOL bStatus;
    HBRUSH hBrushOrg;

    /* Fill in the entire rectangle */
    AlignBrush( hWnd, hDC, hBrushBk );
    hBrushOrg = SelectObject( hDC, hBrushBk );
    bStatus = PatBlt( hDC, lpRect->left, lpRect->top,
            lpRect->right - lpRect->left,
            lpRect->bottom - lpRect->top, PATCOPY );
    SelectObject( hDC, hBrushOrg );
```

Listing 4.4 *continued*

```
    /* Draw the border */
    if ( wStyle )
        {
        return ( CstDraw3DFrame( hWnd, hDC, lpRect, wStyle, hBrushLight,
                 hBrushShadow, iThick ) );
        }

    return ( bStatus );

    }   /* function CstDraw3DRect */
/* End of CST_DRAW.C */
```

Listing 4.5

```c
/*****************************************************************
         File Name: CST_DATA.H
     Expanded Name: Custom Control Data
       Description: Include file for CST_DATA.C
       Portability: Microsoft Windows 3.X
*****************************************************************/

#if !defined ( CST_DATA_DEFINED )
    #define CST_DATA_DEFINED

    /* Flags to specify the area of the control that needs repainting */
    #define AREA_NONE    0
    #define AREA_ALL     1
    #define AREA_BITMAP  2
    #define AREA_TEXT    3

    /* Flags to control the mode of the state function */
    #define STATE_CHECK  0
    #define STATE_GET    1
    #define STATE_RESET  2
    #define STATE_SET    3

    /* Index constants into bitmap array */
    #define CC_BITMAP0  0
    #define CC_BITMAP1  1
    #define CC_BITMAP2  2
    #define CC_BITMAP3  3
    #define CC_BITMAP4  4
    #define CC_BITMAP5  5
    #define CC_NUM_BITMAPS 6

    /* Index constants into brush array */
    #define CC_BRUSH_BACKGROUND 0
    #define CC_BRUSH_BTNFACE    1
    #define CC_BRUSH_3DLIGHT    2
    #define CC_BRUSH_3DSHADOW   3
    #define CC_BRUSH_FRAME      4
    #define CC_NUM_BRUSHS       5

    /* Index constants into color array */
    #define CC_COLOR_BACKGROUND     0
    #define CC_COLOR_BTNFACE        1
    #define CC_COLOR_3DLIGHT        2
    #define CC_COLOR_3DSHADOW       3
    #define CC_COLOR_FRAME          4
    #define CC_COLOR_TEXT           5
    #define CC_COLOR_TEXTBACKGROUND 6
    #define CC_COLOR_GRAYTEXT       7
    #define CC_NUM_COLORS           8

    /* Default default frame thickness */
    #define CC_FRAME 2

    /* Default 3D shadow thickness */
    #define CC_SHADOW 2
```

Listing 4.5 *continued*

```c
/* Default space between bitmap and text */
#define CC_BITMAP_TEXT_SPACE 6

/* Bit flags for WM_CTLCOLOR message response */
#define CTLCOLORMSG_BRUSH        0x01
#define CTLCOLORMSG_COLORTEXT    0x02
#define CTLCOLORMSG_COLORTEXTBK  0x04
#define CTLCOLORMSG_MODETEXTBK   0x08
#define CTLCOLORMSG_FONT         0x10

/* Class and Window extra bytes */
#define CC_CLSEXTRA ( sizeof ( LONG ) + sizeof ( WORD ) )
#define CC_WNDEXTRA ( sizeof ( LONG ) + sizeof ( WORD ) )

/* Offsets into extra bytes */
#define GCL_LPCSTCTLDATA  0
#define GCW_HCSTCTLDATA   ( sizeof ( LONG ) )
#define GWL_LPCSTCTLDATA  0
#define GWW_HCSTCTLDATA   ( sizeof ( LONG ) )

/* Global Memory Flags */
#if defined ( _WINDLL )
#define GMEM_FLAGS \
        ( GMEM_SHARE | GMEM_MOVEABLE | GMEM_NODISCARD | GMEM_ZEROINIT )
#else
#define GMEM_FLAGS ( GMEM_MOVEABLE | GMEM_NODISCARD | GMEM_ZEROINIT )
#endif

/* Instance data interface messages */
#define WM_CSTCTLGETDATA     ( WM_USER + 101 )
#define WM_CSTCTLGETDEFDATA  ( WM_USER + 102 )
#define WM_CSTCTLSETDATA     ( WM_USER + 103 )
#define WM_CSTCTLSETDEFDATA  ( WM_USER + 104 )

/* Ids for instance data members */
#define ID_LCOLOR        1
#define ID_HBITMAP       2
#define ID_HBRUSH        3
#define ID_HFONT         4
#define ID_HWND          5
#define ID_IBKMODE       6
#define ID_IFRAME        7
#define ID_ISHADOW       8
#define ID_RECTBITMAP    9
#define ID_RECTTEXT      10
#define ID_WCTLCOLORMSG  11
#define ID_WSTATE        12
#define ID_WSTYLE        13
#define ID_LVALUE        14

/* Custom control instance data */
typedef struct tagCSTCTLDATA
    {
    COLORREF lColor[CC_NUM_COLORS];  /* Array of Colors */
    HBITMAP hBitmap[CC_NUM_BITMAPS]; /* Array of Bitmaps */
    HBRUSH hBrush[CC_NUM_BRUSHS];    /* Array of Brushes */
    HFONT hFont;           /* Font used by control */
    HWND hWnd;             /* Handle of Window (implementation dependant) */
```

Listing 4.5 *continued*

```c
        int iBkMode;        /* Background mode for displaying text */
        int iFrame;         /* Thickness of default frame */
        int iShadow;        /* Thickness of 3D shadow and highlight */
        RECT RectBitmap;    /* Client area that contains bitmap */
        RECT RectText;      /* Client area that contains text */
        WORD wCtlColorMsg;  /* Response flags to WM_CTLCOLOR message */
        WORD wState;        /* State of control (implementation dependant) */
        WORD wStyle;        /* Auxiliary style (implementation dependant) */
        LONG lValue;        /* Value of control (implementation dependant) */
        } CSTCTLDATA, FAR *LPCSTCTLDATA;
typedef unsigned int HCSTCTLDATA;

/* Prototypes for exported functions in CST_DATA.C */
WORD FAR PASCAL CstCtlColorMsg( HWND hWnd, WORD wState );
DWORD FAR PASCAL CstCtlData( HWND hWnd, UINT wMsg, WPARAM wParam,
        LPARAM lParam );
LPCSTCTLDATA FAR PASCAL CstCtlDataCreate( HWND hWnd );
HCSTCTLDATA FAR PASCAL CstCtlDataDelete( HWND hWnd );
LPCSTCTLDATA FAR PASCAL CstCtlDefDataCreate( HWND hWnd );
HBITMAP FAR PASCAL CstCtlDefGetBitmap( HWND hWnd,
        WORD wBitmapId );
int FAR PASCAL CstCtlDefGetBkMode( HWND hWnd );
HBRUSH FAR PASCAL CstCtlDefGetBrush( HWND hWnd, WORD wBrushId );
COLORREF FAR PASCAL CstCtlDefGetColor( HWND hWnd, WORD wColorId );
int FAR PASCAL CstCtlDefGetFrame( HWND hWnd );
HFONT FAR PASCAL CstCtlDefGetFont( HWND hWnd );
LPCSTCTLDATA FAR PASCAL CstCtlDefGetLpData( HWND hWnd );
int FAR PASCAL CstCtlDefGetShadow( HWND hWnd );
WORD FAR PASCAL CstCtlDefGetState( HWND hWnd );
WORD FAR PASCAL CstCtlDefGetStyle( HWND hWnd );
LONG FAR PASCAL CstCtlDefGetValue( HWND hWnd );
HWND FAR PASCAL CstCtlDefGetWnd( HWND hWnd );
HBITMAP FAR PASCAL CstCtlDefSetBitmap( HWND hWnd, WORD wBitmapId,
        HBITMAP hBitmap );
int FAR PASCAL CstCtlDefSetBkMode( HWND hWnd, int iBkMode );
HBRUSH FAR PASCAL CstCtlDefSetBrush( HWND hWnd, WORD wBrushId,
        HBRUSH hBrush );
COLORREF FAR PASCAL CstCtlDefSetColor( HWND hWnd, WORD wColorId,
        COLORREF lColor );
int FAR PASCAL CstCtlDefSetFrame( HWND hWnd, int iFrame );
HFONT FAR PASCAL CstCtlDefSetFont( HWND hWnd, HFONT hFont );
int FAR PASCAL CstCtlDefSetShadow( HWND hWnd, int wShadow );
WORD FAR PASCAL CstCtlDefSetState( HWND hWnd, WORD wState );
WORD FAR PASCAL CstCtlDefSetStyle( HWND hWnd, WORD wStyle );
LONG FAR PASCAL CstCtlDefSetValue( HWND hWnd, LONG lValue );
HWND FAR PASCAL CstCtlDefSetWnd( HWND hWnd, HWND hWndSet );
HBITMAP FAR PASCAL CstCtlGetBitmap( HWND hWnd, WORD wBitmapId );
int FAR PASCAL CstCtlGetBkMode( HWND hWnd );
HBRUSH FAR PASCAL CstCtlGetBrush( HWND hWnd, WORD wBrushId );
COLORREF FAR PASCAL CstCtlGetColor( HWND hWnd, WORD wColorId );
int FAR PASCAL CstCtlGetFrame( HWND hWnd );
HFONT FAR PASCAL CstCtlGetFont( HWND hWnd );
LPCSTCTLDATA FAR PASCAL CstCtlGetLpData( HWND hWnd );
LPRECT FAR PASCAL CstCtlGetLpRectBitmap( HWND hWnd );
LPRECT FAR PASCAL CstCtlGetLpRectText( HWND hWnd );
int FAR PASCAL CstCtlGetShadow( HWND hWnd );
WORD FAR PASCAL CstCtlGetState( HWND hWnd );
WORD FAR PASCAL CstCtlGetStyle( HWND hWnd );
```

Listing 4.5 *continued*

```
LONG  FAR PASCAL CstCtlGetValue( HWND hWnd );
HWND  FAR PASCAL CstCtlGetWnd( HWND hWnd );
HBITMAP FAR PASCAL CstCtlSetBitmap( HWND hWnd, WORD wBitmapId,
        HBITMAP hBitmap );
int   FAR PASCAL CstCtlSetBkMode( HWND hWnd, int iBkMode );
HBRUSH FAR PASCAL CstCtlSetBrush( HWND hWnd, WORD wBrushId,
        HBRUSH hBrush );
COLORREF FAR PASCAL CstCtlSetColor( HWND hWnd, WORD wColorId,
        COLORREF lColor );
int   FAR PASCAL CstCtlSetFrame( HWND hWnd, int iFrame );
void  FAR PASCAL CstCtlSetRects( HWND hWnd, HBITMAP hBitmap,
        LPRECT lpRectClient, LPRECT lpRectBitmap, LPRECT lpRectText );
HFONT FAR PASCAL CstCtlSetFont( HWND hWnd, HFONT hFont );
int   FAR PASCAL CstCtlSetShadow( HWND hWnd, int wShadow );
WORD  FAR PASCAL CstCtlSetState( HWND hWnd, WORD wState );
WORD  FAR PASCAL CstCtlSetStyle( HWND hWnd, WORD wStyle );
LONG  FAR PASCAL CstCtlSetValue( HWND hWnd, LONG lValue );
HWND  FAR PASCAL CstCtlSetWnd( HWND hWnd, HWND hWndSet );
WORD  FAR PASCAL CstCtlState( HWND hWnd, WORD wState,
        WORD wStateMode, WORD wArea );

/* Macro versions of get functions */
#define CSTCTLDEFGETLPDATA( hWnd ) \
        ( (LPCSTCTLDATA)CSTGETCLASSLONG( hWnd, GCL_LPCSTCTLDATA ) )

#define CSTCTLDEFGETBITMAP( hWnd, hBitmapId ) \
        ( CSTCTLDEFGETLPDATA( hWnd )->hBitmap[hBitmapId] )

#define CSTCTLDEFGETBKMODE( hWnd ) \
        ( CSTCTLDEFGETLPDATA( hWnd )->iBkMode )

#define CSTCTLDEFGETBRUSH( hWnd, hBrushId ) \
        ( CSTCTLDEFGETLPDATA( hWnd )->hBrush[hBrushId] )

#define CSTCTLDEFGETCOLOR( hWnd, lColorId ) \
        ( CSTCTLDEFGETLPDATA( hWnd )->lColor[lColorId] )

#define CSTCTLDEFGETFRAME( hWnd ) \
        ( CSTCTLDEFGETLPDATA( hWnd )->iFrame )

#define CSTCTLDEFGETFONT( hWnd ) \
        ( CSTCTLDEFGETLPDATA( hWnd )->hFont )

#define CSTCTLDEFGETLPRECTBITMAP( hWnd ) \
        ( (LPRECT)&( CSTCTLDEFGETLPDATA( hWnd )->RectBitmap ) )

#define CSTCTLDEFGETLPRECTTEXT( hWnd ) \
        ( (LPRECT)&( CSTCTLDEFGETLPDATA( hWnd )->RectText ) )

#define CSTCTLDEFGETSHADOW( hWnd ) \
        ( CSTCTLDEFGETLPDATA( hWnd )->iShadow )

#define CSTCTLDEFGETSTATE( hWnd ) \
        ( CSTCTLDEFGETLPDATA( hWnd )->wState )

#define CSTCTLDEFGETSTYLE( hWnd ) \
        ( CSTCTLDEFGETLPDATA( hWnd )->wStyle )
```

Listing 4.5 *continued*

```
#define CSTCTLDEFGETVALUE( hWnd ) \
        ( CSTCTLDEFGETLPDATA( hWnd )->lValue )

#define CSTCTLDEFGETWND( hWnd ) \
        ( CSTCTLDEFGETLPDATA( hWnd )->hWnd )

#define CSTCTLGETLPDATA( hWnd ) \
        ( (LPCSTCTLDATA)CSTGETWINDOWLONG( hWnd, GWL_LPCSTCTLDATA ) )

#define CSTCTLGETBITMAP( hWnd, hBitmapId ) \
        ( CSTCTLGETLPDATA( hWnd )->hBitmap[hBitmapId] )

#define CSTCTLGETBKMODE( hWnd ) \
        ( CSTCTLGETLPDATA( hWnd )->iBkMode )

#define CSTCTLGETBRUSH( hWnd, hBrushId ) \
        ( CSTCTLGETLPDATA( hWnd )->hBrush[hBrushId] )

#define CSTCTLGETCOLOR( hWnd, lColorId ) \
        ( CSTCTLGETLPDATA( hWnd )->lColor[lColorId] )

#define CSTCTLGETFRAME( hWnd ) \
        ( CSTCTLGETLPDATA( hWnd )->iFrame )

#define CSTCTLGETFONT( hWnd ) \
        ( CSTCTLGETLPDATA( hWnd )->hFont )

#define CSTCTLGETLPRECTBITMAP( hWnd ) \
        ( (LPRECT)&( CSTCTLGETLPDATA( hWnd )->RectBitmap ) )

#define CSTCTLGETLPRECTTEXT( hWnd ) \
        ( (LPRECT)&( CSTCTLGETLPDATA( hWnd )->RectText ) )

#define CSTCTLGETSHADOW( hWnd ) \
        ( CSTCTLGETLPDATA( hWnd )->iShadow )

#define CSTCTLGETSTATE( hWnd ) \
        ( CSTCTLGETLPDATA( hWnd )->wState )

#define CSTCTLGETSTYLE( hWnd ) \
        ( CSTCTLGETLPDATA( hWnd )->wStyle )

#define CSTCTLGETVALUE( hWnd ) \
        ( CSTCTLGETLPDATA( hWnd )->lValue )

#define CSTCTLGETWND( hWnd_ ) \
        ( CSTCTLGETLPDATA( hWnd_ )->hWnd )

#endif

/* End of CST_DATA.H */
```

Listing 4.6

```
/*****************************************************************************
             File Name: CST_DATA.C
         Expanded Name: Custom Control Data
           Description: Function library for accessing custom control data
 Global Function List: CstCtlColorMsg
                       CstCtlData
                       CstCtlDataCreate
                       CstCtlDataDelete
                       CstCtlDefDataCreate
                       CstCtlDefGetBitmap
                       CstCtlDefGetBkMode
                       CstCtlDefGetBrush
                       CstCtlDefGetColor
                       CstCtlDefGetFrame
                       CstCtlDefGetFont
                       CstCtlDefGetShadow
                       CstCtlDefGetState
                       CstCtlDefGetStyle
                       CstCtlDefGetValue
                       CstCtlDefGetWnd
                       CstCtlDefSetBitmap
                       CstCtlDefSetBkMode
                       CstCtlDefSetBrush
                       CstCtlDefSetColor
                       CstCtlDefSetFrame
                       CstCtlDefSetFont
                       CstCtlDefSetShadow
                       CstCtlDefSetState
                       CstCtlDefSetStyle
                       CstCtlDefSetValue
                       CstCtlDefSetWnd
                       CstCtlGetBitmap
                       CstCtlGetBkMode
                       CstCtlGetBrush
                       CstCtlGetColor
                       CstCtlGetFrame
                       CstCtlGetFont
                       CstCtlGetLpRectBitmap
                       CstCtlGetLpRectText
                       CstCtlGetShadow
                       CstCtlGetState
                       CstCtlGetStyle
                       CstCtlGetValue
                       CstCtlGetWnd
                       CstCtlSetBitmap
                       CstCtlSetBkMode
                       CstCtlSetBrush
                       CstCtlSetColor
                       CstCtlSetFrame
                       CstCtlSetFont
                       CstCtlSetRects
                       CstCtlSetShadow
                       CstCtlSetState
                       CstCtlSetStyle
                       CstCtlSetValue
                       CstCtlSetWnd
           Portability: Microsoft Windows 3.X
```

Listing 4.6 *continued*

```c
**************************************************************************/

/* Microsoft Windows */
#include <windows.h>

/* Types and Prototypes */
#include <cst_xtra.h>

/* Own */
#include <cst_data.h>

/**************************************************************************
         Name: CstCtlColorMsg
Expanded Name: Custom Control Color Message
   Parameters: hWnd - handle to custom control window
               wState - response to WM_CTLCOLOR message
       Return: old state of message
  Description: This is function interface to retrieve and set responses to the
               WM_CTLCOLOR message.
**************************************************************************/
WORD FAR PASCAL CstCtlColorMsg( HWND hWnd, WORD wState )
    {

    WORD wStateOld;
    LPCSTCTLDATA lpCstCtlData = CSTCTLGETLPDATA( hWnd );

    wStateOld = lpCstCtlData->wCtlColorMsg;
    lpCstCtlData->wCtlColorMsg = (WORD)( wState ? wState : 0 );

    return ( wStateOld );

    }   /* function CstCtlColorMsg */


/**************************************************************************
         Name: CstCtlData
Expanded Name: Custom Control Data
   Parameters: hWnd - handle to custom control window
               wMsg - window message
               wParam - instance data structure member id
               lParam - new value of instance data
       Return: old value of instance data
  Description: This is function supports the message interface to set and get
               instance and default data.
**************************************************************************/
DWORD FAR PASCAL CstCtlData( HWND hWnd, UINT wMsg, WPARAM wParam,
        LPARAM lParam )
    {

    DWORD lOldValue = 0;
    switch ( wMsg )
        {
        case WM_CSTCTLGETDATA:
            switch ( LOBYTE( wParam ) )
                {
                case ID_LCOLOR:
                    lOldValue = CSTCTLGETCOLOR( hWnd, HIBYTE( wParam ) );
                    break;
```

Listing 4.6 *continued*

```
            case ID_HBITMAP:
                lOldValue = CSTCTLGETBITMAP( hWnd, HIBYTE( wParam ) );
                break;
            case ID_HBRUSH:
                lOldValue = CSTCTLGETBRUSH( hWnd, HIBYTE( wParam ) );
                break;
            case ID_HFONT:
                lOldValue = CSTCTLGETFONT( hWnd );
                break;
            case ID_HWND:
                lOldValue = CSTCTLGETWND( hWnd );
                break;
            case ID_IBKMODE:
                lOldValue = (DWORD)CSTCTLGETBKMODE( hWnd );
                break;
            case ID_IFRAME:
                lOldValue = (DWORD)CSTCTLGETFRAME( hWnd );
                break;
            case ID_ISHADOW:
                lOldValue = (DWORD)CSTCTLGETSHADOW( hWnd );
                break;
            case ID_RECTBITMAP:
                lOldValue = (DWORD)CSTCTLGETLPRECTBITMAP( hWnd );
                break;
            case ID_RECTTEXT:
                lOldValue = (DWORD)CSTCTLGETLPRECTTEXT( hWnd );
                break;
            case ID_WCTLCOLORMSG:
                lOldValue = CstCtlColorMsg( hWnd, 0 );
                break;
            case ID_WSTATE:
                lOldValue = CSTCTLGETSTATE( hWnd );
                break;
            case ID_WSTYLE:
                lOldValue = CSTCTLGETSTYLE( hWnd );
                break;
            case ID_LVALUE:
                lOldValue = (DWORD)CSTCTLGETVALUE( hWnd );
                break;
            default:
                break;
            }
        break;
    case WM_CSTCTLGETDEFDATA:
        switch ( LOBYTE( wParam ) )
            {
            case ID_LCOLOR:
                lOldValue = CSTCTLDEFGETCOLOR( hWnd, HIBYTE( wParam ) );
                break;
            case ID_HBITMAP:
                lOldValue = CSTCTLDEFGETBITMAP( hWnd, HIBYTE( wParam ) );
                break;
            case ID_HBRUSH:
                lOldValue = CSTCTLDEFGETBRUSH( hWnd, HIBYTE( wParam ) );
                break;
            case ID_HFONT:
                lOldValue = CSTCTLDEFGETFONT( hWnd );
                break;
```

Listing 4.6 *continued*

```
            case ID_HWND:
                lOldValue = CSTCTLDEFGETWND( hWnd );
                break;
            case ID_IBKMODE:
                lOldValue = (DWORD)CSTCTLDEFGETBKMODE( hWnd );
                break;
            case ID_IFRAME:
                lOldValue = (DWORD)CSTCTLDEFGETFRAME( hWnd );
                break;
            case ID_ISHADOW:
                lOldValue = (DWORD)CSTCTLDEFGETSHADOW( hWnd );
                break;
            case ID_WSTATE:
                lOldValue = CSTCTLDEFGETSTATE( hWnd );
                break;
            case ID_WSTYLE:
                lOldValue = CSTCTLDEFGETSTYLE( hWnd );
                break;
            case ID_LVALUE:
                lOldValue = (DWORD)CSTCTLDEFGETVALUE( hWnd );
                break;
            default:
                break;
            }
        break;
    case WM_CSTCTLSETDATA:
        switch ( LOBYTE( wParam ) )
            {
            case ID_LCOLOR:
                lOldValue = CstCtlSetColor( hWnd, HIBYTE( wParam ),
                        (COLORREF)lParam );
                break;
            case ID_HBITMAP:
                lOldValue = CstCtlSetBitmap( hWnd, HIBYTE( wParam ),
                        (HBITMAP)lParam );
                break;
            case ID_HBRUSH:
                lOldValue = CstCtlSetBrush( hWnd, HIBYTE( wParam ),
                        (HBRUSH)lParam );
                break;
            case ID_HFONT:
                lOldValue = CstCtlSetFont( hWnd, (HFONT)lParam );
                break;
            case ID_HWND:
                lOldValue = CstCtlSetWnd( hWnd, (HWND)lParam );
                break;
            case ID_IBKMODE:
                lOldValue = (DWORD)CstCtlSetBkMode( hWnd, (int)lParam );
                break;
            case ID_IFRAME:
                lOldValue = (DWORD)CstCtlSetFrame( hWnd, (int)lParam );
                break;
            case ID_ISHADOW:
                lOldValue = (DWORD)CstCtlSetShadow( hWnd, (int)lParam );
                break;
            case ID_WCTLCOLORMSG:
                lOldValue = CstCtlColorMsg( hWnd, (WORD)lParam );
                break;
```

Listing 4.6 *continued*

```c
            case ID_WSTATE:
                lOldValue = CstCtlSetState( hWnd, (WORD)lParam );
                break;
            case ID_WSTYLE:
                lOldValue = CstCtlSetStyle( hWnd, (WORD)lParam );
                break;
            case ID_LVALUE:
                lOldValue = (DWORD)CstCtlSetValue( hWnd, lParam );
                break;
            default:
                break;
        }
        break;
    case WM_CSTCTLSETDEFDATA:
        switch ( LOBYTE( wParam ) )
        {
            case ID_LCOLOR:
                lOldValue = CstCtlDefSetColor( hWnd, HIBYTE( wParam ),
                        (COLORREF)lParam );
                break;
            case ID_HBITMAP:
                lOldValue = CstCtlDefSetBitmap( hWnd, HIBYTE( wParam ),
                        (HBITMAP)lParam );
                break;
            case ID_HBRUSH:
                lOldValue = CstCtlDefSetBrush( hWnd, HIBYTE( wParam ),
                        (HBRUSH)lParam );
                break;
            case ID_HFONT:
                lOldValue = CstCtlDefSetFont( hWnd, (HFONT)lParam );
                break;
            case ID_HWND:
                lOldValue = CstCtlDefSetWnd( hWnd, (HWND)lParam );
                break;
            case ID_IBKMODE:
                lOldValue = (DWORD)CstCtlDefSetBkMode( hWnd, (int)lParam );
                break;
            case ID_IFRAME:
                lOldValue = (DWORD)CstCtlDefSetFrame( hWnd, (int)lParam );
                break;
            case ID_ISHADOW:
                lOldValue = (DWORD)CstCtlDefSetShadow( hWnd, (int)lParam );
                break;
            case ID_WSTATE:
                lOldValue = CstCtlDefSetState( hWnd, (WORD)lParam );
                break;
            case ID_WSTYLE:
                lOldValue = CstCtlDefSetStyle( hWnd, (WORD)lParam );
                break;
            case ID_LVALUE:
                lOldValue = (DWORD)CstCtlDefSetValue( hWnd, lParam );
                break;
            default:
                break;
        }
        break;
    default:
        break;
```

Listing 4.6 *continued*

```c
            }

        return ( lOldValue );

        }   /* function CstCtlData */


/*****************************************************************************
         Name: CstCtlDataCreate
   Parameters: hWnd - handle to custom control window
       Return: pointer to custom control instance data
  Description: Creates custom control instance data.  Copies the default data
               into the newly created instance data.
*****************************************************************************/
LPCSTCTLDATA FAR PASCAL CstCtlDataCreate( HWND hWnd )
    {

    HCSTCTLDATA  hCstCtlData;
    LPCSTCTLDATA lpCstCtlData = (LPCSTCTLDATA)0;

    hCstCtlData = GlobalAlloc( GMEM_FLAGS, sizeof ( CSTCTLDATA ) );
    if ( hCstCtlData )
        {
        lpCstCtlData = (LPCSTCTLDATA)GlobalLock( hCstCtlData );
        if ( lpCstCtlData )
            {

            LPCSTCTLDATA  lpCstCtlDefData;

            /* Set default information by copying from class data
            ** to the window data */
            lpCstCtlDefData = CSTCTLDEFGETLPDATA( hWnd );
            if ( lpCstCtlDefData )
                {
                *lpCstCtlData = *lpCstCtlDefData;
                }
            CSTSETWINDOWWORD( hWnd, GWW_HCSTCTLDATA, hCstCtlData );
            CSTSETWINDOWLONG( hWnd, GWL_LPCSTCTLDATA, (LONG)lpCstCtlData );
            }
        else
            {
            /* Failed to lock memory */
            GlobalFree( hCstCtlData );
            }
        }

    return ( lpCstCtlData );

    }   /* function CstCtlDataCreate */


/*****************************************************************************
         Name: CstCtlDataDelete
   Parameters: hWnd - handle to custom control window
       Return: handle to custom control instance data (NULL if deleted)
  Description: Deletes (frees) the instance data.
*****************************************************************************/
HCSTCTLDATA FAR PASCAL CstCtlDataDelete( HWND hWnd )
```

Listing 4.6 *continued*

```
    {
    HCSTCTLDATA hCstCtlData;

    hCstCtlData = (HCSTCTLDATA)CSTGETWINDOWWORD( hWnd, GWW_HCSTCTLDATA );
    GlobalUnlock( hCstCtlData );
    hCstCtlData = (HCSTCTLDATA)GlobalFree( hCstCtlData );
    if ( !hCstCtlData )
        {
        CSTSETWINDOWWORD( hWnd, GWW_HCSTCTLDATA, 0 );
        CSTSETWINDOWLONG( hWnd, GWL_LPCSTCTLDATA, 0L );
        }

    return ( hCstCtlData );

    }   /* function CstCtlDataDelete */


/*******************************************************************************
        Name: CstCtlDefDataCreate
  Parameters: hWnd - handle to custom control window
      Return: pointer to custom control class default data
 Description: Creates custom control class default data.
*******************************************************************************/
LPCSTCTLDATA FAR PASCAL CstCtlDefDataCreate( HWND hWnd )
    {

    HCSTCTLDATA  hCstCtlData;
    LPCSTCTLDATA lpCstCtlData = (LPCSTCTLDATA)0;

    hCstCtlData = GlobalAlloc( GMEM_FLAGS, sizeof ( CSTCTLDATA ) );
    if ( !hCstCtlData )
        {
        /* Failed to allocate memory */
        return ( (LPCSTCTLDATA)0 );
        }

    lpCstCtlData = (LPCSTCTLDATA)GlobalLock( hCstCtlData );
    if ( !lpCstCtlData )
        {
        /* Failed to lock memory */
        GlobalFree( hCstCtlData );
        return ( (LPCSTCTLDATA)0 );
        }

    /* Set the class bytes */
    CSTSETCLASSWORD( hWnd, GCW_HCSTCTLDATA, hCstCtlData );
    CSTSETCLASSLONG( hWnd, GCL_LPCSTCTLDATA, (LONG)lpCstCtlData );

    /* Load the default colors */
    lpCstCtlData->lColor[CC_COLOR_BACKGROUND] = (COLORREF)
            GetSysColor( COLOR_WINDOW );
    lpCstCtlData->lColor[CC_COLOR_BTNFACE] = (COLORREF)
            GetSysColor( COLOR_BTNFACE );
#if defined ( COLOR_BTNHIGHLIGHT )
    lpCstCtlData->lColor[CC_COLOR_3DLIGHT] = (COLORREF)
            GetSysColor( COLOR_BTNHIGHLIGHT );
#else
```

Listing 4.6 *continued*

```c
        lpCstCtlData->lColor[CC_COLOR_3DLIGHT] = (COLORREF)
                RGB( 255, 255, 255 );
    #endif
        lpCstCtlData->lColor[CC_COLOR_3DSHADOW] = (COLORREF)
                GetSysColor( COLOR_BTNSHADOW );
        lpCstCtlData->lColor[CC_COLOR_FRAME] = (COLORREF)
                GetSysColor( COLOR_WINDOWFRAME );
        lpCstCtlData->lColor[CC_COLOR_TEXT] = (COLORREF)
                GetSysColor( COLOR_WINDOWTEXT );
        lpCstCtlData->lColor[CC_COLOR_TEXTBACKGROUND] = (COLORREF)
                GetSysColor( COLOR_BTNFACE );
        lpCstCtlData->lColor[CC_COLOR_GRAYTEXT] = (COLORREF)
                GetSysColor( COLOR_GRAYTEXT );

        /* Load the default brushes */
        lpCstCtlData->hBrush[CC_BRUSH_BACKGROUND] = CreateSolidBrush(
                lpCstCtlData->lColor[CC_COLOR_BACKGROUND] );
        lpCstCtlData->hBrush[CC_BRUSH_BTNFACE] = CreateSolidBrush(
                lpCstCtlData->lColor[CC_COLOR_BTNFACE] );
        lpCstCtlData->hBrush[CC_BRUSH_3DLIGHT] = CreateSolidBrush(
                lpCstCtlData->lColor[CC_COLOR_3DLIGHT] );
        lpCstCtlData->hBrush[CC_BRUSH_3DSHADOW] = CreateSolidBrush(
                lpCstCtlData->lColor[CC_COLOR_3DSHADOW] );
        lpCstCtlData->hBrush[CC_BRUSH_FRAME] = CreateSolidBrush(
                lpCstCtlData->lColor[CC_COLOR_FRAME] );

        /* Set default information */
        lpCstCtlData->iBkMode = TRANSPARENT;
        lpCstCtlData->iFrame = CC_FRAME;
        lpCstCtlData->iShadow = CC_SHADOW;

        return ( lpCstCtlData );

        }   /* function CstCtlDefDataCreate */


/*****************************************************************************
          Name: CstCtlDefGet*
    Parameters: hWnd - handle to custom control window
        Return: single data item from CSTCTLDATA structure
   Description: The CstCtlDefGet* functions are a function interface used to
                retrieve default class data.
*****************************************************************************/
HBITMAP FAR PASCAL CstCtlDefGetBitmap( HWND hWnd, WORD wBitmapId )
    {
    return ( CSTCTLDEFGETBITMAP( hWnd, wBitmapId ) );
    }   /* function CstCtlDefGetBitmap */


int FAR PASCAL CstCtlDefGetBkMode( HWND hWnd )
    {
    return ( CSTCTLDEFGETBKMODE( hWnd ) );
    }   /* function CstCtlDefGetBrush */


HBRUSH FAR PASCAL CstCtlDefGetBrush( HWND hWnd, WORD wBrushId )
    {
    return ( CSTCTLDEFGETBRUSH( hWnd, wBrushId ) );
```

Listing 4.6 *continued*

```c
    }   /* function CstCtlDefGetBrush */


COLORREF FAR PASCAL CstCtlDefGetColor( HWND hWnd, WORD wColorId )
    {
    return ( CSTCTLDEFGETCOLOR( hWnd, wColorId ) );
    }   /* function CstCtlDefGetColor */


int FAR PASCAL CstCtlDefGetFrame( HWND hWnd )
    {
    return ( CSTCTLDEFGETFRAME( hWnd ) );
    }   /* function CstCtlDefGetFrame */


HFONT FAR PASCAL CstCtlDefGetFont( HWND hWnd )
    {
    return ( CSTCTLDEFGETFONT( hWnd ) );
    }   /* function CstCtlDefGetFont */


LPCSTCTLDATA FAR PASCAL CstCtlDefGetLpData( HWND hWnd )
    {
    return ( CSTCTLDEFGETLPDATA( hWnd ) );
    }   /* function CstCtlDefGetLpData */


int FAR PASCAL CstCtlDefGetShadow( HWND hWnd )
    {
    return ( CSTCTLDEFGETSHADOW( hWnd ) );
    }   /* function CstCtlDefGetShadow */


WORD FAR PASCAL CstCtlDefGetState( HWND hWnd )
    {
    return ( CSTCTLDEFGETSTATE( hWnd ) );
    }   /* function CstCtlDefGetState */


WORD FAR PASCAL CstCtlDefGetStyle( HWND hWnd )
    {
    return ( CSTCTLDEFGETSTYLE( hWnd ) );
    }   /* function CstCtlDefGetStyle */


LONG FAR PASCAL CstCtlDefGetValue( HWND hWnd )
    {
    return ( CSTCTLDEFGETVALUE( hWnd ) );
    }   /* function CstCtlDefGetValue */


HWND FAR PASCAL CstCtlDefGetWnd( HWND hWnd )
    {
    return ( CSTCTLDEFGETWND( hWnd ) );
    }   /* function CstCtlDefGetWnd */
```

Listing 4.6 *continued*

```
/*****************************************************************************
         Name: CstCtlDefSet*
   Parameters: hWnd - handle to custom control window
               *Id - index id  required for array access of certain data
               * - data value to set
       Return: old data value
  Description: The CstCtlDefSet* functions are a function interface used to set
               values of default class data.
*****************************************************************************/
HBITMAP FAR PASCAL CstCtlDefSetBitmap( HWND hWnd, WORD wBitmapId,
        HBITMAP hBitmap )
    {

    HBITMAP hBitmapOld;
    LPCSTCTLDATA lpCstCtlDefData = CSTCTLDEFGETLPDATA( hWnd );

    hBitmapOld = lpCstCtlDefData->hBitmap[wBitmapId];
    lpCstCtlDefData->hBitmap[wBitmapId] = hBitmap;

    return ( hBitmapOld );

    }   /* function CstCtlDefSetBitmap */


int FAR PASCAL CstCtlDefSetBkMode( HWND hWnd, int iBkMode )
    {

    int iBkModeOld;
    LPCSTCTLDATA lpCstCtlDefData = CSTCTLDEFGETLPDATA( hWnd );

    iBkModeOld = lpCstCtlDefData->iBkMode;
    lpCstCtlDefData->iBkMode = iBkMode;

    return ( iBkModeOld );

    }   /* function CstCtlDefSetBkMode */


HBRUSH FAR PASCAL CstCtlDefSetBrush( HWND hWnd, WORD wBrushId,
        HBRUSH hBrush )
    {

    HBRUSH hBrushOld;
    LPCSTCTLDATA lpCstCtlDefData = CSTCTLDEFGETLPDATA( hWnd );

    hBrushOld = lpCstCtlDefData->hBrush[wBrushId];
    lpCstCtlDefData->hBrush[wBrushId] = hBrush;

    return ( hBrushOld );

    }   /* function CstCtlDefSetBrush */


COLORREF FAR PASCAL CstCtlDefSetColor( HWND hWnd, WORD wColorId,
        COLORREF lColor )
    {

    COLORREF lColorOld;
```

Listing 4.6 continued

```
        LPCSTCTLDATA lpCstCtlDefData = CSTCTLDEFGETLPDATA( hWnd );

        lColorOld = lpCstCtlDefData->lColor[wColorId];
        lpCstCtlDefData->lColor[wColorId] = lColor;

        return ( lColorOld );

        }   /* function CstCtlDefSetColor */

int FAR PASCAL CstCtlDefSetFrame( HWND hWnd, int iFrame )
    {
    int iFrameOld;
    LPCSTCTLDATA lpCstCtlDefData = CSTCTLDEFGETLPDATA( hWnd );

    iFrameOld = lpCstCtlDefData->iFrame;
    lpCstCtlDefData->iFrame = iFrame;

    return ( iFrameOld );

    }   /* function CstCtlDefSetFrame */

HFONT FAR PASCAL CstCtlDefSetFont( HWND hWnd, HFONT hFont )
    {
    HFONT hFontOld;
    LPCSTCTLDATA lpCstCtlDefData = CSTCTLDEFGETLPDATA( hWnd );

    hFontOld = lpCstCtlDefData->hFont;
    lpCstCtlDefData->hFont = hFont;

    return ( hFontOld );

    }   /* function CstCtlDefSetFont */

int FAR PASCAL CstCtlDefSetShadow( HWND hWnd, int iShadow )
    {
    int iShadowOld;
    LPCSTCTLDATA lpCstCtlDefData = CSTCTLDEFGETLPDATA( hWnd );

    iShadowOld = lpCstCtlDefData->iShadow;
    lpCstCtlDefData->iShadow = iShadow;

    return ( iShadowOld );

    }   /* function CstCtlDefSetShadow */

WORD FAR PASCAL CstCtlDefSetState( HWND hWnd, WORD wState )
    {
    WORD wStateOld;
    LPCSTCTLDATA lpCstCtlDefData = CSTCTLDEFGETLPDATA( hWnd );
```

Listing 4.6 *continued*

```
    wStateOld = lpCstCtlDefData->wState;
    lpCstCtlDefData->wState = wState;

    return ( wStateOld );

    }   /* function CstCtlDefSetState */


WORD FAR PASCAL CstCtlDefSetStyle( HWND hWnd, WORD wStyle )
    {

    WORD wStyleOld;
    LPCSTCTLDATA lpCstCtlDefData = CSTCTLDEFGETLPDATA( hWnd );

    wStyleOld = lpCstCtlDefData->wStyle;
    lpCstCtlDefData->wStyle = wStyle;

    return ( wStyleOld );

    }   /* function CstCtlDefSetStyle */


LONG FAR PASCAL CstCtlDefSetValue( HWND hWnd, LONG lValue )
    {

    LONG lValueOld;
    LPCSTCTLDATA lpCstCtlDefData = CSTCTLDEFGETLPDATA( hWnd );

    lValueOld = lpCstCtlDefData->lValue;
    lpCstCtlDefData->lValue = lValue;

    return ( lValueOld );

    }   /* function CstCtlSetDefValue */


HWND FAR PASCAL CstCtlDefSetWnd( HWND hWnd, HWND hWndSet )
    {

    HWND hWndOld;
    LPCSTCTLDATA lpCstCtlDefData = CSTCTLDEFGETLPDATA( hWnd );

    hWndOld = lpCstCtlDefData->hWnd;
    lpCstCtlDefData->hWnd = hWndSet;

    return ( hWndOld );

    }   /* function CstCtlDefSetWnd */


/****************************************************************************
          Name: CstCtlGet*
    Parameters: hWnd - handle to custom control window
        Return: single data item from CSTCTLDATA structure
   Description: The CstCtlGet* functions are a function interface used to
                retrieve instance data.
****************************************************************************/
HBITMAP FAR PASCAL CstCtlGetBitmap( HWND hWnd, WORD wBitmapId )
```

Listing 4.6 *continued*

```
    {
    return ( CSTCTLGETBITMAP( hWnd, wBitmapId ) );
    }   /* function CstCtlGetBitmap */


int FAR PASCAL CstCtlGetBkMode( HWND hWnd )
    {
    return ( CSTCTLGETBKMODE( hWnd ) );
    }   /* function CstCtlGetBrush */


HBRUSH FAR PASCAL CstCtlGetBrush( HWND hWnd, WORD wBrushId )
    {
    return ( CSTCTLGETBRUSH( hWnd, wBrushId ) );
    }   /* function CstCtlGetBrush */


COLORREF FAR PASCAL CstCtlGetColor( HWND hWnd, WORD wColorId )
    {
    return ( CSTCTLGETCOLOR( hWnd, wColorId ) );
    }   /* function CstCtlGetColor */


int FAR PASCAL CstCtlGetFrame( HWND hWnd )
    {
    return ( CSTCTLGETFRAME( hWnd ) );
    }   /* function CstCtlGetFrame */


HFONT FAR PASCAL CstCtlGetFont( HWND hWnd )
    {
    return ( CSTCTLGETFONT( hWnd ) );
    }   /* function CstCtlGetFont */


LPCSTCTLDATA FAR PASCAL CstCtlGetLpData( HWND hWnd )
    {
    return ( CSTCTLGETLPDATA( hWnd ) );
    }   /* function CstCtlGetLpData */


LPRECT FAR PASCAL CstCtlGetLpRectBitmap( HWND hWnd )
    {
    return ( CSTCTLGETLPRECTBITMAP( hWnd ) );
    }   /* function CstCtlGetLpRectBitmap */


LPRECT FAR PASCAL CstCtlGetLpRectText( HWND hWnd )
    {
    return ( CSTCTLGETLPRECTTEXT( hWnd ) );
    }   /* function CstCtlGetLpRectText */


int FAR PASCAL CstCtlGetShadow( HWND hWnd )
    {
    return ( CSTCTLGETSHADOW( hWnd ) );
    }   /* function CstCtlGetShadow */
```

Listing 4.6 *continued*

```c
WORD FAR PASCAL CstCtlGetState( HWND hWnd )
    {
    return ( CSTCTLGETSTATE( hWnd ) );
    }   /* function CstCtlGetState */


WORD FAR PASCAL CstCtlGetStyle( HWND hWnd )
    {
    return ( CSTCTLGETSTYLE( hWnd ) );
    }   /* function CstCtlGetStyle */


LONG FAR PASCAL CstCtlGetValue( HWND hWnd )
    {
    return ( CSTCTLGETVALUE( hWnd ) );
    }   /* function CstCtlGetValue */


HWND FAR PASCAL CstCtlGetWnd( HWND hWnd )
    {
    return ( CSTCTLGETWND( hWnd ) );
    }   /* function CstCtlGetWnd */


/*****************************************************************************
         Name: CstCtlSet*
   Parameters: hWnd - handle to custom control window
               *Id - index id  required for array access of certain data
               *   - data value to set
       Return: old data value
  Description: The CstCtlSet* functions are a function interface used to set
               values of instance data.
*****************************************************************************/
HBITMAP FAR PASCAL CstCtlSetBitmap( HWND hWnd, WORD wBitmapId,
        HBITMAP hBitmap )
    {

    HBITMAP hBitmapOld;
    LPCSTCTLDATA lpCstCtlData = CSTCTLGETLPDATA( hWnd );

    hBitmapOld = lpCstCtlData->hBitmap[wBitmapId];
    lpCstCtlData->hBitmap[wBitmapId] = hBitmap;

    return ( hBitmapOld );

    }   /* function CstCtlSetBitmap */


int FAR PASCAL CstCtlSetBkMode( HWND hWnd, int iBkMode )
    {

    int iBkModeOld;
    LPCSTCTLDATA lpCstCtlData = CSTCTLGETLPDATA( hWnd );

    iBkModeOld = lpCstCtlData->iBkMode;
    lpCstCtlData->iBkMode = iBkMode;
```

Listing 4.6 *continued*

```c
    return ( iBkModeOld );

    }   /* function CstCtlSetBkMode */


HBRUSH FAR PASCAL CstCtlSetBrush( HWND hWnd, WORD wBrushId,
        HBRUSH hBrush )
    {
    HBRUSH hBrushOld;
    LPCSTCTLDATA lpCstCtlData = CSTCTLGETLPDATA( hWnd );

    hBrushOld = lpCstCtlData->hBrush[wBrushId];
    lpCstCtlData->hBrush[wBrushId] = hBrush;

    return ( hBrushOld );

    }   /* function CstCtlSetBrush */


COLORREF FAR PASCAL CstCtlSetColor( HWND hWnd, WORD wColorId,
        COLORREF lColor )
    {
    COLORREF lColorOld;
    LPCSTCTLDATA lpCstCtlData = CSTCTLGETLPDATA( hWnd );

    lColorOld = lpCstCtlData->lColor[wColorId];
    lpCstCtlData->lColor[wColorId] = lColor;

    return ( lColorOld );

    }   /* function CstCtlSetColor */


int FAR PASCAL CstCtlSetFrame( HWND hWnd, int iFrame )
    {
    int iFrameOld;
    LPCSTCTLDATA lpCstCtlData = CSTCTLGETLPDATA( hWnd );

    iFrameOld = lpCstCtlData->iFrame;
    lpCstCtlData->iFrame = iFrame;

    return ( iFrameOld );

    }   /* function CstCtlSetFrame */


HFONT FAR PASCAL CstCtlSetFont( HWND hWnd, HFONT hFont )
    {
    HFONT hFontOld;
    LPCSTCTLDATA lpCstCtlData = CSTCTLGETLPDATA( hWnd );

    hFontOld = lpCstCtlData->hFont;
    lpCstCtlData->hFont = hFont;
```

Listing 4.6 *continued*

```
    return ( hFontOld );

    }   /* function CstCtlSetFont */


/********************************************************************
       Name: CstCtlSetRects
 Parameters: hWnd - window handle to custom control
             hBitmap - bitmap associated with custom control
             lpRectClient - pointer to custom control client rect
             lpRectBitmap - pointer to custom control bitmap area rect
             lpRectText - pointer to custom control text area rect
 Description: Calculates the rectangles for the bitmap and the text areas
              of a custom control that has the text outside the bitmap.
********************************************************************/
void FAR PASCAL CstCtlSetRects( HWND hWnd, HBITMAP hBitmap,
        LPRECT lpRectClient, LPRECT lpRectBitmap, LPRECT lpRectText )
    {

    BITMAP Bitmap;

    GetObject( hBitmap, sizeof ( BITMAP ), (LPSTR)&Bitmap );

    /* Set left and right extents */
    if ( GetWindowLong( hWnd, GWL_STYLE ) & BS_LEFTTEXT )
        {
        /* Text is on the Left */
        lpRectBitmap->right = lpRectClient->right;
        lpRectBitmap->left = lpRectBitmap->right - Bitmap.bmWidth;
        lpRectText->right = lpRectBitmap->left - CC_BITMAP_TEXT_SPACE;
        lpRectText->left = lpRectClient->left + 2;
        }
    else
        {
        /* Text is on the right */
        lpRectBitmap->left = lpRectClient->left;
        lpRectBitmap->right = lpRectBitmap->left + Bitmap.bmWidth;
        lpRectText->left = lpRectBitmap->right + CC_BITMAP_TEXT_SPACE;
        lpRectText->right = lpRectClient->right;
        }

    /* Set the top and bottom extents */
    lpRectBitmap->top = max( lpRectClient->top,
            ( ( lpRectClient->bottom - lpRectClient->top )
            - Bitmap.bmHeight ) / 2 );
    lpRectBitmap->bottom = lpRectBitmap->top + Bitmap.bmHeight;
    lpRectText->top = lpRectClient->top;
    lpRectText->bottom = lpRectClient->bottom;

    }   /* function CstCtlSetRects */


int FAR PASCAL CstCtlSetShadow( HWND hWnd, int iShadow )
    {

    int iShadowOld;
    LPCSTCTLDATA lpCstCtlData = CSTCTLGETLPDATA( hWnd );
```

Listing 4.6 *continued*

```
        iShadowOld = lpCstCtlData->iShadow;
        lpCstCtlData->iShadow = iShadow;

        return ( iShadowOld );

        }   /* function CstCtlSetShadow */


WORD FAR PASCAL CstCtlSetState( HWND hWnd, WORD wState )
        {

        WORD wStateOld;
        LPCSTCTLDATA lpCstCtlData = CSTCTLGETLPDATA( hWnd );

        wStateOld = lpCstCtlData->wState;
        lpCstCtlData->wState = wState;

        return ( wStateOld );

        }   /* function CstCtlSetState */


WORD FAR PASCAL CstCtlSetStyle( HWND hWnd, WORD wStyle )
        {

        WORD wStyleOld;
        LPCSTCTLDATA lpCstCtlData = CSTCTLGETLPDATA( hWnd );

        wStyleOld = lpCstCtlData->wStyle;
        lpCstCtlData->wStyle = wStyle;

        return ( wStyleOld );

        }   /* function CstCtlSetStyle */


LONG FAR PASCAL CstCtlSetValue( HWND hWnd, LONG lValue )
        {

        LONG lValueOld;
        LPCSTCTLDATA lpCstCtlData = CSTCTLGETLPDATA( hWnd );

        lValueOld = lpCstCtlData->lValue;
        lpCstCtlData->lValue = lValue;

        return ( lValueOld );

        }   /* function CstCtlSetValue */


HWND FAR PASCAL CstCtlSetWnd( HWND hWnd, HWND hWndSet )
        {

        HWND hWndOld;
        LPCSTCTLDATA lpCstCtlData = CSTCTLGETLPDATA( hWnd );

        hWndOld = lpCstCtlData->hWnd;
        lpCstCtlData->hWnd = hWndSet;
```

Listing 4.6 continued

```
    return ( hWndOld );

    }   /* function CstCtlSetWnd */


/****************************************************************************
        Name: CstCtlState
  Parameters: hWnd - handle to custom control window
              wState - bit flags of new state to set or reset
              wStateMode - controls whether to set, get, reset or check
              wArea - controls the area of the window to invalidate
      Return: result of the mode operation
 Description: The state bit flags are set, reset, checked or just obtained.
              For operations set and reset, the control is invalidated for
              repainting.  The area to repaint is controlled by the wArea
              parameter.  It is either 0 (AREA_NONE) for no repainting,
              AREA_TEXT for text rectangle only, AREA_BITMAP for bitmap
              rectangle only or AREA_ALL for both bitmap and text rects.
****************************************************************************/
WORD FAR PASCAL CstCtlState( HWND hWnd, WORD wState,
        WORD wStateMode, WORD wArea )
    {

    WORD wCurrState, wPrevState;

    /* Get the state from the instance data */
    wPrevState = CSTCTLGETSTATE( hWnd );

    /* Set or Reset the state bits */
    switch ( wStateMode )
        {
        case STATE_CHECK:
            return ( (WORD)( wPrevState & wState ) );
        case STATE_GET:
            return ( wPrevState );
        case STATE_RESET:
            wCurrState = (WORD)( wPrevState & ~wState );
            break;
        case STATE_SET:
            wCurrState = (WORD)( wPrevState | wState );
            break;
        default:
            return ( FALSE );
        }

    /* Set the state in the instance data */
    CstCtlSetState( hWnd, wCurrState );

    if ( wPrevState != wCurrState )
        {

        LPRECT lpRect = NULL;

        /* If the state has changed repaint the window */
        if ( wArea == AREA_TEXT )
            {
            lpRect = CSTCTLGETLPRECTTEXT( hWnd );
```

Listing 4.6 *continued*

```
            }
        else if ( wArea == AREA_BITMAP )
            {
            lpRect = CSTCTLGETLPRECTBITMAP( hWnd );
            }
        if ( wArea )
            {
            InvalidateRect( hWnd, lpRect, FALSE );
            UpdateWindow( hWnd );
            }

    }   /* if wPrevState */

    return ( wCurrState );

    }   /* function CstCtlState */

/* End of CST_DATA.C */
```

Listing 4.7

```
/*****************************************************************************
        File Name: CST_UTIL.H
    Expanded Name: Custom Control Utilities
      Description: Include file for CST_UTIL.H
      Portability: Microsoft Windows 3.X
*****************************************************************************/

#if !defined ( CST_UTIL_DEFINED )
    #define CST_UTIL_DEFINED

    /* Prototypes for functions in CST_UTIL.C */
    void PASCAL AlignBrush( HWND hWnd, HDC hDC, HBRUSH hBrush );
    BOOL PASCAL PtInWnd( HWND hWnd, POINT Point );
    void PASCAL ResetBrushFix( HDC hDC );

    /* Exported functions */
    BOOL FAR PASCAL SafeDeleteObject( HANDLE hObject );

#endif

/* End of CST_UTIL.H */
```

Listing 4.8

```
/*****************************************************************************
          File Name: CST_UTIL.C
      Expanded Name: Custom Control Utilities
        Description: Library of general utility functions for custom controls
Global Function List: AlignBrush
                     PtInWnd
                     ResetBrushFix
                     SafeDeleteObject
        Portability: Microsoft Windows 3.X
*****************************************************************************/

/* Microsoft Windows */
#include <windows.h>

/* Own */
#include <cst_util.h>

/*****************************************************************************
       Name: AlignBrush
 Parameters: hWnd - handle of window to align brush with origin
             hDC - device context to set new origin
             hBrush - brush to align
Description: The origin for hBrush in hDc is set to the origin of the hWnd
*****************************************************************************/
void PASCAL AlignBrush( HWND hWnd, HDC hDC, HBRUSH hBrush )
    {

    POINT Point;

    Point.x = Point.y = 0;
    UnrealizeObject( hBrush );
    ClientToScreen( hWnd, &Point );
    SetBrushOrg( hDC, Point.x, Point.y );

    }   /* function AlignBrush */


/*****************************************************************************
         Name: PtInWnd
Expanded Name: Point In Window
   Parameters: hWnd - handle to window
               Point - location to check
       Return: nonzero if point is within window, otherwise it is zero
  Description: Determines if a point lies within a window's client area.
*****************************************************************************/
BOOL PASCAL PtInWnd( HWND hWnd, POINT Point )
    {

    RECT Rect;

    GetClientRect( hWnd, &Rect );
    return ( PtInRect( &Rect, Point ) );

    }   /* function PtInWnd */
```

Listing 4.8 *continued*

```
/****************************************************************
       Name: ResetBrushFix
  Parameters: hDC - handle to device context
  Description: This function should be called after a window is moved and it
               is desired to set a new brush origin of the DC after the move.
               This is a fix to a new feature (or bug) in Windows version 3.1.
               Unless this function is called, the origin can not be reset.
****************************************************************/
void PASCAL ResetBrushFix( HDC hDC )
    {

    HBRUSH hBrush;
    HBRUSH hBrushOrg;

    hBrush = CreateSolidBrush( GetSysColor( COLOR_WINDOW ) );
    hBrushOrg = SelectObject( hDC, hBrush );
    SelectObject( hDC, hBrushOrg );
    DeleteObject( hBrush );

    }   /* function ResetBrushFix */


/****************************************************************
       Name: SafeDeleteObject
  Parameters: hObject - handle to resource object
  Description: Safe version of DeleteObject.  It checks to make sure the
               handle to an object is valid before DeleteObject is called.
****************************************************************/
BOOL FAR PASCAL SafeDeleteObject( HANDLE hObject )
    {

    if ( hObject )
        {

        #if ( WINVER >= 0x030a )
        WORD wVer = (WORD)GetVersion();

        if ( HIBYTE( wVer ) )
            {
            if ( IsGDIObject( hObject ) )
                {
                return ( DeleteObject( hObject ) );
                }
            }
        #endif

        return ( DeleteObject( hObject ) );

        }   /* if hObject */

    return ( FALSE );

    }   /* function SafeDeleteObject */

/* End of CST_UTIL.C */
```

# Static Controls

This chapter presents the design and implementation of a custom static control. Because static controls involve only output, they are the simplest to build and explain. Though simple, the static control still uses the same basic structure and still involves the same essential design tasks as its more complex relatives. Thus, the static control makes an excellent starting point for exploring the intricacies of custom controls.

The first part of this chapter will explain the design of the user interface, and the style, data, function, and message portions of the programmer's interface. The later sections of the chapter highlight important coding and implementation details.

The User Interface

Our goal is to create a custom control that behaves just like Windows' standard *STATIC* control, but that gives the programmer much more control over its appearance.

The standard *STATIC* control supports four fundamental styles: frames, icons, rectangles and text (see Figure 5.1). Additionally, frame and rectangle style controls may be drawn in any of the three system colors, normally referred to as black, white, or gray (even though, depending upon the system configuration, these colors might not be displayed as black, white or gray).

While at first, the standard static control seems quite flexible, in practice, it does not give the developer enough control over appearance to satisfy current user expectations for impressive graphics and pleasing aesthetics. The custom control, *CSTSTATIC*, will be "dressier" than the standard control and will add fundamental styles not available in the standard control.

To dress up the appearance of static objects, the *CSTSTATIC* control will add 3-D effects, making individual objects appear raised or lowered with respect to the background. *CSTSTATIC* will accomplish these 3-D effects by drawing frames around objects using highlights and shadows.

Like the standard *STATIC* control, the *CSTSTATIC* will display text, icons, frames, and rectangles, but the custom control will add two new fundamental styles: bitmaps and lines. The line style, together with the frame and rectangle styles, gives the developer a reasonably complete set of drawing primitives. The bitmap style will allow the programmer to specify a bitmap using a protocol that parallels the standard control's method for displaying an icon.

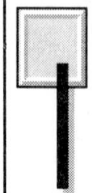

Figure 5.1

These constants from WINDOWS.H set the mapping for the standard static control's style interface.

```
/* Static Control Styles */
#define SS_LEFT             0x00000000L
#define SS_CENTER           0x00000001L
#define SS_RIGHT            0x00000002L
#define SS_ICON             0x00000003L
#define SS_BLACKRECT        0x00000004L
#define SS_GRAYRECT         0x00000005L
#define SS_WHITERECT        0x00000006L
#define SS_BLACKFRAME       0x00000007L
#define SS_GRAYFRAME        0x00000008L
#define SS_WHITEFRAME       0x00000009L
#define SS_SIMPLE           0x0000000BL
#define SS_LEFTNOWORDWRAP   0x0000000CL
#define SS_NOPREFIX         0x00000080L
```

To summarize, the general design specifications for the *CSTSTATIC* control consist of adding a fundamental bitmap style, adding a line style, and dressing up the appearance of the standard frame, icon, rectangle and text styles with 3-D effects.

The Style Interface

This additional functionality will require class specific styles beyond those available in the standard *STATIC* definition. *CSTSTATIC* will need to recognize nine more fundamental and mutually exclusive styles than *STATIC*. Moreover, *CSTSTATIC* will need to expand the supplemental styles to include meaningful options for the new fundamental styles, and to enhance some of the existing fundamental styles. In addition to the existing style controls for color and text handling, the new style interface will support independent vertical and horizontal alignment of text and expansion of text. The new interface will also add styles to control 3-D effects (flat, raised, and lowered) and to specify whether a border is wanted. Table 5.1 summarizes the styles needed for this design. Tables 5.2 and 5.3 detail the behavior associated with each style.

Table 5.1 assigns each of the new styles to one of six groups, based on function. The first group controls the fundamental style or type. The styles in this group are all mutually exclusive. The remaining groups are all supplemental styles. The second group controls the 3-D appearance of the control. The third group specifies whether a border will be drawn around the control. The fourth and fifth groups control the position of the control in the horizontal and vertical directions, respectively. The sixth group contains styles that apply to text objects only.

This design uses a formidable number of styles. The interface is complicated enough that one might be tempted to break it up into several separate custom controls, in keeping with the "single purpose" design goal. Each separate control would support a single fundamental style such as bitmap or text. We've chosen to use a single combined control, because the separate controls would generate lots of redundant code — as you will see when we develop separate control classes for each of the next chapter's button types.

Having decided upon a set of style controls, we are prepared to decide whether to implement the styles by adding to the predefined styles of the standard *STATIC* class, or by designing an entirely new set of class specific styles. The appropriate decision will depend entirely upon how the existing set of styles are coded. If there are enough unused coding options in the existing scheme that you can find sensible and usable codes for the new options, then you can implement the new styles as additions to the existing class. If the existing scheme doesn't leave enough codes

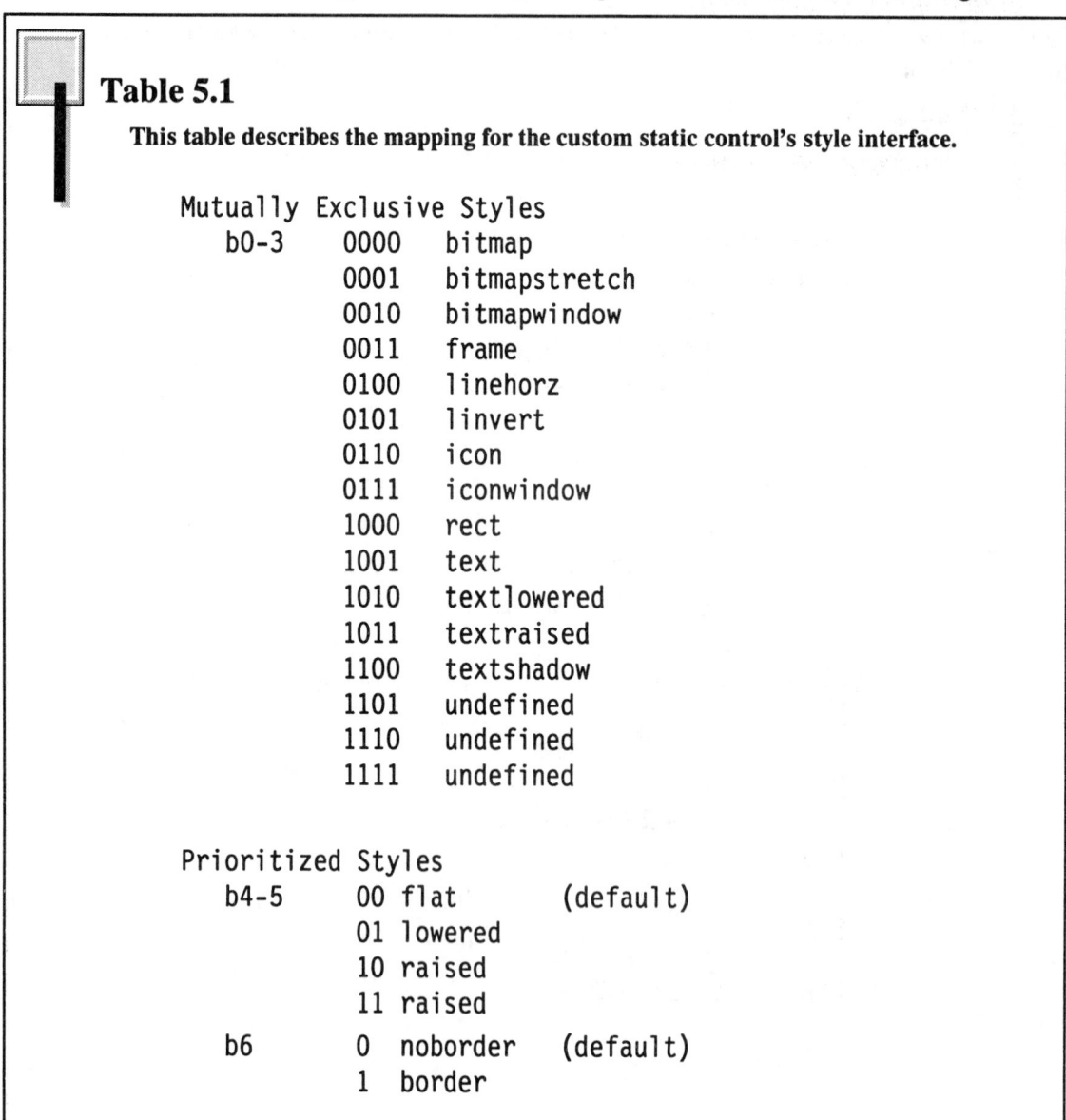

Table 5.1

This table describes the mapping for the custom static control's style interface.

```
Mutually Exclusive Styles
    b0-3    0000   bitmap
            0001   bitmapstretch
            0010   bitmapwindow
            0011   frame
            0100   linehorz
            0101   linvert
            0110   icon
            0111   iconwindow
            1000   rect
            1001   text
            1010   textlowered
            1011   textraised
            1100   textshadow
            1101   undefined
            1110   undefined
            1111   undefined

Prioritized Styles
    b4-5    00 flat        (default)
            01 lowered
            10 raised
            11 raised
    b6      0  noborder    (default)
            1  border
```

Static Controls

unused, or if the structure of the existing scheme doesn't make sense for the new design, then you should start from scratch and design a new set of class-specific style codings.

Figure 5.2 shows the relationship between the existing *STATIC* styles and the new set of styles. The standard *STATIC* styles are implemented as 12 mutually exclusive styles and one combinable style. As the figure

(Text resumes on page 102.)

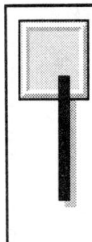

Table 5.1

Continued from facing page.

```
Vertical Position Controls
    b7,b10   00 vert. top
             01 vert. bottom
             10 vert. center
             11 vert. center

Horizontal Position Controls
    b8-9     00 left
             01 center
             10 right
             11 right

Combinable styles
    b11      0
             1 singleline
    b12      0
             1 leftnowordwrap
    b13      0
             1 noprefix
    b14      0
             1 expand tabs
    b15      undefined
```

Table 5.2

This table explains what behavior is associated with each of the fundamental styles of the custom static control.

CSS_BITMAP

This is a mutually exclusive style that displays a bitmap. The supplemental 3-D appearance, vertical position, horizontal position, and border styles, modify the appearance of the enclosing window, and the position of the bitmap within the window. The control loads the bitmap from the resource named in the window text.

CSS_BITMAPSTRETCH

This is the same as *CSS_BITMAP* except the bitmap is stretched to fill the window size. The position styles are meaningless for the *CSS_BITMAPSTRETCH* style.

CSS_BITMAPWINDOW

This is the same as *CSS_BITMAP* except the window is resized to match the size of the bitmap. The position styles are meaningless for the *CSS_BITMAPWINDOW* style.

CSS_FRAME

This is a mutually exclusive style that displays a rectangular frame. The supplemental 3-D appearance and border styles modify the frame's appearance.

CSS_LINEHORZ

This is a mutually exclusive style that displays a horizontal line. The line can appear flat *CSS_FLAT* style (the default) or like a ridge by using the *CSS_RAISED* style or like a groove with the *CSS_LOWERED* style.

CSS_LINEVERT

This is a mutually exclusive style that displays a vertical line. This is the same as the *CSS_LINEHORZ* style except for the orientation of the line.

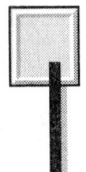

Table 5.2

Continued from the facing page.

CSS_ICON

This mutually exclusive style displays an icon. The supplemental 3-D appearance, border, horizontal position, and vertical position styles control the appearance of the enclosing window, and the position of the icon within the window. The control loads the icon from the resource named in the window text.

CSS_ICONWINDOW

This is the same as *CSS_ICON* except the window is resized to match the size of the icon. The position styles are meaningless for the *CSS_ICONWINDOW* style.

CSS_RECT

This mutually exclusive style displays a rectangle. The supplemental 3-D appearance and border styles control the appearance of the surrounding frame. The control loads a bitmap from the resource named in the window text, builds a brush from the bitmap, and uses the brush to fill the rectangle.

CSS_TEXT

This mutually exclusive style displays text. The supplemental 3-D appearance and border styles control the appearance of the enclosing frame. The horizontal position, vertical position, and text formatting styles modify the position and appearance of the text.

CSS_TEXTLOWERED

This is the same as *CSS_TEXT*, but gives the text a 3-D appearance of being lowered.

CSS_TEXTRAISED

This is the same as *CSS_TEXT*, but gives the text a 3-D appearance of being raised.

CSS_TEXTSHADOW

This is the same as *CSS_TEXT*, but gives the text the appearance of floating above the background and casting a shadow.

Table 5.3

This table explains what behavior is associated with each of the supplemental styles of the custom static control.

3-D Appearance Styles

CSS_FLAT

This style specifies no 3-D effect for windows, frames, rectangles and borders. This is the default appearance style.

CSS_LOWERED

This style uses a highlight and shadow to make a window, frame or rectangle appear lower than the background. If the *CSS_BORDER* style is set, a groove is drawn around the window. When combined with other appearance styles, this style takes priority over the *CSS_FLAT* and *CSS_RAISED* styles.

CSS_RAISED

This style uses a highlight and shadow to make a window, frame or rectangle appear higher than the background. If the *CSS_BORDER* style is set, a raised ridge is drawn around the window. When combined with other appearance styles, this style takes priority over the *CSS_FLAT* style.

Border Styles

CSS_NOBORDER

This, the default border style, specifies a plain control.

CSS_BORDER

This style adds a border to the control. When combined with 3-D appearance styles, the border will appear as either a raised ridge, or a shallow groove. When combined with other border styles, this style takes priority over the *CSS_NOBORDER* style.

Horizontal Position Styles

CSS_HCENTER

This style causes bitmaps, icons, or text, to be centered horizontally within the window. When combined with other horizontal position styles, this style takes priority over *CSS_LEFT* and *CSS_RIGHT*.

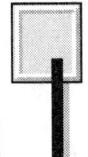

Table 5.3
Continued from the facing page.

CSS_LEFT
This, the default horizontal position style, positions bitmaps, icons, or text at the left side of the window.

CSS_RIGHT
This style positions bitmaps, icons or text, on the right side of the window. When combined with other horizontal position styles, this style takes priority over *CSS_LEFT*.

Vertical Position Styles

CSS_BOTTOM
This style positions bitmaps, icons, or text, at the bottom of the window. When combined with other vertical position styles, this style takes priority over the *CSS_TOP* style.

CSS_TOP
This, the default vertical position style, positions bitmaps, icons, or text at the top of the window.

CSS_VCENTER
This style positions bitmaps, icons, or text in the center of the window. When combined with other vertical position styles, this style takes priority over *CSS_TOP* and *CSS_BOTTOM*.

Text Format Styles

CSS_SINGLELINE
This combinable style applies to text only. It maps into *DrawText()*'s *DT_SINGLELINE* format code.

CSS_LEFTNOWORDWRAP
This combinable style applies to text only. It maps into *DrawText()*'s *DT_LEFTNOWORDWRAP* format code.

shows, one can map all of the class specific styles onto the existing styles, but the result is rather contrived. First, because Microsoft coded all but one style as mutually exclusive, the enlarged scheme must ignore all but six of the standard styles. Worse yet, of those six, five may be combined when used with our control, but not when used with the standard control.

Rather than add to an already baroque system, we chose to use a new coding scheme for the class specific styles. The bit assignments are defined in *CST_STTC.H* (Listing 5.1), and noted in Table 5.1. For uniqueness the *CSTSTATIC* control uses the prefix *CSS_* for class specific styles.

Note that of the supplemental styles, only the styles controlling the border, wordwrap, tab expansion, prefixes, and number of text lines are pure combinable forms. The supplemental styles governing 3-D effects and text placement are each independent sets of mutually exclusive options. Even so, in each of these three sets, the styles may be combined (e.g., *CSS_RAISED | CSS_LOWERED*), even though the combination may be nonsensical. Such combinations will be harmless because each set has been encoded with prioritized styles; all but the most dominant style will be ignored. For example, any combination with *CSS_RAISED* will produce a raised result. Naturally, one shouldn't intentionally write one of the nonsense combinations, but, as we pointed out in Chapter Two,

---

 **Table 5.3**

Continued. This table begins on page 100.

CSS_NOPREFIX

This combinable style applies to text only. It maps into DrawText()'s *DT_NOPREFIX* format code.

CSS_EXPANDTABS

This combinable style applies to text only. It maps into DrawText()'s *DT_EXPANDTABS* format code.

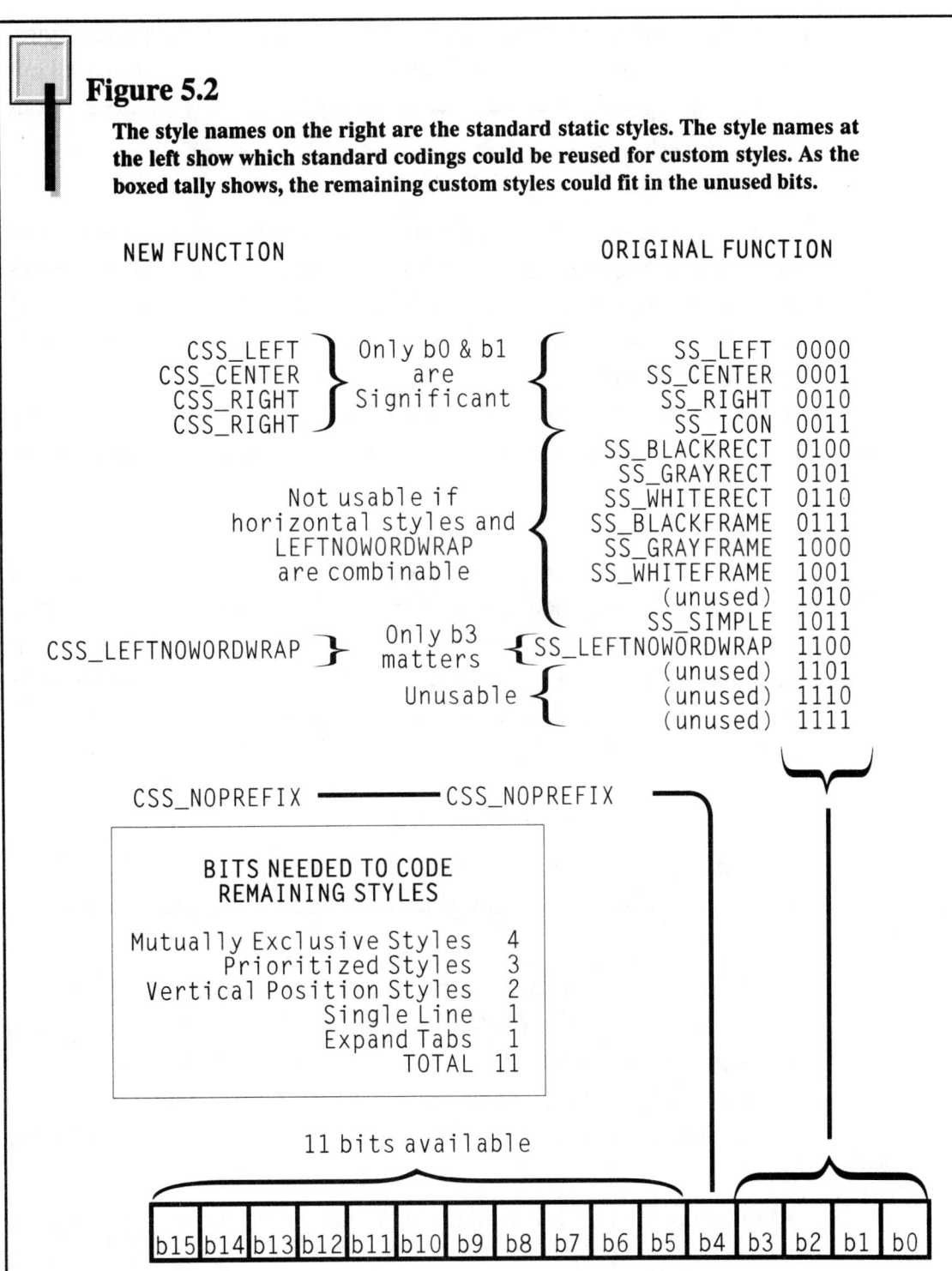

Figure 5.2

The style names on the right are the standard static styles. The style names at the left show which standard codings could be reused for custom styles. As the boxed tally shows, the remaining custom styles could fit in the unused bits.

supplying a defined behavior for otherwise unused codes creates a more robust and programmer friendly class.

The members of the first group, the fundamental styles, are truly mutually exclusive; combining fundamental styles will not produce the intended result.

Besides these class specific styles, there are four class general styles that will have meaning for *CSTSTATIC* controls. First, are the three styles that are implicitly a part of every control: *WS_OVERLAPPED*, *WS_CHILD*, and *WS_VISIBLE*. Additionally, one can use the *WS_CLIPSIBLINGS* style if the static control will be used as a background for other controls. The fundamental rectangle, bitmap, icon, and frame styles will require the *WS_CLIPSIBLINGS* style if the program positions other controls on top of them.

We recommend that the application register the *CSTSTATIC* control with the class styles *CS_DBLCLKS*, *CS_HREDRAW*, and *CS_VREDRAW*. *CS_DBLCLKS* is only needed to support the Dialog Editor. Including *CS_HREDRAW* and *CS_VREDRAW* may not be necessary in all instances, but we prefer to err on the conservative side. The application should register the *CSTSTATIC* control with the class style *CS_GLOBALCLASS* if the control is stored in a DLL.

The Other Interfaces

The static control requires very little definition beyond the common data, function and message interfaces described in Chapters Two, Three, and Four.

CSTSTATIC relies heavily upon the *CSTCTLDATA* structure. This control uses at most one bitmap. *CSTSTATIC* also uses three different brushes for drawing. One for the background, one for the 3-D highlight and one for the 3-D shadow. The text styles also depend upon two colors and a background mode. For more information, see the description in Chapter Two.

In compliance with the suggested naming convention, we've named the window procedure for *CSTSTATIC* *CstStaticWndFn()* (see *CST_STTC.C*, Listing 5.2). Reflecting the relative simplicity of static controls, this window procedure responds to only a handful of messages: the four instance data interface messages, `WM_CREATE`, `WM_DESTROY`, `WM_ERASEBKGND`, `WM_GETDLGCODE`, `WM_PAINT`, `WM_NCHITTEST`, `WM_SETFONT` and `WM_SETTEXT`. `CstStaticWndFn()` sends only two messages: `WM_PARENTNOTIFY` and `WM_CTLCOLOR`.

Separate public functions (CstStaticRegister() and CstStaticUnregister()) manage the registration tasks. Two private (static linkage) functions reduce the size of the window procedure; `CstStaticDraw()` contains the several hundred lines necessary to repaint the control. `GetDrawTextStyle()` translates the window style parameter into the format code required by `DrawText()`.

The header `CST_DATA.H` defines the constants used in the message interface to the instance data (see Chapter 4). To manipulate a specific member item through this interface, the program sends the appropriate message, with the member id in the low byte of *wParam*. If the member is an array, the high byte of *wParam* should hold the array index. With "set" messages, *lParam* should contain the new value for the instance or default data (see Figure 5.3).

Instantiation and Cleanup

Windows sends a `WM_CREATE` message to give the control a chance to create and initialize instance data. `CstStaticWndFn()` responds to this message by calling `CstCtlDataCreate()` to allocate and initialize the instance data. If the window count is zero, the `WM_CREATE` handler first calls `CstStaticDefDataCreate()`, which allocates and initializes the class default data structure, and binds the default data structure to the class by storing its pointer in the class extra bytes. Once a default data structure exists, `CstCtlDataCreate()` copies the values from the default data structure into the new window's `CSTCTLDATA` structure. Finally `CstCtlDataCreate()` binds the instance structure to the *window* by storing the instance data pointer and handle in the window extra bytes.

We chose to lock both the default data and instance data throughout their life so that we wouldn't be forced to lock and unlock a handle each time we access one of these structures. Because the memory is locked, we can access the structure directly through the pointer. Protected mode programs do not suffer any penalty for locking memory. We save the pointer along with the handle in extra byte storage.

CstStaticWndFn() then retrieves the window style (using *GetWindowLong()*) to determine what 3-D style and line thickness to use. Then the window procedure calls *CstCtlSetStyle()* and *CstCtlSetShadow()* to store these values in the instance data.

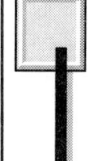

Figure 5.3

These constants define the instance data message interface and the indices of individual instance data members. (These definitions are from CST_DATA.H.)

```
/* Instance data interface messages */

    #define WM_CSTCTLGETDATA    ( WM_USER + 101 )
    #define WM_CSTCTLGETDEFDATA ( WM_USER + 102 )
    #define WM_CSTCTLSETDATA    ( WM_USER + 103 )
    #define WM_CSTCTLSETDEFDATA ( WM_USER + 104 )

/* Ids for instance data members */

    #define ID_LCOLOR       1
    #define ID_HBITMAP      2
    #define ID_HBRUSH       3
    #define ID_HFONT        4
    #define ID_HWND         5
    #define ID_IBKMODE      6
    #define ID_IFRAME       7
    #define ID_ISHADOW      8
    #define ID_RECTBITMAP   9
    #define ID_RECTTEXT     10
    #define ID_WCTLCOLORMSG 11
    #define ID_WSTATE       12
    #define ID_WSTYLE       13
    #define ID_LVALUE       14
```

Next, `CstStaticWndFn()` creates resources. If the fundamental style is one of the bitmap styles or the rectangle style, `CstStaticWndFn()` assumes that the window text specifies the name of a bitmap resource and creates a bitmap. A call to `CstCtlSetBitmap()` stores the bitmap in the instance data. If the style type is `CSS_RECT`, the bitmap represents a pattern for a brush. `CreatePatternBrush()` uses the bitmap to create a brush and `CstCtlSetBrush()` stores the brush in the instance data. The fundamental style types `CSS_LINEHORZ` and `CSS_LINEVERT` require additional style setup.

After setting the styles and allocating and initializing resources, `CstStaticWndFn()` sends a `WM_PARENTNOTIFY` message to the control's parent window. This message gives the parent window an opportunity to override the instance data defaults, either by creating alternate resources or by overwriting part of the instance data.

WM_DESTROY Processing

`CstStaticWinFn()`'s `WM_DESTROY` handler first sends a `WM_PARENTNOTIFY` message to the window's parent. Then, the window procedure deletes resources, which, depending upon the style of the control may include brushes and bitmaps. Finally a call to `CstCtlDataDelete()` frees the instance data storage, decrements the window count, and, if the window counter is zero, calls `CstStaticDefDataDelete()` to free the default data structure. In every case, the code confirms the validity of an object before freeing it.

Painting the Control

Windows sends the `WM_PAINT` message when all or part of the client area of the control needs painting (redrawing). `CstStaticWndFn()` responds by making a `BeginPaint()` call, checking to see if the window is visible, and, if so, calling the private function `CstStaticDraw()`, which hides all the real work.

`CstStaticDraw()` first gives the parent window an opportunity to set colors and define a background brush by sending the parent a `WM_CTLCOLOR` message. A call to `CstCtlColorMsg()` determines whether to use a locally created background brush or the parent's brush (see

Chapter Four). (Except that the `CSS_RECT` style always uses the background brush stored in the control's instance data.)

After constructing the background brush, `CstStaticDraw()` sets up the 3-D highlight and shadow brushes, the border and shadow style and the border and shadow thickness. The function retrieves the window text and extracts the control's fundamental style from the lower four bits of the window style word. A switch statement uses this fundamental style to select the appropriate drawing code. Bitmaps, frames, icons, rectangles and text are all handled separately.

Lines, frames, rectangles, bitmaps, and icons (all with optional 3-D effects), are all drawn using the primitives and support functions in `CST_DRAW.C`. When all the drawing is complete, `CstStaticDraw()` generally restores each device context to its initial state. This step is not necessary with all device contexts, but the program should always restore the initial state if the device context came from the system cache or is a class shared device context.

Miscellaneous Window Management

WM_ERASEBKGND

Windows sends this message whenever the `BeginPaint()` function is called. Because there is no background associated with the `CSTSTATIC` control, the window procedure merely returns a *TRUE* to indicate that the control is ready for painting.

WM_GETDLGCODE

Windows uses this message to ask what type of input the control will process. `CSTSTATIC` notifies Windows that it will process no input by returning the value `DLGC_STATIC`.

WM_NCHITTEST

Windows sends this message whenever the user clicks the mouse on the control. If this message is passed to `DefWndProc()`, it will be interpreted as input for the `CSTSTATIC` control (not likely, since it's an output-only control). By trapping this message and returning `HTTRANSPARENT`, we cause the message to be resent, this time to the window underlying the `CSTSTATIC` control.

WM_SETFONT

The control receives the *WM_SETFONT* messages as a request to use a particular font. *CstStaticWndFn()* responds by recording the new font in the instance data. If *lParam* is nonzero, *CstStaticWndFn()* also generates a *WM_PAINT* message.

WM_SETTEXT

The control receives the *WM_SETTEXT* as a request to change the text associated with the control. *CstStaticWndFn()* first passes this message to the default window procedure, *DefWindowProc()*. It then generates a *WM_PAINT* message to update the display with the new text.

The Demo Program

The program *DEM_STTC*, Listings 5.4 through 5.7, demonstrates most of the possible types and styles of the *CSTSTATIC* control, and how easily the controls can be created. Figures 5.4 through 5.16 show the appearance of the different dialog boxes in *DEM_STTC*.

All of the code in this book has been tested with Borland C++ 3.1, Microsoft Quick C for Windows 1.0, and Microsoft C/C++ 7.0. The listings at the end of this chapter include a make file for Microsoft Quick C. The companion code disk includes a make file for Microsoft PWB and a project file for Borland C++ 3.1. The make files for Chapters 5 through 10 all build statically-linked, standalone applications. Even though our make files (and Table 5.4) use small model, the code is model independent.

To use the PWB make file from within PWB, you must first configure an appropriate template, by setting all the compiler and linker options and saving the resulting configuration to a custom project template. If you attempt to build the project with a misconfigured template, PWB will overwrite the supplied make file. To confirm that the custom template is properly configured, generate a build for some dummy files and check the compiler flags in the resulting *.mak* file. Alternatively, you can bypass PWD and invoke *NMAKE* directly from the command line.

If you write your own make file, we suggest you use the flags in Table 5.4. These flags also include definitions for different preprocessor

110   Windows Custom Controls

Figure 5.4

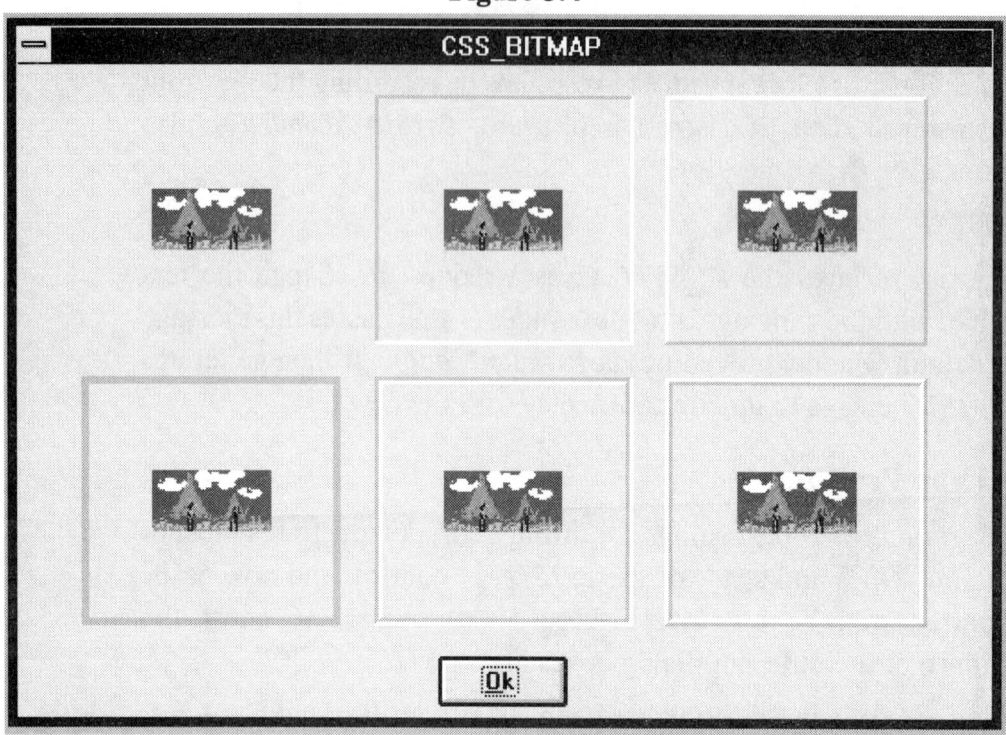

Figure 5.5

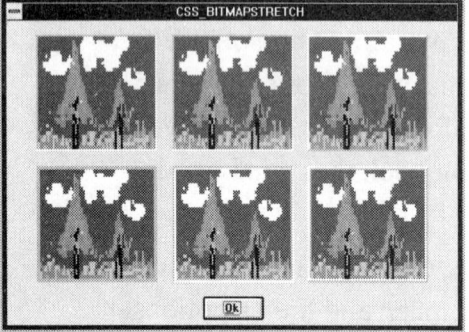

Figure 5.6

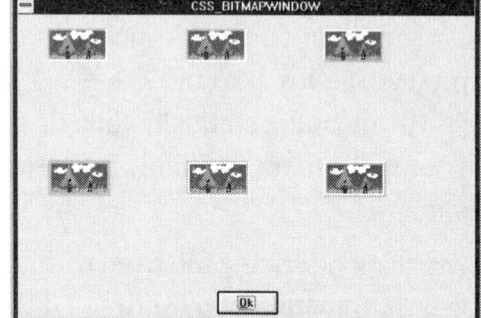

Figure 5.7

Figure 5.8

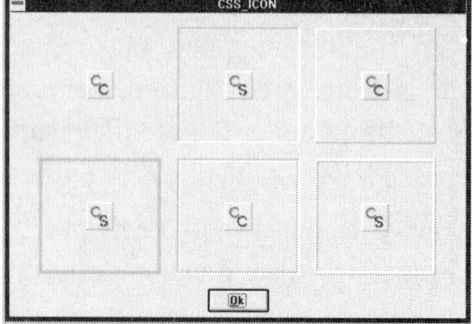

Figure 5.9

Figure 5.10

Figure 5.11

Figure 5.12

These screens, captured from the static demonstration program, show the various capabilities of the custom static control.

112   Windows Custom Controls

Figure 5.13

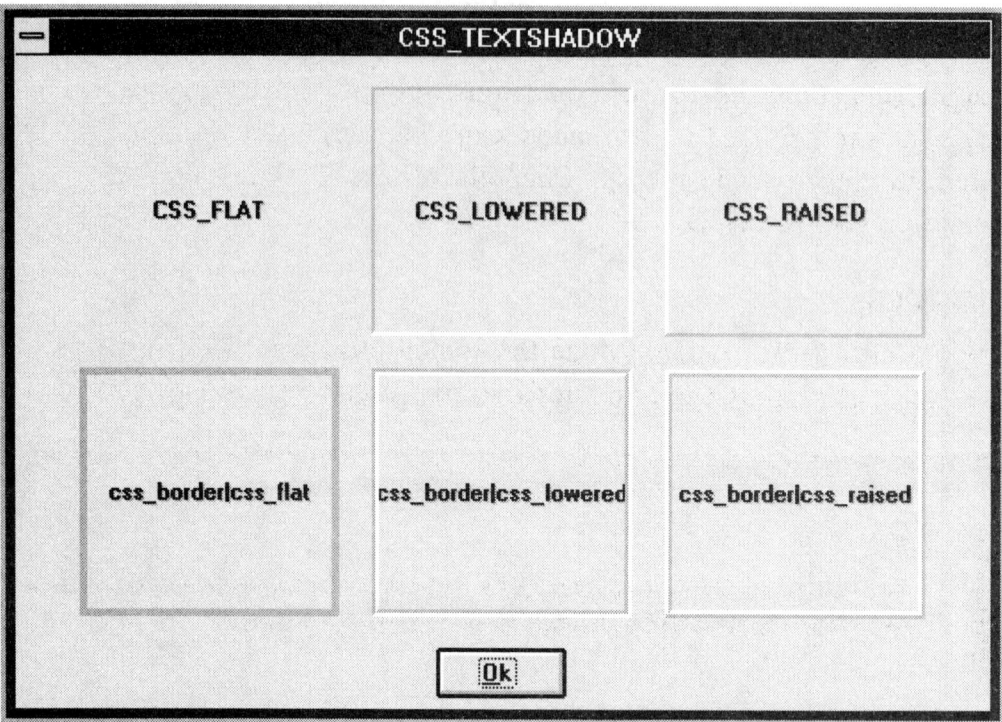

Figure 5.14

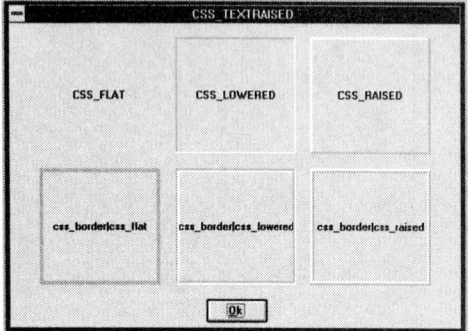

Figure 5.15

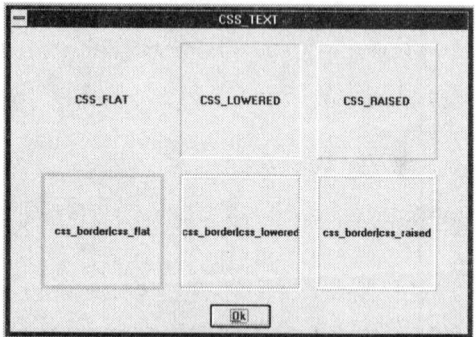

Figure 5.16

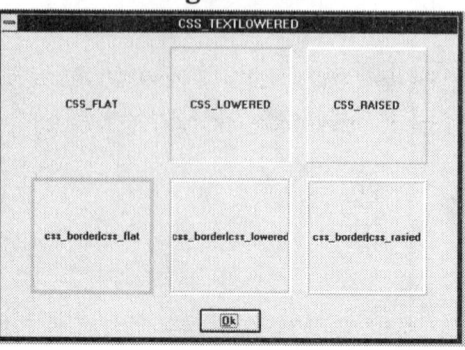

These screens, captured from the static demonstration program, show the various capabilities of the custom static control.

symbols, depending upon whether one is compiling a DLL, a statically linked application, or an application that will use controls stored in a DLL. These symbols control whether classes are registered explicitly by the application (appropriate for standalone, statically linked applications) and whether DLLs are loaded explicitly (necessary in some dynamically linked applications). Chapters 11 and 12 give detailed explanations of these issues.

Conclusion

While the *CSTSTATIC* control avoids the complexities associated with user input, it still requires that the designer pay careful attention to all

Table 5.4

The custom controls are compiled with some combination of these options. Note that DLLs are compiled differently than standalone programs.

Recommended for every build:

    /Asnw /W4 /G2 /DWINVER=0x0300 /Gw /Zp /BATCH

Needed only for CodeView builds:

    /f /Od /Zi /Gs

Recommended only for non-CodeView builds:

    /f- /Os /Ol /Og /Oc /Gs

Needed only when building a DLL:

    /D_WINDLL

Needed only when building a statically-linked, standalone application (such applications do not use *CST_CTLS.DLL*):

    /DNO_DLL

four components of the programmer interface. This control also shows the impact of our implementation strategy: the control is roughly half as large as it would be if it didn't draw upon the common support library and common data structure. Though this is the simplest control we'll build, it's only slightly smaller than average — custom control's just take a certain minimum amount of code.

The resulting control is extremely flexible — so flexible, in fact, that it has the most complex style interface of any of our controls. Even so, *CSTSTATIC* is just as easy to use as the standard *STATIC* control.

Listing 5.1

```
/****************************************************************************
          File Name: CST_STTC.H
      Expanded Name: Custom Static Control
        Description: Include file for CST_STTC.C
        Portability: Microsoft Windows 3.X
****************************************************************************/

#if !defined CST_STTC_DEFINED
    #define CST_STTC_DEFINED

    /* Custom Static Bitmap array access index */
    #define CSS_BITMAP_BITMAP 0

    /* Class specific window styles for custom static control.
    ** There are five groups of styles.
    ** Only 1 style out of the first four groups
    ** should be set.  The fifth group only applies
    ** to text and more than one of the fifth
    ** group styles can be combined. */

    /* These are mutually exclusive types,
    ** they use the lower 4 bits. Only one of these
    ** style can be set and still get meaningful results. */
    #define CSS_BITMAP         0x00L
    #define CSS_BITMAPSTRETCH  0x01L
    #define CSS_BITMAPWINDOW   0x02L
    #define CSS_FRAME          0x03L
    #define CSS_LINEHORZ       0x04L
    #define CSS_LINEVERT       0x05L
    #define CSS_ICON           0x06L
    #define CSS_ICONWINDOW     0x07L
    #define CSS_RECT           0x08L
    #define CSS_TEXT           0x09L
    #define CSS_TEXTLOWERED    0x0AL
    #define CSS_TEXTRAISED     0x0BL
    #define CSS_TEXTSHADOW     0x0CL

    /* These styles control the 3D appearance of the window.
    ** The default styles is CSS_FLAT.  If more than one of
    ** these styles is set, CSS_LOWERED dominates over CSS_RAISED
    ** and CSS_FLAT, CSS_RAISED dominates over CSS_FLAT. */
    #define CSS_FLAT    0x000L
    #define CSS_LOWERED 0x010L
    #define CSS_RAISED  0x020L

    /* These styles control the border around the window.
    ** CSS_NOBORDER is the default and CSS_BORDER dominates
    ** over CSS_NOBORDER if both are set. If CSS_BORDER is set
    ** the 3D appearance style effects the border. */
    #define CSS_BORDER   0x040L
    #define CSS_NOBORDER 0x000L

    /* These styles control the horizontal position of the
    ** object (bitmap, icon or text) in the client window.
    ** CSS_LEFT is the default.  If more than one of these
    ** styles is combined, CSS_HCENTER dominates over CSS_RIGHT
    ** and CSS_RIGHT dominates over CSS_LEFT. */
    #define CSS_HCENTER 0x0100L
    #define CSS_LEFT    0x0000L
```

Listing 5.1 *continued*

```
#define CSS_RIGHT    0x0200L

/* These styles control the vertical position of the
** object (bitmap, icon or text) in the client window.
** CSS_TOP is the default.  If more than one of these
** styles is combined, CSS_VCENTER dominates over CSS_BOTTOM
** and CSS_BOTTOM dominates over CSS_TOP. */
#define CSS_BOTTOM   0x0080L
#define CSS_TOP      0x0000L
#define CSS_VCENTER  0x0400L

/* These styles control how text is displayed.
** They are analogous to the DT_???? format codes
** for the DrawText() function. */
#define CSS_SINGLELINE     0x00800L
#define CSS_LEFTNOWORDWRAP 0x01000L
#define CSS_NOPREFIX       0x02000L
#define CSS_EXPANDTABS     0x04000L

/* Extra byte constants for custom static control */
#define CS_CLSEXTRA ( CC_CLSEXTRA )
#define CS_WNDEXTRA ( CC_WNDEXTRA + sizeof ( LONG ) )

/* WM_CTLCOLOR message for custom static control */
#define CTLCOLOR_CSTSTATIC ( CTLCOLOR_STATIC | 0x010 )

/* Prototypes for exported functions in CST_STTC.C */
int FAR PASCAL CstStaticRegister( HINSTANCE hInstance );
int FAR PASCAL CstStaticUnregister( HINSTANCE hInstance );
LONG FAR PASCAL CstStaticWndFn( HWND hWnd, UINT wMessage, WPARAM wParam,
        LPARAM lParam );

#endif

/* End of CST_STTC.H */
```

Listing 5.2

```
/****************************************************************
         File Name: CST_STTC.C
     Expanded Name: Custom Static
       Description: Library of functions for the static custom control
Global Function List: CstStaticRegister
                     CstStaticUnregister
                     CstStaticWndFn
Static Function List: CstStaticDefDataCreate
                      CstStaticDefDataDelete
                      CstStaticDraw
                      GetDrawTextStyle
       Global Data: _hInstanceCstCtls
       Static Data: _hCstCtlData
                    _lpCstCtlData
       Portability: Microsoft Windows 3.X
****************************************************************/

/* Microsoft Windows */
#include <windows.h>

/* Prototypes and Types */
#include <cst_xtra.h>
#include <cst_data.h>
#include <cst_draw.h>
#include <cst_util.h>

/* Own */
#include <cst_sttc.h>

static int CstStaticDefDataCreate( HWND hWnd );
static void CstStaticDefDataDelete( void );
static void CstStaticDraw( HWND hWnd, HDC hDC );
static WORD GetDrawTextStyle( LONG lStyle );

#if defined ( _WINDLL )
/* DLL Handle */
extern HINSTANCE _hInstanceCstCtls;
#endif

static LPCSTCTLDATA _lpCstCtlData = (LPCSTCTLDATA)0;
static HCSTCTLDATA _hCstCtlData = (HCSTCTLDATA)0;

/****************************************************************
         Name: CstStaticDefDataCreate
Expanded Name: Default Data Create
   Parameters: hWnd - window handle to static control
       Return: TRUE or FALSE
  Description: Creates the default class data
****************************************************************/
static int CstStaticDefDataCreate( HWND hWnd )
    {

    _lpCstCtlData = CstCtlDefDataCreate( hWnd );
    if ( !_lpCstCtlData )
        {
        /* Failed to allocate and initialize data */
        return ( FALSE );
```

Windows Custom Controls

Listing 5.2 *continued*

```
        }
    _hCstCtlData = CSTGETCLASSWORD( hWnd, GCW_HCSTCTLDATA );

    /* Free up the resources we do not need */
    SafeDeleteObject( _lpCstCtlData->hBrush[CC_BRUSH_BTNFACE] );
    _lpCstCtlData->hBrush[CC_BRUSH_BTNFACE] = 0;
    SafeDeleteObject( _lpCstCtlData->hBrush[CC_BRUSH_FRAME] );
    _lpCstCtlData->hBrush[CC_BRUSH_FRAME] = 0;

    return ( TRUE );

    }   /* function CstStaticDefDataCreate */


/*******************************************************************************
        Name: CstStaticDefDataDelete
Expanded Name: Default Data Delete
  Parameters: hWnd - window handle control
 Description: Deletes the default class data
*******************************************************************************/
static void CstStaticDefDataDelete( void )
    {

    if ( _lpCstCtlData )
        {
        SafeDeleteObject( _lpCstCtlData->hBrush[CC_BRUSH_BACKGROUND] );
        SafeDeleteObject( _lpCstCtlData->hBrush[CC_BRUSH_3DLIGHT] );
        SafeDeleteObject( _lpCstCtlData->hBrush[CC_BRUSH_3DSHADOW] );
        _lpCstCtlData = (LPCSTCTLDATA)0;
        }

    if ( _hCstCtlData )
        {
        GlobalUnlock( _hCstCtlData );
        GlobalFree( _hCstCtlData );
        _hCstCtlData = (HCSTCTLDATA)0;
        }

    }   /* function CstStaticDefDataDelete */


/*******************************************************************************
        Name: CstStaticDraw
Expanded Name: Static Draw
  Parameters: hWnd - window handle to static control
              hDC - device context handle
 Description: Draws the static custom control
*******************************************************************************/
static void CstStaticDraw( HWND hWnd, HDC hDC )
    {

    BOOL bFontSelected = FALSE;
    COLORREF lColorHighlight, lColorShadow;
    HANDLE hText;
    HBRUSH hBrushBk = 0, hBrushShadow, hBrushLight;
    HWND hWndParent;
    LONG lFndStyle, lStyle;
    LPRECT lpRectClt, lpRectWnd;
    LPSTR lpstrText;
```

Listing 5.2 *continued*

```
int iThick = 0, iTextLen;
WORD wCtlColorMsg = 0, wStyle;

hWndParent = GetParent( hWnd );
lpRectClt = CSTCTLGETLPRECTBITMAP( hWnd );
lpRectWnd = CSTCTLGETLPRECTTEXT( hWnd );
lStyle = GetWindowLong( hWnd, GWL_STYLE );
lFndStyle = lStyle & 0x0FL;
wStyle = CSTCTLGETSTYLE( hWnd );

if ( hWndParent )
    {
    /* Send message to give parent a chance to change data */
    /* Get the background brush */
    hBrushBk = (HBRUSH)SendMessage( hWndParent, WM_CTLCOLOR, hDC,
            MAKELPARAM( hWnd, CTLCOLOR_CSTSTATIC ) );
    if ( !IsWindow( hWnd ) )
        {
        return;
        }
    wCtlColorMsg = CstCtlColorMsg( hWnd, FALSE );
    if ( !( wCtlColorMsg & CTLCOLORMSG_BRUSH ) )
        {
        /* Use the brush of the parent window */
        if ( lFndStyle != CSS_RECT )
            {
            hBrushBk = GetClassWord( hWndParent, GCW_HBRBACKGROUND );
            }
        else
            {
            hBrushBk = 0;
            }
        }
    }
if ( !hBrushBk )
    {
    /* Still do not have a brush so get the default */
    hBrushBk = CSTCTLGETBRUSH( hWnd, CC_BRUSH_BACKGROUND );
    }

/* Get the border style and thickness */
wStyle = CSTCTLGETSTYLE( hWnd );
iThick = CSTCTLGETSHADOW( hWnd );

/* Get the light and shadow, brushs */
hBrushLight = CSTCTLGETBRUSH( hWnd, CC_BRUSH_3DLIGHT );
hBrushShadow = CSTCTLGETBRUSH( hWnd, CC_BRUSH_3DSHADOW );

/* Get the text */
iTextLen = GetWindowTextLength( hWnd );
hText = GlobalAlloc( GMEM_FLAGS, (DWORD)( iTextLen + 1 ) );
lpstrText = GlobalLock( hText );
GetWindowText( hWnd, lpstrText, iTextLen + 1 );

/* Get size of client and window area */
GetClientRect( hWnd, lpRectClt );
GetWindowRect( hWnd, lpRectWnd );
```

Listing 5.2 *continued*

```
        switch ( lFndStyle )
            {
        case CSS_BITMAP:
        case CSS_BITMAPSTRETCH:
        case CSS_BITMAPWINDOW:
                {

                BITMAP Bitmap;
                HBITMAP hBitmap;

                /* The style is a bitmap */
                hBitmap = CSTCTLGETBITMAP( hWnd, CSS_BITMAP_BITMAP );
                GetObject( hBitmap, sizeof ( BITMAP ), (LPSTR)&Bitmap );
                if ( hBitmap )
                    {
                    if ( lFndStyle == CSS_BITMAPWINDOW )
                        {

                        POINT Point;

                        /* Resize window to match the size of the bitmap */
                        Point.x = lpRectWnd->left;
                        Point.y = lpRectWnd->top;
                        ScreenToClient( hWndParent, &Point );
                        MoveWindow( hWnd, Point.x, Point.y,
                                Bitmap.bmWidth + 2 * iThick,
                                Bitmap.bmHeight + 2 * iThick, FALSE );
                        ResetBrushFix( hDC );
                        GetClientRect( hWnd, lpRectClt );
                        }

                    if ( lFndStyle == CSS_BITMAP )
                        {

                        int iOffsetX, iOffsetY;

                        /* Position bitmap in Y */
                        if ( lStyle & CSS_VCENTER )
                            {
                            /* Centered */
                            iOffsetY = ( lpRectClt->bottom + lpRectClt->top -
                                    Bitmap.bmHeight ) / 2;
                            }
                        else if ( lStyle & CSS_BOTTOM )
                            {
                            /* Bottom justified */
                            iOffsetY = lpRectClt->bottom - iThick -
                                    Bitmap.bmHeight;
                            }
                        else
                            {
                            /* Top justified is default */
                            iOffsetY = lpRectClt->top + iThick;
                            }

                        /* Position bitmap in X */
                        if ( lStyle & CSS_HCENTER )
                            {
```

Listing 5.2 *continued*

```
                /* Centered */
                iOffsetX = ( lpRectClt->right + lpRectClt->left -
                        Bitmap.bmWidth ) / 2;
                }
            else if ( lStyle & CSS_RIGHT )
                {
                /* Left justified */
                iOffsetX = lpRectClt->right - iThick -
                        Bitmap.bmWidth;
                }
            else
                {
                /* Left justified is default */
                iOffsetX = lpRectClt->left + iThick;
                }
            iOffsetX = max( iOffsetX, 0 );
            iOffsetY = max( iOffsetY, 0 );
            CstDraw3DRect( hWndParent, hDC, hBrushBk, lpRectClt, wStyle,
                    hBrushLight, hBrushShadow, iThick );
            CstDrawBitmap( hDC, hBitmap, iOffsetX, iOffsetY, 0, 0 );
            }
        else
            {
            /* Stretch the bitmap to fit in the rectangle */
            CstDraw3DFrame( hWnd, hDC, lpRectClt, wStyle,
                    hBrushLight, hBrushShadow, iThick );
            InflateRect( lpRectClt, -iThick, -iThick );
            CstDrawBitmap( hDC, hBitmap, lpRectClt->left, lpRectClt->top,
                    lpRectClt->right - lpRectClt->left,
                    lpRectClt->bottom - lpRectClt->top );
            }
        }   /* if hBitmap */

    break;

    }   /* case CSS_BITMAP */
case CSS_FRAME:
    CstDraw3DFrame( hWnd, hDC, lpRectClt, wStyle, hBrushLight,
            hBrushShadow, iThick );
    break;
case CSS_LINEHORZ:
case CSS_LINEVERT:
    CstDraw3DLine( hWnd, hDC, lpRectClt, wStyle, hBrushLight,
            hBrushShadow, iThick );
    break;
case CSS_ICON:
case CSS_ICONWINDOW:
    {

    HICON hIcon;

    /* This is an ICON */
    hIcon = LoadIcon( GetWindowWord( hWnd, GWW_HINSTANCE ),
            lpstrText );
    #if defined ( _WINDLL )
    if ( !hIcon )
        {
        hIcon = LoadIcon( _hInstanceCstCtls,"CST_CTLS" );
```

Listing 5.2 *continued*

```
            }
#endif
    if ( hIcon )
        {

        int iMapModeOrg;
        int iIconX, iIconY;
        int iOffsetX = 0, iOffsetY = 0;

        iIconX = GetSystemMetrics( SM_CXICON );
        iIconY = GetSystemMetrics( SM_CYICON );

        if ( lFndStyle == CSS_ICONWINDOW )
            {

            POINT Point;

            /* Resize the window to match the size of the icon */
            Point.x = lpRectWnd->left;
            Point.y = lpRectWnd->top;
            ScreenToClient( hWndParent, &Point );
            MoveWindow( hWnd, Point.x, Point.y, iIconX + 2 * iThick,
                    iIconY + 2 * iThick, FALSE );
            ResetBrushFix( hDC );
            GetClientRect( hWnd, lpRectClt );
            }
        else
            {
            /* Center the icon in Y */

            if ( lStyle & CSS_HCENTER )
                {
                /* Centered */
                iOffsetX = ( lpRectClt->right +
                        lpRectClt->left - iIconX ) / 2;
                }
            else if ( lStyle & CSS_RIGHT )
                {
                /* Right justified */
                iOffsetX = lpRectClt->right - iThick - iIconX;
                }
            else
                {
                /* Left justified is default */
                iOffsetX = lpRectClt->left + iThick;
                }

            /* Position Icon in Y */
            if ( lStyle & CSS_VCENTER )
                {
                /* Centered */
                iOffsetY = ( lpRectClt->bottom +
                        lpRectClt->top - iIconY ) / 2;
                }
            else if ( lStyle & CSS_BOTTOM )
                {
                /* Bottom justified */
                iOffsetY = lpRectClt->bottom - iThick - iIconY;
                }
```

Listing 5.2 *continued*

```
            else
                {
                /* Top justified is default */
                iOffsetY = lpRectClt->top + iThick;
                }
            }

        iOffsetX = max( iOffsetX, iThick );
        iOffsetY = max( iOffsetY, iThick );

        /* Reset the DC origin to align with the parent */
        AlignBrush( hWndParent, hDC, hBrushBk );

        /* Paint the background and draw the icon */
        CstDraw3DRect( hWndParent, hDC, hBrushBk, lpRectClt, wStyle,
                hBrushLight, hBrushShadow, iThick );
        iMapModeOrg = SetMapMode( hDC, MM_TEXT );
        DrawIcon( hDC, iOffsetX, iOffsetY, hIcon );
        SetMapMode( hDC, iMapModeOrg );
        DestroyIcon( hIcon );
        }   /* if hIcon */

    break;

    }   /* case CSS_ICON */
case CSS_RECT:
    CstDraw3DRect( hWndParent, hDC, hBrushBk, lpRectClt, wStyle,
            hBrushLight, hBrushShadow, iThick );
    break;
case CSS_TEXT:
case CSS_TEXTLOWERED:
case CSS_TEXTRAISED:
case CSS_TEXTSHADOW:
    {

    COLORREF lColorText, lColorTextBkOrg, lColorTextOrg;
    HFONT hFont, hFontOrg;
    int iBkModeOrg;
    WORD wFormat;

    /* Paint the background and border */
    if ( !( wStyle & CST_FRAME_FLAT ) ||
            ( wStyle & CST_FRAME_BORDER ) )
        {
        CstDraw3DRect( hWndParent, hDC, hBrushBk, lpRectClt, wStyle, hBrushLight,
                hBrushShadow, iThick );
        }
    InflateRect( lpRectClt, -iThick, -iThick );

    /* Get the font */
    if ( !( wCtlColorMsg & CTLCOLORMSG_FONT ) )
        {
        hFont = CSTCTLGETFONT( hWnd );
        if ( !hFont )
            {
            /* Get the font of the parent window */
            if ( hWndParent )
                {
```

Listing 5.2 continued

```
                    hFont = (HFONT)SendMessage( hWndParent,
                               WM_GETFONT, 0, 0L );
                    CstCtlSetFont( hWnd, hFont );
                    }
                }
        if ( hFont )
            {
            hFontOrg = SelectObject( hDC, hFont );
            bFontSelected = TRUE;
            }
        }   /* if !wCtlColorMsg */

    /* Set the color */
    if ( !( wCtlColorMsg & CTLCOLORMSG_COLORTEXT ) )
        {
        lColorText = CSTCTLGETCOLOR( hWnd, CC_COLOR_TEXT );
        lColorTextOrg = SetTextColor( hDC, lColorText );
        }
    if ( !( wCtlColorMsg & CTLCOLORMSG_COLORTEXTBK ) )
        {
        lColorTextBkOrg = SetBkColor( hDC,
            CSTCTLGETCOLOR( hWnd, CC_COLOR_TEXTBACKGROUND ) );
        }
    if ( !( wCtlColorMsg & CTLCOLORMSG_MODETEXTBK ) )
        {
        iBkModeOrg = SetBkMode( hDC, CSTCTLGETBKMODE( hWnd ) );
        }
    lColorHighlight = CSTCTLGETCOLOR( hWnd, CC_COLOR_3DLIGHT );
    lColorShadow = CSTCTLGETCOLOR( hWnd, CC_COLOR_3DSHADOW );

    /* Draw the text */
    wFormat = GetDrawTextStyle( lStyle );
    if ( lFndStyle == CSS_TEXTLOWERED )
        {
        /* Draw highlight to right and below text */
        lColorText = SetTextColor( hDC, lColorHighlight );
        OffsetRect( lpRectClt, 1, 1 );
        DrawText( hDC, lpstrText, iTextLen, lpRectClt, wFormat );
        OffsetRect( lpRectClt, -1, -1 );
        }
    if ( lFndStyle == CSS_TEXTRAISED )
        {
        /* Draw highlight to left and above text */
        lColorText = SetTextColor( hDC, lColorHighlight );
        OffsetRect( lpRectClt, -1, -1 );
        DrawText( hDC, lpstrText, iTextLen, lpRectClt, wFormat );
        OffsetRect( lpRectClt, 1, 1 );
        }
    if ( lFndStyle == CSS_TEXTSHADOW )
        {
        /* Draw shadow to right and below text */
        lColorText = SetTextColor( hDC, lColorShadow );
        OffsetRect( lpRectClt, 1, 1 );
        DrawText( hDC, lpstrText, iTextLen, lpRectClt, wFormat );
        OffsetRect( lpRectClt, -1, -1 );
        }
    SetTextColor( hDC, lColorText );
    DrawText( hDC, lpstrText, iTextLen, lpRectClt, wFormat );
```

Listing 5.2 *continued*

```
            /* Reset the font */
            if ( bFontSelected )
                {
                SelectObject( hDC, hFontOrg );
                }

            /* Reset the colors and mode */
            if ( !( wCtlColorMsg & CTLCOLORMSG_COLORTEXT ) )
                {
                SetTextColor( hDC, lColorTextOrg );
                }
            if ( !( wCtlColorMsg & CTLCOLORMSG_COLORTEXTBK ) )
                {
                SetBkColor( hDC, lColorTextBkOrg );
                }
            if ( !( wCtlColorMsg & CTLCOLORMSG_MODETEXTBK ) )
                {
                SetBkMode( hDC, iBkModeOrg );
                }
            }   /* case CSS_TEXT */
        default:
            break;
        }   /* switch lFndStyle */

    /* Free the dynamic memory used for the text */
    GlobalUnlock( hText );
    GlobalFree( hText );

    }   /* function CstStaticDraw */


/*****************************************************************************
        Name: CstStaticRegister
  Parameters: hInstance - handle to program or library registering class
      Return: Same as RegisterClass
 Description: Registers the window class for the custom static control
*****************************************************************************/
int FAR PASCAL CstStaticRegister( HINSTANCE hInstance )
    {

    WNDCLASS WndClass;

    WndClass.style = CS_DBLCLKS | CS_HREDRAW | CS_VREDRAW;

    #if defined ( _WINDLL )
    hInstance = _hInstanceCstCtls;
    WndClass.style |= CS_GLOBALCLASS;
    #endif

    WndClass.lpfnWndProc = CstStaticWndFn;
    WndClass.cbClsExtra = CS_CLSEXTRA;
    WndClass.cbWndExtra = CS_WNDEXTRA;
    WndClass.hInstance = hInstance;
    WndClass.hIcon = 0;
    WndClass.hCursor = LoadCursor( 0, IDC_ARROW );
    WndClass.hbrBackground = 0;
    WndClass.lpszMenuName = 0;
```

Listing 5.2 *continued*

```
    WndClass.lpszClassName = "CstStatic";

    return ( RegisterClass( &WndClass ) );

    }   /* function CstStaticRegister */


/******************************************************************************
        Name: CstStaticUnregister
  Parameters: hInstance - handle to program or library that registered class
      Return: Same as UnregisterClass()
 Description: Unregisters the window class for the custom static control
******************************************************************************/
int FAR PASCAL CstStaticUnregister( HINSTANCE hInstance )
    {

    #if defined ( _WINDLL )
    hInstance = _hInstanceCstCtls;
    #endif

    return ( UnregisterClass( "CstStatic", hInstance ) );

    }   /* function CstStaticUnregister */


/******************************************************************************
        Name: CstStaticWndFn
 Expanded Name: Custom Static Window Function
  Description: Window call back function for custom static control
******************************************************************************/
LONG FAR PASCAL CstStaticWndFn( HWND hWnd, UINT wMessage, WPARAM wParam,
        LPARAM lParam )
    {

    static int _WindowCount = 0;

    switch ( wMessage )
        {
        case WM_CREATE:
            {

            int iShadow = 0;
            HWND hWndParent = GetParent( hWnd );
            LONG lStyle = GetWindowLong( hWnd, GWL_STYLE );
            WORD wStyle = 0;

            if ( !_WindowCount )
                {
                if ( !CstStaticDefDataCreate( hWnd ) )
                    {
                    return ( -1 );
                    }
                }

            _WindowCount++;

            /* Turn on WS_CLIPSIBLINGS for frames and rectangles */
            if ( ( lStyle & CSS_FRAME ) || ( lStyle & CSS_RECT ) )
```

Listing 5.2 *continued*

```
            {
            lStyle |= WS_CLIPSIBLINGS;
            SetWindowLong( hWnd, GWL_STYLE, lStyle );
            }

    /* Create instance data */
    CstCtlDataCreate( hWnd );

    /* Get the border style */
    if ( lStyle & CSS_BORDER )
        {
        /* Border style is twice as thick */
        iShadow = 2 * CC_SHADOW;
        wStyle |= CST_FRAME_BORDER;
        if ( lStyle & CSS_LOWERED )
            {
            wStyle |= CST_FRAME_GROOVE;
            }
        else if ( lStyle & CSS_RAISED )
            {
            wStyle |= CST_FRAME_RIDGE;
            }
        else
            {
            wStyle |= CST_FRAME_FLAT;
            }
        }   /* if ( lStyle & CSS_BORDER ) */
    else
        {
        /* No border style */
        if ( lStyle & CSS_LOWERED )
            {
            iShadow = CC_SHADOW;
            wStyle |= CST_FRAME_LOWERED;
            }
        else if ( lStyle & CSS_RAISED )
            {
            iShadow = CC_SHADOW;
            wStyle |= CST_FRAME_RAISED;
            }
        else if ( lStyle & CSS_FRAME )
            {
            /* Flat frame */
            iShadow = CC_SHADOW;
            }
        }   /* else */

    switch ( lStyle & 0x0FL )
        {
        case CSS_BITMAP:
        case CSS_BITMAPSTRETCH:
        case CSS_BITMAPWINDOW:
        case CSS_RECT:
            {

            int    iTextLen;
            HANDLE hText;
            HBITMAP hBitmap = 0;
```

Listing 5.2 continued

```
                     LPSTR  lpstrText;

                     iTextLen = GetWindowTextLength( hWnd );
                     if ( iTextLen )
                         {

                         /* Get the name of the bitmap */
                         hText = GlobalAlloc( GMEM_FLAGS,
                                 (DWORD)( iTextLen + 1 ) );
                         lpstrText = GlobalLock( hText );
                         GetWindowText( hWnd, lpstrText,
                                 iTextLen + 1 );
                         /* Load the bitmap */
                         hBitmap = LoadBitmap( GetWindowWord( hWnd,
                                 GWW_HINSTANCE ), lpstrText );
                         GlobalUnlock( hText );
                         GlobalFree( hText );
                         }    /* if ( iTextLen ) */

                  #if defined ( _WINDLL )
                     if ( !hBitmap )
                         {
                         hBitmap = LoadBitmap( _hInstanceCstCtls,
                                 "CRBGBR00" );
                         }
                  #endif
                     CstCtlSetBitmap( hWnd, CSS_BITMAP_BITMAP, hBitmap );
                     if ( hBitmap && ( lStyle & 0x0FL ) == CSS_RECT )
                         {
                         /* Create background brush for rectangle */
                         CstCtlSetBrush( hWnd, CC_BRUSH_BACKGROUND,
                                 CreatePatternBrush( hBitmap ) );
                         }
                     break;
                     }    /* case CSS_BITMAP */
                  case CSS_LINEHORZ:
                  case CSS_LINEVERT:
                     iShadow = CC_SHADOW;
                     if ( !( lStyle & CSS_BORDER ) )
                         {
                         iShadow /= 2;
                         }
                     if ( lStyle & CSS_LOWERED )
                         {
                         wStyle |= CST_LINE_GROOVE;
                         }
                     else if ( lStyle & CSS_RAISED )
                         {
                         wStyle |= CST_LINE_RIDGE;
                         }
                     else
                         {
                         wStyle |= CST_LINE_FLAT;
                         }
                     if ( ( lStyle & 0x0FL ) == CSS_LINEHORZ )
                         {
                         wStyle |= CST_LINE_HORZ;
                         }
                     else
```

Listing 5.2 continued

```
                    {
                    wStyle |= CST_LINE_VERT;
                    }
                break;
            default:
                break;
            }    /* switch ( lStyle & 0x0FL ) */

        CstCtlSetShadow( hWnd, iShadow );
        CstCtlSetStyle( hWnd, wStyle );

        /* Notify the parent that the control has been created */
        if ( hWndParent )
            {
            SendMessage( hWndParent, WM_PARENTNOTIFY, WM_CREATE,
                    MAKELPARAM( hWnd, GetDlgCtrlID( hWnd ) ) );
            }
        break;
        }    /* case WM_CREATE */
    case WM_CSTCTLGETDATA:
    case WM_CSTCTLGETDEFDATA:
    case WM_CSTCTLSETDATA:
    case WM_CSTCTLSETDEFDATA:
        return ( (LONG)CstCtlData( hWnd, wMessage, wParam, lParam ) );
    case WM_DESTROY:
        {

        HWND hWndParent = GetParent( hWnd );

        /* Notify the parent and then delete the instance data */
        if ( hWndParent )
            {
            SendMessage( hWndParent, WM_PARENTNOTIFY, WM_DESTROY,
                    MAKELPARAM( hWnd, GetDlgCtrlID( hWnd ) ) );
            }
        if ( IsWindow( hWnd ) )
            {

            LONG lStyle = GetWindowLong( hWnd, GWL_STYLE );

            /* Window is still valid so free instance data */
            switch ( lStyle & 0x0FL )
                {
                case CSS_RECT:
                    SafeDeleteObject( CSTCTLGETBRUSH( hWnd,
                            CC_BRUSH_BACKGROUND ) );
                case CSS_BITMAP:
                case CSS_BITMAPSTRETCH:
                case CSS_BITMAPWINDOW:
                    SafeDeleteObject( CSTCTLGETBITMAP( hWnd,
                            CSS_BITMAP_BITMAP ) );
                    break;
                default:
                    break;
                }    /* switch ( lStyle & 0x0FL ) */
            CstCtlDataDelete( hWnd );
            }    /* if ( IsWindow( hWnd ) ) */
```

Listing 5.2 *continued*

```
            _WindowCount-;
            if ( _WindowCount <= 0 )
                {
                CstStaticDefDataDelete();
                }

            break;
            }  /* case WM_DESTROY */
        case WM_ERASEBKGND:
            /* Background is handled during the WM_PAINT message */
            return ( TRUE );
        case WM_GETDLGCODE:
            /* Return to dialog manager that this is a static control */
            return ( DLGC_STATIC );
        case WM_NCHITTEST:
            /* Return HTTRANSPARENT so all sibling windows will
            ** get mouse input */
            return ( HTTRANSPARENT );
        case WM_PAINT:
            {

            PAINTSTRUCT PS;
            HDC hDC = BeginPaint( hWnd, &PS );

            if ( IsWindowVisible( hWnd ) )
                {
                /* Only paint if needed */
                CstStaticDraw( hWnd, hDC );
                }
            EndPaint( hWnd, &PS );
            break;
            }
        case WM_SETFONT:
            if ( wParam )
                {
                CstCtlSetFont( hWnd, wParam );
                }
            if ( lParam )
                {
                /* Send a Paint message */
                InvalidateRect( hWnd, NULL, FALSE );
                UpdateWindow( hWnd );
                }
            break;
        case WM_SETTEXT:
            /* Default processing */
            DefWindowProc( hWnd, wMessage, wParam, lParam );
            /* Send a paint message */
            InvalidateRect( hWnd, NULL, FALSE );
            UpdateWindow( hWnd );
            return ( TRUE );
        default:
            return ( DefWindowProc( hWnd, wMessage, wParam, lParam ) );
        }  /* switch message */

    return ( 0L );

    }  /* function CstStaticWndFn */
```

Listing 5.2 *continued*

```c
/****************************************************************************
         Name: GetDrawTextStyle
   Parameters: lStyle - window style
       Return: format code for DrawText function
  Description: Gets the format code for the DrawText function based upon the
               window style
****************************************************************************/
static WORD GetDrawTextStyle( LONG lStyle )
    {

    WORD wFormat = 0;

    if ( lStyle & CSS_HCENTER )
        {
        wFormat |= DT_CENTER;
        }
    else if ( lStyle & CSS_RIGHT )
        {
        wFormat |= DT_RIGHT;
        }

    if ( lStyle & CSS_VCENTER )
        {
        wFormat |= DT_VCENTER | DT_SINGLELINE;
        }
    else if ( lStyle & CSS_BOTTOM )
        {
        wFormat |= DT_BOTTOM | DT_SINGLELINE;
        }

    if ( lStyle & CSS_LEFTNOWORDWRAP )
        {
        wFormat &= ~DT_WORDBREAK;
        }

    if ( lStyle & CSS_NOPREFIX )
        {
        wFormat |= DT_NOPREFIX;
        }

    if ( lStyle & CSS_SINGLELINE )
        {
        wFormat |= DT_SINGLELINE;
        }

    if ( lStyle & CSS_EXPANDTABS )
        {
        wFormat |= DT_EXPANDTABS;
        }

    return ( wFormat );

    }   /* function GetDrawTextStyle */

/* End of CST_STTC.C */
```

Windows Custom Controls

Listing 5.3

```
/******************************************************************************
            File Name: CST_STTC.RC
        Expanded Name: Custom Static
          Description: Resource file for the static custom control
          Portability: Microsoft Windows 3.X
******************************************************************************/

CRBGBR00 BITMAP BITMAP\CRBGBR00.BMP
CST_CTLS ICON   ICON\CST_CTLS.ICO

/* End of CST_STTC.RC */
```

Listing 5.4

```
/******************************************************************************
            File Name: DEM_STTC.H
        Expanded Name: Demo Static
          Description: Include file for DEM_STTC.C & DEM_STTC.RC
          Portability: Microsoft Windows 3.X
******************************************************************************/

#define IDM_BITMAP          101
#define IDM_BITMAPSTRETCH   102
#define IDM_BITMAPWINDOW    103
#define IDM_FRAME           104
#define IDM_ICON            105
#define IDM_ICONWINDOW      106
#define IDM_LINEHORZ        107
#define IDM_LINEVERT        108
#define IDM_RECT            109
#define IDM_TEXT            110
#define IDM_TEXTLOWERED     111
#define IDM_TEXTRAISED      112
#define IDM_TEXTSHADOW      113
#define IDM_EXIT            114

/* End of DEM_STTC.H */
```

Listing 5.5

```
/*****************************************************************************
        File Name: DEM_STTC.C
    Expanded Name: Demo Static
      Description: Demo program for custom static control
     Program List: DEM_STTC.C
                   DEM_STTC.RC
                   DEM_STTC.DEF
                   CST_DATA.C
                   CST_DRAW.C
                   CST_STTC.C
                   CST_UTIL.C
                   CST_XTRA.C
                   or
                   DEM_STTC.C
                   DEM_STTC.RC
                   DEM_STTC.DEF
                   CST_CTLS.LIB,DLL
Global Function List: WinMain
                   DemoDialog
                   StaticDemoDialogProc
                   MainWindowProc
      Portability: Microsoft Windows 3.X
*****************************************************************************/

/* Microsoft Windows */
#include <windows.h>

/* Types and prototypes */
#include <cst_data.h>
#include <cst_draw.h>
#include <cst_sttc.h>
#include <cst_util.h>

/* Own */
#include <dem_sttc.h>

int PASCAL WinMain( HINSTANCE hInstance, HINSTANCE hPrevInstance,
        LPSTR lpCmdLine, int nCmdShow );
BOOL PASCAL DemoDialog( HINSTANCE hInstance, HWND hWndParent,
        LPSTR DialogName );
LONG FAR PASCAL MainWindowProc( HWND hwnd, UINT wMessage,
        WPARAM wParam, LPARAM lParam );
BOOL FAR PASCAL StaticDemoDialogProc( HWND hDlg, UINT wMessage,
        WPARAM wParam, LPARAM lParam );

/*****************************************************************************
        Name: WinMain
  Description: Main window function
*****************************************************************************/
int PASCAL WinMain( HINSTANCE hInstance, HINSTANCE hPrevInstance,
        LPSTR lpCmdLine, int nCmdShow )
    {

    #if !defined ( NO_DLL )
    HINSTANCE hInstanceDll;
    #endif
    HWND hWnd;
    MSG Msg;
    static char _Name[] = "DEM_STTC";
```

Listing 5.5 *continued*

```
    WNDCLASS WndClass;

    lpCmdLine = lpCmdLine;
    nCmdShow = nCmdShow;

    #if defined ( NO_DLL )
    CstStaticRegister( hInstance );
    #else
    hInstanceDll = LoadLibrary( "CST_CTLS.DLL" );
    #endif

    if ( !hPrevInstance )
        {
        WndClass.style = 0;
        WndClass.lpfnWndProc = MainWindowProc;
        WndClass.cbClsExtra = 0;
        WndClass.cbWndExtra = 0;
        WndClass.hInstance = hInstance;
        WndClass.hIcon = LoadIcon( hInstance, _Name );
        WndClass.hCursor = LoadCursor( NULL, IDC_ARROW );
        WndClass.hbrBackground = COLOR_WINDOW + 1;
        WndClass.lpszMenuName = _Name;
        WndClass.lpszClassName = _Name;
        RegisterClass( &WndClass );
        }

    hWnd = CreateWindow( _Name, "Custom Stattic Control Demo",
            WS_OVERLAPPEDWINDOW, CW_USEDEFAULT, CW_USEDEFAULT,
            CW_USEDEFAULT, CW_USEDEFAULT, NULL, NULL, hInstance, NULL );

    ShowWindow( hWnd, nCmdShow );
    UpdateWindow( hWnd );

    while ( GetMessage( &Msg, NULL, 0, 0 ) )
        {
        TranslateMessage( &Msg );
        DispatchMessage ( &Msg );
        }

    #if !defined ( NO_DLL )
    FreeLibrary( hInstanceDll );
    #endif

    return ( (int)Msg.wParam );

    }   /* function WinMain */

/********************************************************************
        Name: DemoDialog
  Description: Function for invoking dialog boxes
********************************************************************/
BOOL PASCAL DemoDialog( HINSTANCE hInstance, HWND hWndParent,
        LPSTR DialogName )
    {

    BOOL bStatus;
    FARPROC lpfnProc;

    lpfnProc = MakeProcInstance( StaticDemoDialogProc, hInstance );
```

Listing 5.5 *continued*

```
    bStatus = DialogBox( hInstance, DialogName, hWndParent, lpfnProc );
    FreeProcInstance( lpfnProc );

    return ( bStatus );

    }   /* function DemoDialog */

/*****************************************************************************
        Name: StaticDemoDialogProc
 Description: Dialog call back function for custom static control demo
*****************************************************************************/
BOOL FAR PASCAL StaticDemoDialogProc( HWND hDlg, UINT wMessage,
        WPARAM wParam, LPARAM lParam )
    {

    lParam = lParam;

    switch( wMessage )
        {
        case WM_INITDIALOG:
            return ( TRUE );
        case WM_CLOSE:
            EndDialog( hDlg, 0 );
            return ( FALSE );
        case WM_COMMAND:
            switch ( wParam )
                {
                case IDOK:
                    EndDialog( hDlg, 0 );
                    return ( TRUE );
                default:
                    break;
                }
            return ( TRUE );
        default:
            break;
        }   /* switch wMessage */

    return ( FALSE );

    }   /* function StaticDemoDialogProc */

/*****************************************************************************
        Name: MainWindowProc
 Description: Window call back function for main window
*****************************************************************************/
LONG FAR PASCAL MainWindowProc( HWND hWnd, UINT wMessage,
        WPARAM wParam, LPARAM lParam )
    {
    switch( wMessage )
        {
        case WM_COMMAND:
            {

            HINSTANCE hInstance = GetWindowWord( hWnd, GWW_HINSTANCE );

            switch( wParam )
                {
                case IDM_BITMAP:
```

Listing 5.5 *continued*

```
                    DemoDialog( hInstance, hWnd, "BITMAP" );
                    break;
                case IDM_BITMAPSTRETCH:
                    DemoDialog( hInstance, hWnd, "BITMAPSTRETCH" );
                    break;
                case IDM_BITMAPWINDOW:
                    DemoDialog( hInstance, hWnd, "BITMAPWINDOW" );
                    break;
                case IDM_FRAME:
                    DemoDialog( hInstance, hWnd, "FRAME" );
                    break;
                case IDM_ICON:
                    DemoDialog( hInstance, hWnd, "ICON" );
                    break;
                case IDM_ICONWINDOW:
                    DemoDialog( hInstance, hWnd, "ICONWINDOW" );
                    break;
                case IDM_LINEHORZ:
                    DemoDialog( hInstance, hWnd, "LINEHORZ" );
                    break;
                case IDM_LINEVERT:
                    DemoDialog( hInstance, hWnd, "LINEVERT" );
                    break;
                case IDM_RECT:
                    DemoDialog( hInstance, hWnd, "RECT" );
                    break;
                case IDM_TEXT:
                    DemoDialog( hInstance, hWnd, "TEXT" );
                    break;
                case IDM_TEXTLOWERED:
                    DemoDialog( hInstance, hWnd, "TEXTLOWERED" );
                    break;
                case IDM_TEXTRAISED:
                    DemoDialog( hInstance, hWnd, "TEXTRAISED" );
                    break;
                case IDM_TEXTSHADOW:
                    DemoDialog( hInstance, hWnd, "TEXTSHADOW" );
                    break;
                case IDM_EXIT:
                    DestroyWindow( hWnd );
                    break;
                default:
                    break;
            }
            return ( FALSE );
            }
        case WM_DESTROY:
            PostQuitMessage( 0 );
            return ( FALSE );
        default:
            break;
        }

    return ( DefWindowProc( hWnd, wMessage, wParam, lParam ) );

    }   /* function MainWindowProc */

/* End of DEM_STTC.C */
```

Listing 5.6

```
/*****************************************************************
        File Name: DEM_STTC.RC
    Expanded Name: Demo Static
      Description: Resource file for the custom static control demo
      Portability: Microsoft Windows 3.X
*****************************************************************/

#include <windows.h>
#include <dem_sttc.h>
#include <cst_sttc.h>

DEM_STTC ICON ICON\DEM_STTC.ICO
CST_CTLS ICON ICON\CST_CTLS.ICO

DEM_STTC MENU
BEGIN
    POPUP "&Demo"
    BEGIN
        MENUITEM "Bitmap...",          IDM_BITMAP
        MENUITEM "BitmapStretch...",   IDM_BITMAPSTRETCH
        MENUITEM "BitmapWindow...",    IDM_BITMAPWINDOW
        MENUITEM "Frame...",           IDM_FRAME
        MENUITEM "Icon...",            IDM_ICON
        MENUITEM "IconWindow...",      IDM_ICONWINDOW
        MENUITEM "LineHorz...",        IDM_LINEHORZ
        MENUITEM "LineVert...",        IDM_LINEVERT
        MENUITEM "Rect...",            IDM_RECT
        MENUITEM "Text...",            IDM_TEXT
        MENUITEM "TextLowered...",     IDM_TEXTLOWERED
        MENUITEM "TextRaised...",      IDM_TEXTRAISED
        MENUITEM "TextShadow...",      IDM_TEXTSHADOW
        MENUITEM SEPARATOR
        MENUITEM "E&xit",              IDM_EXIT
    END
END

BITMAP DIALOG 10, 10, 300, 210
CAPTION "CSS_BITMAP"
STYLE DS_MODALFRAME | WS_CAPTION | WS_SYSMENU
FONT 8, "Helv"
BEGIN
    CONTROL "trees", -1, "CstStatic", CSS_BITMAP | CSS_FLAT    |
            CSS_VCENTER | CSS_HCENTER | CSS_NOBORDER,  20,  10, 80, 80
    CONTROL "trees", -1, "CstStatic", CSS_BITMAP | CSS_LOWERED |
            CSS_VCENTER | CSS_HCENTER | CSS_NOBORDER, 110,  10, 80, 80
    CONTROL "trees", -1, "CstStatic", CSS_BITMAP | CSS_RAISED  |
            CSS_VCENTER | CSS_HCENTER | CSS_NOBORDER, 200,  10, 80, 80
    CONTROL "trees", -1, "CstStatic", CSS_BITMAP | CSS_FLAT    |
            CSS_VCENTER | CSS_HCENTER | CSS_BORDER,    20, 100, 80, 80
    CONTROL "trees", -1, "CstStatic", CSS_BITMAP | CSS_LOWERED |
            CSS_VCENTER | CSS_HCENTER | CSS_BORDER,   110, 100, 80, 80
    CONTROL "trees", -1, "CstStatic", CSS_BITMAP | CSS_RAISED  |
            CSS_VCENTER | CSS_HCENTER | CSS_BORDER,   200, 100, 80, 80
    CONTROL "&Ok",   IDOK, "button",    WS_TABSTOP | BS_DEFPUSHBUTTON,
                                                      130, 190, 40, 16
END

BITMAPSTRETCH DIALOG 10, 10, 300, 210
```

Listing 5.6 *continued*

```
CAPTION "CSS_BITMAPSTRETCH"
STYLE DS_MODALFRAME | WS_CAPTION | WS_SYSMENU
FONT 8, "Helv"
BEGIN
    CONTROL "trees", -1, "CstStatic", CSS_BITMAPSTRETCH | CSS_FLAT    |
            CSS_NOBORDER,  20,  10, 80, 80
    CONTROL "trees", -1, "CstStatic", CSS_BITMAPSTRETCH | CSS_LOWERED |
            CSS_NOBORDER, 110,  10, 80, 80
    CONTROL "trees", -1, "CstStatic", CSS_BITMAPSTRETCH | CSS_RAISED  |
            CSS_NOBORDER, 200,  10, 80, 80
    CONTROL "trees", -1, "CstStatic", CSS_BITMAPSTRETCH | CSS_FLAT    |
            CSS_BORDER,    20, 100, 80, 80
    CONTROL "trees", -1, "CstStatic", CSS_BITMAPSTRETCH | CSS_LOWERED |
            CSS_BORDER,   110, 100, 80, 80
    CONTROL "trees", -1, "CstStatic", CSS_BITMAPSTRETCH | CSS_RAISED  |
            CSS_BORDER,   200, 100, 80, 80
    CONTROL "&Ok",   IDOK, "button",   WS_TABSTOP | BS_DEFPUSHBUTTON,
                      130, 190, 40, 16
END

BITMAPWINDOW DIALOG 10, 10, 300, 210
CAPTION "CSS_BITMAPWINDOW"
STYLE DS_MODALFRAME | WS_CAPTION | WS_SYSMENU
FONT 8, "Helv"
BEGIN
    CONTROL "trees", -1, "CstStatic", CSS_BITMAPWINDOW | CSS_FLAT    |
            CSS_NOBORDER,  20,  10, 80, 80
    CONTROL "trees", -1, "CstStatic", CSS_BITMAPWINDOW | CSS_LOWERED |
            CSS_NOBORDER, 110,  10, 80, 80
    CONTROL "trees", -1, "CstStatic", CSS_BITMAPWINDOW | CSS_RAISED  |
            CSS_NOBORDER, 200,  10, 80, 80
    CONTROL "trees", -1, "CstStatic", CSS_BITMAPWINDOW | CSS_FLAT    |
            CSS_BORDER,    20, 100, 80, 80
    CONTROL "trees", -1, "CstStatic", CSS_BITMAPWINDOW | CSS_LOWERED |
            CSS_BORDER,   110, 100, 80, 80
    CONTROL "trees", -1, "CstStatic", CSS_BITMAPWINDOW | CSS_RAISED  |
            CSS_BORDER,   200, 100, 80, 80
    CONTROL "&Ok",   IDOK, "button",   WS_TABSTOP | BS_DEFPUSHBUTTON,
                      130, 190, 40, 16
END

FRAME DIALOG 10, 10, 300, 210
CAPTION "CSS_FRAME"
STYLE DS_MODALFRAME | WS_CAPTION | WS_SYSMENU
FONT 8, "Helv"
BEGIN
    CONTROL "",   -1, "CstStatic", CSS_FRAME | CSS_FLAT    |
            CSS_NOBORDER,  20,  10, 80, 80
    CONTROL "",   -1, "CstStatic", CSS_FRAME | CSS_LOWERED |
            CSS_NOBORDER, 110,  10, 80, 80
    CONTROL "",   -1, "CstStatic", CSS_FRAME | CSS_RAISED  |
            CSS_NOBORDER, 200,  10, 80, 80
    CONTROL "",   -1, "CstStatic", CSS_FRAME | CSS_FLAT    |
            CSS_BORDER,    20, 100, 80, 80
    CONTROL "",   -1, "CstStatic", CSS_FRAME | CSS_LOWERED |
            CSS_BORDER,   110, 100, 80, 80
    CONTROL "",   -1, "CstStatic", CSS_FRAME | CSS_RAISED  |
            CSS_BORDER,   200, 100, 80, 80
```

Listing 5.6 *continued*

```
    CONTROL "&Ok", IDOK, "button",    WS_TABSTOP | BS_DEFPUSHBUTTON,
            130, 190, 40, 16
END

ICON DIALOG 10, 10, 300, 210
CAPTION "CSS_ICON"
STYLE DS_MODALFRAME | WS_CAPTION | WS_SYSMENU
FONT 8, "Helv"
BEGIN
    CONTROL "cst_ctls", -1, "CstStatic", CSS_ICON | CSS_FLAT    |
            CSS_VCENTER | CSS_HCENTER | CSS_NOBORDER, 20, 10, 80, 80
    CONTROL "dem_sttc", -1, "CstStatic", CSS_ICON | CSS_LOWERED |
            CSS_VCENTER | CSS_HCENTER | CSS_NOBORDER, 110, 10, 80, 80
    CONTROL "cst_ctls", -1, "CstStatic", CSS_ICON | CSS_RAISED  |
            CSS_VCENTER | CSS_HCENTER | CSS_NOBORDER, 200, 10, 80, 80
    CONTROL "dem_sttc", -1, "CstStatic", CSS_ICON | CSS_FLAT    |
            CSS_VCENTER | CSS_HCENTER | CSS_BORDER,   20, 100, 80, 80
    CONTROL "cst_ctls", -1, "CstStatic", CSS_ICON | CSS_LOWERED |
            CSS_VCENTER | CSS_HCENTER | CSS_BORDER,  110, 100, 80, 80
    CONTROL "dem_sttc", -1, "CstStatic", CSS_ICON | CSS_RAISED  |
            CSS_VCENTER | CSS_HCENTER | CSS_BORDER,  200, 100, 80, 80
    CONTROL "&Ok",     IDOK, "button",    WS_TABSTOP | BS_DEFPUSHBUTTON,
            130, 190, 40, 16
END

ICONWINDOW DIALOG 10, 10, 300, 210
CAPTION "CSS_ICONWINDOW"
STYLE DS_MODALFRAME | WS_CAPTION | WS_SYSMENU
FONT 8, "Helv"
BEGIN
    CONTROL "dem_sttc", -1, "CstStatic", CSS_ICONWINDOW | CSS_FLAT    |
            CSS_NOBORDER,  20,  10, 80, 80
    CONTROL "cst_ctls", -1, "CstStatic", CSS_ICONWINDOW | CSS_LOWERED |
            CSS_NOBORDER, 110,  10, 80, 80
    CONTROL "dem_sttc", -1, "CstStatic", CSS_ICONWINDOW | CSS_RAISED  |
            CSS_NOBORDER, 200,  10, 80, 80
    CONTROL "cst_ctls", -1, "CstStatic", CSS_ICONWINDOW | CSS_FLAT    |
            CSS_BORDER,    20, 100, 80, 80
    CONTROL "dem_sttc", -1, "CstStatic", CSS_ICONWINDOW | CSS_LOWERED |
            CSS_BORDER,   110, 100, 80, 80
    CONTROL "cst_ctls", -1, "CstStatic", CSS_ICONWINDOW | CSS_RAISED  |
            CSS_BORDER,   200, 100, 80, 80
    CONTROL "&Ok",     IDOK, "button",    WS_TABSTOP | BS_DEFPUSHBUTTON,
            130, 190, 40, 16
END

LINEHORZ DIALOG 10, 10, 300, 210
CAPTION "CSS_LINEHORZ"
STYLE DS_MODALFRAME | WS_CAPTION | WS_SYSMENU
FONT 8, "Helv"
BEGIN
    CONTROL "",   -1,  "CstStatic", CSS_LINEHORZ | CSS_FLAT    |
            CSS_NOBORDER,  20,  10, 80, 80
    CONTROL "",   -1,  "CstStatic", CSS_LINEHORZ | CSS_LOWERED |
            CSS_NOBORDER, 110,  10, 80, 80
    CONTROL "",   -1,  "CstStatic", CSS_LINEHORZ | CSS_RAISED  |
            CSS_NOBORDER, 200,  10, 80, 80
    CONTROL "",   -1,  "CstStatic", CSS_LINEHORZ | CSS_FLAT    |
            CSS_BORDER,    20, 100, 80, 80
```

Listing 5.6 *continued*

```
        CONTROL "",      -1, "CstStatic", CSS_LINEHORZ | CSS_LOWERED |
                CSS_BORDER,   110, 100, 80, 80
        CONTROL "",      -1, "CstStatic", CSS_LINEHORZ | CSS_RAISED |
                CSS_BORDER,   200, 100, 80, 80
        CONTROL "&Ok", IDOK, "button",    WS_TABSTOP | BS_DEFPUSHBUTTON,
                        130, 190, 40, 16
END

LINEVERT DIALOG 10, 10, 300, 210
CAPTION "CSS_LINEVERT"
STYLE DS_MODALFRAME | WS_CAPTION | WS_SYSMENU
FONT 8, "Helv"
BEGIN
        CONTROL "",      -1, "CstStatic", CSS_LINEVERT | CSS_FLAT    |
                CSS_NOBORDER, 20, 10, 80, 80
        CONTROL "",      -1, "CstStatic", CSS_LINEVERT | CSS_LOWERED |
                CSS_NOBORDER, 110, 10, 80, 80
        CONTROL "",      -1, "CstStatic", CSS_LINEVERT | CSS_RAISED  |
                CSS_NOBORDER, 200, 10, 80, 80
        CONTROL "",      -1, "CstStatic", CSS_LINEVERT | CSS_FLAT    |
                CSS_BORDER,   20, 100, 80, 80
        CONTROL "",      -1, "CstStatic", CSS_LINEVERT | CSS_LOWERED |
                CSS_BORDER,   110, 100, 80, 80
        CONTROL "",      -1, "CstStatic", CSS_LINEVERT | CSS_RAISED  |
                CSS_BORDER,   200, 100, 80, 80
        CONTROL "&Ok", IDOK, "button",    WS_TABSTOP | BS_DEFPUSHBUTTON,
                        130, 190, 40, 16
END

RECT DIALOG 10, 10, 300, 210
CAPTION "CSS_RECT"
STYLE DS_MODALFRAME | WS_CAPTION | WS_SYSMENU
FONT 8, "Helv"
BEGIN
        CONTROL "cdbgbr00", -1, "CstStatic", CSS_RECT | CSS_FLAT    |
                CSS_NOBORDER, 20, 10, 80, 80
        CONTROL "cdbgbr00", -1, "CstStatic", CSS_RECT | CSS_LOWERED |
                CSS_NOBORDER, 110, 10, 80, 80
        CONTROL "cdbgbr00", -1, "CstStatic", CSS_RECT | CSS_RAISED  |
                CSS_NOBORDER, 200, 10, 80, 80
        CONTROL "cdbgbr00", -1, "CstStatic", CSS_RECT | CSS_FLAT    |
                CSS_BORDER,   20, 100, 80, 80
        CONTROL "cdbgbr00", -1, "CstStatic", CSS_RECT | CSS_LOWERED |
                CSS_BORDER,   110, 100, 80, 80
        CONTROL "cdbgbr00", -1, "CstStatic", CSS_RECT | CSS_RAISED  |
                CSS_BORDER,   200, 100, 80, 80
        CONTROL "&Ok",    IDOK, "button",   WS_TABSTOP | BS_DEFPUSHBUTTON,
                        130, 190, 40, 16
END

TEXT DIALOG 10, 10, 300, 210
CAPTION "CSS_TEXT"
STYLE DS_MODALFRAME | WS_CAPTION | WS_SYSMENU
FONT 8, "Helv"
BEGIN
        CONTROL "CSS_FLAT",    -1,   "CstStatic", CSS_TEXT | CSS_FLAT    |
                CSS_HCENTER | CSS_VCENTER | CSS_NOBORDER, 20, 10, 80, 80
        CONTROL "CSS_LOWERED", -1,   "CstStatic", CSS_TEXT | CSS_LOWERED |
                CSS_HCENTER | CSS_VCENTER | CSS_NOBORDER, 110, 10, 80, 80
```

Listing 5.6 *continued*

```
    CONTROL "CSS_RAISED", -1,   "CstStatic", CSS_TEXT | CSS_RAISED |
            CSS_HCENTER | CSS_VCENTER | CSS_NOBORDER, 200, 10, 80, 80
    CONTROL "css_border|css_flat", -1,   "CstStatic", CSS_TEXT | CSS_FLAT |
            CSS_HCENTER | CSS_VCENTER | CSS_BORDER,    20, 100, 80, 80
    CONTROL "css_border|css_lowered", -1,"CstStatic", CSS_TEXT | CSS_LOWERED |
            CSS_HCENTER | CSS_VCENTER | CSS_BORDER,   110, 100, 80, 80
    CONTROL "css_border|css_raised", -1, "CstStatic", CSS_TEXT | CSS_RAISED |
            CSS_HCENTER | CSS_VCENTER | CSS_BORDER,   200, 100, 80, 80
    CONTROL "&Ok",  IDOK, "button",    WS_TABSTOP | BS_DEFPUSHBUTTON,
                                                   130, 190, 40, 16
END

TEXTLOWERED DIALOG 10, 10, 300, 210
CAPTION "CSS_TEXTLOWERED"
STYLE DS_MODALFRAME | WS_CAPTION | WS_SYSMENU
FONT 8, "Helv"
BEGIN
    CONTROL "CSS_FLAT", -1,   "CstStatic", CSS_TEXTLOWERED | CSS_FLAT    |
            CSS_HCENTER | CSS_VCENTER | CSS_NOBORDER, 20, 10, 80, 80
    CONTROL "CSS_LOWERED", -1,   "CstStatic", CSS_TEXTLOWERED | CSS_LOWERED |
            CSS_HCENTER | CSS_VCENTER | CSS_NOBORDER, 110, 10, 80, 80
    CONTROL "CSS_RAISED", -1,   "CstStatic", CSS_TEXTLOWERED | CSS_RAISED |
            CSS_HCENTER | CSS_VCENTER | CSS_NOBORDER, 200, 10, 80, 80
    CONTROL "css_border|css_flat", -1,   "CstStatic", CSS_TEXTLOWERED |
            CSS_FLAT    |
            CSS_HCENTER | CSS_VCENTER | CSS_BORDER,    20, 100, 80, 80
    CONTROL "css_border|css_lowered", -1, "CstStatic", CSS_TEXTLOWERED |
            CSS_LOWERED |
            CSS_HCENTER | CSS_VCENTER | CSS_BORDER,   110, 100, 80, 80
    CONTROL "css_border|css_rasied", -1,   "CstStatic", CSS_TEXTLOWERED |
            CSS_RAISED  |
            CSS_HCENTER | CSS_VCENTER | CSS_BORDER,   200, 100, 80, 80
    CONTROL "&Ok",  IDOK, "button",    WS_TABSTOP | BS_DEFPUSHBUTTON,
                                                   130, 190, 40, 16
END

TEXTRAISED DIALOG 10, 10, 300, 210
CAPTION "CSS_TEXTRAISED"
STYLE DS_MODALFRAME | WS_CAPTION | WS_SYSMENU
FONT 8, "Helv"
BEGIN
    CONTROL "CSS_FLAT", -1,   "CstStatic", CSS_TEXTRAISED | CSS_FLAT    |
            CSS_HCENTER | CSS_VCENTER | CSS_NOBORDER, 20, 10, 80, 80
    CONTROL "CSS_LOWERED", -1,   "CstStatic", CSS_TEXTRAISED | CSS_LOWERED |
            CSS_HCENTER | CSS_VCENTER | CSS_NOBORDER, 110, 10, 80, 80
    CONTROL "CSS_RAISED", -1,   "CstStatic", CSS_TEXTRAISED | CSS_RAISED |
            CSS_HCENTER | CSS_VCENTER | CSS_NOBORDER, 200, 10, 80, 80
    CONTROL "css_border|css_flat", -1,   "CstStatic", CSS_TEXTRAISED |
            CSS_FLAT    |
            CSS_HCENTER | CSS_VCENTER | CSS_BORDER,    20, 100, 80, 80
    CONTROL "css_border|css_lowered", -1,   "CstStatic", CSS_TEXTRAISED |
            CSS_LOWERED |
            CSS_HCENTER | CSS_VCENTER | CSS_BORDER,   110, 100, 80, 80
    CONTROL "css_border|css_raised", -1,   "CstStatic", CSS_TEXTRAISED |
            CSS_RAISED  |
            CSS_HCENTER | CSS_VCENTER | CSS_BORDER,   200, 100, 80, 80
    CONTROL "&Ok",  IDOK, "button",    WS_TABSTOP | BS_DEFPUSHBUTTON,
                                                   130, 190, 40, 16
END
```

Windows Custom Controls

Listing 5.6 *continued*

```
TEXTSHADOW DIALOG 10, 10, 300, 210
CAPTION "CSS_TEXTSHADOW"
STYLE DS_MODALFRAME | WS_CAPTION | WS_SYSMENU
FONT 8, "Helv"
BEGIN
    CONTROL "CSS_FLAT", -1,   "CstStatic", CSS_TEXTSHADOW | CSS_FLAT    |
            CSS_HCENTER | CSS_VCENTER | CSS_NOBORDER,  20,  10, 80, 80
    CONTROL "CSS_LOWERED", -1,   "CstStatic", CSS_TEXTSHADOW | CSS_LOWERED |
            CSS_HCENTER | CSS_VCENTER | CSS_NOBORDER, 110,  10, 80, 80
    CONTROL "CSS_RAISED", -1,   "CstStatic", CSS_TEXTSHADOW | CSS_RAISED  |
            CSS_HCENTER | CSS_VCENTER | CSS_NOBORDER, 200,  10, 80, 80
    CONTROL "css_border|css_flat", -1,   "CstStatic", CSS_TEXTSHADOW |
            CSS_FLAT    |
            CSS_HCENTER | CSS_VCENTER | CSS_BORDER,    20, 100, 80, 80
    CONTROL "css_border|css_lowered", -1,   "CstStatic", CSS_TEXTSHADOW |
            CSS_LOWERED |
            CSS_HCENTER | CSS_VCENTER | CSS_BORDER,   110, 100, 80, 80
    CONTROL "css_border|css_raised", -1,   "CstStatic", CSS_TEXTSHADOW |
            CSS_RAISED  |
            CSS_HCENTER | CSS_VCENTER | CSS_BORDER,   200, 100, 80, 80
    CONTROL "&Ok",   IDOK, "button",    WS_TABSTOP | BS_DEFPUSHBUTTON,
                                                          130, 190, 40, 16
END

TREES    BITMAP BITMAP\TREES.BMP
CDBGBR00 BITMAP BITMAP\CDBGBR00.BMP

/* End of DEM_STTC.RC */
```

Listing 5.7

```
NAME DEM_STTC
DESCRIPTION 'Custom Static Control Demo Program'
EXETYPE WINDOWS
CODE PRELOAD MOVEABLE
DATA PRELOAD MOVEABLE MULTIPLE
HEAPSIZE 1024
STACKSIZE 5120
EXPORTS
        MainWindowProc
        StaticDemoDialogProc
        CstStaticWndFn
```

Listing 5.8

```
ORIGIN   = QCWIN
ORIGIN_VER = 1.00

PROJ =DEM_STTC
DEBUG    =0
PROGTYPE =1
CALLER   =
ARGS =
DLLS =
CVPACK   =1
CC   =cl -qc
RC   =rc
CFLAGS_G_WEXE=/AS /W4 /Ze /D_WINDOWS /DNO_DLL /G2w /Zp /Aw
CFLAGS_D_WEXE=/Zi /Od
CFLAGS_R_WEXE=/O /Os /Gs /DNDEBUG
CFLAGS_G_WDLL=/AS /G2w /Zp /Aw /W3 /D_WINDOWS /D_WINDLL
CFLAGS_D_WDLL=/Gi /Od /Zi
CFLAGS_R_WDLL=/O /Os /DNDEBUG
CFLAGS_G_WTTY=/AS /G2w /W3 /D_WINDOWS
CFLAGS_D_WTTY=/Gi /Od /Zi
CFLAGS_R_WTTY=/O /Os /DNDEBUG
CFLAGS_G_DEXE=/AS /W2
CFLAGS_D_DEXE=/Gi /Od /Zi
CFLAGS_R_DEXE=/O /Ot /DNDEBUG
CFLAGS   =$(CFLAGS_G_WEXE) $(CFLAGS_R_WEXE)
LFLAGS_G_WEXE=/NOE/A:16/ST:10240
LFLAGS_D_WEXE=/CO
LFLAGS_R_WEXE=
LFLAGS_G_WDLL=/ST:5120 /A:16
LFLAGS_D_WDLL=/CO
LFLAGS_R_WDLL=
LFLAGS_G_WTTY=/ST:5120 /A:16
LFLAGS_D_WTTY=/CO
LFLAGS_R_WTTY=
LFLAGS_G_DEXE=/NOI /ST:2048
LFLAGS_D_DEXE=/CO
LFLAGS_R_DEXE=
LFLAGS   =$(LFLAGS_G_WEXE) $(LFLAGS_R_WEXE)
RCFLAGS =/DNO_DLL
RESFLAGS =
RUNFLAGS =
DEFFILE =     DEMSSTTC.DEF
OBJS_EXT =
LIBS_EXT =

.rc.res: ; $(RC) $(RCFLAGS) -r $*.rc

all: $(PROJ).EXE

DEM_STTC.OBJ: DEM_STTC.C $(H)

DEM_STTC.RES: DEM_STTC.RC $(RESFILES) $(H)

CST_DATA.OBJ: CST_DATA.C $(H)

CST_DRAW.OBJ: CST_DRAW.C $(H)

CST_STTC.OBJ: CST_STTC.C $(H)
```

Listing 5.8 *continued*

```
CST_UTIL.OBJ:CST_UTIL.C $(H)

$(PROJ).EXE: DEM_STTC.OBJ CST_DATA.OBJ CST_DRAW.OBJ CST_STTC.OBJ CST_UTIL.OBJ
$(OBJS_EXT) $(DEFFILE)
    echo >NUL @<<$(PROJ).CRF
DEM_STTC.OBJ +
CST_DATA.OBJ +
CST_DRAW.OBJ +
CST_STTC.OBJ +
CST_UTIL.OBJ +
$(OBJS_EXT)
$(PROJ).EXE

C:\PRGLNG\QCW\LIB\+
/NOD slibcew oldnames  libw
$(DEFFILE);
<<
    link $(LFLAGS) @$(PROJ).CRF
    rc $(RESFLAGS) DEM_STTC.RES $(PROJ).EXE

$(PROJ).EXE: DEM_STTC.RES
    rc $(RESFLAGS) DEM_STTC.RES $(PROJ).EXE

run: $(PROJ).EXE
    $(PROJ) $(RUNFLAGS)
```

6 Dynamic Controls

This chapter introduces custom controls capable of simple action/selection user interaction. The three custom button controls introduced here illustrate how to manage the keyboard and mouse interface and how to enhance appearance with bitmaps. The instance data interface and the registration methodology are the same as those used for the *CSTSTATIC* control.

Each of these three new custom controls corresponds to one of the fundamental styles of the standard *BUTTON* control. Thus, *CSTCHECKBOX* is a functional copy of a check box style *BUTTON* control. *CSTPUSHBTN* copies the pushbutton style. *CSTRADIOBTN* copies the radio button style. However, because the custom versions are drawn with bitmaps, the programmer has much greater control over their appearance.

The Standard *BUTTON* Control

Windows' built-in *BUTTON* control is the simplest standard dynamic control. Even so, this action/selection control is an important part of the Windows interface; nearly every dialog box has at least one *BUTTON* control. Since the custom button controls aim to emulate the functionality of the standard *BUTTON* control, the user interface will be a copy of the *BUTTON* interface. Similarly, the custom button controls will use *BUTTON*'s class specific window styles and messages.

Class Specific Window Styles for the *BUTTON* Control

There are four major types of *BUTTON* control: the check box, group box, pushbutton, and radio button controls. Some of these have more than one fundamental style. Table 6.1 lists the four types of *BUTTON* controls and the fundamental styles that apply to each type.

Windows defines eleven class specific window styles for the *BUTTON* Control, each prefixed with *BS_*. With one exception, these are mutually exclusive fundamental styles and are mapped into the first four bits of the style parameter. The one combinable style (*BS_LEFTTEXT*) designates the position of the control's text for the check box and radio button styles. It is mapped onto a separate bit (See Figure 6.1).

We won't build an analog for the group box style button control, because it behaves more like a static control than a dynamic control. Group boxes are rectangles with text, which are used to group controls (usually check boxes or radio buttons) — not to process user interaction. This functionality can be simulated by putting custom text controls on top of a custom *3D* frame.

Table 6.1 omits one of the standard *BUTTON* fundamental styles: *BS_OWNERDRAW*. The owner-draw style is Windows' answer for developers who want to change the appearance of the *BUTTON* control, by creating a style that will be drawn by the parent! This approach is fine for unique cases, but because owner-draw controls are neither modular nor reusable, they aren't appropriate for the general case.

Our custom controls won't implement the *OWNERDRAW* style. It makes more sense to teach your children to dress themselves than to be always spending time dressing them. So it is with custom controls. A custom control that takes care of its own drawing is easier to use and puts a smaller burden on the developer.

Implementation Strategy

Since the *CSTCHECKBOX*, *CSTPUSHBTN* and *CSTRADIOBTN* controls copy the behavior of the *BUTTON* control, an ideal solution would be to enhance the source code of the standard *BUTTON* control. Unfortunately, Windows does not make the source code for its built-in control classes available.

Table 6.1
The standard BUTTON control supports four types. This table itemizes the styles associated with each button type.

Type	Fundamental Styles
Check Box	BS_AUTOCHECKBOX BS_AUTO3STATE BS_CHECKBOX BS_3STATE
Group Box	BS_GROUPBOX
Pushbutton	BS_DEFPUSHBUTTON BS_PUSHBUTTON
Radio Button	BS_AUTORADIOBUTTON BS_RADIOBUTTON

Figure 6.1
With one exception, the standard BUTTON control styles are mutually exclusive, fundamental styles. Only BS_LEFTTEXT is coded as a combinable style.

```
#define BS_PUSHBUTTON         0x00000000L
#define BS_DEFPUSHBUTTON      0x00000001L
#define BS_CHECKBOX           0x00000002L
#define BS_AUTOCHECKBOX       0x00000003L
#define BS_RADIOBUTTON        0x00000004L
#define BS_3STATE             0x00000005L
#define BS_AUTO3STATE         0x00000006L
#define BS_GROUPBOX           0x00000007L
#define BS_USERBUTTON         0x00000008L
#define BS_AUTORADIOBUTTON    0x00000009L
#define BS_OWNERDRAW          0x0000000BL
#define BS_LEFTTEXT           0x00000020L
```

Alternatively, we could reuse *BUTTON*'s object code, by *subclassing* the standard control. The next chapter covers subclassing; to illustrate the tradeoffs, this chapter will develop each control from scratch.

Starting from scratch sounds worse than it is. Drawing operations account for a large fraction of each control's code. This code is exactly the new and different functionality the custom control adds over the standard control. Only the code that sets states and handles user interactions is duplicated in the custom and standard controls. This functionality is a small fraction of the total amount of code. Thus, there is less motivation for subclassing than one might expect.

Developing each control individually will highlight the differences in how the controls handle their user interaction — and that is the main focus of this chapter.

Besides, when the controls are finished, you *will* have the source code to three types of *BUTTON* controls. It may not be Microsoft's source code, but it can still serve as the basis for future enhancements.

Bitmaps

Microsoft draws the standard *BUTTON* control using the GDI line drawing functions. Our code will draw the custom controls using bitmaps. Bitmaps have the advantage of being fast, flexible and potentially striking in appearance. They have the distinct disadvantage of being device dependent.

The device dependence of bitmaps requires different bitmaps optimized for different resolution display devices. The bitmaps used by the custom button controls in this book are optimized for standard color VGA adapters with 640x480 resolution. These bitmaps will work fine for slightly higher resolution of 800x600, but may be too small for 1024x768 and greater resolution. For very high resolution displays and for displays with a lower resolution than the standard VGA, you should create new bitmaps. An ideal implementation would include a different set of bitmaps for each different display resolution expected. The control could then determine the display capabilities by a call to the Windows function `GetSystemMetrics()`, and, based on this information, select an appropriate set of bitmaps.

We chose to use bitmaps despite their device dependence, because they allow one to modify the appearance of a control very easily. Custom controls that have multiple states require this flexibility, because they need a different appearance to represent each state. When the control is drawn with bitmaps, each appearance is simply a different bitmap.

Moreover, if all the control's states are represented by bitmaps, it's a simple matter to substitute an entirely different set of bitmaps. Thus, a bitmap-based control is nearly as flexible as the owner-draw style, without the programming overhead.

In the controls presented in this chapter, the window class registration code automatically loads a default set of bitmaps and then binds these to the control. The programmer can override the defaults either on an instance or class basis by changing the binding in the instance data structure or in the class default data structure.

Even though these controls use bitmaps, the drawing requirements aren't significantly different from those of the *CSTSTATIC* control. The utility drawing functions in *CST_DRAW.C* provide the tools to draw bitmaps and controls with 3-D shading. The most significant differences relate to how the controls process user input, select the appropriate bitmap, and keep track of their internal state. The next section details how the *CSTCHECKBOX* control resolves these issues. The later sections focus on how *CSTPUSHBTN* and *CSTRADIOBTN* differ from *CSTCHECKBOX*.

The Custom Check Box Control

The *CSTCHECKBOX* control, Listings 6.1, 6.2 and 6.3, emulates the standard *BUTTON* control for the styles *BS_3STATE*, *BS_AUTOCHECKBOX*, *BS_CHECKBOX*, but uses bitmaps to dress up its appearance.

The standard check box is a very simple square frame that can contain an "X" when checked. A text label normally appears to the right of the control, but can be forced to the left by using the *BS_LEFTTEXT* style.

CSTCHECKBOX can take on six states, implying that it also requires six bitmaps. The new control has different appearances for up, down, up checked, down checked, disabled, and checked disabled. Like the standard control, the custom control will also draw a rectangle around the text of the control to indicate focus.

Figure 6.2 shows the six bitmaps, which are defined in resource file *CST_CKBX.RC* (Listing 6.3). Since its functionality isn't different from the standard control, the *CSTCHECKBOX* control does not require any new class specific styles. *CSTCHECKBOX* will support five of the eleven *BUTTON* class specific styles (Table 6.2).

Registration

CSTCHECKBOX's registration and unregistration functions, *CstCheckBoxRegister()* and *CstCheckBoxUnregister()*, are very similar to the parallel functions described in Chapter Five. *CSTCHECKBOX* also uses a very typical (for a control) set of class styles, namely *CS_HREDRAW, CS_VREDRAW, CS_DBLCLKS* and *CS_PARENTDC*. *CstCheckBoxRegister()* adds the *CS_GLOBALCLASS* if *_WINDLL* is defined. These are nearly the same styles used for the *CSTSTATIC* control.

Instance Data

Unlike static controls, dynamic controls change state as the user interacts with them. Thus, besides information about drawing options, the *CSTCHECKBOX* control must keep track of its present state.

This state information is recorded in six independent, on/off state flags. Table 6.3 lists and describes the constants (defined in *CST_CKBX.H*, Listing 6.1) used to represent the state information. (Consistent with Windows naming practice, all *CSTCHECKBOX* constants begin with the prefix *CCB_*.)

Note that these states *do not* directly correspond to the appearance of the control. Only some of these state flags affect appearance.

CSTCHECKBOX Message Handling

In addition to the general window management messages that a static control responds to, *CSTCHECKBOX* responds to user mouse input messages, keyboard event messages, and state control messages. The

Table 6.2
The custom check box control supports five of the 11 standard BUTTON class specific styles

Style	Description
BS_AUTOCHECKBOX	Same as BS_CHECKBOX with auto toggle of state
BS_AUTO3STATE	Same as BS_AUTOCHECKBOX with ability to be grayed
BS_CHECKBOX	Box button that can be checked
BS_LEFTTEXT	Designates text to left of button, right is default
BS_3STATE	Same as BS_CHECKBOX with ability to be grayed

Figure 6.2
Each of the check box states requires a different bitmap. These are the bitmaps used in the control library.

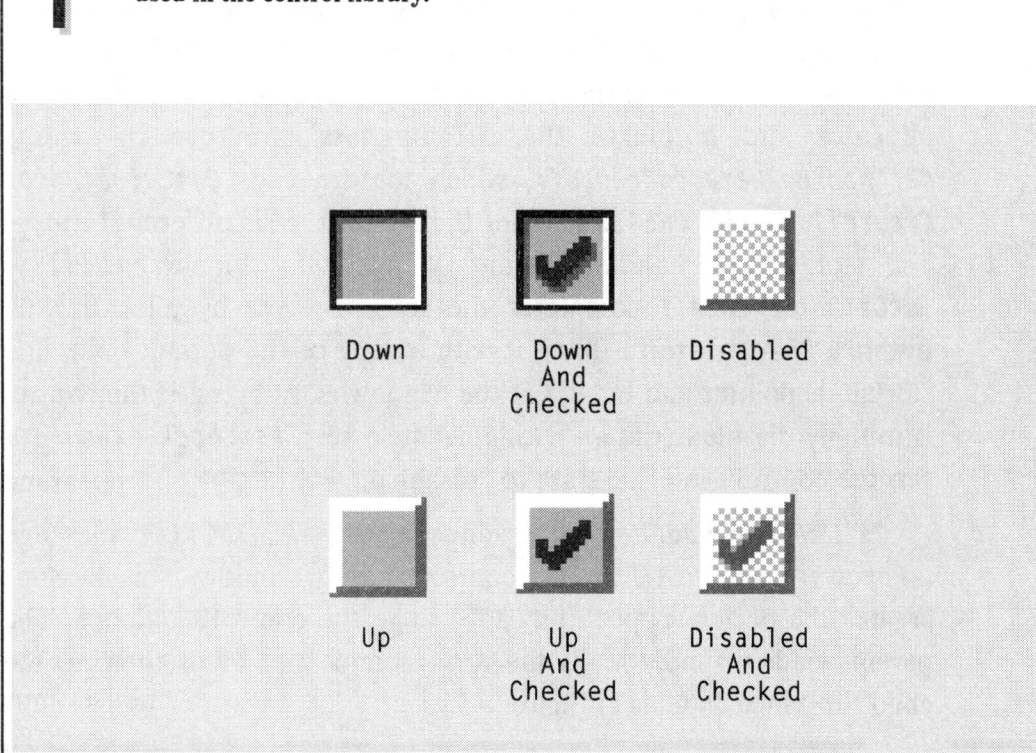

keyboard interface requires monitoring the *WM_KEYDOWN* and *WM_KEYUP* messages. The mouse interface requires responding to the *WM_LBUTTONDOWN*, *WM_LBUTTONUP* and *WM_MOUSEMOVE* messages. The state control messages are:

BM_GETCHECK,
BM_SETCHECK,
BM_GETSTATE,
BM_SETSTATE,
BM_GETSTYLE,
BM_SETSTYLE,
WM_KILLFOCUS,
WM_SETFOCUS and
WM_ENABLE.

Each custom button control responds to a subset of these control messages.

Instantiation and Cleanup

The *CSTCHECKBOX* window function, *CstCheckBoxWndFn()*, responds to the *WM_CREATE* message by loading the six bitmaps, allocating and initializing all the instance and (if needed) default data, and setting the control's initial state. If the window counter is zero, the create handler allocates and initializes the default data structure by calling *CstCheckBoxDefDataCreate()*, which in turn calls *CstCtlDefDataCreate()*. The *WM_CREATE* handler then loads the six different bitmaps and stores their handles in the default data. Finally, a call to *CstCtlDataCreate()* completes the setup process by allocating an instance data structure, filling it with a copy of the default data, and storing its pointer and handle in the window extra bytes. If the control is initially disabled (the *WS_DISABLED* style set), *CstCheckBoxWndFn()* sets the control's internal state to "disabled."

CstCheckBoxWndFn() next sends a *WM_PARENTNOTIFY* message (*wParam* == *WM_CREATE*) to the control's parent window. This message creates the perfect opportunity to change the control's bitmaps. The parent window simply loads the new bitmaps and binds them to the child's instance data, as in Figure 6.3.

WM_DESTROY

Just like the *CSTSTATIC* control, *CstCheckBoxWndFn()* responds to the *WM_DESTROY* message by first notifying the parent window that the control is about to be destroyed. The control then frees the dynamic memory associated with the instance data and deletes the bitmaps loaded by *WM_CREATE*. The *WM_DESTROY* handler then decrements the window counter, and, if necessary, frees the default data structure.

Figure 6.3
Because the checkbox is drawn with bitmaps, its appearance can be changed easily by loading different bitmaps. This code example shows how.

```
.
.
.
case WM_PARENTNOTIFY:
    {
    HWND hCtl = LOWORD( lParam );
    HINSTANCE hInstance = GetWindowWord( hDlg, GWW_HINSTANCE );
    switch ( wParam )
        {
        case WM_CREATE:
            switch ( HIWORD( lParam ) )
                {
                case IDD_LEFTBITMAP:
                    CstCtlSetBitmap( hCtl, CPB_BITMAP_DOWN,
                        LoadBitmap( hInstance, "GCDW1616" ) );
                    CstCtlSetBitmap( hCtl, CPB_BITMAP_UP,
                        LoadBitmap( hInstance, "GCUP1616" ) );
                    CstCtlSetBitmap( hCtl, CPB_BITMAP_UPFOCUS,
                        CSTCTLGETBITMAP( hCtl, CPB_BITMAP_UP ) );
                    break;
                case IDD_:
                    .
                    .
                    .
        case WM_DESTROY:
            .
            .
            .
```

If the parent window created any resources when it first created the control, it should delete those resources when it receives the WM_PARENTNOTIFY message. Figure 6.4 illustrates the appropriate response. If the parent window replaced any of the default bitmaps, it must also free the original versions of these resources.

Drawing the Control

CstCheckBoxWndFn() responds to the *WM_PAINT* message by calling the *CstCheckBoxDraw()* function, which obtains an index to the appropriate bitmap by calling *CstCheckBoxBitmapIndex()*. *CstCheckBoxBitmapIndex()* hides all the logic required to decide which bitmap goes with the current state.

CstCheckBoxDraw() retrieves the bitmap and divides the control's client area into two regions: one for the bitmap and the other for text. The function *CstCtlSetRects()* copies the boundaries of these regions

Figure 6.4

If the parent window creates any resources (like replacement bitmaps), it must delete those resources before it is destroyed.

```
        .
        .
        .
case WM_DESTROY
    switch( HIWORD( lParam )
        {
        case IDD_LEFTBITMAP:
            SafeDeleteObject( CSTCTLGETBITMAP( hCtl,
                    CPB_BITMAP_DOWN ) );
            SafeDeleteObject( CSTCTLGETBITMAP( hCtl,
                    CPB_BITMAP_UP ) );
            break;
        case IDD_
                .
                .
                .
        }
        .
        .
        .
```

into the instance data *RECT* structure. *CstCheckBoxDraw()* then displays the bitmap with a call to *BitBlt()*.

CstCheckBoxDraw() sets text colors and font and draws the text portion of the control. If the control is in focus, *CstCheckBoxDraw()* draws a focus rectangle around the text.

Manipulating States

We have implemented both a function and a message interface to the state information. The support function *CstCtlState()* (in *CST_DATA.C*) retrieves, sets, gets, and checks the state of a control. This function takes four parameters: a window handle, a state value, a command code, and an area. The state value can be any combination of the states in Table 6.3. Commands and areas are represented by constants (Table 6.4). Depending upon the state change, all, just the bitmap, or just the text area will need redrawing. The area parameter allows *CstCtlState()* to invalidate only the part of the control area that needs redrawing.

The messages in Table 6.5 and the messages related to mouse and keyboard input can all affect the control's state. Table 6.5 describes all but the mouse and keyboard messages; those are discussed below.

Table 6.3

The check box control uses state flags to keep track of whether the control is disabled, in focus, depressed, or checked and whether the mouse is captured.

State Flag Constant	Description
CCB_STATE_CAPTURE	Mouse is captured
CCB_STATE_DISABLED	Control is disabled
CCB_STATE_DOWN	Control is being held down
CCB_STATE_FOCUS	Control is in focus
CCB_STATE_INSIDE	Mouse is inside control
CCB_STATE_CHECK	Control is checked

User Interaction

Users may interact with the control through either the keyboard or the mouse. Each device has a separate message interface. The keyboard interface consists of the *WM_KEYDOWN* and *WM_KEYUP* messages; the mouse interface, of the *WM_LBUTTONDOWN*, *WM_LBUTTONUP* and *WM_MOUSEMOVE* messages. Under certain conditions these user interaction messages also generate a state change.

The *WM_KEYDOWN* message indicates that the user has pressed a key when the control has the input focus. The pushbutton control ignores all keys except the space bar. If the user depresses the space bar, *CstCheckBoxWndFn()* toggles the state to "down." The *WM_KEYUP* message indicates that the user has released a key when the control had the input focus. If the key was the space bar, *CstCheckBoxWndFn()* toggles the state to "up." The Windows internal dialog code processes any "Enter" keystrokes by translating the key into a selection.

Controls of style *BS_AUTOCHECKBOX* or *BS_AUTO3STATE* automatically toggle the check state to the opposite of the current state. *CstCheckBoxWndFn()* does this by sending the *BM_SETCHECK* message to itself. Whatever the style, if the control is in focus, either a *WM_KEYUP* or a *WM_LBUTTONUP* event will cause *CstCheckBoxWndFn()* to send the message

Table 6.4

To update state information, the programmer calls CstCtlState() with one of these command codes.

Flags to specify the area of the control that needs repainting

```
#define AREA_NONE    0
#define AREA_ALL     1
#define AREA_BITMAP  2
#define AREA_TEXT    3
```

Flags to control the mode of the state function

```
#define STATE_CHECK  0
#define STATE_GET    1
#define STATE_RESET  2
#define STATE_SET    3
```

Table 6.5

This table describes how each of the following messages can affect the custom control's status.

State Interface Messages

This set of messages interrogates or manipulates the state flags.

BM_GETCHECK

The *BM_GETCHECK* message is a request for the checked state of the control. If the control is currently in a checked state, *CstCheckBoxWndFn()* returns *TRUE*. If the control is not currently in a checked state, *CstCheckBoxWndFn()* returns *FALSE*. *CstCheckBoxWndFn()* accesses the check state with the function *CstCtlState()*.

BM_GETSTATE

The *BM_GETSTATE* message is a request for the up/down state of the control. *CstCheckBoxWndFn()* returns *TRUE* if the control is in the down state. Otherwise it returns *FALSE*.

BM_SETCHECK

The *BM_SETCHECK* message sets or resets the checked state of the control. Based on *wParam*, the response is:

```
        zero:    Check <- unchecked
                 area  <- bitmap
        nonzero: Check <- checked
                 area  <- bitmap
```

Table 6.5
Continued from the preceding page.

If the control supports a disabled state (styles *BS_3STATE* or *BS_AUTO3STATE*), the *BM_SETCHECK* also controls the disabled state:

```
0: check <- unchecked
   area  <- bitmap
1: check <- checked
   area  <- bitmap
2: state <- disabled
   area  <- all
```

BM_SETSTATE
The *BM_SETSTATE* message sets or resets the up/down state of the control. If *wParam* is non-zero the state is set to down. If *wParam* is zero the state is reset to up. The bitmap portion of the control is redrawn.

Window Management Messages

WM_ENABLE
The *WM_ENABLE* message sets (*wParam* non-zero) or resets (*wParam* zero) the disabled state of the control. This forces a redraw of the bitmap and text areas of the control.

WM_KILLFOCUS
The *WM_KILLFOCUS* message indicates that the control has lost the input focus. This requires the state to be set and the entire control to be redrawn.

WM_SETFOCUS
The *WM_SETFOCUS* message indicates that the control now has the input focus. This requires the state to be set and the entire control to be redrawn.

```
SendMessage(GetParent(hWnd),WM_COMMAND, (WPARAM)GetDlgCtrlID( hWnd ),
        MAKELPARAM( hWnd, BN_CLICKED ) );
```

to notify the control's parent window of a button click.

The *WM_LBUTTONDOWN* message indicates that the user pressed the left mouse button when the mouse cursor was over the control. Following this message, the window procedure should capture the mouse with a call to *SetCapture()*, so that the corresponding button up and other mouse messages (i.e., *WM_MOUSEMOVE*) won't be missed just because the mouse was inadvertently moved off the control before the mouse button was released. Once the mouse is captured, *CstCheckBoxWndFn()* sets the state to indicate that: the mouse cursor is captured, the mouse cursor is inside the control, the control is in a down state, and the bitmap needs redrawing. The call to *CstCheckBoxWndFn()* is:

```
CstCtlState( hWnd, CCB_STATE_CAPTURE | CCB_STATE_DOWN | CCB_STATE_IN-
SIDE,
        STATE_SET, AREA_BITMAP );
```

If a *WM_LBUTTONDOWN* message is received while the control does not have the focus, *CstCheckBoxWndFn()* calls *SetFocus()* to assign focus to the control.

Table 6.5

Continued. This table begins on page 157.

These messages also affect the control's state:
    WM_KEYUP
    WM_KEYDOWN
    WM_LBUTTONUP
    WM_LBUTTONDOWN
    WM_MOUSEMOVE
See the narrative for details.

The *WM_LBUTTONUP* message indicates that the user has released the left mouse button while the mouse cursor was either inside the control or captured by the control. *CstCheckBoxWndFn()* responds by releasing the mouse capture with a call to *ReleaseCapture()*. If the state *CCB_STATE_INSIDE* is set, *CstCheckBoxWndFn()* responds as if the user had released the space bar.

The *WM_MOUSEMOVE* message indicates that the user has moved the mouse when the mouse cursor was either captured or inside the control's client rectangle. If the control has captured the mouse, *CstCheckBoxWndFn()* updates the state *CCB_STATE_INSIDE* depending upon the new mouse position.

Window Maintenance & Data Interface

CstCheckBoxWndFn()'s response to the following messages exactly parallels those of *CstStaticWndFn()*, described in Chapter Five: *WM_ERASEBKGND*, *WM_PAINT*, *WM_SETFONT*, *WM_CSTCTLGETDATA()*, *WM_SETTEXT*, *WM_CSTCTLGETDEFDATA()*, *WM_CSTCTLSETDATA()*, *WM_CSTCTLSETDEFDATA()*.

Custom Pushbutton Control

The *CSTPUSHBTN* control, Listings 6.4 and 6.5, is an appearance enhancing replacement of the standard *BUTTON* control with styles *BS_PUSHBUTTON* or *BS_DEFPUSHBUTTON*. *CSTPUSHBTN* behaves in the same way as *BUTTON*; it just looks better and offers more flexibility and control over its appearance.

Unlike the *CSTCHECKBOX* control described above, the *CSTPUSHBTN* control requires some new class specific window styles. Table 6.6 lists the standard styles and Table 6.7 lists the nine new styles. Figure 6.5 shows how the styles are coded. Generally these styles control the positioning of text and bitmaps, and the drawing of borders, shadows and focus rectangles.

Another fundamental difference between the *CSTPUSHBTN* control and the *CSTCHECKBOX* control is that *CSTPUSHBTN* does not have a set of default bitmaps. Instead, *CSTPUSHBTN*'s default appearance is an empty pushbutton frame drawn using the GDI. The custom pushbutton still supports bitmaps, but they must be set at run time. *CSTPUSHBTN* supports five different appearances, thus it needs five separate bitmaps. Table 6.8 describes the different state flags for *CSTPUSHBTN*.

Because pushbuttons can have a default style (i.e., an individual instance can be marked as the default response for the containing dialog box), the code that reacts to the *WM_KILLFOCUS* message is different from that of *CSTCHECKBOX*. The default style also complicates the state information.

Table 6.6

The CSTPUSHBTN control supports two of the standard pushbutton class specific window styles.

Style	Description
BS_DEFPUSHBUTTON	Pushbutton with default activation
BS_PUSHBUTTON	Pushbutton

Table 6.7

The CSTPUSHBTN control also responds to nine new class specific window styles.

Style	Description
CPBS_LEFTTEXT	Left justifies text inside button
CPBS_RIGHTTEXT	Right justifies text inside button
CPBS_NOFOCUS	Prevents drawing of focus rectangle
CPBS_NOFRAME	Prevents drawing of frame rectangle
CPBS_NOSHADOW	Prevents drawing of 3D shadow
CPBS_STRETCHBITMAP	Stretches bitmap to fit the button size
CPBS_LEFTBITMAP	Left justifies bitmap inside button
CPBS_RIGHTBITMAP	Right justifies bitmap inside button
CPBS_STRETCHBUTTON	Stretches button to fit the bitmap size

Figure 6.5

This fragment from CST_PBTN.H shows how the custom pushbutton styles are mapped.

```
#define CPBS_LEFTTEXT      0x0040L
#define CPBS_RIGHTTEXT     0x0080L
#define CPBS_NOFOCUS       0x0100L
#define CPBS_NOFRAME       0x0200L
#define CPBS_NOSHADOW      0x0400L
#define CPBS_STRETCHBITMAP 0x0800L
#define CPBS_LEFTBITMAP    0x1000L
#define CPBS_RIGHTBITMAP   0x2000L
#define CPBS_STRETCHBUTTON 0x4000L
```

Table 6.8

Except for two extra flags related to identifying the default pushbutton, the custom pushbutton control maintains the same state information as the custom check box control.

State Flag Constant	Description
CPB_STATE_CAPTURE	Mouse is captured
CPB_STATE_DISABLED	Control is disabled
CPB_STATE_DOWN	Control is being held down
CPB_STATE_FOCUS	Control is in focus
CPB_STATE_INSIDE	Mouse is inside control
CPB_STATE_CHECK	Control is checked
CPB_STATE_DEFAULT	Control is current default pushbutton
CPB_STATE_DEFAULTORG	Control is the original default pushbutton

Two new messages, `BM_GETSTYLE` and `BM_SETSTYLE`, allow the program to designate a different default button by changing styles in the appropriate buttons.

Also, the control's window procedure now has two possible responses to the `WM_GETDLGCODE`; `DLGC_DEFPUSHBUTTON` if the current control is the default button, `DLGC_PUSHBUTTON` otherwise.

Being able to control the position of the text inside the control with the `CPBS_TEXTLEFT` or `CPBS_TEXTRIGHT` styles complicates the drawing chores for `CSTPUSHBTN`. Two supporting functions, `CstPushBtnDrawFocus()` and `CstPushBtnDrawText()`, handle these complications. These functions properly position the text and the focus rectangle for the different text positioning styles.

The file `CST_PBTN.C` contains the functions required to support the `CSTPUSHBTN` control. The file `CST_PBTN.H` contains the style definitions, the state codes, and prototypes for the functions in `CST_PBTN.C`. Since there are no default bitmaps, there are no resource or bitmap files.

A Custom Radio Button

The similarities between the `CSTRADIOBTN` control, Listings 6.6, 6.7, and 6.8, and the `CSTCHECKBOX` control are even more striking than the similarities between `CSTPUSHBTN` and `CSTCHECKBOX`.

The `BM_SETCHECK` message handler must manipulate additional state information because radio buttons are mutually exclusive, rather than combinable like check boxes. The draw functions are slightly different because the radio button does not support a disabled state. Thus the radio button needs only four different bitmaps, and never needs to display grayed text. Since a radio button can never be disabled, the control also does not need to react to the `WM_ENABLE` message.

Because setting the input focus to a radio button is the same as clicking the radio button, the code that responds to the `WM_SETFOCUS` must send a `BN_CLICKED` notification message to its parent. If the radio button style is `BS_AUTORADIOBUTTON`, `CstRadioBtnWndFn()` sets the checked state of the button, and searches through all sibling controls in the same group, resetting all other buttons which have *BS_AUTORADIOBUTTON* style.

Table 6.9 contains the standard button styles that *CSTRADIOBTN* supports. Table 6.10 lists the state flags for the *CSTRADIOBTN*. Figure 6.6 shows the four appearances for both the standard and the custom control.

Design Tradeoffs

Why create three custom controls, to mimic functionality that Windows packed into a single, multiple style control — especially considering the degree of similarity among the *CSTCHECKBOX*, *CSTPUSHBTN*, and *CSTRADIOBTN* controls?

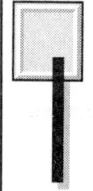

Table 6.9

The CSTRADIOBTN control responds to these three standard BUTTON class specific styles.

Style	Description
BS_RADIOBUTTON	Radio button
BS_AUTORADIOBUTTON	Radio button with auto set/reset of check state
BS_LEFTTEXT	Position text to left of button

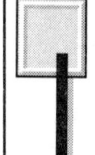

Table 6.10

The custom radio button control needs the same state information as the custom check box control.

State Flag Constant	Description
CRB_STATE_CAPTURE	Mouse is captured
CRB_STATE_DOWN	Control is being held down
CRB_STATE_FOCUS	Control is in focus
CRB_STATE_INSIDE	Mouse is inside control
CRB_STATE_CHECK	Control is checked

You could create one control that does it all. Since one control eliminates a lot of duplicate code, the total amount of code would be significantly less. But, because the control is no longer single purpose, the resulting code would also be significantly more complex. For example, virtually every portion of the window procedure would need to determine the style of the current control before it could select an appropriate response.

Our feeling was that even though the similarities are significant, the differences — differences in appearance, defaults, and states — are great enough to warrant treating each variant as a separate control.

Possible Enhancements

Our implementations faithfully mimic the functionality of the corresponding standard controls. With source code as a base, you can produce your own enhanced versions of the standard controls.

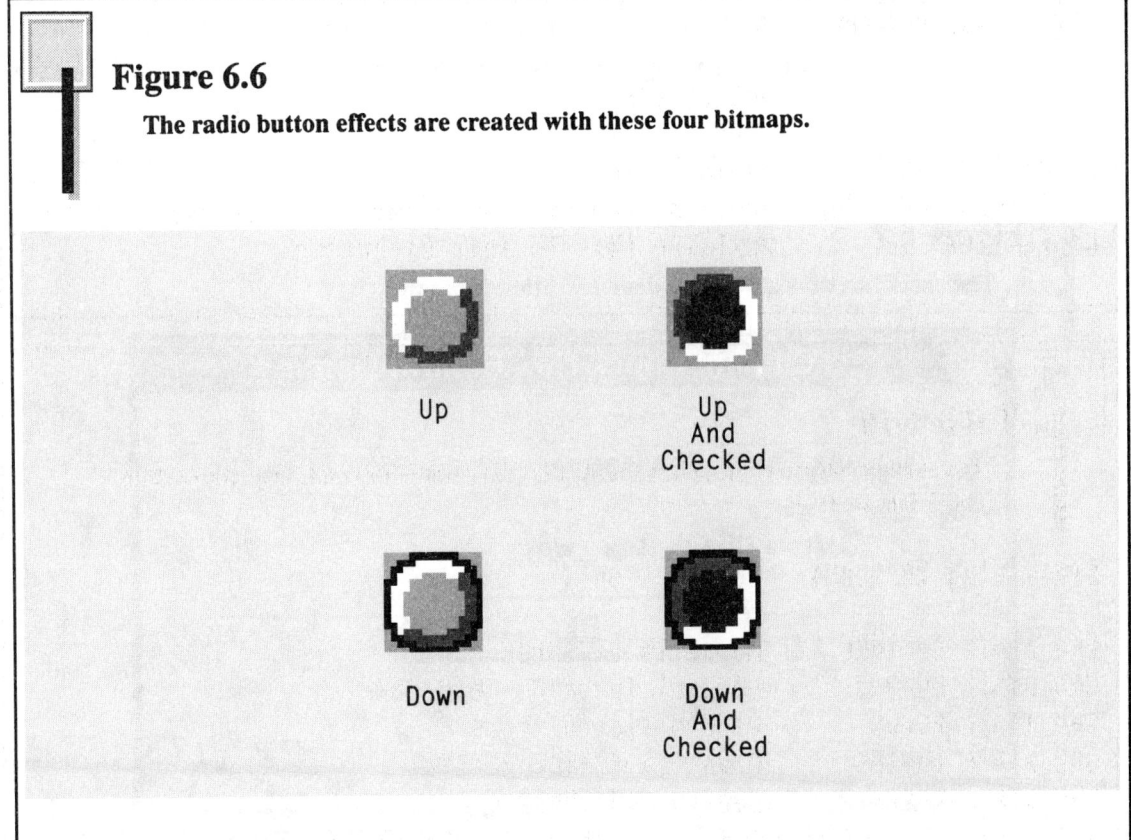

Figure 6.6
The radio button effects are created with these four bitmaps.

For example, by enhancing the notification interface, the parent can better manage which control has the input focus and how the cursor moves between controls (in response to keyboard input).

You can add such functionality by requesting the tab and arrow keys when responding to the WM_GETDLGCODE message and by defining more notification messages. The control sends a more specific notification message to the parent when processing a control navigation key such as a tab or shift tab. The control could also notify the parent when it receives or loses the input focus.

Alternatively, you could add new appearance styles. For example, you might create a pushbutton style that locates the text outside the button, making it more consistent with the CSTCHECKBOX and DSTRADIOBTN controls. As a starting point, you might approximate this effect by using the styles CPBS_NOFRAME, CPBS_NOSHADOW and a small bitmap (left or right justified) inside the control. A static text control combined with a pushbutton control also yields the same result.

Finally, you might consider creating a button control that can handle multiple lines of text. Such a button would let you choose your label for its readability instead of for its horizontal dimensions.

Figure 6.7
The check box dialog from the demonstration program.

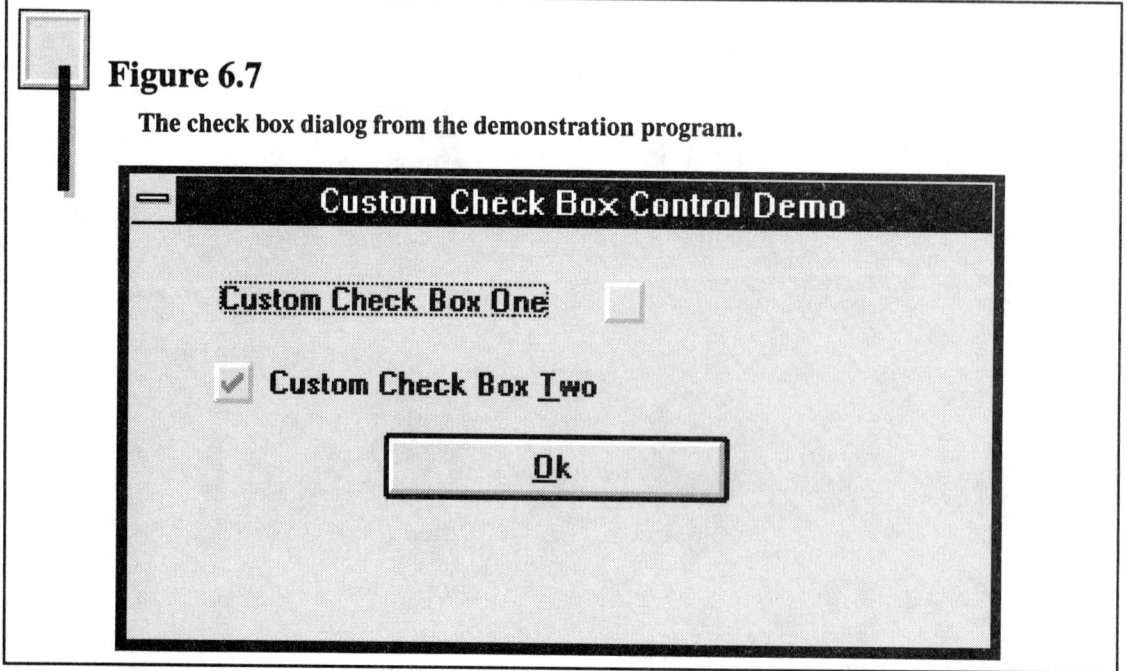

Program for CSTCHECKBOX, CSTPUSHBTN and CSTRADIOBTN

The program DEM_BTTN, Listings 6.9, 6.10, 6.11 and 6.12, displays all three types of custom button. The program generates three dialog boxes, each containing a different type of custom button control and displaying examples of most of the possible styles. Figures 6.7 through 6.9 show the three dialog boxes in DEM_BTTN.

Conclusion

Separating radio buttons, check boxes, and pushbuttons into three separate controls keeps each control's window procedure simple, but results in a lot of redundant code. The registration code, the WM_CREATE and WM_DESTROY handlers, and even some of the drawing code is nearly duplicated in several places. Total code size would probably shrink by 50 percent if we were to implement all three behaviors as a single control. But, the window procedure would be much uglier, because many message handlers would be forced to include multiple, style-controlled responses.

These controls show how to manage state information using our common data structure, and demonstrate how simply you can build and

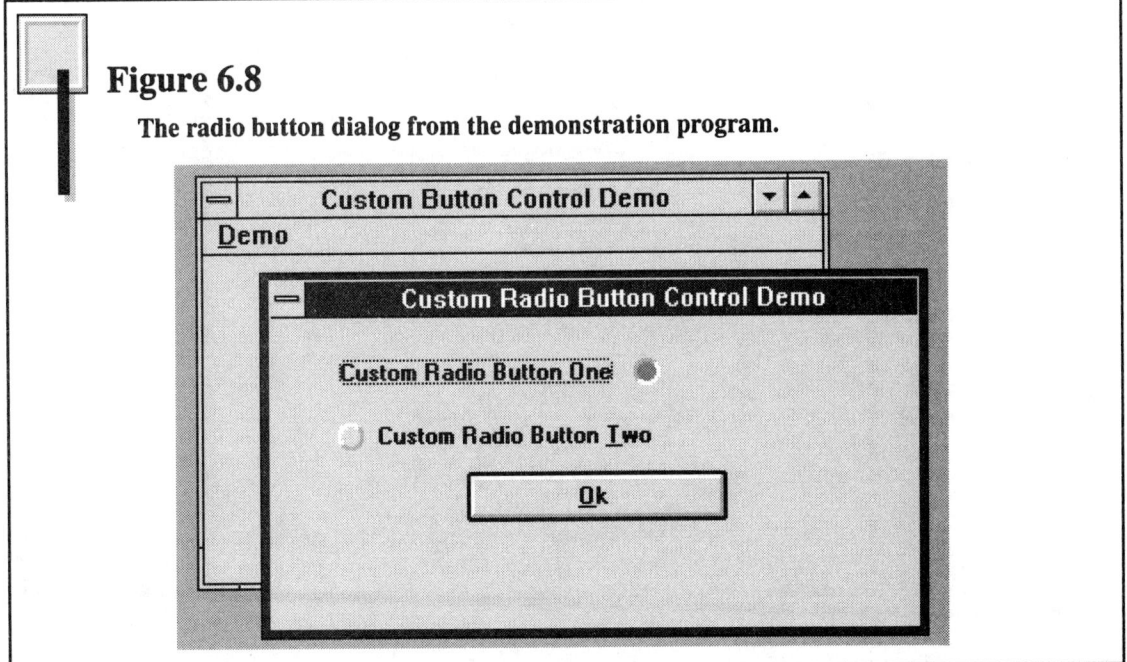

Figure 6.8
The radio button dialog from the demonstration program.

modify creative visual effects using bitmaps. When run on a device with unusual characteristics, these controls will also demonstrate the major disadvantage of bitmaps (as compared to GDI drawings): device dependence.

By itself, each of these controls seems a relatively minor departure from the standard versions, but as the screen shots in the preface clearly illustrate, collectively they can significantly improve a dialog's appearance.

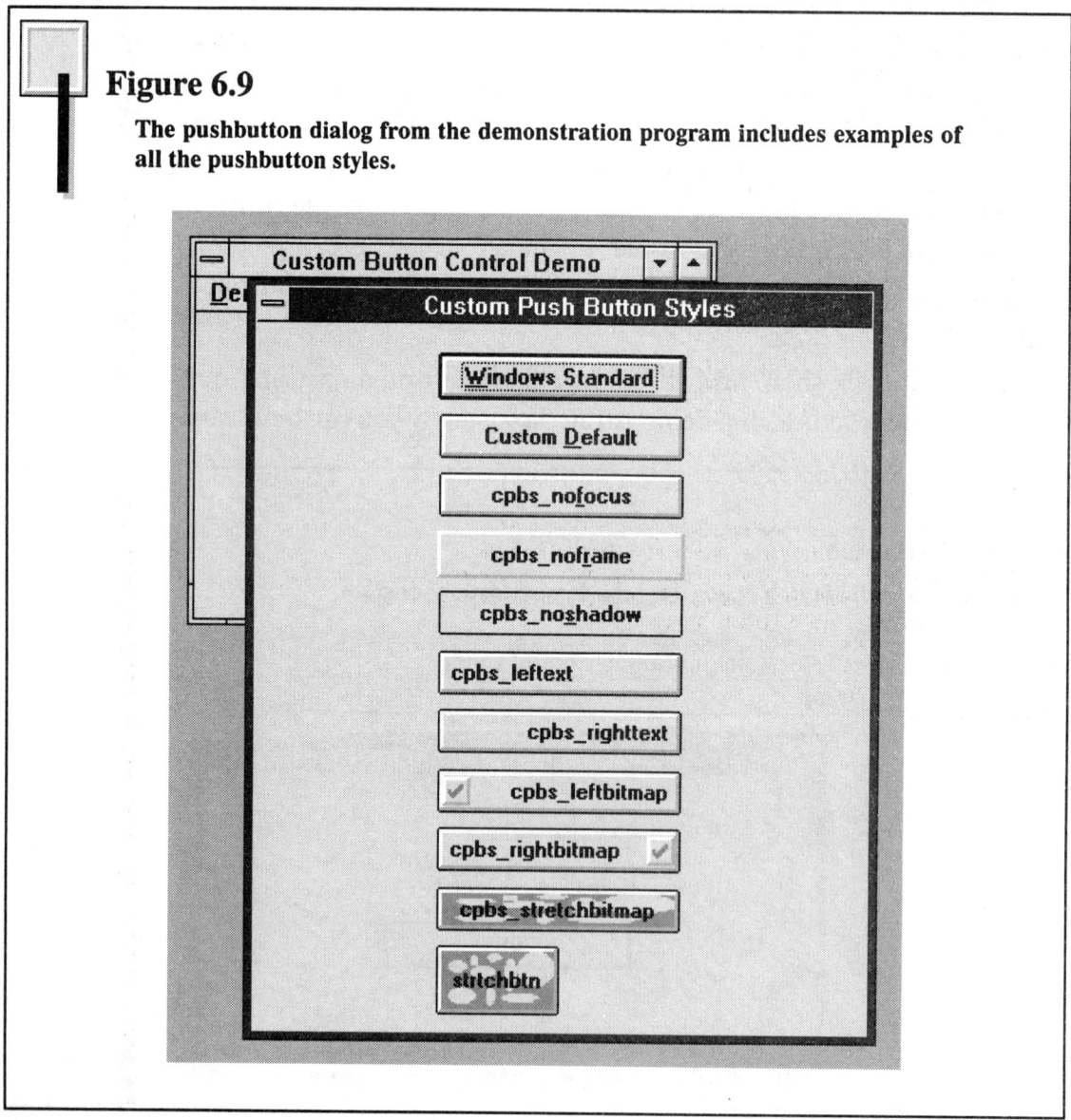

Figure 6.9

The pushbutton dialog from the demonstration program includes examples of all the pushbutton styles.

Listing 6.1

```c
/****************************************************************
          File Name: CST_CKBX.H
      Expanded Name: Custom Check Box
        Description: Include file for CST_CKBX.C
        Portability: Microsoft Windows 3.X
****************************************************************/

#if !defined ( CST_CKBX_DEFINED )
    #define CST_CKBX_DEFINED

    /* Custom Check Box Bitmap array access index */
    #define CCB_BITMAP_DOWN             0
    #define CCB_BITMAP_DOWNCHECK        1
    #define CCB_BITMAP_UP               2
    #define CCB_BITMAP_UPCHECK          3
    #define CCB_BITMAP_DISABLED         4
    #define CCB_BITMAP_DISABLEDCHECK    5

    /* Custom Check Box State bit flags */
    #define CCB_STATE_CAPTURE  0x01
    #define CCB_STATE_CHECK    0x02
    #define CCB_STATE_DISABLED 0x04
    #define CCB_STATE_DOWN     0x08
    #define CCB_STATE_FOCUS    0x10
    #define CCB_STATE_INSIDE   0x20

    /* Extra byte constants for custom check box control */
    #define CCB_CLSEXTRA ( CC_CLSEXTRA )
    #define CCB_WNDEXTRA ( CC_WNDEXTRA + sizeof ( LONG ) )

    /* WM_CTLCOLOR type for custom check box control */
    #define CTLCOLOR_CSTCHECKBOX ( CTLCOLOR_BTN | 0x020 )

    /* Prototypes for exported functions in CST_CKBX.C */
    int FAR PASCAL CstCheckBoxRegister( HINSTANCE hInstance );
    int FAR PASCAL CstCheckBoxUnregister( HINSTANCE hInstance );
    LONG FAR PASCAL CstCheckBoxWndFn( HWND hWnd, UINT wMessage,
            WPARAM wParam, LPARAM lParam );

#endif

/* End of CST_CKBX.H */
```

Listing 6.2

```c
/******************************************************************************
            File Name: CST_CKBX.C
        Expanded Name: Custom Check Box
          Description: Library of functions for the check box custom control
 Global Function List: CstCheckBoxRegister
                       CstCheckBoxUnregister
                       CstCheckBoxWndFn
 Static Function List: CstCheckBoxBitmapIndex
                       CstCheckBoxDefDataCreate
                       CstCheckBoxDefDataDelete
                       CstCheckBoxDraw
          Static Data: _hCstCtlData
                       _lpCstCtlData
          Global Data: _hInstanceCstCtls
          Portability: Microsoft Windows 3.X
******************************************************************************/

/* Microsoft Windows */
#include <windows.h>

/* Prototypes and Types */
#include <cst_xtra.h>
#include <cst_data.h>
#include <cst_util.h>

/* Own */
#include <cst_ckbx.h>

/* Prototypes of local static functions */
static WORD CstCheckBoxBitmapIndex( WORD wState );
static int  CstCheckBoxDefDataCreate( HWND hWnd );
static void CstCheckBoxDefDataDelete( void );
static void CstCheckBoxDraw( HWND hWnd, HDC hDC );

#if defined ( _WINDLL )
/* DLL Handle */
extern HINSTANCE _hInstanceCstCtls;
#endif

static HCSTCTLDATA  _hCstCtlData  = (HCSTCTLDATA)0;
static LPCSTCTLDATA _lpCstCtlData = (LPCSTCTLDATA)0;

/******************************************************************************
           Name: CstCheckBoxBitmapIndex
  Expanded Name: Get Check Box Bitmap Index
     Parameters: wState - instance state bit flags
         Return: Index into bitmap array
    Description: Gets the index into bitmap array depending on the button state.
******************************************************************************/
static WORD CstCheckBoxBitmapIndex( WORD wState )
    {

    WORD wBitmapIndex;

    if ( wState & CCB_STATE_DOWN )
        {
        if ( wState & CCB_STATE_CHECK )
```

Listing 6.2 *continued*

```
                {
                wBitmapIndex = CCB_BITMAP_DOWNCHECK;
                }
            else
                {
                wBitmapIndex = CCB_BITMAP_DOWN;
                }
            }
    else
        {
        if ( wState & CCB_STATE_CHECK )
            {
            if ( wState & CCB_STATE_DISABLED )
                {
                wBitmapIndex = CCB_BITMAP_DISABLEDCHECK;
                }
            else
                {
                wBitmapIndex = CCB_BITMAP_UPCHECK;
                }
            }
        else
            {
            if ( wState & CCB_STATE_DISABLED )
                {
                wBitmapIndex = CCB_BITMAP_DISABLED;
                }
            else
                {
                wBitmapIndex = CCB_BITMAP_UP;
                }
            }
        }   /* else */

    return ( wBitmapIndex );

    }   /* function CstCheckBoxBitmapIndex */

/******************************************************************************
         Name: CstCheckBoxDefDataCreate
Expanded Name: Default Data Create
   Parameters: hWnd - window handle to CheckBox control
       Return: TRUE or FALSE
  Description: Creates the default class data
******************************************************************************/
static int CstCheckBoxDefDataCreate( HWND hWnd )
    {

    HINSTANCE hInstanceClass;

    #if defined ( _WINDLL )
    hInstanceClass = _hInstanceCstCtls;
    #else
    hInstanceClass = GetWindowWord( hWnd, GWW_HINSTANCE );
    #endif

    _lpCstCtlData = CstCtlDefDataCreate( hWnd );
    if ( ! _lpCstCtlData )
```

Listing 6.2 continued

```
        {
        /* Failed to allocate and initialize data */
        return ( FALSE );
        }
    _hCstCtlData = CSTGETCLASSWORD( hWnd, GCW_HCSTCTLDATA );

    /* Free up the resources we do not need */
    SafeDeleteObject( _lpCstCtlData->hBrush[CC_BRUSH_BTNFACE] );
    _lpCstCtlData->hBrush[CC_BRUSH_BTNFACE] = 0;
    SafeDeleteObject( _lpCstCtlData->hBrush[CC_BRUSH_3DLIGHT] );
    _lpCstCtlData->hBrush[CC_BRUSH_3DLIGHT] = 0;
    SafeDeleteObject( _lpCstCtlData->hBrush[CC_BRUSH_3DSHADOW] );
    _lpCstCtlData->hBrush[CC_BRUSH_3DSHADOW] = 0;
    SafeDeleteObject( _lpCstCtlData->hBrush[CC_BRUSH_FRAME] );
    _lpCstCtlData->hBrush[CC_BRUSH_FRAME] = 0;

    /* Create the default bitmaps */
    _lpCstCtlData->hBitmap[CCB_BITMAP_DOWN] =
            LoadBitmap( hInstanceClass, "CBD_1616" );
    _lpCstCtlData->hBitmap[CCB_BITMAP_DOWNCHECK] =
            LoadBitmap( hInstanceClass, "CBDC1616" );
    _lpCstCtlData->hBitmap[CCB_BITMAP_UP] =
            LoadBitmap( hInstanceClass, "CBU_1616" );
    _lpCstCtlData->hBitmap[CCB_BITMAP_UPCHECK] =
            LoadBitmap( hInstanceClass, "CBUC1616" );
    _lpCstCtlData->hBitmap[CCB_BITMAP_DISABLED] =
            LoadBitmap( hInstanceClass, "CBS_1616" );
    _lpCstCtlData->hBitmap[CCB_BITMAP_DISABLEDCHECK] =
            LoadBitmap( hInstanceClass, "CBSC1616" );

    return ( TRUE );

    }   /* function CstCheckBoxDefDataCreate */


/******************************************************************************
        Name: CstCheckBoxDefDataDelete
Expanded Name: Default Data Delete
   Parameters: hWnd - window handle control
  Description: Deletes the default class data
******************************************************************************/
static void CstCheckBoxDefDataDelete( void )
    {

    if ( _lpCstCtlData )
        {
        SafeDeleteObject( _lpCstCtlData->hBrush[CC_BRUSH_BACKGROUND] );
        SafeDeleteObject( _lpCstCtlData->hBitmap[CCB_BITMAP_DOWN] );
        SafeDeleteObject( _lpCstCtlData->hBitmap[CCB_BITMAP_DOWNCHECK] );
        SafeDeleteObject( _lpCstCtlData->hBitmap[CCB_BITMAP_UP] );
        SafeDeleteObject( _lpCstCtlData->hBitmap[CCB_BITMAP_UPCHECK] );
        SafeDeleteObject( _lpCstCtlData->hBitmap[CCB_BITMAP_DISABLED] );
        SafeDeleteObject( _lpCstCtlData->hBitmap[CCB_BITMAP_DISABLEDCHECK] );
        _lpCstCtlData = (LPCSTCTLDATA)0;
        }

    if ( _hCstCtlData )
        {
        GlobalUnlock( _hCstCtlData );
```

Listing 6.2 continued

```
            GlobalFree( _hCstCtlData );
            _hCstCtlData = (HCSTCTLDATA)0;
            }

    }   /* function CstCheckBoxDefDataDelete */

/********************************************************************
        Name: CstCheckBoxDraw
Expanded Name: Check Box Draw
  Parameters: hWnd - window handle to check box control
              hDC - device context of check box control
 Description: Draws the check box custom control
********************************************************************/
static void CstCheckBoxDraw( HWND hWnd, HDC hDC )
    {

    BOOL bFontSelected = FALSE;
    COLORREF lColorTextBkOrg, lColorTextOrg;
    HANDLE hText;
    HBITMAP hBitmap;
    HBRUSH hBrushBk = 0;
    HDC hDCMem;
    HFONT hFont, hFontOrg;
    HWND hWndParent;
    int iBkModeOrg, iTextHeight, iTextLen;
    LPRECT lpRectBitmap, lpRectText;
    LPSTR lpstrText;
    RECT Rect, RectDrawText;
    WORD wBitmapIndex, wState, wCtlColorMsg = 0;

    hWndParent = GetParent( hWnd );
    if ( hWndParent )
        {
        /* Send message to give parent a chance to change data */
        hBrushBk = (HBRUSH)SendMessage( hWndParent, WM_CTLCOLOR, hDC,
                MAKELPARAM( hWnd, CTLCOLOR_CSTCHECKBOX ) );
        wCtlColorMsg = CstCtlColorMsg( hWnd, FALSE );
        if ( !( wCtlColorMsg & CTLCOLORMSG_BRUSH ) )
            {
            /* Use the brush of the parent window */
            hBrushBk = GetClassWord( hWndParent, GCW_HBRBACKGROUND );
            }
        }
    if ( !hBrushBk )
        {
        /* Still do not have a brush so get the default */
        hBrushBk = CSTCTLGETBRUSH( hWnd, CC_BRUSH_BACKGROUND );
        }

    /* Get the bitmap based on state of button */
    wState = CSTCTLGETSTATE( hWnd );
    wBitmapIndex = CstCheckBoxBitmapIndex( wState );
    hBitmap = CSTCTLGETBITMAP( hWnd, wBitmapIndex );

    /* Paint the background */
    GetClientRect( hWnd, &Rect );
    AlignBrush( hWndParent, hDC, hBrushBk );
    FillRect( hDC, &Rect, hBrushBk );
    lpRectText = CSTCTLGETLPRECTTEXT( hWnd );
```

Listing 6.2 *continued*

```
hDCMem = CreateCompatibleDC( hDC );
if ( SelectObject( hDCMem, hBitmap ) )
    {

    BITMAP Bitmap;

    /* Display the bitmap */
    lpRectBitmap = CSTCTLGETLPRECTBITMAP( hWnd );
    CstCtlSetRects( hWnd, hBitmap, &Rect, lpRectBitmap, lpRectText );
    GetObject( hBitmap, sizeof ( BITMAP ), (LPSTR)&Bitmap );
    BitBlt( hDC, lpRectBitmap->left, lpRectBitmap->top, Bitmap.bmWidth,
            Bitmap.bmHeight, hDCMem, 0, 0, SRCCOPY );
    }

/* Free the DC for the bitmap */
DeleteDC( hDCMem );

/* Get the text */
iTextLen = GetWindowTextLength( hWnd );
hText = GlobalAlloc( GMEM_FLAGS, (DWORD)( iTextLen + 1 ) );
lpstrText = GlobalLock( hText );
GetWindowText( hWnd, lpstrText, iTextLen + 1 );

/* Get the font */
if ( !( wCtlColorMsg & CTLCOLORMSG_FONT ) )
    {
    hFont = CSTCTLGETFONT( hWnd );
    if ( !hFont )
        {
        /* Get the font of the parent window */
        if ( hWndParent )
            {
            hFont = (HFONT)SendMessage( hWndParent, WM_GETFONT, 0, 0L );
            CstCtlSetFont( hWnd, hFont );
            }
        }
    if ( hFont )
        {
        hFontOrg = SelectObject( hDC, hFont );
        bFontSelected = TRUE;
        }
    }   /* if !wCtlColorMsg */

/* Set the color */
if ( !( wCtlColorMsg & CTLCOLORMSG_COLORTEXT ) )
    {
    lColorTextOrg = SetTextColor( hDC,
            CSTCTLGETCOLOR( hWnd, CC_COLOR_TEXT ) );
    }
if ( !( wCtlColorMsg & CTLCOLORMSG_COLORTEXTBK ) )
    {
    lColorTextBkOrg = SetBkColor( hDC,
            CSTCTLGETCOLOR( hWnd, CC_COLOR_TEXTBACKGROUND ) );
    }
if ( !( wCtlColorMsg & CTLCOLORMSG_MODETEXTBK ) )
    {
    iBkModeOrg = SetBkMode( hDC, CSTCTLGETBKMODE( hWnd ) );
    }
```

Listing 6.2 *continued*

```c
    /* Center the text vertically and then display the text */
    RectDrawText = *lpRectText;
    iTextHeight = DrawText( hDC, lpstrText, -1, &RectDrawText,
            DT_LEFT | DT_SINGLELINE | DT_CALCRECT );
    OffsetRect( &RectDrawText, 0,
            max( 0, ( ( Rect.bottom - Rect.top) - iTextHeight ) / 2 ) );
    DrawText( hDC, lpstrText, -1, &RectDrawText, DT_SINGLELINE );

    if ( ( GetFocus() == hWnd ) && ( iTextLen > 0 ) )
        {
        /* The window is in focus with text so draw focus rect */
        DrawFocusRect( hDC, &RectDrawText );
        }

    /* Free the memory for text */
    GlobalUnlock( hText );
    GlobalFree( hText );

    /* Reset the font */
    if ( bFontSelected )
        {
        SelectObject( hDC, hFontOrg );
        }

    /* Reset the colors and mode */
    if ( !( wCtlColorMsg & CTLCOLORMSG_COLORTEXT ) )
        {
        SetTextColor( hDC, lColorTextOrg );
        }
    if ( !( wCtlColorMsg & CTLCOLORMSG_COLORTEXTBK ) )
        {
        SetBkColor( hDC, lColorTextBkOrg );
        }
    if ( !( wCtlColorMsg & CTLCOLORMSG_MODETEXTBK ) )
        {
        SetBkMode( hDC, iBkModeOrg );
        }

    }   /* function CstCheckBoxDraw */

/*******************************************************************************
        Name: CstCheckBoxRegister
  Parameters: hInstance - handle to program or library registering class
      Return: Same as RegisterClass
 Description: Registers the window class for the custom Check Box control
*******************************************************************************/
int FAR PASCAL CstCheckBoxRegister( HINSTANCE hInstance )
    {

    WNDCLASS WndClass;

    WndClass.style = CS_HREDRAW | CS_VREDRAW | CS_PARENTDC;

    #if defined ( _WINDLL )
    hInstance = _hInstanceCstCtls;
    WndClass.style |= CS_GLOBALCLASS;
    #endif

    WndClass.lpfnWndProc = CstCheckBoxWndFn;
```

Listing 6.2 continued

```
    WndClass.cbClsExtra = CCB_CLSEXTRA;
    WndClass.cbWndExtra = CCB_WNDEXTRA;
    WndClass.hInstance = hInstance;
    WndClass.hIcon = 0;
    WndClass.hCursor = LoadCursor( 0, IDC_ARROW );
    WndClass.hbrBackground = 0;
    WndClass.lpszMenuName = 0;
    WndClass.lpszClassName = (LPSTR)"CstCheckBox";

    return ( RegisterClass( &WndClass ) );

    }   /* function CstCheckBoxRegister */


/*****************************************************************************
        Name: CstCheckBoxUnregister
  Parameters: hInstance - handle to program or library that registered class
      Return: Same as UnregisterClass
 Description: Unregisters the window class for the custom Check Box control
*****************************************************************************/
int FAR PASCAL CstCheckBoxUnregister( HINSTANCE hInstance )
    {

    #if defined ( _WINDLL )
    hInstance = _hInstanceCstCtls;
    #endif

    return ( UnregisterClass( "CstCheckBox", hInstance ) );

    }   /* function CstCheckBoxUnregister */



/*****************************************************************************
         Name: CstCheckBoxWndFn
 Expanded Name: Custom Check Box Window Callback Function
  Description: Window call back function for the custom check box control
*****************************************************************************/
LONG FAR PASCAL CstCheckBoxWndFn( HWND hWnd, UINT wMessage,
        WPARAM wParam, LPARAM lParam )
    {

    static int _WindowCount = 0;

    switch ( wMessage )
        {
        case BM_GETCHECK:
            /* Return whether the control is checked (TRUE) or not (FALSE) */
            return ( CstCtlState( hWnd, CCB_STATE_CHECK,
                    STATE_CHECK, AREA_NONE ) );
        case BM_GETSTATE:
            /* Returns nonzero if the button is down */
            return ( CstCtlState( hWnd, CCB_STATE_DOWN,
                    STATE_CHECK, AREA_NONE ) );
        case BM_SETCHECK:
            {


            DWORD dwStyle;
```

Listing 6.2 *continued*

```
            dwStyle = (DWORD)GetWindowLong( hWnd, GWL_STYLE ) & 0x0FL;
            /* Sets or resets the check box check state */
            if ( ( dwStyle == BS_3STATE ) || ( dwStyle == BS_AUTO3STATE ) )
                {
                switch ( wParam )
                    {
                    case 0:
                        CstCtlState( hWnd, CCB_STATE_CHECK, STATE_RESET,
                                AREA_BITMAP );
                        break;
                    case 1:
                        CstCtlState( hWnd, CCB_STATE_CHECK, STATE_SET,
                                AREA_BITMAP );
                        break;
                    case 2:
                        CstCtlState( hWnd, CCB_STATE_DISABLED, STATE_SET,
                                AREA_ALL );
                        break;
                    default:
                        break;
                    }  /* switch wParam */
                }   /* if dwStyle */
            else
                {
                CstCtlState( hWnd, CCB_STATE_CHECK, (WORD)( wParam ?
                        STATE_SET : STATE_RESET ), AREA_BITMAP );
                }
            break;
            }
        case BM_SETSTATE:
            /* Sets or resets the check box down state */
            CstCtlState( hWnd, CCB_STATE_DOWN, (WORD)( wParam ?
                    STATE_SET : STATE_RESET ), AREA_BITMAP );
            break;
        case WM_CREATE:
            {

            HWND hWndParent = GetParent( hWnd );

            if ( !_WindowCount )
                {
                if ( !CstCheckBoxDefDataCreate( hWnd ) )
                    {
                    return ( -1 );
                    }
                }
            _WindowCount++;

            /* Create instance data */
            CstCtlDataCreate( hWnd );

            /* Set initial states */
            if ( ( (LPCREATESTRUCT)lParam )->style & WS_DISABLED )
                {
                CstCtlState( hWnd, CCB_STATE_DISABLED,
                        STATE_SET, AREA_NONE );
                }
            /* Notify the parent that the button has been created */
```

Windows Custom Controls

Listing 6.2 *continued*

```
            if ( hWndParent )
                {
                SendMessage( hWndParent, WM_PARENTNOTIFY, WM_CREATE,
                        MAKELPARAM( hWnd, GetDlgCtrlID( hWnd ) ) );
                }
            break;
            }   /* case WM_CREATE */
    case WM_CSTCTLGETDATA:
    case WM_CSTCTLGETDEFDATA:
    case WM_CSTCTLSETDATA:
    case WM_CSTCTLSETDEFDATA:
            return ( (LONG)CstCtlData( hWnd, wMessage, wParam, lParam ) );
    case WM_DESTROY:
            {

            HWND hWndParent = GetParent( hWnd );

            /* Notify the parent and then delete the instance data */
            if ( hWndParent )
                {
                SendMessage( hWndParent, WM_PARENTNOTIFY,
                        WM_DESTROY, MAKELPARAM( hWnd,
                        GetDlgCtrlID( hWnd ) ) );
                }
            if ( IsWindow( hWnd ) )
                {
                CstCtlDataDelete( hWnd );
                }

            _WindowCount--;
            if ( _WindowCount <= 0 )
                {
                CstCheckBoxDefDataDelete();
                }
            break;
            }   /* case WM_DESTROY */
    case WM_ENABLE:
            /* Set or Reset enable state */
            CstCtlState( hWnd, CCB_STATE_DISABLED, (WORD)( wParam ?
                    STATE_RESET : STATE_SET ), AREA_ALL );
            break;
    case WM_ERASEBKGND:
            /* Background is handled during the WM_PAINT message */
            return ( TRUE );
    case WM_GETDLGCODE:
            /* Return to dialog manager that this is a button */
            return ( DLGC_BUTTON );
    case WM_KEYDOWN:
            if ( ( wParam == ' ' ) &&
                    !( HIBYTE( HIWORD( lParam ) ) & 0x40 ) )
                {
                /* Space bar toggles to the down state */
                CstCtlState( hWnd, CCB_STATE_DOWN, STATE_SET, AREA_BITMAP );
                }
            break;
    case WM_KEYUP:
            if ( wParam == ' ' )
                {
```

Listing 6.2 *continued*

```
            DWORD dwStyle;

            /* Space bar toggles to the up state */
            CstCtlState( hWnd, CCB_STATE_DOWN, STATE_RESET, AREA_BITMAP );
            dwStyle = (DWORD)GetWindowLong( hWnd, GWL_STYLE ) & 0x0FL;
            if ( ( dwStyle == BS_AUTOCHECKBOX ) ||
                    ( dwStyle == BS_AUTO3STATE ) )
                {
                SendMessage( hWnd, BM_SETCHECK,
                        (WPARAM)!CstCtlState( hWnd, CCB_STATE_CHECK,
                        STATE_CHECK, AREA_NONE ), 0L );
                if ( !IsWindow( hWnd ) )
                    {
                    break;
                    }
                }
            if ( CstCtlState( hWnd, CCB_STATE_FOCUS,
                    STATE_CHECK, AREA_NONE ) )
                {

                HWND hWndParent = GetParent( hWnd );

                /* Button is in focus so send message to parent */
                if ( hWndParent )
                    {
                    SendMessage( hWndParent, WM_COMMAND,
                            (WPARAM)GetDlgCtrlID( hWnd ),
                            MAKELPARAM( hWnd, BN_CLICKED ) );
                    }
                }
            }   /* if wParam */
        break;
    case WM_KILLFOCUS:
        /* Reset states */
        CstCtlState( hWnd, CCB_STATE_FOCUS | CCB_STATE_DOWN,
                STATE_RESET, AREA_ALL );
        break;
    case WM_LBUTTONDOWN:
        /* Left mouse button is down, capture the mouse, focus
        ** and update instance status */
        SetCapture( hWnd );
        CstCtlState( hWnd, CCB_STATE_CAPTURE | CCB_STATE_DOWN |
                CCB_STATE_INSIDE, STATE_SET, AREA_BITMAP );
        if ( GetFocus() != hWnd )
            {
            SetFocus( hWnd );
            }
        break;
    case WM_LBUTTONUP:
        ReleaseCapture();
        if ( CstCtlState( hWnd, CCB_STATE_INSIDE,
                STATE_CHECK, AREA_NONE ) )
            {

            DWORD dwStyle;
            HWND hWndParent = GetParent( hWnd );

            /* The mouse was inside button so send message to parent */
```

Listing 6.2 continued

```
            dwStyle = (DWORD)GetWindowLong( hWnd, GWL_STYLE ) & 0x0FL;
            if ( ( dwStyle == BS_AUTOCHECKBOX ) ||
                 ( dwStyle == BS_AUTO3STATE ) )
                {
                SendMessage( hWnd, BM_SETCHECK,
                         (WPARAM)!CstCtlState( hWnd, CCB_STATE_CHECK,
                             STATE_CHECK, AREA_NONE ), 0L );
                if ( !IsWindow( hWnd ) )
                    {
                    break;
                    }
                }
            if ( hWndParent )
                {
                SendMessage( hWndParent, WM_COMMAND,
                    (WPARAM)GetDlgCtrlID( hWnd ),
                    MAKELPARAM( hWnd, BN_CLICKED ) );
                }
            if ( !IsWindow( hWnd ) )
                {
                break;
                }
            }
        CstCtlState( hWnd, CCB_STATE_DOWN | CCB_STATE_CAPTURE |
                CCB_STATE_INSIDE, STATE_RESET, AREA_BITMAP );
        break;
    case WM_MOUSEMOVE:
        {

        WORD wState = CSTCTLGETSTATE( hWnd );

        if ( wState & CCB_STATE_CAPTURE )
            {

            POINT Point;

            /* Mouse has been captured so check the location */
            Point.x = (int)LOWORD( lParam );
            Point.y = (int)HIWORD( lParam );
            if ( PtInWnd( hWnd, Point ) )
                {
                /* Inside the control */
                if ( !( wState & CCB_STATE_INSIDE ) )
                    {
                    /* Was outside control, change states */
                    CstCtlState( hWnd, CCB_STATE_DOWN |
                            CCB_STATE_INSIDE, STATE_SET, AREA_BITMAP );
                    }
                }
            else
                {
                /* Outside the control */
                if ( wState & CCB_STATE_INSIDE )
                    {
                    /* Was inside control, change states */
                    CstCtlState( hWnd, CCB_STATE_DOWN |
                            CCB_STATE_INSIDE, STATE_RESET, AREA_BITMAP );
                    }
```

Listing 6.2 *continued*

```
                    }
            }    /* if wState */
        break;
        }    /* case WM_MOUSEMOVE */
    case WM_PAINT:
        {

        PAINTSTRUCT PS;
        HDC hDC = BeginPaint( hWnd, &PS );

        if ( IsWindowVisible( hWnd ) )
            {
            /* Only paint if needed */
            CstCheckBoxDraw( hWnd, hDC );
            }
        EndPaint( hWnd, &PS );
        break;
        }
    case WM_SETFOCUS:
        CstCtlState( hWnd, CCB_STATE_FOCUS, STATE_SET, AREA_ALL );
        break;
    case WM_SETFONT:
        if ( wParam )
            {
            CstCtlSetFont( hWnd, wParam );
            }
        if ( lParam )
            {
            /* Send a Paint message */
            InvalidateRect( hWnd, NULL, FALSE );
            UpdateWindow( hWnd );
            }
        break;
    case WM_SETTEXT:
        /* Default processing */
        DefWindowProc( hWnd, wMessage, wParam, lParam );
        /* Send a paint message */
        InvalidateRect( hWnd, NULL, FALSE );
        UpdateWindow( hWnd );
        return ( TRUE );
    default:
        return ( DefWindowProc( hWnd, wMessage, wParam, lParam ) );
    }    /* switch wMessage */

    return ( 0L );

    }    /* function CstCheckBoxWndFn */

/* End of CST_CKBX.C */
```

Listing 6.3

```
/*****************************************************************************
          File Name: CST_CKBX.RC
      Expanded Name: Custom Check Box
        Description: Resource file for the check box custom control
        Portability: Microsoft Windows 3.X
*****************************************************************************/

CBD_1616 BITMAP BITMAP\CBD_1616.BMP    /* Down State */
CBDC1616 BITMAP BITMAP\CBDC1616.BMP    /* Down & Checked State */
CBU_1616 BITMAP BITMAP\CBU_1616.BMP    /* Up State */
CBUC1616 BITMAP BITMAP\CBUC1616.BMP    /* UP & Checked State */
CBS_1616 BITMAP BITMAP\CBS_1616.BMP    /* Disabled State */
CBSC1616 BITMAP BITMAP\CBSC1616.BMP    /* Disabled & Checked Stated */

/* End of CST_CKBX.RC */
```

Listing 6.4

```c
/****************************************************************************
         File Name: CST_PBTN.H
     Expanded Name: Custom Push Button
       Description: Include file for CST_PBTN.C
       Portability: Microsoft Windows 3.X
****************************************************************************/

#if !defined ( CST_PBTN_DEFINED )
    #define CST_PBTN_DEFINED

    /* Custom Push Button Bitmap array access index */
    #define CPB_BITMAP_DOWN          0
    #define CPB_BITMAP_UP            1
    #define CPB_BITMAP_UPFOCUS       2
    #define CPB_BITMAP_DISABLED      3
    #define CPB_BITMAP_DISABLEDFOCUS 4

    /* Custom Push Button State bit flags */
    #define CPB_STATE_CAPTURE     0x01
    #define CPB_STATE_DISABLED    0x04
    #define CPB_STATE_DOWN        0x08
    #define CPB_STATE_FOCUS       0x10
    #define CPB_STATE_INSIDE      0x20
    #define CPB_STATE_DEFAULT     0x40
    #define CPB_STATE_DEFAULTORG  0x80

    /* Class specific window styles for custom push button control */
    #define CPBS_LEFTTEXT      0x0040L
    #define CPBS_RIGHTTEXT     0x0080L
    #define CPBS_NOFOCUS       0x0100L
    #define CPBS_NOFRAME       0x0200L
    #define CPBS_NOSHADOW      0x0400L
    #define CPBS_STRETCHBITMAP 0x0800L
    #define CPBS_LEFTBITMAP    0x1000L
    #define CPBS_RIGHTBITMAP   0x2000L
    #define CPBS_STRETCHBUTTON 0x4000L

    /* Extra byte constants for custom push button control */
    #define CPB_CLSEXTRA ( CC_CLSEXTRA )
    #define CPB_WNDEXTRA ( CC_WNDEXTRA + sizeof ( LONG ) )

    /* WM_CTLCOLOR type for custom push button control */
    #define CTLCOLOR_CSTPUSHBTN ( CTLCOLOR_BTN | 0x040 )

    /* Prototypes for exported functions in CST_PBTN.C */
    int FAR PASCAL CstPushBtnRegister( HINSTANCE hInstance );
    int FAR PASCAL CstPushBtnUnregister( HINSTANCE hInstance );
    LONG FAR PASCAL CstPushBtnWndFn( HWND hWnd, UINT wMessage, WPARAM wParam,
            LPARAM lParam );

#endif

/* End of CST_PBTN.H */
```

Listing 6.5

```
/*****************************************************************************
         File Name: CST_PBTN.C
     Expanded Name: Custom Push Button
       Description: Library of functions for the push button custom control
Global Function List: CstPushBtnRegister
                    CstPushBtnUnregister
                    CstPushBtnWndFn
Static Function List: CstPushBtnBitmapIndex
                    CstPushBtnDefDataCreate
                    CstPushBtnDefDataDelete
                    CstPushBtnDraw
                    CstPushBtnDrawFocus
                    CstPushBtnDrawText
                    RectInRect
       Global Data: _hInstanceCstCtls
       Static Data: _hCstCtlData
                    _lpCstCtlData
       Portability: Microsoft Windows 3.X
*****************************************************************************/

/* Microsoft Windows */
#include <windows.h>

/* Standard C */
#include <stdlib.h>
#include <string.h>

/* Types and Prototypes */
#include <cst_xtra.h>
#include <cst_data.h>
#include <cst_draw.h>
#include <cst_util.h>

/* Own */
#include <cst_pbtn.h>

/* Prototypes of static functions */
static WORD CstPushBtnBitmapIndex( WORD wState );
static int  CstPushBtnDefDataCreate( HWND hWnd );
static void CstPushBtnDefDataDelete( void );
static void CstPushBtnDraw( HWND hWnd, HDC hDC );
static void CstPushBtnDrawFocus( HWND hWnd, HDC hDC, LPRECT lpRect,
        LPSTR lpstrText, WORD wFormat );
static void CstPushBtnDrawText( HWND hWnd, HDC hDC, int iWidth, int iHeight,
        WORD wCtlColorMsg );
static BOOL RectInRect( LPRECT lpRectIn, LPRECT lpRectOut );

#if defined ( _WINDLL )
/* DLL Handle */
extern HINSTANCE _hInstanceCstCtls;
#endif

static HCSTCTLDATA  _hCstCtlData  = (HCSTCTLDATA)0;
static LPCSTCTLDATA _lpCstCtlData = (LPCSTCTLDATA)0;

/*****************************************************************************
         Name: CstPushBtnBitmapIndex
Expanded Name: Get Push Button Bitmap Index
   Parameters: wState - instance state bit flags
```

Listing 6.5 *continued*

```
        Return: Index into bitmap array
   Description: Gets the index into bitmap array depending on the button state.
****************************************************************************/
static WORD CstPushBtnBitmapIndex( WORD wState )
    {

    WORD wBitmapIndex;

    if ( wState & CPB_STATE_DOWN )
        {
        wBitmapIndex = CPB_BITMAP_DOWN;
        }
    else if ( wState & CPB_STATE_DISABLED )
        {
        if ( wState & CPB_STATE_FOCUS )
            {
            wBitmapIndex = CPB_BITMAP_DISABLEDFOCUS;
            }
        else
            {
            wBitmapIndex = CPB_BITMAP_DISABLED;
            }
        }
    else
        {
        if ( wState & CPB_STATE_FOCUS )
            {
            wBitmapIndex = CPB_BITMAP_UPFOCUS;
            }
        else
            {
            wBitmapIndex = CPB_BITMAP_UP;
            }
        }

    return ( wBitmapIndex );

    }   /* function CstPushBtnBitmapIndex */


/****************************************************************************
          Name: CstPushBtnDefDataCreate
 Expanded Name: Default Data Create
    Parameters: hWnd - window handle to CstPushBtn control
        Return: TRUE or FALSE
   Description: Creates the default class data
****************************************************************************/
static int CstPushBtnDefDataCreate( HWND hWnd )
    {

    _lpCstCtlData = CstCtlDefDataCreate( hWnd );
    if ( !_lpCstCtlData )
        {
        /* Failed to allocate and initialize data */
        return ( FALSE );
        }
    _hCstCtlData = CSTGETCLASSWORD( hWnd, GCW_HCSTCTLDATA );
```

Listing 6.5 continued

```c
    /* Change the default text color for this particular control */
    _lpCstCtlData->lColor[CC_COLOR_TEXT] = (COLORREF)
            GetSysColor( COLOR_BTNTEXT );
    _lpCstCtlData->lColor[CC_COLOR_TEXTBACKGROUND] = (COLORREF)
            GetSysColor( COLOR_BTNFACE );

    return ( TRUE );

    }   /* function CstPushBtnDefDataCreate */


/*****************************************************************************
         Name: CstPushBtnDefDataDelete
Expanded Name: Default Data Delete
   Parameters: hWnd - window handle control
  Description: Deletes the default class data
*****************************************************************************/
static void CstPushBtnDefDataDelete( void )
    {

    if ( _lpCstCtlData )
        {
        SafeDeleteObject( _lpCstCtlData->hBrush[CC_BRUSH_BACKGROUND] );
        SafeDeleteObject( _lpCstCtlData->hBrush[CC_BRUSH_BTNFACE] );
        SafeDeleteObject( _lpCstCtlData->hBrush[CC_BRUSH_3DLIGHT] );
        SafeDeleteObject( _lpCstCtlData->hBrush[CC_BRUSH_3DSHADOW] );
        SafeDeleteObject( _lpCstCtlData->hBrush[CC_BRUSH_FRAME] );
        _lpCstCtlData = (LPCSTCTLDATA)0;
        }

    if ( _hCstCtlData )
        {
        GlobalUnlock( _hCstCtlData );
        GlobalFree( _hCstCtlData );
        _hCstCtlData = (HCSTCTLDATA)0;
        }

    }   /* function CstPushBtnDefDataDelete */


/*****************************************************************************
         Name: CstPushBtnDraw
Expanded Name: Push Button Draw
   Parameters: hWnd - window handle of push button control
               hDC - device context push button control
  Description: Draws the push button custom control
*****************************************************************************/
static void CstPushBtnDraw( HWND hWnd, HDC hDC )
    {

    BITMAP Bitmap;
    HBITMAP hBitmap;
    HBRUSH hBrushBk = 0, hBrushBtnFace, hBrushFrame, hBrushLight, hBrushShadow;
    HWND hWndParent;
    int iFrame = 0, iShadow = 0;
    LONG lStyle;
    RECT Rect;
    WORD wBitmapIndex, wState, wCtlColorMsg = 0;
```

Listing 6.5 *continued*

```
hWndParent = GetParent( hWnd );
if ( hWndParent )
    {
    /* Send message to give parent a chance to change data */
    hBrushBk = (HBRUSH)SendMessage( hWndParent, WM_CTLCOLOR, hDC,
            MAKELPARAM( hWnd, CTLCOLOR_CSTPUSHBTN ) );
    wCtlColorMsg = CstCtlColorMsg( hWnd, FALSE );
    if ( !( wCtlColorMsg & CTLCOLORMSG_BRUSH ) )
        {
        /* Use the brush of the parent window */
        hBrushBk = GetClassWord( hWndParent, GCW_HBRBACKGROUND );
        }
    }
if ( !hBrushBk )
    {
    /* Still do not have a brush so get the default */
    hBrushBk = CSTCTLGETBRUSH( hWnd, CC_BRUSH_BACKGROUND );
    }

/* Get the bitmap based on state of button */
wState = CSTCTLGETSTATE( hWnd );
wBitmapIndex = CstPushBtnBitmapIndex( wState );
hBitmap = CSTCTLGETBITMAP( hWnd, wBitmapIndex );

/* Get the style of the push button */
lStyle = GetWindowLong( hWnd, GWL_STYLE );
if ( !( lStyle & CPBS_NOFRAME ) )
    {
    /* Get the thickness of the default frame to draw */
    iFrame = CSTCTLGETFRAME( hWnd );
    }
if ( !( lStyle & CPBS_NOSHADOW ) )
    {
    /* Get the thickness of the 3D shadow to draw */
    iShadow = CSTCTLGETSHADOW( hWnd );
    }

/* Get the brushs of the button */
hBrushLight   = CSTCTLGETBRUSH( hWnd, CC_BRUSH_3DLIGHT );
hBrushBtnFace = CSTCTLGETBRUSH( hWnd, CC_BRUSH_BTNFACE );
hBrushShadow  = CSTCTLGETBRUSH( hWnd, CC_BRUSH_3DSHADOW );
hBrushFrame   = CSTCTLGETBRUSH( hWnd, CC_BRUSH_FRAME );

if ( hBitmap )
    {

    /* There is a bitmap */
    GetObject( hBitmap, sizeof ( BITMAP ), (LPSTR)&Bitmap );

    if ( lStyle & CPBS_STRETCHBUTTON )
        {

        POINT Point;

        /* Size the window to the bitmap */
        GetWindowRect( hWnd, &Rect );
        Point.x = Rect.left;
        Point.y = Rect.top;
        ScreenToClient( hWndParent, &Point );
```

Listing 6.5 *continued*

```
            MoveWindow( hWnd, Point.x, Point.y,
                    Bitmap.bmWidth + ( 2 * ( iFrame + iShadow ) ),
                    Bitmap.bmHeight + ( 2 * ( iFrame + iShadow ) ),
                    FALSE );
            ResetBrushFix( hDC );
            }   /* if lStyle */

        }   /* if hBitmap */

    GetClientRect( hWnd, &Rect );
    if ( iFrame )
        {

        int iBackground = iFrame;

        /* Draw the background */
        CstDraw3DFrame( hWndParent, hDC, (LPRECT)&Rect,
                CST_FRAME_FLAT, hBrushBk, hBrushBk, iBackground );

        if ( !( wState & CPB_STATE_DEFAULT ) )
            {
            /* Decrease the rectangle by the background size
            ** for non-default state */
            iBackground = iFrame / 2;
            InflateRect( &Rect, -iBackground, -iBackground );
            }

        /* Draw the frame */
        CstDraw3DFrame( hWnd, hDC, (LPRECT)&Rect,
                CST_FRAME_FLAT | CST_FRAME_NOCORNERS,
                hBrushFrame, hBrushFrame, iBackground );

        /* Decrease the rectangle by the frame size */
        InflateRect( &Rect, -iBackground, -iBackground );
        }   /* if iFrame */

    /* Paint the button highlight, face, and shadow */
    CstDraw3DRect( hWnd, hDC, hBrushBtnFace, (LPRECT)&Rect,
            (WORD)( ( wState & CPB_STATE_DOWN ) ?
            CST_RECT_LOWERED : CST_RECT_RAISED ),
            hBrushLight, hBrushShadow, iShadow );

    if ( hBitmap )
        {

        if ( !( lStyle & CPBS_STRETCHBITMAP ) )
            {

            int iOffsetX, iOffsetY;

            /* Center the bitmap in Y */
            iOffsetY = ( Rect.bottom + Rect.top - Bitmap.bmHeight ) / 2;
            if ( lStyle & CPBS_LEFTBITMAP )
                {
                iOffsetX = Rect.left + iShadow;
                }
            else if ( lStyle & CPBS_RIGHTBITMAP )
                {
                iOffsetX = Rect.right - iShadow - Bitmap.bmWidth;
```

Listing 6.5 *continued*

```
                }
            else
                {
                /* Centered is the default */
                iOffsetX = ( Rect.right + Rect.left - Bitmap.bmWidth ) / 2;
                }
            iOffsetX = max( iOffsetX, 0 );
            iOffsetY = max( iOffsetY, 0 );
            CstDrawBitmap( hDC, hBitmap, iOffsetX, iOffsetY, 0, 0 );
            }
        else
            {
            /* Stretch the bitmap to fit in the rectangle */
            InflateRect( &Rect, -iShadow, -iShadow );
            CstDrawBitmap( hDC, hBitmap, Rect.left, Rect.top,
                    Rect.right - Rect.left, Rect.bottom - Rect.top );
            }
        }   /* if hBitmap */

    if ( GetWindowTextLength( hWnd ) )
        {
        /* Display the text and focus rectangle around it
        ** if needed */
        CstPushBtnDrawText( hWnd, hDC, iFrame, iShadow, wCtlColorMsg );
        }
    else if ( ( wState & CPB_STATE_FOCUS ) && !( lStyle & CPBS_NOFOCUS ) )
        {
        DrawFocusRect( hDC, &Rect );
        }

    }   /* function CstPushBtnDraw */


/*****************************************************************************
        Name: CstPushBtnDrawFocus
  Parameters: hWnd - handle of push button control
              hDC - device context of push button control
              lpRect - client rect. of push button control
              lpstrText - text of push button control
              wFormat - DrawText format code
 Description: A focus rectangle is drawn around the controls text to indicate
              that the control has the input focus.
*****************************************************************************/
static void CstPushBtnDrawFocus( HWND hWnd, HDC hDC, LPRECT lpRect,
        LPSTR lpstrText, WORD wFormat )
    {

    RECT RectFocus = *lpRect;

    if ( lpstrText )
        {

        DWORD dwTextExtent;
        int iTemp;
        LPSTR lpstrTemp;
        POINT TextExtent;

        /* Get the size of the text */
        lpstrTemp = _fstrchr( lpstrText, '&' );
```

Listing 6.5 *continued*

```
            if ( !lpstrTemp )
                {
                iTemp = (int)lstrlen( lpstrText );
                lpstrText[iTemp] = '&';
                lpstrText[iTemp + 1] = '\0';
                }
            dwTextExtent = GetTextExtent( hDC, lpstrText,
                    (int)lstrlen( lpstrText ) );
            TextExtent = MAKEPOINT( dwTextExtent );

            /* Center in y direction */
            iTemp = ( lpRect->bottom - RectFocus.top - TextExtent.y ) / 2;
            RectFocus.top += iTemp;
            RectFocus.bottom -= iTemp;

            /* Center or shift in the x direction */
            iTemp = RectFocus.right - RectFocus.left - TextExtent.x;
            if ( wFormat == DT_LEFT )
                {
                RectFocus.right -= iTemp;
                }
            else if ( wFormat == DT_RIGHT )
                {
                RectFocus.left += iTemp;
                }
            else
                {
                /* Centered is default */
                iTemp /= 2;
                RectFocus.left += iTemp;
                RectFocus.right -= iTemp;
                }
            RectFocus.top--;
            RectFocus.bottom++;
            }   /* if lpstrText */

    /* Draw the smallest of either the focus or client rectangle */
    GetClientRect( hWnd, lpRect );
    if ( RectInRect( &RectFocus, lpRect ) )
        {
        lpRect = &RectFocus;
        }
    DrawFocusRect( hDC, lpRect );

    }   /* function CstPushBtnDrawFocus */


/****************************************************************************
        Name: CstPushBtnDrawText
  Parameters: hWnd - handle to push button control
              hDC - device context of push button control
              iFrame - thickness of default frame
              iShadow - thickness of shadow
              wCtlColorMsg - message response to WM_CTLCOLOR message
 Description: The text for a push button control is drawn.  The position
              depends upon the window style.  The DrawText function is used
              to draw the formatted text.
****************************************************************************/
```

Listing 6.5 *continued*

```
static void CstPushBtnDrawText( HWND hWnd, HDC hDC, int iFrame, int iShadow,
        WORD wCtlColorMsg )
    {

    BOOL bFontSelected = FALSE;
    COLORREF lColorTextOrg, lColorTextBkOrg;
    HANDLE hText = 0;
    HFONT hFont, hFontOrg;
    int iBkModeOrg, iTextLen;
    LONG lStyle;
    LPSTR lpstrText = 0;
    RECT Rect;
    WORD wFormat, wState;

    /* Get the font */
    if ( !( wCtlColorMsg & CTLCOLORMSG_FONT ) )
        {
        hFont = CSTCTLGETFONT( hWnd );
        if ( !hFont )
            {

            HWND hWndParent = GetParent( hWnd );

            /* Get the font of the parent window */
            if ( hWndParent )
                {
                hFont = (HFONT)SendMessage( hWndParent, WM_GETFONT, 0, 0L );
                CstCtlSetFont( hWnd, hFont );
                }
            }

        if ( hFont )
            {
            hFontOrg = SelectObject( hDC, hFont );
            bFontSelected = TRUE;
            }
        }

    /* Set the color */
    wState = CSTCTLGETSTATE( hWnd );
    if ( !( wCtlColorMsg & CTLCOLORMSG_COLORTEXT ) )
        {
        if ( wState & CPB_STATE_DISABLED )
            {
            lColorTextOrg = SetTextColor( hDC,
                    CSTCTLGETCOLOR( hWnd, CC_COLOR_GRAYTEXT ) );
            }
        else
            {
            lColorTextOrg = SetTextColor( hDC,
                    CSTCTLGETCOLOR( hWnd, CC_COLOR_TEXT ) );
            }
        }
    if ( !( wCtlColorMsg & CTLCOLORMSG_COLORTEXTBK ) )
        {
        lColorTextBkOrg = SetBkColor( hDC,
                CSTCTLGETCOLOR( hWnd, CC_COLOR_TEXTBACKGROUND ) );
        }
    if ( !( wCtlColorMsg & CTLCOLORMSG_MODETEXTBK ) )
```

Listing 6.5 *continued*

```
        {
        iBkModeOrg = SetBkMode( hDC, CSTCTLGETBKMODE( hWnd ) );
        }

    /* Get the draw text style */
    lStyle = GetWindowLong( hWnd, GWL_STYLE );
    if ( lStyle & CPBS_LEFTTEXT )
        {
        wFormat = DT_LEFT;
        }
    else if ( lStyle & CPBS_RIGHTTEXT )
        {
        wFormat = DT_RIGHT;
        }
    else
        {
        /* This is the default */
        wFormat = DT_CENTER;
        }


    /* Get the text */
    iTextLen = GetWindowTextLength( hWnd );
    if ( iTextLen )
        {
        hText = GlobalAlloc( GMEM_FLAGS, (DWORD)( iTextLen + 1 ) );
        if ( hText )
            {
            lpstrText = GlobalLock( hText );
            if ( lpstrText )
                {
                GetWindowText( hWnd, lpstrText, iTextLen + 1 );
                }
            }
        }


    /* Compensate for the shadow */
    GetClientRect( hWnd, &Rect );
    Rect.left += 2 * ( iShadow + iFrame );
    Rect.right -= 2 * ( iShadow + iFrame );

    /* Draw the text */
    if ( wState & CPB_STATE_DOWN )
        {
        /* If the button is down, move the text right and down */
        iShadow /= 2;
        OffsetRect( &Rect, iShadow, iShadow );
        iShadow *= 2;
        }
    DrawText( hDC, lpstrText, iTextLen, &Rect,
            ( wFormat | DT_VCENTER | DT_SINGLELINE ) );

    if ( ( wState & CPB_STATE_FOCUS ) && !( lStyle & CPBS_NOFOCUS ) )
        {

        int iDirection, iTemp;
```

Listing 6.5 *continued*

```
        /* Shift back the rect and draw the focus around text */
        if ( wFormat == DT_LEFT )
            {
            iDirection = -1;
            }
        else if ( wFormat == DT_RIGHT )
            {
            iDirection = 1;
            }
        else
            {
            /* Default center */
            iDirection = 0;
            }

        /* Shift the rectangle to center focus around text */
        iTemp = 3 * ( iDirection * iShadow ) / 2;
        if ( ( iTemp >= 0 ) || ( abs( iTemp ) < Rect.left ) )
            {
            Rect.left += iTemp;
            }
        if ( ( iTemp >= 0 ) || ( abs( iTemp ) < Rect.right ) )
            {
            Rect.right += iTemp;
            }
        CstPushBtnDrawFocus( hWnd, hDC, &Rect, lpstrText, wFormat );

        }   /* if wState */

/* Free the memory for text */
if ( lpstrText )
    {
    GlobalUnlock( hText );
    }
if ( hText )
    {
    GlobalFree( hText );
    }

/* Reset the font */
if ( bFontSelected )
    {
    SelectObject( hDC, hFontOrg );
    }

/* Reset the colors and mode */
if ( !( wCtlColorMsg & CTLCOLORMSG_COLORTEXT ) )
    {
    SetTextColor( hDC, lColorTextOrg );
    }
if ( !( wCtlColorMsg & CTLCOLORMSG_COLORTEXTBK ) )
    {
    SetBkColor( hDC, lColorTextBkOrg );
    }
if ( !( wCtlColorMsg & CTLCOLORMSG_MODETEXTBK ) )
    {
    SetBkMode( hDC, iBkModeOrg );
    }
```

Listing 6.5 *continued*

```
    }   /* function CstPushBtnDrawText */


/******************************************************************************
        Name: CstPushBtnRegister
   Parameters: hInstance - handle to program or library registering class
       Return: Same as RegisterClass
  Description: Registers the window class for the custom push button control
******************************************************************************/
int FAR PASCAL CstPushBtnRegister( HINSTANCE hInstance )
    {

    WNDCLASS WndClass;

    WndClass.style = CS_DBLCLKS | CS_HREDRAW | CS_VREDRAW | CS_PARENTDC;

    #if defined ( _WINDLL )
    hInstance = _hInstanceCstCtls;
    WndClass.style |= CS_GLOBALCLASS;
    #endif

    WndClass.lpfnWndProc = CstPushBtnWndFn;
    WndClass.cbClsExtra = CPB_CLSEXTRA;
    WndClass.cbWndExtra = CPB_WNDEXTRA;
    WndClass.hInstance = hInstance;
    WndClass.hIcon = 0;
    WndClass.hCursor = LoadCursor( 0, IDC_ARROW );
    WndClass.hbrBackground = 0;
    WndClass.lpszMenuName = 0;
    WndClass.lpszClassName = "CstPushBtn";

    return ( RegisterClass( &WndClass ) );

    }   /* function CstPushBtnRegister */


/******************************************************************************
        Name: CstPushBtnUnregister
   Parameters: hInstance - handle to program or library that registered class
       Return: Same as UnregisterClass
  Description: Unregisters the window class for the custom push button type
******************************************************************************/
int FAR PASCAL CstPushBtnUnregister( HINSTANCE hInstance )
    {

    #if defined ( _WINDLL )
    hInstance = _hInstanceCstCtls;
    #endif

    return ( UnregisterClass( "CstPushBtn", hInstance ) );

    }   /* function CstPushBtnUnregister */


/******************************************************************************
        Name: CstPushBtnWndFn
Expanded Name: Custom Push Button Window Function
  Description: Window call back function for custom push button control
******************************************************************************/
```

Listing 6.5 *continued*

```
LONG FAR PASCAL CstPushBtnWndFn( HWND hWnd, UINT wMessage, WPARAM wParam,
        LPARAM lParam )
    {

    static int _WindowCount = 0;

    switch ( wMessage )
        {
        case BM_GETSTATE:
            /* Returns nonzero if the button is down */
            return ( CstCtlState( hWnd, CPB_STATE_DOWN,
                    STATE_CHECK, AREA_NONE ) );
        case BM_SETSTATE:
            /* Sets or resets the push button down state */
            CstCtlState( hWnd, CPB_STATE_DOWN, (WORD)( wParam ?
                    STATE_SET : STATE_RESET ), AREA_ALL );
            break;
        case BM_SETSTYLE:
            /* Change the button style to or from BS_DEFPUSHBUTTON */
            CstCtlState( hWnd, CPB_STATE_DEFAULTORG,
                    (WORD)( wParam == BS_DEFPUSHBUTTON ?
                    STATE_SET : STATE_RESET ), AREA_ALL );
            break;
        case WM_CREATE:
            {

            HWND hWndParent = GetParent( hWnd );

            if ( !_WindowCount )
                {
                if ( !CstPushBtnDefDataCreate( hWnd ) )
                    {
                    return ( -1 );
                    }
                }
            _WindowCount++;

            /* Create instance data */
            CstCtlDataCreate( hWnd );

            /* If the button is a default, set state */
            if ( ( (LPCREATESTRUCT)lParam )->style & BS_DEFPUSHBUTTON )
                {
                CstCtlState( hWnd,
                        CPB_STATE_DEFAULTORG | CPB_STATE_DEFAULT,
                        STATE_SET, AREA_NONE );
                }
            /* If the button is disabled, set state */
            if ( ( (LPCREATESTRUCT)lParam )->style & WS_DISABLED )
                {
                CstCtlState( hWnd, CPB_STATE_DISABLED,
                        STATE_SET, AREA_NONE );
                }
            /* Notify the parent that the button has been created */
            if ( hWndParent )
                {
                SendMessage( hWndParent, WM_PARENTNOTIFY, WM_CREATE,
                        MAKELPARAM( hWnd, GetDlgCtrlID( hWnd ) ) );
                }
```

Listing 6.5 *continued*

```
            break;
        }   /* case WM_CREATE */
    case WM_CSTCTLGETDATA:
    case WM_CSTCTLGETDEFDATA:
    case WM_CSTCTLSETDATA:
    case WM_CSTCTLSETDEFDATA:
        return ( (LONG)CstCtlData( hWnd, wMessage, wParam, lParam ) );
    case WM_DESTROY:
        {

        HWND hWndParent = GetParent( hWnd );

        /* Notify the parent and then delete the instance data */
        if ( hWndParent )
            {
            SendMessage( hWndParent, WM_PARENTNOTIFY, WM_DESTROY,
                    MAKELPARAM( hWnd, GetDlgCtrlID( hWnd ) ) );
            }
        if ( IsWindow( hWnd ) )
            {
            CstCtlDataDelete( hWnd );
            }

        _WindowCount--;
        if ( _WindowCount <= 0 )
            {
            CstPushBtnDefDataDelete();
            }

        break;
        }   /* case WM_DESTROY */
    case WM_ENABLE:
        /* Set or Reset enable state */
        CstCtlState( hWnd, CPB_STATE_DISABLED, (WORD)( wParam ?
                STATE_RESET : STATE_SET ), AREA_ALL );
        break;
    case WM_ERASEBKGND:
        /* Background is handled during the WM_PAINT message */
        return ( TRUE );
    case WM_GETDLGCODE:
        /* Return to dialog manager that this is a push button and
        ** is or is not a default push button */
        return ( DLGC_BUTTON | CstCtlState( hWnd,
                CPB_STATE_DEFAULTORG, STATE_CHECK, AREA_NONE ) ?
                DLGC_DEFPUSHBUTTON : DLGC_UNDEFPUSHBUTTON );
    case WM_KEYDOWN:
        if ( ( wParam == ' ' ) &&
                !( HIBYTE( HIWORD( lParam ) ) & 0x40 ) )
            {
            /* Space bar toggles to the down state */
            CstCtlState( hWnd, CPB_STATE_DOWN, STATE_SET, AREA_ALL );
            }
        break;
    case WM_KEYUP:
        if ( wParam == ' ' )
            {
            /* Space bar toggles to the up state */
            CstCtlState( hWnd, CPB_STATE_DOWN, STATE_RESET, AREA_ALL );
            if ( CstCtlState( hWnd, CPB_STATE_FOCUS,
```

Listing 6.5 *continued*

```
                    STATE_CHECK, AREA_NONE ) )
                {
                HWND hWndParent = GetParent( hWnd );

                /* Button is in focus so send message to parent */
                if ( hWndParent )
                    {
                    SendMessage( hWndParent, WM_COMMAND,
                        (WPARAM)GetDlgCtrlID( hWnd ),
                        MAKELPARAM( hWnd, BN_CLICKED ) );
                    }
                }
            }   /* if wParam */
        break;
    case WM_KILLFOCUS:
        /* Button is now out of focus, reset states */
        CstCtlState( hWnd,
                CPB_STATE_FOCUS | CPB_STATE_DOWN | CPB_STATE_DEFAULT,
                STATE_RESET, AREA_ALL );
        if ( ( wParam ) && ( GetParent( wParam ) == GetParent( hWnd ) ) )
            {

            LONG lType = SendMessage( wParam, WM_GETDLGCODE, 0, 0L );

            if ( !( ( lType & DLGC_DEFPUSHBUTTON ) ||
                    ( lType & DLGC_UNDEFPUSHBUTTON ) ) )
                {

                HWND hWndCtl;
                HWND hWndDlg = GetParent( hWnd );

                /* Another non-pushbutton control in same dialog
                ** has focus so the original default is now the
                ** default push button and needs to be redrawn
                ** search through all the tab items to find it */
                hWndCtl = hWnd;
                while ( ( hWndCtl =
                        GetNextDlgTabItem( hWndDlg, hWndCtl, FALSE ) )
                        != NULL )
                    {
                    lType = SendMessage( hWndCtl, WM_GETDLGCODE, 0, 0L );
                    if ( lType & DLGC_DEFPUSHBUTTON )
                        {
                        CstCtlState( hWnd, CPB_STATE_DEFAULT,
                                STATE_SET, AREA_ALL );
                        hWndCtl = hWndDlg;
                        break;
                        }
                    }   /* while */
                if ( hWndCtl == hWndDlg )
                    {
                    break;
                    }
                hWndCtl = hWnd;
                while ( ( hWndCtl =
                        GetNextDlgTabItem( hWndDlg, hWndCtl, TRUE ) )
                        != NULL )
                    {
```

Listing 6.5 continued

```
                            lType = SendMessage( hWndCtl, WM_GETDLGCODE, 0, 0L );
                            if ( lType & DLGC_DEFPUSHBUTTON )
                                {
                                CstCtlState( hWnd, CPB_STATE_DEFAULT,
                                        STATE_SET, AREA_ALL );
                                }
                            }   /* while */
                        }   /* if lType */
                    }   /* if wParam */
                break;
            case WM_LBUTTONDOWN:
                /* Left mouse button is down, capture the mouse, set focus
                ** and update instance status */
                SetCapture( hWnd );
                CstCtlState( hWnd, CPB_STATE_CAPTURE | CPB_STATE_DOWN |
                        CPB_STATE_INSIDE, STATE_SET, AREA_ALL );
                if ( GetFocus() != hWnd )
                    {
                    SetFocus( hWnd );
                    }
                break;
            case WM_LBUTTONUP:
                /* Release mouse and reset down state */
                ReleaseCapture();
                if ( CstCtlState( hWnd, CPB_STATE_INSIDE,
                        STATE_CHECK, AREA_NONE ) )
                    {

                    HWND hWndParent = GetParent( hWnd );

                    /* The mouse was inside button so send message to parent */
                    if ( hWndParent )
                        {
                        SendMessage( hWndParent, WM_COMMAND,
                                (WPARAM)GetDlgCtrlID( hWnd ),
                                MAKELPARAM( hWnd, BN_CLICKED ) );
                        }
                    if ( !IsWindow( hWnd ) )
                        {
                        /* Window is no longer valid */
                        break;
                        }
                    }
                CstCtlState( hWnd, CPB_STATE_DOWN | CPB_STATE_CAPTURE |
                        CPB_STATE_INSIDE, STATE_RESET, AREA_ALL );
                break;
            case WM_MOUSEMOVE:
                {

                WORD wState = CSTCTLGETSTATE( hWnd );

                if ( wState & CPB_STATE_CAPTURE )
                    {

                    POINT Point;

                    /* Mouse has been captured so check the location */
                    Point.x = (int)LOWORD( lParam );
                    Point.y = (int)HIWORD( lParam );
```

Listing 6.5 *continued*

```c
                if ( PtInWnd( hWnd, Point ) )
                    {
                    /* Inside the control */
                    if ( !( wState & CPB_STATE_INSIDE ) )
                        {
                        /* Was outside control, change states */
                        CstCtlState( hWnd, CPB_STATE_DOWN |
                                CPB_STATE_INSIDE, STATE_SET, AREA_ALL );
                        }
                    }
                else
                    {
                    /* Outside the control */
                    if ( wState & CPB_STATE_INSIDE )
                        {
                        /* Was inside control, change states */
                        CstCtlState( hWnd, CPB_STATE_DOWN |
                                CPB_STATE_INSIDE, STATE_RESET, AREA_ALL );
                        }
                    }
                }   /* if wState */
            break;
            }   /* case WM_MOUSEMOVE */
        case WM_PAINT:
            {

            PAINTSTRUCT PS;
            HDC hDC = BeginPaint( hWnd, &PS );

            if ( IsWindowVisible( hWnd ) )
                {
                /* Only paint if needed */
                CstPushBtnDraw( hWnd, hDC );
                }
            EndPaint( hWnd, &PS );
            break;
            }   /* case WM_PAINT */
        case WM_SETFOCUS:
            /* Button is now in focus, set state */
            CstCtlState( hWnd, CPB_STATE_FOCUS | CPB_STATE_DEFAULT,
                    STATE_SET, AREA_ALL );
            break;
        case WM_SETFONT:
            if ( wParam )
                {
                CstCtlSetFont( hWnd, wParam );
                }
            if ( lParam )
                {
                /* Send a Paint message */
                InvalidateRect( hWnd, NULL, FALSE );
                UpdateWindow( hWnd );
                }
            break;
        default:
            return ( DefWindowProc( hWnd, wMessage, wParam, lParam ) );
        }   /* switch wMessage */

    return ( 0L );
```

Listing 6.5 *continued*

```
    }   /* function CstPushBtnWndFn */


/*******************************************************************************
         Name: RectInRect
Expanded Name: Rectangle In Rectangle
   Parameters: lpRectIn - inside rectangle
               lpRectOut - outside rectangle
       Return: nonzero if RectIn is within RectOut, otherwise it is zero
  Description: Determines if a rectangle is inside another rectangle
*******************************************************************************/
static BOOL RectInRect( LPRECT lpRectIn, LPRECT lpRectOut )
    {

    if ( ( lpRectIn->top < lpRectOut->top ) ||
           ( lpRectIn->left < lpRectOut->left ) ||
           ( lpRectIn->bottom > lpRectOut->bottom ) ||
           ( lpRectIn->right > lpRectOut->right ) )
        {
        return ( FALSE );
        }

    return ( TRUE );

    }   /* function RectInRect */

/* End of CST_PBTN.C */
```

Listing 6.6

```
/*****************************************************************************
        File Name: CST_RBTN.H
    Expanded Name: Custom Radio Button
      Description: Include file for CST_RBTN.C
      Portability: Microsoft Windows 3.X
*****************************************************************************/

#if !defined ( CST_RBTN_DEFINED )
    #define CST_RBTN_DEFINED

    /* Custom Radio Button Bitmap array access index */
    #define CRB_BITMAP_DOWN        0
    #define CRB_BITMAP_DOWNCHECK   1
    #define CRB_BITMAP_UP          2
    #define CRB_BITMAP_UPCHECK     3

    /* Custom Push Button State bit flags */
    #define CRB_STATE_CAPTURE  0x01
    #define CRB_STATE_CHECK    0x02
    #define CRB_STATE_DOWN     0x08
    #define CRB_STATE_FOCUS    0x10
    #define CRB_STATE_INSIDE   0x20

    /* Extra byte constants for custom radio button control */
    #define CRB_CLSEXTRA ( CC_CLSEXTRA )
    #define CRB_WNDEXTRA ( CC_WNDEXTRA + sizeof ( LONG ) )

    /* WM_CTLCOLOR type for custom radio button control */
    #define CTLCOLOR_CSTRADIOBTN ( CTLCOLOR_BTN | 0x080 )

    /* Prototypes for exported functions in CST_RBTN.C */
    int FAR PASCAL CstRadioBtnRegister( HINSTANCE hInstance );
    int FAR PASCAL CstRadioBtnUnregister( HINSTANCE hInstance );
    LONG FAR PASCAL CstRadioBtnWndFn( HWND hWnd, UINT wMessage, WPARAM wParam,
            LPARAM lParam );

#endif

/* End of CST_RBTN.H */
```

Listing 6.7

```c
/*****************************************************************************
          File Name: CST_RBTN.C
      Expanded Name: Custom Radio Button
        Description: Library of functions for the radio button custom control
Global Function List: CstRadioBtnRegister
                     CstRadioBtnUnregerister
                     CstRadioBtnWndFn
Static Function List: CstRadioBtnBitmapIndex
                     CstRadioBtnDefDataCreate
                     CstRadioBtnDefDataDelete
                     CstRadioBtnDraw
        Global Data: _hInstanceCstCtls
        Static Data: _hCstCtlData
                     _lpCstCtlData
        Portability: Microsoft Windows 3.X
*****************************************************************************/

/* Microsoft Windows */
#include <windows.h>

/* Prototypes and Types */
#include <cst_xtra.h>
#include <cst_data.h>
#include <cst_util.h>

/* Own */
#include <cst_rbtn.h>

/* Prototypes of static functions */
static WORD CstRadioBtnBitmapIndex( WORD wState );
static int  CstRadioBtnDefDataCreate( HWND hWnd );
static void CstRadioBtnDefDataDelete( void );
static void CstRadioBtnDraw( HWND hWnd, HDC hDC );

#if defined ( _WINDLL )
/* DLL Handle */
extern HINSTANCE _hInstanceCstCtls;
#endif

static HCSTCTLDATA  _hCstCtlData  = (HCSTCTLDATA)0;
static LPCSTCTLDATA _lpCstCtlData = (LPCSTCTLDATA)0;

/*****************************************************************************
         Name: CstRadioBtnBitmapIndex
 Expanded Name: Get Radio Button Bitmap Index
   Parameters: wState - instance state bit flags
       Return: Index into bitmap array
  Description: Gets the index into bitmap array depending on the button state.
*****************************************************************************/
static WORD CstRadioBtnBitmapIndex( WORD wState )
    {

    WORD wBitmapIndex;

    if ( wState & CRB_STATE_DOWN )
        {
        if ( wState & CRB_STATE_CHECK )
            {
            wBitmapIndex = CRB_BITMAP_DOWNCHECK;
```

Listing 6.7 *continued*

```
                }
        else
            {
            wBitmapIndex = CRB_BITMAP_DOWN;
            }
        }
    else
        {
        if ( wState & CRB_STATE_CHECK )
            {
            wBitmapIndex = CRB_BITMAP_UPCHECK;
            }
        else
            {
            wBitmapIndex = CRB_BITMAP_UP;
            }
        }  /* else */

    return ( wBitmapIndex );

    }   /* function CstRadioBtnBitmapIndex */


/*******************************************************************************
        Name: CstRadioBtnDefDataCreate
Expanded Name: Default Data Create
   Parameters: hWnd - window handle to CstRadioBtn control
       Return: TRUE or FALSE
  Description: Creates the default class data
*******************************************************************************/
static int CstRadioBtnDefDataCreate( HWND hWnd )
    {

    HINSTANCE hInstanceClass;

    #if defined ( _WINDLL )
    hInstanceClass = _hInstanceCstCtls;
    #else
    hInstanceClass = GetWindowWord( hWnd, GWW_HINSTANCE );
    #endif

    _lpCstCtlData = CstCtlDefDataCreate( hWnd );
    if ( !_lpCstCtlData )
        {
        /* Failed to allocate and initialize data */
        return ( FALSE );
        }
    _hCstCtlData = CSTGETCLASSWORD( hWnd, GCW_HCSTCTLDATA );

    /* Free up the resources we do not need */
    SafeDeleteObject( _lpCstCtlData->hBrush[CC_BRUSH_BTNFACE] );
    _lpCstCtlData->hBrush[CC_BRUSH_BTNFACE] = 0;
    SafeDeleteObject( _lpCstCtlData->hBrush[CC_BRUSH_3DLIGHT] );
    _lpCstCtlData->hBrush[CC_BRUSH_3DLIGHT] = 0;
    SafeDeleteObject( _lpCstCtlData->hBrush[CC_BRUSH_3DSHADOW] );
    _lpCstCtlData->hBrush[CC_BRUSH_3DSHADOW] = 0;
    SafeDeleteObject( _lpCstCtlData->hBrush[CC_BRUSH_FRAME] );
    _lpCstCtlData->hBrush[CC_BRUSH_FRAME] = 0;
```

Listing 6.7 *continued*

```c
    /* Create the default bitmaps */
    _lpCstCtlData->hBitmap[CRB_BITMAP_DOWN] =
            LoadBitmap( hInstanceClass, "RBD_1616" );
    _lpCstCtlData->hBitmap[CRB_BITMAP_DOWNCHECK] =
            LoadBitmap( hInstanceClass, "RBDC1616" );
    _lpCstCtlData->hBitmap[CRB_BITMAP_UP] =
            LoadBitmap( hInstanceClass, "RBU_1616" );
    _lpCstCtlData->hBitmap[CRB_BITMAP_UPCHECK] =
            LoadBitmap( hInstanceClass, "RBUC1616" );

    return ( TRUE );

    }   /* function CstRadioBtnDefDataCreate */


/*******************************************************************************
        Name: CstRadioBtnDefDataDelete
Expanded Name: Default Data Delete
   Parameters: hWnd - window handle control
  Description: Deletes the default class data
*******************************************************************************/
static void CstRadioBtnDefDataDelete( void )
    {

    if ( _lpCstCtlData )
        {
        SafeDeleteObject( _lpCstCtlData->hBrush[CC_BRUSH_BACKGROUND] );
        SafeDeleteObject( _lpCstCtlData->hBitmap[CRB_BITMAP_DOWN] );
        SafeDeleteObject( _lpCstCtlData->hBitmap[CRB_BITMAP_DOWNCHECK] );
        SafeDeleteObject( _lpCstCtlData->hBitmap[CRB_BITMAP_UP] );
        SafeDeleteObject( _lpCstCtlData->hBitmap[CRB_BITMAP_UPCHECK] );
        _lpCstCtlData = (LPCSTCTLDATA)0;
        }

    if ( _hCstCtlData )
        {
        GlobalUnlock( _hCstCtlData );
        GlobalFree( _hCstCtlData );
        _hCstCtlData = (HCSTCTLDATA)0;
        }

    }   /* function CstRadioBtnDefDataDelete */


/*******************************************************************************
        Name: CstRadioBtnDraw
Expanded Name: Radio Button Draw
   Parameters: hWnd - window handle of radio button control
               hDC - device context of radio button control
  Description: Draws the radio button custom control
*******************************************************************************/
static void CstRadioBtnDraw( HWND hWnd, HDC hDC )
    {

    BOOL bFontSelected = FALSE;
    COLORREF lColorTextBkOrg, lColorTextOrg;
    HANDLE hText;
    HBITMAP hBitmap;
```

Listing 6.7 *continued*

```
    HBRUSH hBrushBk = 0;
HDC hDCMem;
HFONT hFont, hFontOrg;
HWND hWndParent;
int iBkModeOrg, iTextHeight, iTextLen;
LPRECT lpRectBitmap, lpRectText;
LPSTR lpstrText;
RECT Rect, RectDrawText;
WORD wBitmapIndex, wState, wCtlColorMsg = 0;

hWndParent = GetParent( hWnd );
if ( hWndParent )
    {
    /* Send message to give parent a chance to change data */
    hBrushBk = (HBRUSH)SendMessage( hWndParent, WM_CTLCOLOR, hDC,
            MAKELPARAM( hWnd, CTLCOLOR_CSTRADIOBTN ) );
    wCtlColorMsg = CstCtlColorMsg( hWnd, FALSE );
    if ( !( wCtlColorMsg & CTLCOLORMSG_BRUSH ) )
        {
        /* Use the brush of the parent window */
        hBrushBk = GetClassWord( hWndParent, GCW_HBRBACKGROUND );
        }
    }
if ( !hBrushBk )
    {
    /* Still do not have a brush so get the default */
    hBrushBk = CSTCTLGETBRUSH( hWnd, CC_BRUSH_BACKGROUND );
    }

/* Get the bitmap based on state of button */
wState = CSTCTLGETSTATE( hWnd );
wBitmapIndex = CstRadioBtnBitmapIndex( wState );
hBitmap = CSTCTLGETBITMAP( hWnd, wBitmapIndex );

/* Paint the background */
GetClientRect( hWnd, &Rect );
AlignBrush( hWndParent, hDC, hBrushBk );
FillRect( hDC, &Rect, hBrushBk );

hDCMem = CreateCompatibleDC( hDC );
lpRectText = CSTCTLGETLPRECTTEXT( hWnd );
if ( SelectObject( hDCMem, hBitmap ) )
    {

    BITMAP Bitmap;

    /* Display the bitmap */
    lpRectBitmap = CSTCTLGETLPRECTBITMAP( hWnd );
    CstCtlSetRects( hWnd, hBitmap, &Rect, lpRectBitmap, lpRectText );
    GetObject( hBitmap, sizeof ( BITMAP ), (LPSTR)&Bitmap );
    BitBlt( hDC, lpRectBitmap->left, lpRectBitmap->top, Bitmap.bmWidth,
            Bitmap.bmHeight, hDCMem, 0, 0, SRCCOPY );
    }

/* Free the DC for the bitmap */
DeleteDC( hDCMem );

/* Get the text */
iTextLen = GetWindowTextLength( hWnd );
```

Listing 6.7 continued

```
hText = GlobalAlloc( GMEM_FLAGS, (DWORD)( iTextLen + 1 ) );
lpstrText = GlobalLock( hText );
GetWindowText( hWnd, lpstrText, iTextLen + 1 );

/* Get the font */
if ( !( wCtlColorMsg & CTLCOLORMSG_FONT ) )
    {
    hFont = CSTCTLGETFONT( hWnd );
    if ( !hFont )
        {
        /* Get the font of the parent window */
        if ( hWndParent )
            {
            hFont = (HFONT)SendMessage( hWndParent, WM_GETFONT, 0, 0L );
            CstCtlSetFont( hWnd, hFont );
            }
        }
    if ( hFont )
        {
        hFontOrg = SelectObject( hDC, hFont );
        bFontSelected = TRUE;
        }
    }   /* if !wCtlColorMsg */

/* Set the color */
if ( !( wCtlColorMsg & CTLCOLORMSG_COLORTEXT ) )
    {
    lColorTextOrg = SetTextColor( hDC,
            CSTCTLGETCOLOR( hWnd, CC_COLOR_TEXT ) );
    }
if ( !( wCtlColorMsg & CTLCOLORMSG_COLORTEXTBK ) )
    {
    lColorTextBkOrg = SetBkColor( hDC,
            CSTCTLGETCOLOR( hWnd, CC_COLOR_TEXTBACKGROUND ) );
    }
if ( !( wCtlColorMsg & CTLCOLORMSG_MODETEXTBK ) )
    {
    iBkModeOrg = SetBkMode( hDC, CSTCTLGETBKMODE( hWnd ) );
    }

/* Center the text vertically and then display the text */
RectDrawText = *lpRectText;
iTextHeight = DrawText( hDC, lpstrText, -1, &RectDrawText,
        DT_LEFT | DT_SINGLELINE | DT_CALCRECT );
OffsetRect( &RectDrawText, 0,
        max( 0, ( ( Rect.bottom - Rect.top) - iTextHeight ) / 2 ) );
DrawText( hDC, lpstrText, -1, &RectDrawText, DT_SINGLELINE );

if ( ( GetFocus() == hWnd ) && ( iTextLen > 0 ) )
    {
    /* The window is in focus with text so draw focus rect */
    DrawFocusRect( hDC, &RectDrawText );
    }


/* Free the memory for text */
GlobalUnlock( hText );
GlobalFree( hText );
```

Listing 6.7 *continued*

```
    /* Reset the font */
    if ( bFontSelected )
        {
        SelectObject( hDC, hFontOrg );
        }

    /* Reset the colors and mode */
    if ( !( wCtlColorMsg & CTLCOLORMSG_COLORTEXT ) )
        {
        SetTextColor( hDC, lColorTextOrg );
        }
    if ( !( wCtlColorMsg & CTLCOLORMSG_COLORTEXTBK ) )
        {
        SetBkColor( hDC, lColorTextBkOrg );
        }
    if ( !( wCtlColorMsg & CTLCOLORMSG_MODETEXTBK ) )
        {
        SetBkMode( hDC, iBkModeOrg );
        }

    }   /* function CstRadioBtnDraw */


/*****************************************************************************
        Name: CstRadioBtnRegister
   Parameters: hInstance - handle to program or library registering class
       Return: Number of register counts or 0 if failure
  Description: Registers the window class for the custom Radio button control
*****************************************************************************/
int FAR PASCAL CstRadioBtnRegister( HINSTANCE hInstance )
    {

    WNDCLASS WndClass;

    WndClass.style = CS_HREDRAW | CS_VREDRAW | CS_PARENTDC;

    #if defined ( _WINDLL )
    hInstance = _hInstanceCstCtls;
    WndClass.style |= CS_GLOBALCLASS;
    #endif

    WndClass.lpfnWndProc = CstRadioBtnWndFn;
    WndClass.cbClsExtra = CRB_CLSEXTRA;
    WndClass.cbWndExtra = CRB_WNDEXTRA;
    WndClass.hInstance = hInstance;
    WndClass.hIcon = 0;
    WndClass.hCursor = LoadCursor( 0, IDC_ARROW );
    WndClass.hbrBackground = 0;
    WndClass.lpszMenuName = 0;
    WndClass.lpszClassName = "CstRadioBtn";

    return ( RegisterClass( &WndClass ) );

    }   /* function CstRadioBtnRegister */
```

Listing 6.7 *continued*

```
/******************************************************************************
      Name: CstRadioBtnUnregister
 Parameters: hInstance - handle to program or library that registered class
     Return: Number of remaining register counts
Description: Unregisters the window class for the CstRadioBtn control
******************************************************************************/
int FAR PASCAL CstRadioBtnUnregister( HINSTANCE hInstance )
    {

    #if defined ( _WINDLL )
    hInstance = _hInstanceCstCtls;
    #endif

    return ( UnregisterClass( "CstRadioBtn", hInstance ) );

    }  /* function CstRadioBtnUnregister */

/******************************************************************************
      Name: CstRadioBtnWndFn
Expanded Name: Custom Radio Button Window Function
Description: Window call back function for custom radio button control
******************************************************************************/
LONG FAR PASCAL CstRadioBtnWndFn( HWND hWnd, UINT wMessage, WPARAM wParam,
         LPARAM lParam )
    {

    static int _WindowCount = 0;

    switch ( wMessage )
        {
        case BM_GETCHECK:
            /* Return whether the control is checked (TRUE) or not (FALSE) */
            return ( CstCtlState( hWnd, CRB_STATE_CHECK,
                    STATE_CHECK, AREA_NONE ) );
        case BM_GETSTATE:
            /* Returns nonzero if the button is down */
            return ( CstCtlState( hWnd, CRB_STATE_DOWN,
                    STATE_CHECK, AREA_NONE ) );
        case BM_SETCHECK:
            if ( wParam )
                {

                DWORD dwStyle;

                /* Sets or resets the radio button check state */
                CstCtlState( hWnd, CRB_STATE_CHECK, STATE_SET, AREA_BITMAP );
                SetWindowLong( hWnd, GWL_STYLE,
                        GetWindowLong( hWnd, GWL_STYLE ) | WS_TABSTOP );
                dwStyle = (DWORD)GetWindowLong( hWnd, GWL_STYLE ) & 0x0FL;
                if ( dwStyle == BS_AUTORADIOBUTTON )
                    {

                    HWND hWndCtl = hWnd;

                    /* The control is auto style so send a BM_SETCHECK
                    ** message to all the other controls in this group
                    ** that are auto radio buttons to uncheck them */
                    while ( ( hWndCtl = GetNextDlgGroupItem( GetParent( hWnd ),
                            hWndCtl, FALSE ) ) != hWnd )
```

Listing 6.7 *continued*

```
                    {
                    dwStyle = (DWORD)GetWindowLong( hWndCtl,
                            GWL_STYLE ) & 0x0FL;
                    if ( dwStyle == BS_AUTORADIOBUTTON )
                        {
                        SendMessage( hWndCtl, BM_SETCHECK, FALSE, 0L );
                        }
                    }  /* while hWndCtl */
                }  /* if dwStyle */
            }  /* if wParam */
        else
            {
            CstCtlState( hWnd, CRB_STATE_CHECK, STATE_RESET, AREA_BITMAP );
            }
        break;
    case BM_SETSTATE:
        /* Sets or resets the radio button down state */
        CstCtlState( hWnd, CRB_STATE_DOWN, (WORD)( wParam ?
                STATE_SET : STATE_RESET ), AREA_BITMAP );
        break;
    case WM_CREATE:
        {

        HWND hWndParent = GetParent( hWnd );

        if ( !_WindowCount )
            {
            if ( !CstRadioBtnDefDataCreate( hWnd ) )
                {
                return ( -1 );
                }
            }
        _WindowCount++;

        /* Create instance data */
        CstCtlDataCreate( hWnd );
        /* Notify the parent that the button has been created */
        if ( hWndParent )
            {
            SendMessage( hWndParent, WM_PARENTNOTIFY, WM_CREATE,
                    MAKELPARAM( hWnd, GetDlgCtrlID( hWnd ) ) );
            }
        break;
        }  /* case WM_CREATE */
    case WM_CSTCTLGETDATA:
    case WM_CSTCTLGETDEFDATA:
    case WM_CSTCTLSETDATA:
    case WM_CSTCTLSETDEFDATA:
        return ( (LONG)CstCtlData( hWnd, wMessage, wParam, lParam ) );
    case WM_DESTROY:
        {

        HWND hWndParent = GetParent( hWnd );

        /* Notify the parent and then delete the instance data */
        if ( hWndParent )
            {
            SendMessage( hWndParent, WM_PARENTNOTIFY, WM_DESTROY,
                    MAKELPARAM( hWnd, GetDlgCtrlID( hWnd ) ) );
```

Listing 6.7 continued

```
            }
        if ( IsWindow( hWnd ) )
            {
            CstCtlDataDelete( hWnd );
            }

        _WindowCount--;
        if ( _WindowCount <= 0 )
            {
            CstRadioBtnDefDataDelete();
            }

        break;
        }   /* case WM_DESTROY */
    case WM_ERASEBKGND:
        /* Background is handled during the WM_PAINT message */
        return ( TRUE );
    case WM_GETDLGCODE:
        /* Return to dialog manager that this is a radio button */
        return ( DLGC_RADIOBUTTON );
    case WM_KEYDOWN:
        if ( ( wParam == ' ' ) &&
                !( HIBYTE( HIWORD( lParam ) ) & 0x40 ) )
            {
            /* Space bar toggles to the down state */
            CstCtlState( hWnd, CRB_STATE_DOWN, STATE_SET, AREA_BITMAP );
            }
        break;
    case WM_KEYUP:
        if ( wParam == ' ' )
            {

            DWORD dwStyle;

            /* Space bar toggles to the up state */
            CstCtlState( hWnd, CRB_STATE_DOWN, STATE_RESET, AREA_BITMAP );
            dwStyle = (DWORD)GetWindowLong( hWnd, GWL_STYLE ) & 0x0FL;
            if ( dwStyle == BS_AUTORADIOBUTTON )
                {
                SendMessage( hWnd, BM_SETCHECK, TRUE, 0L );
                if ( !IsWindow( hWnd ) )
                    {
                    break;
                    }
                }
            if ( CstCtlState( hWnd, CRB_STATE_FOCUS,
                    STATE_CHECK, AREA_NONE ) )
                {

                HWND hWndParent = GetParent( hWnd );

                /* Button is in focus so send message to parent */
                if ( hWndParent )
                    {
                    SendMessage( hWndParent, WM_COMMAND,
                        (WPARAM)GetDlgCtrlID( hWnd ),
                        MAKELPARAM( hWnd, BN_CLICKED ) );
                    }
```

Listing 6.7 *continued*

```
            }
        }   /* if wParam */
    break;
case WM_KILLFOCUS:
    /* Reset states */
    CstCtlState( hWnd, CRB_STATE_FOCUS | CRB_STATE_DOWN,
            STATE_RESET, AREA_ALL );
    break;
case WM_LBUTTONDOWN:
    /* Left mouse button is down, capture the mouse, focus
    ** and update instance status */
    SetCapture( hWnd );
    CstCtlState( hWnd, CRB_STATE_CAPTURE | CRB_STATE_DOWN |
            CRB_STATE_INSIDE, STATE_SET, AREA_BITMAP );
    if ( GetFocus() != hWnd )
        {
        SetFocus( hWnd );
        }
    break;
case WM_LBUTTONUP:
    /* Release mouse and reset down state */
    ReleaseCapture();
    if ( CstCtlState( hWnd, CRB_STATE_INSIDE,
            STATE_CHECK, AREA_NONE ) )
        {

        DWORD dwStyle;
        HWND hWndParent = GetParent( hWnd );

        /* The mouse was inside button so send message to parent */
        dwStyle = (DWORD)GetWindowLong( hWnd, GWL_STYLE ) & 0x0FL;
        if ( dwStyle == BS_AUTORADIOBUTTON )
            {
            SendMessage( hWnd, BM_SETCHECK, TRUE, 0L );
            if ( !IsWindow( hWnd ) )
                {
                break;
                }
            }
        if ( hWndParent )
            {
            SendMessage( hWndParent, WM_COMMAND,
                    (WPARAM)GetDlgCtrlID( hWnd ),
                    MAKELPARAM( hWnd, BN_CLICKED ) );
            }
        if ( !IsWindow( hWnd ) )
            {
            break;
            }
        }
    CstCtlState( hWnd, CRB_STATE_DOWN | CRB_STATE_CAPTURE |
            CRB_STATE_INSIDE, STATE_RESET, AREA_BITMAP );
    break;
case WM_MOUSEMOVE:
    {

    WORD wState = CSTCTLGETSTATE( hWnd );
```

Listing 6.7 *continued*

```
                    if ( wState & CRB_STATE_CAPTURE )
                        {

                        POINT Point;

                        /* Mouse has been captured so check the location */
                        Point.x = (int)LOWORD( lParam );
                        Point.y = (int)HIWORD( lParam );
                        if ( PtInWnd( hWnd, Point ) )
                            {
                            /* Inside the control */
                            if ( !( wState & CRB_STATE_INSIDE ) )
                                {
                                /* Was outside control, change states */
                                CstCtlState( hWnd, CRB_STATE_DOWN |
                                        CRB_STATE_INSIDE, STATE_SET, AREA_BITMAP );
                                }
                            }
                        else
                            {
                            /* Outside the control */
                            if ( wState & CRB_STATE_INSIDE )
                                {
                                /* Was inside control, change states */
                                CstCtlState( hWnd, CRB_STATE_DOWN |
                                        CRB_STATE_INSIDE, STATE_RESET, AREA_BITMAP );
                                }
                            }
                        }   /* if wState */
                    break;
                    }   /* case WM_MOUSEMOVE */
                case WM_PAINT:
                    {

                    PAINTSTRUCT PS;
                    HDC hDC = BeginPaint( hWnd, &PS );

                    if ( IsWindowVisible( hWnd ) )
                        {
                        /* Only paint if needed */
                        CstRadioBtnDraw( hWnd, hDC );
                        }
                    EndPaint( hWnd, &PS );
                    break;
                    }
                case WM_SETFOCUS:
                    CstCtlState( hWnd, CRB_STATE_FOCUS, STATE_SET, AREA_ALL );
                    if ( !CstCtlState( hWnd, CRB_STATE_DOWN, STATE_CHECK, AREA_NONE ) )
                        {

                        DWORD dwStyle;
                        HWND hWndParent = GetParent( hWnd );

                        dwStyle = (DWORD)GetWindowLong( hWnd, GWL_STYLE ) & 0x0FL;
                        if ( dwStyle == BS_AUTORADIOBUTTON )
                            {
                            SendMessage( hWnd, BM_SETCHECK, TRUE, 0L );
                            if ( !IsWindow( hWnd ) )
                                {
```

Listing 6.7 continued

```
                    break;
                }
            }
        if ( hWndParent )
            {
            SendMessage( hWndParent, WM_COMMAND,
                    (WPARAM)GetDlgCtrlID( hWnd ),
                    MAKELPARAM( hWnd, BN_CLICKED ) );
            }
        }
        break;
    case WM_SETFONT:
        if ( wParam )
            {
            CstCtlSetFont( hWnd, wParam );
            }
        if ( lParam )
            {
            /* Send a Paint message */
            InvalidateRect( hWnd, NULL, FALSE );
            UpdateWindow( hWnd );
            }
        break;
    default:
        return ( DefWindowProc( hWnd, wMessage, wParam, lParam ) );
    }   /* switch wMessage */

    return ( 0L );

}   /* function CstRadioBtnWndFn */

/* End of CST_RBTN.C */
```

Listing 6.8

```
/*****************************************************************************
        File Name: CST_RBTN.RC
    Expanded Name: Custom Radio Button
      Description: Resource file for the radio button custom control
      Portability: Microsoft Windows 3.X
*****************************************************************************/

RBD_1616 BITMAP BITMAP\RBD_1616.BMP   /* Down State */
RBDC1616 BITMAP BITMAP\RBDC1616.BMP   /* Down & Checked State */
RBU_1616 BITMAP BITMAP\RBU_1616.BMP   /* Up State */
RBUC1616 BITMAP BITMAP\RBUC1616.BMP   /* Up & Checked State */

/* End of CST_RBTN.RC */
```

Listing 6.9

```
/*****************************************************************************
        File Name: DEM_BTTN.H
    Expanded Name: Demo Button
      Description: Include file for DEM_BTTN.C & DEM_BTTN.RC
      Portability: Microsoft Windows 3.X
*****************************************************************************/

#define IDM_CHECKBOX 108
#define IDM_PUSHBTN 109
#define IDM_RADIOBTN 110
#define IDM_STATIC 111
#define IDM_EXIT 112

#define IDD_STANDARD 201
#define IDD_DEFAULT 202
#define IDD_NOFOCUS 203
#define IDD_NOFRAME 204
#define IDD_NOSHADOW 205
#define IDD_LEFTTEXT 206
#define IDD_RIGHTTEXT 207
#define IDD_LEFTBITMAP 208
#define IDD_RIGHTBITMAP 209
#define IDD_STRETCHBITMAP 210
#define IDD_STRETCHBUTTON 211

#define IDD_CHECKBOX1 301
#define IDD_CHECKBOX2 302

#define IDD_RADIOBTN1 401
#define IDD_RADIOBTN2 402

/* End of DEM_BTTN.H */
```

Listing 6.10

```c
/*****************************************************************************
          File Name: DEM_BTTN.C
      Expanded Name: Demo Button
        Description: Demo program for custom button controls
       Program List: DEM_BTTN.C
                     DEM_BTTN.RC
                     DEM_BTTN.DEF
                     CST_DATA.C
                     CST_DRAW.C
                     CST_CKBX.C
                     CST_PBTN.C
                     CST_RBTN.C
                     CST_UTIL.C
                     CST_XTRA.C
                     or
                     DEM_BTTN.C
                     DEM_BTTN.RC
                     DEM_BTTN.DEF
                     CST_CTLS.LIB,DLL
Global Function List: WinMain
                     CheckBoxDemoDialogProc
                     RadioBtnDemoDialogProc
                     PushBtnDemoDialogProc
                     MainWindowProc
        Portability: Microsoft Windows 3.X
*****************************************************************************/

/* Microsoft Windows */
#include <windows.h>

/* Types and prototypes */
#include <cst_ctls.h>

/* Own */
#include <dem_bttn.h>

int PASCAL WinMain( HANDLE hInstance, HANDLE hPrevInstance, LPSTR lpCmdLine,
        int nCmdShow );
BOOL FAR PASCAL CheckBoxDemoDialogProc( HWND hDlg, UINT wMessage,
        WPARAM wParam, LPARAM lParam );
BOOL FAR PASCAL PushBtnDemoDialogProc( HWND hDlg, UINT wMessage,
        WPARAM wParam, LPARAM lParam );
BOOL FAR PASCAL RadioBtnDemoDialogProc( HWND hDlg, UINT wMessage,
        WPARAM wParam, LPARAM lParam );
LONG FAR PASCAL MainWindowProc( HWND hwnd, UINT wMessage, WPARAM wParam,
        LPARAM lParam );

/*****************************************************************************
       Name: WinMain
Description: Main Window function
*****************************************************************************/
int PASCAL WinMain( HINSTANCE hInstance, HINSTANCE hPrevInstance,
        LPSTR lpCmdLine, int nCmdShow )
    {

    HWND hWnd;
    MSG Msg;
    static char _Name[] = "DEM_BTTN";
    WNDCLASS WndClass;
```

Listing 6.10 *continued*

```
        lpCmdLine = lpCmdLine;
        nCmdShow = nCmdShow;

        #if defined ( NO_DLL )
        CstCheckBoxRegister( hInstance );
        CstPushBtnRegister( hInstance );
        CstRadioBtnRegister( hInstance );
        #endif

        if ( !hPrevInstance )
            {
            WndClass.style = 0;
            WndClass.lpfnWndProc = MainWindowProc;
            WndClass.cbClsExtra = 0;
            WndClass.cbWndExtra = 0;
            WndClass.hInstance = hInstance;
            WndClass.hIcon = LoadIcon( hInstance, _Name );
            WndClass.hCursor = LoadCursor( NULL, IDC_ARROW );
            WndClass.hbrBackground = COLOR_WINDOW + 1;
            WndClass.lpszMenuName = _Name;
            WndClass.lpszClassName = _Name;
            RegisterClass( &WndClass );
            }

        hWnd = CreateWindow( _Name, "Custom Button Control Demo",
                WS_OVERLAPPEDWINDOW, CW_USEDEFAULT, CW_USEDEFAULT,
                CW_USEDEFAULT, CW_USEDEFAULT, NULL, NULL, hInstance, NULL );

        ShowWindow( hWnd, nCmdShow );
        UpdateWindow( hWnd );

        while ( GetMessage( &Msg, NULL, 0, 0 ) )
            {
            TranslateMessage( &Msg );
            DispatchMessage ( &Msg );
            }

        return ( (int)Msg.wParam );

        }   /* function WinMain */


/*****************************************************************************
        Name: CheckBoxDemoDialogProc
    Description: Dialog Proc to demonstrate custom check box control
*****************************************************************************/
BOOL FAR PASCAL CheckBoxDemoDialogProc( HWND hDlg, UINT wMessage,
        WPARAM wParam, LPARAM lParam )
    {

    lParam = lParam;

    switch( wMessage )
        {
        case WM_INITDIALOG:
            return ( TRUE );
        case WM_CLOSE:
```

Listing 6.10 *continued*

```
                EndDialog( hDlg, 0 );
                return ( FALSE );
            case WM_COMMAND:
                switch ( wParam )
                    {
                    case IDD_CHECKBOX1:
                    case IDD_CHECKBOX2:
                        {

                        LONG lState;

                        lState = SendMessage( GetDlgItem( hDlg, (int)wParam ),
                                BM_GETCHECK, 0, 0L );
                        SendMessage( GetDlgItem( hDlg, (int)wParam ),
                                BM_SETCHECK, lState ? FALSE : TRUE, 0L );
                        break;
                        }
                    case IDD_STANDARD:
                        EndDialog( hDlg, 0 );
                        return ( TRUE );
                    default:
                        break;
                    }
                return ( TRUE );
            default:
                break;
            }   /* switch wMessage */

        return ( FALSE );

        }   /* function CheckBoxDemoDialogProc */


/*******************************************************************************
        Name: RadioBtnDemoDialogProc
 Description: Dialog Proc to demonstrate custom radio button control
*******************************************************************************/
BOOL FAR PASCAL RadioBtnDemoDialogProc( HWND hDlg, UINT wMessage,
        WPARAM wParam, LPARAM lParam )
    {

    lParam = lParam;

    switch( wMessage )
        {
        case WM_INITDIALOG:
            return ( TRUE );
        case WM_CLOSE:
            EndDialog( hDlg, 0 );
            return ( FALSE );
        case WM_COMMAND:
            switch ( wParam )
                {
                case IDD_RADIOBTN1:
                    {

                    LONG lState;

                    lState = SendMessage( GetDlgItem( hDlg, IDD_RADIOBTN1 ),
```

Listing 6.10 *continued*

```
                            BM_GETCHECK, 0, 0L );
                    SendMessage( GetDlgItem( hDlg, IDD_RADIOBTN1 ),
                            BM_SETCHECK, lState ? FALSE : TRUE, 0L );
                    if ( !lState )
                        {
                        SendMessage( GetDlgItem( hDlg, IDD_RADIOBTN2 ),
                                BM_SETCHECK, FALSE, 0L );
                        }
                    break;
                    }
                case IDD_RADIOBTN2:
                    {

                    LONG lState;

                    lState = SendMessage( GetDlgItem( hDlg, IDD_RADIOBTN2 ),
                            BM_GETCHECK, 0, 0L );
                    SendMessage( GetDlgItem( hDlg, IDD_RADIOBTN2 ),
                            BM_SETCHECK, lState ? FALSE : TRUE, 0L );
                    if ( !lState )
                        {
                        SendMessage( GetDlgItem( hDlg, IDD_RADIOBTN1 ),
                                BM_SETCHECK, FALSE, 0L );
                        }
                    break;
                    }
                case IDD_STANDARD:
                    EndDialog( hDlg, 0 );
                    return ( TRUE );
                default:
                    break;
                }
            return ( TRUE );
        default:
            break;
        }   /* switch wMessage */

    return ( FALSE );

    }   /* function RadioBtnDemoDialogProc */


/******************************************************************************
        Name: PushBtnDemoDialogProc
 Description: Dialog Proc to demonstrate custom push button control
******************************************************************************/
BOOL FAR PASCAL PushBtnDemoDialogProc( HWND hDlg, UINT wMessage,
        WPARAM wParam, LPARAM lParam )
    {

    switch( wMessage )
        {
        case WM_INITDIALOG:
            return ( TRUE );
        case WM_CLOSE:
            EndDialog( hDlg, 0 );
            return ( FALSE );
        case WM_COMMAND:
            switch ( wParam )
```

Listing 6.10 *continued*

```
            {
            case IDD_STANDARD:
            case IDD_DEFAULT:
            case IDD_NOFOCUS:
            case IDD_NOFRAME:
            case IDD_NOSHADOW:
            case IDD_LEFTTEXT:
            case IDD_RIGHTTEXT:
            case IDD_LEFTBITMAP:
            case IDD_RIGHTBITMAP:
            case IDD_STRETCHBITMAP:
            case IDD_STRETCHBUTTON:
                EndDialog( hDlg, 0 );
                return ( TRUE );
            default:
                break;
            }
        return ( TRUE );
    case WM_PARENTNOTIFY:
        {
        HWND hCtl = LOWORD( lParam );
        HANDLE hInstance = GetWindowWord( hDlg, GWW_HINSTANCE );
        switch ( wParam )
            {
            case WM_CREATE:
                switch ( HIWORD( lParam ) )
                    {
                    case IDD_LEFTBITMAP:
                        CstCtlSetBitmap( hCtl, CPB_BITMAP_DOWN,
                                LoadBitmap( hInstance, "GCDW1616" ) );
                        CstCtlSetBitmap( hCtl, CPB_BITMAP_UP,
                                LoadBitmap( hInstance, "GCUP1616" ) );
                        CstCtlSetBitmap( hCtl, CPB_BITMAP_UPFOCUS,
                                CSTCTLGETBITMAP( hCtl, CPB_BITMAP_UP ) );
                        break;
                    case IDD_RIGHTBITMAP:
                        {
                        HWND hSib = GetDlgItem( hDlg, IDD_LEFTBITMAP );
                        CstCtlSetBitmap( hCtl, CPB_BITMAP_DOWN,
                                CSTCTLGETBITMAP( hSib, CPB_BITMAP_DOWN ) );
                        CstCtlSetBitmap( hCtl, CPB_BITMAP_UP,
                                CSTCTLGETBITMAP( hSib, CPB_BITMAP_UP ) );
                        CstCtlSetBitmap( hCtl, CPB_BITMAP_UPFOCUS,
                                CSTCTLGETBITMAP( hSib, CPB_BITMAP_UPFOCUS ) );
                        break;
                        }
                    case IDD_STRETCHBITMAP:
                        CstCtlSetBitmap( hCtl, CPB_BITMAP_DOWN,
                                LoadBitmap( hInstance, "STRETCH" ) );
                        CstCtlSetBitmap( hCtl, CPB_BITMAP_UP,
                                CSTCTLGETBITMAP( hCtl, CPB_BITMAP_DOWN ) );
                        CstCtlSetBitmap( hCtl, CPB_BITMAP_UPFOCUS,
                                CSTCTLGETBITMAP( hCtl, CPB_BITMAP_DOWN ) );
                        break;
                    case IDD_STRETCHBUTTON:
                        {
                        HWND hSib = GetDlgItem( hDlg, IDD_STRETCHBITMAP );
                        CstCtlSetBitmap( hCtl, CPB_BITMAP_DOWN,
                                CSTCTLGETBITMAP( hSib, CPB_BITMAP_DOWN ) );
```

Listing 6.10 *continued*

```
                                CstCtlSetBitmap( hCtl, CPB_BITMAP_UP,
                                    CSTCTLGETBITMAP( hSib, CPB_BITMAP_UP ) );
                                CstCtlSetBitmap( hCtl, CPB_BITMAP_UPFOCUS,
                                    CSTCTLGETBITMAP( hSib, CPB_BITMAP_UPFOCUS ) );
                                break;
                                }
                            default:
                                break;
                            }
                        break;
                    case WM_DESTROY:
                        switch ( HIWORD( lParam ) )
                            {
                            case IDD_LEFTBITMAP:
                                SafeDeleteObject( CSTCTLGETBITMAP( hCtl,
                                    CPB_BITMAP_DOWN ) );
                                SafeDeleteObject( CSTCTLGETBITMAP( hCtl,
                                    CPB_BITMAP_UP ) );
                                break;
                            case IDD_STRETCHBITMAP:
                                SafeDeleteObject( CSTCTLGETBITMAP( hCtl,
                                    CPB_BITMAP_UP ) );
                                break;
                            default:
                                break;
                            }
                        break;
                    default:
                        break;
                    }   /* switch wParam */
                return ( TRUE );
                }   /* case WM_PARENTNOTIFY */
            default:
                break;
            }   /* switch wMessage */

        return ( FALSE );

        }   /* function PushBtnDemoDialogProc */


/*****************************************************************************
        Name: MainWindowProc
    Description: Window procedure for main window
*****************************************************************************/
LONG FAR PASCAL MainWindowProc( HWND hWnd, UINT wMessage,
        WPARAM wParam, LPARAM lParam )
        {

    switch( wMessage )
        {
        case WM_COMMAND:
            {

            FARPROC lpfnProc;
            HINSTANCE hInstance;

            hInstance = (HINSTANCE)GetWindowWord( hWnd, GWW_HINSTANCE );
```

Listing 6.10 *continued*

```
            switch( wParam )
                {
                case IDM_CHECKBOX:
                    lpfnProc = MakeProcInstance( CheckBoxDemoDialogProc,
                                hInstance );
                    DialogBox( hInstance, "CHECKBOX", hWnd, lpfnProc );
                    FreeProcInstance( lpfnProc );
                    break;
                case IDM_PUSHBTN:
                    lpfnProc = MakeProcInstance( PushBtnDemoDialogProc,
                                hInstance );
                    DialogBox( hInstance, "PUSHBTN", hWnd, lpfnProc );
                    FreeProcInstance( lpfnProc );
                    break;
                case IDM_RADIOBTN:
                    lpfnProc = MakeProcInstance( RadioBtnDemoDialogProc,
                                hInstance );
                    DialogBox( hInstance, "RADIOBTN", hWnd, lpfnProc );
                    FreeProcInstance( lpfnProc );
                    break;
                case IDM_EXIT:
                    DestroyWindow( hWnd );
                    break;
                default:
                    break;
                }
            return ( FALSE );
            }
        case WM_DESTROY:
            PostQuitMessage( 0 );
            return ( FALSE );
        default:
            break;
        }

    return ( DefWindowProc( hWnd, wMessage, wParam, lParam ) );

    }   /* function MainWindowProc */

/* End of DEM_BTTN.C */
```

Listing 6.11

```
NAME DEM_BTTN
DESCRIPTION 'Custom Button Control Demo Program'
EXETYPE WINDOWS
CODE PRELOAD MOVEABLE
DATA PRELOAD MOVEABLE MULTIPLE
HEAPSIZE 1024
STACKSIZE 5120
EXPORTS
        MainWindowProc
        CheckBoxDemoDialogProc
        PushBtnDemoDialogProc
        RadioBtnDemoDialogProc
        CstCheckBoxWndFn
        CstPushBtnWndFn
        CstRadioBtnWndFn
```

Listing 6.12

```
ORIGIN    = QCWIN
ORIGIN_VER    = 1.00

PROJ =DEM_BTTN
DEBUG    =0
PROGTYPE =1
CALLER    =
ARGS =
DLLS =
CVPACK    =1
CC    =cl -qc
RC    =rc
CFLAGS_G_WEXE =/AS /W4 /Ze /D_WINDOWS /DNO_DLL /G2w /Zp /Aw
CFLAGS_D_WEXE =/Zi /Od
CFLAGS_R_WEXE =/O /Os /Gs /DNDEBUG
CFLAGS_G_WDLL =/AS /G2w /Zp /Aw /W3 /D_WINDOWS /D_WINDLL
CFLAGS_D_WDLL =/Gi /Od /Zi
CFLAGS_R_WDLL =/O /Os /DNDEBUG
CFLAGS_G_WTTY =/AS /G2w /W3 /D_WINDOWS
CFLAGS_D_WTTY =/Gi /Od /Zi
CFLAGS_R_WTTY =/O /Os /DNDEBUG
CFLAGS_G_DEXE =/AS /W2
CFLAGS_D_DEXE =/Gi /Od /Zi
CFLAGS_R_DEXE =/O /Ot /DNDEBUG
CFLAGS    =$(CFLAGS_G_WEXE) $(CFLAGS_R_WEXE)
LFLAGS_G_WEXE =/NOE/A:16/ST:10240
LFLAGS_D_WEXE =/CO
LFLAGS_R_WEXE =
LFLAGS_G_WDLL =/ST:5120 /A:16
LFLAGS_D_WDLL =/CO
LFLAGS_R_WDLL =
LFLAGS_G_WTTY =/ST:5120 /A:16
LFLAGS_D_WTTY =/CO
LFLAGS_R_WTTY =
LFLAGS_G_DEXE =/NOI /ST:2048
LFLAGS_D_DEXE =/CO
LFLAGS_R_DEXE =
LFLAGS    =$(LFLAGS_G_WEXE) $(LFLAGS_R_WEXE)
RCFLAGS   =/DNO_DLL
RESFLAGS =
RUNFLAGS =
DEFFILE =       DEMSBTTN.DEF
OBJS_EXT =
LIBS_EXT =

.rc.res: ; $(RC) $(RCFLAGS) -r $*.rc

all: $(PROJ).EXE

DEM_BTTN.OBJ: DEM_BTTN.C $(H)

DEM_BTTN.RES: DEM_BTTN.RC $(RESFILES) $(H)

CST_CKBX.OBJ: CST_CKBX.C $(H)

CST_DATA.OBJ: CST_DATA.C $(H)

CST_DRAW.OBJ: CST_DRAW.C $(H)
```

Listing 6.12 *continued*

```
CST_PBTN.OBJ: CST_PBTN.C $(H)

CST_RBTN.OBJ: CST_RBTN.C $(H)

CST_UTIL.OBJ: CST_UTIL.C $(H)

$(PROJ).EXE:  DEM_BTTN.OBJ CST_CKBX.OBJ CST_DATA.OBJ CST_DRAW.OBJ CST_PBTN.OBJ CST_RBTN.OBJ \
    CST_UTIL.OBJ $(OBJS_EXT) $(DEFFILE)
    echo >NUL @<<$(PROJ).CRF
DEM_BTTN.OBJ +
CST_CKBX.OBJ +
CST_DATA.OBJ +
CST_DRAW.OBJ +
CST_PBTN.OBJ +
CST_RBTN.OBJ +
CST_UTIL.OBJ +
$(OBJS_EXT)
$(PROJ).EXE

C:\PRGLNG\QCW\LIB\+
/NOD slibcew oldnames libw
$(DEFFILE);
<<
    link $(LFLAGS) @$(PROJ).CRF
    rc $(RESFLAGS) DEM_BTTN.RES $(PROJ).EXE

$(PROJ).EXE:  DEM_BTTN.RES
    rc $(RESFLAGS) DEM_BTTN.RES $(PROJ).EXE

run: $(PROJ).EXE
    $(PROJ) $(RUNFLAGS)
```

Subclassed Controls

The previous two chapters created custom controls by creating all new code for the window class. This chapter will create a custom control that borrows code from existing standard controls, using a method known as subclassing. Subclassing allows a programmer to create a new window class (or control) that uses a previously defined class's window function as the default message processor for the new window class.

Subclassing is best suited to custom controls with functionality that differs only slightly from that of an existing control. The more complex the parent class and the more functionality the controls have in common, the more development time subclassing will save.

The User, Data, & Style Interfaces

In this chapter we use subclassing to create a data entry table custom control which combines the functionality of the standard *LISTBOX* and *EDIT* controls. The new control class, *CSTTABLE* will be a subclass of the *LISTBOX* control and will use a supporting window class, *CSTTABLEEDIT*, which is a subclass of the standard *EDIT* control.

When displayed, this control will look just like the standard *LISTBOX* control, but, the user will be able to add new items and edit or delete existing items. Tables 7.1 through 7.4 describe the new keyboard and mouse interface for the *CSTTABLE* control.

Windows Custom Controls

Because the control *CSTTABLE* incorporates the functionality of more than one class, it is a *hybrid* control. In this regard, it is like the standard Windows combobox, which combines the functionality of the list box with that of an edit control in a single hybrid control. The *CSTTABLE* control looks like, and for the most part behaves like a standard list box control, but unlike a standard control, with *CSTTABLE* the user can easily edit, delete, and insert cells.

With one exception, namely *LBS_MULTIPLESEL*, the *CSTTABLE* control supports all the window styles defined for the standard *LISTBOX* control. *CSTTABLE* also responds to all the *LISTBOX* class specific messages exactly as a standard *LISTBOX* control would. Thus, when using the *CSTTABLE* control in a dialog box function, the programmer may treat it just like a standard listbox control.

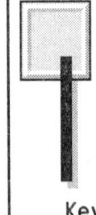

Table 7.1
When the edit mode is active, CSTTABLE responds to this keyboard interface.

Key Stroke	Action
Backspace	If cell is empty, deletes cell
Backspace	If caret is at beginning of cell moves to end of previous cell
Delete	If cell is empty, deletes cell is cell is empty
Insert	Creates a new cell
Return	Exits edit mode and moves to next cell
Left	If caret is at beginning of cell moves to end of previous cell
Right	If caret is at end of cell, moves to beginning of next cell

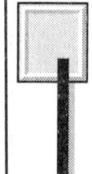

Table 7.2
When the edit mode is inactive, CSTTABLE responds to these keys.

Key Stroke	Action
Backspace	Deletes previous cell
Delete	Deletes current cell
Insert	Create a new cell
Return	Enters Edit mode

The *CSTTABLE* control uses the same instance data interface as our other controls. In particular, *CSTTABLE* records the current cell index in the *wState* member, stores the handle of a supporting window (an instance of the *CSTTABLEEDIT* class) in the *hWnd* member, and uses the frame field to limit the length of each list entry. *CSTTABLEEDIT* does not use the instance data interface at all.

Extra Byte Complications

In a sense, each instance of a subclass control has two window procedures that share access to a single window structure: the subclass window procedure and the original (base) class procedure. The subclass window procedure will intercept and respond to selected messages (those associated with the difference in functionality between the base class and

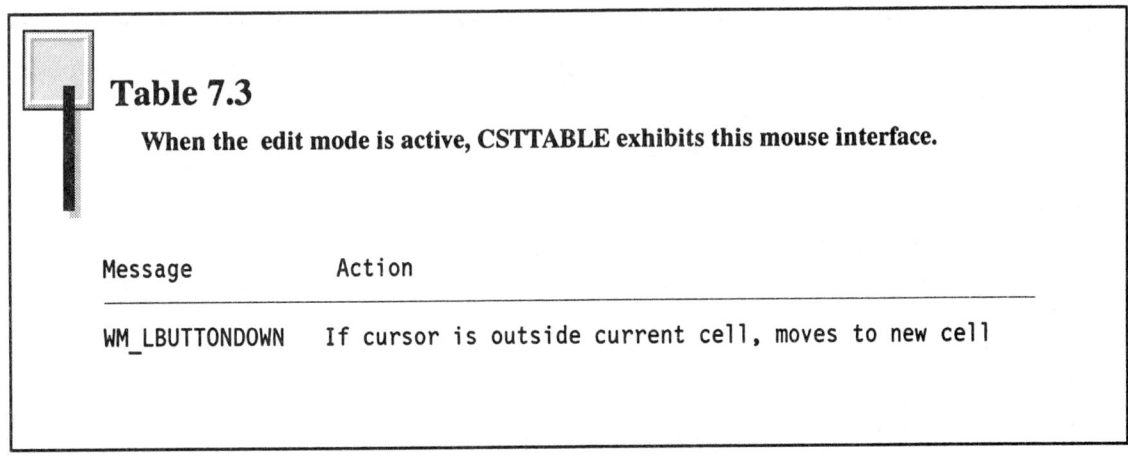

Table 7.3

When the edit mode is active, CSTTABLE exhibits this mouse interface.

Message	Action
WM_LBUTTONDOWN	If cursor is outside current cell, moves to new cell

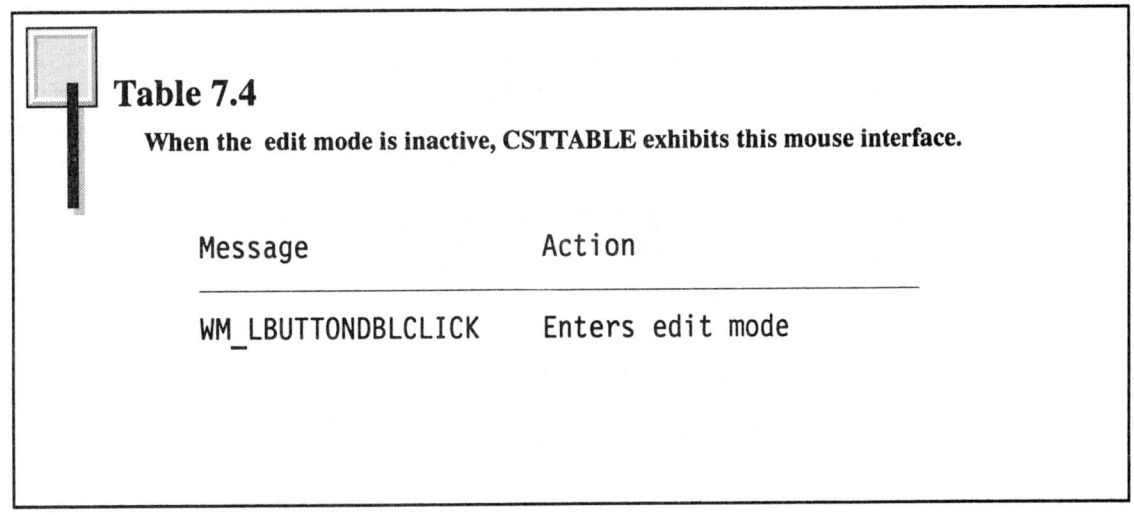

Table 7.4

When the edit mode is inactive, CSTTABLE exhibits this mouse interface.

Message	Action
WM_LBUTTONDBLCLICK	Enters edit mode

subclass) but will forward most of its messages to the base class procedure. The base class procedure can't distinguish between its normal messages and messages forwarded from the subclass procedure.

Even though the base class and subclass procedures share the same window structure, the two procedures *will* have a different understanding of the layout and extent of that structure. At a minimum, the subclass procedure will need to augment the window structure or the associated instance data with storage for a pointer to the parent window procedure. This difference in the view of the instance data and our desire to have a common data interface for all classes, create some serious design issues.

Our common data interface will be easiest to implement and use if the pointer to (and handle for) the instance data structure are positioned at the same offset within the extra bytes in *every* class. This constraint is easy to meet if we create the class, or base the subclass on a class we have created. In these cases *we* alone determine how the extra bytes are used.

Figure 7.1

If both the base class and the derived class always observed the same conventions, the instance data pointer could be stored at the beginning of the extra bytes.

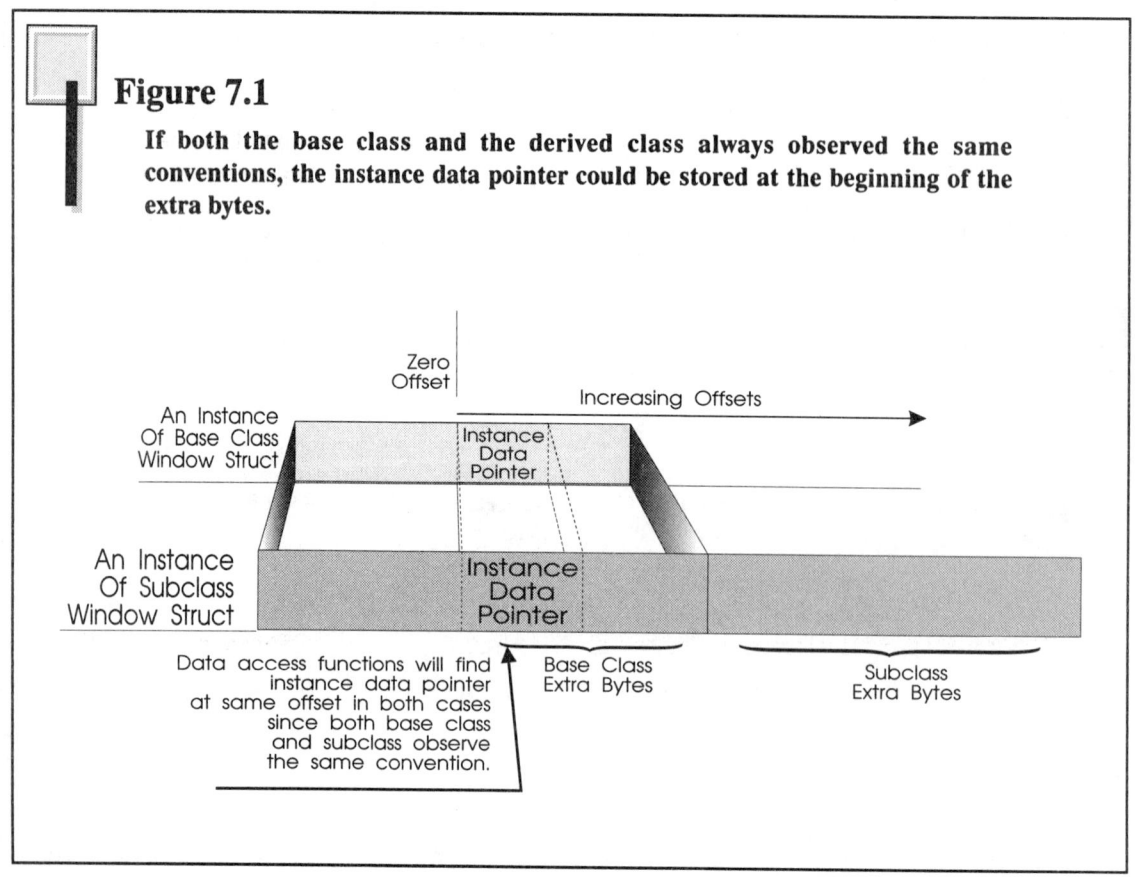

For example, in our own classes, we could just choose always to place the pointers first (see Figure 7.1).

Unfortunately, such simple schemes fail when one subclasses a *standard* control, because the standard control may *already* use those extra bytes for something else (See Figure 7.2).

We solved this problem by *logically* (as opposed to physically) reversing the order of the extra bytes so that all our custom controls can pretend that the extra bytes used by the standard controls always fall *after* those used by our controls. (See Figure 7.3.) In other words, instead of always placing the instance data pointers at the same offset relative to the *beginning* of the extra bytes, we always place the pointers at the same offset relative to the *end* of the extra bytes.

Because a subclass window procedure can have a different view of the window structure than the associated parent window procedure,

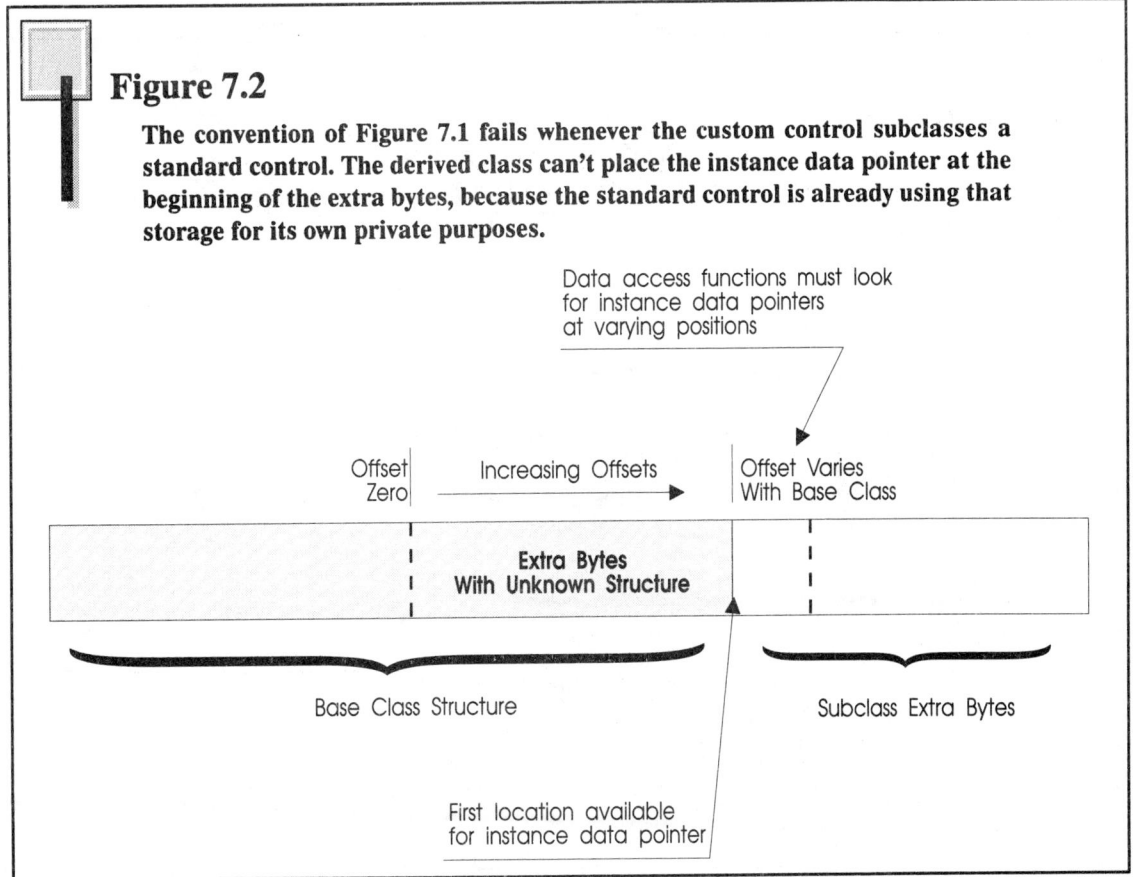

Figure 7.2

The convention of Figure 7.1 fails whenever the custom control subclasses a standard control. The derived class can't place the instance data pointer at the beginning of the extra bytes, because the standard control is already using that storage for its own private purposes.

230 Windows Custom Controls

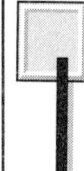

Figure 7.3

In contrast to Figure 7.1, a custom control can always store the instance data pointer at the end of the extra bytes, even if the control subclasses a standard control.

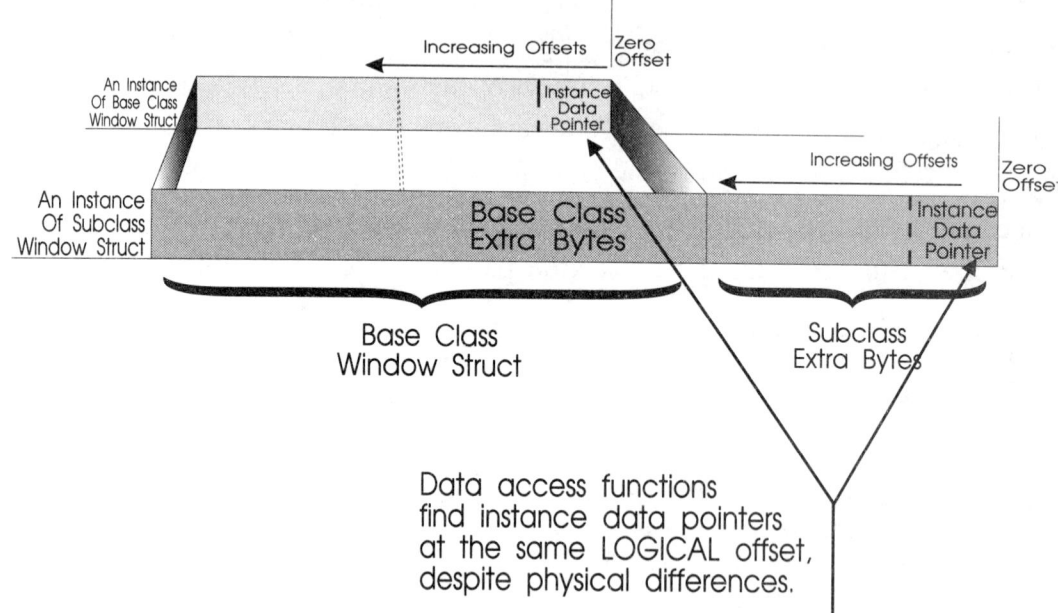

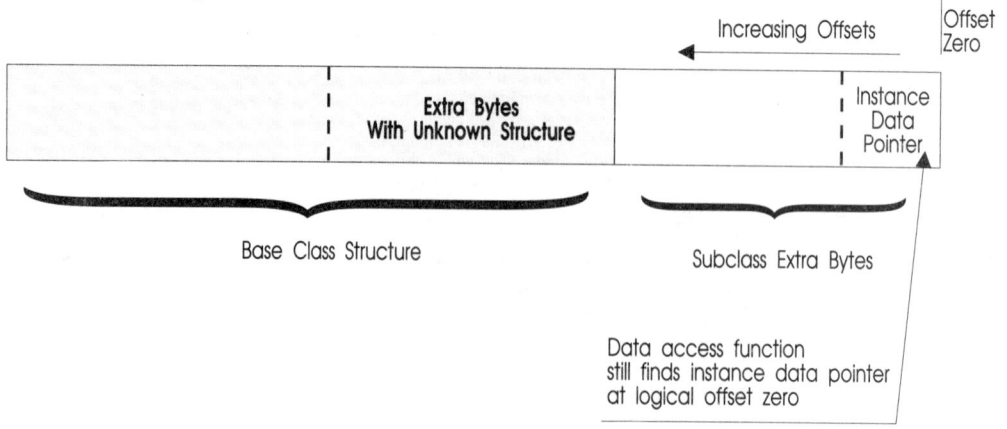

subclassing imposes a nonobvious requirement on the implementation of this "reverse indexing" mechanism. Namely, the end of the extra bytes must be computed dynamically at runtime. As Figures 7.4 and 7.5 show, when a base class window procedure has been subclassed, the number of extra bytes in the window structure may vary from call to call, depending on whether the procedure is processing a message from an instance of the base class or from an instance of a subclass. Because of this runtime variation in where the extra bytes end, offsets relative to the end of the extra bytes must also be resolved at runtime. Fortunately, the length of the extra byte area is stored in the window structure, making the calculation simple.

The eight functions in `CST_XTRA.C` (Listing 4.2) access the extra bytes using this "end-based" indexing scheme. These functions mimic the functionality of the windows standard functions `GetClassLong()` through `SetWindowWord()`, but take an offset relative to the end of the extra byte region. We have named each function by adding a `Cst` prefix to each of the corresponding standard function names. Those developing in C or C++, can use the macro versions of these functions, `CSTGETCLASSLONG()` through `CSTSETWINDOWWORD()`. Listing 4.1, `CST_XTRA.H`, defines these macros and declares prototypes for all the functions in Listing 4.2.

Programs must use these custom functions *only* to access members of the extra bytes, and *only* using constant offsets defined by the custom control. For all offsets defined by Windows (e.g., `GCL_MENUNAME`) the program must use the standard `GetClassWord()`, etc., functions.

Creating a Subclass

The `WNDCLASS` structure used to register a subclass control is not created "from scratch" — instead, the subclass structure is created by modifying a copy of the base class structure. The registration code calls `GetClassInfo()` to retrieve the copy. For example, this line loads `WndClass` with the standard `EDIT` control's class information:

```
GetClassInfo( NULL, "EDIT", &WndClass );
```

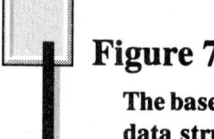

Figure 7.4

The base class window procedure receives messages with different sized instance data structures. (Compare the sequence in this figure with that in Figure 7.5.) When the message is forwarded from a subclass, the instance data will have additional extra byte space.

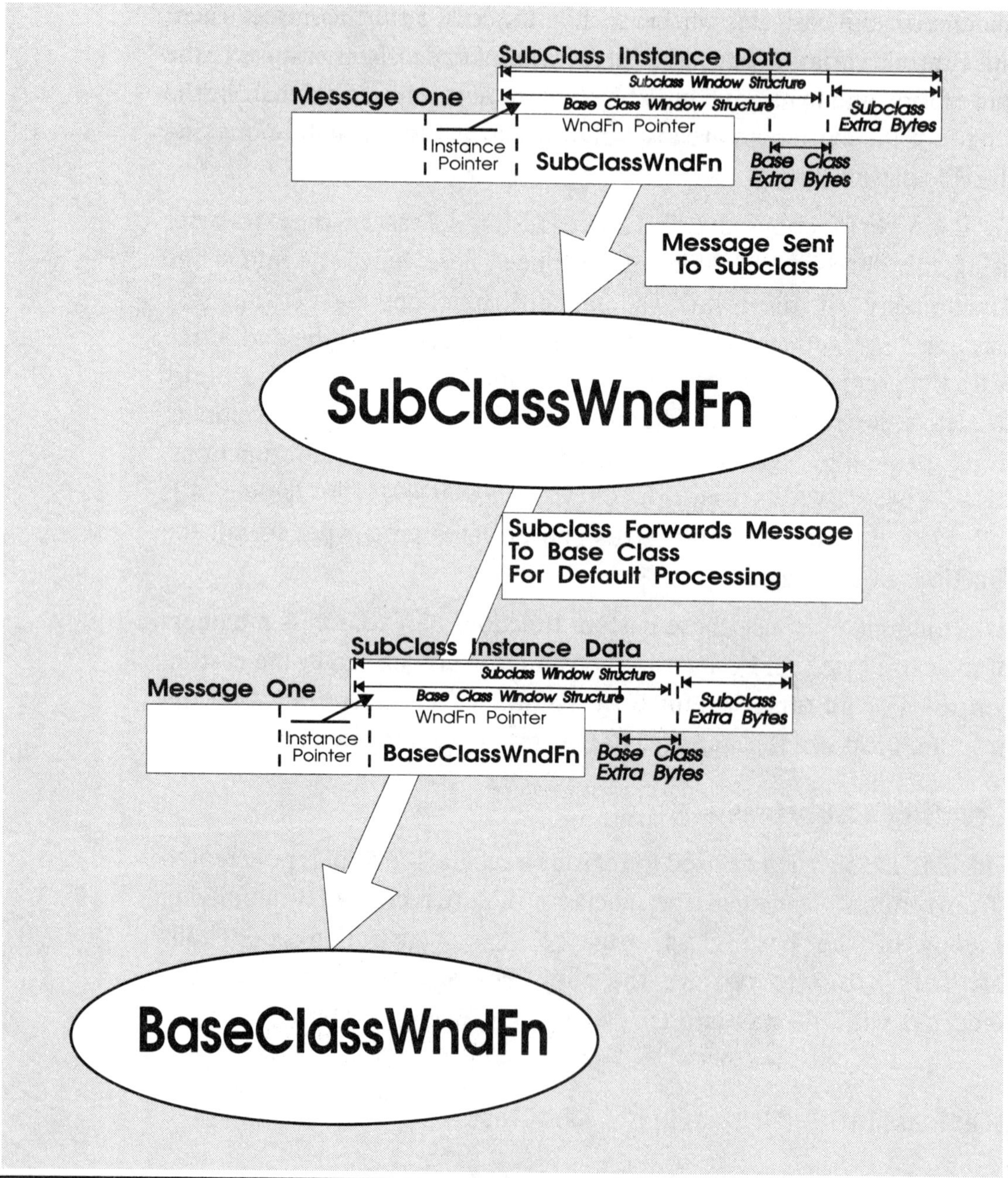

The first parameter to `GetClassInfo()` is the instance handle of the application that registered the class — `NULL` for the standard Windows controls.

The registration code then modifies those `WNDCLASS` structure members that will be different for the subclassed control. Every subclassed control will change at least the class name, window procedure, and instance handle. If the subclass needs additional class or

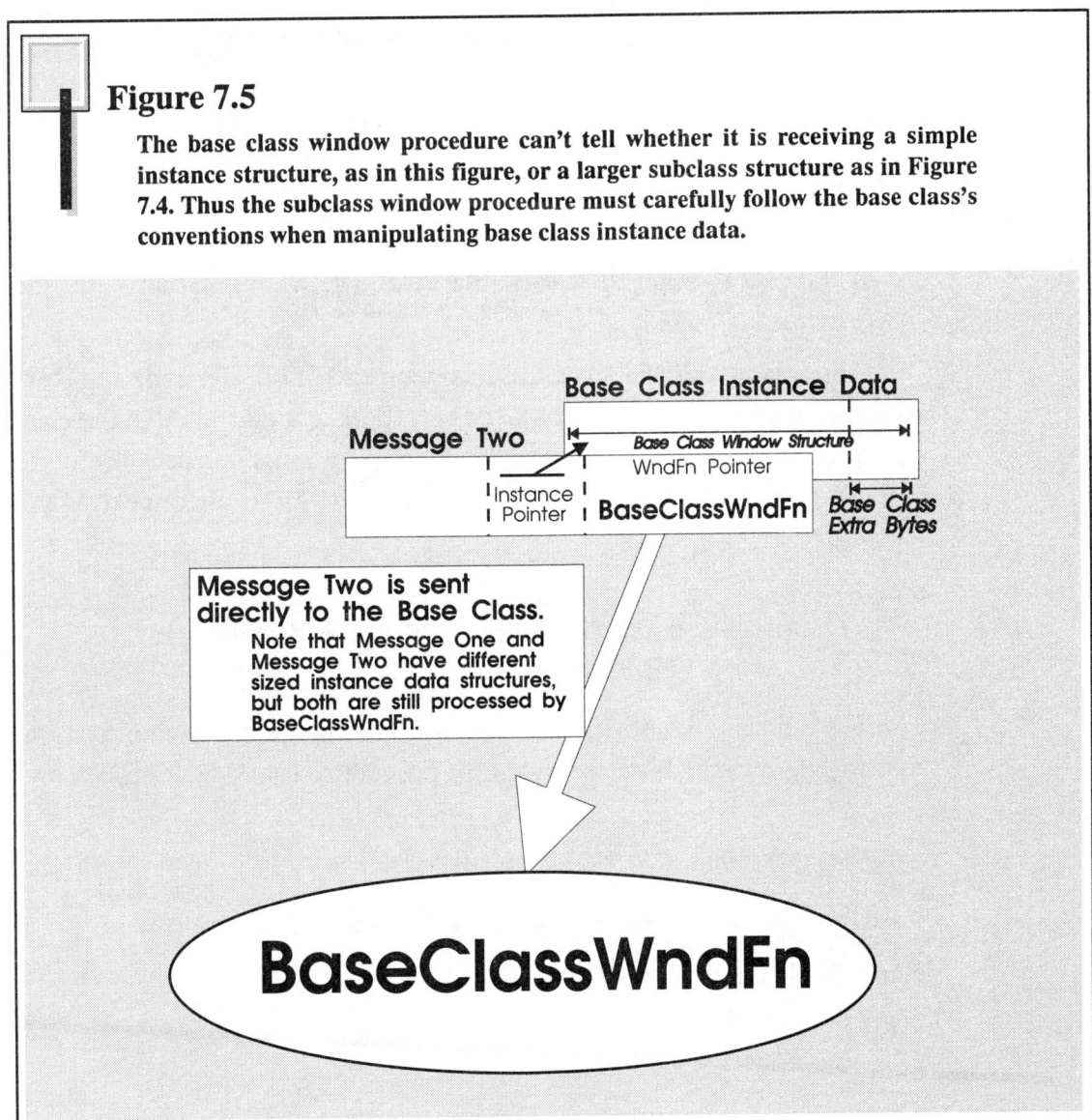

Figure 7.5

The base class window procedure can't tell whether it is receiving a simple instance structure, as in this figure, or a larger subclass structure as in Figure 7.4. Thus the subclass window procedure must carefully follow the base class's conventions when manipulating base class instance data.

window extra bytes (most of ours will) the values in the *cbClsExtra()* and *cbWndExtra()* members also must be increased accordingly:

```
WndClass.cbClsExtra += SUBCLASS_CLSEXTRA;

WndClass.cbWndExtra += SUBCLASS_WNDEXTRA;
```

Since the subclassed window will call the base window procedure as a default message handler, the registration code must save a pointer to the base window procedure before installing the new procedure:

```
lpfnParentWndFn = (LONG)WndClass.lpfnWndProc;

WndClass.lpfnWndProc = SubClassWndFn;
```

If the subclass will be stored in a DLL, the code must also add the class style, *CS_GLOBALCLASS*.

Once the *WNDCLASS* structure has been modified, the code registers the class with a call to *RegisterClass()*. Before an instance of the class is used, the pointer to the base class procedure must be copied into the subclass class extra bytes. Our code does this with the custom extra byte function:

```
CSTSETCLASSLONG( hWnd, GCL_WNDPROCPARENT, lpfnParentWndFn );
```

The subclass window procedure will use this pointer when passing messages on to the base class window procedure for default processing:

```
lpfnParentWndFn = (FARPROC)CSTGETCLASSLONG( hWnd, GCL_WNDPROCPARENT );

CallWindowProc( lpfnListBoxWndFn, hWnd, wMessage, wParam, lParam );
```

Our Implementation

Our code avoids the need to save the base window procedure function pointer, by performing a second `GetClassInfo()` call (if needed) at the beginning of the window procedure. The window procedure then saves the base class window procedure pointer in the class extra bytes, positioning it relative to the end of the extra bytes. This pointer, however, does not always fall at a fixed logical offset within the extra bytes. Its position will vary depending upon how much extra byte storage the class uses. As a consequence, each subclass control must declare a unique constant (`GCL_WNDPROCPARENT` above). Since these constants are necessary only in subclass window procedures, and since their use is confined to the subclass within which they are defined, we felt this was a reasonable implementation.

(Don't be misled by our use of "parent" in the `GCL_WNDPROCPARENT()` constant. The base class is the parent of the subclass in only one sense: the subclass "inherits" behavior from the base class. Instances of subclass windows are very rarely child windows of an instance of their base class.)

Hybrid Controls

A hybrid control uses more than one window class and more than one window to perform a single functionality. The *CSTTABLE* control actually uses four window classes. *CSTTABLE* is a hybrid of itself and *CSTTABLEEDIT*. *CSTTABLE* is a subclass of *LISTBOX*. *CSTTABLEEDIT* is a subclass of *EDIT*.

During its life cycle, a hybrid control will create and destroy windows of its component classes. *CSTTABLE* creates and destroys windows of class type *CSTTABLEEDIT*, which in turn creates and destroys windows of class type *CSTTABLEEDIT*. Figure 7.6 shows the ownership (parent/child) relationships among these windows. This figure also incorporates inheritance information.

Basically, *CSTTABLE* relies upon the *LISTBOX* window procedure for it's behavior until the user selects an item. When an item is selected, *CSTTABLE* overlays the item with a *CSTTABLEEDIT* window, and copies the item into the new window. The *CSTTABLEEDIT* window is just a specialized version of the standard *EDIT* control, and relies upon the standard *EDIT* window procedure for most of its functionality. Once the user signals that all edits are complete, the edited item is copied from the *CSTTABLEEDIT* window back into the *CSTTABLE* list, and the edit window is destroyed.

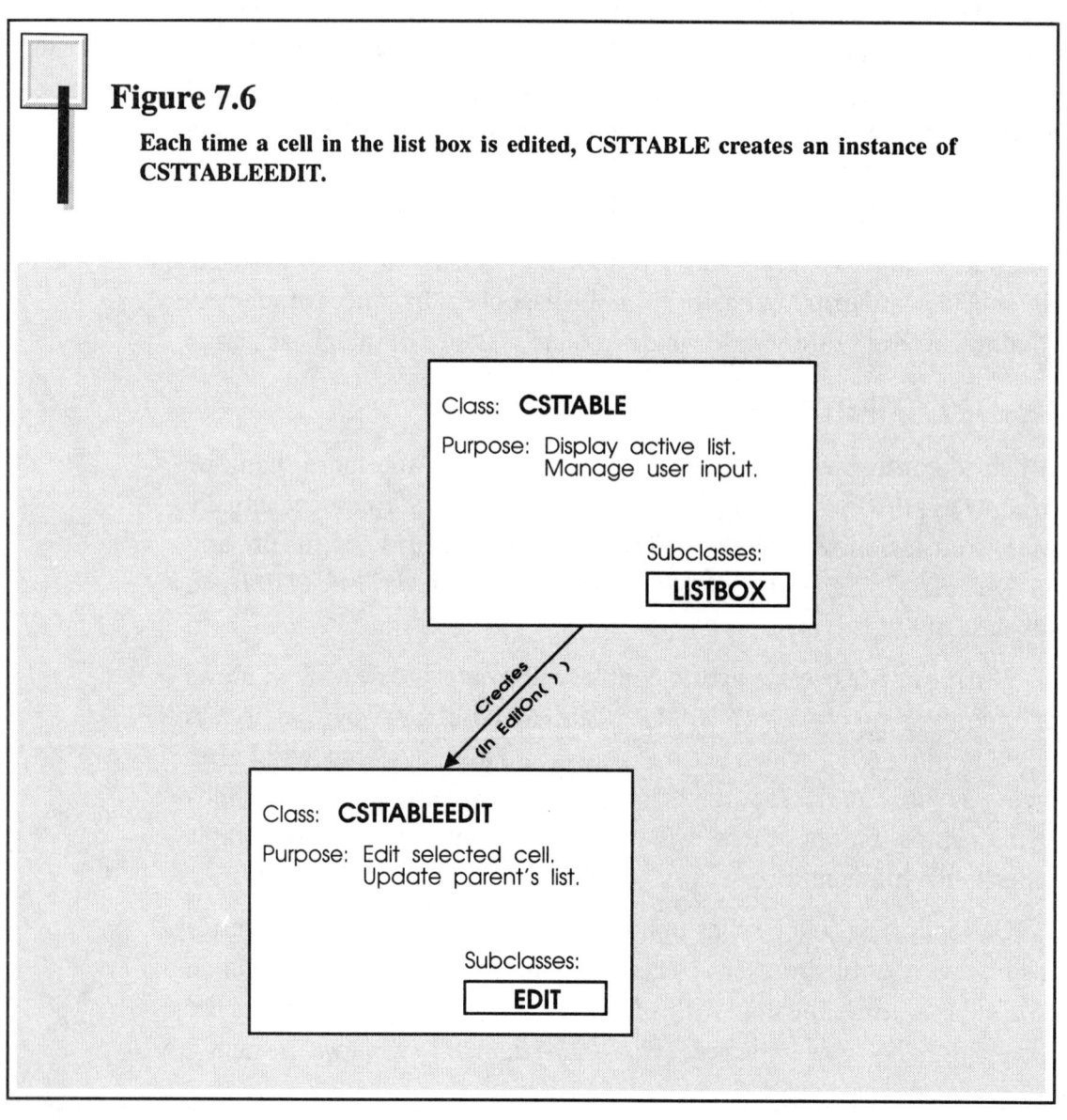

Figure 7.6

Each time a cell in the list box is edited, CSTTABLE creates an instance of CSTTABLEEDIT.

Registering Hybrid Controls

Since a hybrid control uses more than one window class, registering the hybrid control class may require registering multiple classes. The cleanest implementation is to create one registration function which registers both the hybrid class and all its component classes. This strategy requires only one public registration function.

In the case of *CSTTABLE*, the public function *CstTableRegister()* (in *CST_TABL.C*, Listing 7.2) registers both the *CSTTABLE* and *CSTTABLEEDIT* controls. *CstTableRegister()*, in turn, calls the private function *CstTableEditRegister()*. *CstTableWndFn()* and *CstTableEditWndFn()* test the class extra bytes for a valid base class window procedure pointer. If they don't find a valid pointer, they obtain a window procedure pointer for the appropriate base class (via *GetClassInfo()*) and copy it to the class extra bytes. This code excerpt from *CstTableWndFn()* shows the process:

```
FARPROC lpfnListBoxWndFn =
   (FARPROC)CSTGETCLASSLONG( hWnd, GCL_WNDPROCLISTBOX );
if ( !lpfnListBoxWndFn )
 {
 WNDCLASS WndClass;
 if ( GetClassInfo( NULL, "ListBox", &WndClass ) )
   {
   lpfnListBoxWndFn = (FARPROC)WndClass.lpfnWndProc;
   CSTSETCLASSLONG( hWnd, GCL_WNDPROCLISTBOX, (LONG)lpfnListBoxWndFn );
   }
 }
```

For robustness, the window function for *CSTTABLE* always turns off the unsupported *LBS_MULTIPLESEL* style when processing the *WM_CREATE* message.

Listing 7.2 contains the *CstTableWndFn()*, the window function for the *CSTTABLE* class, and *CstTableEditWndFn()*, the window function for the *CSTTABLEEDIT* class.

Controlling Appearance

Both *CstTableEditWndFn()* and *CstTableWndFn()* respond to most of the messages they receive (including even the *WM_PAINT* message) by passing the message on to their base class window function. *CstTableEditWndFn()* even forwards the *WM_CREATE* and *WM_DESTROY* messages to its base class window function. This heavy reliance upon the base class procedures gives *CSTTABLE* and *CSTTABLEEDIT* nearly identical appearance and behavior as the standard *LISTBOX* and *EDIT* controls.

Since the subclass functions refer the *WM_PAINT* messages to the appropriate base class, the *WM_CTLCOLOR* message is our only opportunity for modifying the appearance of the control. Thus the code that controls the appearance of the *CSTTABLEEDIT* window resides in its parent's window procedure, *CstTableWndFn()*.

CstTableWndFn() uses the values in the instance data to set the colors for the *CSTTABLEEDIT* window as follows:

```
   .
   .
   .
case WM_CTLCOLOR:
    if ( HIWORD( lParam ) == CTLCOLOR_EDIT )
        {
        /* Set up drawing attributes for the edit control */
        SetBkMode( wParam, CSTCTLGETBKMODE( hWnd ) );
        SetTextColor( wParam, CSTCTLGETCOLOR( hWnd, CC_COLOR_TEXT ) );
        SetBkColor( wParam,
                CSTCTLGETCOLOR( hWnd, CC_COLOR_TEXTBACKGROUND ) );
        return ( CSTCTLGETBRUSH( hWnd, CC_BRUSH_BACKGROUND ) );
        }
    break;
   .
   .
   .
```

Handling User Interactions

Most of the code for *CSTTABLE* is devoted to responding to user interactions, in the form of mouse, keyboard, focus and instance data interface messages.

To force Windows to send all keystrokes to *CstTableWndFn()* and *CstTableEditWndFn()*, both functions respond to the *WM_GETDLGCODE* message by requesting all keys:

```
case WM_GETDLGCODE:
    return ( DLGC_WANTALLKEYS );
```

Without this request, the dialog manager would not give the custom control a chance to process certain keys (such as the return key). By processing these keys in the subclass window procedure, we can redefine the default behavior. For example, in this case the return key exits the edit mode instead of selecting the default push button for the dialog box.

CSTTABLE responds to user interactions by repetitively creating and destroying *CSTTABLEEDIT* windows. This process is managed by the two functions *CstTableEditOff()* and *CstTableEditOn()* (see Listing 7.1).

CstTableEditOn() uses standard listbox messages to identify the display boundaries of the selected list item and then creates an *CSTTABLEEDIT* edit window that overlaps that area. Using both standard edit control messages and list box messages, *CstTableEditOn()* then copies the existing list item into the edit window.

CstTableEditOff() has the tricky job of updating the *CSTTABLE* window once the selected item has been edited. To prevent unwanted painting and the accompanying flash, *CstTableEditOff()* uses the *WM_SETREDRAW* message to turn off automatic updating. Once all the changes have been to *CSTTABLE* only the area that needs repainting is updated. This skeletal code outlines the process:

```
/* Turn off redrawing */
SendMessage( hWndTable, WM_SETREDRAW, FALSE, 0L );
    .
    .
    .
/* Make changes to table */
    .
    .
    .
/* Turn on redrawing */
SendMessage( hWndTable, WM_SETREDRAW, TRUE, 0L );
```

CstTableEditOff() must also copy the edited text from the *CSTTABLEEDIT* window into the appropriate slot within the *CSTTABLE* list.

Demonstration Program

The program *DEM_TABL* is a demonstration of a single and multicolumn *CSTTABLE* control. The files *DEM_TABL.C*, Listing 7.4, *DEM_TABL.H*, Listing 7.3 and *DEM_TABL.RC*, Listing 7.5 contain the source to this program.

As in the previous demonstrations, we rely upon a resource script to attach the controls to a dialog box, causing them to be created as a side effect of creating an instance of the dialog box.

This program defines two different dialog boxes: one for the single column data entry table, and a second for the multiple column data entry table. Initially the tables will be blank; the first operation must be an insertion initiated by the insert key.

Possible Enhancements

A relatively simple enhancement would be to improve the control's appearance by drawing a grid to separate rows and columns, and by adding a border that identifies each row and column. This change would require the subclass function to trap the *WM_PAINT* message, but it could still rely upon the base class procedure to do most of the work. Just change *CstTableWndFn()* so that it responds to the *WM_PAINT* message first by sending the *WM_PAINT* message to the base class procedure, and *then* by drawing rectangles around all the newly updated list cells. Trapping the *WM_NCPAINT* message will give the program an additional opportunity to change the appearance.

Those interested in a more challenging project might add the ability to associate different types of controls with each cell. Besides edit controls, one might associate buttons, or comboboxes with cells. Given the appropriate subordinate controls, this line of development could yield a full-fledged spreadsheet control.

Since the *CSTTABLE* control uses the standard *LISTBOX* control, it inherits all its capacity limits; some of these are onerous. For example, Windows limits the contents of a *LISTBOX* control to 64K of data, and

8160 items. One can overcome these limits by adding a buffering and paging scheme to the control. This extra capability would require an adjustable (and possibly virtualized) scroll range. The next chapter, develops a virtual memory custom control that virtualizes the scroll range.

Most users would probably appreciate an undo feature. This change would require storage for some history, and a trap for the undo key.

Summary

It seems an obvious waste to begin from scratch when a new control differs only slightly from some existing control, or when a proposed control merely combines features from various existing controls. Subclassing is an important Windows technique, both because it allows the programmer to reuse code, and because it is central to the construction of hybrid controls.

As the code for *CSTTABLE* illustrates, an effective plan for accessing subclass extra bytes is a key issue in building a usable and maintainable subclass control. Indexing from the end of the extra bytes offers an effective and space efficient solution.

Listing 7.1

```
/*******************************************************************************
            File Name: CST_TABL.H
        Expanded Name: Custom Table
          Description: Include file for CST_TABL.C
          Portability: Microsoft Windows 3.X
*******************************************************************************/

#if !defined ( CST_TABL_DEFINED )
    #define CST_TABL_DEFINED

    /* Default edit buffer size */
    #define CT_TABLEEDITLEN 1024

    /* Extra byte constants for custom table control */
    #define CT_CLSEXTRA         ( CC_CLSEXTRA + sizeof ( FARPROC ) )
    #define CT_WNDEXTRA         ( CC_WNDEXTRA )
    #define GCL_WNDPROCLISTBOX  ( CC_CLSEXTRA )

    /* Extra byte constants for custom table edit control */
    #define CTE_CLSEXTRA        ( sizeof ( FARPROC ) )
    #define CTE_WNDEXTRA        0
    #define GCL_WNDPROCEDIT     0

    /* Prototypes for exported functions in CST_TABL.C */
    LONG FAR PASCAL CstTableEditWndFn( HWND hWnd, UINT wMessage, WPARAM wParam,
            LPARAM lParam );
    int FAR PASCAL CstTableRegister( HINSTANCE hInstance );
    int FAR PASCAL CstTableUnregister( HINSTANCE hInstance );
    LONG FAR PASCAL CstTableWndFn( HWND hWnd, UINT wMessage, WPARAM wParam,
            LPARAM lParam );

#endif

/* End of CST_TABL.H */
```

Listing 7.2

```
/***************************************************************************
         File Name: CST_TABL.C
     Expanded Name: Custom Data Entry Table
       Description: Library of functions for the entry table custom control
Global Function List: CstTableEditWndFn
                      CstTableRegister
                      CstTableUnregister
                      CstTableWndFn
Static Function List: CstTableDefDataCreate
                      CstTableDefDataDelete
                      CstTableEditOff
                      CstTableEditOn
                      CstTableEditRegister
                      CstTableEditUnregister
       Global Data: _hInstanceCstCtls
       Static Data: _hCstCtlData
                    _lpCstCtlData
       Portability: Microsoft Windows 3.X
***************************************************************************/

/* Microsoft Windows */
#include <windows.h>

/* Prototypes and Types */
#include <cst_xtra.h>
#include <cst_data.h>
#include <cst_util.h>

/* Own */
#include <cst_tabl.h>

/* Prototypes for static functions */
static int CstTableDefDataCreate( HWND hWnd );
static void CstTableDefDataDelete( void );
static int CstTableEditRegister( HINSTANCE hInstance );
static int CstTableEditUnregister( HINSTANCE hInstance );
static void CstTableEditOff( HWND hWndTable, HWND hWndTableEdit, WPARAM wKey );
static HWND CstTableEditOn( HWND hWndTable, DWORD dwCurPos );

#define SEL_LAST  0x7FFF7FFFL
#define SEL_FIRST 0x00000000L

#if defined ( _WINDLL )
/* DLL Handle */
extern HINSTANCE _hInstanceCstCtls;
#endif

static HCSTCTLDATA  _hCstCtlData = (HCSTCTLDATA)0;
static LPCSTCTLDATA _lpCstCtlData = (LPCSTCTLDATA)0;

/***************************************************************************
          Name: CstTableDefDataCreate
 Expanded Name: Default Data Create
    Parameters: hWnd - window handle to Table control
        Return: TRUE or FALSE
   Description: Creates the default class data
***************************************************************************/
static int CstTableDefDataCreate( HWND hWnd )
   {
```

Listing 7.2 *continued*

```
    _lpCstCtlData = CstCtlDefDataCreate( hWnd );
    if ( !_lpCstCtlData )
        {
        /* Failed to allocate and initialize data */
        return ( FALSE );
        }
    _hCstCtlData = CSTGETCLASSWORD( hWnd, GCW_HCSTCTLDATA );

    /* Free up the resources we do not need */
    SafeDeleteObject( _lpCstCtlData->hBrush[CC_BRUSH_BTNFACE] );
    _lpCstCtlData->hBrush[CC_BRUSH_BTNFACE] = 0;
    SafeDeleteObject( _lpCstCtlData->hBrush[CC_BRUSH_3DLIGHT] );
    _lpCstCtlData->hBrush[CC_BRUSH_3DLIGHT] = 0;
    SafeDeleteObject( _lpCstCtlData->hBrush[CC_BRUSH_3DSHADOW] );
    _lpCstCtlData->hBrush[CC_BRUSH_3DSHADOW] = 0;
    SafeDeleteObject( _lpCstCtlData->hBrush[CC_BRUSH_FRAME] );
    _lpCstCtlData->hBrush[CC_BRUSH_FRAME] = 0;

    /* Set colors and mode for the edit control */
    _lpCstCtlData->lColor[CC_COLOR_TEXTBACKGROUND] = (COLORREF)
            GetSysColor( COLOR_WINDOW );
    CstCtlDefSetBkMode( hWnd, OPAQUE );

    /* Set the default length of text for a edit */
    CstCtlDefSetFrame( hWnd, CT_TABLEEDITLEN );

    /* Set the current selected item */
    CstCtlDefSetState( hWnd, (WORD)LB_ERR );

    return ( TRUE );

    }   /* function CstTableDefDataCreate */


/*******************************************************************************
         Name: CstTableDefDataDelete
Expanded Name: Default Data Delete
   Parameters: hWnd - window handle control
  Description: Deletes the default class data
*******************************************************************************/
static void CstTableDefDataDelete( void )
    {

    if ( _lpCstCtlData )
        {
        SafeDeleteObject( _lpCstCtlData->hBrush[CC_BRUSH_BACKGROUND] );
        _lpCstCtlData = (LPCSTCTLDATA)0;
        }

    if ( _hCstCtlData )
        {
        GlobalUnlock( _hCstCtlData );
        GlobalFree( _hCstCtlData );
        _hCstCtlData = (HCSTCTLDATA)0;
        }

    }   /* function CstTableDefDataDelete */
```

Listing 7.2 *continued*

```c
/*****************************************************************************
         Name: CstTableEditOff
   Parameters: hWndTable - handle to table window
               hWndTableEdit - handle to table edit window
               wKey - key code that generated this call
  Description: Turns off editing for a table cell.  The edit window is
               destroyed and the list box repainted.
*****************************************************************************/
static void CstTableEditOff( HWND hWndTable, HWND hWndTableEdit, WPARAM wKey )
    {

    int iTextLen;
    WORD wTableIndex;
    HANDLE hText;
    LPSTR lpstrText;
    RECT RectCell;

    if ( !IsWindow( hWndTable ) || !IsWindow( hWndTableEdit ) ||
            hWndTableEdit != CSTCTLGETWND( hWndTable ) )
        {
        /* There was not a valid window handle */
        return;
        }

    /* Turn off drawing and set the table text */
    SendMessage( hWndTable, WM_SETREDRAW, FALSE, 0L );
    wTableIndex = CSTCTLGETSTATE( hWndTable );
    if ( wTableIndex == (WORD)LB_ERR )
        {
        wTableIndex = (WORD)SendMessage( hWndTable, LB_GETCURSEL, 0, 0L );
        }
    if ( wTableIndex == (WORD)LB_ERR )
        {
        /* No cell is selected so set it to the first one */
        wTableIndex = 0;
        }
    CstCtlSetState( hWndTable, wTableIndex );
    SendMessage( hWndTable, LB_SETCURSEL, wTableIndex, 0L );
    iTextLen = GetWindowTextLength( hWndTableEdit );
    hText = GlobalAlloc( GMEM_FLAGS, (DWORD)( iTextLen + 1 ) );
    if ( hText )
        {
        lpstrText = GlobalLock( hText );
        if ( lpstrText )
            {
            GetWindowText( hWndTableEdit, lpstrText, iTextLen + 1 );
            SendMessage( hWndTable, LB_INSERTSTRING, wTableIndex,
                    (LPARAM)lpstrText );
            GlobalUnlock( hText );
            }
        GlobalFree( hText );
        }
    DestroyWindow( hWndTableEdit );
    SetFocus( NULL );
    CstCtlSetWnd( hWndTable, 0 );
    SendMessage( hWndTable, LB_DELETESTRING, wTableIndex + 1, 0L );
```

Listing 7.2 *continued*

```c
        SendMessage( hWndTable, LB_SETCURSEL, (WPARAM)-1, 0L );
        SendMessage( hWndTable, WM_SETREDRAW, TRUE, 0L );
        ValidateRect( hWndTable, NULL );

        /* Draw the cell, the cell above and the cell below */
        SendMessage( hWndTable, LB_GETITEMRECT, wTableIndex,
                (LPARAM)( (LPRECT)&RectCell ) );
        InvalidateRect( hWndTable, &RectCell, TRUE );
        if ( wKey != VK_UP )
            {
            SendMessage( hWndTable, LB_GETITEMRECT, wTableIndex - 1,
                    (LPARAM)( (LPRECT)&RectCell ) );
            InvalidateRect( hWndTable, &RectCell, TRUE );
            }
        if ( wKey != VK_DOWN )
            {
            SendMessage( hWndTable, LB_GETITEMRECT, wTableIndex + 1,
                    (LPARAM)( (LPRECT)&RectCell ) );
            InvalidateRect( hWndTable, &RectCell, TRUE );
            }
        UpdateWindow( hWndTable );

        /* Set the current selected item */
        SendMessage( hWndTable, WM_SETREDRAW, FALSE, 0L );
        SendMessage( hWndTable, LB_SETCURSEL, wTableIndex, 0L );
        CstCtlSetState( hWndTable, (WORD)LB_ERR );
        SendMessage( hWndTable, WM_SETREDRAW, TRUE, 0L );

    }   /* function CstTableEditOff */


/*******************************************************************************
        Name: CstTableEditOn
  Parameters: hWndTable - handle to table window
              dwCurPos - start and end of select zone in edit window
      Return: handle to table edit window
 Description: Turns on editing for a table cell.  A edit window is created
              on top of the table cell and the edit window is given the
              input focus.
*******************************************************************************/
static HWND CstTableEditOn( HWND hWndTable, DWORD dwCurPos )
    {

    HWND hWndTableEdit;
    int iHeightEdit, iHeightList;
    RECT RectCell;
    WORD wTableIndex, wTableItems;

    /* Get the index to the current cell in the table */
    if ( !IsWindow( hWndTable ) )
        {
        /* The table window is not valid */
        return ( 0 );
        }

    wTableIndex = (WORD)SendMessage( hWndTable, LB_GETCURSEL, 0, 0L );
    if ( wTableIndex == (WORD)LB_ERR )
        {
        /* No cell is selected so set it to the first one */
```

Listing 7.2 *continued*

```
    wTableIndex = 0;
    SendMessage( hWndTable, LB_SETCURSEL, wTableIndex, 0L );
    }
wTableItems = (WORD)SendMessage( hWndTable, LB_GETCOUNT, 0, 0L );
if ( !wTableItems )
    {
    /* Create an empty cell */
    SendMessage( hWndTable, LB_INSERTSTRING, wTableIndex,
            (LPARAM)(LPSTR)"" );
    }

/* Turn off drawing and set current item */
SendMessage( hWndTable, WM_SETREDRAW, FALSE, 0L );
CstCtlSetState( hWndTable, wTableIndex );

/* Get the size of the table cell */
SendMessage( hWndTable, LB_GETITEMRECT, wTableIndex,
        (LPARAM)( (LPRECT)&RectCell ) );
iHeightList = RectCell.bottom - RectCell.top;
iHeightEdit = 3 * iHeightList / 2;

/* Create the edit window */
hWndTableEdit = CreateWindow( "CstTableEdit", "",
        ES_AUTOHSCROLL | ES_LEFT | WS_CHILD | WS_VISIBLE | WS_BORDER,
        RectCell.left, RectCell.top - ( iHeightEdit - iHeightList ) / 2,
        RectCell.right - RectCell.left, iHeightEdit,
        hWndTable, 0, GetWindowWord( hWndTable, GWW_HINSTANCE ), 0L );

if ( hWndTableEdit )
    {

    HFONT hFont;
    int iTextLen;

    SetFocus( hWndTableEdit );

    /* Load the edit window with the text from the table */
    CstCtlSetWnd( hWndTable, hWndTableEdit );
    hFont = (HFONT)SendMessage( hWndTable, WM_GETFONT, 0, 0L );
    SendMessage( hWndTableEdit, WM_SETFONT, hFont, 0L );
    SendMessage( hWndTableEdit, EM_LIMITTEXT,
            (WPARAM)CSTCTLGETFRAME( hWndTable ), 0L );
    iTextLen = (int)SendMessage( hWndTable, LB_GETTEXTLEN,
            wTableIndex, 0L );
    if ( iTextLen )
        {

        HANDLE hText;
        LPSTR lpstrText = NULL;

        hText = GlobalAlloc( GMEM_FLAGS, (DWORD)( iTextLen + 1 ) );
        if ( hText )
            {
            lpstrText = GlobalLock( hText );
            if ( lpstrText )
                {
                SendMessage( hWndTable, LB_GETTEXT, wTableIndex,
                        (LPARAM)lpstrText );
```

Listing 7.2 *continued*

```
                    SetWindowText( hWndTableEdit, lpstrText );
                    GlobalUnlock( hText );
                    }
                GlobalFree( hText );
                }
            }

        SendMessage( hWndTableEdit, EM_SETSEL, 0, (LPARAM)dwCurPos );

        }   /* if hWndTableEdit */

    /* Deselect current item and turn on drawing */
    SendMessage( hWndTable, LB_SETCURSEL, (WPARAM)( -1 ), 0L );
    SendMessage( hWndTable, WM_SETREDRAW, TRUE, 0L );

    return ( hWndTableEdit );

    }   /* function CstTableEditOn */


/*******************************************************************************
        Name: CstTableEditRegister
  Parameters: hInstance - handle to program or library registering class
      Return: Number of register counts or 0 if failure
 Description: Registers the window class for the custom Check Box control
*******************************************************************************/
static int CstTableEditRegister( HINSTANCE hInstance )
    {

    WNDCLASS WndClass;

    GetClassInfo( NULL, "EDIT", &WndClass );

    #if defined ( _WINDLL )
    hInstance = _hInstanceCstCtls;
    WndClass.style |= CS_GLOBALCLASS;
    #endif

    WndClass.lpfnWndProc = CstTableEditWndFn;
    WndClass.cbClsExtra += (int)CTE_CLSEXTRA;
    WndClass.cbWndExtra += (int)CTE_WNDEXTRA;
    WndClass.hInstance = hInstance;
    WndClass.lpszClassName = "CstTableEdit";

    return ( RegisterClass( &WndClass ) );

    }   /* function CstTableEditRegister */


/*******************************************************************************
        Name: CstTableEditUnregister
  Parameters: hInstance - handle to program or library that registered class
      Return: same as UnregisterClass()
 Description: Unregisters the window class for the table edit control
*******************************************************************************/
static int CstTableEditUnregister( HINSTANCE hInstance )
    {

    #if defined ( _WINDLL )
```

Listing 7.2 *continued*

```
    hInstance = _hInstanceCstCtls;
#endif

    return ( UnregisterClass( "CstTableEdit", hInstance ) );

    }   /* function CstTableEditUnregister */


/*****************************************************************************
        Name: CstTableEditWndFn
Expanded Name: Custom Table Edit Window Function
  Description: Window call back function for custom data entry table control
*****************************************************************************/
LONG FAR PASCAL CstTableEditWndFn( HWND hWnd, UINT wMessage, WPARAM wParam,
        LPARAM lParam )
    {

    FARPROC lpfnEditWndFn =
            (FARPROC)CSTGETCLASSLONG( hWnd, GCL_WNDPROCEDIT );
    HWND hWndTable = GetParent( hWnd );

    if ( !lpfnEditWndFn )
        {

        WNDCLASS WndClass;

        if ( GetClassInfo( NULL, "EDIT", &WndClass ) )
            {
            lpfnEditWndFn = (FARPROC)WndClass.lpfnWndProc;
            CSTSETCLASSLONG( hWnd, GCL_WNDPROCEDIT, (LONG)lpfnEditWndFn );
            }
        }

    switch ( wMessage )
        {
        case WM_GETDLGCODE:
            /* Return to dialog manager that control wants all keys */
            return ( DLGC_WANTALLKEYS );
        case WM_KEYDOWN:
            switch ( wParam )
                {
                case VK_BACK:
                    {

                    DWORD dwCurSel;

                    if ( !GetWindowTextLength( hWnd ) )
                        {
                        /* Empty cell same as delete key */
                        SendMessage( hWnd, WM_KEYDOWN, VK_DELETE, 0L );
                        return ( 0L );
                        }
                    dwCurSel = (DWORD)SendMessage( hWnd, EM_GETSEL, 0, 0L );
                    if ( HIWORD( dwCurSel ) == 0 )
                        {
                        /* Beginning of cell same as left arrow key */
                        SendMessage( hWnd, WM_KEYDOWN, VK_LEFT, 0L );
                        return ( 0L );
                        }
```

Listing 7.2 *continued*

```
            break;
        }
    case VK_DELETE:
        if ( !GetWindowTextLength( hWnd ) )
            {
            /* If the cell is empty, delete the entire cell */
            CstTableEditOff( hWndTable, hWnd, wParam );
            SendMessage( hWndTable, wMessage, wParam, lParam );
            CstTableEditOn( hWndTable, SEL_LAST );
            return ( 0L );
            }
        break;
    case VK_INSERT:
        /* Close edit window and send message to the table */
        CstTableEditOff( hWndTable, hWnd, wParam );
        SetFocus( hWndTable );
        SendMessage( hWndTable, wMessage, wParam, lParam );
        return ( 0L );
    case VK_RETURN:
        {

        WORD wTableIndex, wTableItems;

        /* Close this edit window and move to next cell */
        CstTableEditOff( hWndTable, hWnd, wParam );
        SendMessage( hWndTable, WM_KEYDOWN, VK_DOWN, 0L );
        wTableIndex = (WORD)SendMessage( hWndTable,
                LB_GETCURSEL, 0, 0L );
        wTableItems = (WORD)SendMessage( hWndTable,
                LB_GETCOUNT, 0, 0L );
        if ( wTableIndex == (WORD)LB_ERR )
            {
            wTableIndex = 0;
            }
        if ( ( wTableIndex == 0 ) ||
                ( wTableIndex == ( wTableItems - 1 ) ) )
            {
            SendMessage( hWndTable, LB_SETCURSEL,
                    wTableIndex, 0L );
            }
        SetFocus( hWndTable );
        return ( 0L );
        }   /* case VK_RETURN */
    case VK_LEFT:
        {

        DWORD dwCurSel;

        /* If the cursor is at the beginning of the field
        ** send the message on to the table. */
        dwCurSel = (DWORD)SendMessage( hWnd, EM_GETSEL, 0, 0L );
        if ( HIWORD( dwCurSel ) == 0 )
            {
            CstTableEditOff( hWndTable, hWnd, wParam );
            SendMessage( hWndTable, WM_SETREDRAW, FALSE, 0L );
            SendMessage( hWndTable, wMessage, wParam, lParam );
            SendMessage( hWndTable, WM_SETREDRAW, TRUE, 0L );
            CstTableEditOn( hWndTable, SEL_LAST );
```

Listing 7.2 *continued*

```
                    return ( 0L );
                    }
                break;
                }
            case VK_RIGHT:
                {

                DWORD dwCurSel;
                int iTextLen;

                /* If the cursor is at the end of the field
                ** send the message on the the table. */
                iTextLen = GetWindowTextLength( hWnd );
                dwCurSel = (DWORD)SendMessage( hWnd, EM_GETSEL, 0, 0L );
                if ( LOWORD( dwCurSel ) >= (WORD)iTextLen )
                    {
                    CstTableEditOff( hWndTable, hWnd, wParam );
                    SendMessage( hWndTable, WM_SETREDRAW, FALSE, 0L );
                    SendMessage( hWndTable, wMessage, wParam, lParam );
                    SendMessage( hWndTable, WM_SETREDRAW, TRUE, 0L );
                    CstTableEditOn( hWndTable, SEL_FIRST );
                    return ( 0L );
                    }
                break;
                }
            case VK_DOWN:
            case VK_UP:
            case VK_PRIOR:
            case VK_NEXT:
                {

                DWORD dwCurSel;

                /* Get position of current edit window and close it */
                dwCurSel = (DWORD)SendMessage( hWnd, EM_GETSEL, 0, 0L );
                CstTableEditOff( hWndTable, hWnd, wParam );
                SendMessage( hWndTable, WM_SETREDRAW, FALSE, 0L );
                SendMessage( hWndTable, wMessage, wParam, lParam );
                SendMessage( hWndTable, WM_SETREDRAW, TRUE, 0L );
                CstTableEditOn( hWndTable, dwCurSel );
                return ( 0L );
                }
            case VK_TAB:
                SendMessage( hWndTable, wMessage, wParam, lParam );
                return ( 0L );
            default:
                break;
            }   /* switch ( wParam ) */
        break;
    case WM_LBUTTONDBLCLK:
        CstTableEditOff( hWndTable, hWnd, VK_RIGHT );
        SendMessage( hWndTable, LB_SETCURSEL, (WPARAM)SendMessage(
                hWndTable, LB_GETCURSEL, 0, 0L ), 0L );
        SetFocus( hWndTable );
        return ( 0L );
    default:
        break;
    }   /* switch ( wMessage ) */
```

Listing 7.2 *continued*

```
    if ( lpfnEditWndFn )
        {
        return ( CallWindowProc( lpfnEditWndFn, hWnd, wMessage, wParam,
                lParam ) );
        }

    return ( 0L );

    }   /* function CstTableEditWndFn */


/******************************************************************************
        Name: CstTableRegister
  Parameters: hInstance - handle to program or library registering class
      Return: Number of register counts or 0 if failure
 Description: Registers the window class for the custom Check Box control
******************************************************************************/
int FAR PASCAL CstTableRegister( HINSTANCE hInstance )
    {

    WNDCLASS WndClass;

    GetClassInfo( NULL, "LISTBOX", &WndClass );

    #if defined ( _WINDLL )
    hInstance = _hInstanceCstCtls;
    WndClass.style |= CS_GLOBALCLASS;
    #endif

    WndClass.lpfnWndProc = CstTableWndFn;
    WndClass.cbClsExtra += (int)CT_CLSEXTRA;
    WndClass.cbWndExtra += (int)CT_WNDEXTRA;
    WndClass.hInstance = hInstance;
    WndClass.lpszClassName = "CstTable";

    if ( !CstTableEditRegister( hInstance ) )
        {
        /* Failed to register */
        return ( FALSE );
        }

    return ( RegisterClass( &WndClass ) );

    }   /* function CstTableRegister */


/******************************************************************************
        Name: CstTableUnregister
  Parameters: hInstance - handle to program or library that registered class
      Return: Number of remaining register counts
 Description: Unregisters the window class for the custom Check Box control
******************************************************************************/
int FAR PASCAL CstTableUnregister( HINSTANCE hInstance )
    {

    #if defined ( _WINDLL )
    hInstance = _hInstanceCstCtls;
    #endif
```

Listing 7.2 *continued*

```
    CstTableEditUnregister( hInstance );

    return ( UnregisterClass( "CstTable", hInstance ) );

    }   /* function CstTableUnregister */


/******************************************************************************
        Name: CstTableWndFn
Expanded Name: Custom Table Window Function
  Description: Window call back function for custom data entry table control
******************************************************************************/
LONG FAR PASCAL CstTableWndFn( HWND hWnd, UINT wMessage, WPARAM wParam,
        LPARAM lParam )
    {

    static int _WindowCount = 0;

    FARPROC lpfnListBoxWndFn =
            (FARPROC)CSTGETCLASSLONG( hWnd, GCL_WNDPROCLISTBOX );

    if ( !lpfnListBoxWndFn )
        {

        WNDCLASS WndClass;

        if ( GetClassInfo( NULL, "ListBox", &WndClass ) )
            {
            lpfnListBoxWndFn = (FARPROC)WndClass.lpfnWndProc;
            CSTSETCLASSLONG( hWnd, GCL_WNDPROCLISTBOX, (LONG)lpfnListBoxWndFn );
            }
        }

    switch ( wMessage )
        {
        case WM_CREATE:
            {

            HWND hWndParent = GetParent( hWnd );

            if ( !_WindowCount )
                {
                if ( !CstTableDefDataCreate( hWnd ) )
                    {
                    return ( -1 );
                    }
                }
            _WindowCount++;

            /* Create instance data */
            CstCtlDataCreate( hWnd );

            /* Notify the parent that the control has been created */
            if ( hWndParent )
                {
                SendMessage( hWndParent, WM_PARENTNOTIFY, WM_CREATE,
                        MAKELPARAM( hWnd, GetDlgCtrlID( hWnd ) ) );
                }
```

Listing 7.2 continued

```c
            /* Turn off the LBS_MULTIPLESEL style */
            SetWindowLong( hWnd, GWL_STYLE,
                    GetWindowLong( hWnd, GWL_STYLE ) & ~LBS_MULTIPLESEL );
            break;
            }   /* case WM_CREATE */
        case WM_CTLCOLOR:
            if ( HIWORD( lParam ) == CTLCOLOR_EDIT )
                {
                /* Set up drawing attributes for the edit control */
                SetBkMode( wParam, CSTCTLGETBKMODE( hWnd ) );
                SetTextColor( wParam, CSTCTLGETCOLOR( hWnd, CC_COLOR_TEXT ) );
                SetBkColor( wParam,
                        CSTCTLGETCOLOR( hWnd, CC_COLOR_TEXTBACKGROUND ) );
                return ( CSTCTLGETBRUSH( hWnd, CC_BRUSH_BACKGROUND ) );
                }
            break;
        case WM_DESTROY:
            {

            HWND hWndParent = GetParent( hWnd );

            /* Notify the parent and then delete the instance data */
            if ( hWndParent )
                {
                SendMessage( hWndParent, WM_PARENTNOTIFY, WM_DESTROY,
                        MAKELPARAM( hWnd, GetDlgCtrlID( hWnd ) ) );
                }
            if ( IsWindow( hWnd ) )
                {
                CstCtlDataDelete( hWnd );
                }

            _WindowCount--;
            if ( _WindowCount <= 0 )
                {
                CstTableDefDataDelete();
                }

            break;
            }   /* case WM_DESTROY */
        case WM_GETDLGCODE:
            /* Return to dialog manager that control wants all keys */
            return ( DLGC_WANTALLKEYS );
        case WM_LBUTTONDBLCLK:
            if ( !CSTCTLGETWND( hWnd ) )
                {
                CstTableEditOn( hWnd, SEL_LAST );
                return ( 0L );
                }
            break;
        case WM_LBUTTONDOWN:
            if ( CSTCTLGETWND( hWnd ) )
                {

                DWORD dwCurSel;
                HWND hWndEdit = CSTCTLGETWND( hWnd );

                /* Get position in edit window */
                dwCurSel = (DWORD)SendMessage( hWndEdit, EM_GETSEL, 0, 0L );
```

Listing 7.2 continued

```
            CstTableEditOff( hWnd, hWndEdit, VK_RIGHT );
            /* Pass message on */
            CallWindowProc( lpfnListBoxWndFn, hWnd, wMessage, wParam,
                    lParam );
            CstTableEditOn( hWnd, dwCurSel );
            return ( 0L );
            }
      break;
case WM_KEYDOWN:
      switch ( wParam )
          {
          case VK_BACK:
              {
              SendMessage( hWnd, WM_KEYDOWN, VK_LEFT, 0L );
              SendMessage( hWnd, WM_KEYDOWN, VK_DELETE, 0L );
              return ( 0L );
              }
          case VK_DELETE:
              {

              WORD wTableIndex, wTableItems;

              wTableIndex = (WORD)SendMessage( hWnd,
                      LB_GETCURSEL, 0, 0L );
              wTableItems = (WORD)SendMessage( hWnd,
                      LB_GETCOUNT, 0, 0L );

              if ( !wTableItems )
                  {
                  /* Empty table */
                  break;
                  }
              if( wTableIndex == (WORD)LB_ERR )
                  {
                  /* Use the first cell */
                  wTableIndex = 0;
                  }
              SendMessage( hWnd, LB_DELETESTRING, wTableIndex, 0L );
              if ( wTableIndex == ( wTableItems - 1 ) )
                  {
                  /* Last item */
                  if ( wTableIndex != 0 )
                      {
                      wTableIndex--;
                      }
                  }
              SendMessage( hWnd, LB_SETCURSEL, wTableIndex, 0L );
              return ( 0L );
              }  /* case VK_DELETE */
          case VK_INSERT:
              {

              WORD wTableIndex;

              wTableIndex = (WORD)SendMessage( hWnd,
                      LB_GETCURSEL, 0, 0L );
              if ( wTableIndex == (WORD)LB_ERR )
                  {
                  wTableIndex = 0;
```

Listing 7.2 continued

```
                    }
                SendMessage( hWnd, LB_INSERTSTRING, wTableIndex,
                        (LPARAM)(LPSTR)"" );
                CstTableEditOn( hWnd, SEL_FIRST );
                return ( 0L );
                }   /* case VK_INSERT */
            case VK_TAB:
                if ( GetKeyState( VK_SHIFT ) < 0 )
                    {
                    SetFocus( GetNextDlgTabItem( GetParent( hWnd ),
                        hWnd, TRUE ) );
                    }
                else
                    {
                    SetFocus( GetNextDlgTabItem( GetParent( hWnd ),
                        hWnd, TRUE ) );
                    }
                return ( 0L );
            case VK_RETURN:
                CstTableEditOn( hWnd, SEL_LAST );
                return ( 0L );
            default:
                break;
            }   /* switch ( wParam ) */
        break;
    case WM_SETFOCUS:
        if ( CSTCTLGETWND( hWnd ) )
            {
            /* Set focus to the edit window */
            SetFocus( CSTCTLGETWND( hWnd ) );
            return ( 0L );
            }
        break;
    case WM_CSTCTLGETDATA:
    case WM_CSTCTLGETDEFDATA:
    case WM_CSTCTLSETDATA:
    case WM_CSTCTLSETDEFDATA:
        return ( (LONG)CstCtlData( hWnd, wMessage, wParam, lParam ) );
    default:
        break;
    }   /* switch ( wMessage ) */

if ( lpfnListBoxWndFn )
    {
    return ( CallWindowProc( lpfnListBoxWndFn, hWnd, wMessage, wParam,
            lParam ) );
    }

return ( 0L );

}   /* function CstTableWndFn */

/* End of CST_TABL.C */
```

Listing 7.3

```
/*****************************************************************************
        File Name: DEM_TABL.H
    Expanded Name: Demo Table
      Description: Include file for DEM_TABL.C & DEM_TABL.RC
      Portability: Microsoft Windows 3.X
*****************************************************************************/

#define IDM_SINGLE      101
#define IDM_MULTIPLE    102
#define IDM_EXIT        114

/* End of DEM_TABL.H */
```

Listing 7.4

```
/******************************************************************************
        File Name: DEM_TABL.C
    Expanded Name: Demo Table
      Description: Demo program for custom table control
     Program List: DEM_TABL.C
                   DEM_TABL.RC
                   DEM_TABL.DEF
                   CST_DATA.C
                   CST_TABL.C
                   CST_XTRA.C
                   or
                   DEM_TABL.C
                   DEM_TABL.RC
                   DEM_TABL.DEF
                   CST_CTLS.LIB,DLL
Global Function List: WinMain
                      DemoDialog
                      TableDemoDialogProc
                      MainWindowProc
      Portability: Microsoft Windows 3.X
******************************************************************************/

/* Microsoft Windows */
#include <windows.h>

/* Types and prototypes */
#include <cst_data.h>
#include <cst_tabl.h>

/* Own */
#include <dem_tabl.h>

int PASCAL WinMain( HINSTANCE hInstance, HINSTANCE hPrevInstance,
        LPSTR lpCmdLine, int nCmdShow );
BOOL PASCAL DemoDialog( HINSTANCE hInstance, HWND hWndParent,
        LPSTR DialogName );
LONG FAR PASCAL MainWindowProc( HWND hwnd, UINT wMessage,
        WPARAM wParam, LPARAM lParam );
BOOL FAR PASCAL TableDemoDialogProc( HWND hDlg, UINT wMessage,
        WPARAM wParam, LPARAM lParam );

/******************************************************************************
        Name: WinMain
 Description: Main Window function
******************************************************************************/
int PASCAL WinMain( HINSTANCE hInstance, HINSTANCE hPrevInstance,
        LPSTR lpCmdLine, int nCmdShow )
    {

    #if !defined ( NO_DLL )
    HINSTANCE hInstanceDll;
    #endif
    HWND hWnd;
    MSG Msg;
    static char _Name[] = "DEM_TABL";
    WNDCLASS WndClass;

    lpCmdLine = lpCmdLine;
    nCmdShow = nCmdShow;
```

Listing 7.4 *continued*

```
    #if defined ( NO_DLL )
    CstTableRegister( hInstance );
    #else
    hInstanceDll = LoadLibrary( "CST_CTLS.DLL" );
    #endif

    if ( !hPrevInstance )
        {
        WndClass.style = 0;
        WndClass.lpfnWndProc = MainWindowProc;
        WndClass.cbClsExtra = 0;
        WndClass.cbWndExtra = 0;
        WndClass.hInstance = hInstance;
        WndClass.hIcon = LoadIcon( hInstance, _Name );
        WndClass.hCursor = LoadCursor( NULL, IDC_ARROW );
        WndClass.hbrBackground = COLOR_WINDOW + 1;
        WndClass.lpszMenuName = _Name;
        WndClass.lpszClassName = _Name;
        RegisterClass( &WndClass );
        }

    hWnd = CreateWindow( _Name, "Custom Table Control Demo",
            WS_OVERLAPPEDWINDOW, CW_USEDEFAULT, CW_USEDEFAULT,
            CW_USEDEFAULT, CW_USEDEFAULT, NULL, NULL, hInstance, NULL );

    ShowWindow( hWnd, nCmdShow );
    UpdateWindow( hWnd );

    while ( GetMessage( &Msg, NULL, 0, 0 ) )
        {
        TranslateMessage( &Msg );
        DispatchMessage ( &Msg );
        }

    #if !defined ( NO_DLL )
    FreeLibrary( hInstanceDll );
    #endif

    return ( (int)Msg.wParam );

    }    /* function WinMain */


/***************************************************************************
       Name: DemoDialog
Description: Function for invoking dialog boxes
***************************************************************************/
BOOL PASCAL DemoDialog( HINSTANCE hInstance, HWND hWndParent, LPSTR DialogName )
    {

    BOOL bStatus;
    FARPROC lpfnProc;

    lpfnProc = MakeProcInstance( TableDemoDialogProc, hInstance );
    bStatus = DialogBox( hInstance, DialogName, hWndParent, lpfnProc );
    FreeProcInstance( lpfnProc );
```

Listing 7.4 continued

```
        return ( bStatus );

    }   /* function DemoDialog */


/*****************************************************************************
        Name: TableDemoDialogProc
 Description: Dialog call back function for custom table control demo
*****************************************************************************/
BOOL FAR PASCAL TableDemoDialogProc( HWND hDlg, UINT wMessage,
        WPARAM wParam, LPARAM lParam )
    {

    lParam = lParam;

    switch( wMessage )
        {
        case WM_INITDIALOG:
            return ( TRUE );
        case WM_CLOSE:
            EndDialog( hDlg, 0 );
            return ( FALSE );
        case WM_COMMAND:
            switch ( wParam )
                {
                case IDOK:
                    EndDialog( hDlg, 0 );
                    return ( TRUE );
                default:
                    break;
                }
            return ( TRUE );
        default:
            break;
        }   /* switch wMessage */

    return ( FALSE );

    }   /* function TableDemoDialogProc */


/*****************************************************************************
        Name: MainWindowProc
 Description: Window call back function for main window
*****************************************************************************/
LONG FAR PASCAL MainWindowProc( HWND hWnd, UINT wMessage,
        WPARAM wParam, LPARAM lParam )
    {

    switch( wMessage )
        {
        case WM_COMMAND:
            {

            HINSTANCE hInstance = GetWindowWord( hWnd, GWW_HINSTANCE );

            switch( wParam )
                {
```

Listing 7.4 *continued*

```
            case IDM_SINGLE:
                DemoDialog( hInstance, hWnd, "SINGLE" );
                break;
            case IDM_MULTIPLE:
                DemoDialog( hInstance, hWnd, "MULTIPLE" );
                break;
            case IDM_EXIT:
                DestroyWindow( hWnd );
                break;
            default:
                break;
            }
        return ( FALSE );
        }
    case WM_DESTROY:
        PostQuitMessage( 0 );
        return ( FALSE );
    default:
        break;
    }

    return ( DefWindowProc( hWnd, wMessage, wParam, lParam ) );

    }   /* function MainWindowProc */

/* End of DEM_TABL.C */
```

Listing 7.5

```
/****************************************************************************
           File Name: DEM_TABL.RC
       Expanded Name: Demo Table
         Description: Resource file for the custom table control demo
         Portability: Microsoft Windows 3.X
****************************************************************************/

#include <windows.h>
#include <dem_tabl.h>

DEM_TABL ICON ICON\DEM_TABL.ICO

DEM_TABL MENU
BEGIN
    POPUP "&Demo"
    BEGIN
        MENUITEM "Single Column...",    IDM_SINGLE
        MENUITEM "Multiple Column...",  IDM_MULTIPLE
        MENUITEM SEPARATOR
        MENUITEM "E&xit",               IDM_EXIT
    END
END

SINGLE DIALOG 10, 10, 300, 210
CAPTION "Single Column Table"
STYLE DS_MODALFRAME | WS_CAPTION | WS_SYSMENU
FONT 8, "Helv"
BEGIN
    CONTROL "",     100,  "CstTable", WS_TABSTOP | LBS_HASSTRINGS | LBS_NOTIFY |
             WS_BORDER | WS_VSCROLL | WS_CHILD, 20, 20, 260, 150
    CONTROL "&Ok", IDOK, "button",   WS_TABSTOP | BS_DEFPUSHBUTTON,
                                                130, 190, 40, 16
END

MULTIPLE DIALOG 10, 10, 300, 210
CAPTION "Multiple Column Table"
STYLE DS_MODALFRAME | WS_CAPTION | WS_SYSMENU
FONT 8, "Helv"
BEGIN
    CONTROL "",     100,  "CstTable", WS_TABSTOP | LBS_HASSTRINGS | LBS_NOTIFY |
             WS_BORDER | WS_VSCROLL | WS_CHILD | LBS_MULTICOLUMN,
             20, 20, 260, 150
    CONTROL "&Ok", IDOK, "button",   WS_TABSTOP | BS_DEFPUSHBUTTON,
             130, 190, 40, 16
END

/* End of DEM_TABL.RC */
```

Listing 7.6

```
NAME DEM_TABL
DESCRIPTION 'Custom Table Control Demo Program'
EXETYPE WINDOWS
CODE PRELOAD MOVEABLE
DATA PRELOAD MOVEABLE MULTIPLE
HEAPSIZE 1024
STACKSIZE 5120
EXPORTS
        MainWindowProc
        TableDemoDialogProc
        CstTableWndFn
        CstTableEditWndFn
```

Listing 7.7

```
ORIGIN    = QCWIN
ORIGIN_VER   = 1.00

PROJ =DEM_TABL
DEBUG   =0
PROGTYPE =1
CALLER  =
ARGS =
DLLS =
CVPACK   =1
CC   =cl -qc
RC   =rc
CFLAGS_G_WEXE =/AS /W4 /Ze /D_WINDOWS /DNO_DLL /G2w /Zp /Aw
CFLAGS_D_WEXE =/Zi /Od
CFLAGS_R_WEXE =/O /Os /Gs /DNDEBUG
CFLAGS_G_WDLL =/AS /G2w /Zp /Aw /W3 /D_WINDOWS /D_WINDLL
CFLAGS_D_WDLL =/Gi /Od /Zi
CFLAGS_R_WDLL =/O /Os /DNDEBUG
CFLAGS_G_WTTY =/AS /G2w /W3 /D_WINDOWS
CFLAGS_D_WTTY =/Gi /Od /Zi
CFLAGS_R_WTTY =/O /Os /DNDEBUG
CFLAGS_G_DEXE =/AS /W2
CFLAGS_D_DEXE =/Gi /Od /Zi
CFLAGS_R_DEXE =/O /Ot /DNDEBUG
CFLAGS    =$(CFLAGS_G_WEXE) $(CFLAGS_R_WEXE)
LFLAGS_G_WEXE =/NOE/A:16/ST:10240
LFLAGS_D_WEXE =/CO
LFLAGS_R_WEXE =
LFLAGS_G_WDLL =/ST:5120 /A:16
LFLAGS_D_WDLL =/CO
LFLAGS_R_WDLL =
LFLAGS_G_WTTY =/ST:5120 /A:16
LFLAGS_D_WTTY =/CO
LFLAGS_R_WTTY =
LFLAGS_G_DEXE =/NOI /ST:2048
LFLAGS_D_DEXE =/CO
LFLAGS_R_DEXE =
LFLAGS    =$(LFLAGS_G_WEXE) $(LFLAGS_R_WEXE)
RCFLAGS  =/DNO_DLL
RESFLAGS =
RUNFLAGS =
DEFFILE =     DEMSTABL.DEF
OBJS_EXT =
LIBS_EXT =

.rc.res: ; $(RC) $(RCFLAGS) -r $*.rc

all: $(PROJ).EXE

DEM_TABL.OBJ: DEM_TABL.C $(H)

DEM_TABL.RES: DEM_TABL.RC $(RESFILES) $(H)

CST_DATA.OBJ: CST_DATA.C $(H)

CST_UTIL.OBJ: CST_UTIL.C $(H)
```

Listing 7.7 *continued*

```
CST_TABL.OBJ: CST_TABL.C $(H)

$(PROJ).EXE:  DEM_TABL.OBJ CST_DATA.OBJ CST_UTIL.OBJ CST_TABL.OBJ $(OBJS_EXT)
$(DEFFILE)
    echo >NUL @<<$(PROJ).CRF
DEM_TABL.OBJ +
CST_DATA.OBJ +
CST_UTIL.OBJ +
CST_TABL.OBJ +
$(OBJS_EXT)
$(PROJ).EXE

C:\PRGLNG\QCW\LIB\+
/NOD slibcew oldnames  libw
$(DEFFILE);
<<
    link $(LFLAGS) @$(PROJ).CRF
    rc $(RESFLAGS) DEM_TABL.RES $(PROJ).EXE

$(PROJ).EXE:  DEM_TABL.RES
    rc $(RESFLAGS) DEM_TABL.RES $(PROJ).EXE

run: $(PROJ).EXE
    $(PROJ) $(RUNFLAGS)
```

8 Virtual Memory Controls

The lack of a decent file browsing utility is one of Windows' more noticeable deficiencies. As we explain in more detail later, the standard *EDIT* control (even though it has a read-only mode) can handle only relatively small files. The standard *NOTEPAD* utility is little more than a multiline edit control. In this chapter we develop a custom file browser control that can be used with very large files. With this control, creating a convenient standalone browsing utility becomes a relatively trivial task. More importantly, though, you can embed this control in any application, making it easy to display program results, configurations, input data, or any other information that might be stored in a file.

While describing the *CSTFILEVIEW* control, this chapter covers the topics of buffering, scrolling, and class specific messages.

The User Interface

The *CSTFILEVIEW* control creates a window that displays a file and allows the application to append lines to the file. If the length of the file exceeds the size of the window, the user can scroll the text to access the areas not currently displayed. The control includes facilities for wrapping long lines, adjusting tab stops, and changing the display font. The user can control scrolling features via either the mouse or the keyboard. The control's other functions (loading files, adjusting tab stops, adjusting word wrap) are accessed through a class specific message interface. Table 8.1 details the keyboard interface.

This is a simple definition of functionality, yet this control requires more code than any other custom control in this book. The source for the *CSTFILEVIEW* control is in the files *CST_FLVW.H*, Listing 8.1, *CST_FLVW.C*, Listing 8.2, and *CST_FLVW.RC*, Listing 8.3. About half the code in Listing 8.2 supports buffering the file.

Style Interface

There are no class specific window styles for *CSTFILEVIEW*, but it does respond to a broad range of window general styles.

Table 8.1
The CSTFILEVIEW control intercepts and responds to all the keys in this table.

Key Stroke	Scroll Action Through File
Home	Horizontal to Beginning of Current Line
Up Arrow	Vertical One Line Up
Page Up	Vertical One Page Up
Left Arrow	Horizontal One Character Left
Right Arrow	Horizontal One Character Right
End	Horizontal to End of Current Line
Down Arrow	Vertical One Line Down
Page Down	Vertical One Page Down
Cntrl + Home	Horizontal and Vertical to Beginning
Cntrl + Up Arrow	Same as Page Up
Cntrl + Page Up	Vertical to Beginning
Cntrl + Left Arrow	Horizontal One Tab Stop to Left
Cntrl + Right Arrow	Horizontal One Tab Stop to Right
Cntrl + End	Horizontal and Vertical to End
Cntrl + Down Arrow	Same as Page Down
Cntrl + Page Down	Vertical to End

One can control the nonclient area of the window with `WS_CAPTION` and `WS_SYSMENU` styles. The Developer may want to limit the user's ability to close the window before its parent is destroyed, especially if the control is in a dialog box. (See the box **Disabling System "Close."**) If you specify `WS_THICKFRAME`, `WS_MINIMIZEBOX`, and `WS_MAXIMIZEBOX` the user can change the size of the window. The `WS_POPUP` style (which is incompatible with the `WS_CHILD` style) will allow the custom control to be moved outside its parent window.

When minimized, `CSTFILEVIEW` is represented by the icon defined in the resource file, `CST_FLVW.RC`, Listing 8.3.

Design Overview

The file browser control will be written from scratch (as opposed to created by subclassing a standard control), because none of the standard Windows controls offers a suitable base for subclassing. The most likely candidate, the Windows `EDIT` control, is too limited to serve as a base. The Windows `EDIT` control has an absolute limit of 64K bytes of data, and the practical limit is usually substantially less. Thus a file viewer based on the `EDIT` control could manipulate only files smaller than 64K.

Disabling System "Close"

If you use the `WS_SYSMENU` style the user will be able to close the window. When using the `CSTFILEVIEW` control with a dialog box you may wish to disable the Close option on the system menu, to prevent the user from closing the `CSTFILEVIEW` window before its parent, the dialog box, is destroyed. There are two ways to disable the Close menu item: you can register the class with a `CS_NOCLOSE` style, or you can disable the close item in the system menu. To disable the close menu option, you must get the handle to the system menu and tell Windows to disable the Close item:

```
hFVSysMenu = GetSystemMenu( hFVWnd, FALSE );
EnableMenuItem( hFVSysMenu, SC_CLOSE, MF_DISABLED );
```

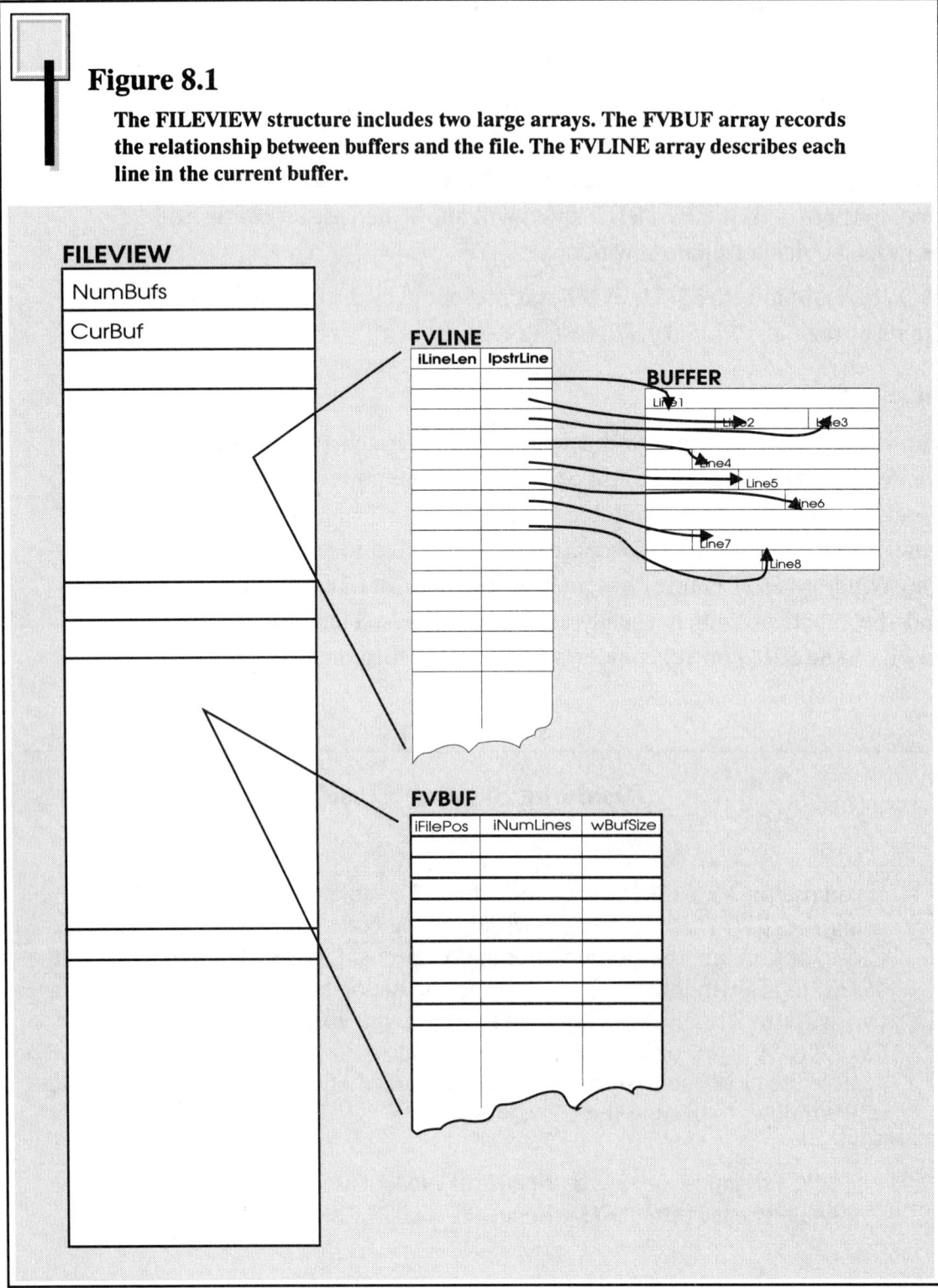

Figure 8.1
The FILEVIEW structure includes two large arrays. The FVBUF array records the relationship between buffers and the file. The FVLINE array describes each line in the current buffer.

Even if one could load more than 64K into the *EDIT* control, it still wouldn't be a suitable base. The standard control uses an unscaled standard SCROLLBAR, preventing the manipulation of files longer than 32,767 lines.

The *CSTFILEVIEW* control overcomes these limitations with a simple buffering scheme and scaled scroll controls. Instead of loading the entire file into memory, *CSTFILEVIEW* loads only one buffer into memory. When the user scrolls beyond the part of the file that is in memory, *CSTFILEVIEW* reads the desired part of the file into memory and displays it.

CSTFILEVIEW uses a single 60K buffer, allocated from the global heap. The buffer is indexed through a fixed length array of line descriptors (*FVLINE* structures). Each descriptor contains the line's character count (length) and a pointer to the beginning of the line.

Though the browser keeps only one buffer of text in memory at any time, it reads the entire file before displaying the first buffer. During this initial read, *CSTFILEVIEW* counts lines and collects information about each buffer it might need to load later. (On large files, this initial read can cause a noticeable delay, but, knowing the exact line count makes it very easy to scale the scroll bar.) The individual buffer descriptors are kept in a fixed length array of *FVBUF* structures. These buffer descriptors consist of a file offset, a line count, and a character count. Both these descriptor arrays and other important information are declared as members of a single large structure. This allows all the buffering information to be associated with the control by installing just one pointer in the instance data. Figure 8.1 shows the buffering scheme.

Of course, using fixed length arrays to hold line and buffer descriptors limits the number of lines and the size of file which the custom browser can view. Even so, *CSTFILEVIEW* can handle a much larger file than the *EDIT* control. In this implementation, we've sized the *FVBUF* array at 5,000 elements, and the *FVLINE* array at 300 elements. To guarantee that the 60,000 character buffer can always hold 300 lines, we've limited each line to a maximum of 200 characters. (Figure 8.2 defines constants that set the limits for the *CSTFILEVIEW* control.) Thus

CSTFILEVIEW can handle any file that has fewer than 1,500,000 lines (5,000 buffers * 300 lines/buffer) and fewer than 300,000,000 characters (1,500,000 lines * 200 characters/line). To make the scroll bars work appropriately, the control scales the scroll bar range to match the number of lines in the file. For example, if a file had 70,000 lines, each scroll bar click would correspond to three lines (70,000/32,767 rounded up).

While we would have preferred to close the file between reads, reopening the file for append operations greatly slowed the program. For that reason we leave the file open until the parent requests a new file or the window is destroyed.

This is a very simple buffering scheme, but it performs surprisingly well.

Data Interface

For all of the usual window attributes, *CSTFILEVIEW* uses the same instance data interface and responds to the same instance data messages as the other controls in this book. As mentioned earlier, all the more specialized data is declared as members of a single large *FILEVIEW* structure. The control installs a pointer and handle for this structure in the window extra bytes. In addition to the buffer and line descriptors described earlier, this structure keeps the window's scroll position and

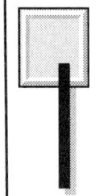

Figure 8.2

These constants determine the limits for the CSTFILEVIEW control.

```
#define FV_MAXBUFS           5000    /* Size of FVBUF array */
#define FV_MAXLINESPERBUF     300    /* Size of FVLINE array */
#define FV_MAXLINELEN         200
#define FV_MINLINELEN          20
#define FV_MAXBUFSIZE       60000
#define FV_MAXVERTSCRL      32700
#define FV_MAXNUMTABS           8
```

scroll range in the *SCRL* member, information about the open file in the standard Windows structure *OFSTRUCT*, and records the number of tab positions in the *iNumTabPos* member. Figure 8.3 defines the *FILEVIEW* structure.

Class Specific Messages

Besides responding to the required system and user interaction messages, the *CSTFILEVIEW* control also responds to its own set of class

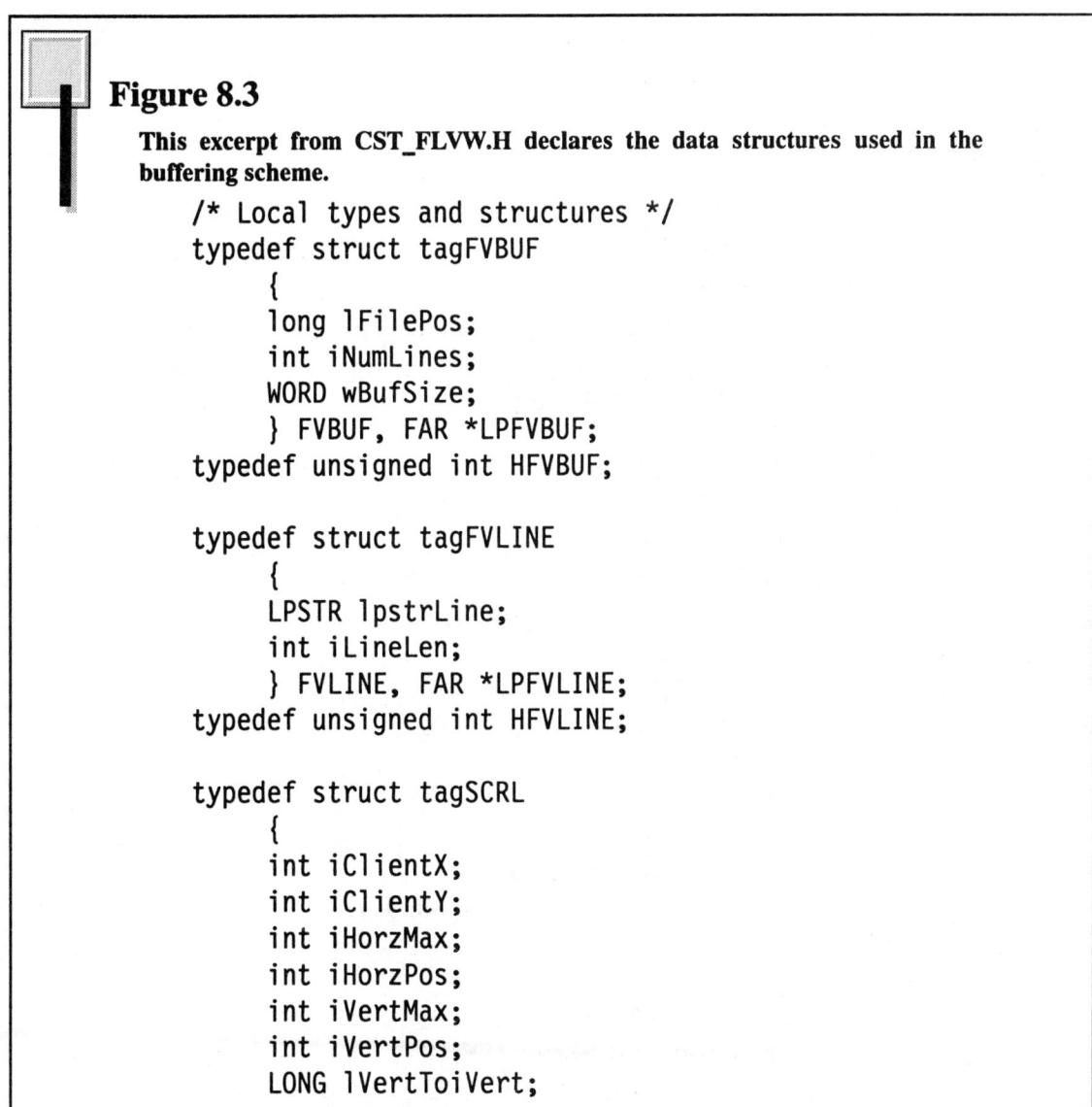

Figure 8.3

This excerpt from CST_FLVW.H declares the data structures used in the buffering scheme.

```
/* Local types and structures */
typedef struct tagFVBUF
    {
    long lFilePos;
    int iNumLines;
    WORD wBufSize;
    } FVBUF, FAR *LPFVBUF;
typedef unsigned int HFVBUF;

typedef struct tagFVLINE
    {
    LPSTR lpstrLine;
    int iLineLen;
    } FVLINE, FAR *LPFVLINE;
typedef unsigned int HFVLINE;

typedef struct tagSCRL
    {
    int iClientX;
    int iClientY;
    int iHorzMax;
    int iHorzPos;
    int iVertMax;
    int iVertPos;
    LONG lVertToiVert;
```

specific messages, which: cause the control to load or unload a file; append lines to a file; and control how *CSTFILEVIEW* displays the file. Table 8.2 contains the messages and a description of what each message does. The second part of Table 8.2 also details the *wParam*, *lParam*, and return values for each message.

As suggested by Microsoft, we have assigned these messages numbers following *WM_USER* (see Figure 8.4).

Figure 8.3

Continued from the preceding page.

```
        LONG lVertMax;
        LONG lVertPos;
        int iWidthChar;
        int iHeightChar;
        } SCRL, FAR *LPSCRL;
typedef unsigned int HSCRL;

typedef struct tagFILEVIEW
        {
        HANDLE hstrBuf;
        LPSTR lpstrBuf;
        LONG lNumLines;
        int iNumBufs;
        int iCurBuf;
        int iMaxLineLen;
        int iWrapLineLen;
        int iNumTabPos;
        int FAR *iTabPos;
        FVBUF fvBuf[FV_MAXBUFS];
        FVLINE fvLine[FV_MAXLINESPERBUF];
        SCRL scrl;
        OFSTRUCT of;
        } FILEVIEW, FAR *LPFILEVIEW;
typedef unsigned int HFILEVIEW;
```

Table 8.2

These messages are specific to the CSTFILEVIEW class. This table describes how each is used and gives appropriate lParam values.

Message	Description
CFVM_LOADFILE	Loads a new file
CFVM_GETNUMTABS	Gets number of tab positions
CFVM_SETNUMTABS	Sets number of tab positions
CFVM_GETTABPOS	Gets tab positions
CFVM_SETTABPOS	Sets tab position
CFVM_GETWRAPLINELEN	Gets maximum line length
CFVM_SETWRAPLINELEN	Sets maximum line length
CFVM_APPENDLINE	appends a line to the end of the file

Message	wParam	lParam	Return
CFVM_CLEARFILE	Not used	Not used	0
CFVM_LOADFILE	Not used	LPSTR file name	0
CFVM_GETNUMTABS	Not used	Not used	Number of tabs
CFVM_SETNUMTABS	Number of tabs	Not used	0
CFVM_GETTABPOS	Not used	Not used	Tab pos array
CFVM_SETTABPOS	Not used	Tab pos array	0
CFVM_GETWRAPLINELEN	Not used	Not used	Max line len
CFVM_SETWRAPLINELEN	Max line len	Not used	0
CFVM_APPENDLINE	Not used	Pointer to string	0

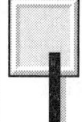

Figure 8.4

The CSTFILEVIEW class specific messages are assigned numbers beginning at WM_USER + 1.

```
#define CFVM_CLEARFILE        ( WM_USER + 1 )
#define CFVM_LOADFILE         ( WM_USER + 2 )
#define CFVM_GETNUMTABS       ( WM_USER + 3 )
#define CFVM_SETNUMTABS       ( WM_USER + 4 )
#define CFVM_GETTABPOS        ( WM_USER + 5 )
#define CFVM_SETTABPOS        ( WM_USER + 6 )
#define CFVM_GETWRAPLINELEN   ( WM_USER + 7 )
#define CFVM_SETWRAPLINELEN   ( WM_USER + 8 )
#define CFVM_APPENDLINE       ( WM_USER + 9 )
```

Implementation and Function Interface

The function *CstFileViewLoadFile()* allocates the dynamic memory for the *FILEVIEW* structure and buffer via a call to *CstFileViewCreateData()*. *CstFileViewLoadFile()* then opens the file and calls the function *CstFileViewLoadBuf()* once for one buffer after another, until it has read the entire file. *CstFileViewLoadBuf()*, in turn, calls *CstFileViewParseBuf()* to break the buffer into lines. As *CstFileViewParseBuf()* identifies line endings, it sets the appropriate *FVLINE* structure members.

Once the file has been fully analyzed, the draw function can obtain a pointer to any line, and the line's length, by calling *CstFileViewGetLine()* with the relevant line number. If the target line isn't in the current buffer, *CstFileViewGetLine()* will call *CstFileViewLoadBuf()* to load the appropriate buffer. Thus, *CstFileViewGetLine()* creates a logical interface to the file which completely hides the buffering mechanism from the rest of the window class code.

We also provide a create window function for this class. You can use the *CreateWindow()* function directly, or you can use the more convenient *CstFileViewCreateWindow()*.

Instantiation and Cleanup

When a new browser window is created, the *CstFileViewWndFn()* window function will respond to the *WM_CREATE* message by creating the instance data and loading the target file. If the control was created by the dialog manager (via a resource script), *CstFileViewWndFn()* will use the window text as the target file's name. If the control was created by a call to *CstFileViewCreateWindow()*, the window text will be blank. In this instance, *CstFileViewWndFn()* will not load a file until it receives a *CFVM_LOADFILE* message. In response to this message, the control will load the file whose name is available as the *lpCreateParams* member of the window's *CREATESTRUCT*.

Once *CstFileViewWndFn()* has found a string that it can use as a filename, it calls *CstFileViewLoadFile()* to load the file into the buffering system. After `CstFileViewWndFn()` attempts to load a file, it notifies its parent window that it has been created.

We register the `CSTFILEVIEW` control *without* the `CS_HREDRAW` and `CS_VREDRAW` styles, because these styles cause too much unnecessary painting for this control.

In response to the `WM_DESTROY` message, `CstFileViewWndFn()` must not only delete the instance data, but also free the dynamic memory used for buffering the file. After first notifying its parent window that it is being destroyed, `CstFileViewWndFn()` calls the function `CstFileViewClearFile()` to deallocate the buffering memory and calls `CstCtlDataDelete()` to free the instance data.

Display Operations

All of the code for a paint response is encapsulated in the function `CstFileViewDraw()`. Before doing any drawing, `CstFileViewDraw()` gives the parent window an opportunity to adjust the colors by sending a `WM_CTLCOLOR` message to the parent window. If the parent traps the message, `CstFileViewDraw()` will use the new colors, otherwise it will use the default colors. (See the discussion of `WM_CTLCOLOR` in Chapter 4 for more details.)

Once the colors are known and brushes created, `CstFileViewDraw()` checks entries in the `FILEVIEW` structure to determine which line numbers to redraw. It gets an appropriate pointer through `CstFileViewGetLine()`, and paints the line by passing the pointer to either `TextOut()` or `TabbedTextOut()` (depending upon whether any tab stops have been specified in the `iNumTabPos` member of the `FILEVIEW` structure). If `iNumTabPos` is negative, `CstFileViewDraw()` uses `TextOut()`, which does not expand tabs. If `iNumTabPos` is zero then `CstFileViewDraw()` uses the default of tabs every eight characters. Otherwise `CstFileViewDraw()` assumes that `iNumTabPos` contains the number of tab stops and `iTabPos` is an array of the positions.

This implementation provides for only eight tab stops. One can easily change this limit by changing size of the `iTabPos` array.

Scrolling

Since both type size and window size have a direct effect on the amount of text displayed, these two parameters also affect how the scroll controls are scaled. Consequently, in addition to setting the scroll bar scale factors when the file is first loaded, *CstFileViewWndFn()* must also trap the *WM_SIZE* and *WM_SETFONT* messages, and adjust the scale factors accordingly.

CstFileViewWndFn() determines how many lines fit vertically in the client window and how many characters fit horizontally in the client window. The function *CstFileViewInitScrl()* determines the height and width of a character.

The function *CstFileViewInitScrl()* uses information obtained through the *GetTextMetrics()* function to determine the height and width of a character. Other functions use this information, to calculate how many lines will fit vertically and how many characters will fit horizontally in the client window.

Since the number of lines in the buffered file can exceed the maximum scroll range of the Windows SCROLLBAR control, *CstFileViewWndFn()* must determine both the true (file units) scroll range and position and the scaled (scroll-bar units) scroll range and position. The *SCRL* structure contains both long (true) and integer (scaled) values of the vertical scroll range and position. *CstFileViewWndFn()* determines the integer (scaled) values based upon the ratio between the true range and the maximum range.

Key Stroke Conversion

The *CSTFILEVIEW* control must respond to scrolling messages generated by the mouse and also map keyboard interaction into scrolling messages.

CstFileViewWndFn() converts key strokes into scroll operations by trapping *WM_KEYDOWN* messages and sending the appropriate scroll messages to itself. Table 8.3 lists the virtual key codes which *CstFileViewWndFn()* responds to, the associated *wParam* value, and the scroll message each key code generates.

Note that the virtual key code does not always distinguish between normal key strokes and control-shifted key strokes. `CstFileViewWndFn()` must call the Windows function `GetKeyState()` to detect a control-shift key stroke. The code in Figure 8.5 shows how to perform this test.

Table 8.3

This table lists the virtual key codes to which CstFileViewWndFn() responds, the associated wParam value, and the scroll message each key code generates.

wParam for WM_KEYDOWN	VK_CONTROL	Scroll Messages	wParam
VK_HOME	Down	WM_VSCROLL WM_HSCROLL	SB_TOP SB_TOP
VK_HOME	Up	WM_HSCROLL	SB_TOP
VK_END	Down	WM_VSCROLL WM_HSCROLL	SB_BOTTOM SB_BOTTOM
VK_END	Up	WM_HSCROLL	SB_BOTTOM
VK_PRIOR	Down	WM_VSCROLL	SB_TOP
VK_PRIOR	Up	WM_VSCROLL	SB_PAGEUP
VK_NEXT	Down	WM_VSCROLL	SB_BOTTOM
VK_NEXT	Up	WM_VSCROLL	SB_PAGEDOWN
VK_UP	Down or Up	WM_VSCROLL	SB_LINEUP
VK_DOWN	Down or Up	WM_HSCROLL	SB_LINEDOWN
VK_LEFT	Down	WM_HSCROLL	SB_PAGEUP
VK_LEFT	Up	WM_HSCROLL	SB_LINEUP
VK_RIGHT	Down	WM_HSCROLL	SB_PAGEDOWN
VK_RIGHT	Up	WM_HSCROLL	SB_LINEDOWN

The Demonstration Program

The demonstration program (*DEM_FLVW.C*, Listing 8.5), demonstrates both top-level and child-window instances of the file viewer, and allows the user to exercise the append capability. If *DEM_FLVW* finds an argument on the command line, it opens the corresponding file and displays it in a top-level window. *DEM_FLVW* immediately overlays this window with the main application window.

The main application window offers four menu choices. The first choice acts as a toggle, alternately creating and destroying instances of the file view control. This control always loads and displays the source file, *CST_FLVW.C*. The second choice opens another instance of the file

Figure 8.5

The key stroke handler must perform this test to distinguish between a normal key stroke and a control-shifted key stroke.

```
.
.
.
case WM_KEYDOWN:
    {
    switch ( wParam )
        {
        case VK_HOME:
            if ( GetKeyState( VK_CONTROL ) < 0 )
                {
                SendMessage( hWnd, WM_VSCROLL, SB_TOP, 0 );
                SendMessage( hWnd, WM_HSCROLL, SB_TOP, 0 );
                }
            else
                {
                SendMessage( hWnd, WM_HSCROLL, SB_TOP, 0 );
                }
            break;
            .
            .
            .
```

view control and appends 100 lines to the new window. The third choice closes the append window. The fourth choice exits the program.

Possible Enhancements

A browser for large files needs more sophisticated navigation controls than just forward and backward scrolls. We suggest adding a search capability, and a *goto* line number capability. To help orient the user, each of these features should also mark the target string or line, perhaps by displaying it in a different color or font. Another helpful display feature might be optional line numbering. Alternatively, a status bar at the bottom of the window could display the current cursor position.

You could avoid the delay associated with the initial loading of the file by loading only as much as necessary to display each buffer. This change would require some additional state information to keep track of where the last file read stopped. With careful design, this additional complexity could be hidden entirely in the `CstFileViewGetLine()` and `CstFileViewLoadFile()` functions. Be aware, though, that this modification will force you to base scrollbar scaling on something other than total line count, since total line count will usually not be available. Character count, or an estimated line count (based on an average line length), might be workable alternatives.

Finally, if you are really ambitious, you can make the control handle even larger files, by paying careful attention to segment boundaries, or by demand paging the buffer and line descriptors.

Listing 8.1

```
/****************************************************************************
            File Name: CST_FLVW.H
        Expanded Name: Custom File View
          Description: Include file for CST_FLVW.C
          Portability: Microsoft Windows 3.X
****************************************************************************/

#if !defined ( CST_FLVW_DEFINED )
    #define CST_FLVW_DEFINED

    /* Class specific messages for custom file view control */
    #define CFVM_CLEARFILE      ( WM_USER + 1 )
    #define CFVM_LOADFILE       ( WM_USER + 2 )
    #define CFVM_GETNUMTABS     ( WM_USER + 3 )
    #define CFVM_SETNUMTABS     ( WM_USER + 4 )
    #define CFVM_GETTABPOS      ( WM_USER + 5 )
    #define CFVM_SETTABPOS      ( WM_USER + 6 )
    #define CFVM_GETWRAPLINELEN ( WM_USER + 7 )
    #define CFVM_SETWRAPLINELEN ( WM_USER + 8 )
    #define CFVM_APPENDLINE     ( WM_USER + 9 )

    /* Extra byte constants for file view control */
    #define CFV_CLSEXTRA   ( CC_CLSEXTRA )
    #define CFV_WNDEXTRA   ( CC_WNDEXTRA + (int)sizeof ( LONG ) + \
            (int)sizeof ( WORD ) )
    #define GWL_LPFILEVIEW ( CC_WNDEXTRA )
    #define GWW_HFILEVIEW  ( CC_WNDEXTRA + (int)sizeof ( LONG ) )

    /* WM_CTLCOLOR type for custom file view control */
    #define CTLCOLOR_CSTFILEVIEW 400

    /* Prototypes for exported functions in CST_FLVW.C */
    HWND FAR PASCAL CstFileViewCreateWindow( DWORD dwStyle,
            int X, int Y, int iWidth, int iHeight, HWND hWndParent,
            HINSTANCE hInstance, LPSTR lpstrFileName );
    int FAR PASCAL CstFileViewRegister( HINSTANCE hInstance );
    int FAR PASCAL CstFileViewUnregister( HINSTANCE hInstance );
    LONG FAR PASCAL CstFileViewWndFn( HWND hWnd, UINT wMessage, WPARAM wParam,
            LPARAM lParam );

#endif

/* End of CST_FLVW.H */
```

Listing 8.2

```
/***************************************************************************
            File Name: CST_FLVW.C
        Expanded Name: Custom File View
          Description: Library of functions for the check box custom control
 Global Function List: CstFileViewCreateWindow
                       CstFileViewRegister
                       CstFileViewUnregister
                       CstFileViewWndFn
 Static Function List: CstFileViewAppendLine
                       CstFileViewClearFile
                       CstFileViewCreateData
                       CstFileViewDefDataCreate
                       CstFileViewDefDataDelete
                       CstFileViewDraw
                       CstFileViewGetLine
                       CstFileViewLoadBuf
                       CstFileViewLoadFile
                       CstFileViewParseBuf
          Global Data: _hInstanceCstCtls
          Static Data: _hCstCtlData
                       _lpCstCtlData
          Portability: Microsoft Windows 3.X
***************************************************************************/

/* Microsoft Windows */
#include <windows.h>

/* Standard C */
#include <stdio.h>
#include <string.h>

/* Microsoft C */
#include <io.h>

/* Prototypes and Types */
#include <cst_xtra.h>
#include <cst_data.h>
#include <cst_util.h>

/* Own */
#include <cst_flvw.h>

/* Constants defining limits and ranges */
#define FV_MAXBUFS              5000    /* Size of FVBUF array */
#define FV_MAXLINESPERBUF       300     /* Size of FVLINE array */
#define FV_MAXLINELEN           200
#define FV_MINLINELEN           20
#define FV_MAXBUFSIZE           60000u
#define FV_MAXVERTSCRL          32700
#define FV_MAXNUMTABS           8

/* Local types and structures */
typedef struct tagFVBUF
    {
    long lFilePos;
    int iNumLines;
    WORD wBufSize;
    } FVBUF, FAR *LPFVBUF;
typedef unsigned int HFVBUF;
```

Listing 8.2 *continued*

```c
typedef struct tagFVLINE
    {
    LPSTR lpstrLine;
    int iLineLen;
    } FVLINE, FAR *LPFVLINE;
typedef unsigned int HFVLINE;

typedef struct tagSCRL
    {
    int iClientX;
    int iClientY;
    int iHorzMax;
    int iHorzPos;
    int iVertMax;
    int iVertPos;
    LONG lVertToiVert;
    LONG lVertMax;
    LONG lVertPos;
    int iWidthChar;
    int iHeightChar;
    } SCRL, FAR *LPSCRL;
typedef unsigned int HSCRL;

typedef struct tagFILEVIEW
    {
    HANDLE hstrBuf;
    LPSTR lpstrBuf;
    LONG lNumLines;
    int hf;
    int iNumBufs;
    int iCurBuf;
    int iMaxLineLen;
    int iWrapLineLen;
    int iNumTabPos;
    int FAR *iTabPos;
    FVBUF fvBuf[FV_MAXBUFS];
    FVLINE fvLine[FV_MAXLINESPERBUF];
    SCRL scrl;
    OFSTRUCT of;
    } FILEVIEW, FAR *LPFILEVIEW;
typedef unsigned int HFILEVIEW;

/* Prototypes of local static functions. */
static int CstFileViewAppendLine( HWND hWnd, LPSTR Line );
static void CstFileViewClearFile( HWND hWnd );
static LPFILEVIEW CstFileViewCreateData( HWND hWnd );
static int CstFileViewDefDataCreate( HWND hWnd );
static void CstFileViewDefDataDelete( void );
static void CstFileViewDraw( HWND hWnd, HDC hDC, LPPAINTSTRUCT lpPs,
        LPFILEVIEW lpFV );
static LPSTR CstFileViewGetLine( HWND hWnd, LONG lLineNum, int FAR *iLineLen,
        int FAR *Status );
static WORD CstFileViewLoadBuf( LPFILEVIEW lpFV, int iBufNum );
static int CstFileViewLoadFile( HWND hWnd, LPSTR lpstrFileName, int Create );
static WORD CstFileViewParseBuf( LPFILEVIEW lpFV, WORD wBufSize );
```

Listing 8.2 *continued*

```c
#if defined ( _WINDLL )
/* DLL Handle */
extern HINSTANCE _hInstanceCstCtls;
#endif

static HCSTCTLDATA _hCstCtlData = (HCSTCTLDATA)0;
static LPCSTCTLDATA _lpCstCtlData = (LPCSTCTLDATA)0;

/****************************************************************************
          Name: CstFileViewAppendLine
    Parameters: hWnd - handle to file view window
                Line - pointer to line to add to file
        Return: TRUE (line added) or FALSE (line not added)
   Description: Appends a line unto the end of a file being viewed
****************************************************************************/
static int CstFileViewAppendLine( HWND hWnd, LPSTR Line )
    {

    int iLineLen, iCrPos, iBuf;
    long lFilePos, lParam;
    char CrStr[2];
    char WorkLine[FV_MAXLINELEN];
    RECT Rect;
    LPFILEVIEW lpFV = (LPFILEVIEW)CSTGETWINDOWLONG( hWnd, GWL_LPFILEVIEW );

    if ( !lpFV )
        {
        /* Bad data */
        return ( FALSE );
        }

    if ( lpFV->hf <= 0 )
        {
        lpFV->hf = OpenFile( (LPSTR)lpFV->of.szPathName, &( lpFV->of ),
                OF_READWRITE );
        if (lpFV->hf == -1 )
            {
            /* Error condition could not open the file */
            return ( FALSE );
            }
        }

    /* Move to the end of the file */
    lFilePos = lseek( lpFV->hf, 0L, SEEK_END );
    if ( lFilePos < 0 )
        {
        /* File error */
        _lclose( lpFV->hf );
        lpFV->hf = 0;
        return ( FALSE );
        }

    /* Write the new data */
    _fstrncpy( WorkLine, Line, FV_MAXLINELEN );
    WorkLine[FV_MAXLINELEN - 1] = '\0';
    iLineLen = lstrlen( WorkLine );
    iLineLen = min( iLineLen, lpFV->iWrapLineLen );
    CrStr[0] = 13;
    CrStr[1] = 0;
```

Listing 8.2 *continued*

```
iCrPos = (int)_fstrcspn( WorkLine, CrStr );
if ( iCrPos < 0 )
    {
    /* did not find a c.r. */
    iCrPos = lpFV->iWrapLineLen;
    }
if ( iCrPos < iLineLen - 2 )
    {
    /* c.r. encountered before end of string */
    iLineLen = iCrPos + 2;
    }
if ( ( WorkLine[iLineLen - 2] != 13 ) && ( WorkLine[iLineLen - 2] != 10 ) )
    {
    if ( ( WorkLine[iLineLen - 1] != 13 ) &&
         ( WorkLine[iLineLen - 1] != 10 ) )
        {
        /* Need to add a c.r./l.f. pair at end of string */
        WorkLine[iLineLen++] = 13;
        WorkLine[iLineLen++] = 10;
        }
    else
        {
        /* add a l.f. at end of string */
        WorkLine[iLineLen - 1] = 13;
        WorkLine[iLineLen++] = 10;
        }
    }
else
    {
    /* Make sure l.f. follows c.r. */
    WorkLine[iLineLen - 2] = 13;
    WorkLine[iLineLen - 1] = 10;
    }
_lwrite( lpFV->hf, WorkLine, iLineLen );

/* Close the file */
/* _lclose( lpFV->hf ); */

/* Get the last buffer number */
if ( lpFV->iNumBufs == 0 )
    {
    /* Have not read in a file yet */
    iBuf = 0;
    lpFV->iNumBufs = 1;
    }
else
    {
    iBuf = lpFV->iNumBufs - 1;
    }

if ( ( lpFV->fvBuf[iBuf].iNumLines >= FV_MAXLINESPERBUF ) ||
     ( lpFV->fvBuf[iBuf].wBufSize >= FV_MAXBUFSIZE ) )
    {
    /* Create a new buffer */
    iBuf++;
    lpFV->iNumBufs++;
    lpFV->fvBuf[iBuf].lFilePos = lFilePos;
    }
```

Listing 8.2 *continued*

```c
    /* Increment the number of buffer lines and the buffer size */
    lpFV->fvBuf[iBuf].iNumLines++;
    lpFV->fvBuf[iBuf].wBufSize += (WORD)iLineLen;

    /* Increment the total number of lines */
    lpFV->lNumLines++;

    if ( iBuf == lpFV->iCurBuf )
        {
        /* Reload the current buffer with new data */
        if ( !CstFileViewLoadBuf( lpFV, iBuf ) )
            {
            return ( FALSE );
            }
        }

    /* Adjust the scroll ranges and scroll to bottom */
    GetClientRect( hWnd, &Rect );
    lParam = (DWORD)( (WORD)Rect.bottom );
    lParam = lParam << 16;
    lParam += (DWORD)( (WORD)Rect.right );
    SendMessage( hWnd, WM_SIZE, 0, (LPARAM)lParam );
    if ( CSTCTLGETSTATE( hWnd ) )
        {
        SendMessage( hWnd, WM_VSCROLL, SB_BOTTOM, 0L );
        if ( !lpFV->scrl.lVertPos )
            {
            /* Redraw the entire window */
            InvalidateRect( hWnd, NULL, TRUE );
            }
        else
            {
            /* Redraw the last two text lines on the screen */
            Rect.top = Rect.bottom - 3 * lpFV->scrl.iHeightChar;
            Rect.bottom -= lpFV->scrl.iHeightChar;
            InvalidateRect( hWnd, &Rect, TRUE );
            }
        UpdateWindow( hWnd );
        }   /* if CSTCTLGETSTATE( hWnd ) */

    return ( TRUE );

    }   /* function CstFileViewAppendLine */


/*****************************************************************************
        Name: CstFileViewClearFile
   Parameters: hWnd - handle to file view window
  Description: frees the dynamic memory used for a file view window
*****************************************************************************/
static void CstFileViewClearFile( HWND hWnd )
    {

    HFILEVIEW  hFV;
    LPFILEVIEW lpFV;

    hFV  = (HFILEVIEW)CSTGETWINDOWWORD( hWnd, GWW_HFILEVIEW );
    lpFV = (LPFILEVIEW)CSTGETWINDOWLONG( hWnd, GWL_LPFILEVIEW );
```

Windows Custom Controls

Listing 8.2 continued

```
        if ( lpFV )
           {
           if ( lpFV->hf > 0 )
              {
              _lclose( lpFV->hf );
              }
           if ( lpFV->lpstrBuf )
              {
              GlobalUnlock( lpFV->hstrBuf );
              GlobalFree( lpFV->hstrBuf );
              }
           GlobalUnlock( hFV );
           GlobalFree( hFV );
           CSTSETWINDOWWORD( hWnd, GWW_HFILEVIEW, 0 );
           CSTSETWINDOWLONG( hWnd, GWL_LPFILEVIEW, 0L );
           }

        SetWindowText( hWnd, "" );

        if ( CSTCTLGETSTATE( hWnd ) )
           {
           InvalidateRect( hWnd, NULL, TRUE );
           UpdateWindow( hWnd );
           }

        }   /* function CstFileViewClearFile */


/********************************************************************
       Name: CstFileViewCreateData
 Parameters: hWnd - handle to file view custom control window
     Return: pointer to FILEVIEW structure or NULL if out of memory
Description: Allocates the memory for the FILEVIEW structure and buffer
********************************************************************/
static LPFILEVIEW CstFileViewCreateData( HWND hWnd )
    {

    HFILEVIEW hFV;

    hFV = GlobalAlloc( GMEM_FLAGS, (DWORD)sizeof ( FILEVIEW ) );
    if ( hFV )
       {

       LPFILEVIEW lpFV;

       lpFV = (LPFILEVIEW)GlobalLock( hFV );

       if ( lpFV )
          {
          lpFV->hstrBuf = GlobalAlloc( GMEM_FLAGS, (DWORD)FV_MAXBUFSIZE );
          if ( lpFV->hstrBuf )
             {
             lpFV->lpstrBuf = GlobalLock( lpFV->hstrBuf );
             if ( lpFV->lpstrBuf )
                {
                CSTSETWINDOWWORD( hWnd, GWW_HFILEVIEW, hFV );
                CSTSETWINDOWLONG( hWnd, GWL_LPFILEVIEW, lpFV );
                lpFV->iWrapLineLen = CSTCTLGETFRAME( hWnd );
                lpFV->iWrapLineLen =
```

Listing 8.2 *continued*

```
                                min( lpFV->iWrapLineLen, FV_MAXLINELEN );
                    lpFV->iWrapLineLen =
                                max( lpFV->iWrapLineLen, FV_MINLINELEN );
                    CstCtlSetFrame( hWnd, lpFV->iWrapLineLen );
                    lpFV->iNumTabPos = (int)CSTCTLGETSTYLE( hWnd );
                    lpFV->iTabPos = (int FAR *)CSTCTLGETLPRECTBITMAP( hWnd );
                    return ( lpFV );
                    }
                GlobalFree( lpFV->hstrBuf );
                }
            }
        GlobalFree( hFV );
        }

    return ( NULL );

    }   /* function CstFileViewCreateData */

/********************************************************************
        Name: CstFileViewCreateWindow
  Parameters: Similar to CreateWindow function
      Return: handle to CstFileView window
 Description: Creates a window of class CstFileView
********************************************************************/
HWND FAR PASCAL CstFileViewCreateWindow( DWORD dwStyle, int X, int Y,
        int iWidth, int iHeight, HWND hWndParent, HINSTANCE hInstance,
        LPSTR lpstrFileName )
    {

    HWND hWndFileView;
    HWND hWnd = hWndParent;

    if ( hWndParent == NULL )
        {
        if ( hInstance == NULL )
            {
            return ( FALSE );
            }
        hWndParent = GetDesktopWindow();
        }
    else
        {
        hInstance = GetWindowWord( hWndParent, GWW_HINSTANCE );
        }

    if ( X == CW_USEDEFAULT && Y == CW_USEDEFAULT &&
            iWidth != CW_USEDEFAULT && iHeight != CW_USEDEFAULT )
        {

        RECT Rect;

        /* Calculate the location of the window */
        GetWindowRect( hWndParent, &Rect );
        X = Rect.left + ( Rect.right - Rect.left ) / 2;
        X -= iWidth / 2;
        if ( X < 0 )
            {
            X = 0;
            }
```

Listing 8.2 continued

```
            Y = Rect.top + ( Rect.bottom - Rect.top ) / 2;
            Y -= iHeight / 2;
            if ( Y < 0 )
                {
                Y = 0;
                }
            }

        hWndFileView = CreateWindow( "CstFileView", NULL, dwStyle,
                X, Y, iWidth, iHeight, hWnd, NULL, hInstance, lpstrFileName );

        if ( hWndFileView )
            {
            CstFileViewLoadFile( hWndFileView, lpstrFileName, TRUE );
            }
        return ( hWndFileView );

        }   /* function CstFileViewCreateWindow */

/********************************************************************************
        Name: CstFileViewDefDataCreate
Expanded Name: Default Data Create
   Parameters: hWnd - window handle to FileView control
        Return: TRUE or FALSE
  Description: Creates the default class data
********************************************************************************/
static int CstFileViewDefDataCreate( HWND hWnd )
    {

    _lpCstCtlData = CstCtlDefDataCreate( hWnd );
    if ( !_lpCstCtlData )
        {
        /* Failed to allocate and initialize data */
        return ( FALSE );
        }
    _hCstCtlData = CSTGETCLASSWORD( hWnd, GCW_HCSTCTLDATA );

    /* Free up the resources we do not need */
    SafeDeleteObject( _lpCstCtlData->hBrush[CC_BRUSH_BTNFACE] );
    _lpCstCtlData->hBrush[CC_BRUSH_BTNFACE] = 0;
    SafeDeleteObject( _lpCstCtlData->hBrush[CC_BRUSH_3DLIGHT] );
    _lpCstCtlData->hBrush[CC_BRUSH_3DLIGHT] = 0;
    SafeDeleteObject( _lpCstCtlData->hBrush[CC_BRUSH_3DSHADOW] );
    _lpCstCtlData->hBrush[CC_BRUSH_3DSHADOW] = 0;
    SafeDeleteObject( _lpCstCtlData->hBrush[CC_BRUSH_FRAME] );
    _lpCstCtlData->hBrush[CC_BRUSH_FRAME] = 0;

    /* Initialize some data */
    _lpCstCtlData->iFrame = FV_MAXLINELEN;
    _lpCstCtlData->hFont = GetStockObject( OEM_FIXED_FONT );
    _lpCstCtlData->wState = TRUE;
    _lpCstCtlData->wStyle = (WORD)( -1 );
    _lpCstCtlData->iBkMode = OPAQUE;
    _lpCstCtlData->lColor[CC_COLOR_TEXTBACKGROUND] = (COLORREF)
            GetSysColor( COLOR_WINDOW );

    return ( TRUE );

    }   /* function CstFileViewDefDataCreate */
```

Listing 8.2 *continued*

```c
/****************************************************************************
        Name: CstFileViewDefDataDelete
Expanded Name: Default Data Delete
   Parameters: hWnd - window handle control
  Description: Deletes the default class data
****************************************************************************/
static void CstFileViewDefDataDelete( void )
    {

    if ( _lpCstCtlData )
        {
        SafeDeleteObject( _lpCstCtlData->hBrush[CC_BRUSH_BACKGROUND] );
        SafeDeleteObject( _lpCstCtlData->hFont );
        _lpCstCtlData = (LPCSTCTLDATA)0;
        }

    if ( _hCstCtlData )
        {
        GlobalUnlock( _hCstCtlData );
        GlobalFree( _hCstCtlData );
        _hCstCtlData = (HCSTCTLDATA)0;
        }

    }   /* function CstFileViewDefDataDelete */


/****************************************************************************
       Name: CstFileViewDraw
  Parameters: hWnd - handle to file view window
              hDC  - handle to drawing device
              lpPs - pointer to paint struct
              lpFV - pointer to file view struct
  Description: Draws the file view window
****************************************************************************/
static void CstFileViewDraw( HWND hWnd, HDC hDC, LPPAINTSTRUCT lpPs,
        LPFILEVIEW lpFV )
    {

    COLORREF lColorTextBkOrg, lColorTextOrg;
    HFONT hFont, hFontOrg;
    HWND hWndParent;
    int iBkModeOrg;
    WORD wCtlColorMsg = 0;

    hWndParent = GetParent( hWnd );
    if ( hWndParent )
        {

        HBRUSH hBrushBk;

        /* Send message to give parent a chance to change data */
        hBrushBk = (HBRUSH)SendMessage( hWndParent, WM_CTLCOLOR, hDC,
                MAKELPARAM( hWnd, CTLCOLOR_CSTFILEVIEW ) );
        wCtlColorMsg = CstCtlColorMsg( hWnd, FALSE );
        if ( ( wCtlColorMsg & CTLCOLORMSG_BRUSH ) && hBrushBk )
            {
            SetClassWord( hWnd, GCW_HBRBACKGROUND, (WORD)hBrushBk );
```

Listing 8.2 *continued*

```
                CstCtlSetBrush( hWnd, CC_BRUSH_BACKGROUND, hBrushBk );
                }
        }
    /* Get the font */
    hFont = CSTCTLGETFONT( hWnd );
    if ( !hFont )
        {
        /* Get the default font */
        hFont = GetStockObject( OEM_FIXED_FONT );
        CstCtlSetFont( hWnd, hFont );
        }
    hFontOrg = SelectObject( hDC, hFont );

    /* Set the color */
    if ( !( wCtlColorMsg & CTLCOLORMSG_COLORTEXT ) )
        {
        lColorTextOrg = SetTextColor( hDC,
                CSTCTLGETCOLOR( hWnd, CC_COLOR_TEXT ) );
        }
    if ( !( wCtlColorMsg & CTLCOLORMSG_COLORTEXTBK ) )
        {
        lColorTextBkOrg = SetBkColor( hDC,
                CSTCTLGETCOLOR( hWnd, CC_COLOR_TEXTBACKGROUND ) );
        }
    if ( !( wCtlColorMsg & CTLCOLORMSG_MODETEXTBK ) )
        {
        iBkModeOrg = SetBkMode( hDC, CSTCTLGETBKMODE( hWnd ) );
        }

    if ( lpFV )
        {

        int x, y, Status, iLineLen;
        LONG lLineNum, lPaintBeg, lPaintEnd;
        LPSCRL Scrl;
        LPSTR lpstrLine;

        Scrl = (LPSCRL)&lpFV->scrl;

        lPaintBeg = Scrl->lVertPos +
                (LONG)( ( lpPs->rcPaint.top / Scrl->iHeightChar ) - 1 );
        lPaintBeg = max( 0L, lPaintBeg );

        lPaintEnd = Scrl->lVertPos +
                (LONG)( lpPs->rcPaint.bottom / Scrl->iHeightChar );
        lPaintEnd = min( lpFV->lNumLines + 1, lPaintEnd );

        for ( lLineNum = lPaintBeg; lLineNum < lPaintEnd; lLineNum++ )
            {

            lpstrLine = CstFileViewGetLine( hWnd,
                    lLineNum, &iLineLen, &Status );

            if ( !Status )
                {
                break;
                }   /* if !Status */
```

Listing 8.2 *continued*

```c
            if ( lpstrLine == NULL )
               {
               continue;
               }

            x = Scrl->iWidthChar * ( 1 - Scrl->iHorzPos );
            y = Scrl->iHeightChar * (int)( 1L - Scrl->lVertPos + lLineNum );
            if ( lpFV->iNumTabPos < 0 )
               {
               TextOut( hDC, x, y, lpstrLine, iLineLen );
               }
            else
               {
               TabbedTextOut( hDC, x, y, lpstrLine, iLineLen,
                       lpFV->iNumTabPos, lpFV->iTabPos,
                       Scrl->iWidthChar );
               }
            }  /* for lLineNum */
       }  /* if lpFV */

   /* Reset the font */
   SelectObject( hDC, hFontOrg );

   /* Reset the colors and mode */
   if ( !( wCtlColorMsg & CTLCOLORMSG_COLORTEXT ) )
      {
      SetTextColor( hDC, lColorTextOrg );
      }
   if ( !( wCtlColorMsg & CTLCOLORMSG_COLORTEXTBK ) )
      {
      SetBkColor( hDC, lColorTextBkOrg );
      }
   if ( !( wCtlColorMsg & CTLCOLORMSG_MODETEXTBK ) )
      {
      SetBkMode( hDC, iBkModeOrg );
      }

   }  /* function CstFileViewDraw */


/****************************************************************************
       Name: CstFileViewGetLine
  Parameters: hWnd - handle to file view window
              lLineNum - number of line to get
              iLineLen - length of line to get
              Status - error code
      Return: line
 Description: gets the line for a give line number
****************************************************************************/
static LPSTR CstFileViewGetLine( HWND hWnd, LONG lLineNum, int FAR *iLineLen,
       int FAR *Status )
   {

   int iBufNum, iLineNum;
   LPFILEVIEW lpFV;

   lpFV = (LPFILEVIEW)CSTGETWINDOWLONG( hWnd, GWL_LPFILEVIEW );
   *Status = FALSE;
   *iLineLen = 0;
```

Listing 8.2 *continued*

```c
        if ( !lpFV )
            {
            /* Bad Data */
            return ( NULL );
            }

        /* Get the buffer number */
        iBufNum = (int)( lLineNum / (LONG)FV_MAXLINESPERBUF );
        if ( iBufNum >= lpFV->iNumBufs )
            {
            /* Error condition */
            return ( NULL );
            }

        if ( iBufNum != lpFV->iCurBuf )
            {

            if ( !CstFileViewLoadBuf( lpFV, iBufNum ) )
                {
                return ( NULL );
                }
            }

        iLineNum = (int)( lLineNum - ( (LONG)iBufNum * (LONG)FV_MAXLINESPERBUF ) );
        if ( iLineNum >= lpFV->fvBuf[iBufNum].iNumLines )
            {
            return ( NULL );
            }

        *Status = TRUE;
        *iLineLen = lpFV->fvLine[iLineNum].iLineLen;

        return ( lpFV->fvLine[iLineNum].lpstrLine );

        }   /* function CstFileViewGetLine */


/*******************************************************************************
        Name: CstFileViewInitScrl
   Parameters: hWnd - handle to file view window
               lpFV - pointer to file view data
  Description: Initializes the scroll information
*******************************************************************************/
static void CstFileViewInitScrl( HWND hWnd, LPFILEVIEW lpFV )
    {

    if ( lpFV )
        {

        TEXTMETRIC Tm;
        DWORD lParam;
        RECT Rect;
        LPSCRL Scrl = (LPSCRL)&lpFV->scrl;
        HFONT hFontOld, hFont = CSTCTLGETFONT( hWnd );
        HDC hDC = GetDC( hWnd );

        hFontOld = (HFONT)SelectObject( hDC, hFont );
        GetTextMetrics( hDC, &Tm );
```

Listing 8.2 *continued*

```
        SelectObject( hDC, hFontOld );
        ReleaseDC( hWnd, hDC );

        Scrl->iWidthChar = Tm.tmAveCharWidth;
        Scrl->iHeightChar = Tm.tmHeight + Tm.tmExternalLeading;
        Scrl->iHorzPos = 0;
        Scrl->iVertPos = 0;
        Scrl->lVertPos = 0L;

        GetClientRect( hWnd, &Rect );
        lParam = (DWORD)( (WORD)Rect.bottom );
        lParam = lParam << 16;
        lParam += (DWORD)( (WORD)Rect.right );
        SendMessage( hWnd, WM_SIZE, 0, (LPARAM)lParam );

        }  /* if lpFV */

    }  /* function CstFileViewInitScrl */

/*****************************************************************************
        Name: CstFileViewLoadBuf
  Parameters: lpFV - pointer to file view struct
              iBufNum - number of buffer to load
      Return: -1 if buffer not loaded, else the number of chars loaded
 Description: loads the file view buffer with contents from the file
*****************************************************************************/
static WORD CstFileViewLoadBuf( LPFILEVIEW lpFV, int iBufNum )
    {

    WORD wBufSize;

    if ( !lpFV )
        {
        return ( FALSE );
        }
    if ( lpFV->hf <= 0 )
        {
        lpFV->hf = OpenFile( (LPSTR)lpFV->of.szPathName, &( lpFV->of ),
                OF_READWRITE );
        if ( lpFV->hf == -1 )
            {
            /* Error condition */
            return ( FALSE );
            }
        }

    if ( lseek( lpFV->hf, lpFV->fvBuf[iBufNum].lFilePos, SEEK_SET ) < 0 )
        {
        /* Error condition */
        _lclose( lpFV->hf );
        lpFV->hf = 0;
        return ( FALSE );
        }

    /* Read in the buffer */
    if ( !lpFV->fvBuf[iBufNum].wBufSize )
        {
        lpFV->fvBuf[iBufNum].wBufSize = FV_MAXBUFSIZE;
        }
```

Listing 8.2 *continued*

```
        wBufSize = (WORD)_lread( lpFV->hf, lpFV->lpstrBuf,
                lpFV->fvBuf[iBufNum].wBufSize );
        /* _lclose( lpFV->hf ); */

        if ( wBufSize == (WORD)-1 )
            {
            /* Error condition */
            wBufSize = 0;
            }

        if ( wBufSize > 0 )
            {
            lpFV->iCurBuf = iBufNum;
            wBufSize = CstFileViewParseBuf( lpFV, wBufSize );
            }
        lpFV->fvBuf[iBufNum].wBufSize = wBufSize;

        return ( wBufSize );

        }   /* CstFileViewLoadBuf */


/*******************************************************************************
            Name: CstFileViewParseBuf
      Parameters: lpFV - pointer to file view struct
                  wBufSize - size of buffer to parse
     Description: parses the lines of a buffer by setting pointers to each line
                  in the buffer and saving the length of each line
*******************************************************************************/
static WORD CstFileViewParseBuf( LPFILEVIEW lpFV, WORD wBufSize )
    {

    int iLineNum, iLineLen, iCharLastSpace;
    WORD wCharTotal;
    LPSTR lpstrLoc, lpstrLastSpace;

    lpFV->fvBuf[lpFV->iCurBuf].iNumLines = FV_MAXLINESPERBUF;
    lpFV->iMaxLineLen = 0;

    /* Loop through the buffer setting the line pointers and line lengths */
    for ( iLineNum = 0, wCharTotal = 0, lpstrLoc = lpFV->lpstrBuf;
            iLineNum < FV_MAXLINESPERBUF; iLineNum++ )
        {

        lpFV->fvLine[iLineNum].lpstrLine = lpstrLoc;
        iLineLen = 0;
        iCharLastSpace = 0;
        lpstrLastSpace = NULL;

        while ( *lpstrLoc != 13 )
            {

            if ( *lpstrLoc == ' ' )
                {
                iCharLastSpace = iLineLen;
                lpstrLastSpace = lpstrLoc;
                }
```

Listing 8.2 *continued*

```
            if ( iLineLen > lpFV->iWrapLineLen )
                {
                /* Move back to the last space */
                if ( lpstrLastSpace )
                    {
                    lpstrLoc = lpstrLastSpace;
                    wCharTotal -= (WORD)( iLineLen - iCharLastSpace );
                    iLineLen = iCharLastSpace;
                    wCharTotal++;
                    iLineLen++;
                    lpstrLoc++;
                    }
                break;
                }
            iLineLen++;
            lpstrLoc++;
            wCharTotal++;
            if ( wCharTotal == FV_MAXBUFSIZE || wCharTotal == wBufSize )
                {
                /* Terminate the loop */
                lpFV->fvLine[iLineNum].iLineLen = iLineLen;
                lpFV->fvBuf[lpFV->iCurBuf].iNumLines = iLineNum + 1;
                return ( wCharTotal );
                }
            }   /* while *lpstrLoc */

        lpFV->fvLine[iLineNum].iLineLen = iLineLen;
        lpFV->iMaxLineLen = max( lpFV->iMaxLineLen, iLineLen );
        if ( *lpstrLoc == 13 )
            {
            lpstrLoc++;
            wCharTotal++;
            if ( wCharTotal == FV_MAXBUFSIZE || wCharTotal == wBufSize )
                {
                /* Terminate the loop */
                lpFV->fvLine[iLineNum].iLineLen = iLineLen;
                lpFV->fvBuf[lpFV->iCurBuf].iNumLines = iLineNum + 1;
                return ( wCharTotal );
                }
            }
        if ( *lpstrLoc == 10 )
            {
            /* Move past the line feed */
            lpstrLoc++;
            wCharTotal++;
            if ( wCharTotal == FV_MAXBUFSIZE || wCharTotal == wBufSize )
                {
                /* Terminate the loop */
                lpFV->fvLine[iLineNum].iLineLen = iLineLen;
                lpFV->fvBuf[lpFV->iCurBuf].iNumLines = iLineNum + 1;
                return ( wCharTotal );
                }
            }

        }   /* for iLineNum */

    return ( wCharTotal );

    }   /* function CstFileViewParseBuf */
```

Listing 8.2 *continued*

```
/******************************************************************************
        Name: CstFileViewLoadFile
  Parameters: hWnd - handle to file view window
              lpstrFileName - name of the file to load
      Return: TRUE if file loaded, FALSE if not loaded
 Description: loads a file by counting the number of lines in the file
              and setting up information for each buffer in the file
******************************************************************************/
static int CstFileViewLoadFile( HWND hWnd, LPSTR lpstrFileName, int Create )
    {

    int iBufNum;
    /* int hf; */
    LONG lFileSize, lFileSizeCalc = 0;
    LPFILEVIEW lpFV;
    WORD wBufSize;

    lpFV = (LPFILEVIEW)CSTGETWINDOWLONG( hWnd, GWL_LPFILEVIEW );

    /* If a file is already loaded - dump the file */
    if ( lpFV )
        {
        CstFileViewClearFile( hWnd );
        }

    lpFV = CstFileViewCreateData( hWnd );

    if ( !lpFV )
        {
        return ( FALSE );
        }

    /* See if the file can be opened and if it exists */
    if ( Create < 0 )
        {
        /* Force the creation */
        Create = TRUE;
        lpFV->hf = OpenFile( lpstrFileName, &( lpFV->of ), OF_CREATE );
        _lclose( lpFV->hf );
        }
    lpFV->hf = OpenFile( lpstrFileName, &( lpFV->of ), OF_READWRITE );
    if ( lpFV->hf < 0 )
        {
        if ( Create )
            {
            lpFV->hf = OpenFile( lpstrFileName, &( lpFV->of ), OF_CREATE );
            }
        if ( lpFV->hf < 0 )
            {
            CstFileViewClearFile( hWnd );
            return ( FALSE );
            }
        else
            {
            _lclose( lpFV->hf );
            lpFV->hf = OpenFile( lpstrFileName, &( lpFV->of ), OF_READWRITE );
            }
        }  /* if ( lpFV->hf < 0 ) */
```

Listing 8.2 *continued*

```c
    /* Get the size of the file */
    lFileSize = filelength( lpFV->hf );
    /* _lclose( lpFV->hf ); */

    /* Load the caption text with the file name */
    SetWindowText( hWnd, lpstrFileName );

    /* Read in the file, get the total number of lines
    ** set the buffers */
    lpFV->lNumLines = 0L;
    for ( iBufNum = 0; iBufNum < FV_MAXBUFS; iBufNum++ )
        {
        wBufSize = CstFileViewLoadBuf( lpFV, iBufNum );
        lpFV->lNumLines += (LONG)lpFV->fvBuf[iBufNum].iNumLines;
        if ( !wBufSize )
            {
            lpFV->iNumBufs = iBufNum;
            break;
            }
        lFileSizeCalc += (LONG)wBufSize;
        if ( lFileSizeCalc >= lFileSize )
            {
            lpFV->iNumBufs = iBufNum + 1;
            break;
            }
        if ( iBufNum + 1 < FV_MAXBUFS )
            {
            lpFV->fvBuf[iBufNum + 1].lFilePos =
                    lpFV->fvBuf[iBufNum].lFilePos + wBufSize;
            }
        }

    /* Re-read the first file buffer if needed */
    if ( lpFV->iNumBufs > 1 )
        {
        CstFileViewLoadBuf( lpFV, 0 );
        }

    CstFileViewInitScrl( hWnd, lpFV );

    return ( TRUE );

    }   /* function CstFileViewLoadFile */

/*****************************************************************************
        Name: CstFileViewRegister
  Parameters: hInstance - handle to program or library registering class
      Return: Number of register counts or 0 if failure
 Description: Registers the window class for the custom file view control
*****************************************************************************/
int FAR PASCAL CstFileViewRegister( HINSTANCE hInstance )
    {

    WNDCLASS WndClass;

    WndClass.style = CS_DBLCLKS;
```

Listing 8.2 *continued*

```c
#if defined ( _WINDLL )
hInstance = _hInstanceCstCtls;
WndClass.style |= CS_GLOBALCLASS;
#endif

WndClass.lpfnWndProc = CstFileViewWndFn;
WndClass.cbClsExtra = CFV_CLSEXTRA;
WndClass.cbWndExtra = CFV_WNDEXTRA;
WndClass.hInstance = hInstance;
WndClass.hIcon = LoadIcon( hInstance, "CstFileView" );
WndClass.hCursor = LoadCursor( 0, IDC_ARROW );
WndClass.hbrBackground = COLOR_WINDOW + 1;
WndClass.lpszMenuName = 0;
WndClass.lpszClassName = "CstFileView";

return ( RegisterClass( &WndClass ) );

}   /* function CstFileViewRegister */


/*****************************************************************************
       Name: CstFileViewUnregister
 Parameters: hInstance - handle to program or library that registered class
     Return: Number of remaining register counts
Description: Unregisters the window class for the custom Check Box control
*****************************************************************************/
int FAR PASCAL CstFileViewUnregister( HINSTANCE hInstance )
    {

    #if defined ( _WINDLL )
    hInstance = _hInstanceCstCtls;
    #endif

    return ( UnregisterClass( "CstFileView", hInstance ) );

    }   /* function CstFileViewUnregister */



/*****************************************************************************
       Name: CstFileViewWndFn
Description: Window call back function for custom file view control
*****************************************************************************/
LONG FAR PASCAL CstFileViewWndFn( HWND hWnd, UINT wMessage, WPARAM wParam,
        LPARAM lParam )
    {

    static int _WindowCount = 0;

    LPSCRL lpScrl = NULL;
    LPFILEVIEW lpFV = NULL;

    lpFV = (LPFILEVIEW)CSTGETWINDOWLONG( hWnd, GWL_LPFILEVIEW );
    if ( lpFV )
        {
        lpScrl = (LPSCRL)&lpFV->scrl;
        }
```

Listing 8.2 *continued*

```
switch ( wMessage )
    {
    case CFVM_APPENDLINE:
        CstFileViewAppendLine( hWnd, (LPSTR)lParam );
        break;
    case CFVM_CLEARFILE:
        CstFileViewClearFile( hWnd );
        break;
    case CFVM_LOADFILE:
        CstFileViewLoadFile( hWnd, (LPSTR)lParam, wParam );
        break;
    case CFVM_GETNUMTABS:
        if ( lpFV )
            {
            return ( (LONG)lpFV->iNumTabPos );
            }
        return ( 0L );
    case CFVM_SETNUMTABS:
        if ( lpFV )
            {

            int iNumTabsOld = lpFV->iNumTabPos;

            lpFV->iNumTabPos = min( (int)wParam, FV_MAXNUMTABS );
            return ( (LONG)iNumTabsOld );
            }
        return ( 0L );
    case CFVM_GETTABPOS:
        if ( lpFV )
            {
            return ( (LONG)lpFV->iTabPos );
            }
        return ( 0L );
    case CFVM_SETTABPOS:
        if ( lpFV )
            {

            int i, FAR *iTabPos = (int FAR *)lParam;

            for ( i = 0; i < lpFV->iNumTabPos; i++ )
                {
                lpFV->iTabPos[i] = iTabPos[i];
                }
            return ( (LONG)lpFV->iTabPos   );
            }
        return ( 0L );
    case CFVM_GETWRAPLINELEN:
        if ( lpFV )
            {
            return ( (LONG)lpFV->iWrapLineLen );
            }
        return ( 0L );
    case CFVM_SETWRAPLINELEN:
        CstCtlSetFrame( hWnd, (int)wParam );
        if ( lpFV )
            {

            int iTextLen;
```

Listing 8.2 *continued*

```
                    iTextLen = GetWindowTextLength( hWnd );
                    if ( iTextLen )
                        {

                        HANDLE hText;

                        hText = GlobalAlloc( GMEM_FLAGS,
                                (DWORD)( iTextLen + 1 ) );
                        if ( hText )
                            {

                            LPSTR lpstrFileName;

                            lpstrFileName = GlobalLock( hText );
                            if ( lpstrFileName )
                                {
                                CstFileViewLoadFile( hWnd, lpstrFileName, FALSE );
                                }
                            }
                        }
                    }   /* if lpFV */
        case WM_CREATE:
            {

            HWND hWndParent;
            int iTextLen;

            if ( !_WindowCount )
                {
                if ( !CstFileViewDefDataCreate( hWnd ) )
                    {
                    return ( -1 );
                    }
                }
            _WindowCount++;

            CstCtlDataCreate( hWnd );

            iTextLen = GetWindowTextLength( hWnd );
            if ( iTextLen )
                {

                HANDLE hText;

                hText = GlobalAlloc( GMEM_FLAGS,
                        (DWORD)( iTextLen + 1 ) );
                if ( hText )
                    {

                    LPSTR lpstrFileName = GlobalLock( hText );

                    if ( lpstrFileName )
                        {
                        GetWindowText( hWnd,
                                lpstrFileName, iTextLen + 1 );
                        CstFileViewLoadFile( hWnd,
                                lpstrFileName, TRUE );
                        }
                    GlobalUnlock( hText );
```

Listing 8.2 *continued*

```
            GlobalFree( hText );
            }
        }   /* if ( iTextLen ) */

    hWndParent = GetParent( hWnd );
    if ( hWndParent )
        {
        /* Notify the parent that the window has been created */
        SendMessage( hWndParent, WM_PARENTNOTIFY, WM_CREATE,
                MAKELPARAM( hWnd, GetDlgCtrlID( hWnd ) ) );
        }
    break;
    }   /* case WM_CREATE */
case WM_CSTCTLGETDATA:
case WM_CSTCTLGETDEFDATA:
case WM_CSTCTLSETDATA:
case WM_CSTCTLSETDEFDATA:
    return ( (LONG)CstCtlData( hWnd, wMessage, wParam, lParam ) );
case WM_DESTROY:
    {

    HWND hWndParent = GetParent( hWnd );

    /* Notify the parent and then delete the instance data */
    if ( hWndParent )
        {
        SendMessage( hWndParent, WM_PARENTNOTIFY,
                WM_DESTROY, MAKELPARAM( hWnd,
                GetDlgCtrlID( hWnd ) ) );
        }
    if ( IsWindow( hWnd ) )
        {
        CstFileViewClearFile( hWnd );
        CstCtlDataDelete( hWnd );
        }

    _WindowCount--;
    if ( _WindowCount <= 0 )
        {
        CstFileViewDefDataDelete();
        }

    break;
    }   /* case WM_DESTROY */
case WM_GETDLGCODE:
    return ( DLGC_WANTALLKEYS );
case WM_HSCROLL:
    {

    int HscrollInc;

    if ( lpScrl == NULL )
        {
        break;
        }

    switch ( wParam )
        {
        case SB_TOP:
```

Listing 8.2 continued

```
                HscrollInc = -lpScrl->iHorzPos;
                break;
            case SB_BOTTOM:
                HscrollInc = lpScrl->iHorzMax - lpScrl->iHorzPos;
                break;
            case SB_LINEUP:
                HscrollInc = -1;
                break;
            case SB_LINEDOWN:
                HscrollInc = 1;
                break;
            case SB_PAGEUP:
                HscrollInc = -8;
                break;
            case SB_PAGEDOWN:
                HscrollInc = 8;
                break;
            case SB_THUMBTRACK:
                HscrollInc = (int)LOWORD( lParam ) - lpScrl->iHorzPos;
                break;
            default:
                HscrollInc = 0;
                break;
            }   /* switch wParam */
        if ( ( HscrollInc = max( -lpScrl->iHorzPos, min( HscrollInc,
                ( lpScrl->iHorzMax - lpScrl->iHorzPos ) ) ) ) != 0 )
            {
            lpScrl->iHorzPos += HscrollInc;
            ScrollWindow( hWnd, -lpScrl->iWidthChar *
                    HscrollInc, 0, NULL, NULL );
            SetScrollPos( hWnd, SB_HORZ,
                    lpScrl->iHorzPos, TRUE );
            if ( CSTCTLGETSTATE( hWnd ) )
                {
                if ( lpFV->iNumTabPos >= 0 )
                    {
                    InvalidateRect( hWnd, NULL, TRUE );
                    }
                UpdateWindow( hWnd );
                }
            }   /* if HscrollInc */
        break;
        }   /* case WM_HSCROLL */
    case WM_KEYDOWN:
        {
        switch ( wParam )
            {
            case VK_HOME:
                if ( GetKeyState( VK_CONTROL ) < 0 )
                    {
                    SendMessage( hWnd, WM_VSCROLL, SB_TOP, 0 );
                    SendMessage( hWnd, WM_HSCROLL, SB_TOP, 0 );
                    }
                else
                    {
                    SendMessage( hWnd, WM_HSCROLL, SB_TOP, 0 );
                    }
                break;
            case VK_END:
```

Listing 8.2 *continued*

```
        if ( GetKeyState( VK_CONTROL ) < 0 )
            {
            SendMessage( hWnd, WM_VSCROLL, SB_BOTTOM, 0 );
            SendMessage( hWnd, WM_HSCROLL, SB_BOTTOM, 0 );
            }
        else
            {
            SendMessage( hWnd, WM_HSCROLL, SB_BOTTOM, 0 );
            }
        break;
    case VK_PRIOR: /* Page up */
        if ( GetKeyState( VK_CONTROL ) < 0 )
            {
            SendMessage( hWnd, WM_VSCROLL, SB_TOP, 0 );
            }
        else
            {
            SendMessage( hWnd, WM_VSCROLL, SB_PAGEUP, 0 );
            }
        break;
    case VK_NEXT: /* Page down */
        if ( GetKeyState( VK_CONTROL ) < 0 )
            {
            SendMessage( hWnd, WM_VSCROLL, SB_BOTTOM, 0 );
            }
        else
            {
            SendMessage( hWnd, WM_VSCROLL, SB_PAGEDOWN, 0 );
            }
        break;
    case VK_UP: /* Up arrow */
        SendMessage( hWnd, WM_VSCROLL, SB_LINEUP, 0 );
        break;
    case VK_DOWN: /* Down arrow */
        SendMessage( hWnd, WM_VSCROLL, SB_LINEDOWN, 0 );
        break;
    case VK_LEFT: /* Left arrow */
        if ( GetKeyState( VK_CONTROL ) < 0 )
            {
            SendMessage( hWnd, WM_HSCROLL, SB_PAGEUP, 0 );
            }
        else
            {
            SendMessage( hWnd, WM_HSCROLL, SB_LINEUP, 0 );
            }
        break;
    case VK_RIGHT: /* Right arrow */
        if ( GetKeyState( VK_CONTROL ) < 0 )
            {
            SendMessage( hWnd, WM_HSCROLL, SB_PAGEDOWN, 0 );
            }
        else
            {
            SendMessage( hWnd, WM_HSCROLL, SB_LINEDOWN, 0 );
            }
        break;
default:
    break;
    } /* switch wParam */
```

Listing 8.2 *continued*

```
        return ( 0L );

        }   /* case WM_KEYDOWN */
case WM_PAINT:
    {

    PAINTSTRUCT Ps;
    HDC hDC = BeginPaint( hWnd, &Ps );

    if ( IsWindowVisible( hWnd ) )
        {
        if ( !IsIconic( hWnd ) )
            {
            if ( CSTCTLGETSTATE( hWnd ) )
                {
                /* Only paint if needed */
                CstFileViewDraw( hWnd, hDC, &Ps, lpFV );
                }
            }
        }
    EndPaint( hWnd, &Ps );
    break;
    }
case WM_SETFONT:
    if ( wParam )
        {
        CstCtlSetFont( hWnd, wParam );
        CstFileViewInitScrl( hWnd, lpFV );
        }
    if ( lParam )
        {
        /* Send a Paint message */
        if ( CSTCTLGETSTATE( hWnd ) )
            {
            InvalidateRect( hWnd, NULL, TRUE );
            UpdateWindow( hWnd );
            }
        }
    break;
case WM_SETREDRAW:
    {

    WORD wState;

    wState = CstCtlSetState( hWnd, (WORD)wParam );
    if ( wParam && !wState )
        {
        InvalidateRect( hWnd, NULL, TRUE );
        UpdateWindow( hWnd );
        }
    break;
    }
case WM_SIZE:
    {

    int iOldY;
    int iOldX;
```

Listing 8.2 *continued*

```c
            if ( lpScrl == NULL )
                {
                break;
                }
            iOldY = lpScrl->iClientY;
            iOldX = lpScrl->iClientX;
            lpScrl->iClientY = (int)HIWORD( lParam );
            lpScrl->iClientX = (int)LOWORD( lParam );
            if ( lpFV )
                {
                lpScrl->lVertMax = max( 0L, lpFV->lNumLines + 2L -
                        (LONG)( lpScrl->iClientY / lpScrl->iHeightChar ) );
                if ( lpScrl->lVertMax > FV_MAXVERTSCRL )
                    {
                    lpScrl->iVertMax = FV_MAXVERTSCRL;
                    }
                else
                    {
                    lpScrl->iVertMax = max( 0, (int)lpFV->lNumLines +
                            2 - ( lpScrl->iClientY /
                            lpScrl->iHeightChar ) );
                    }
                if ( ( lpScrl->iVertMax == 0 ) || ( lpScrl->lVertMax == 0 ) )
                    {
                    lpScrl->lVertToiVert = 1L;
                    }
                else
                    {
                    lpScrl->lVertToiVert = lpScrl->lVertMax /
                            (LONG)lpScrl->iVertMax;
                    }
                lpScrl->iHorzMax = max( 0, (int)lpFV->iMaxLineLen +
                        2 - ( lpScrl->iClientX / lpScrl->iWidthChar ) );
                }   /* if lpFV */
            lpScrl->lVertToiVert = max( 1L, lpScrl->lVertToiVert );
            lpScrl->lVertPos = min( lpScrl->lVertPos, lpScrl->lVertMax );
            lpScrl->iVertPos = (int)( lpScrl->lVertPos /
                    lpScrl->lVertToiVert );
            if ( lpScrl->iVertPos < 0 )
                {
                lpScrl->iVertPos = FV_MAXVERTSCRL;
                }
            lpScrl->iHorzPos = min( lpScrl->iHorzPos, lpScrl->iHorzMax );
            SetScrollRange( hWnd, SB_VERT, 0, lpScrl->iVertMax, FALSE );
            SetScrollPos( hWnd, SB_VERT, lpScrl->iVertPos, TRUE );
            SetScrollRange( hWnd, SB_HORZ, 0, lpScrl->iHorzMax, FALSE );
            SetScrollPos( hWnd, SB_HORZ, lpScrl->iHorzPos, TRUE );
            if ( CSTCTLGETSTATE( hWnd ) )
                {
                if ( ( ( iOldY < lpScrl->iClientY ) &&
                        ( lpScrl->lVertPos == lpScrl->lVertMax ) ) ||
                        ( ( iOldX < lpScrl->iClientX ) &&
                        ( lpScrl->iHorzPos == lpScrl->iHorzMax ) ) )
                    {
                    InvalidateRect( hWnd, NULL, TRUE );
                    UpdateWindow( hWnd );
                    }
                }
            break;
```

Listing 8.2 continued

```
        }   /* case WM_SIZE */
case WM_VSCROLL:
    {

    LONG VscrollInc;

    if ( lpScrl == NULL )
        {
        break;
        }
    switch ( wParam )
        {
        case SB_TOP:
            VscrollInc = -lpScrl->lVertPos;
            break;
        case SB_BOTTOM:
            VscrollInc = lpScrl->lVertMax - lpScrl->lVertPos;
            break;
        case SB_LINEUP:
            VscrollInc = -1;
            break;
        case SB_LINEDOWN:
            VscrollInc = 1;
            break;
        case SB_PAGEUP:
            VscrollInc = min( -1,
                    -lpScrl->iClientY / lpScrl->iHeightChar );
            break;
        case SB_PAGEDOWN:
            VscrollInc = max( 1,
                    lpScrl->iClientY / lpScrl->iHeightChar );
            break;
        case SB_THUMBTRACK:
            VscrollInc = lpScrl->lVertToiVert * (LONG)
                    ( (int)LOWORD( lParam ) - lpScrl->iVertPos );
            break;
        default:
            VscrollInc = 0;
        }   /* switch wParam */
    if ( ( VscrollInc = max( -lpScrl->lVertPos, min( VscrollInc,
            ( lpScrl->lVertMax - lpScrl->lVertPos ) ) ) != 0 )
        {
        lpScrl->lVertPos += VscrollInc;
        lpScrl->iVertPos =
                (int)( lpScrl->lVertPos / lpScrl->lVertToiVert );
        if ( lpScrl->iVertPos < 0 )
            {
            lpScrl->iVertPos = FV_MAXVERTSCRL;
            }
        if ( ( VscrollInc > (LONG)FV_MAXVERTSCRL ) ||
                ( VscrollInc < -(LONG)FV_MAXVERTSCRL ) )
            {
            VscrollInc /= lpScrl->lVertToiVert;
            }
        ScrollWindow( hWnd, 0, -lpScrl->iHeightChar *
                (int)VscrollInc, NULL, NULL );
        SetScrollPos( hWnd, SB_VERT,
                lpScrl->iVertPos, TRUE );
        if ( CSTCTLGETSTATE( hWnd ) )
```

Listing 8.2 *continued*

```
                {
                UpdateWindow( hWnd );
                }
            }    /* if VscrollInc */
        break;
        }    /* case WM_VSCROLL */
    default:
        return ( DefWindowProc( hWnd, wMessage, wParam, lParam ) );
    }   /* switch wMessage */

    return ( 0L );

    }   /* function CstFileViewWndFn */

/* End of CST_FLVW.C */
```

Listing 8.3

```
/*****************************************************************************
            File Name: CST_FLVW.RC
        Expanded Name: Custom File View
          Description: Resource file for the file view custom control
          Portability: Microsoft Windows 3.X
*****************************************************************************/

CSTFILEVIEW ICON ICON\CST_FLVW.ICO

/* End of CST_FLVW.RC */
```

Listing 8.4

```
/*****************************************************************************
         File Name: DEM_FLVW.H
     Expanded Name: Demo File View
       Description: Include file for DEM_FLVW.C & DEM_FLVW.RC
       Portability: Microsoft Windows 3.X
*****************************************************************************/

#define IDM_VIEW 101
#define IDM_APPEND 102
#define IDM_CLEAR 103
#define IDM_DIALOG 104
#define IDM_EXIT 105

/* End of DEM_FLVW.H */
```

Listing 8.5

```
/******************************************************************************
         File Name: DEM_FLVW.C
     Expanded Name: Demo File View
       Description: Demo of custom file view control, CSTFILEVIEW
      Program List: DEM_FLVW.C
                    DEM_FLVW.RC
                    DEM_FLVW.DEF
                    CST_DATA.C
                    CST_FLVW.C
                    CST_UTIL.C
                    CST_XTRA.C
                    or
                    DEM_FLVW.C
                    DEM_FLVW.RC
                    DEM_FLVW.DEF
                    CST_CTLS.LIB,DLL
Global Function List: WinMain
       Portability: Microsoft Windows 3.X
******************************************************************************/

/* Microsoft Windows */
#include <windows.h>

/* Types and prototypes */
#include <cst_flvw.h>

/* Own */
#include <dem_flvw.h>

BOOL PASCAL DemoDialog( HINSTANCE hInstance, HWND hWndParent,
        LPSTR DialogName );
BOOL FAR PASCAL FileViewDemoDialogProc( HWND hDlg, UINT wMessage,
        WPARAM wParam, LPARAM lParam );
LONG FAR PASCAL MainWindowProc( HWND hwnd, UINT wMessage,
        WPARAM wParam, LPARAM lParam );

/******************************************************************************
         Name: WinMain
  Description: Main Window function
******************************************************************************/
int PASCAL WinMain( HINSTANCE hInstance, HINSTANCE hPrevInstance,
        LPSTR lpCmdLine, int nCmdShow )
    {

    HWND hWnd;
    HWND hWndFileView;
    MSG Msg;
    static char _Name[] = "DEM_FLVW";
    WNDCLASS WndClass;

    lpCmdLine = lpCmdLine;
    nCmdShow = nCmdShow;

    #if defined ( NO_DLL )
    CstFileViewRegister( hInstance );
    #endif

    if ( !hPrevInstance )
        {
```

Listing 8.5 *continued*

```
        WndClass.style = 0;
        WndClass.lpfnWndProc = MainWindowProc;
        WndClass.cbClsExtra = 0;
        WndClass.cbWndExtra = 0;
        WndClass.hInstance = hInstance;
        WndClass.hIcon = LoadIcon( hInstance, _Name );
        WndClass.hCursor = LoadCursor( NULL, IDC_ARROW );
        WndClass.hbrBackground = COLOR_WINDOW + 1;
        WndClass.lpszMenuName = _Name;
        WndClass.lpszClassName = _Name;
        RegisterClass( &WndClass );
        }
    else
        {
        hWnd = FindWindow( _Name, NULL );
        if ( hWnd )
            {
            BringWindowToTop( hWnd );
            }
        return ( FALSE );
        }


    if ( lpCmdLine && *lpCmdLine )
        {

        hWndFileView = CstFileViewCreateWindow( WS_OVERLAPPEDWINDOW,
                CW_USEDEFAULT, CW_USEDEFAULT, CW_USEDEFAULT, CW_USEDEFAULT,
                NULL, hInstance, lpCmdLine );
        ShowWindow( hWndFileView, SW_SHOW );
        UpdateWindow( hWndFileView );

        }

    hWnd = CreateWindow( _Name, "Custom File View  Control Demo",
            WS_OVERLAPPEDWINDOW, CW_USEDEFAULT, CW_USEDEFAULT,
            CW_USEDEFAULT, CW_USEDEFAULT, NULL, NULL, hInstance, NULL );

    ShowWindow( hWnd, nCmdShow );
    UpdateWindow( hWnd );

    while ( GetMessage( &Msg, NULL, 0, 0 ) )
        {
        TranslateMessage( &Msg );
        DispatchMessage ( &Msg );
        }


    if ( IsWindow( hWndFileView ) )
        {
        DestroyWindow( hWndFileView );
        }

    return ( 0 );

    }   /* WinMain */
```

Listing 8.5 continued

```
/*************************************************************************
         Name: MainWindowProc
  Description: Window procedure for main window
*************************************************************************/
LONG FAR PASCAL MainWindowProc( HWND hWnd, UINT wMessage,
        WPARAM wParam, LPARAM lParam )
    {

    static HWND hWndView, hWndAppend;

    switch( wMessage )
        {
        case WM_COMMAND:
            {

            HINSTANCE hInstance;

            hInstance = (HINSTANCE)GetWindowWord( hWnd, GWW_HINSTANCE );

            switch( wParam )
                {
                case IDM_VIEW:
                    if ( !IsWindow( hWndView ) )
                        {
                        hWndView = CstFileViewCreateWindow(
                                WS_CHILD | WS_CAPTION | WS_THICKFRAME |
                                WS_MINIMIZEBOX | WS_MAXIMIZEBOX,
                                CW_USEDEFAULT, CW_USEDEFAULT,
                                CW_USEDEFAULT,   CW_USEDEFAULT,
                                hWnd, hInstance, "CST_FLVW.C" );
                        ShowWindow( hWndView, SW_SHOW );
                        UpdateWindow( hWndView );
                        }
                    else
                        {
                        DestroyWindow( hWndView );
                        hWndView = (HWND)0;
                        }
                    break;
                case IDM_APPEND:
                    {

                    int i;
                    char Buf[64];

                    if ( !IsWindow ( hWndAppend ) )
                        {
                        hWndAppend = CstFileViewCreateWindow(
                                WS_OVERLAPPEDWINDOW,
                                CW_USEDEFAULT, CW_USEDEFAULT,
                                CW_USEDEFAULT,   CW_USEDEFAULT,
                                hWnd, hInstance, "DEM_FLVW.APD" );
                        ShowWindow( hWndAppend, SW_SHOW );
                        UpdateWindow( hWndAppend );
                        }

                    BringWindowToTop( hWndAppend );
                    SendMessage( hWndAppend, WM_SETREDRAW, FALSE, 0L );
```

Listing 8.5 continued

```c
                    for ( i = 1; i <= 100; i++ )
                        {
                        wsprintf( Buf, "This is line number %d\n", i );
                        SendMessage( hWndAppend, CFVM_APPENDLINE, 0,
                                (LPARAM)(LPSTR)Buf );
                        }
                    SendMessage( hWndAppend, WM_VSCROLL, SB_BOTTOM, 0L );
                    SendMessage( hWndAppend, WM_SETREDRAW, TRUE, 0L );

                    break;
                    }   /* case IDM_APPEND */
                case IDM_CLEAR:
                    {

                    if ( IsWindow( hWndAppend ) )
                        {
                        SendMessage( hWndAppend, CFVM_CLEARFILE, 0, 0L );
                        SendMessage( hWndAppend, CFVM_LOADFILE, (WPARAM)-1,
                                (LPARAM)(LPSTR)"DEM_FLVW.APD" );
                        }

                    break;


                    }   /* case IDM_CLEAR */
                case IDM_DIALOG:
                    {
                    DemoDialog( hInstance, hWnd, "FILEVIEW" );
                    break;
                    }
                case IDM_EXIT:
                    if ( IsWindow( hWndView ) )
                        {
                        DestroyWindow( hWndView );
                        }
                    if ( IsWindow( hWndAppend ) )
                        {
                        DestroyWindow( hWndAppend );
                        }
                    DestroyWindow( hWnd );
                    break;
                default:
                    break;
                }
            return ( FALSE );
            }
        case WM_DESTROY:
            PostQuitMessage( 0 );
            return ( FALSE );
        default:
            break;
        }

    return ( DefWindowProc( hWnd, wMessage, wParam, lParam ) );

    }   /* function MainWindowProc */
```

Windows Custom Controls

Listing 8.5 *continued*

```
/********************************************************************
        Name: DemoDialog
  Description: Function for invoking dialog boxes
********************************************************************/
BOOL PASCAL DemoDialog( HINSTANCE hInstance, HWND hWndParent, LPSTR DialogName )
    {

    BOOL bStatus;
    FARPROC lpfnProc;

    lpfnProc = MakeProcInstance( FileViewDemoDialogProc, hInstance );
    bStatus = DialogBox( hInstance, DialogName, hWndParent, lpfnProc );
    FreeProcInstance( lpfnProc );

    return ( bStatus );

    }   /* function DemoDialog */


/********************************************************************
        Name: FileViewDemoDialogProc
  Description: Dialog call back function for custom FileView control demo
********************************************************************/
BOOL FAR PASCAL FileViewDemoDialogProc( HWND hDlg, UINT wMessage,
        WPARAM wParam, LPARAM lParam )
    {

    lParam = lParam;

    switch( wMessage )
        {
        case WM_INITDIALOG:
            return ( TRUE );
        case WM_CLOSE:
            EndDialog( hDlg, 0 );
            return ( FALSE );
        case WM_COMMAND:
            switch ( wParam )
                {
                case IDOK:
                    EndDialog( hDlg, 0 );
                    return ( TRUE );
                default:
                    break;
                }
            return ( TRUE );
        default:
            break;
        }   /* switch wMessage */

    return ( FALSE );

    }   /* function FileViewDemoDialogProc */


/* End of DEM_FLVW.C */
```

Listing 8.6

```
/*****************************************************************************
          File Name: DEM_FLVW.RC
      Expanded Name: Demo File View
        Description: Resource file for custom file view control demo
        Portability: Microsoft Windows 3.X
*****************************************************************************/

#include <windows.h>
#include <dem_flvw.h>

DEM_FLVW ICON ICON\CST_CTLS.ICO

DEM_FLVW MENU
BEGIN
    POPUP "&Demo"
    BEGIN
        MENUITEM "View CST_FLVW.C in Child Window", IDM_VIEW
        MENUITEM "Append 100 Lines to DEM_FLVW.APD in Popup Window", IDM_APPEND
        MENUITEM "Clear DEM_FLVW.APD", IDM_CLEAR
        MENUITEM "View DEM_FLVW.APD in Dialog Control", IDM_DIALOG
        MENUITEM SEPARATOR
        MENUITEM "E&xit", IDM_EXIT
    END
END

FILEVIEW DIALOG 10, 10, 300, 210
CAPTION "File View Control in Dialog"
STYLE DS_MODALFRAME | WS_CAPTION | WS_SYSMENU
FONT 8, "Helv"
BEGIN
    CONTROL "DEM_FLVW.APD", 100, "CstFileView", WS_TABSTOP | WS_CHILD |
            WS_BORDER | WS_VSCROLL | WS_HSCROLL, 20, 20, 260, 150
    CONTROL "&Ok", IDOK, "button",   WS_TABSTOP | BS_DEFPUSHBUTTON,
                                     130, 190, 40, 16
END

#if defined ( NO_DLL )
#include <cst_flvw.rc>
#endif

/* End of DEM_FLVW.RC */
```

Listing 8.7

```
NAME DEM_FLVW
DESCRIPTION 'Custom File View Control Demo Program'
EXETYPE WINDOWS
CODE PRELOAD MOVEABLE
DATA PRELOAD MOVABLE MULTIPLE
HEAPSIZE 1024
STACKSIZE  16384
EXPORTS
      MainWindowProc
      FileViewDemoDialogProc
      CstFileViewWndFn
```

Listing 8.8

```
ORIGIN     = QCWIN
ORIGIN_VER = 1.00

PROJ =DEM_FLVW
DEBUG    =0
PROGTYPE =1
CALLER   =
ARGS =dem_flvw.c
DLLS =
CVPACK   =1
CC  =cl -qc
RC  =rc
CFLAGS_G_WEXE =/AS /W4 /Ze /D_WINDOWS /DNO_DLL /G2w /Zp /Aw
CFLAGS_D_WEXE =/Zi /Od
CFLAGS_R_WEXE =/O /Os /Gs /DNDEBUG
CFLAGS_G_WDLL =/AS /G2w /Zp /Aw /W3 /D_WINDOWS /D_WINDLL
CFLAGS_D_WDLL =/Gi /Od /Zi
CFLAGS_R_WDLL =/O /Os /DNDEBUG
CFLAGS_G_WTTY =/AS /G2w /W3 /D_WINDOWS
CFLAGS_D_WTTY =/Gi /Od /Zi
CFLAGS_R_WTTY =/O /Os /DNDEBUG
CFLAGS_G_DEXE =/AS /W2
CFLAGS_D_DEXE =/Gi /Od /Zi
CFLAGS_R_DEXE =/O /Ot /DNDEBUG
CFLAGS   =$(CFLAGS_G_WEXE) $(CFLAGS_R_WEXE)
LFLAGS_G_WEXE =/NOE/A:16/ST:16384
LFLAGS_D_WEXE =/CO
LFLAGS_R_WEXE =
LFLAGS_G_WDLL =/ST:5120 /A:16
LFLAGS_D_WDLL =/CO
LFLAGS_R_WDLL =
LFLAGS_G_WTTY =/ST:5120 /A:16
LFLAGS_D_WTTY =/CO
LFLAGS_R_WTTY =
LFLAGS_G_DEXE =/NOI /ST:2048
LFLAGS_D_DEXE =/CO
LFLAGS_R_DEXE =
LFLAGS   =$(LFLAGS_G_WEXE) $(LFLAGS_R_WEXE)
RCFLAGS  =/DNO_DLL
RESFLAGS =
RUNFLAGS =
DEFFILE =     DEMSFLVW.DEF
OBJS_EXT =
LIBS_EXT =

.rc.res: ; $(RC) $(RCFLAGS) -r $*.rc

all: $(PROJ).EXE

DEM_FLVW.OBJ: DEM_FLVW.C $(H)

DEM_FLVW.RES: DEM_FLVW.RC $(RESFILES) $(H)

CST_DATA.OBJ: CST_DATA.C $(H)

CST_FLVW.OBJ: CST_FLVW.C $(H)

CST_UTIL.OBJ: CST_UTIL.C $(H)
```

Listing 8.8 continued

```
$(PROJ).EXE: DEM_FLVW.OBJ CST_DATA.OBJ CST_FLVW.OBJ CST_UTIL.OBJ $(OBJS_EXT) $(DEFFILE)
    echo >NUL @<<$(PROJ).CRF
DEM_FLVW.OBJ +
CST_DATA.OBJ +
CST_FLVW.OBJ +
CST_UTIL.OBJ +
$(OBJS_EXT)
$(PROJ).EXE

C:\PRGLNG\QCW\LIB\+
/NOD slibcew oldnames  libw
$(DEFFILE);
<<
    link $(LFLAGS) @$(PROJ).CRF
    rc $(RESFLAGS) DEM_FLVW.RES $(PROJ).EXE

$(PROJ).EXE: DEM_FLVW.RES
    rc $(RESFLAGS) DEM_FLVW.RES $(PROJ).EXE

run: $(PROJ).EXE
    $(PROJ) $(RUNFLAGS)
```

Custom Toolbox Class

No matter what you call it — toolbox, tool bar, or button bar — an array of bitmaps provides a visual and convenient way for a user to select a feature. Many popular commercial products (e.g., Microsoft Word and Microsoft Excel) have a horizontal "tool bar" fixed in place just below the main window's menu. Other applications (e.g., the dialog editor) have a free-floating "toolbox" window that can be positioned anywhere on the desktop.

This chapter presents a custom toolbox. Technically, our toolbox isn't a control: the toolbox can be created as a nonchild window, and you can't create it in a resource script. Even so, for convenience's sake, we'll call the toolbox a control. At the end of the chapter, we'll even comment on ways to convert our toolbox into a true control.

User Interface

Unlike a menu or dialog box, a toolbox is always available to the user. This ready access makes the toolbox a very convenient interface for capabilities that require frequent user interaction. But, since the toolbox is always visible,

- the user must be able to move it out of the way or
- tile another window on top of it, for certain operations.

Depending on the window style, our toolbox control can be free-floating or anchored. The anchored version may be locked at a fixed

322 Windows Custom Controls

point on the screen or attached to a spot in the parent window's client area.

The user selects a tool from the toolbox by clicking the mouse on the appropriate tool cell. When selected, the tool changes from a raised to a lowered appearance. With one style of control, selecting one tool automatically de-selects all others (as with radio buttons). With the other style, any number of tools can be selected simultaneously (much like check boxes).

Clicking on any part of the toolbox causes it to be brought back to the top of the desktop. Thus, if another window has partially overlaid the toolbox, the user can force the toolbox to be redisplayed, without selecting a tool, by clicking on the caption bar.

Programmer Interface

Our design goal was to create a control that was easy for the programmer to use, yet flexible enough to meet a wide range of needs. To create an instance of the control, the programmer makes a single call to *CstToolBoxCreateWindow()*, specifying the number of rows and

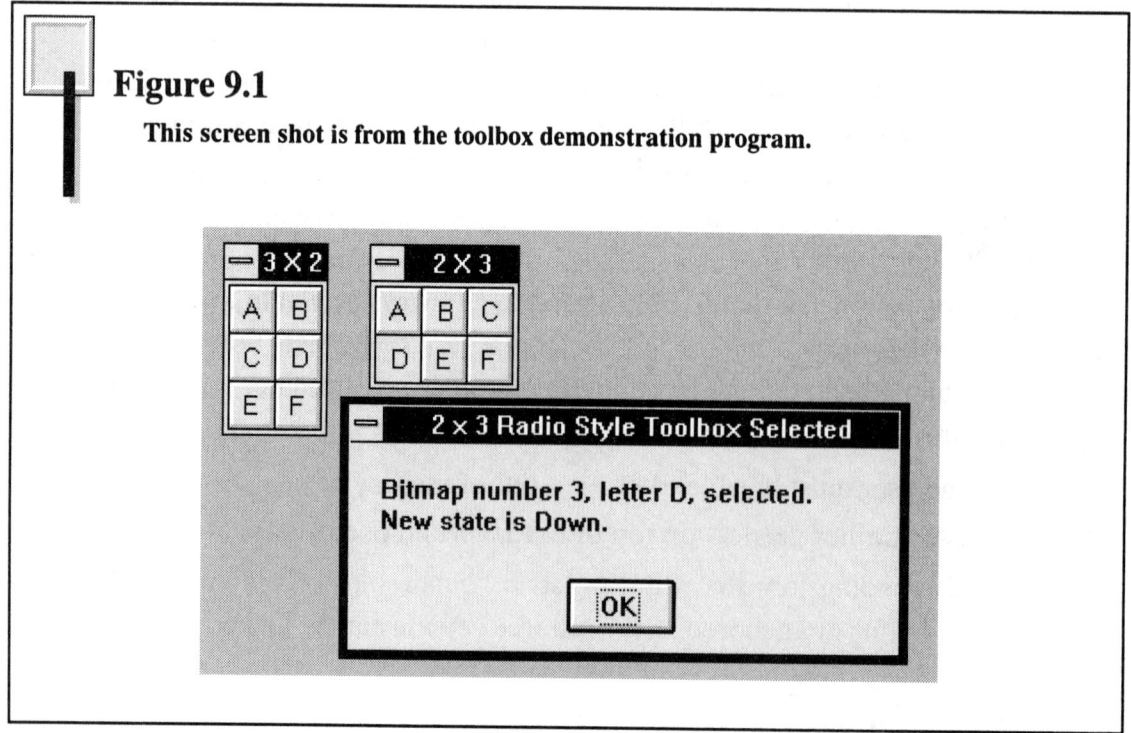

Figure 9.1
This screen shot is from the toolbox demonstration program.

columns in the matrix of tool cells. All of the other details of construction — loading and sizing of bitmaps, sizing of the window, shape of the control, and positioning of the bitmaps — are handled automatically. When a tool is selected, the toolbox control sends its parent window a message identifying the selected tool. Thus, the toolbox doesn't need to know anything about what response the selection triggers, and remains unaffected by changes in the application response. To add another tool to an existing toolbox, the programmer simply adds another case to the parent window procedure and adjusts the row and column arguments in the create call. None of the control code changes.

When created with the `WS_CAPTION` style, the toolbox can be moved anywhere on the screen. When organized as one or two vertical columns, such a free-floating toolbox behaves much like the toolbox in Windows Paint. If created with `WS_SYSMENU`, the user can even close the toolbox.

When created as a child window, the toolbox becomes confined to the client area of the parent window. This style is appropriate to "tool bar" applications, where the tool cells appear in a single line at the top of a window's client area.

The bitmaps that contain the tool icons are specified in a resource script. This allows the bitmaps to be changed without changing *any* program code. Their resource names must form a sequence — a sequence that the program can build at runtime by substituting sequential integers into a `wsprintf()` format string. Similarly, the programmer can change the order of the tool in the toolbox by changing the order of the bitmaps in the resource script. Moreover, the bitmaps may be of varied sizes; the toolbox will automatically rescale all bitmaps to match the dimensions of the first bitmap in the resource list. There must be two bitmaps for every tool cell: one for the up state and one for the down state.

Special messages even allow the parent window to change the bitmaps dynamically, perhaps to indicate that certain tools are temporarily unavailable.

Style and Data Interfaces

With only two window specific styles, the style interface is trivial. (See Table 9.1.) *CTBS_CHECK* is the default (all zeros) style, and evokes check box behavior. *CTBS_RADIO* (one bit set) triggers radio button behavior.

The data interface is only slightly more complicated. Besides the common data interface, we use an array of *TBDATA* structures to keep track of the bitmaps and current state associated with each tool cell, and an *LPTBCREATE* structure (see Table 9.2) to communicate the toolbox dimensions and other information to the control's *WM_CREATE* handler.

Unfortunately, the common instance data doesn't include storage for row and column information. Since none of our other controls need this kind of information, we decided to "overload" existing unused fields, rather than increase the size of the common structure. The row and column data are stored in the unused *iBkMode* and *iShadow* fields. Two macros, *CSTTOOLBOXGETROWS()* and *CSTTOOLBOXGETCOLS()*, help hide this kludge from the programmer.

Instantiation and Cleanup

To create a toolbox, the programmer calls *CstToolBoxCreateWindow()*, passing parameters that set the caption, style, location, grid size (rows and columns), frame size, parent window, bitmap name template, and application instance. Using the bitmap name template,

Table 9.1

The toolbox control has only two window specific styles, making the style interface trivial.

Style	Description
CTBS_CHECK	Makes bitmaps act like check boxes (default)
CTBS_RADIO	Makes bitmaps act like radio buttons

CstToolBoxCreateWindow() loads the first bitmap, so that it can determine the bitmap size. *CstToolBoxCreateWindow()* then computes a size for the window, based upon the grid size and the size of the first bitmap. Next, *CstToolBoxCreateWindow()* allocates a *TBCREATE* structure, copies the appropriate arguments into the new structure, and calls *CreateWindow()*, passing a pointer to the *TBCREATE* structure in *lParam*. *CstToolBoxCreateWindow()* first creates the toolbox window with the *WS_VISIBLE* style forced off. Once the window exists, *CstToolBoxCreateWindow()* adjusts the size and makes it visible if the *WS_VISIBLE* style was originally on.

When the toolbox window is initialized, the *WM_CREATE* handler copies the information in the *TBCREATE* structure into the window

Table 9.2

The toolbox control uses an array of TBDATA structures to keep track of bitmaps and state information. The control uses the TBCREATE structure to communicate with the WM_CREATE handler.

```
/* Local structure needed to keep track of tool info. */
typedef struct tagTBDATA
   {
   HBITMAP hBitmap[2];
   int iState;
   } TBDATA, FAR * LPTBDATA;
typedef unsigned int HTBDATA;

/* Local structure used to pass information to window proc. */
typedef struct tagTBCREATE
   {
   HWND hWndParent;
   int nRows;
   int nCols;
   int iFrame;
   RECT Rect;
   LPSTR lpstrBitmapFormat;
   } TBCREATE, FAR *LPTBCREATE;
```

instance data as shown in Figure 9.2. Note that the window handle installed in *hWnd()* is copied from *TBCREATE* — not acquired through *GetParent()*! Because the toolbox can be created as a nonchild window, it might not have a parent. Thus, we use the *TBCREATE* structure to pass in a handle to the window that created the toolbox — i.e., the window which should be notified whenever a tool is selected.

After the *WM_CREATE* handler has created all the class and instance data structures, it uses the bitmap name template to create a sequence of resource names (e.g., *TB1*, *TB2*, *TB3* ...), and loads the corresponding bitmaps. The bitmap handles are saved in the array *TBDATA*, and a pointer to *TBDATA* is saved in the instance data structure.

The *WM_DESTROY* handler destroys all the bitmap resources, frees the *TBDATA* array, frees the instance data, and, if needed, frees the default data structure.

Message Interface

Besides the common window management messages (*WM_CREATE*, *WM_DESTROY*, etc.), the toolbox responds to two seldom used messages, *WM_GETMINMAXINFO* and *WM_NCACTIVATE*, and several class specific messages. (See Table 9.3.) The response to the *WM_GETMINMAXINFO* message limits how large or small the window can become as it is resized.

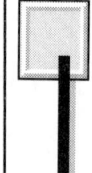

Figure 9.2

CstToolBoxCreateWindow() initializes a TBCREATE structure with information that describes the toolbox and its parent. This information is passed to the toolbox by passing a pointer in the lParam of a CreateWindow() call. This code excerpt shows what information goes into the TBCREATE structure.

```
lpCstCtlData->hWnd       = lpTBCreate->hWndParent;
lpCstCtlData->hFont      = hTBData;
lpCstCtlData->RectBitmap = lpTBCreate->Rect;
lpCstCtlData->iBkMode    = nRows;
lpCstCtlData->iShadow    = nCols;
lpCstCtlData->iFrame     = lpTBCreate->iFrame;
lpCstCtlData->lValue     = (LONG)lpTBData;
```

Unfortunately, the minimum size returned by *DefWndProc()* is far too large for most toolbox applications. By trapping *WM_GETMINMAXINFO*, we can override this minimum, so that the window will be exactly the right size for the toolbox.

If we didn't trap the *WM_NCACTIVATE* message, the toolbox caption bar would be drawn as "inactive" whenever some other window has the focus. As a practical matter, the toolbox is always available to its only source of input, namely the mouse. By always responding *TRUE* to the *WM_NCACTIVATE* message we force the toolbox caption to always be drawn as "active," thereby eliminating some unnecessary "visual noise."

The calling interface for the five class specific toolbox messages are outlined in Table 9.4. A toolbox window sends a *CTBM_CLICKED* message to its parent window when the user has selected a tool. The parent window can use *CTBM_GETCHECK* and *CTBM_SETCHECK* to manipulate the state of individual tools. Using the *CTBM_GETBITMAP* and *CTBM_SETBITMAP* messages, the parent window can dynamically change the bitmap associated with a particular tool cell. If the parent window does change a bit map, then it becomes responsible for releasing the old bitmap resource.

The *WM_LBUTTONDOWN* handler calls *CstToolBoxSelect()* to determine which tool has been selected. *CstToolBoxSelect()* uses the bitmap size and the mouse coordinates to determine which tool was selected.

Table 9.3
The CSTTOOLBOX control responds to these class specific messages.

Message	Description
CTBM_CLICKED	Tells the parent window the user clicked on the tool box
CTBM_GETCHECK	Gets the check state of the tool box
CTBM_SETCHECK	Sets the check state of the tool box
CTBM_GETBITMAP	Gets the current specified bitmap handle
CTBM_SETBITMAP	Sets the specified bitmap handle and returns previous

The Demonstration Program

The menu entries in the toolbox demonstration program, *DEM_TLBX.C*, will create a six-cell, free-floating toolbox, with either radio button or check box behavior. Clicking on a tool cell, generates a dialog box that announces which cell was selected.

Possible Enhancements

The current implementation forces all tool bitmaps to be the same size and shape. With only a little extra effort, one can make certain cells appear to be twice as large as others (by using the same handler for two adjacent cells and drawing the icon for the combined cell in two pieces), but applications with lots of tools could benefit from a more flexible cell size. One alternative might be to allow the bitmap size to determine the cell size.

Our toolbox isn't really a control, but it isn't very difficult to convert it into a pure control. One need only find a way to embed the row, column, and bitmap-naming information into the resource script. One alternative would be to code the rows and columns in all the unused style bits, and to put the bitmap name template in the window text. With these

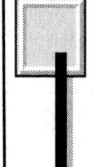

Table 9.4

This table summarizes the calling interface for the five class specific messages.

```
Message          wParam           lParam                    Return

CTBM_CLICKED     Tool Box hWnd    Bitmap ID                 Do not care
CTBM_GETCHECK    Not used         Bitmap ID or -1           TRUE FALSE or Bitmap ID
CTBM_SETCHECK    TRUE or FALSE    Bitmap ID                 0
CTBM_GETBITMAP   Not used         0,up 1,down in HIWORD     Bitmap Handle
                                  Bitmap ID in LOWORD
CTBM_SETBITMAP   Bitmap Handle    0,up 1,down in HIWORD     Previous Bitmap Handle
                                  Bitmap ID in LOWORD
```

changes, the toolbox could be created directly from the resource script, like any other custom control.

Conclusions

The toolbox is an example of a control that gains much of its versatility from class general window styles, rather than class specific styles. Our implementation also illustrates how to use the *lParam* to communicate special information to the WM_CREATE handler, and a simple trick for loading bitmaps. Although our common data structure wasn't designed with the tool bar in mind, we were still able to use our common support routines.

All in all, the toolbox is a pleasant addition to our stock of custom components — pleasant for the user, and equally pleasant for the developer.

Listing 9.1

```
/****************************************************************************
            File Name: CST_TLBX.H
        Expanded Name: Custom Tool Box
          Description: Include file for CST_TLBX.C
          Portability: Microsoft Windows 3.X
****************************************************************************/

#if !defined ( CST_TLBX_DEFINED )
    #define CST_TLBX_DEFINED

    /* Class specific messages for custom tool box control */
    #define CTBM_CLICKED      ( WM_USER + 1 )
    #define CTBM_GETCHECK     ( WM_USER + 2 )
    #define CTBM_SETCHECK     ( WM_USER + 3 )
    #define CTBM_GETBITMAP    ( WM_USER + 4 )
    #define CTBM_SETBITMAP    ( WM_USER + 5 )

    /* Class specific window styles for custom tool box control */
    #define CTBS_CHECK 0x00L
    #define CTBS_RADIO 0x01L

    /* Extra byte constants for custom tool box control */
    #define CTB_CLSEXTRA    ( CC_CLSEXTRA )
    #define CTB_WNDEXTRA    ( CC_WNDEXTRA )

    /* WM_CTLCOLOR type for custom tool box control */
    #define CTLCOLOR_CSTTOOLBOX 500

    /* Prototypes for exported functions in CST_TLBX.C */
    HWND FAR PASCAL CstToolBoxCreateWindow( LPSTR lpstrCaption, DWORD dwStyle,
            int xLoc, int yLoc, int nRows, int nCols, int iFrame,
            LPSTR lpstrBitmapForma, HWND hWndParent, HINSTANCE hInstance );
    int FAR PASCAL CstToolBoxRegister( HINSTANCE hInstance );
    int FAR PASCAL CstToolBoxUnregister( HINSTANCE hInstance );
    LONG FAR PASCAL CstToolBoxWndFn( HWND hWnd, UINT wMessage, WPARAM wParam,
            LPARAM lParam );

    /* Macros for custom tool box control */
    #define CSTTOOLBOXGETROWS( hWnd ) CSTCTLGETBKMODE( hWnd )
    #define CSTTOOLBOXGETCOLS( hWnd ) CSTCTLGETSHADOW( hWnd )

#endif

/* End of CST_TLBX.H */
```

Listing 9.2

```c
/*****************************************************************************
           File Name: CST_TLBX.C
       Expanded Name: Custom Tool Box
         Description: Library of functions for the tool box custom control
Global Function List: CstToolBoxCreateWindow
                      CstToolBoxRegister
                      CstToolBoxUnregister
                      CstToolBoxWndFn
Static Function List: CstToolBoxDefDataCreate
                      CstToolBoxDefDataDelete
                      CstToolBoxDraw
                      CstToolBoxSelect
                      CstToolBoxState
         Global Data: _hInstanceCstCtls
         Static Data: _hCstCtlData
                      _lpCstCtlData
         Portability: Microsoft Windows 3.X
*****************************************************************************/

/* Microsoft Windows */
#include <windows.h>

/* Prototypes and Types */
#include <cst_xtra.h>
#include <cst_data.h>
#include <cst_draw.h>
#include <cst_util.h>

/* Own */
#include <cst_tlbx.h>

/* Prototypes of local static functions */
static int CstToolBoxDefDataCreate( HWND hWnd );
static void CstToolBoxDefDataDelete( void );
static int CstToolBoxDraw( HWND hWnd, HDC hDC );
static int CstToolBoxRect( HWND hWnd, int iBitmap, LPRECT lpRect );
static int CstToolBoxSelect( HWND hWnd, int x, int y );
static int CstToolBoxState( HWND hWnd, int iBitmap, int iCheck );

#if defined ( _WINDLL )
/* DLL Handle */
extern HINSTANCE _hInstanceCstCtls;
#endif

static HCSTCTLDATA _hCstCtlData = (HCSTCTLDATA)0;
static LPCSTCTLDATA _lpCstCtlData = (LPCSTCTLDATA)0;

/* Local structure needed to keep track of tool info. */
typedef struct tagTBDATA
    {
    HBITMAP hBitmap[2];
    int iState;
    } TBDATA, FAR * LPTBDATA;
typedef unsigned int HTBDATA;

/* Local structure used to pass information to window proc. */
typedef struct tagTBCREATE
    {
    HWND hWndParent;
```

Listing 9.2 continued

```
    int nRows;
    int nCols;
    int iFrame;
    RECT Rect;
    LPSTR lpstrBitmapFormat;
    } TBCREATE, FAR *LPTBCREATE;

/***************************************************************************
         Name: CstToolBoxCreate
   Parameters: lpstrCaption - String to load in window caption bar
               dwStyle - window style of tool box
               xLoc - x location of tool box
               yLoc - y location of tool box
               nRows - number of rows of tools
               nCols - number of colomns of tools
               iFrame - thickness of window frame
               lpstrBitmapFormat - format string to create bitmap names
               hWndParent - handle to parent window
               hInstance - handle to instance
       Return: CreateWindow
  Description: Creates a window of class CstToolBox
***************************************************************************/
HWND FAR PASCAL CstToolBoxCreateWindow( LPSTR lpstrCaption, DWORD dwStyle,
        int xLoc, int yLoc, int nRows, int nCols, int iFrame,
        LPSTR lpstrBitmapFormat, HWND hWndParent, HINSTANCE hInstance )
    {

    HWND hWnd;
    HBITMAP hBitmap;
    BITMAP Bitmap;
    RECT Rect;
    TBCREATE TBCreate;
    char BitmapName[40];

    /* Get the size of the first bitmap */
    wsprintf( BitmapName, lpstrBitmapFormat, 0 );
    hBitmap = LoadBitmap( hInstance, BitmapName );
    GetObject( hBitmap, sizeof ( BITMAP ), (LPSTR)&Bitmap );
    SafeDeleteObject( hBitmap );
    Rect.left = Rect.top = 0;
    Rect.right = nCols * ( Bitmap.bmWidth + 1 ) + 1 + iFrame * 2;
    Rect.bottom = nRows * ( Bitmap.bmHeight + 1 ) + 1 + iFrame * 2;
    AdjustWindowRect( &Rect, dwStyle, FALSE );

    /* Load the Create data */
    TBCreate.hWndParent = hWndParent;
    TBCreate.Rect.left = TBCreate.Rect.top = 0;
    TBCreate.Rect.right = Bitmap.bmWidth;
    TBCreate.Rect.bottom = Bitmap.bmHeight;
    TBCreate.nCols = nCols;
    TBCreate.nRows = nRows;
    TBCreate.iFrame = iFrame;
    TBCreate.lpstrBitmapFormat = lpstrBitmapFormat;

    hWnd = CreateWindow( "CstToolBox", lpstrCaption, ( dwStyle & ~WS_VISIBLE ),
            xLoc, yLoc, ( Rect.right - Rect.left ), ( Rect.bottom - Rect.top ),
            hWndParent, NULL, hInstance, (LPSTR)&TBCreate );
```

Listing 9.2 continued

```
    if ( hWnd )
        {
        int iWidth, iHeight;
        RECT cRect;
        RECT wRect;

        GetClientRect( hWnd, &cRect );
        GetWindowRect( hWnd, &wRect );

        iWidth  = wRect.right  - wRect.left - ( cRect.right  - Rect.right );
        iHeight = wRect.bottom - wRect.top  - ( cRect.bottom - Rect.bottom );

        MoveWindow( hWnd, wRect.left, wRect.top, iWidth, iHeight, FALSE );

        if ( dwStyle & WS_VISIBLE )
            {
            ShowWindow( hWnd, SW_SHOWNA );
            UpdateWindow( hWnd );
            }

        }   /* if hWnd */

    return ( hWnd );

    }   /* function CstToolBoxCreateWindow */


/*****************************************************************************
         Name: CstToolBoxDefDataCreate
Expanded Name: Default Data Create
   Parameters: hWnd - window handle to ToolBox control
       Return: TRUE or FALSE
  Description: Creates the default class data
*****************************************************************************/
static int CstToolBoxDefDataCreate( HWND hWnd )
    {

    _lpCstCtlData = CstCtlDefDataCreate( hWnd );
    if ( !_lpCstCtlData )
        {
        /* Failed to allocate and initialize data */
        return ( FALSE );
        }
    _hCstCtlData = CSTGETCLASSWORD( hWnd, GCW_HCSTCTLDATA );

    /* Free up the resources we do not need */
    SafeDeleteObject( _lpCstCtlData->hBrush[CC_BRUSH_BACKGROUND] );
    _lpCstCtlData->hBrush[CC_BRUSH_BACKGROUND] = 0;
    SafeDeleteObject( _lpCstCtlData->hBrush[CC_BRUSH_3DLIGHT] );
    _lpCstCtlData->hBrush[CC_BRUSH_3DLIGHT] = 0;
    SafeDeleteObject( _lpCstCtlData->hBrush[CC_BRUSH_3DSHADOW] );
    _lpCstCtlData->hBrush[CC_BRUSH_3DSHADOW] = 0;

    return ( TRUE );

    }   /* function CstToolBoxDefDataCreate */
```

Listing 9.2 continued

```c
/*****************************************************************************
        Name: CstToolBoxDefDataDelete
Expanded Name: Default Data Delete
   Parameters: hWnd - window handle control
  Description: Deletes the default class data
*****************************************************************************/
static void CstToolBoxDefDataDelete( void )
    {

    if ( _lpCstCtlData )
        {
        SafeDeleteObject( _lpCstCtlData->hBrush[CC_BRUSH_BTNFACE] );
        SafeDeleteObject( _lpCstCtlData->hBrush[CC_BRUSH_FRAME] );
        _lpCstCtlData = (LPCSTCTLDATA)0;
        }

    if ( _hCstCtlData )
        {
        GlobalUnlock( _hCstCtlData );
        GlobalFree( _hCstCtlData );
        _hCstCtlData = (HCSTCTLDATA)0;
        }

    }   /* function CstToolBoxDefDataDelete */


/*****************************************************************************
        Name: CstToolBoxDraw
   Parameters: hWnd - handle to tool box window
               hDC  - handle to device context
       Return: number of tool bitmaps drawn
  Description: Unregisters the window class for the custom Tool Box control
*****************************************************************************/
static int CstToolBoxDraw( HWND hWnd, HDC hDC )
    {

    int iBitmap;
    int iFrame;
    int iRow, nRows;
    int iCol, nCols;
    LPTBDATA lpTBData;
    RECT Rect;
    HBITMAP hBitmap;
    HBRUSH hBrushBk, hBrushFrame;

    /* Get the background and frame bushes */
    hBrushBk = CSTCTLGETBRUSH( hWnd, CC_BRUSH_FRAME );
    hBrushFrame = CSTCTLGETBRUSH( hWnd, CC_BRUSH_BTNFACE );

    /* Draw the border  and the background */
    iFrame = CSTCTLGETFRAME( hWnd );
    GetClientRect( hWnd, &Rect );
    CstDraw3DRect( hWnd, hDC, hBrushBk, &Rect,
            ( CST_RECT_BORDER | CST_RECT_FLAT ),
            hBrushFrame, hBrushFrame, iFrame );

    /* Loop though all the bitmaps */
    lpTBData = (LPTBDATA)CSTCTLGETVALUE( hWnd );
    nRows = CSTTOOLBOXGETROWS( hWnd );
```

Listing 9.2 *continued*

```
    nCols = CSTTOOLBOXGETCOLS( hWnd );
    for ( iRow = 0; iRow < nRows; iRow++ )
        {
        for ( iCol = 0; iCol < nCols; iCol++ )
            {
            iBitmap = iRow * nCols + iCol;
            CstToolBoxRect( hWnd, iBitmap, &Rect );
            hBitmap = lpTBData[iBitmap].hBitmap[lpTBData[iBitmap].iState];
            if ( hBitmap )
                {
                CstDrawBitmap( hDC, hBitmap, Rect.left, Rect.top,
                        Rect.right - Rect.left, Rect.bottom - Rect.top );
                }
            }   /* for iCol */
        }   /* for iRow */

    return ( iBitmap );

    }   /* function CstToolBoxDraw */


/******************************************************************************
        Name: CstToolBoxRect
  Parameters: hWnd - handle to tool box window
              iBitmap - tool bitmap id
              lpRect - rectangle to store coordinates int
      Return: iBitmap or -1 if failure
 Description: Registers the window class for the custom Tool Box control
******************************************************************************/
static int CstToolBoxRect( HWND hWnd, int iBitmap, LPRECT lpRect )
    {

    int Row;
    int nCols, Col;
    int iFrame;
    LPRECT lpRectBitmap;

    lpRectBitmap = CSTCTLGETLPRECTBITMAP( hWnd );
    nCols = CSTTOOLBOXGETCOLS( hWnd );
    iFrame = CSTCTLGETFRAME( hWnd );
    Row = iBitmap / ( nCols );
    Col = iBitmap - ( Row * nCols );
    if ( Row < 0 || Col < 0 )
        {
        /* Failure of some kind */
        iBitmap = -1;
        }

    lpRect->left = iFrame + 1 + ( Col * ( lpRectBitmap->right + 1 ) );
    lpRect->right = lpRect->left + lpRectBitmap->right;
    lpRect->top = iFrame + 1 + ( Row * ( lpRectBitmap->bottom + 1 ) );
    lpRect->bottom = lpRect->top + lpRectBitmap->bottom;

    return ( iBitmap );

    }   /* function CstToolBoxRect */
```

Listing 9.2 continued

```
/*****************************************************************************
         Name: CstToolBoxRegister
   Parameters: hInstance - handle to program or library registering class
       Return: Number of register counts or 0 if failure
  Description: Registers the window class for the custom Tool Box control
*****************************************************************************/
int FAR PASCAL CstToolBoxRegister( HINSTANCE hInstance )
    {

    WNDCLASS WndClass;

    WndClass.style = CS_HREDRAW | CS_VREDRAW;

    #if defined ( _WINDLL )
    hInstance = _hInstanceCstCtls;
    WndClass.style |= CS_GLOBALCLASS;
    #endif

    WndClass.lpfnWndProc = CstToolBoxWndFn;
    WndClass.cbClsExtra = CTB_CLSEXTRA;
    WndClass.cbWndExtra = CTB_WNDEXTRA;
    WndClass.hInstance = hInstance;
    WndClass.hIcon = 0;
    WndClass.hCursor = LoadCursor( 0, IDC_ARROW );
    WndClass.hbrBackground = 0;
    WndClass.lpszMenuName = 0;
    WndClass.lpszClassName = (LPSTR)"CstToolBox";

    return ( RegisterClass( &WndClass ) );

    }   /* function CstToolBoxRegister */



/*****************************************************************************
         Name: CstToolBoxSelect
   Parameters: hWnd - handle to tool box window
               x - x location of mouse click
               y - y location of mouse click
       Return: id number of bitmap clicked on or -1 if none
  Description: gets the id number of a bitmap clicked on
*****************************************************************************/
static int CstToolBoxSelect( HWND hWnd, int x, int y )
    {

    int nRows, Row;
    int nCols, Col;
    int iBitmap;
    LPRECT lpRectBitmap;

    lpRectBitmap = CSTCTLGETLPRECTBITMAP( hWnd );
    Row = y / ( lpRectBitmap->bottom + 1 );
    Col = x / ( lpRectBitmap->right + 1 );
    nRows = CSTTOOLBOXGETROWS( hWnd );
    nCols = CSTTOOLBOXGETCOLS( hWnd );
    iBitmap = Row * nCols + Col;
    if ( iBitmap >= ( nCols * nRows ) )
        {
```

Listing 9.2 *continued*

```
        /* Failure of some kind */
        iBitmap = -1;
        }

    return ( iBitmap );

    }   /* function CstToolBoxSelect */
/****************************************************************************
        Name: CstToolBoxState
  Parameters: hWnd - handle to tool box window
              iBitmap - id number of bitmap to toggle state
      Return: id number of previous bitmap in down state
 Description: Changes the state of a tool bitmap
****************************************************************************/
static int CstToolBoxState( HWND hWnd, int iBitmap, int iCheck )
    {

    RECT Rect;
    LPTBDATA lpTBData = (LPTBDATA)CSTCTLGETVALUE( hWnd );
    DWORD dwStyle = (DWORD)GetWindowLong( hWnd, GWL_STYLE );
    int iBitmapPrev = (int)CSTCTLGETSTATE( hWnd );
    int iCurState = lpTBData[iBitmap].iState;

    if ( dwStyle & CTBS_RADIO )
        {

        /* Turn off the previous tool */
        if ( ( iBitmapPrev >= 0 ) && ( iBitmapPrev != iBitmap ) )
            {

            if ( lpTBData[iBitmapPrev].iState == TRUE )
                {

                lpTBData[iBitmapPrev].iState = FALSE;
                CstToolBoxRect( hWnd, iBitmapPrev, &Rect );
                InvalidateRect( hWnd, &Rect, FALSE );

                }   /* if lpTBData */

            }   /* if iBitmap */

        }   /* if dwStyle */

    CstToolBoxRect( hWnd, iBitmap, &Rect );

    if ( iCheck == -TRUE )
        {
        /* Just toggle the current state */
        iCheck = !iCurState;
        }   /* if dwStyle */

    if ( iCurState != iCheck )
        {
        lpTBData[iBitmap].iState = iCheck;
        InvalidateRect( hWnd, &Rect, FALSE );
        }
```

Listing 9.2 continued

```c
        CstCtlSetState( hWnd, (WORD)iBitmap );

    return ( iBitmapPrev );

    }   /* function CstToolBoxState */


/*****************************************************************************
        Name: CstToolBoxUnregister
  Parameters: hInstance - handle to program or library that registered class
      Return: Number of remaining register counts
 Description: Unregisters the window class for the custom Tool Box control
*****************************************************************************/
int FAR PASCAL CstToolBoxUnregister( HINSTANCE hInstance )
    {

    #if defined ( _WINDLL )
    hInstance = _hInstanceCstCtls;
    #endif

    return ( UnregisterClass( "CstToolBox", hInstance ) );

    }   /* function CstToolBoxUnregister */


/*****************************************************************************
        Name: CstToolBoxWndFn
Expanded Name: Custom Tool Box Window Callback Function
 Description: Window call back function for the custom tool box control
*****************************************************************************/
LONG FAR PASCAL CstToolBoxWndFn( HWND hWnd, UINT wMessage,
        WPARAM wParam, LPARAM lParam )
    {

    static int _WindowCount = 0;

    switch ( wMessage )
        {
        case CTBM_GETBITMAP:
            {

            int iBitmap = (int)LOWORD( lParam );

            if ( ( iBitmap < 0 ) || ( iBitmap >
                    ( CSTTOOLBOXGETROWS( hWnd ) *
                      CSTTOOLBOXGETCOLS( hWnd ) ) ) )
                {
                break;
                }
            else
                {

                LPTBDATA lpTBData = (LPTBDATA)CSTCTLGETVALUE( hWnd );

                return ( lpTBData[iBitmap].hBitmap[HIWORD( lParam )] );
                }

            }   /* case CTBM_GETBITMAP */
```

Listing 9.2 *continued*

```
case CTBM_GETCHECK:
    {

    int iBitmap;

    iBitmap = (int)LOWORD( lParam );
    if ( iBitmap < 0 )
        {
        return ( CSTCTLGETSTATE( hWnd ) );
        }
    else
        {

        LPTBDATA lpTBData = (LPTBDATA)CSTCTLGETVALUE( hWnd );

        return ( lpTBData[iBitmap].iState );
        }
    }   /* case CTBM_GETCHECK */
case CTBM_SETBITMAP:
    {

    int iBitmap = (int)LOWORD( lParam );

    if ( ( iBitmap < 0 ) || ( iBitmap >
            ( CSTTOOLBOXGETROWS( hWnd ) *
            CSTTOOLBOXGETCOLS( hWnd ) ) ) )
        {
        break;
        }
    else
        {

        HBITMAP hBitmapOld;
        LPTBDATA lpTBData = (LPTBDATA)CSTCTLGETVALUE( hWnd );

        hBitmapOld = lpTBData[iBitmap].hBitmap[HIWORD( lParam )];
        lpTBData[iBitmap].hBitmap[HIWORD( lParam )] = (HBITMAP)wParam;
        return ( (LONG)hBitmapOld );
        }
    }   /* case CTBM_SETBITMAP */
case CTBM_SETCHECK:
    CstToolBoxState( hWnd, (int)LOWORD( lParam ), (int)wParam );
    break;
case WM_CREATE:
    {

    int i, nCols, nRows;
    HTBDATA hTBData;
    LPTBDATA lpTBData;
    LPTBCREATE lpTBCreate;
    LPCSTCTLDATA lpCstCtlData;
    HWND hWndParent;

    if ( !_WindowCount )
        {
        if ( !CstToolBoxDefDataCreate( hWnd ) )
            {
            return ( -1 );
            }
```

Listing 9.2 continued

```
        }
    _WindowCount++;

    CstCtlDataCreate( hWnd );
    lpCstCtlData = CSTCTLGETLPDATA( hWnd );

    lpTBCreate = (LPTBCREATE)
            ( (LPCREATESTRUCT)lParam )->lpCreateParams;

    if ( lpTBCreate )
        {
        char BitmapName[40];
        HINSTANCE hInstance;

        /* Allocate memory for all the tools */
        nRows = lpTBCreate->nRows;
        nCols = lpTBCreate->nCols;
        hTBData = GlobalAlloc( GMEM_FLAGS,
                (DWORD)( nCols * nRows ) * sizeof ( TBDATA ) );
        if ( !hTBData )
            {
            break;
            }
        lpTBData = (LPTBDATA)GlobalLock( hTBData );
        if ( !lpTBData )
            {
            GlobalFree( hTBData );
            break;
            }
        hInstance = GetWindowWord( hWnd, GWW_HINSTANCE );
        for ( i = 0; i < nCols * nRows; i++ )
            {
            wsprintf( BitmapName,
                    lpTBCreate->lpstrBitmapFormat, i * 2 );
            lpTBData[i].hBitmap[0] =
                    LoadBitmap( hInstance, BitmapName );
            wsprintf( BitmapName,
                    lpTBCreate->lpstrBitmapFormat, i * 2 + 1 );
            lpTBData[i].hBitmap[1] =
                    LoadBitmap( hInstance, BitmapName );
            }
        /* Window handle in instance data holds handle to TB data */
        hWndParent = lpCstCtlData->hWnd = lpTBCreate->hWndParent;
        lpCstCtlData->hFont = hTBData;
        lpCstCtlData->RectBitmap = lpTBCreate->Rect;
        lpCstCtlData->iBkMode = nRows;
        lpCstCtlData->iShadow = nCols;
        lpCstCtlData->iFrame = lpTBCreate->iFrame;
        lpCstCtlData->lValue = (LONG)lpTBData;

        /* Notify the parent that the tool box has been created */
        if ( hWndParent )
            {
            SendMessage( hWndParent, WM_PARENTNOTIFY, WM_CREATE,
                    MAKELPARAM( hWnd, 0 ) );
            }
        }  /* if lpTBCreate */
    break;
```

Listing 9.2 continued

```
        }   /* case WM_CREATE */
case WM_CSTCTLGETDATA:
case WM_CSTCTLGETDEFDATA:
case WM_CSTCTLSETDATA:
case WM_CSTCTLSETDEFDATA:
    return ( (LONG)CstCtlData( hWnd, wMessage, wParam, lParam ) );
case WM_DESTROY:
    {

    HWND hWndParent = CSTCTLGETWND( hWnd );

    /* Notify the parent and then delete the instance data */
    if ( hWndParent )
        {
        SendMessage( hWndParent, WM_PARENTNOTIFY,
                WM_DESTROY, MAKELPARAM( hWnd, 0 ) );
        }

    if ( IsWindow( hWnd ) )
        {

        int i;
        HTBDATA hTBData = CSTCTLGETFONT( hWnd );
        LPTBDATA lpTBData = (LPTBDATA)CSTCTLGETVALUE( hWnd );
        int nRows = CSTTOOLBOXGETROWS( hWnd );
        int nCols = CSTTOOLBOXGETCOLS( hWnd );

        if ( lpTBData )
            {
            for ( i = 0; i < nCols * nRows; i++ )
                {
                SafeDeleteObject( lpTBData[i].hBitmap[0] );
                SafeDeleteObject( lpTBData[i].hBitmap[1] );
                }
            }

        if ( hTBData )
            {
            GlobalUnlock( hTBData );
            GlobalFree( hTBData );
            }
        CstCtlDataDelete( hWnd );

        }   /* if IsWindow */

    _WindowCount--;
    if ( _WindowCount <= 0 )
        {
        CstToolBoxDefDataDelete();
        }

    break;
    }   /* case WM_DESTROY */
case WM_ERASEBKGND:
    /* Background is handled during the WM_PAINT message */
    return ( TRUE );
case WM_GETMINMAXINFO:
    {
```

Listing 9.2 *continued*

```
        MINMAXINFO FAR *lpMinMaxInfo;

        lpMinMaxInfo = (MINMAXINFO FAR *)lParam;
        lpMinMaxInfo->ptMinTrackSize.x = 2;
        lpMinMaxInfo->ptMinTrackSize.y = 2;
        break;
        }   /* case WM_GETMINMAXINFO */
    case WM_LBUTTONDOWN:
    case WM_LBUTTONDBLCLK:
        {

        int iBitmap;

        /* Bring the toolbox window to the top of window order */
        BringWindowToTop( hWnd );

        /* Determine which if any bitmap has been checked */
        iBitmap = CstToolBoxSelect( hWnd,
                (int)LOWORD( lParam ), (int)HIWORD( lParam ) );

        if ( iBitmap >= 0 )
            {

            HWND hWndParent = CSTCTLGETWND( hWnd );

            CstToolBoxState( hWnd, iBitmap, -TRUE );
            if ( hWndParent )
                {
                SendMessage( hWndParent, CTBM_CLICKED, hWnd,
                        (LONG)iBitmap );
                }
            }   /* if iBitmap */

        break;
        }   /* case WM_LBUTTONDOWN */
    case WM_PAINT:
        {

        PAINTSTRUCT PS;
        HDC hDC;

        /* Keep the window caption appearance active */
        SendMessage( hWnd, WM_NCACTIVATE, 1, 0L );
        hDC = BeginPaint( hWnd, &PS );
        if ( IsWindowVisible( hWnd ) )
            {
            /* Only paint if needed */
            CstToolBoxDraw( hWnd, hDC );
            }
        EndPaint( hWnd, &PS );
        break;
        }   /* case WM_PAINT */
    case WM_NCACTIVATE:
        /* Force active window appearance */
        wParam = TRUE;
    default:
        return ( DefWindowProc( hWnd, wMessage, wParam, lParam ) );
    }   /* switch ( wMessage ) */
```

Listing 9.2 *continued*

```
    return ( 0L );
    }    /* function CstToolBoxWndFn */
/* End of CST_TLBX.C */
```

Listing 9.3

```
/******************************************************************
            File Name: DEM_TLBX.H
        Expanded Name: Demo Tool Box
          Description: Include file for DEM_TLBX.C & DEM_TLBX.RC
          Portability: Microsoft Windows 3.X
******************************************************************/

#define IDM_TOOLBOX3X2 101
#define IDM_TOOLBOX2X3 102
#define IDM_TOOLBOX6X1 103
#define IDM_EXIT 104

/* End of DEM_TLBX.H */
```

Listing 9.4

```
/****************************************************************
         File Name: DEM_TLBX.C
     Expanded Name: Demo Tool Box
       Description: Demo program for custom tool box control
      Program List: DEM_TLBX.C
                    DEM_TLBX.RC
                    DEM_TLBX.DEF
                    CST_DATA.C
                    CST_DRAW.C
                    CST_UTIL.C
                    CST_TLBX.C
                    CST_XTRA.C
                    or
                    DEM_TLBX.C
                    DEM_TLBX.RC
                    DEM_TLBX.DEF
                    CST_CTLS.LIB,DLL
Global Function List: WinMain
                      MainWindowProc
       Portability: Microsoft Windows 3.X
****************************************************************/

/* Microsoft Windows */
#include <windows.h>

/* Types and prototypes */
#include <cst_xtra.h>
#include <cst_data.h>
#include <cst_tlbx.h>
#include <cst_util.h>

/* Own */
#include <dem_tlbx.h>
int PASCAL WinMain( HANDLE hInstance, HANDLE hPrevInstance, LPSTR lpCmdLine,
        int nCmdShow );
LONG FAR PASCAL MainWindowProc( HWND hwnd, UINT wMessage, WPARAM wParam,
        LPARAM lParam );
#define BITMAP_FORMAT "TB%d2424"

/****************************************************************
       Name: WinMain
Description: Main Window function
****************************************************************/
int PASCAL WinMain( HINSTANCE hInstance, HINSTANCE hPrevInstance,
        LPSTR lpCmdLine, int nCmdShow )
    {

    HWND hWnd;
    MSG Msg;
    static char _Name[] = "DEM_TLBX";
    WNDCLASS WndClass;

    lpCmdLine = lpCmdLine;
    nCmdShow = nCmdShow;

    #if defined ( NO_DLL )
    CstToolBoxRegister( hInstance );
    #endif
```

Listing 9.4 *continued*

```c
    if ( !hPrevInstance )
        {
        WndClass.style = 0;
        WndClass.lpfnWndProc = MainWindowProc;
        WndClass.cbClsExtra = 0;
        WndClass.cbWndExtra = 0;
        WndClass.hInstance = hInstance;
        WndClass.hIcon = LoadIcon( hInstance, _Name );
        WndClass.hCursor = LoadCursor( NULL, IDC_ARROW );
        WndClass.hbrBackground = COLOR_WINDOW + 1;
        WndClass.lpszMenuName = _Name;
        WndClass.lpszClassName = _Name;
        RegisterClass( &WndClass );
        }
    else
        {
        hWnd = FindWindow( _Name, NULL );
        if ( hWnd )
            {
            BringWindowToTop( hWnd );
            }
        return ( FALSE );
        }

    hWnd = CreateWindow( _Name, "Custom Tool Box Control Demo",
            WS_OVERLAPPEDWINDOW, CW_USEDEFAULT, CW_USEDEFAULT,
            CW_USEDEFAULT, CW_USEDEFAULT, NULL, NULL, hInstance, NULL );

    ShowWindow( hWnd, nCmdShow );
    UpdateWindow( hWnd );

    while ( GetMessage( &Msg, NULL, 0, 0 ) )
        {
        TranslateMessage( &Msg );
        DispatchMessage ( &Msg );
        }

    return ( (int)Msg.wParam );

    }   /* function WinMain */


/******************************************************************************
        Name: MainWindowProc
 Description: Window procedure for main window
******************************************************************************/
LONG FAR PASCAL MainWindowProc( HWND hWnd, UINT wMessage,
        WPARAM wParam, LPARAM lParam )
    {

    static HWND hWnd3x2, hWnd2x3, hWnd6x1;

    switch( wMessage )
        {
        case CTBM_CLICKED:
            {

            char Caption[64];
```

Listing 9.4 *continued*

```
    char Message[128];
    char State[8];
    int iNewState;

    if ( (HWND)wParam == hWnd3x2 )
        {
        lstrcpy( Caption, "3 x 2 Check Style Toolbox Selected" );
        }
    else if ( (HWND)wParam == hWnd2x3 )
        {
        lstrcpy( Caption, "2 x 3 Radio Style Toolbox Selected" );
        }
    else if ( (HWND)wParam == hWnd6x1 )
        {
        lstrcpy( Caption, "6 x 1 Radio Style Toolbox Selected" );
        }
    else
        {
        break;
        }
    iNewState = (int)SendMessage( (HWND)wParam, CTBM_GETCHECK, 0,
            lParam );
    if ( iNewState )
        {
        lstrcpy( State, "Down" );
        }
    else
        {
        lstrcpy( State, "Up" );
        }
    wsprintf( Message, "Bitmap number %d, letter %c, selected.\n"
            "New state is %s.",
            (int)lParam, (char)( 65 + (int)lParam ), (LPSTR)State );
    MessageBox( hWnd, Message, Caption, MB_OK );

    break;

    } /* case CTBM_CLICKED */
case WM_COMMAND:
    {

    HINSTANCE hInstance;

    hInstance = (HINSTANCE)GetWindowWord( hWnd, GWW_HINSTANCE );
    switch( wParam )
        {
        case IDM_TOOLBOX3X2:
            if ( !IsWindow( hWnd3x2 ) )
                {
                hWnd3x2 = CstToolBoxCreateWindow( "3 X 2",
                        WS_SYSMENU | WS_VISIBLE | WS_OVERLAPPED |
                        CTBS_CHECK,
                        CW_USEDEFAULT, CW_USEDEFAULT, 3, 2, 2,
                        BITMAP_FORMAT, hWnd, hInstance );
                }
            else
                {
                DestroyWindow( hWnd3x2 );
                hWnd3x2 = (HWND)0;
```

Listing 9.4 continued

```
                    }
                    break;
                case IDM_TOOLBOX2X3:
                    if ( !IsWindow ( hWnd2x3 ) )
                        {
                        hWnd2x3 = CstToolBoxCreateWindow( "2 X 3",
                                WS_SYSMENU | WS_VISIBLE | WS_OVERLAPPED |
                                CTBS_RADIO,
                                CW_USEDEFAULT, CW_USEDEFAULT, 2, 3, 2,
                                BITMAP_FORMAT, hWnd, hInstance );
                        }
                    else
                        {
                        DestroyWindow( hWnd2x3 );
                        hWnd2x3 = (HWND)0;
                        }
                    break;
                case IDM_TOOLBOX6X1:
                    if ( !IsWindow ( hWnd6x1 ) )
                        {
                        hWnd6x1 = CstToolBoxCreateWindow( "6x1",
                                WS_VISIBLE | WS_OVERLAPPED | CTBS_RADIO,
                                CW_USEDEFAULT, CW_USEDEFAULT, 6, 1, 2,
                                BITMAP_FORMAT, hWnd, hInstance );
                        }
                    else
                        {
                        DestroyWindow( hWnd6x1 );
                        hWnd6x1 = (HWND)0;
                        }
                    break;
                case IDM_EXIT:
                    if ( IsWindow( hWnd3x2 ) )
                        {
                        DestroyWindow( hWnd3x2 );
                        }
                    if ( IsWindow( hWnd2x3 ) )
                        {
                        DestroyWindow( hWnd2x3 );
                        }
                    if ( IsWindow( hWnd5x1 ) )
                        {
                        DestroyWindow( hWnd6x1 );
                        }
                    DestroyWindow( hWnd );
                    break;
                default:
                    break;
                }
            return ( FALSE );
            }
        case WM_DESTROY:
            PostQuitMessage( 0 );
            return ( FALSE );
        default:
            break;
        }
```

Listing 9.4 *continued*

```
    return ( DefWindowProc( hWnd, wMessage, wParam, lParam ) );
    }    /* function MainWindowProc */
/* End of DEM_TLBX.C */
```

Listing 9.5

```
/*****************************************************************************
            File Name: DEM_TLBX.RC
        Expanded Name: Demo Tool Box
          Description: Resource file for the custom tool box control demo
          Portability: Microsoft Windows 3.X
*****************************************************************************/

#include <windows.h>
#include <dem_tlbx.h>

DEM_TLBX ICON ICON\DEM_TLBX.ICO

DEM_TLBX MENU
BEGIN
    POPUP "&Demo"
    BEGIN
        MENUITEM "3 X 2 Tool Box Check Style...", IDM_TOOLBOX3X2
        MENUITEM "2 X 3 Tool Box Radio Style...", IDM_TOOLBOX2X3
        MENUITEM "6 X 1 Tool Box Radio Style...", IDM_TOOLBOX6X1
        MENUITEM SEPARATOR
        MENUITEM "E&xit", IDM_EXIT
    END
END

TB02424  BITMAP BITMAP\TB02424.BMP
TB12424  BITMAP BITMAP\TB12424.BMP
TB22424  BITMAP BITMAP\TB22424.BMP
TB32424  BITMAP BITMAP\TB32424.BMP
TB42424  BITMAP BITMAP\TB42424.BMP
TB52424  BITMAP BITMAP\TB52424.BMP
TB62424  BITMAP BITMAP\TB62424.BMP
TB72424  BITMAP BITMAP\TB72424.BMP
TB82424  BITMAP BITMAP\TB82424.BMP
TB92424  BITMAP BITMAP\TB92424.BMP
TB102424 BITMAP BITMAP\TB102424.BMP
TB112424 BITMAP BITMAP\TB112424.BMP

/* End of DEM_TLBX.RC */
```

Listing 9.6

```
NAME DEM_TLBX
DESCRIPTION 'Custom Tool Box Demo Program'
EXETYPE WINDOWS
CODE PRELOAD MOVEABLE
DATA PRELOAD MOVEABLE MULTIPLE
HEAPSIZE 1024
STACKSIZE 5120
EXPORTS
      MainWindowProc
      CstToolBoxWndFn
```

Listing 9.7

```
ORIGIN   = QCWIN
ORIGIN_VER   = 1.00

PROJ =DEM_TLBX
DEBUG    =0
PROGTYPE =1
CALLER   =
ARGS =
DLLS =
CVPACK   =1
CC   =cl -qc
RC   =rc
CFLAGS_G_WEXE =/AS /W4 /Ze /D_WINDOWS /DNO_DLL /G2w /Zp /Aw
CFLAGS_D_WEXE =/Zi /Od
CFLAGS_R_WEXE =/O /Os /Gs /DNDEBUG
CFLAGS_G_WDLL =/AS /G2w /Zp /Aw /W3 /D_WINDOWS /D_WINDLL
CFLAGS_D_WDLL =/Gi /Od /Zi
CFLAGS_R_WDLL =/O /Os /DNDEBUG
CFLAGS_G_WTTY =/AS /G2w /W3 /D_WINDOWS
CFLAGS_D_WTTY =/Gi /Od /Zi
CFLAGS_R_WTTY =/O /Os /DNDEBUG
CFLAGS_G_DEXE =/AS /W2
CFLAGS_D_DEXE =/Gi /Od /Zi
CFLAGS_R_DEXE =/O /Ot /DNDEBUG
CFLAGS   =$(CFLAGS_G_WEXE) $(CFLAGS_R_WEXE)
LFLAGS_G_WEXE =/NOE/A:16/ST:10240
LFLAGS_D_WEXE =/CO
LFLAGS_R_WEXE =
LFLAGS_G_WDLL =/ST:5120 /A:16
LFLAGS_D_WDLL =/CO
LFLAGS_R_WDLL =
LFLAGS_G_WTTY =/ST:5120 /A:16
LFLAGS_D_WTTY =/CO
LFLAGS_R_WTTY =
LFLAGS_G_DEXE =/NOI /ST:2048
LFLAGS_D_DEXE =/CO
LFLAGS_R_DEXE =
LFLAGS   =$(LFLAGS_G_WEXE) $(LFLAGS_R_WEXE)
RCFLAGS  =/DNO_DLL
RESFLAGS =
RUNFLAGS =
DEFFILE =       DEMSTLBX.DEF
OBJS_EXT =
LIBS_EXT =

.rc.res: ; $(RC) $(RCFLAGS) -r $*.rc

all: $(PROJ).EXE

DEM_TLBX.OBJ: DEM_TLBX.C $(H)

DEM_TLBX.RES: DEM_TLBX.RC $(RESFILES) $(H)

CST_DATA.OBJ: CST_DATA.C $(H)

CST_DRAW.OBJ: CST_DRAW.C $(H)
```

Listing 9.7 *continued*

```
CST_TLBX.OBJ: CST_TLBX.C $(H)

CST_UTIL.OBJ: CST_UTIL.C $(H)

$(PROJ).EXE:  DEM_TLBX.OBJ CST_DATA.OBJ CST_DRAW.OBJ CST_TLBX.OBJ CST_UTIL.OBJ $(OBJS_EXT)
$(DEFFILE)
    echo >NUL @<<$(PROJ).CRF
DEM_TLBX.OBJ +
CST_DATA.OBJ +
CST_DRAW.OBJ +
CST_TLBX.OBJ +
CST_UTIL.OBJ +
$(OBJS_EXT)
$(PROJ).EXE

C:\PRGLNG\QCW\LIB\+
/NOD slibcew oldnames  libw
$(DEFFILE);
<<
    link $(LFLAGS) @$(PROJ).CRF
    rc $(RESFLAGS) DEM_TLBX.RES $(PROJ).EXE

$(PROJ).EXE:  DEM_TLBX.RES
    rc $(RESFLAGS) DEM_TLBX.RES $(PROJ).EXE

run: $(PROJ).EXE
    $(PROJ) $(RUNFLAGS)
```

10 Custom Dialog Classes

The preceding chapters have been devoted to customizing controls. This chapter will show you how to create a custom dialog class. Dialog boxes and controls form an important relationship in Windows. Normally, each dialog box functions as the parent window for several controls (child windows). The preceding chapters have focused on altering the controls. This chapter concentrates on altering the parent dialog class. The custom dialog class we create, `CSTDIALOG`, will allow you to alter the appearance of the dialog box background.

The Message Process

The call back function for a dialog box is significantly different from the call back function for other window classes because the dialog box occupies a different spot in the message processing hierarchy. Normal window call back procedures receive their messages *before* the message is passed to the default handler. Dialog box call back procedures, on the other hand, receive their messages *after* the default handler. A custom dialog class inserts an *additional* call-back procedure in this chain.

The Window Call Back Function

Normally Windows first sends messages to the window function. The window function invokes default processing for messages by invoking *DefWindowProc()*, explicitly:

```
/* Invoke default processing for window function */
return ( DefWindowProc( hWnd, wMessage, wParam, lParam ) );
```

Unless the message requires return information, the window function returns a zero. The return value of a window function does not affect default processing. Figure 10.1 contains a block diagram illustrating the flow of messages for a window call back function.

The Dialog Call Back Function

The call back function for a *dialog* window, though, receives its messages differently. Messages sent to a dialog box are *first* sent to the default

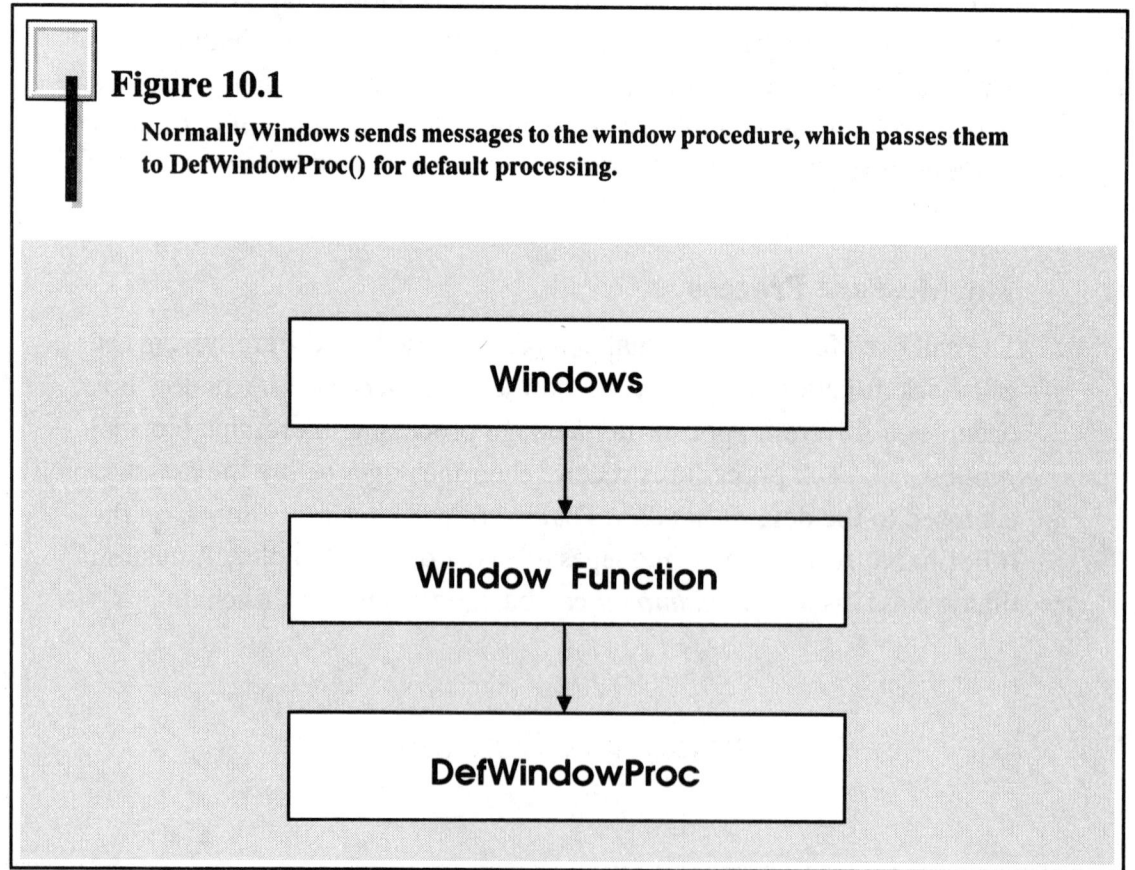

Figure 10.1

Normally Windows sends messages to the window procedure, which passes them to DefWindowProc() for default processing.

dialog window function, *DefDlgProc()*. *DefDlgProc()* first responds to the message by immediately passing it on to your dialog box function. If your dialog box function returns *FALSE*, *DefDlgProc()* supplies the standard default response to the message. However, if your dialog box function returns *TRUE*, *DefDlgProc()* exits without doing any further processing.

Thus, in a window call back function, the function must explicitly request default processing, but in a dialog box, the call back function need merely "defer" to the calling process, by returning *FALSE*:

```
/* Invoke default processing for dialog box function */
return ( FALSE );
```

Figure 10.2 contains a block diagram illustrating the flow of messages for a dialog box function.

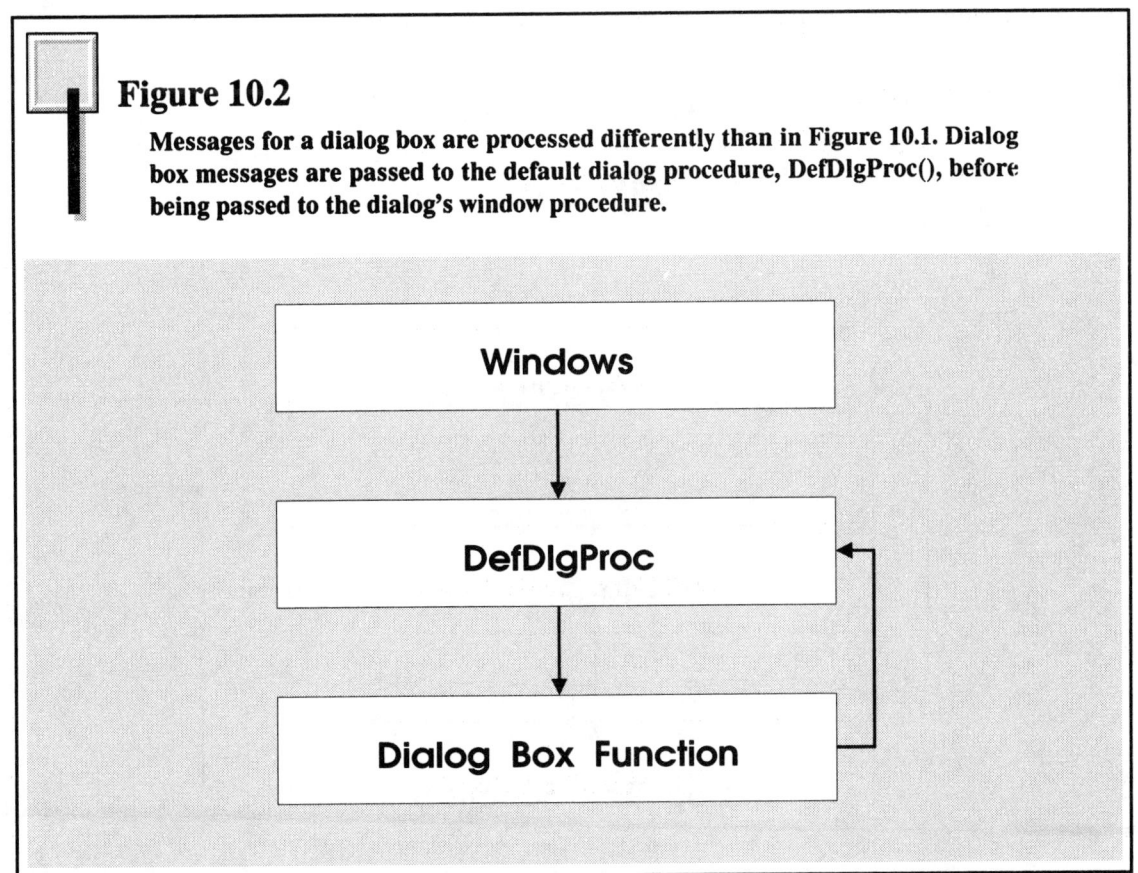

Figure 10.2

Messages for a dialog box are processed differently than in Figure 10.1. Dialog box messages are passed to the default dialog procedure, DefDlgProc(), before being passed to the dialog's window procedure.

Custom Dialog Class Call Back Functions

Custom dialog class call back functions are window functions — *not* dialog box functions. But unlike normal call back functions, the dialog class call back function invokes *DefDlgProc()* for default processing instead of *DefWindowProc()*. Thus, a custom dialog class "inserts" another call back function into the normal dialog box message processing hierarchy. The custom dialog class window function gets a chance to act in response to messages targeted for your dialog procedure first, before *DefDlgProc()* and before your dialog box function. Figure 10.3 diagrams the flow of messages for a custom dialog class function.

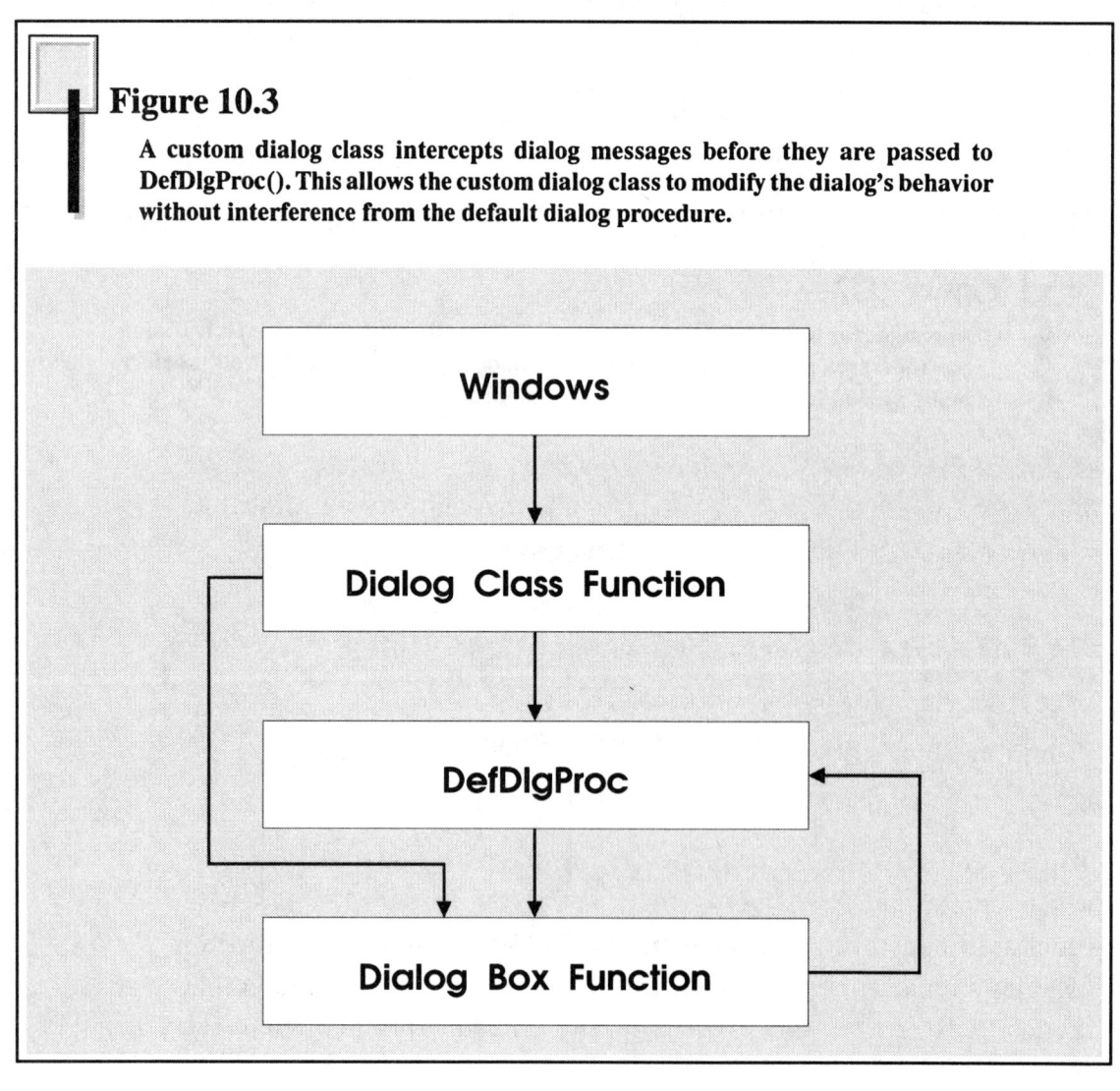

Figure 10.3

A custom dialog class intercepts dialog messages before they are passed to DefDlgProc(). This allows the custom dialog class to modify the dialog's behavior without interference from the default dialog procedure.

Custom dialog classes are most commonly used to dress up the appearance of the dialog box background. Other uses include :

- controlling the movement of the input focus between controls
- and taking over some drawing chores of controls to increase display speed.

Our example, CSTDIALOG does not attempt to do anything more than customize the appearance of the dialog box background.

Function Interface

The code for the CSTDIALOG class is the simplest of all the custom controls in this book. The file CST_DILG.C, Listing 10.2, contains only three functions: the registration function, CstDialogRegister(); the unregistration function, CstDialogUnregister(); and the window function CstDialogWndFn(). The registration and unregistration functions are nearly identical with the other custom controls in this book. The window function is much simpler than the call back functions for the other custom controls.

Data Interface

Because instances of a custom dialog class will be processed by standard dialog functions, the class *must* declare as many window extra bytes as a standard dialog would. Windows declares the constant, DLGWINDOWEXTRA, for just this reason. You must add this value to the number of window extra bytes that your dialog class uses:

```
/* Extra byte constants for custom dialog class */
#define CD_CLSEXTRA ( CC_CLSEXTRA )
#define CD_WNDEXTRA ( CC_WNDEXTRA + DLGWINDOWEXTRA )
```

You should treat these extra bytes as the private domain of Windows, which creates problems very much like those we encountered with subclassed controls. Again, the reverse indexing scheme described in Chapter 7 comes in handy. Since the instance data interface assumes that the last part of the extra bytes contain the handle and pointer to the instance data, you can still use the instance data interface for custom dialog classes.

Class Specific Styles

Besides the standard window styles and dialog styles, *CSTDIALOG* supports five new class specific window styles, which control the appearance of the dialog box client area. These new dialog class styles are similar to some of the styles for the *CSTSTATIC* control covered in Chapter 5. Two styles control the appearance of a border around the dialog box client area. Three styles control the appearance of the client area or the border.

Since these are class specific styles, they must be mapped onto the lower 16 bits of the style parameter. The developer must also be careful to select a mapping that does not conflict with the existing class specific (prefix *DS_*) styles for dialog boxes. This requirement is easily met, since there are only four existing class specific styles for dialog boxes: *DS_LOCALEDIT*, *DS_MODALFRAME*, *DS_NOIDLEMSG*, and *DS_SYSMODAL*. Table 10.1 and Table 10.2 list the new class specific window styles for the *CSTDIALOG* class.

Window Function for *CSTDIALOG*

Listing 10.2 contains the window call back function, *CstDialogWndFn()* for *CSTDIALOG*. Besides the instance data interface messages, *CstDialogWndFn()* responds to only three system messages: *WM_CREATE*, *WM_DESTROY*, and *WM_ERASEBKGND*. *CstDialogWndFn()* sends all other messages to *DefDlgProc()* for default processing.

In response to the *WM_CREATE* message, *CstDialogWndFn()* allocates the instance data and sets the *wStyle()* member in the instance data based upon the window style. This value controls the 3-D and border appearance of the dialog box. In response to the *WM_DESTROY* message, *CstDialogWndFn()* deletes the instance data.

Unlike the custom control window functions, *CstDialogWndFn()* does not notify its parent window when it has been created or is being destroyed. You could send the *WM_PARENTNOTIFY* message to the current instance and eventually the dialog box function will get the message. This

Table 10.1

These styles control 3-D effects in the CSTDIALOG control.

CDS_FLAT
When combined with the CDS_BORDER style, this style causes the window to be drawn without any 3-D effects. This is the default appearance style.

CDS_LOWERED
This style uses highlights and shadows to make the dialog box client area or border appear lowered. If you set the CDS_BORDER style, a groove is drawn around the client area of the dialog box. If you specify more than one 3-D style, this style dominates over the CDS_FLAT and CDS_RAISED styles.

CDS_RAISED
This style uses highlights and shadows to make the dialog box client area or border appear to be raised. If the CDS_BORDER style is set, a ridge is drawn around the client area of the dialog box. If you specify more than one 3-D style, this style dominates over the CDS_FLAT style.

Table 10.2

These styles enable and disable the border around the CSTDIALOG control.

CDS_NOBORDER
This style causes the dialog box client area to be drawn without a border. This is the default style.

CDS_BORDER
This style causes the dialog box client area to be drawn with a border. In windows with this style, the 3-D appearance styles will apply to the border instead of the window. The result is a border that is raised or lowered with respect to the background. The dialog box client area appears to be left at the same level as the background. If you specify more than one border style, the CDS_BORDER style dominates over the CDS_NOBORDER style.

360 *Windows Custom Controls*

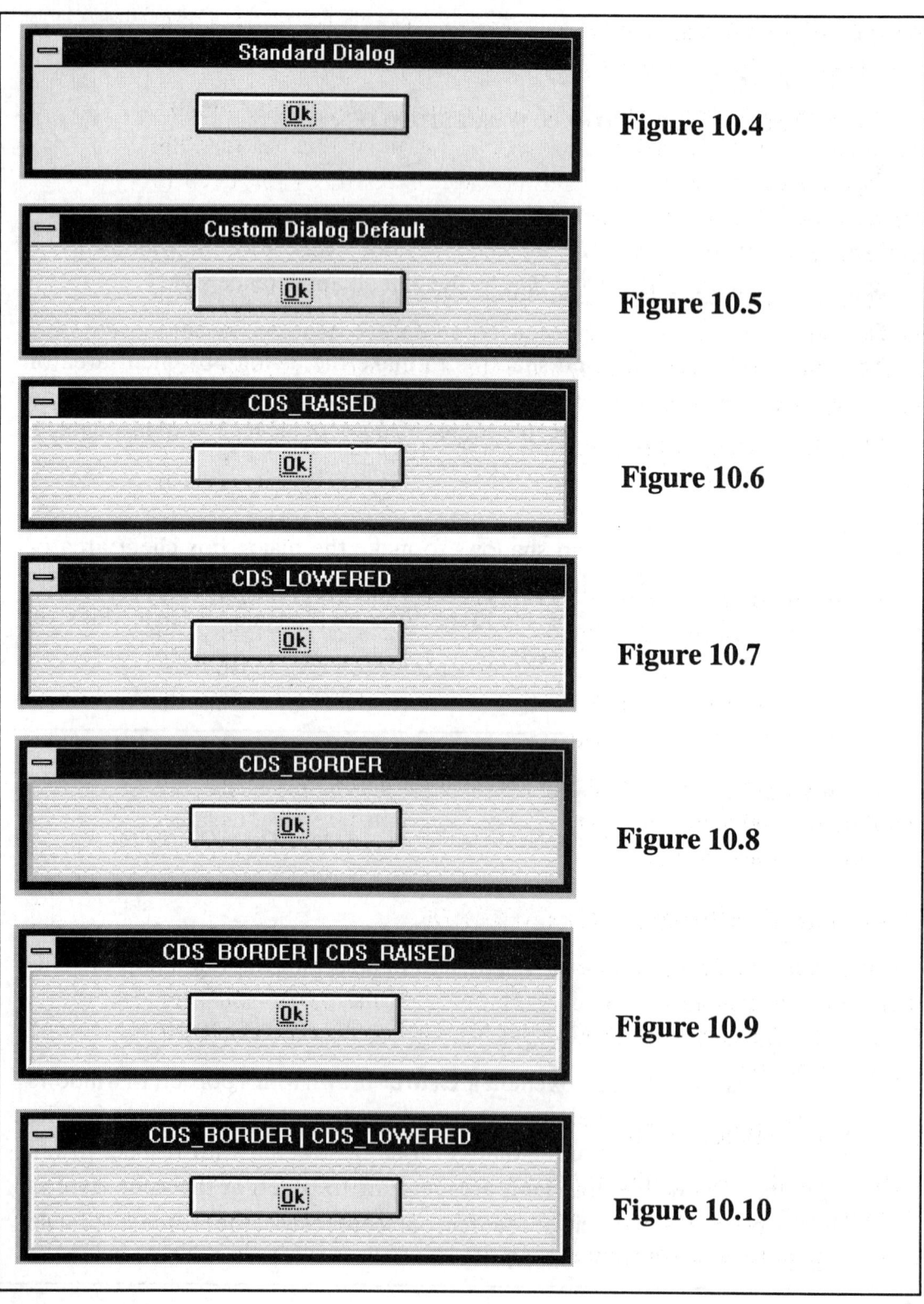

Figure 10.4

Figure 10.5

Figure 10.6

Figure 10.7

Figure 10.8

Figure 10.9

Figure 10.10

may get a bit confusing and is not necessary. The dialog box function already knows when it is being created or destroyed.

If you need to create any resources or allocate memory to support the dialog box's functionality, you can do so in the dialog box function in response to the WM_INITDIALOG message. Later when you need to delete resources or dynamic memory, you can do it right before you call EndDialog().

CstDialogWndFn() responds to the WM_ERASEBKGND to carry out all its drawing needs. It first sends the WM_CTLCOLOR to itself, because CstDialogWndFn() forwards the WM_CTLCOLOR message to DefDlgProc() which, in turn, forwards it to the dialog box function.

This gives the dialog box function a chance to change the background brush. If the dialog box function does not set a new brush, CstDialogWndFn() uses the default brush (a pattern brush) out of the instance data.

In our example, the default brush is a bitmap that the resource file CST_DILG.RC, Listing 10.3, loads. CstDialogWndFn() extracts the shadow and highlight brushes from the instance data. CstDialogWndFn() draws the background with a border and 3-D effects by calling the function CstDraw3DRect(), Listing 4.4.

If you wish to override the default brushes for the dialog background, shadow, and highlight, you can use the instance data interface to change the values of these brushes.

Demonstration Program for CSTDIALOG

The program DEM_DILG, Listings 10.4, 10.5, and 10.6, is a simple program that demonstrates all of the possible styles of the CSTDIALOG class. Figures 10.4 through 10.10 show the appearance of the different dialog boxes in DEM_DILG.

Enhancement Ideas for CSTDIALOG

Besides just dressing up the appearance of dialog boxes, you can use a custom dialog class to enhance functionality. One possibility is to change how the input focus is switched among child controls. In some situations you can accelerate the drawing of a child control by creating a custom dialog class that takes over some drawing responsibilities. This technique can eliminate some messages, but requires a lot of programming. The speed increase will probably be noticeable only on low end hardware.

Before doing anything very aggressive with custom dialog classes, we recommend that you study the source for *DefDlgProc()* and *DefWndProc()*. Microsoft includes the source for both these functions as part of the Windows SDK.

Listing 10.1

```
/*******************************************************************
        File Name: CST_DILG.H
    Expanded Name: Custom Control Dialog
      Description: Include file for CST_DILG.C
      Portability: Microsoft Windows 3.X
*******************************************************************/

#if !defined ( CST_DILG_DEFINED )
    #define CST_DILG_DEFINED

    /* Class specific window styles for custom dialog class */

    /* These styles control the border around the window.
    ** CDS_NOBORDER is the default and CDS_BORDER dominates
    ** over CDS_NOBORDER if both are set. If CDS_BORDER is set
    ** the 3D appearance style effects the border. */
    #define CDS_NOBORDER 0x0000L
    #define CDS_BORDER   0x02000L

    /* These styles control the 3D appearance of the dialog box.
    ** The default styles is CDS_FLAT.  If more than one of
    ** these styles is set, CDS_LOWERED dominates over CDS_RAISED
    ** and CDS_FLAT, CDS_RAISED dominates over CSS_FLAT. */
    #define CDS_FLAT     0x00000L
    #define CDS_LOWERED  0x04000L
    #define CDS_RAISED   0x08000L

    /* Default bitmap for background brush */
    #define CD_DEFBITMAP_3DBACKGROUND "cdbgbr00"
    #define CD_BITMAP_BACKGROUND      0

    /* Extra byte constants for custom dialog class */
    #define CD_CLSEXTRA ( CC_CLSEXTRA )
    #define CD_WNDEXTRA ( CC_WNDEXTRA + DLGWINDOWEXTRA )

    /* WM_CTLCOLOR type for custom dialog class */
    #define CTLCOLOR_CSTDIALOG ( CTLCOLOR_DLG | 0x010 )

    /* Prototypes of exported functions in CST_DILG.C */
    int FAR PASCAL CstDialogRegister( HINSTANCE hInstance );
    int FAR PASCAL CstDialogUnregister( HINSTANCE hInstance );
    LONG FAR PASCAL CstDialogWndFn( HWND hWnd, UINT wMessage, WPARAM wParam,
            LPARAM lParam );

#endif

/* End of CST_DILG.H */
```

Listing 10.2

```c
/*****************************************************************************
          File Name: CST_DILG.C
      Expanded Name: Custom Control Dialog
        Description: Function library for custom control dialog type
Global Function List: CstDialogRegister
                     CstDialogUnregister
                     CstDialogWndFn
Static Function List: CstDialogDefDataCreate
                     CstDialogDefDataDelete
         Global Data: _hInstanceCstCtls
         Static Data: _hCstCtlData
                     _lpCstCtlData
        Portability: Microsoft Windows 3.X
*****************************************************************************/

/* Microsoft Windows */
#include <windows.h>

/* Types and Prototypes */
#include <cst_xtra.h>
#include <cst_data.h>
#include <cst_draw.h>
#include <cst_util.h>

/* Own */
#include <cst_dilg.h>

/* Prototypes of local static functions */
static int CstDialogDefDataCreate( HWND hWnd );
static void CstDialogDefDataDelete( void );

#if defined ( _WINDLL )
/* DLL Handle */
extern HINSTANCE _hInstanceCstCtls;
#endif

static HCSTCTLDATA  _hCstCtlData  = (HCSTCTLDATA)0;
static LPCSTCTLDATA _lpCstCtlData = (LPCSTCTLDATA)0;

/*****************************************************************************
         Name: CstDialogDefDataCreate
 Expanded Name: Default Data Create
    Parameters: hWnd - window handle to Dialog control
        Return: TRUE or FALSE
   Description: Creates the default class data
*****************************************************************************/
static int CstDialogDefDataCreate( HWND hWnd )
    {

    HINSTANCE hInstanceClass;

    #if defined ( _WINDLL )
    hInstanceClass = _hInstanceCstCtls;
    #else
    hInstanceClass = GetWindowWord( hWnd, GWW_HINSTANCE );
    #endif

    _lpCstCtlData = CstCtlDefDataCreate( hWnd );
    if ( !_lpCstCtlData )
```

Listing 10.2 *continued*

```
        {
        /* Failed to allocate and initialize data */
        return ( FALSE );
        }
    _hCstCtlData = CSTGETCLASSWORD( hWnd, GCW_HCSTCTLDATA );

    /* Free up the resources we do not need */
    SafeDeleteObject( _lpCstCtlData->hBrush[CC_BRUSH_BTNFACE] );
    _lpCstCtlData->hBrush[CC_BRUSH_BTNFACE] = 0;
    SafeDeleteObject( _lpCstCtlData->hBrush[CC_BRUSH_FRAME] );
    _lpCstCtlData->hBrush[CC_BRUSH_FRAME] = 0;
    SafeDeleteObject( _lpCstCtlData->hBrush[CC_BRUSH_BACKGROUND] );

    /* Create and set the background brush */
    _lpCstCtlData->hBitmap[CD_BITMAP_BACKGROUND] = LoadBitmap( hInstanceClass,
            CD_DEFBITMAP_3DBACKGROUND );
    _lpCstCtlData->hBrush[CC_BRUSH_BACKGROUND] = CreatePatternBrush(
            _lpCstCtlData->hBitmap[CD_BITMAP_BACKGROUND] );
    SetClassWord( hWnd, GCW_HBRBACKGROUND,
            (WORD)_lpCstCtlData->hBrush[CC_BRUSH_BACKGROUND] );

    return ( TRUE );

    }   /* function CstDialogDefDataCreate */



/*****************************************************************************
        Name: CstDialogDefDataDelete
Expanded Name: Default Data Delete
   Parameters: hWnd - window handle control
  Description: Deletes the default class data
*****************************************************************************/
static void CstDialogDefDataDelete( void )
    {

    if ( _lpCstCtlData )
        {
        /* Background brush is already deleted - it is the class brush */
        /*
        SafeDeleteObject( lpCstCtlData->hBrush[CC_BRUSH_BACKGROUND] );
        */
        SafeDeleteObject( _lpCstCtlData->hBitmap[CD_BITMAP_BACKGROUND] );
        SafeDeleteObject( _lpCstCtlData->hBrush[CC_BRUSH_3DLIGHT] );
        SafeDeleteObject( _lpCstCtlData->hBrush[CC_BRUSH_3DSHADOW] );
        _lpCstCtlData = (LPCSTCTLDATA)0;
        }

    if ( _hCstCtlData )
        {
        GlobalUnlock( _hCstCtlData );
        GlobalFree( _hCstCtlData );
        _hCstCtlData = (HCSTCTLDATA)0;
        }

    }   /* function CstDialogDefDataDelete */
```

Windows Custom Controls

Listing 10.2 *continued*

```
/*****************************************************************************
         Name: CstDialogRegister
   Parameters: hInstance - handle to program or library registering class
       Return: Same as RegisterClass
  Description: Registers the window class for the custom dialog type
*****************************************************************************/
int FAR PASCAL CstDialogRegister( HINSTANCE hInstance )
    {

    WNDCLASS WndClass;

    WndClass.style = CS_DBLCLKS | CS_HREDRAW | CS_VREDRAW;

    #if defined ( _WINDLL )
    hInstance = _hInstanceCstCtls;
    WndClass.style |= CS_GLOBALCLASS;
    #endif

    WndClass.lpfnWndProc = CstDialogWndFn;
    WndClass.cbClsExtra = CD_CLSEXTRA;
    WndClass.cbWndExtra = CD_WNDEXTRA;
    WndClass.hInstance = hInstance;
    WndClass.hIcon = 0;
    WndClass.hCursor = LoadCursor( 0, IDC_ARROW );
    WndClass.hbrBackground = 0;
    WndClass.lpszMenuName = 0;
    WndClass.lpszClassName = "CstDialog";

    return ( RegisterClass( &WndClass ) );

    }   /* function CstDialogRegister */


/*****************************************************************************
         Name: CstDialogUnregister
   Parameters: hInstance - handle to program or library that registered class
       Return: Same as UnregisterClass
  Description: Unregisters the window class for the custom dialog type
*****************************************************************************/
int FAR PASCAL CstDialogUnregister( HINSTANCE hInstance )
    {

    #if defined ( _WINDLL )
    hInstance = _hInstanceCstCtls;
    #endif

    return ( UnregisterClass( "CstDialog", hInstance ) );

    }   /* function CstDialogUnregister */



/*****************************************************************************
         Name: CstDialogWndFn
 Expanded Name: Custom Dialog Window Callback Function
  Description: Window callback function custom dialog class
*****************************************************************************/
LONG FAR PASCAL CstDialogWndFn( HWND hWnd, UINT wMessage, WPARAM wParam,
        LPARAM lParam )
```

Listing 10.2 *continued*

```
{
static int _WindowCount = 0;

switch ( wMessage )
    {
    case WM_CREATE:
        {
        LONG lStyle = GetWindowLong( hWnd, GWL_STYLE );
        WORD wStyle = 0;

        if ( !_WindowCount )
            {
            if ( !CstDialogDefDataCreate( hWnd ) )
                {
                return ( -1 );
                }
            }
        _WindowCount++;

        /* Create instance data */
        CstCtlDataCreate( hWnd );

        /* Set the style */
        if ( lStyle & CDS_BORDER )
            {
            wStyle |= CST_RECT_BORDER;
            if ( lStyle & CDS_LOWERED )
                {
                wStyle |= CST_RECT_GROOVE;
                }
            else if ( lStyle & CDS_RAISED )
                {
                wStyle |= CST_RECT_RIDGE;
                }
            else
                {
                wStyle |= CST_RECT_FLAT;
                }
            }
        else
            {
            if ( lStyle & CDS_LOWERED )
                {
                wStyle |= CST_RECT_LOWERED;
                }
            else if ( lStyle & CDS_RAISED )
                {
                wStyle |= CST_RECT_RAISED;
                }
            }
        CstCtlSetStyle( hWnd, wStyle );
        break;
        }   /* case WM_CREATE */
    case WM_CSTCTLGETDATA:
    case WM_CSTCTLGETDEFDATA:
    case WM_CSTCTLSETDATA:
    case WM_CSTCTLSETDEFDATA:
```

Listing 10.2 continued

```
                return ( (LONG)CstCtlData( hWnd, wMessage, wParam, lParam ) );
        case WM_DESTROY:
            /* Free attribute data */
            CstCtlDataDelete( hWnd );

            _WindowCount--;
            if ( _WindowCount <= 0 )
                {
                CstDialogDefDataDelete();
                }

            break;
        case WM_ERASEBKGND:
            {
            /* Redraw background */

            HBRUSH hBrushBk, hBrushLight, hBrushShadow;
            int iThick;
            RECT Rect;
            WORD wStyle;

            /* Send messages to give dialog a chance to change the
            ** drawing attributes */
            hBrushBk = (HBRUSH)SendMessage( hWnd, WM_CTLCOLOR,
                    (HDC)wParam, MAKELPARAM( hWnd, CTLCOLOR_DLG ) );
            if ( !CstCtlColorMsg( hWnd, FALSE ) || hBrushBk == 0 )
                {
                /* Get the default brush */
                hBrushBk = CSTCTLGETBRUSH( hWnd, CC_BRUSH_BACKGROUND );
                }

            /* Get Data */
            hBrushLight = CSTCTLGETBRUSH( hWnd, CC_BRUSH_3DLIGHT );
            hBrushShadow = CSTCTLGETBRUSH( hWnd, CC_BRUSH_3DSHADOW );
            wStyle = CSTCTLGETSTYLE( hWnd );
            iThick = CSTCTLGETSHADOW( hWnd );
            if ( wStyle & CST_RECT_BORDER )
                {
                iThick *= 2;
                }

            GetClientRect( hWnd, &Rect );
            return ( CstDraw3DRect( hWnd, (HDC)wParam, hBrushBk,
                    (LPRECT)&Rect, wStyle, hBrushLight, hBrushShadow,
                    iThick ) );
            }   /* case WM_ERASEBKGND */
        default:
            break;
        }   /* switch message */

    return ( DefDlgProc( hWnd, wMessage, wParam, lParam ) );

    }   /* function CstDialogWndFn */

/* End of CST_DILG.C */
```

Listing 10.3

```
/*****************************************************************
         File Name: CST_DILG.RC
     Expanded Name: Custom Dialog
       Description: Resource file for the custom dialog class
       Portability: Microsoft Windows 3.X
*****************************************************************/

CDBGBR00 BITMAP BITMAP\CDBGBR00.BMP

/* End of CST_DILG.RC */
```

Listing 10.4

```
/*****************************************************************
         File Name: DEM_DILG.H
     Expanded Name: Demo Dialog
       Description: Include file for DEM_DILG.C & DEM_DILG.RC
       Portability: Microsoft Windows 3.X
*****************************************************************/

#define IDD_STANDARD 200

#define IDM_STANDARD 101
#define IDM_DEFAULT 102
#define IDM_BORDER 103
#define IDM_LOWERED 104
#define IDM_RAISED 105
#define IDM_BORDER_LOWERED 106
#define IDM_BORDER_RAISED 107
#define IDM_EXIT 112

/* End of DEM_DILG.H */
```

Listing 10.5

```c
/****************************************************************************
        File Name: DEM_DILG.C
    Expanded Name: Demo Dialog
      Description: Demo program for custom dialog class
     Program List: DEM_DILG.C
                   DEM_DILG.RC
                   DEM_DILG.DEF
                   CST_DATA.C
                   CST_DILG.C
                   CST_DRAW.C
                   CST_UTIL.C
                   CST_XTRA.C
                   or
                   DEM_DILG.C
                   DEM_DILG.RC
                   DEM_DILG.DEF
                   CST_CTLS.LIB,DLL
Global Function List: WinMain
                      DemoDialog
                      DemoDialogProc
                      MainWindowProc
      Portability: Microsoft Windows 3.X
****************************************************************************/

/* Microsoft Windows */
#include <windows.h>

#if !defined ( USE_CST_CTLS_DLL )
#include <cst_dilg.h>
#endif

/* Own */
#include <dem_dilg.h>

int PASCAL WinMain( HINSTANCE hInstance, HINSTANCE hPrevInstance, LPSTR lpCmdLine,
        int nCmdShow );
BOOL PASCAL DemoDialog( HINSTANCE hInstance, HWND hWndParent, LPSTR DialogName );
BOOL FAR PASCAL DialogDemoDialogProc( HWND hDlg, UINT wMessage,
        WPARAM wParam, LPARAM lParam );
LONG FAR PASCAL MainWindowProc( HWND hwnd, UINT wMessage,
        WPARAM wParam, LPARAM lParam );

/****************************************************************************
        Name: WinMain
  Description: Main Window function
****************************************************************************/
int PASCAL WinMain( HINSTANCE hInstance, HINSTANCE hPrevInstance,
        LPSTR lpCmdLine, int nCmdShow )
    {

    #if !defined ( NO_DLL )
    HINSTANCE hInstanceDll;
    #endif
    HWND hWnd;
    MSG Msg;
    static char _Name[] = "DEM_DILG";
    WNDCLASS WndClass;

    lpCmdLine = lpCmdLine;
```

Listing 10.5 *continued*

```
    nCmdShow = nCmdShow;

#if defined ( NO_DLL )
CstDialogRegister( hInstance );
#else
hInstanceDll = LoadLibrary( "CST_CTLS.DLL" );
#endif

    if ( !hPrevInstance )
        {
        WndClass.style = 0;
        WndClass.lpfnWndProc = MainWindowProc;
        WndClass.cbClsExtra = 0;
        WndClass.cbWndExtra = 0;
        WndClass.hInstance = hInstance;
        WndClass.hIcon = LoadIcon( hInstance, _Name );
        WndClass.hCursor = LoadCursor( NULL, IDC_ARROW );
        WndClass.hbrBackground = COLOR_WINDOW + 1;
        WndClass.lpszMenuName = _Name;
        WndClass.lpszClassName = _Name;
        RegisterClass( &WndClass );
        }

    hWnd = CreateWindow( _Name, "Custom Dialog Class Demo",
            WS_OVERLAPPEDWINDOW, CW_USEDEFAULT, CW_USEDEFAULT,
            CW_USEDEFAULT, CW_USEDEFAULT, NULL, NULL, hInstance, NULL );

    ShowWindow( hWnd, nCmdShow );
    UpdateWindow( hWnd );

    while ( GetMessage( &Msg, NULL, 0, 0 ) )
        {
        TranslateMessage( &Msg );
        DispatchMessage ( &Msg );
        }

#if !defined ( NO_DLL )
FreeLibrary( hInstanceDll );
#endif

    return ( (int)Msg.wParam );

    }    /* function WinMain */


/******************************************************************
        Name: DemoDialog
 Description: Function for invoking dialog boxes
 ******************************************************************/
BOOL PASCAL DemoDialog( HINSTANCE hInstance, HWND hWndParent, LPSTR DialogName )
    {

    BOOL bStatus;
    FARPROC lpfnProc;

    lpfnProc = MakeProcInstance( DialogDemoDialogProc, hInstance );
    bStatus = DialogBox( hInstance, DialogName, hWndParent, lpfnProc );
    FreeProcInstance( lpfnProc );
```

Listing 10.5 *continued*

```c
    return ( bStatus );

}   /* function DemoDialog */


/*****************************************************************************
        Name: DialogDemoDialogProc
 Description: Dialog call back function for custom dialog class demo
*****************************************************************************/
BOOL FAR PASCAL DialogDemoDialogProc( HWND hDlg, UINT wMessage,
        WPARAM wParam, LPARAM lParam )
    {

    lParam = lParam;

    switch( wMessage )
        {
        case WM_INITDIALOG:
            return ( TRUE );
        case WM_CLOSE:
            EndDialog( hDlg, 0 );
            return ( FALSE );
        case WM_COMMAND:
            switch ( wParam )
                {
                case IDD_STANDARD:
                    EndDialog( hDlg, 0 );
                    return ( TRUE );
                default:
                    break;
                }
            return ( TRUE );
        default:
            break;
        }   /* switch wMessage */

    return ( FALSE );

    }   /* function DialogDemoDialogProc */


/*****************************************************************************
        Name: MainWindowProc
 Description: Window call back function for main window
*****************************************************************************/
LONG FAR PASCAL MainWindowProc( HWND hWnd, UINT wMessage,
        WPARAM wParam, LPARAM lParam )
    {

    switch( wMessage )
        {
        case WM_COMMAND:
            {

            HINSTANCE hInstance = GetWindowWord( hWnd, GWW_HINSTANCE );

            switch( wParam )
```

Listing 10.5 *continued*

```c
            {
            case IDM_STANDARD:
                DemoDialog( hInstance, hWnd, "STANDARD" );
                break;
            case IDM_DEFAULT:
                DemoDialog( hInstance, hWnd, "CDS_DEFAULT" );
                break;
            case IDM_BORDER:
                DemoDialog( hInstance, hWnd, "BORDER" );
                break;
            case IDM_LOWERED:
                DemoDialog( hInstance, hWnd, "LOWERED" );
                break;
            case IDM_RAISED:
                DemoDialog( hInstance, hWnd, "RAISED" );
                break;
            case IDM_BORDER_LOWERED:
                DemoDialog( hInstance, hWnd, "CDS_BORDER_LOWERED" );
                break;
            case IDM_BORDER_RAISED:
                DemoDialog( hInstance, hWnd, "CDS_BORDER_RAISED" );
                break;
            case IDM_EXIT:
                DestroyWindow( hWnd );
                break;
            default:
                break;
            }
            return ( FALSE );
            }
        case WM_DESTROY:
            PostQuitMessage( 0 );
            return ( FALSE );
        default:
            break;
        }

    return ( DefWindowProc( hWnd, wMessage, wParam, lParam ) );

    }   /* function MainWindowProc */

/* End of DEM_DILG.C */
```

Listing 10.6

```c
/******************************************************************************
            File Name: DEM_DILG.RC
        Expanded Name: Demo Dialog
          Description: Resource file for the custom dialog class demo
          Portability: Microsoft Windows 3.X
******************************************************************************/

#include <windows.h>

#include <cst_dilg.h>
#include <dem_dilg.h>

DEM_DILG ICON ICON\DEM_DILG.ICO

DEM_DILG MENU
BEGIN
    POPUP "&Demo"
    BEGIN
        MENUITEM "&Standard Dialog...", IDM_STANDARD
        MENUITEM "Custom Dialog &Default...", IDM_DEFAULT
        MENUITEM "Custom Dialog CDS_&BORDER...", IDM_BORDER
        MENUITEM "Custom Dialog CDS_&LOWERED...", IDM_LOWERED
        MENUITEM "Custom Dialog CDS_&RAISED...", IDM_RAISED
        MENUITEM "Custom Dialog CDS_BORDER | CDS_LOWERED...", IDM_BORDER_LOWERED
        MENUITEM "Custom Dialog CDS_BORDER | CDS_RAISED...", IDM_BORDER_RAISED
        MENUITEM SEPARATOR
        MENUITEM "E&xit", IDM_EXIT
    END
END

STANDARD DIALOG 20, 20, 200, 40
CAPTION "Standard Dialog"
STYLE DS_MODALFRAME | WS_CAPTION | WS_SYSMENU
FONT 8, "Helv"
BEGIN
    CONTROL "&Ok", IDD_STANDARD, "button",  WS_TABSTOP | BS_DEFPUSHBUTTON,
            60, 10, 80, 16
END

CDS_DEFAULT DIALOG 20, 20, 200, 40
CAPTION "Custom Dialog Default"
CLASS "CstDialog"
STYLE DS_MODALFRAME | WS_CAPTION | WS_SYSMENU
FONT 8, "Helv"
BEGIN
    CONTROL "&Ok", IDD_STANDARD, "button",  WS_TABSTOP | BS_DEFPUSHBUTTON,
            60, 10, 80, 16
END

BORDER DIALOG 20, 20, 200, 40
CAPTION "CDS_BORDER"
CLASS "CstDialog"
STYLE DS_MODALFRAME | WS_CAPTION | WS_SYSMENU | CDS_BORDER
FONT 8, "Helv"
BEGIN
    CONTROL "&Ok", IDD_STANDARD, "button",  WS_TABSTOP | BS_DEFPUSHBUTTON,
            60, 10, 80, 16
END
```

Listing 10.6 *continued*

```
LOWERED DIALOG 20, 20, 200, 40
CAPTION "CDS_LOWERED"
CLASS "CstDialog"
STYLE DS_MODALFRAME | WS_CAPTION | WS_SYSMENU | CDS_LOWERED
FONT 8, "Helv"
BEGIN
    CONTROL "&Ok", IDD_STANDARD, "button",  WS_TABSTOP | BS_DEFPUSHBUTTON,
            60, 10, 80, 16
END

RAISED DIALOG 20, 20, 200, 40
CAPTION "CDS_RAISED"
CLASS "CstDialog"
STYLE DS_MODALFRAME | WS_CAPTION | WS_SYSMENU | CDS_RAISED
FONT 8, "Helv"
BEGIN
    CONTROL "&Ok", IDD_STANDARD, "button",  WS_TABSTOP | BS_DEFPUSHBUTTON,
            60, 10, 80, 16
END

CDS_BORDER_LOWERED DIALOG 20, 20, 200, 40
CAPTION "CDS_BORDER | CDS_LOWERED"
CLASS "CstDialog"
STYLE DS_MODALFRAME | WS_CAPTION | WS_SYSMENU | CDS_BORDER | CDS_LOWERED
FONT 8, "Helv"
BEGIN
    CONTROL "&Ok", IDD_STANDARD, "button",  WS_TABSTOP | BS_DEFPUSHBUTTON,
            60, 10, 80, 16
END

CDS_BORDER_RAISED DIALOG 20, 20, 200, 40
CAPTION "CDS_BORDER | CDS_RAISED"
CLASS "CstDialog"
STYLE DS_MODALFRAME | WS_CAPTION | WS_SYSMENU | CDS_BORDER | CDS_RAISED
FONT 8, "Helv"
BEGIN
    CONTROL "&Ok", IDD_STANDARD, "button",  WS_TABSTOP | BS_DEFPUSHBUTTON,
            60, 10, 80, 16
END

#if defined ( NO_DLL )
#include <cst_dilg.rc>
#endif

/* End of DEM_DILG.RC */
```

Listing 10.7

```
NAME DEM_DILG
DESCRIPTION 'Custom Dialog Class Demo Program'
EXETYPE WINDOWS
CODE PRELOAD MOVEABLE
DATA PRELOAD MOVEABLE MULTIPLE
HEAPSIZE 1024
STACKSIZE 5120
EXPORTS
        MainWindowProc
        DialogDemoDialogProc
        CstDialogWndFn
```

Listing 10.8

```
ORIGIN   = QCWIN
ORIGIN_VER = 1.00

PROJ =DEM_DILG
DEBUG    =0
PROGTYPE =1
CALLER   =
ARGS =
DLLS =
CVPACK   =1
CC  =cl -qc
RC  =rc
CFLAGS_G_WEXE =/AS /W4 /Ze /D_WINDOWS /DNO_DLL /G2w /Zp /Aw
CFLAGS_D_WEXE =/Zi /Od
CFLAGS_R_WEXE =/O /Os /Gs /DNDEBUG
CFLAGS_G_WDLL =/AS /G2w /Zp /Aw /W3 /D_WINDOWS /D_WINDLL
CFLAGS_D_WDLL =/Gi /Od /Zi
CFLAGS_R_WDLL =/O /Os /DNDEBUG
CFLAGS_G_WTTY =/AS /G2w /W3 /D_WINDOWS
CFLAGS_D_WTTY =/Gi /Od /Zi
CFLAGS_R_WTTY =/O /Os /DNDEBUG
CFLAGS_G_DEXE =/AS /W2
CFLAGS_D_DEXE =/Gi /Od /Zi
CFLAGS_R_DEXE =/O /Ot /DNDEBUG
CFLAGS   =$(CFLAGS_G_WEXE) $(CFLAGS_R_WEXE)
LFLAGS_G_WEXE =/NOE/A:16/ST:10240
LFLAGS_D_WEXE =/CO
LFLAGS_R_WEXE =
LFLAGS_G_WDLL =/ST:5120 /A:16
LFLAGS_D_WDLL =/CO
LFLAGS_R_WDLL =
LFLAGS_G_WTTY =/ST:5120 /A:16
LFLAGS_D_WTTY =/CO
LFLAGS_R_WTTY =
LFLAGS_G_DEXE =/NOI /ST:2048
LFLAGS_D_DEXE =/CO
LFLAGS_R_DEXE =
LFLAGS   =$(LFLAGS_G_WEXE) $(LFLAGS_R_WEXE)
RCFLAGS  =/DNO_DLL
RESFLAGS =
RUNFLAGS =
DEFFILE =       DEMSDILG.DEF
OBJS_EXT =
LIBS_EXT =

.rc.res: ; $(RC) $(RCFLAGS) -r $*.rc

all: $(PROJ).EXE

DEM_DILG.OBJ: DEM_DILG.C $(H)

DEM_DILG.RES: DEM_DILG.RC $(RESFILES) $(H)

CST_DILG.OBJ: CST_DILG.C $(H)

CST_DRAW.OBJ: CST_DRAW.C $(H)

CST_DATA.OBJ: CST_DATA.C $(H)
```

Listing 10.8 *continued*

```
CST_UTIL.OBJ: CST_UTIL.C $(H)

$(PROJ).EXE:  DEM_DILG.OBJ CST_DILG.OBJ CST_DRAW.OBJ CST_DATA.OBJ CST_UTIL.OBJ $(OBJS_EXT)
$(DEFFILE)
    echo >NUL @<<$(PROJ).CRF
DEM_DILG.OBJ +
CST_DILG.OBJ +
CST_DRAW.OBJ +
CST_DATA.OBJ +
CST_UTIL.OBJ +
$(OBJS_EXT)
$(PROJ).EXE

C:\PRGLNG\QCW\LIB\+
/NOD slibcew oldnames  libw
$(DEFFILE);
<<
    link $(LFLAGS) @$(PROJ).CRF
    rc $(RESFLAGS) DEM_DILG.RES $(PROJ).EXE

$(PROJ).EXE:  DEM_DILG.RES
    rc $(RESFLAGS) DEM_DILG.RES $(PROJ).EXE

run: $(PROJ).EXE
    $(PROJ) $(RUNFLAGS)
```

11 DLL Requirements

In most situations, to gain the full benefit from a custom control, it should be placed in a DLL. One can more easily incorporate the control into new applications if it is in a DLL. Moreover, if you plan to interface the control to the dialog editor, you must store it in a DLL.

Functions in a DLL must observe certain coding conventions. Since multiple applications can share DLLs, all the code in a DLL must be reentrant. Data references must be handled carefully, since DLLs do not have their own stack segment. Finally, because DLL functions always reside in a different segment than the application, any functions that a DLL exports must be designated *FAR*.

In practice, these restrictions are relatively easy to meet. In fact, all the custom controls we've presented already meet these requirements. In this chapter we'll explain our approach to meeting these requirements and how to construct the DLL.

Static Linking Versus Dynamic Linking

There are two methods of linking code for custom controls (any code for that matter) to a Windows program: static and dynamic. Static linking binds the code into the linked program. Dynamic linking produces a module that can be "connected" to the rest of a program *while the program is executing*.

Dynamic linking has the advantage of sharing a single copy of a library between multiple applications. This can yield significant space savings. Multiple applications need to store just one copy of a library on disk and one copy of a library in memory.

Data References

When used to compile standalone DOS programs, most compilers assume that the application will have a single stack and that the stack and data will reside in the same segment (i.e., *SS* = *DS*). This assumption simplifies code generation and generally makes data references execute faster.

This assumption won't work with shared code (e.g., a DLL), because each application using the code needs to maintain a separate stack. Since each application might reside in a different segment, the various stacks may also reside in different segments. Thus, data and function references appearing in a DLL must be fully specified, i.e., they must include a segment descriptor as part of every pointer.

While this requirement makes DLL code more verbose, it doesn't make the code any harder to write. In fact, programmers can insure that their code is DLL competent, simply by observing these four rules:

- Treat all data as *FAR*
- Use only *FAR* versions of C standard library functions
- Declare all public functions as *FAR*, and export each
- Set the *GMEM_SHARE* flag for shared global heap memory.

Treat All Data As *FAR*

Code written in the small or medium memory models, must declare all data pointers using the *FAR* keyword. In the large or huge models, pointers are *FAR* by default. For greatest flexibility, we recommend always using the *FAR* keyword.

Use Only *FAR* Versions of C Standard Library Functions

The normal standard library functions also assume that *SS* = *DS*. Thus, a function stored in a DLL will also be unable to pass an appropriate data pointer to the normal standard library functions. Both Borland and Microsoft supply special versions of the standard library routines that accept *FAR* pointers. Microsoft uses the _*f* prefix to designate their *FAR* version. Depending upon the version, Borland prefixes their *FAR* versions with *far*. There are Windows versions of some of standard library functions such as *lstrcpy()* and *wsprintf()*. You can use these instead of _*fstrcpy()* and _*fsprintf()*. Programs which use *lstrcpy()* instead of _*fstrcopy()* will be smaller because *lstrcpy()* is part of windows and is dynamically linked. Because it is part of the standard library, _*fstrcpy* will be statically linked, adding to the size of the application.

Declare All Public Functions as *FAR*, and Export Each

To make a DLL's functions available to other applications, the developer must declare them as *FAR* and "export" their names. To export the function name use the __*export* keyword in the function declaration or list the function name in the *EXPORTS* section of the linker definition file.

Set the *GMEM_SHARE()* Flag

Any global heap memory that a DLL dynamically allocates (using *GlobalAlloc()*) and that client applications will need to access from outside the DLL, must be given the *GMEM_SHARE()* attribute when allocated. To specify this attribute, combine the *GMEM_SHARE()* flag with other appropriate attribute flags in the *GlobalAlloc()* call.

Using Large Model

Windows programming authors have almost unanimously discouraged the use of the large memory model for Windows programming. Much of this attitude can be attributed to carry over from the older versions of windows which supported real mode. But even with those problems behind us, the large model still has drawbacks for Windows programming, none of which are a liability for DLL programmers. In fact, the large model makes things easier for DLLs. If you use the large memory model when compiling and linking your DLL, you automatically meet the first three memory model requirements for DLLs.

The first complaint against the large model is that it is slow. Since every data and procedure call is *FAR*, the large model adds overhead to every data access and function call. *FAR* calls aren't a significant liability for DLL developers, because virtually every DLL data reference and procedure call must be *FAR* anyway.

The second drawback has to do with multiple data segments and fixed memory. Windows limits any program that has multiple data segments to a single instance. The data space of a large model DLL function that uses a large data structure, may grow to require more than one data segment.

Neither of these two problems has much impact upon DLLs. DLLs are single instance by definition and must be marked as single instance in the linker definition file. Use the *SINGLE* keyword in the *DATA* statement in the linker definition file. The *CST_CTLS* library uses the following statement in the linker definition file to designate it as single instance.

```
DATA PRELOAD MOVEABLE SINGLE
```

Since DLLs are single instance and DLLs treat all calls to functions outside the DLL as *FAR*, using the large memory model has no significant negative effects on DLLs. The large memory model is actually a good match for DLLs, because it simplifies the memory model issues. Table 11.1 summarizes the issues for large memory model programming.

Required Library Functions

In addition to the application-related functions, each DLL must include three DLL support functions: *LibEntry()*, *LibMain()*, and *WEP()*. Windows will call these functions just after loading and just before unloading the DLL. *LibEntry()* is the assembly language entry point for the DLL initialization. *LibEntry()* performs some fundamental setup and then calls *LibMain()*, which is the entry point for the C portion of the library initialization code. *WEP()* is meant to be the library cleanup function.

Microsoft Windows SDK provides the (memory model independent) code for *LibEntry()* in the assembly file *LIBENTRY.ASM*. Most compilers that can generate DLLs also include a copy of *LIBENTRY.ASM*. For convenience, most compilers also include a precompiled object file, *LIBENTRY.OBJ*. You just statically link this file with your DLL. (Some compilers, such as Microsoft Quick C for Windows, include a generic *LibEntry()* in commonly used libraries, making it unnecessary to specify *LIBENTRY.OBJ* in the make list.)

Windows calls *LibEntry()* (or for all practical purposes, *LibMain()*) once just after the library is loaded, and calls *WEP()* once just before the library is destroyed. Unfortunately, because these functions are nontasked, these calls occur with only a *partial* application context, limiting the kinds of calls one can make from *LibMain()* and *WEP()*. In particular, when Windows loads a library automatically (as the result of

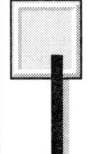

Table 11.1

Because DLLs must be reentrant, the large memory model offers more advantages than disadvantages for the DLL developer.

Drawbacks	Advantages
Slow	Good Match for DLLs
Multiple Data Segments	Eliminates DS != SS Issue
Single Instance Applications	Pointers are FAR by default
	Uses FAR Versions of C Library Functions

implicitly or explicitly importing one of the library functions), the library will be loaded *before* the application's messaging queue has been created. Thus `LibMain()` cannot call any API function that would cause a message to be sent (e.g., `CreateWindow()`).

The situation is even worse with `WEP()`. While `LibMain()` is at least called on the task and stack of the application, `WEP()` is called with a special, smaller-than-normal stack provided by the kernal. You must avoid not only functions that generate messages, but also any calls that perform global memory allocation. `WEP() can` unregister the class, but, ironically, doesn't need to — classes created by a DLL are automatically destroyed when the DLL is unloaded. To be safe, `WEP()` should do nothing; all cleanup actions can be done outside `WEP()`.

Implementation Issues

Since all of our controls allocate and deallocate their own instance and class data in the `WM_CREATE` and `WM_DESTROY` handlers, our `LibMain()` is also nearly a do-nothing function. It merely unlocks the data segment, sets a global data value to the instance handle for the library, and registers the classes. (See Figure 11.1)

Similarly, our custom control library has a "do-nothing" `WEP()` function:

```
int FAR PASCAL WEP( int nSystemExit )
    {
    return ( TRUE );
    }
```

This arrangement allows the controls to be used with almost no overhead. Once the DLL is loaded, the controls are registered and ready to be used. Unfortunately, Windows does not load the DLL when it loads the application unless the application directly references a function that resides in the DLL. If Windows doesn't load the library automatically, the programmer must do so with an explicit call to `LoadLibrary()`. If the program attempts to use one of our controls by calling *CreateWindow()*, before the library has been loaded, the create call will fail. Applications that link correctly without specifying an import from the DLL, must call *LoadLibrary()* explicitly.

Because *LibMain()* and *WEP()* are needed only when controls are being packaged in a DLL, we recommend storing *LibMain()* and *WEP()* in a separate module (source file). If these functions are in a separate file, you can easily exclude them if you ever wish to statically link the custom control code with an application.

The file *CST_CTLS.C*, Listing 11.2, contains the code for *LibMain()* and *WEP()*.

DLL Linkage

To establish linkage between a function stored in a DLL and an application that wishes to use that function, you must export the DLL

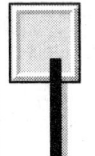

Figure 11.1
Because all of our controls manage their own resources, they need only this simple LibMain().

```
int FAR PASCAL LibMain( HINSTANCE hInstance, WORD wDataSeg, WORD wHeapSize,
    LPSTR lpstrCmd )
{

lpstrCmd = lpstrCmd;

if ( wHeapSize )
    {
    /* LibEntry called LocalInit - so unlock data segment */
    UnlockSegment( wDataSeg );
    }

/* Set the external data value */
_hInstanceCstCtls = hInstance;

return ( CstCtlRegister( hInstance ) );

}   /* function LibMain */
```

function, and include some kind of import linkage within the application. Exporting a function makes its name visible to other applications, and tells the compiler to generate function prologues and epilogues that are appropriate for a function that always uses the caller's stack and data segment. The import linkage is the code that allows Windows to find the function when it is called (and if necessary, reload it and fix inaccurate references).

To designate a function for export, you may either:

- use the export tag as part of the function prototype and definition, or
- list the exported functions in the module definition file for the DLL.

We think it's good coding practice to use the export tag, regardless of whether the function will also be listed in a module definition file.

In particular, you must export the `LibMain()` and `WEP()` functions. No matter how it is tagged, you must also list `WEP()` in the exports section of the DLL's linker definition file and give it the `RESIDENTNAME` qualifier. For best performance each function in the DLL should be listed in the module definition file and assigned an ordinal value. You *must* associate `WEP()` with an ordinal value, for example:

```
EXPORTS WEP @1 RESIDENTNAME
```

Any ordinal value except two through six (which are reserved for other standard DLL support functions) is acceptable. Standard practice is to use *@1* as in the example.

One may generate the import linkage implicitly (using an import library), explicitly (with an appropriate statement in the module definition file), or dynamically (by calling `GetProcAddress()` at runtime). Implicit linkage is, by far, the most convenient and transparent for the application programmer. When an import library is available, the application programmer references the DLL function as he would any static library function, and then includes the import mechanism by naming the import library during the normal link operation.

The *IMPLIB.EXE* program creates an import library from a module definition file. When you build a DLL file using the project builder in either the Microsoft or Borland development, the make file automatically invokes *IMPLIB*. The import library for our custom controls is *CST_CTLS.LIB*.

Besides making sure you export functions that are in a DLL, it is convenient to also create a single include file that supports all the function prototypes, message *define*s and other macros. Listing 11.1, *CST_CTLS.H*, is the include file for the custom controls library. Since each custom control already has its own include file, *CST_CTLS.H* just includes all these include files. Any application that uses the custom control library needs to include just one file, *CST_CTLS.H*.

Using the DLL

Before using any of our custom controls, an application must:

- load the library, and
- initialize the library.

Any call to a DLL function will cause Windows to automatically load the library, if the imports were created implicitly (by linking to the import library) or explicitly (with entries in the module definition file). Alternatively, the application can load the library dynamically by calling *LoadLibrary()* with the library's name. Table 11.2 summarizes the steps required to use a DLL.

DLLs and Code Sharing

Besides being convenient, DLLs are necessary to properly support code sharing between applications. While you can establish global visibility for a control that has been statically linked (by registering the control with the *CS_GLOBALCLASS* style), Windows does not properly handle references from other applications *unless* the code is stored in a DLL.

While the owner application is in memory, the window class call back function will be available and other applications will be able to successfully share a statically linked custom control class. But, when the application exits and the code for the call back function is removed from memory, the custom control's code will also be removed, even though it may still be needed by the other applications.

To avoid this problem, only controls that are stored in a DLL should be registered with the CS_GLOBALCLASS style.

DLL Support in Our Code

All the source code in this book is written to compile either as a DLL, or as part of a statically linked application.

If the constant _WINDLL is defined, the code is compiled as a DLL. Microsoft defines this constant internally if the compiler is invoked with the /GD flag. Other compilers may require that you explicitly define the _WINDLL. We use this constant throughout our code to control conditional compilation directives that select constants and attributes appropriate for a DLL function.

For example, the directive

```
#if defined ( _WINDLL )
WndClass.style |= CS_GLOBALCLASS;
#endif
```

causes the controls to have CS_GLOBALCLASS if _WINDLL is defined. Similar conditionals adjust the attributes used when allocating dynamic memory from the global heap:

```
/* Global Memory Flags */
#if defined ( _WINDLL )
#define GMEM_FLAGS \
    ( GMEM_SHARE | GMEM_MOVEABLE | GMEM_NODISCARD | GMEM_ZEROINIT )
#else
#define GMEM_FLAGS ( GMEM_MOVEABLE | GMEM_NODISCARD | GMEM_ZEROINIT )
#endif
```

The code for all the different custom controls in this book is memory model independent. Because the code declares all pointers as *FAR* and uses *FAR* versions of standard library functions, it may be compiled without modification in any memory model.

Conclusion

Given some care in the initial coding, adapting a control for inclusion in a DLL is not a particularly difficult task, and offers some significant advantages. When stored in a DLL, the control is easier to reuse, is easier to share among applications, and takes less space when shared among applications. Moreover, the control can never be fully integrated into the development environment unless it is stored in a DLL. Only a DLL can be interfaced to the dialog editor.

Table 11.2

This table summarizes the steps required to successfully build and use a custom control which is stored in a DLL.

Step	Description	Specific Step for CST_CTLS
1	Resolve External References	Link with CST_CTLS.LIB
2	Load and Initialize Library	Automatic
3	Register Custom Control Classes	> CstCtlRegister()
4	Initialize Custom Control Data	/
5	Create Custom Control Instances	CreateWindow(), Dialog Resource
6	Destroy Custom Control Instances	DestroyWindow()
7	Release Custom Control Data	> CstCtlUnregister()
8	Unregister Custom Control Classes	/
9	Unload Library	Automatic

Listing 11.1

```
/******************************************************************************
         File Name: CST_CTLS.H
     Expanded Name: Custom Controls Library
       Description: Include file for custom control dynamic link library
       Portability: Microsoft Windows 3.X
******************************************************************************/

#if !defined ( CST_CTLS_DEFINED )
    #define CST_CTLS_DEFINED

    #include <cst_xtra.h>
    #include <cst_data.h>
    #include <cst_ckbx.h>
    #include <cst_dilg.h>
    #include <cst_draw.h>
    #include <cst_flvw.h>
    #include <cst_pbtn.h>
    #include <cst_rbtn.h>
    #include <cst_rgst.h>
    #include <cst_sttc.h>
    #include <cst_tabl.h>
    #include <cst_tlbx.h>
    #include <cst_util.h>

#endif

/* End of CST_CTLS.H */
```

Listing 11.2

```
/*****************************************************************************
        File Name: CST_CTLS.C
    Expanded Name: Custom Controls Library
      Description: Main module for custom control dynamic link library
     Program List: CST_CTLS.C
                   CST_CTLS.RC
                   CST_CTLS.DEF
                   CST_CKBX.C
                   CST_DATA.C
                   CST_DILG.C
                   CST_DRAW.C
                   CST_FLVW.C
                   CST_PBTN.C
                   CST_RBTN.C
                   CST_RGST.C
                   CST_STTC.C
                   CST_TABL.C
                   CST_TLBX.C
                   CST_UTIL.C
                   CST_XTRA.C
Global Function List: LibMain
                   WEP
      Global Data: _hInstanceCstCtls
      Portability: Microsoft Windows 3.X
*****************************************************************************/

/* Microsoft Window */
#include <windows.h>

/* Prototypes and Types */
#include <cst_rgst.h>

HINSTANCE _hInstanceCstCtls;

/*****************************************************************************
        Name: LibMain
      Return: TRUE
 Description: DLL main function
*****************************************************************************/
int FAR PASCAL LibMain( HINSTANCE hInstance, WORD wDataSeg, WORD wHeapSize,
        LPSTR lpstrCmd )
    {

    lpstrCmd = lpstrCmd;

    if ( wHeapSize )
        {
        /* LibEntry called LocalInit - so unlock data segment */
        UnlockSegment( wDataSeg );
        }

    /* Set the external data value */
    _hInstanceCstCtls = hInstance;

    return ( CstCtlRegister( hInstance ) );

    }   /* function LibMain */
```

Listing 11.2 *continued*

```
/******************************************************************************
         Name: WEP
       Return: TRUE
  Description: DLL exit function
******************************************************************************/
int FAR PASCAL WEP( int nSystemExit )
    {

    nSystemExit = nSystemExit;

    return ( TRUE );

    }   /* function WEP */

/* End of CST_CTLS.C */
```

Listing 11.3

```
/******************************************************************
        File Name: CST_CTLS.RC
    Expanded Name: Custom Controls
      Description: Resource file for the custom controls library
      Portability: Microsoft Windows 3.X
*******************************************************************/

rcinclude cst_ckbx.rc
rcinclude cst_dilg.rc
rcinclude cst_flvw.rc
rcinclude cst_rbtn.rc
rcinclude cst_sttc.rc

/* End of CST_CTLS.RC */
```

Listing 11.4

```
LIBRARY CST_CTLS
DESCRIPTION 'Custom Control DLL'
EXETYPE WINDOWS
CODE PRELOAD MOVEABLE SHARED DISCARDABLE
DATA PRELOAD MOVEABLE SINGLE
HEAPSIZE 1024
EXPORTS
        WEP                       @1    RESIDENTNAME
        CstCheckBoxRegister       @2
        CstCheckBoxUnregister     @3
        CstCheckBoxWndFn          @4
        CstCtlColorMsg            @5
        CstCtlData                @6
        CstCtlDataCreate          @7
        CstCtlDataDelete          @8
        CstCtlDefDataCreate       @9
        CstCtlDefGetBitmap        @10
        CstCtlDefGetBkMode        @11
        CstCtlDefGetBrush         @12
        CstCtlDefGetColor         @13
        CstCtlDefGetFrame         @14
        CstCtlDefGetFont          @15
        CstCtlDefGetLpData        @16
        CstCtlDefGetShadow        @17
        CstCtlDefGetState         @18
        CstCtlDefGetStyle         @19
        CstCtlDefGetValue         @20
        CstCtlDefGetWnd           @21
        CstCtlDefSetBitmap        @22
        CstCtlDefSetBkMode        @23
        CstCtlDefSetBrush         @24
        CstCtlDefSetColor         @25
        CstCtlDefSetFrame         @26
        CstCtlDefSetFont          @27
        CstCtlDefSetShadow        @28
        CstCtlDefSetState         @29
        CstCtlDefSetStyle         @30
        CstCtlDefSetValue         @31
        CstCtlDefSetWnd           @32
        CstCtlGetBitmap           @33
        CstCtlGetBkMode           @34
        CstCtlGetBrush            @35
        CstCtlGetColor            @36
        CstCtlGetFrame            @37
        CstCtlGetFont             @38
        CstCtlGetLpData           @39
        CstCtlGetLpRectBitmap     @40
        CstCtlGetLpRectText       @41
        CstCtlGetShadow           @42
        CstCtlGetState            @43
        CstCtlGetStyle            @44
        CstCtlGetValue            @45
        CstCtlGetWnd              @46
        CstCtlRegister            @47
        CstCtlSetBitmap           @48
        CstCtlSetBkMode           @49
        CstCtlSetBrush            @50
        CstCtlSetColor            @51
        CstCtlSetFrame            @52
```

Listing 11.4 *continued*

```
CstCtlSetRects          @53
CstCtlSetFont           @54
CstCtlSetShadow         @55
CstCtlSetState          @56
CstCtlSetStyle          @57
CstCtlSetValue          @58
CstCtlSetWnd            @59
CstCtlState             @60
CstCtlUnregister        @61
CstDialogRegister       @62
CstDialogUnregister     @63
CstDialogWndFn          @64
CstFileViewCreateWindow @65
CstFileViewRegister     @66
CstFileViewUnregister   @67
CstFileViewWndFn        @68
CstGetClassLong         @69
CstGetClassWord         @70
CstGetWindowLong        @71
CstGetWindowWord        @72
CstPushBtnRegister      @73
CstPushBtnUnregister    @74
CstPushBtnWndFn         @75
CstRadioBtnRegister     @76
CstRadioBtnUnregister   @77
CstRadioBtnWndFn        @78
CstSetClassLong         @79
CstSetClassWord         @80
CstSetWindowLong        @81
CstSetWindowWord        @82
CstStaticRegister       @83
CstStaticUnregister     @84
CstStaticWndFn          @85
CstTableEditWndFn       @86
CstTableRegister        @87
CstTableUnregister      @88
CstTableWndFn           @89
CstToolBoxCreateWindow  @90
CstToolBoxRegister      @91
CstToolBoxUnregister    @92
CstToolBoxWndFn         @93
SafeDeleteObject        @94
```

Listing 11.5

```
ORIGIN   = QCWIN
ORIGIN_VER   = 1.00

PROJ =CST_CTLS
DEBUG    =1
PROGTYPE =2
CALLER   =
ARGS =
DLLS =
CVPACK   =1
CC   =cl
RC   =rc
CFLAGS_G_WEXE =/AS /W3 /Ze /D_WINDOWS /DQC_FOR_WINDOWS /G2w /Zp
CFLAGS_D_WEXE =/Zi /Od
CFLAGS_R_WEXE =/O /Os /Gs /DNDEBUG
CFLAGS_G_WDLL =/AS /W4 /Ze /D_WINDOWS /D_WINDLL /G2w /Zp /Aw
CFLAGS_D_WDLL =/Zi /Od
CFLAGS_R_WDLL =/O /Os /Gs /DNDEBUG
CFLAGS_G_WTTY =/AS /G2w /W3 /D_WINDOWS
CFLAGS_D_WTTY =/Gi /Od /Zi
CFLAGS_R_WTTY =/O /Os /DNDEBUG
CFLAGS_G_DEXE =/AS /W2
CFLAGS_D_DEXE =/Gi /Od /Zi
CFLAGS_R_DEXE =/O /Ot /DNDEBUG
CFLAGS   =$(CFLAGS_G_WDLL) $(CFLAGS_D_WDLL)
LFLAGS_G_WEXE =/A:16/ST:10240
LFLAGS_D_WEXE =/CO
LFLAGS_R_WEXE =
LFLAGS_G_WDLL =/NOE/A:16/ST:5120
LFLAGS_D_WDLL =/CO
LFLAGS_R_WDLL =
LFLAGS_G_WTTY =/ST:5120 /A:16
LFLAGS_D_WTTY =/CO
LFLAGS_R_WTTY =
LFLAGS_G_DEXE =/NOI /ST:2048
LFLAGS_D_DEXE =/CO
LFLAGS_R_DEXE =
LFLAGS   =$(LFLAGS_G_WDLL) $(LFLAGS_D_WDLL)
RCFLAGS  =
RESFLAGS =
RUNFLAGS =
DEFFILE =    CST_CTLS.DEF
OBJS_EXT =
LIBS_EXT =

.rc.res: ; $(RC) $(RCFLAGS) -r $*.rc

all: $(PROJ).DLL

CST_CKBX.OBJ: CST_CKBX.C $(H)

CST_CTLS.OBJ: CST_CTLS.C $(H)

CST_DATA.OBJ: CST_DATA.C $(H)

CST_DILG.OBJ: CST_DILG.C $(H)

CST_DRAW.OBJ: CST_DRAW.C $(H)
```

Listing 11.5 *continued*

```
CST_FLVW.OBJ: CST_FLVW.C $(H)

CST_PBTN.OBJ: CST_PBTN.C $(H)

CST_RBTN.OBJ: CST_RBTN.C $(H)

CST_RGST.OBJ: CST_RGST.C $(H)

CST_STTC.OBJ: CST_STTC.C $(H)

CST_TABL.OBJ: CST_TABL.C $(H)

CST_TLBX.OBJ: CST_TLBX.C $(H)

CST_UTIL.OBJ: CST_UTIL.C $(H)

CST_XTRA.OBJ: CST_XTRA.C $(H)

CST_CTLS.RES: CST_CTLS.RC $(RESFILES) $(H)

$(PROJ).DLL:  CST_CKBX.OBJ CST_CTLS.OBJ CST_DATA.OBJ CST_DILG.OBJ CST_DRAW.OBJ CST_FLVW.OBJ \
    CST_PBTN.OBJ CST_RBTN.OBJ CST_RGST.OBJ CST_STTC.OBJ CST_TABL.OBJ CST_TLBX.OBJ
CST_UTIL.OBJ \
    CST_XTRA.OBJ $(OBJS_EXT) $(DEFFILE)
    echo >NUL @<<$(PROJ).CRF
CST_CKBX.OBJ +
CST_CTLS.OBJ +
CST_DATA.OBJ +
CST_DILG.OBJ +
CST_DRAW.OBJ +
CST_FLVW.OBJ +
CST_PBTN.OBJ +
CST_RBTN.OBJ +
CST_RGST.OBJ +
CST_STTC.OBJ +
CST_TABL.OBJ +
CST_TLBX.OBJ +
CST_UTIL.OBJ +
CST_XTRA.OBJ +
$(OBJS_EXT)
$(PROJ).DLL

F:\PRGLNG\QCWIN\LIB\+
/NOD sdllcew oldnames  libw
$(DEFFILE);
<<
    link $(LFLAGS) @$(PROJ).CRF
    rc $(RESFLAGS) CST_CTLS.RES $(PROJ).DLL

$(PROJ).DLL:  CST_CTLS.RES
    rc $(RESFLAGS) CST_CTLS.RES $(PROJ).DLL

run: $(PROJ).DLL
    $(PROJ) $(RUNFLAGS)
```

Dialog Editor Requirements

Once a custom control has been packaged in a DLL, you can name it in a resource script, just as if it were a standard control — if you are willing to keyboard or edit the text of the resource file.

We would prefer to create the resource script using a resource editor, such as the Dialog Editor, or Borland's Resource Workshop. The task of interfacing a custom control with the Dialog Editor is the most unpleasant chore in the whole process of creating custom controls. It requires lots of uninteresting, repetitive code, but it has its rewards, too. Controls that have a Dialog Editor interface, can be selected and manipulated just like a standard control. This ability greatly expands the usefulness of the Dialog Editor and simplifies the building of impressive Dialog Boxes.

A good Dialog Editor interface is especially important to a commercial custom control library. The Dialog Editor not only makes it easier for a developer to use your custom control, but also makes a good place to show off your custom control.

This chapter interfaces six of the eight custom components from the previous chapters. The remaining two would not normally be part of a dialog box. When the dialog interface is complete, each custom control will have its own DLL. Each of these DLLs will link to *CST_CTLS.DLL*, the DLL created in the previous chapter. Table 12.1 lists all the custom controls and dynamic link libraries. Table 12.2 lists the files contained in the Dialog Editor interface DLLs.

The Dialog Editor

This chapter will interface the custom controls of the previous chapters with the Microsoft Dialog Editor. While the Dialog Editor was the first resource tool available to Windows developers, its functionality has now been eclipsed by other resource tools (in particular, by Borland's Resource Workshop). Nonetheless, Dialog Editor still represents the lowest common denominator among most of the resource tools. While tools from other vendors may use a different interface, these differences usually represent an optional superset. Thus, by conforming to the Microsoft interface and a few additional requirements, you can build controls that will integrate well with many resource tools.

The Dialog Editor provides two mechanisms for using a custom control: a "temporary" method, which operates without any knowledge of the control's special characteristics; and a quasi-permanent method, which uses custom support routines to provide specialized support for each control.

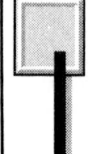

Table 12.1

The dialog editor interface requires a separate DLL for every true custom control. The controls proper are stored in a sixth DLL.

Custom Control	Custom Control DLL	Dialog Editor Interface DLL
CSTCHECKBOX	CST_CTLS.DLL	DEI_CKBX.DLL
CSTDIALOG	CST_CTLS.DLL	Not Applicable
CSTFILEVIEW	CST_CTLS.DLL	DEI_FLVW.DLL
CSTPUSHBTN	CST_CTLS.DLL	DEI_PBTN.DLL
CSTRADIOBTN	CST_CTLS.DLL	DEI_RBTN.DLL
CSTSTATIC	CST_CTLS.DLL	DEI_STTC.DLL
CSTTABLE	CST_CTLS.DLL	DEI_TABL.DLL
CSTTOOLBOX	CST_CTLS.DLL	Not Applicable

The temporary method requires no programming support, but is very inconvenient. Each time a programmer starts a session with the Dialog Editor they must reinform the dialog editor of the window class name for every custom control they wish to use. Since the Dialog Editor knows *only* the control's class name, it can supply only generic support for the control and its styles. Instead of drawing the actual control, the dialog editor will substitute a generic box. Instead of editing styles through a dialog filled with appropriate check boxes or buttons, the programmer is forced to specify styles numerically. These limitations make this

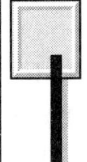

Table 12.2

Each interface DLL requires several files. All but the files for the check box DLL appear in Appendix A.

```
DEI_CKBX.DLL                              DEI_STTC.DLL
    DEI_CKBX.H,    Listing 12.1               DEI_STTC.H,    Listing A.11
    DEI_CKBX.C,    Listing 12.2               DEI_STTC.C,    Listing A.12
    DEI_CKBX.RC,   Listing 12.3               DEI_STTC.RC,   Listing A.13
    DEI_CKBX.DLG,  Listing 12.4               DEI_STTC.DLG,  Listing A.14
    DEI_CKBX.DEF,  Listing 12.5               DEI_STTC.DEF,  Listing A.15
    DEI_CTLS.H,    Listing 12.7               DEI_CTLS.H,    Listing 12.7
    DEI_CTLS.C,    Listing 12.8               DEI_CTLS.C,    Listing 12.8

DEI_PBTN.DLL                              DEI_TABL.DLL
    DEI_PBTN.H,    Listing A.1                DEI_TABL.H,    Listing A.16
    DEI_PBTN.C,    Listing A.2                DEI_TABL.C,    Listing A.17
    DEI_PBTN.RC,   Listing A.3                DEI_TABL.RC,   Listing A.18
    DEI_PBTN.DLG,  Listing A.4                DEI_TABL.DLG,  Listing A.19
    DEI_PBTN.DEF,  Listing A.5                DEI_TABL.DEF,  Listing A.20
    DEI_CTLS.H,    Listing 12.7               DEI_CTLS.H,    Listing 12.7
    DEI_CTLS.C,    Listing 12.8               DEI_CTLS.C,    Listing 12.8

DEI_RBTN.DLL                              DEI_FLVW.DLL
    DEI_RBTN.H,    Listing A.6                DEI_FLVW.H,    Listing A.21
    DEI_RBTN.C,    Listing A.7                DEI_FLVW.C,    Listing A.22
    DEI_RBTN.RC,   Listing A.8                DEI_FLVW.RC,   Listing A.23
    DEI_RBTN.DLG,  Listing A.9                DEI_FLVW.DLG,  Listing A.24
    DEI_RBTN.DEF,  Listing A.10               DEI_FLVW.DEF,  Listing A.25
    DEI_CTLS.H,    Listing 12.7               DEI_CTLS.H,    Listing 12.7
    DEI_CTLS.C,    Listing 12.8               DEI_CTLS.C,    Listing 12.8
```

method totally unsuited for any custom control that will be used more than once or twice.

The permanent method, on the other hand, seamlessly integrates the custom control into the Dialog Editor. Once this interface is built, the programmer need enter the name of the control's DLL *only once*; the Dialog Editor will save the name in its .INI file, and automatically load the custom control DLL for subsequent Dialog Editor sessions. Moreover, the Dialog Editor will display the actual control, and will offer a custom dialog box when the control's styles are edited.

The Interface

Each control that is to be "permanently" interfaced with the Dialog Editor must be packaged, along with some special interface functions, in a separate DLL. (Other resource tools relax this restriction and allow the programmer to put multiple controls in the same DLL.) The Dialog Editor calls special functions in the DLL to extract information about the custom control, to display the control and an appropriate style edit dialog box, and to translate style information into strings appropriate for a resource script.

Besides these interface routines, the dialog editor interface requires two data structures for each custom control: one to keep track of the control's status (*CTLSTYLE*), and one to supply defaults and display labels for the control (*CTLINFO*). These structures are defined in *CUSTCNTL.H* (supplied with the Windows SDK).

Table 12.3 describes the six members of the *CTLINFO* structure. The dialog editor uses information from this structure to control the initial display of a control instance and to expand the list of controls associated with the custom control option in the dialog editor's tool box. The *wVersion* member should reflect the revision level of the custom control. Typically the *szTitle* member is set to the window class name, but if the class name is cryptic or abbreviated, one can use an expanded description.

The Type member points to a list of "style variants," which should have a separate entry in the Dialog Editor's list of custom controls;

wCtlTypes tells how many entries are in the list. Unfortunately, the dialog editor doesn't know how to handle more than one type, so only the first member in this list is significant.

Each entry in the list is a structure of type *CTLTYPE* (see Table 12.4). This structure includes: the nonfunctional control type (it must be set to zero), the default size of the control(*wWidth* and *wHeight*), the name of the control class (*szClass*), the style word that will produce the associated control, and a descriptive text string *szDescr*. Unfortunately, the Dialog editor ignores the description member, *szDescr*. Borland's Resource Workshop uses this string as the name of the control when it displays a list of available custom controls. The Dialog Editor always lists the control (regardless of style variations) by the control's class name.

Table 12.3

The dialog editor uses information from the CTLINFO structure to control the initial display of a control. CTLINFO has these members:

Member	Type	Description
wVersion	UINT	Version of control, typically 100 for first version
wCtlTypes	UINT	Number of fundamental types, 1 to CTLTYPES
szClass	char	String containing the control's window class name
szTitle	char	Title, Copyright or usually the class name again
Type	CTLTYPE	Array of CTLTYPE structures

Table 12.4

The CTLTYPE structure is used to create multiple "standard flavors" of a single control. The members record the default style and size information for each variant of the control.

Member	Type	Description
wType	UINT	The type of control
wWidth	UINT	Default width of control in dialog coordinates
hHeight	UINT	Default height of control in dialog coordinates
dwStyle	DWORD	Default style flags
szDescr	char	String containing descriptive name of control

The string and array members in *CTLINFO* have fixed lengths, determined by constants defined in *CUSTCNTL.H* (see Table 12.5).

The height and width specified in the *CTLTYPE* structure, should be consistent with the standard controls. Table 12.6 lists the sizes of some standard controls in dialog units. To specify a control's size in pixels instead of dialog units, use the function *GetDialogBaseUnits()* and convert from pixels into dialog units.

The *CTLSTYLE* structure contains information that describes a specific instance of a custom control window. It contains the current values of the size, location, styles and text for a custom control (see Table 12.7).

The Interface Functions

Besides the *LibEntry()*, *LibMain()* and *WEP()* functions required for every DLL, the Dialog Editor interface requires the five functions in Table 12.8. These functions are either called by the Dialog Editor or are call back functions.

The *Info()* Function

When you first install a new custom control or when you first start up the Dialog Editor with a custom control already installed, the Dialog Editor calls the *ClassNameInfo()* function by ordinal number (where *ClassName()* is replaced by the name of the custom control) to retrieve information about a custom control. The *Info()* function must allocate and initialize a *CTLINFO* structure in the global heap. The initialization

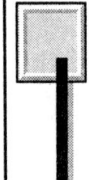

Table 12.5

The string and array members of CTLINFO have these fixed lengths:

Constant	Value	Description
CTLCLASS	20	Maximum length of class name string + 1;
CTLTITLE	94	Maximum length of title string + 1;
CTLTYPES	12	Maximum number of fundamental types or class styles
CTLDESCR	22	Maximum length of fundamental type description sting + 1

includes building a `CTLTYPE` array. The `Info()` function then passes the structure memory handle back to the Dialog Editor.

Other tools, in particular Borland's Resource Workshop, infer information from the function names. The Resource Workshop, for example, determines whether a DLL contains a Borland interface, a

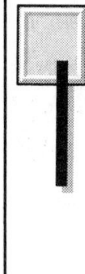

Table 12.6

Initially the Dialog Editor will display the custom controls in these sizes (all in dialog units):

Control	Width	Height
Check Box	NA	12
Pushbutton	NA	14
Combo Box	NA	12
Combo Box, Owner Draw	NA	17
Edit	NA	12
Scroll Bar, Vertical	9	NA
Scroll Bar, Horizontal	NA	9
Static Text	NA	8

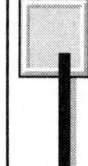

Table 12.7

The CTLSTYLE structure contains information that describes a specific instance of a custom control. It has these members:

Member	Type	Description
wX	UINT	X origin of control in dialog units
wY	UINT	Y origin of control in dialog units
wCx	UINT	Width of control in dialog units
wCy	UINT	Height of control in dialog units
wId	UINT	Id of control
dwStyle	DWORD	Style of control
szClass	char	Control window class name
szTitle	char	Control's window text

Microsoft interface, or no interface by looking for specific function names. See the **Windows/DOS Developer's Journal** article by Ron Burk (Appendix B) for more details.

The *Style()* Function

Whenever the user asks to edit the styles of a custom control, the Dialog Editor calls the *ClassNameStyle()* function. This function must invoke the style dialog box for the custom control, pass information about current style settings to the dialog box, and return a value indicating whether the user desires to change the style. The Dialog Editor passes four parameters (see Table 12.9) to the *Style()* function.

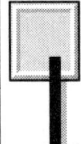

Table 12.8

The Dialog Editor interface requires that these functions be assigned specific ordinal numbers.

Suggested Name	Ordinal	Description
ClassNameInfo	2	Passes information about control to Dialog Editor
ClassNameStyle	3	Invokes the style dialog box
ClassNameFlags	4	Expands style value into string for resource file
ClassNameDlgFn	5	Dialog box callback function for specifying styles
ClassNameWndFn	6	Window callback function for custom control class

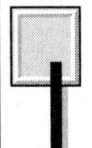

Table 12.9

The ClassNameStyle() function takes these parameters:

Parameter	Type	Description
hWnd	HWND	Handle to the Dialog Editor Window
hCtlStyle	GLOBALHANDLE	Global memory handle of CTLSTYLE structure
lpfnStrToId	LPFNSTRTOID	Function pointer to convert string to id
lpfnIdToStr	LPFNIDTOSTR	Function pointer to convert id to string

The style dialog box is your one opportunity for creativity in the otherwise rigidly defined chore of interfacing custom controls with the Dialog Editor. Typically, a style dialog box gives the developer/user a chance to set the id, text and styles for a control. The rest of the controls in the style dialog box are usually a combination of check boxes and radio buttons, one control for each possible style.

By default, the Dialog Editor only calls the *Style()* function when the user selects the "Styles..." menu item from the Dialog Editor's Edit menu. However, if the custom control has the *CS_DBLCLKS* style, the Dialog Editor will also call the *ClassNameStyle()* function when the user double clicks on the custom control's window.

The *DlgFn()* Function

The *ClassNameDlgFn()*, is the windows call back function that handles all user interaction with the style dialog box. At a minimum the *ClassNameDlgFn()* must respond to three messages: *WM_INITDIALOG*, *WM_COMMAND*, and *WM_DESTROY*. Since *WM_COMMAND* can be accompanied by a value *IDC_OK* (indicating the styles have been changed), or *IDC_CANCEL* (indicating the styles have not been changed), the function actually responds to four separate events.

In response the *WM_INITDIALOG* message, *DlgFn()* should set the initial state of the various buttons and controls in the style dialog, and allocate any data structures it may need.

If the *IDC_OK* command is received, *DlgFn()* must interrogate all the controls in the style dialog and use the results to construct a new style word (and possibly window text) for the custom control.

DlgFn() then calls the standard Windows function *EndDialog()* to destroy the dialog. All other *WM_COMMAND* messages simply call *EndDialog()*.

On the *WM_DESTROY* message, *DlgFn()* releases any resources it may have acquired in response to the *WM_INITDIALOG* message.

The *WndFn()* Function

ClassNameWndFn() is the control's call back function. This function must process all messages to the control, just as if the control were being used by an application, and not by the Dialog Editor.

The *Flags()* Function

The Dialog Editor calls the *ClassNameFlags()* function when the user saves the dialog resource file (typically at the end of an editing session). This function expands the control's current style word into a string of style identifiers.

Implementation Strategy

One could package all of the application code for a custom control together with the Dialog Editor interface in a single DLL. This packaging alternative would have the advantage of being simple to maintain, but would have the major disadvantage of forcing both developer and end user to allocate disk storage for all the Dialog Editor interface code. Alternatively, one could create two different DLLs, one for the developer (with the interface code) and one for the end user (without the interface code). This second packaging alternative reduces the size of the end user's DLL, but forces the implementor to duplicate all the code of the custom control call back function in both DLLs, creating potential maintenance problems.

Our implementation avoids both problems by putting all the interface code *except the control's call back function* in a separate interface DLL. In place of the call back function, the interface DLL uses a simple "wrapper function" to link to the call back function in the standard end user DLL. This minimizes the size of the end user DLL, avoids duplication of the call back function in the interface DLL, and insures that both the Dialog Editor and the application are using *exactly* the same implementation of the control.

To minimize the effort required to interface a new custom control to the Dialog Editor, we also push as much code as possible into a common interface support library. The programming interface for this library is patterned after a similar library by Jeffery Richter (See Appendix B). To support communication among these common routines, our interface libraries require a *CSTCTLSTYLE* structure in addition to those required by the Dialog Editor. Both the *ClassNameStyle()* and *ClassNameDlg-Fn()* functions use the *CSTCTLSTYLE* structure defined in *DEI_CTLS.H*, Listing 12.7, to transport data into the styles dialog box for a custom control. This structure is bound to the appropriate dialog box window by saving its handle as a window property.

As a result, all but the style dialog call back function and the flags function become trivial. Considering that the flags function is always just a big case statement that maps bit patterns onto strings, one could easily argue that, while not small, it too, is trivial.

Finally, we have tried to make our style dialog boxes consistent with the Dialog Editor's standard dialog boxes. Our dialogs are structured and positioned much like the standard ones. The biggest difference is that our dialogs all use our custom versions of the standard controls.

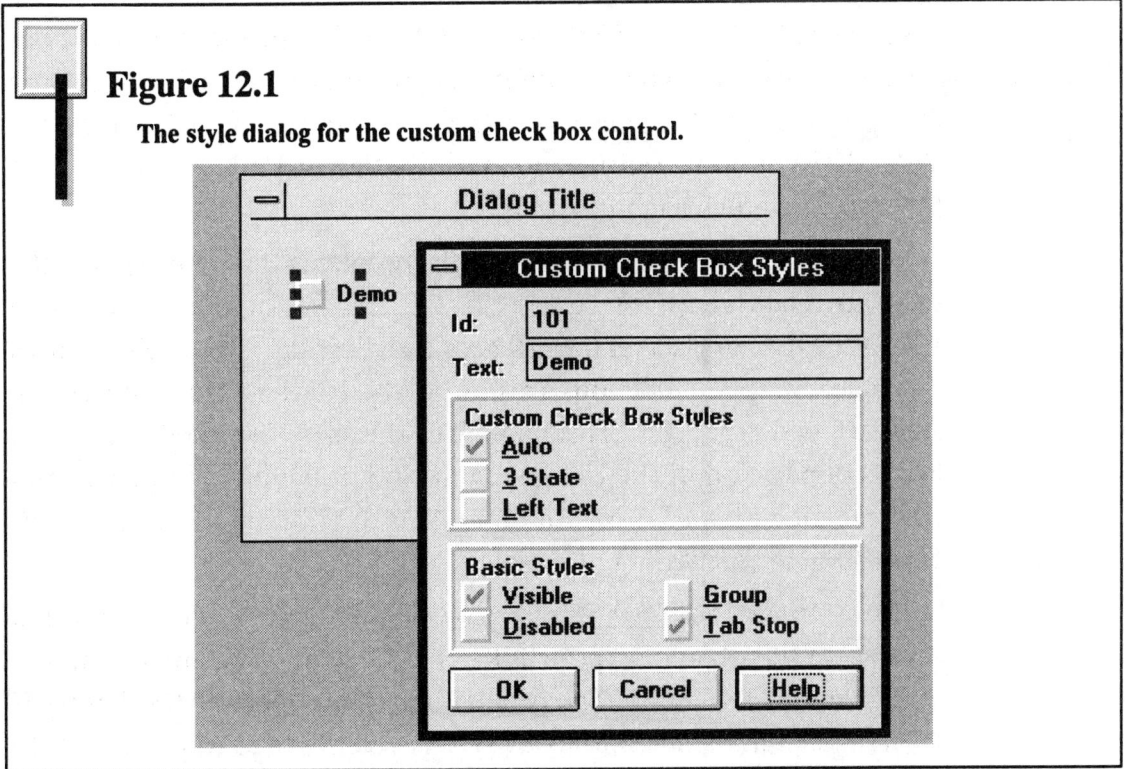

Figure 12.1
The style dialog for the custom check box control.

Figure 12.1 through 12.5 and Figure II in the Preface show each of the dialog boxes.

The *Info()* Function

Again in the interface DLL, we must solve the problem of when to register the control. *LibMain()* is still unreliable, and since we don't have access to the Dialog Editor source, we can't put the registration call in *WinMain()*. The answer is to put the registration call in the *Info()* function: the Dialog Editor must call the *Info()* function to have enough information to create an instance of the control, and the message loop will be running. As before, we use a registration counter to avoid multiple registrations. Notice that the call to our registration function has the nonobvious side effect of forcing windows to load the *CST_CTLS.DLL*. This call assures that the control's call back function will be available before it is called.

After registering the control class, *Info()* calls the utility function *CtlInfoCreate()* which builds a *CTLINFO* structure, which has a blank

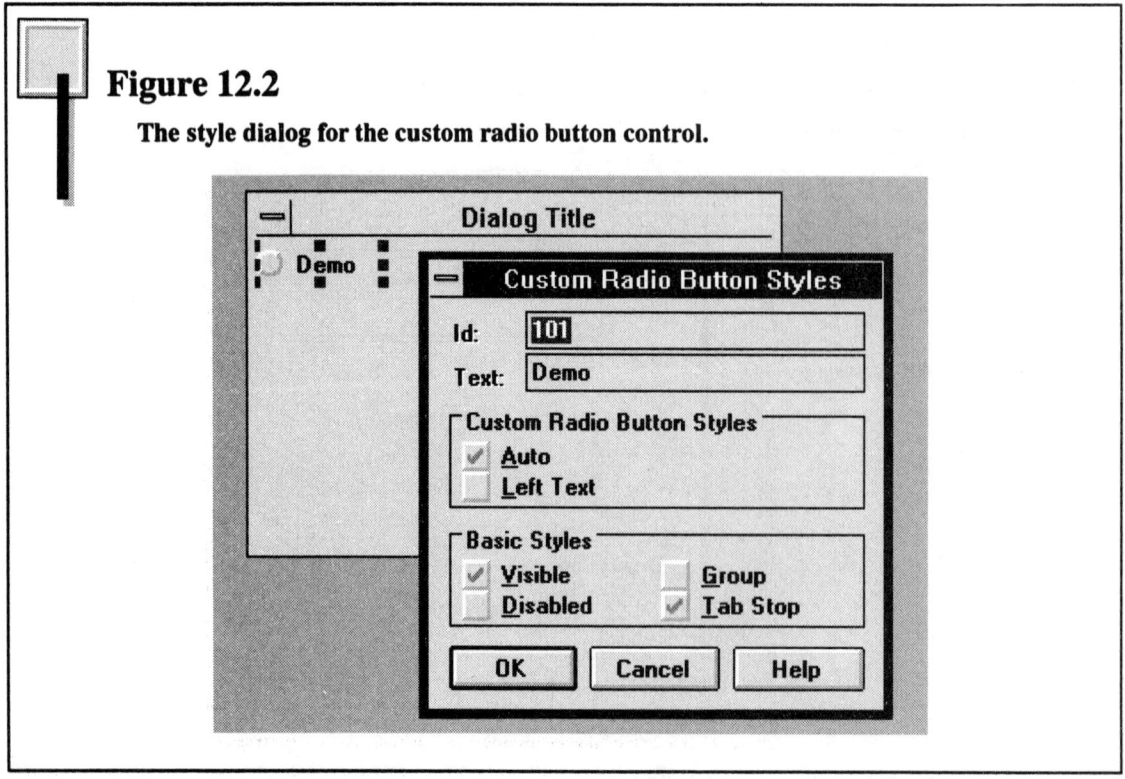

Figure 12.2
The style dialog for the custom radio button control.

type list, but is complete otherwise. Finally, *Info()* constructs appropriate entries (default sizes, style, and description of the control) in the type list.

The *Info()* function for the custom check box control appears in Figure 12.6.

The Style Function

Because all our style dialogs are created from resource templates (see the *.dlg files), we can use a common utility function to display each of the style dialogs. Thus, *CstCheckBoxStyle()* does nothing more than call the function *CstCtlDlg()*.

CstCtlDlg() first allocates memory for a *CSTCTLSTYLE* structure, which will be used to pass information into the style dialog box function. This structure will contain a handle to the control's *CTLSTYLE* structure, a pointer to the function for converting strings to ids, and a pointer to the function for converting ids to strings.

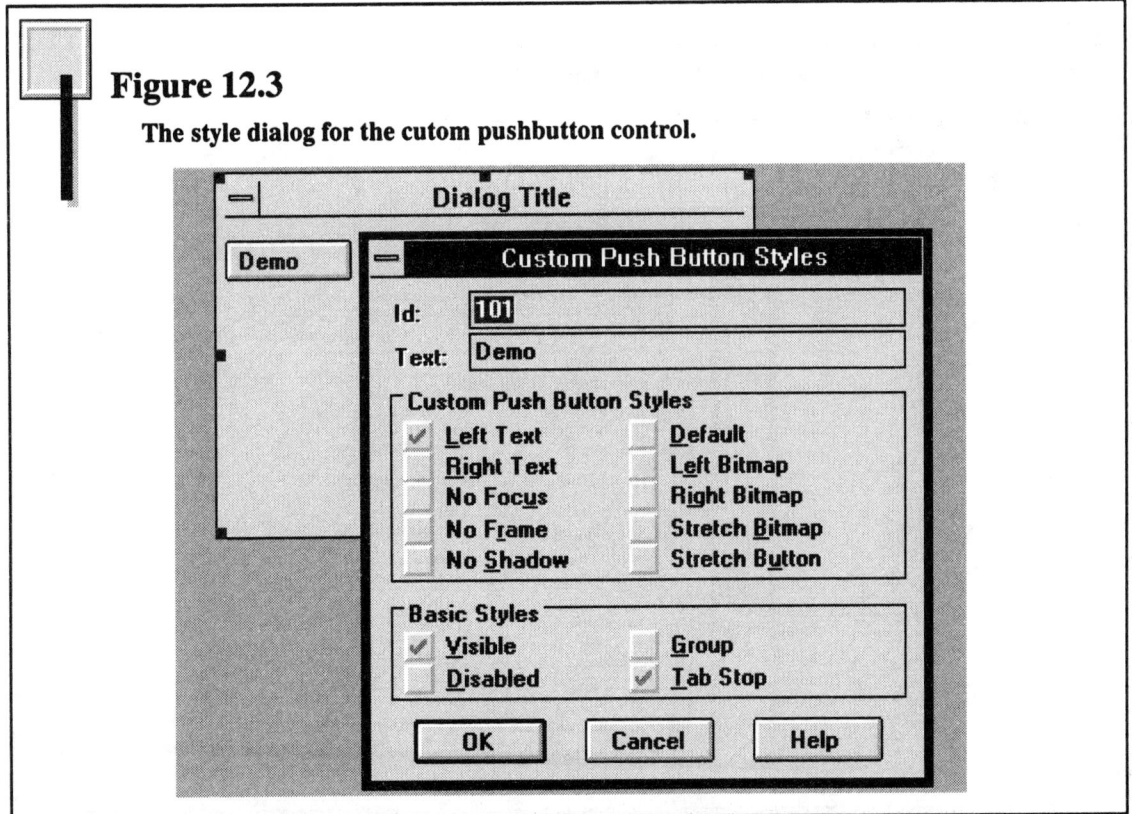

Figure 12.3
The style dialog for the cutom pushbutton control.

CstCtlDlg() will supply the dialog function with a handle to this structure indirectly, through the *WM_INITDIALOG* message. *CstCtlDlg()* creates the style dialog box by calling the standard Windows function *DialogBoxParam()*. The last parameter to *DialogBoxParam()* is a long which will be passed to the new window as the *lParam* for the *WM_INITDIALOG* message. *CstCtlDlg()* sets this parameter to the handle of the *CSTCTLSTYLE* structure. This handle is then bound to the dialog box window by setting a window property and the window style for the custom control retrieved.

The Dialog Function

In response to the *WM_INITDIALOG* message, the *DlgFn()* function copies the handle to the *CSTCTLSTYLE* structure from its *lParam()* into a window property. *DlgFn()* then calls *CenterWindow()* from the support library to reposition the style dialog. While it's not strictly necessary to center

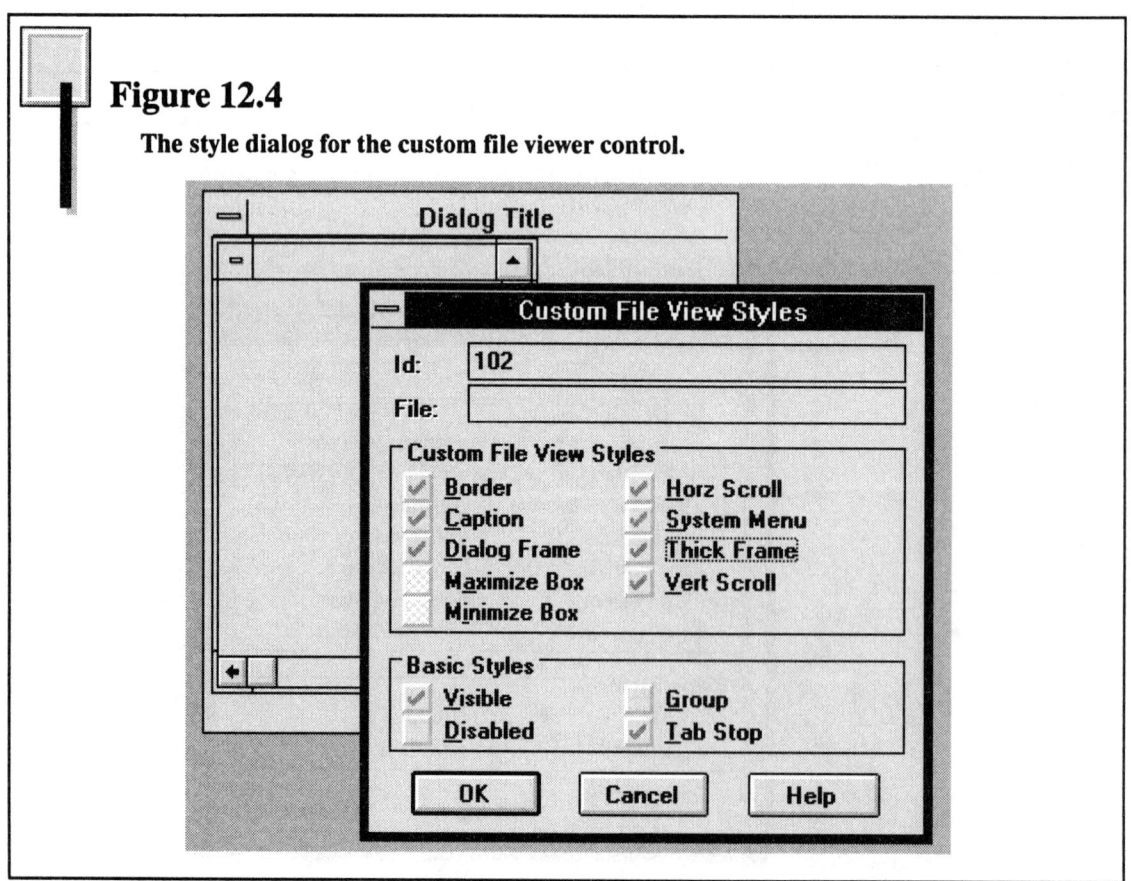

Figure 12.4

The style dialog for the custom file viewer control.

the dialog, doing so keeps the user interface more consistent across controls. Finally, *DlgFn()* sets the state of all the controls to reflect the currently selected style.

DlgFn() responds to the *WM_COMMAND* when the developer selects the *Ok* or *Cancel* push button. In response to an *"Ok" WM_COMMAND* message, *ClassNameDlgFn()* polls all the controls in the dialog box and sets the information in the *CTLSTYLE* structure. It also returns *TRUE* through the *EndDialog()* function indicating that the styles have changed. When a *WM_COMMAND* contains *"Cancel"*, *DlgFn()* calls *EndDialog()* and indicates that the styles have not changed. *CstCtlDlg()* passes the return value of the dialog box back up through the *ClassNameStyle()* function to the Dialog Editor.

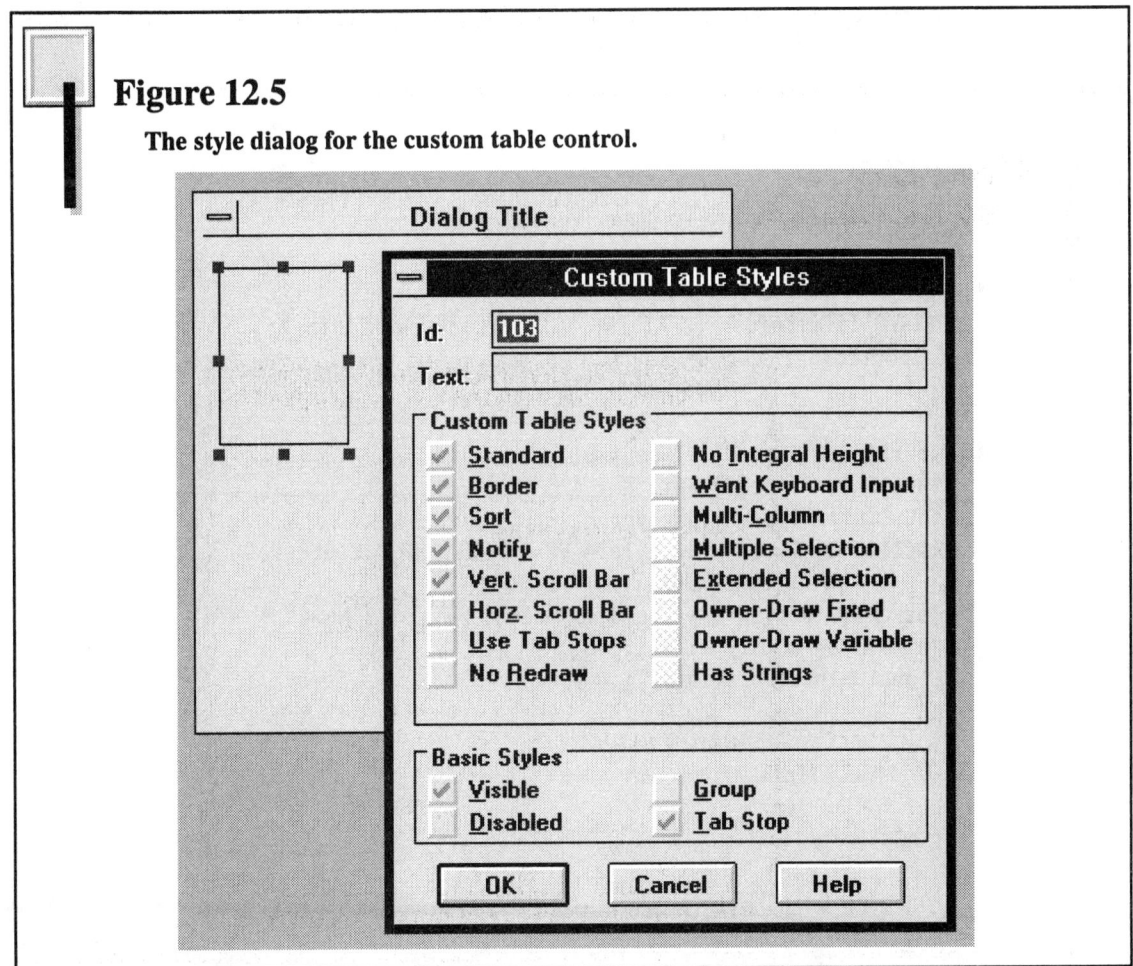

Figure 12.5
The style dialog for the custom table control.

In response to the WM_DESTROY message, ClassNameDlgFn() removes the window property. The ClassNameDlgFn() uses the function CenterWindow() to position the dialog box in the center of the Dialog Editor. The Dialog Editor does not require this operation, but it gives consistency and predictability to the user interface for a custom control. Each style dialog invokes the Windows help engine if the Help button is pushed.

Figure 12.6

Our interface DLLs register the controls in the Info() function.

```
GLOBALHANDLE FAR PASCAL Dei_CkBxInfo( void )
  {

  GLOBALHANDLE hCtlInfo = NULL;

  hCtlInfo = CtlInfoCreate( 100, _szCstCtlName, _szCstCtlName );
  if ( hCtlInfo )
      {

      LPCTLINFO lpCtlInfo = (LPCTLINFO)GlobalLock( hCtlInfo );
      if ( lpCtlInfo )
         {

         lpCtlInfo->Type[0].wType = 0;
         lpCtlInfo->Type[0].wWidth = 40;
         lpCtlInfo->Type[0].wHeight = 12;
         lpCtlInfo->Type[0].dwStyle = WS_CHILD | WS_VISIBLE |
                 BS_AUTOCHECKBOX | WS_TABSTOP;
         lstrcpy( lpCtlInfo->Type[0].szDescr, _szCstCtlName );
         lpCtlInfo->wCtlTypes = 1;
         GlobalUnlock( hCtlInfo );

         }   /* if lpCtlInfo */
      }   /* if hCtlInfo */

  return ( hCtlInfo );

  }   /* function Dei_CkBxInfo */
```

Figure 12.7 shows the style function for the *CstCheckBox* class.

The *Flags()* Function

The *Flags()* function needs a plethora of strings. These strings can be saved in the string table, and retrieved using the style constants as string identifiers. Even though window style constants are long values and string identifiers in the resource script are integers, this technique works,

Figure 12.7

As this style function from the custom check box interface illustrates, the utility function CstCtlStyleDlg() does all the real work.

```
BOOL FAR PASCAL CstCheckBoxStyle( HWND hWnd, GLOBALHANDLE hCtlStyle,
    LPFNSTRTOID lpfnStrToId, LPFNIDTOSTR lpfnIdToStr )
{

return ( CstCtlStyleDlg( _hInstanceDLL, _szCstCtlName,
        (FARPROC)CstCheckBoxDlgFn,
        hWnd, hCtlStyle, lpfnStrToId, lpfnIdToStr ) );

}   /* function CstCheckBoxStyle */
```

Figure 12.8

All of the strings for the Flags() function are saved in the string table, and created with resource scripts such as this:

```
STRINGTABLE
BEGIN
      BS_CHECKBOX,     "BS_CHECKBOX"
      BS_AUTOCHECKBOX, "BS_AUTOCHECKBOX"
      BS_3STATE,       "BS_3STATE"
      BS_AUTO3STATE,   "BS_AUTO3STATE"
      BS_LEFTTEXT,     "BS_LEFTTEXT"
END
```

because widening the value has no negative consequences — the class specific styles are always confined to the low word of the window style.

Figure 12.8 is an excerpt from Listing 12.3, *DEI_CKBX.RC*. This is the string table from the resource file for the DLL that interfaces the *CstCheckBox* control with the Dialog Editor. The resource file for each custom control has a string table of the class specific window styles.

The *WndFn()* Function

The wrapper function resides in the Dialog Editor interface DLL, *DEI_NAME.DLL* (where *NAME* designates the custom control). The wrapper function in *DEI_NAME.DLL* is a call back function that does nothing more than invoke the window class function that resides in *CST_CTLS.DLL*.

```
LONG FAR PASCAL DeiClassNameWndFn( HWND hWnd, UINT wMessage,
        WPARAM wParam,
     LPARAM lParam )
   {
   return ( ClassNameWndFn( hWnd, wMessage, wParam, lParam ) );
   }
```

The window function can call *ClassNameWndFn()* directly, without calling *MakeProcInstance()*, because *ClassNameWndFn()* is an exported function that resides in a DLL.

Note that our use of a wrapper forces us to violate the *ClassName???()* naming convention we've observed so carefully everywhere else. This exception will have no consequence for the Dialog Editor, because the Dialog Editor links to the interface functions using only the ordinal numbers. (Which implies that you *must* declare the functions using the right ordinal numbers. See Table 12.8 for the required values.)

Custom Dialog Classes

You can also use custom dialog classes within the dialog editor, but you can't "install" them as you can a custom control. To incorporate a custom dialog class into your application, change the class entry for dialog boxes in the styles dialog. If your resource tool does not allow you to set the class for a dialog box, you will need to edit the resource script. Simply use a text editor to insert the class specification after the dialog name and before the *BEGIN* keyword:

```
DialogName DIALOG 32768, 0, 32768, 32768
CLASS "ClassName"
CAPTION "Caption"
STYLE WS_OVERLAPPEDWINDOW
FONT 8, "Helv"
MENU DialogMenu
BEGIN
    .
    .
    .
END
```

Conclusion

Using the code from this chapter, you can create six new DLLs that will allow you to conveniently develop dialogs using the controls from the DLL created in the previous chapter. Placing the interface in a separate DLL allows you to share code among the various controls (by using a common support library within the control DLL) and allows you to distribute separate products to developers and end users without maintaining two versions of the same code.

With the control fully integrated into the dialog editor, you can create customized dialogs just as easily as standard dialogs. The result can be a much richer, more intuitive user interface.

Listing 12.1

```
/*****************************************************************************
            File Name: DEI_CKBX.H
        Expanded Name: Dialog Editor Interface for CSTCHECKBOX
          Description: Include file for DEI_CKBX.C & DEI_CKBX.RC
          Portability: Microsoft Windows 3.X
*****************************************************************************/

#define IDC_AUTO        101
#define IDC_3STATE      102
#define IDC_LEFTTEXT    103

#define IDC_VISIBLE     201
#define IDC_DISABLED    202
#define IDC_GROUP       203
#define IDC_TABSTOP     204

#define IDC_EDIT_ID     300
#define IDC_EDIT_TEXT   301

#define IDC_OK            1
#define IDC_CANCEL        2
#define IDC_HELP          8

/* End of DEI_CKBX.H */
```

Listing 12.2

```
/****************************************************************************
          File Name: DEI_CKBX.C
      Expanded Name: Dialog Editor Interface for Custom Check Box Control
        Description: Library of functions for interfacing the CSTCHECKBOX
                    control with the Dialog Editor.
       Program List: DEI_CKBX.C
                    DEI_CKBX.RC
                    DEI_CKBX.DEF
                    DEI_CTLS.C
                    CST_CTLS.LIB,DLL
Global Function List: CstCheckBoxDlgFn
                    CstCheckBoxFlags
                    CstCheckBoxStyle
                    Dei_CkBxInfo
                    Dei_CkBxWndFn
                    LibMain
                    WEP
        Static Data: _hInstanceDLL
                    _szCstCtlName
        Portability: Microsoft Windows 3.X
****************************************************************************/

/* Microsoft Windows */
#include <windows.h>

/* Custom Control Interface */
#include <custcntl.h>

/* Standard C */
#include <stdlib.h>

/* Prototypes and Types */
#include <cst_ckbx.h>
#include <dei_ctls.h>


/* Own */
#include <dei_ckbx.h>

/* Library instance handle */
static HINSTANCE _hInstanceDLL = 0;

static char _szCstCtlName[] = "CstCheckBox";

/* Prototypes of functions */
BOOL FAR PASCAL CstCheckBoxDlgFn( HWND hDlg, WORD wMessage, WORD wParam,
        LONG lParam );
WORD FAR PASCAL CstCheckBoxFlags( DWORD dwFlags, LPSTR szString,
        WORD wMaxString );
BOOL FAR PASCAL CstCheckBoxStyle( HWND hWnd, GLOBALHANDLE hCtlStyle,
        LPFNSTRTOID lpfnStrToId, LPFNIDTOSTR lpfnIdToStr );
GLOBALHANDLE FAR PASCAL Dei_CkBxInfo( void );
LONG FAR PASCAL Dei_CkBxBoxWndFn( HWND hWnd, UINT wMessage, WPARAM wParam,
        LPARAM lParam );
```

Listing 12.2 continued

```
/******************************************************************************
       Name: CstCheckBoxDlgFn
 Description: Dialog box callback function for style selection.
******************************************************************************/
BOOL FAR PASCAL CstCheckBoxDlgFn( HWND hDlg, WORD wMsg, WORD wParam,
       LONG lParam )
    {

    switch ( wMsg )
        {
        case WM_INITDIALOG:
            {

            char szIdStr[CTLTITLE];

            /* Set the property */
            HCSTCTLSTYLE hCstCtlStyle = LOWORD( lParam );
            LPCSTCTLSTYLE lpCstCtlStyle =
                    (LPCSTCTLSTYLE)GlobalLock( hCstCtlStyle );
            LPCTLSTYLE lpCtlStyle =
                    (LPCTLSTYLE)GlobalLock( lpCstCtlStyle->hCtlStyle );
            DWORD dwStyle = lpCtlStyle->dwStyle;
            DWORD dwType = dwStyle & 0x0FL;

            SetProp( hDlg, _szCstCtlStyle, hCstCtlStyle );

            /* Center Dialog Box */
            CenterWindow( GetParent( hDlg ), hDlg, 0 );

            /* Text */
            SetDlgItemText( hDlg, IDC_EDIT_TEXT, lpCtlStyle->szTitle );

            /* Id */
            if ( !(*lpCstCtlStyle->lpfnIdToStr)( lpCtlStyle->wId, szIdStr,
                    CTLTITLE ) )
                {
                wsprintf( szIdStr, "%n", lpCtlStyle->wId );
                }
            SetDlgItemText( hDlg, IDC_EDIT_ID, szIdStr );
            GlobalUnlock( lpCstCtlStyle->hCtlStyle );
            GlobalUnlock( hCstCtlStyle );

            /* Check Box styles */
            if ( ( dwType == BS_AUTOCHECKBOX ) ||
                    ( dwType == BS_AUTO3STATE ) )
                {
                CheckDlgButton( hDlg, IDC_AUTO, TRUE );
                }
            if ( ( dwType == BS_AUTO3STATE ) ||
                    ( dwType == BS_3STATE ) )
                {
                CheckDlgButton( hDlg, IDC_3STATE, TRUE );
                }
            if ( dwStyle & BS_LEFTTEXT )
                {
                CheckDlgButton( hDlg, IDC_LEFTTEXT, TRUE );
                }
```

Listing 12.2 *continued*

```c
        /* Basic styles */
        if ( dwStyle & WS_VISIBLE )
            {
            CheckDlgButton( hDlg, IDC_VISIBLE, TRUE );
            }
        if ( dwStyle & WS_DISABLED )
            {
            CheckDlgButton( hDlg, IDC_DISABLED, TRUE );
            }
        if ( dwStyle & WS_GROUP )
            {
            CheckDlgButton( hDlg, IDC_GROUP, TRUE );
            }
        if ( dwStyle & WS_TABSTOP )
            {
            CheckDlgButton( hDlg, IDC_TABSTOP, TRUE );
            }
        break;
        }
    case WM_COMMAND:
        switch ( wParam )
            {
            case IDC_HELP:
                WinHelp( hDlg, "CST_CTLS.HLP", HELP_KEY,
                    (DWORD)(LPSTR)"CstCheckBox" );
                break;
            case IDC_OK:
                {
                char szIdStr[32];
                DWORD dwStyle, dwId;
                HCSTCTLSTYLE hCstCtlStyle;
                LPCSTCTLSTYLE lpCstCtlStyle;
                LPCTLSTYLE lpCtlStyle;

                hCstCtlStyle = GetProp( hDlg, _szCstCtlStyle );
                lpCstCtlStyle = (LPCSTCTLSTYLE)GlobalLock(
                        hCstCtlStyle );
                lpCtlStyle = (LPCTLSTYLE)GlobalLock(
                        lpCstCtlStyle->hCtlStyle );
                dwStyle = lpCtlStyle->dwStyle & 0xFFFF0000L;

                /* Text */
                GetDlgItemText( hDlg, IDC_EDIT_TEXT,
                        lpCtlStyle->szTitle, CTLTITLE );

                /* Id */
                GetDlgItemText( hDlg, IDC_EDIT_ID, szIdStr,
                        sizeof ( szIdStr ) );
                dwId = (*lpCstCtlStyle->lpfnStrToId)( szIdStr );
                if ( LOWORD( dwId ) == 0 )
                    {
                    lpCtlStyle->wId = max( (WORD)atoi( szIdStr ),
                            lpCtlStyle->wId );
                    }
                else
                    {
                    lpCtlStyle->wId = HIWORD( dwId );
                    }
```

Listing 12.2 *continued*

```
        /* Check Box Styles */
        if ( IsDlgButtonChecked( hDlg, IDC_AUTO ) )
            {
            if ( IsDlgButtonChecked( hDlg, IDC_3STATE ) )
                {
                dwStyle |= BS_AUTO3STATE;
                }
            else
                {
                dwStyle |= BS_AUTOCHECKBOX;
                }
            }
        else if ( IsDlgButtonChecked( hDlg, IDC_3STATE ) )
            {
            dwStyle |= BS_3STATE;
            }
        /*
        else
            {
            dwStyle |= BS_CHECKBOX;
            }
        */
        if ( IsDlgButtonChecked( hDlg, IDC_LEFTTEXT ) )
            {
            dwStyle |= BS_LEFTTEXT;
            }

        /* Basic Styles */
        if ( IsDlgButtonChecked( hDlg, IDC_VISIBLE ) )
            {
            dwStyle |= WS_VISIBLE;
            }
        else
            {
            dwStyle &= ~WS_VISIBLE;
            }
        if ( IsDlgButtonChecked( hDlg, IDC_DISABLED ) )
            {
            dwStyle |= WS_DISABLED;
            }
        else
            {
            dwStyle &= ~WS_DISABLED;
            }
        if ( IsDlgButtonChecked( hDlg, IDC_GROUP ) )
            {
            dwStyle |= WS_GROUP;
            }
        else
            {
            dwStyle &= ~WS_GROUP;
            }
        if ( IsDlgButtonChecked( hDlg, IDC_TABSTOP ) )
            {
            dwStyle |= WS_TABSTOP;
            }
        else
            {
```

Listing 12.2 *continued*

```
                    dwStyle &= ~WS_TABSTOP;
                    }

                lpCtlStyle->dwStyle = dwStyle;
                GlobalUnlock( lpCstCtlStyle->hCtlStyle );
                GlobalUnlock( hCstCtlStyle );
                EndDialog( hDlg, TRUE );
                break;
                }
            case IDC_CANCEL:
                EndDialog( hDlg, FALSE );
                break;
            default:
                return ( FALSE );
            }   /* switch wParam */
        break;
    case WM_DESTROY:
        WinHelp( hDlg, "CST_CTLS.HLP", HELP_QUIT, 0L );
        RemoveProp( hDlg, _szCstCtlStyle );
        break;
    default:
        return ( FALSE );
    }   /* switch wMsg */

return ( TRUE );

}   /* function CstCheckBoxDlgFn */

/****************************************************************************
        Name: CstCheckBoxFlags
  Parameters: dwFlags - current style of control
              lpstrStyle - buffer to store style string
              wMaxLen - maximum length of style string
      Return: length of style string
 Description: Converts a style into a string of style flags of all the
              class specific window styles for a control.  The basic, or
              class general styles are concatenated onto these by the dialog
              editor.
****************************************************************************/
WORD FAR PASCAL CstCheckBoxFlags( DWORD dwFlags, LPSTR lpstrStyle,
        WORD wMaxLen )
    {

    UINT uiType;
    char szBuf[32];
    int iBufLen = 32;

    wMaxLen = wMaxLen;

    /* Check Box Type */
    uiType = (UINT)( dwFlags & 0x0FL );
    LoadString( _hInstanceDLL, uiType, szBuf, iBufLen );
    lstrcpy( lpstrStyle, szBuf );

    /* Check Box Style */
    if ( dwFlags & BS_LEFTTEXT )
        {
        LoadString( _hInstanceDLL, (UINT)BS_LEFTTEXT, szBuf, iBufLen );
        lstrcat( lpstrStyle, " | " );
```

Listing 12.2 continued

```c
            lstrcat( lpstrStyle, szBuf );
            }

        return ( (WORD)lstrlen( lpstrStyle ) );

        }   /* function CstCheckBoxFlags */

/*****************************************************************************
          Name: CstCheckBoxStyle
    Parameters: hWnd - handle of dialog editor window
                hCtlStyle - global handle of CTLSTYLE structure
                lpfnStrToId - pointer to func to convert string to control id
                lpfnIdToStr - pointer to func to convert control id to string
        Return: TRUE if style has changed, FALSE if no change
   Description: Invokes the style dialog box for a custom control.
*****************************************************************************/
BOOL FAR PASCAL CstCheckBoxStyle( HWND hWnd, GLOBALHANDLE hCtlStyle,
        LPFNSTRTOID lpfnStrToId, LPFNIDTOSTR lpfnIdToStr )
    {

    return ( CstCtlStyleDlg( _hInstanceDLL, _szCstCtlName,
            (FARPROC)CstCheckBoxDlgFn,
            hWnd, hCtlStyle, lpfnStrToId, lpfnIdToStr ) );

    }   /* function CstCheckBoxStyle */


/*****************************************************************************
         Name: Dei_CkBxInfo
       Return: global handle to CTLINFO structure
  Description: Allocates a CTLINFO structure in the global heap.  Loads the
               structure with information about the custom control.
*****************************************************************************/
GLOBALHANDLE FAR PASCAL Dei_CkBxInfo( void )
    {

    GLOBALHANDLE hCtlInfo = NULL;

    hCtlInfo = CtlInfoCreate( 100, _szCstCtlName, _szCstCtlName );
    if ( hCtlInfo )
        {
        LPCTLINFO lpCtlInfo = (LPCTLINFO)GlobalLock( hCtlInfo );
        if ( lpCtlInfo )
            {
            lpCtlInfo->Type[0].wType = 0;
            lpCtlInfo->Type[0].wWidth = 40;
            lpCtlInfo->Type[0].wHeight = 12;
            lpCtlInfo->Type[0].dwStyle = WS_CHILD | WS_VISIBLE |
                    BS_AUTOCHECKBOX | WS_TABSTOP;
            lstrcpy( lpCtlInfo->Type[0].szDescr, _szCstCtlName );
            lpCtlInfo->wCtlTypes = 1;
            GlobalUnlock( hCtlInfo );

            }   /* if lpCtlInfo */
        }   /* if hCtlInfo */

    return ( hCtlInfo );

    }   /* function Dei_CkBxInfo */
```

Listing 12.2 continued

```c
/*****************************************************************************
        Name: Dei_CkBxWndFn
      Return: Same as CstCheckBoxWndFn
 Description: Windows call back function for custom control.  This is a
              wrapper function for the existing function that resides in the
              CST_CTLS.DLL.
*****************************************************************************/
LONG FAR PASCAL Dei_CkBxWndFn( HWND hWnd, UINT wMessage, WPARAM wParam,
        LPARAM lParam )
    {

    return ( CstCheckBoxWndFn( hWnd, wMessage, wParam, lParam ) );

    }   /* function Dei_CkBxWndFn */


/*****************************************************************************
        Name: LibMain
      Return: TRUE
 Description: DLL main function
*****************************************************************************/
int FAR PASCAL LibMain( HINSTANCE hInstance, WORD wDataSeg, WORD wHeapSize,
        LPSTR lpstrCmd )
    {

    lpstrCmd = lpstrCmd;

    if ( wHeapSize )
        {
        /* LibEntry called LocalInit - so unlock data segment */
        UnlockSegment( wDataSeg );
        }

    /* Set the external data value */
    _hInstanceDLL = hInstance;

    return ( TRUE );

    }   /* function LibMain */


/*****************************************************************************
        Name: WEP
      Return: TRUE
 Description: DLL exit function
*****************************************************************************/
int FAR PASCAL WEP( int nSystemExit )
    {

    nSystemExit = nSystemExit;

    return ( TRUE );

    }   /* function WEP */

/* End of DEI_CKBX.C */
```

Listing 12.3

```
/*****************************************************************************
           File Name: DEI_CKBX.RC
       Expanded Name: Dialog Editor Interface for CSTCHECKBOX
         Description: Resource file for DEI_CKBX.DLL.
         Portability: Microsoft Windows 3.X
*****************************************************************************/

#include <windows.h>
#include <cst_ctls.h>

#include <dei_ckbx.h>
#include <dei_ckbx.dlg>

STRINGTABLE
BEGIN
    BS_CHECKBOX,      "BS_CHECKBOX"
    BS_AUTOCHECKBOX,  "BS_AUTOCHECKBOX"
    BS_3STATE,        "BS_3STATE"
    BS_AUTO3STATE,    "BS_AUTO3STATE"
    BS_LEFTTEXT,      "BS_LEFTTEXT"
END

/* End of DEI_CKBX.RC */
```

Listing 12.4

```
/*****************************************************************************
        File Name: DEI_CKBX.DLG
    Expanded Name: Dialog Editor Interface for CSTCHECKBOX
      Description: Style Dialog file for DEI_CKBX.DLL.
      Portability: Microsoft Windows 3.X
*****************************************************************************/

CstCheckBox DIALOG LOADONCALL MOVEABLE DISCARDABLE 16, 16, 140, 142
STYLE DS_MODALFRAME | WS_POPUP | WS_VISIBLE | WS_CAPTION | WS_SYSMENU |
      CDS_BORDER | CDS_RAISED
CAPTION "Custom Check Box Styles"
FONT 8, "Helv"
BEGIN
    CONTROL "Id:" -1, "cststatic", CSS_TEXTLOWERED | WS_GROUP, 6, 6, 20, 10
    CONTROL "", IDC_EDIT_ID, "EDIT", ES_LEFT | ES_AUTOHSCROLL | WS_BORDER |
        WS_GROUP | WS_TABSTOP, 30, 4, 104, 12
    CONTROL "Text:", -1, "cststatic", CSS_TEXTLOWERED | WS_GROUP, 6, 20, 20, 10
    CONTROL "", IDC_EDIT_TEXT, "EDIT", ES_LEFT | ES_AUTOHSCROLL | WS_BORDER |
        WS_GROUP | WS_TABSTOP, 30, 18, 104, 12

    CONTROL "Custom Check Box Styles", -1, "CstStatic", CSS_TEXTLOWERED,
        10, 36, 100, 10
    CONTROL "Custom Check Box Styles", -1, "CstStatic", WS_GROUP |
        CSS_FRAME | CSS_BORDER | CSS_RAISED, 6, 34, 128, 44
    CONTROL "&Auto", IDC_AUTO, "cstcheckbox", BS_AUTOCHECKBOX | WS_GROUP |
        WS_TABSTOP, 10, 46, 28, 10
    CONTROL "&3 State", IDC_3STATE, "cstcheckbox", BS_AUTOCHECKBOX |
        WS_TABSTOP, 10, 56, 38, 10
    CONTROL "&Left Text", IDC_LEFTTEXT, "cstcheckbox", BS_AUTOCHECKBOX |
        WS_TABSTOP, 10, 66, 44, 10

    CONTROL "Basic Styles", -1, "CstStatic", CSS_TEXTLOWERED,
        10, 84, 64, 10
    CONTROL "Basic Styles", -1, "CstStatic", WS_GROUP |
        CSS_FRAME | CSS_BORDER | CSS_RAISED, 6, 82, 128, 36
    CONTROL "&Visible", IDC_VISIBLE, "cstcheckbox", BS_AUTOCHECKBOX | WS_GROUP |
        WS_TABSTOP, 10, 94, 36, 10
    CONTROL "&Disabled", IDC_DISABLED, "cstcheckbox", BS_AUTOCHECKBOX |
        WS_TABSTOP, 10, 104, 42, 10
    CONTROL "&Group", IDC_GROUP, "cstcheckbox", BS_AUTOCHECKBOX | WS_TABSTOP,
        72, 94, 34, 10
    CONTROL "&Tab Stop", IDC_TABSTOP, "cstcheckbox", BS_AUTOCHECKBOX |
        WS_TABSTOP, 72, 104, 46, 10

    CONTROL "OK", IDC_OK, "BUTTON", BS_DEFPUSHBUTTON | WS_GROUP | WS_TABSTOP,
        6, 122, 40, 14
    CONTROL "Cancel", IDC_CANCEL, "BUTTON", BS_PUSHBUTTON | WS_TABSTOP, 50,
        122, 40, 14
    CONTROL "Help", IDC_HELP, "BUTTON", BS_PUSHBUTTON | WS_TABSTOP,
        94, 122, 40, 14
END

/* End of DEI_CKBX.DLG */
```

Windows Custom Controls

Listing 12.5

```
LIBRARY DEI_CKBX
DESCRIPTION 'Dialog Editor - CSTCHECKBOX DLL
EXETYPE WINDOWS
CODE PRELOAD MOVEABLE SHARED DISCARDABLE
DATA PRELOAD MOVEABLE SINGLE
HEAPSIZE 1024
EXPORTS
        WEP                 @1      RESIDENTNAME
        Dei_CkBxInfo        @2
        CstCheckBoxStyle    @3
        CstCheckBoxFlags    @4
        Dei_CkBxWndFn       @5
        CstCheckBoxDlgFn    @6
```

Listing 12.6

```
ORIGIN     = QCWIN
ORIGIN_VER = 1.00

PROJ =DEI_CKBX
DEBUG    =0
PROGTYPE =2
CALLER   =
ARGS =
DLLS =
CVPACK    =1
CC  =cl -qc
RC  =rc
CFLAGS_G_WEXE=/AS /W4 /Ze /D_WINDOWS /G2w /Zp  /Aw
CFLAGS_D_WEXE=/Zi /Od
CFLAGS_R_WEXE=/O /Os /Gs /DNDEBUG
CFLAGS_G_WDLL=/AS /W4 /Ze /D_WINDOWS /D_WINDLL /G2w /Zp /Aw
CFLAGS_D_WDLL=/Zi /Od
CFLAGS_R_WDLL=/O /Os /Gs /DNDEBUG
CFLAGS_G_WTTY=/AS /G2w /W3 /D_WINDOWS
CFLAGS_D_WTTY=/Gi /Od /Zi
CFLAGS_R_WTTY=/O /Os /DNDEBUG
CFLAGS_G_DEXE=/AS /W2
CFLAGS_D_DEXE=/Gi /Od /Zi
CFLAGS_R_DEXE=/O /Ot /DNDEBUG
CFLAGS    =$(CFLAGS_G_WDLL) $(CFLAGS_R_WDLL)
LFLAGS_G_WEXE=/NOE/A:16/ST:10240
LFLAGS_D_WEXE=/CO
LFLAGS_R_WEXE=
LFLAGS_G_WDLL=/NOE/A:16/ST:5120
LFLAGS_D_WDLL=/CO
LFLAGS_R_WDLL=
LFLAGS_G_WTTY=/ST:5120 /A:16
LFLAGS_D_WTTY=/CO
LFLAGS_R_WTTY=
LFLAGS_G_DEXE=/NOI /ST:2048
LFLAGS_D_DEXE=/CO
LFLAGS_R_DEXE=
LFLAGS    =$(LFLAGS_G_WDLL) $(LFLAGS_R_WDLL)
RCFLAGS  =
RESFLAGS =
RUNFLAGS =
DEFFILE =     DEI_CKBX.DEF
OBJS_EXT =
LIBS_EXT =    CST_CTLS.LIB

.rc.res: ; $(RC) $(RCFLAGS) -r $*.rc

all: $(PROJ).DLL

DEI_CKBX.OBJ: DEI_CKBX.C $(H)

DEI_CKBX.RES: DEI_CKBX.RC $(RESFILES) $(H)

DEI_CTLS.OBJ: DEI_CTLS.C $(H)

$(PROJ).DLL: DEI_CKBX.OBJ DEI_CTLS.OBJ $(OBJS_EXT) $(DEFFILE)
    echo >NUL @<<$(PROJ).CRF
DEI_CKBX.OBJ +
DEI_CTLS.OBJ +
```

Listing 12.6 continued

```
$(OBJS_EXT)
$(PROJ).DLL

C:\PRGLNG\QCW\LIB\+
/NOD sdllcew oldnames  libw+
CST_CTLS.LIB
$(DEFFILE);
<<
    link $(LFLAGS) @$(PROJ).CRF
    rc $(RESFLAGS) DEI_CKBX.RES $(PROJ).DLL

$(PROJ).DLL: DEI_CKBX.RES
    rc $(RESFLAGS) DEI_CKBX.RES $(PROJ).DLL

run: $(PROJ).DLL
    $(PROJ)  $(RUNFLAGS)
```

Listing 12.7

```
/****************************************************************************
        File Name: DEI_CTLS.H
    Expanded Name: Dialog Editor Interface for Custom Controls
      Description: Include file for DEI_CTLS.C
      Portability: Microsoft Windows 3.X
****************************************************************************/

#if !defined ( DEI_CTLS_DEFINED )
    #define DEI_CTLS_DEFINED

    /* Data used to get information into the style dialog box function. */
    typedef struct
        {
        GLOBALHANDLE hCtlStyle;    /* Mem. handle of CTLSTYLE for control */
        LPFNSTRTOID lpfnStrToId;   /* Func. to cnvrt. string ID to number */
        LPFNIDTOSTR lpfnIdToStr;   /* Func. to cnvrt. numeric ID to string */
        } CSTCTLSTYLE, FAR *LPCSTCTLSTYLE, NEAR *NPCSTCTLSTYLE;
    typedef unsigned int HCSTCTLSTYLE;

    /* Prototypes of functions in DEI_CTLS.C */
    void PASCAL CenterWindow( HWND hWndParent, HWND hWndCenter,
            BOOL bRepaint );
    void PASCAL CenterWindowRect( HWND hWndParent,
            HWND hWndCenter, LPRECT RectCenter );
    int PASCAL CstCtlStyleDlg( HINSTANCE hInstance, LPSTR szCstCtlStyleDlgName,
            FARPROC fpCstCtlStyleDlgProc, HWND hWndParent,
            GLOBALHANDLE hCtlStyle, LPFNSTRTOID lpfnStrToId,
            LPFNIDTOSTR lpfnIdToStr );
    GLOBALHANDLE PASCAL CtlInfoCreate( WORD wVersion,
            LPSTR szClass, LPSTR szTitle );
    WORD PASCAL GetIdString( HWND hDlg, LPSTR szId, WORD wIdMaxLen );
    DWORD PASCAL SetIdValue( HWND hDlg, LPSTR szId );

    extern char _szCstCtlStyle[];

#endif

/* End of DEI_CTLS.H */
```

Windows Custom Controls

Listing 12.8

```
/*****************************************************************************
           File Name: DEI_CTLS.C
       Expanded Name: Dialog Editor Interface for Custom Controls
         Description: Library of functions for interfacing custom controls
                      with the dialog editor.
Global Function List: CenterWindow
                      CenterWindowRect
                      CtlInfoCreate
                      GetIdString
                      SetIdValue
                      CstCtlStyleDlg
Static Function List: CtlStyleLock
                      CtlStyleUnlock
         Global Data: _szCtlProp[]
         Portability: Microsoft Windows 3.X
*****************************************************************************/

/* Microsoft Windows */
#include <windows.h>

/* Custom Control Interface */
#include <custcntl.h>

/* Own */
#include <dei_ctls.h>

/* Macro for CenterWindow */
#define BYTE_ALIGN( x )  ( ( x + 4 ) & ~ 7 )

/* Property name used to store handle of CSTCTLSTYLE data structure. */
char _szCstCtlStyle[] = "CstCtlStyle";

/* Prototypes for static functions */
static LPCTLSTYLE PASCAL CtlStyleLock( HWND hDlg );
static BOOL PASCAL CtlStyleUnlock( HWND hDlg );

/*****************************************************************************
        Name: CenterWindow
  Parameters: hWndParent - handle of parent window
              hWndCenter - handle of window to center
              bRepaint - Flag to specify repainting after moving.  If bRepaint
                         is 0, the window is not painted.
 Description: Moves a window to the center of the
              specified parent window.  If parent
              window is NULL, the desktop window is
              used.  Also sends a WM_PAINT message
              if bRepaint is non-zero.
*****************************************************************************/
void PASCAL CenterWindow( HWND hWndParent, HWND hWndCenter,
      BOOL bRepaint )
   {

   RECT RectCenter;

   CenterWindowRect( hWndParent, hWndCenter, &RectCenter );

   MoveWindow( hWndCenter, RectCenter.left, RectCenter.top,
            ( RectCenter.right - RectCenter.left ),
            ( RectCenter.bottom - RectCenter.top ), bRepaint );
```

Listing 12.8 *continued*

```
    }   /* function CenterWindow */

/*******************************************************************************
        Name: CenterWindowRect
  Parameters: hWndParent - handle of parent window
              hWndCenter - handle of parent window
              RectCenter - pointer to RECT struct
      Return: Indirectly returns the values of the calculated center position
              in RectCenter
 Description: Gets the X and Y location in screen coordinates of the window to
              center.  If the center window handle is NULL, the values in the
              RECT struct that RectCenter points to are assumed to be the
              valid current values for the center window. They are used to
              calculate the height and width of the center window.
*******************************************************************************/
void PASCAL CenterWindowRect( HWND hWndParent, HWND hWndCenter,
        LPRECT RectCenter )
    {

    RECT RectParent;
    int CenterX, CenterY, Height, Width;

    if ( hWndParent == NULL )
        {
        hWndParent = GetDesktopWindow();
        }

    GetWindowRect( hWndParent, &RectParent );

    if ( hWndCenter != NULL )
        {
        GetWindowRect( hWndCenter, RectCenter );
        }

    Width = ( RectCenter->right - RectCenter->left );
    Height = ( RectCenter->bottom - RectCenter->top );
    CenterX = ( ( RectParent.right - RectParent.left ) - Width ) / 2;
    CenterY = ( ( RectParent.bottom - RectParent.top ) - Height ) / 2;

    if ( ( CenterX < 0 ) || ( CenterY < 0 ) )
        {

        /* The Center Window is smaller than the
        ** parent window. */

        if ( hWndParent != GetDesktopWindow() )
            {
            /* If the parent window is not the
            ** desktop use the desktop size. */
            CenterX = ( GetSystemMetrics( SM_CXSCREEN ) - Width ) / 2;
            CenterY = ( GetSystemMetrics( SM_CYSCREEN ) - Height ) / 2;
            }

        CenterX = ( CenterX < 0 ) ? 0: CenterX;
        CenterY = ( CenterY < 0 ) ? 0: CenterY;
```

Listing 12.8 *continued*

```
        }     /* if CenterX */
    else
        {
        CenterX += RectParent.left;
        CenterY += RectParent.top;
        }

    /* Byte Align in the x direction for speed. */
    CenterX = BYTE_ALIGN( CenterX );

    /* Copy the values into RectCenter. */
    RectCenter->left = CenterX;
    RectCenter->right = CenterX + Width;
    RectCenter->top = CenterY;
    RectCenter->bottom = CenterY + Height;

    }    /* function CenterWindowRect */


/*****************************************************************************
         Name: CstCtlStyleDlg
   Parameters: szCstCtlStyleDlgName - style dialog box resource name
               fpCstCtlStyleDlgProc - pntr to style dialog box callback proc
               hWndParent - parent window of style dialog box
               hCtlStyle - global heap handle of CTLSTYLE structure
               lpfnStrToId - function pointer to convert string to id
               lpfnIdToStr - function pointer to convert id to string
       Return: TRUE if CTLSTYLE data changed, else FALSE
  Description: This function displays the control's style dialog box. It is
               should be called from the ClassStyle function.
*****************************************************************************/
int PASCAL CstCtlStyleDlg( HINSTANCE hInstance, LPSTR szCstCtlStyleDlgName,
        FARPROC fpCstCtlStyleDlgProc, HWND hWndParent,
        GLOBALHANDLE hCtlStyle, LPFNSTRTOID lpfnStrToId,
        LPFNIDTOSTR lpfnIdToStr )
    {

    HCSTCTLSTYLE hCstCtlStyle;
    int iDialogReturn = FALSE;

    hCstCtlStyle = GlobalAlloc( GMEM_MOVEABLE | GMEM_NODISCARD |
            GMEM_ZEROINIT | GMEM_SHARE, sizeof ( CSTCTLSTYLE ) );
    if ( hCstCtlStyle )
        {

        LPCSTCTLSTYLE lpCstCtlStyle = (LPCSTCTLSTYLE)GlobalLock( hCstCtlStyle );

        if ( lpCstCtlStyle )
            {

            HWND hWndFocus = GetFocus();
            LPARAM lParam = MAKELPARAM( hCstCtlStyle, 0 );

            lpCstCtlStyle->hCtlStyle = hCtlStyle;
            lpCstCtlStyle->lpfnStrToId = lpfnStrToId;
            lpCstCtlStyle->lpfnIdToStr = lpfnIdToStr;
            GlobalUnlock( hCstCtlStyle );
```

Listing 12.8 *continued*

```
             /* Display control's Styles Dialog Box. */
             iDialogReturn = DialogBoxParam( hInstance,
                    szCstCtlStyleDlgName, hWndParent, fpCstCtlStyleDlgProc,
                    lParam );

             if ( hWndFocus )
                 {
                 /* Reset the focus */
                 SetFocus( hWndFocus );
                 }

             }   /* if lpCstCtlStyle */

        GlobalFree( hCstCtlStyle );

        }   /* if hCstCtlStyle */

    /* Return whether CTLSTYLE structure has been changed. */
    return ( iDialogReturn == IDOK );

    }   /* function CstCtlStyleDlg */


/*******************************************************************************
        Name: CtlInfoCreate
  Parameters: wVersion - version of control
              szClass - custom control window class name
              szTitle - custom control expanded name
      Return: Global heap handle to CTLINFO structure
 Description: This allocates a CTLINFO structure and loads it with the
              information about the control passed to it as parameters.
*******************************************************************************/
GLOBALHANDLE PASCAL CtlInfoCreate( WORD wVersion, LPSTR szClass,
        LPSTR szTitle )
    {

    GLOBALHANDLE hCtlInfo;

    hCtlInfo = GlobalAlloc( GMEM_MOVEABLE | GMEM_NODISCARD |
            GMEM_ZEROINIT | GMEM_SHARE, (DWORD)sizeof ( CTLINFO ) );
    if ( hCtlInfo )
        {

        LPCTLINFO lpCtlInfo = (LPCTLINFO)GlobalLock( hCtlInfo );

        if ( lpCtlInfo )
            {
            lpCtlInfo->wVersion = wVersion;
            lstrcpy( lpCtlInfo->szClass, szClass );
            lstrcpy( lpCtlInfo->szTitle, szTitle );
            GlobalUnlock( hCtlInfo );
            }

        }   /* if hCstInfo */

    return ( hCtlInfo );

    }   /* function CtlInfoCreate */
```

Listing 12.8 continued

```
/*****************************************************************************
        Name: CtlStyleLock
  Parameters: hDlg - handle to style dialog box window
      Return: pointer to CTLSTYLE structure
 Description: This is a helper function used to retrieve a pointer to the
              CTLSTYLE structure from a window property and a wrapping
              structure, CSTCTLSTYLE.
*****************************************************************************/
static LPCTLSTYLE PASCAL CtlStyleLock( HWND hDlg )
    {

    HCSTCTLSTYLE hCstCtlStyle = GetProp( hDlg, _szCstCtlStyle );
    LPCTLSTYLE lpCtlStyle = NULL;

    if ( hCstCtlStyle )
        {

        LPCSTCTLSTYLE lpCstCtlStyle = (LPCSTCTLSTYLE)GlobalLock( hCstCtlStyle );

        if ( lpCstCtlStyle )
            {
            lpCtlStyle = (LPCTLSTYLE)GlobalLock( lpCstCtlStyle->hCtlStyle );
            GlobalUnlock( hCstCtlStyle );
            }

        }   /* if hCstCtlStyle */

    return ( lpCtlStyle );

    }   /* function CtlStyleLock */


/*****************************************************************************
        Name: CtlStyleUnlock
  Parameters: hDlg - handle to style dialog box window
      Return: TRUE or FALSE
 Description: This is a helper function used to unlock the memory that
              contains a CTLSTYLE structure.
*****************************************************************************/
static BOOL PASCAL CtlStyleUnlock( HWND hDlg )
    {

    BOOL bResult = FALSE;
    HCSTCTLSTYLE hCstCtlStyle = GetProp( hDlg, _szCstCtlStyle );

    if ( hCstCtlStyle )
        {

        LPCSTCTLSTYLE lpCstCtlStyle = (LPCSTCTLSTYLE)GlobalLock( hCstCtlStyle );

        if ( lpCstCtlStyle )
            {
            bResult = GlobalUnlock( lpCstCtlStyle->hCtlStyle );
            GlobalUnlock( hCstCtlStyle );
            }

        }   /* if hCstCtlStyle */
```

Listing 12.8 *continued*

```
    return ( bResult );

    }   /* function CtlStyleUnlock */
/********************************************************************
        Name: GetIdString
  Parameters: hDlg - handle to style dialog box window
              szId - string buffer to contain string identifier
              wIdMaxLen - maximum length of string buffer
      Return: Number of characters in string
 Description: This function converts a control ID value into a string.  It
              stores the string in the buffer passed as a parameter.
********************************************************************/
WORD PASCAL GetIdString( HWND hDlg, LPSTR szId, WORD wIdMaxLen )
    {
    HCSTCTLSTYLE hCstCtlStyle = GetProp( hDlg, _szCstCtlStyle );
    UINT wIdLen = 0;

    if ( hCstCtlStyle )
        {
        LPCSTCTLSTYLE lpCstCtlStyle = (LPCSTCTLSTYLE)GlobalLock( hCstCtlStyle );

        if ( lpCstCtlStyle )
            {
            LPCTLSTYLE lpCtlStyle = (LPCTLSTYLE)GlobalLock(
                    lpCstCtlStyle->hCtlStyle );
            if ( lpCtlStyle )
                {
                /* Convert numeric ID to string */
                wIdLen = ( *lpCstCtlStyle->lpfnIdToStr )( lpCtlStyle->wId,
                        szId, wIdMaxLen );
                GlobalUnlock( lpCstCtlStyle->hCtlStyle );
                }

            GlobalUnlock( hCstCtlStyle );

            }   /* if lpCstCtlStyle */
        }   /* if hCstCtlStyle */

    return ( (WORD)wIdLen );

    }   /* function GetIdString */


/********************************************************************
        Name: SetIdValue
  Parameters: hDlg - handle to style dialog box window
              szId - string Id
      Return: Numeric value of Id and flag indicating success, 1 or fail 0.
 Description: This function converts an ID string value into its numeric
              equivalent and stores the numeric value in the CTLSTYLE
              structure for the control.  If the LOWORD of the result is 0,
```

Listing 12.8 *continued*

```
              the ID is invalid, otherwise, the HIWORD contains the numeric
              value of the ID.
****************************************************************************/
DWORD PASCAL SetIdValue( HWND hDlg, LPSTR szId )
    {

    HCSTCTLSTYLE hCstCtlStyle = GetProp( hDlg, _szCstCtlStyle );
    DWORD dwResult = 0;

    if ( hCstCtlStyle )
        {

        LPCTLSTYLE  lpCtlStyle;
        LPCSTCTLSTYLE lpCstCtlStyle = (LPCSTCTLSTYLE)GlobalLock( hCstCtlStyle );

        if ( lpCstCtlStyle )
            {
            /* Convert string to numeric ID */
            dwResult = ( *lpCstCtlStyle->lpfnStrToId )( szId );
            GlobalUnlock( hCstCtlStyle );
            }

        if ( LOWORD( dwResult ) == 0 )
            {
            /* String not found */
            return ( dwResult );
            }

        lpCtlStyle = CtlStyleLock( hDlg );
        if ( lpCtlStyle )
            {
            /* Numeric ID is in HIWORD */
            lpCtlStyle->wId = HIWORD( dwResult );
            CtlStyleUnlock( hDlg );
            }

        }  /* if hCstCtlStyle */

    return ( dwResult );

    }  /* function SetIdValue */

/* End of DEI_CTLS.C */
```

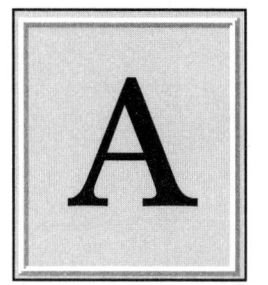

Editor Interface Modules

Appendix A lists all of the files required by the dialog editor interface, except the interface files related to the custom check box control. The custom check box files appear at the end of Chapter 12. The interface files are summarized in Table 12.2. In addition, the make files for the DLLs are given in Listings A.27 through A.30.

Listing A.1

```
/***************************************************************************
         File Name: DEI_PBTN.H
     Expanded Name: Dialog Editor Interface for CSTPUSHBTN
       Description: Include file for DEI_PBTN.C & DEI_PBTN.RC
       Portability: Microsoft Windows 3.X
***************************************************************************/

#define IDC_LEFTTEXT        101
#define IDC_RIGHTTEXT       102
#define IDC_NOFOCUS         103
#define IDC_NOFRAME         104
#define IDC_NOSHADOW        105
#define IDC_DEFAULT         106
#define IDC_LEFTBITMAP      107
#define IDC_RIGHTBITMAP     108
#define IDC_STRETCHBITMAP   109
#define IDC_STRETCHBUTTON   110

#define IDC_VISIBLE         201
#define IDC_DISABLED        202
#define IDC_GROUP           203
#define IDC_TABSTOP         204

#define IDC_EDIT_ID         301
#define IDC_EDIT_TEXT       302

#define IDC_OK                1
#define IDC_CANCEL            2
#define IDC_HELP              8

/* End of DEI_PBTN.H */
```

Listing A.2

```
/*****************************************************************************
        File Name: DEI_PBTN.C
    Expanded Name: Dialog Editor Interface for Custom Pushbutton Control
      Description: Library of functions for interfacing the CSTPUSHBTN
                   control with the Dialog Editor.
     Program List: DEI_PBTN.C
                   DEI_PBTN.RC
                   DEI_PBTN.DEF
                   DEI_CTLS.C
                   CST_CTLS.LIB,DLL
Global Function List: CstPushBtnDlgFn
                   CstPushBtnFlags
                   CstPushBtnStyle
                   Dei_PBtnInfo
                   Dei_PBtnWndFn
                   LibMain
                   WEP
      Static Data: _hInstanceDLL
                   _szCstCtlName
      Portability: Microsoft Windows 3.X
*****************************************************************************/

/* Microsoft Windows */
#include <windows.h>

/* Custom Control Interface */
#include <custcntl.h>

/* Standard C */
#include <stdlib.h>

/* Prototypes and Types */
#include <cst_pbtn.h>
#include <dei_ctls.h>

/* Own */
#include <dei_pbtn.h>

/* Library instance handle */
static HINSTANCE _hInstanceDLL = 0;

static char _szCstCtlName[] = "CstPushBtn";

/* Prototypes of functions */
BOOL FAR PASCAL CstPushBtnDlgFn( HWND hDlg, WORD wMessage, WORD wParam,
        LONG lParam );
WORD FAR PASCAL CstPushBtnFlags( DWORD dwFlags, LPSTR szString,
        WORD wMaxString );
BOOL FAR PASCAL CstPushBtnStyle( HWND hWnd, GLOBALHANDLE hCtlStyle,
        LPFNSTRTOID lpfnStrToId, LPFNIDTOSTR lpfnIdToStr );
GLOBALHANDLE FAR PASCAL Dei_PBtnInfo( void );
LONG FAR PASCAL Dei_PBtnWndFn( HWND hWnd, UINT wMessage, WPARAM wParam,
        LPARAM lParam );
```

Listing A.2 *continued*

```
/******************************************************************************
        Name: CstPushBtnDlgFn
  Description: Dialog box callback function for style selection.
******************************************************************************/
BOOL FAR PASCAL CstPushBtnDlgFn( HWND hDlg, WORD wMsg, WORD wParam,
        LONG lParam )
    {

    switch ( wMsg )
        {
        case WM_INITDIALOG:
            {

            char szIdStr[CTLTITLE];

            /* Set the property */
            HCSTCTLSTYLE hCstCtlStyle = LOWORD( lParam );
            LPCSTCTLSTYLE lpCstCtlStyle =
                    (LPCSTCTLSTYLE)GlobalLock( hCstCtlStyle );
            LPCTLSTYLE lpCtlStyle =
                    (LPCTLSTYLE)GlobalLock( lpCstCtlStyle->hCtlStyle );
            DWORD dwStyle = lpCtlStyle->dwStyle;

            SetProp( hDlg, _szCstCtlStyle, hCstCtlStyle );

            /* Center Dialog Box */
            CenterWindow( GetParent( hDlg ), hDlg, 0 );

            /* Text */
            SetDlgItemText( hDlg, IDC_EDIT_TEXT, lpCtlStyle->szTitle );

            /* Id */
            if ( !(*lpCstCtlStyle->lpfnIdToStr)( lpCtlStyle->wId, szIdStr,
                    CTLTITLE ) )
                {
                wsprintf( szIdStr, "%n", lpCtlStyle->wId );
                }
            SetDlgItemText( hDlg, IDC_EDIT_ID, szIdStr );
            GlobalUnlock( lpCstCtlStyle->hCtlStyle );
            GlobalUnlock( hCstCtlStyle );

            /* Custom Push Button Styles */
            if ( dwStyle & CPBS_LEFTTEXT )
                {
                CheckDlgButton( hDlg, IDC_LEFTTEXT, TRUE );
                }
            else if ( dwStyle & CPBS_RIGHTTEXT )
                {
                CheckDlgButton( hDlg, IDC_RIGHTTEXT, TRUE );
                }
            if ( dwStyle & CPBS_NOFOCUS )
                {
                CheckDlgButton( hDlg, IDC_NOFOCUS, TRUE );
                }
            if ( dwStyle & CPBS_NOFRAME )
                {
                CheckDlgButton( hDlg, IDC_NOFRAME, TRUE );
                }
            if ( dwStyle & CPBS_NOSHADOW )
```

Listing A.2 continued

```
            {
            CheckDlgButton( hDlg, IDC_NOSHADOW, TRUE );
            }
        if ( dwStyle & BS_DEFPUSHBUTTON )
            {
            CheckDlgButton( hDlg, IDC_DEFAULT, TRUE );
            }
        if ( dwStyle & CPBS_LEFTBITMAP )
            {
            CheckDlgButton( hDlg, IDC_LEFTBITMAP, TRUE );
            }
        else if ( dwStyle & CPBS_RIGHTBITMAP )
            {
            CheckDlgButton( hDlg, IDC_RIGHTBITMAP, TRUE );
            }
        if ( dwStyle & CPBS_STRETCHBITMAP )
            {
            CheckDlgButton( hDlg, IDC_STRETCHBITMAP, TRUE );
            }
        else if ( dwStyle & CPBS_STRETCHBUTTON )
            {
            CheckDlgButton( hDlg, IDC_STRETCHBUTTON, TRUE );
            }

        /* Basic styles */
        if ( dwStyle & WS_VISIBLE )
            {
            CheckDlgButton( hDlg, IDC_VISIBLE, TRUE );
            }
        if ( dwStyle & WS_DISABLED )
            {
            CheckDlgButton( hDlg, IDC_DISABLED, TRUE );
            }
        if ( dwStyle & WS_GROUP )
            {
            CheckDlgButton( hDlg, IDC_GROUP, TRUE );
            }
        if ( dwStyle & WS_TABSTOP )
            {
            CheckDlgButton( hDlg, IDC_TABSTOP, TRUE );
            }

        break;
        }
    case WM_COMMAND:
        switch ( wParam )
            {
            case IDC_HELP:
                WinHelp( hDlg, "CST_CTLS.HLP", HELP_KEY,
                         (DWORD)(LPSTR)"CstPushBtn" );
                break;
            case IDC_OK:
                {

                char szIdStr[32];
                DWORD dwStyle, dwId;
                HCSTCTLSTYLE hCstCtlStyle;
                LPCSTCTLSTYLE lpCstCtlStyle;
```

Listing A.2 *continued*

```
LPCTLSTYLE lpCtlStyle;

hCstCtlStyle = GetProp( hDlg, _szCstCtlStyle );
lpCstCtlStyle = (LPCSTCTLSTYLE)GlobalLock(
        hCstCtlStyle );
lpCtlStyle = (LPCTLSTYLE)GlobalLock(
        lpCstCtlStyle->hCtlStyle );
dwStyle = lpCtlStyle->dwStyle & 0xFFFF0000L;

/* Text */
GetDlgItemText( hDlg, IDC_EDIT_TEXT,
        lpCtlStyle->szTitle, CTLTITLE );

/* Id */
GetDlgItemText( hDlg, IDC_EDIT_ID, szIdStr,
        sizeof ( szIdStr ) );
dwId = (*lpCstCtlStyle->lpfnStrToId)( szIdStr );
if ( LOWORD( dwId ) == 0 )
    {
    lpCtlStyle->wId = max( (WORD)atoi( szIdStr ),
            lpCtlStyle->wId );
    }
else
    {
    lpCtlStyle->wId = HIWORD( dwId );
    }

/* Custom Push Button Styles */
if ( IsDlgButtonChecked( hDlg, IDC_LEFTTEXT ) )
    {
    dwStyle |= CPBS_LEFTTEXT;
    }
else if ( IsDlgButtonChecked( hDlg, IDC_RIGHTTEXT ) )
    {
    dwStyle |= CPBS_RIGHTTEXT;
    }
if ( IsDlgButtonChecked( hDlg, IDC_NOFOCUS ) )
    {
    dwStyle |= CPBS_NOFOCUS;
    }
if ( IsDlgButtonChecked( hDlg, IDC_NOFRAME ) )
    {
    dwStyle |= CPBS_NOFRAME;
    }
if ( IsDlgButtonChecked( hDlg, IDC_NOSHADOW ) )
    {
    dwStyle |= CPBS_NOSHADOW;
    }
if ( IsDlgButtonChecked( hDlg, IDC_DEFAULT ) )
    {
    dwStyle |= BS_DEFPUSHBUTTON;
    }
if ( IsDlgButtonChecked( hDlg, IDC_LEFTBITMAP ) )
    {
    dwStyle |= CPBS_LEFTBITMAP;
    }
else if ( IsDlgButtonChecked( hDlg, IDC_RIGHTBITMAP ) )
    {
    dwStyle |= CPBS_RIGHTBITMAP;
```

Listing A.2 *continued*

```
                }
            if ( IsDlgButtonChecked( hDlg, IDC_STRETCHBITMAP ) )
                {
                dwStyle |= CPBS_STRETCHBITMAP;
                }
            else if ( IsDlgButtonChecked( hDlg, IDC_STRETCHBUTTON ) )
                {
                dwStyle |= CPBS_STRETCHBUTTON;
                }

            /* Basic Styles */
            if ( IsDlgButtonChecked( hDlg, IDC_VISIBLE ) )
                {
                dwStyle |= WS_VISIBLE;
                }
            else
                {
                dwStyle &= ~WS_VISIBLE;
                }
            if ( IsDlgButtonChecked( hDlg, IDC_DISABLED ) )
                {
                dwStyle |= WS_DISABLED;
                }
            else
                {
                dwStyle &= ~WS_DISABLED;
                }
            if ( IsDlgButtonChecked( hDlg, IDC_GROUP ) )
                {
                dwStyle |= WS_GROUP;
                }
            else
                {
                dwStyle &= ~WS_GROUP;
                }
            if ( IsDlgButtonChecked( hDlg, IDC_TABSTOP ) )
                {
                dwStyle |= WS_TABSTOP;
                }
            else
                {
                dwStyle &= ~WS_TABSTOP;
                }

            lpCtlStyle->dwStyle = dwStyle;
            GlobalUnlock( lpCstCtlStyle->hCtlStyle );
            GlobalUnlock( hCstCtlStyle );
            EndDialog( hDlg, TRUE );
            break;
            }
        case IDC_CANCEL:
            EndDialog( hDlg, FALSE );
            break;
        default:
            return ( FALSE );
        } /* switch wParam */
    break;
case WM_DESTROY:
```

Listing A.2 *continued*

```c
            WinHelp( hDlg, "CST_CTLS.HLP", HELP_QUIT, 0L );
            RemoveProp( hDlg, _szCstCtlStyle );
            break;
        default:
            return ( FALSE );
    }   /* switch wMsg */

    return ( TRUE );

    }  /* function CstPushBtnDlgFn */


/******************************************************************************
       Name: CstPushBtnFlags
 Parameters: dwFlags - current style of control
             lpstrStyle - buffer to store style string
             wMaxLen - maximum length of style string
     Return: length of style string
Description: Converts a style into a string of style flags of all the
             class specific window styles for a control.  The basic, or
             class general styles are concatenated onto these by the dialog
             editor.
******************************************************************************/
WORD FAR PASCAL CstPushBtnFlags( DWORD dwFlags, LPSTR lpstrStyle,
        WORD wMaxLen )
    {

    UINT uiType;
    char szBuf[32];
    int iBufLen = 32;

    wMaxLen = wMaxLen;

    /* Type */
    uiType = (UINT)( dwFlags & 0x0FL );
    LoadString( _hInstanceDLL, uiType, szBuf, iBufLen );
    lstrcpy( lpstrStyle, szBuf );

    /* Custom Push Button Styles */
    if ( dwFlags & CPBS_LEFTTEXT )
        {
        LoadString( _hInstanceDLL, (UINT)CPBS_LEFTTEXT, szBuf, iBufLen );
        lstrcat( lpstrStyle, " | " );
        lstrcat( lpstrStyle, szBuf );
        }
    else if ( dwFlags & CPBS_RIGHTTEXT )
        {
        LoadString( _hInstanceDLL, (UINT)CPBS_RIGHTTEXT, szBuf, iBufLen );
        lstrcat( lpstrStyle, " | " );
        lstrcat( lpstrStyle, szBuf );
        }
    if ( dwFlags & CPBS_NOFOCUS )
        {
        LoadString( _hInstanceDLL, (UINT)CPBS_NOFOCUS, szBuf, iBufLen );
        lstrcat( lpstrStyle, " | " );
        lstrcat( lpstrStyle, szBuf );
        }
    if ( dwFlags & CPBS_NOFRAME )
        {
```

Listing A.2 *continued*

```
        LoadString( _hInstanceDLL, (UINT)CPBS_NOFRAME, szBuf, iBufLen );
        lstrcat( lpstrStyle, " | " );
        lstrcat( lpstrStyle, szBuf );
        }
    if ( dwFlags & CPBS_NOSHADOW )
        {
        LoadString( _hInstanceDLL, (UINT)CPBS_NOSHADOW, szBuf, iBufLen );
        lstrcat( lpstrStyle, " | " );
        lstrcat( lpstrStyle, szBuf );
        }
    if ( dwFlags & CPBS_LEFTBITMAP )
        {
        LoadString( _hInstanceDLL, (UINT)CPBS_LEFTBITMAP, szBuf, iBufLen );
        lstrcat( lpstrStyle, " | " );
        lstrcat( lpstrStyle, szBuf );
        }
    else if ( dwFlags & CPBS_RIGHTBITMAP )
        {
        LoadString( _hInstanceDLL, (UINT)CPBS_RIGHTBITMAP, szBuf, iBufLen );
        lstrcat( lpstrStyle, " | " );
        lstrcat( lpstrStyle, szBuf );
        }
    if ( dwFlags & CPBS_STRETCHBITMAP )
        {
        LoadString( _hInstanceDLL, (UINT)CPBS_STRETCHBITMAP, szBuf, iBufLen );
        lstrcat( lpstrStyle, " | " );
        lstrcat( lpstrStyle, szBuf );
        }
    else if ( dwFlags & CPBS_STRETCHBUTTON )
        {
        LoadString( _hInstanceDLL, (UINT)CPBS_STRETCHBUTTON, szBuf, iBufLen );
        lstrcat( lpstrStyle, " | " );
        lstrcat( lpstrStyle, szBuf );
        }

    return ( (WORD)lstrlen( lpstrStyle ) );

    }   /* function CstPushBtnFlags */


/****************************************************************************
        Name: CstPushBtnStyle
  Parameters: hWnd - handle of dialog editor window
              hCtlStyle - global handle of CTLSTYLE structure
              lpfnStrToId - pointer to func to convert string to control id
              lpfnIdToStr - pointer to func to convert control id to string
      Return: TRUE if style has changed, FALSE if no change
 Description: Invokes the style dialog box for a custom control.
****************************************************************************/
BOOL FAR PASCAL CstPushBtnStyle( HWND hWnd, GLOBALHANDLE hCtlStyle,
        LPFNSTRTOID lpfnStrToId, LPFNIDTOSTR lpfnIdToStr )
    {

    return ( CstCtlStyleDlg( _hInstanceDLL, _szCstCtlName,
            (FARPROC)CstPushBtnDlgFn,
            hWnd, hCtlStyle, lpfnStrToId, lpfnIdToStr ) );

    }   /* function CstPushBtnStyle */
```

Listing A.2 continued

```
/****************************************************************************
         Name: Dei_PBtnInfo
       Return: global handle to CTLINFO structure
  Description: Allocates a CTLINFO structure in the global heap.  Loads the
               structure with information about the custom control.
****************************************************************************/
GLOBALHANDLE FAR PASCAL Dei_PBtnInfo( void )
    {

    GLOBALHANDLE hCtlInfo = NULL;

    hCtlInfo = CtlInfoCreate( 100, _szCstCtlName, _szCstCtlName );
    if ( hCtlInfo )
        {

        LPCTLINFO lpCtlInfo = (LPCTLINFO)GlobalLock( hCtlInfo );
        if ( lpCtlInfo )
            {

            lpCtlInfo->Type[0].wType = 0;
            lpCtlInfo->Type[0].wWidth = 40;
            lpCtlInfo->Type[0].wHeight = 14;
            lpCtlInfo->Type[0].dwStyle = WS_CHILD | WS_VISIBLE |
                    BS_PUSHBUTTON | WS_TABSTOP;
            lstrcpy( lpCtlInfo->Type[0].szDescr, _szCstCtlName );
            lpCtlInfo->wCtlTypes = 1;
            GlobalUnlock( hCtlInfo );

            }   /* if lpCtlInfo */
        }   /* if hCtlInfo */

    return ( hCtlInfo );

    }   /* function Dei_PBtnInfo */


/****************************************************************************
         Name: Dei_PBtnWndFn
       Return: Same as CstPushBtnWndFn
  Description: Windows call back function for custom control.  This is a
               wrapper function for the existing function that resides in the
               CST_CTLS.DLL.
****************************************************************************/
LONG FAR PASCAL Dei_PBtnWndFn( HWND hWnd, UINT wMessage, WPARAM wParam,
        LPARAM lParam )
    {

    return ( CstPushBtnWndFn( hWnd, wMessage, wParam, lParam ) );

    }   /* function Dei_PBtnWndFn */
```

Listing A.2 *continued*

```c
/****************************************************************
        Name: LibMain
      Return: TRUE
 Description: DLL main function
****************************************************************/
int FAR PASCAL LibMain( HINSTANCE hInstance, WORD wDataSeg, WORD wHeapSize,
        LPSTR lpstrCmd )
    {

    lpstrCmd = lpstrCmd;

    if ( wHeapSize )
        {
        /* LibEntry called LocalInit - so unlock data segment */
        UnlockSegment( wDataSeg );
        }

    /* Set the external data value */
    _hInstanceDLL = hInstance;

    return ( TRUE );

    }  /* function LibMain */


/****************************************************************
        Name: WEP
      Return: TRUE
 Description: DLL exit function
****************************************************************/
int FAR PASCAL WEP( int nSystemExit )
    {

    nSystemExit = nSystemExit;

    return ( TRUE );

    }  /* function WEP */

/* End of DEI_PBTN.C */
```

Listing A.3

```
/******************************************************************************
            File Name: DEI_PBTN.RC
        Expanded Name: Dialog Editor Interface for CSTPUSHBTN
          Description: Resource file for DEI_PBTN.DLL
          Portability: Microsoft Windows 3.X
******************************************************************************/

#include <windows.h>
#include <cst_ctls.h>

#include <dei_pbtn.h>
#include <dei_pbtn.dlg>

STRINGTABLE
BEGIN
    BS_DEFPUSHBUTTON,    "BS_DEFPUSHBUTTON"
    BS_PUSHBUTTON,       "BS_PUSHBUTTON"
    CPBS_LEFTTEXT,       "CPBS_LEFTTEXT"
    CPBS_RIGHTTEXT,      "CPBS_RIGHTTEXT"
    CPBS_NOFOCUS,        "CPBS_NOFOCUS"
    CPBS_NOFRAME,        "CPBS_NOFRAME"
    CPBS_NOSHADOW,       "CPBS_NOSHADOW"
    CPBS_STRETCHBITMAP,  "CPBS_STRETCHBITMAP"
    CPBS_LEFTBITMAP,     "CPBS_LEFTBITMAP"
    CPBS_RIGHTBITMAP,    "CPBS_RIGHTBITMAP"
    CPBS_STRETCHBUTTON,  "CPBS_STRETCHBUTTON"
END

/* End of DEI_PBTN.RC */
```

Listing A.4

```
/****************************************************************
        File Name: DEI_PBTN.DLG
    Expanded Name: Dialog Editor Interface for CSTPUSHBTN
      Description: Style Dialog file for DEI_PBTN.DLL.
      Portability: Microsoft Windows 3.X
****************************************************************/
CstPushBtn DIALOG 16, 16, 170, 162
STYLE DS_MODALFRAME | WS_POPUP | WS_VISIBLE | WS_CAPTION | WS_SYSMENU
CAPTION "Custom Push Button Styles"
FONT 8, "Helv"
BEGIN
    CONTROL "Id:" -1, "cststatic", CSS_TEXTLOWERED | WS_GROUP, 6, 6, 20, 10
    CONTROL "", IDC_EDIT_ID, "EDIT", ES_LEFT | ES_AUTOHSCROLL | WS_BORDER |
            WS_GROUP | WS_TABSTOP, 30, 4, 134, 12
    CONTROL "Text:", -1, "cststatic", CSS_TEXTLOWERED | WS_GROUP, 6, 20, 20, 10
    CONTROL "", IDC_EDIT_TEXT, "EDIT", ES_LEFT | ES_AUTOHSCROLL | WS_BORDER |
            WS_GROUP | WS_TABSTOP, 30, 18, 134, 12
    CONTROL "Custom Push Button Styles", -1, "BUTTON", BS_GROUPBOX | WS_GROUP,
            6, 34, 158, 64
    CONTROL "&Left Text", IDC_LEFTTEXT, "cstcheckbox", BS_AUTOCHECKBOX |
            WS_GROUP | WS_TABSTOP, 10, 46, 42, 10
    CONTROL "&Right Text", IDC_RIGHTTEXT, "cstcheckbox", BS_AUTOCHECKBOX |
            WS_TABSTOP, 10, 56, 64, 10
    CONTROL "No Foc&us", IDC_NOFOCUS, "cstcheckbox", BS_AUTOCHECKBOX |
            WS_TABSTOP, 10, 66, 64, 10
    CONTROL "No F&rame", IDC_NOFRAME, "cstcheckbox", BS_AUTOCHECKBOX |
            WS_TABSTOP, 10, 76, 64, 10
    CONTROL "No &Shadow", IDC_NOSHADOW, "cstcheckbox", BS_AUTOCHECKBOX |
            WS_TABSTOP, 10, 86, 64, 10
    CONTROL "&Default", IDC_DEFAULT, "cstcheckbox", BS_AUTOCHECKBOX |
            WS_TABSTOP, 79, 46, 75, 10
    CONTROL "L&eft Bitmap", IDC_LEFTBITMAP, "cstcheckbox", BS_AUTOCHECKBOX |
            WS_TABSTOP, 79, 56, 84, 10
    CONTROL "R&ight Bitmap", IDC_RIGHTBITMAP, "cstcheckbox", BS_AUTOCHECKBOX |
            WS_TABSTOP, 79, 66, 54, 10
    CONTROL "Stretch &Bitmap", IDC_STRETCHBITMAP, "cstcheckbox",
            BS_AUTOCHECKBOX | WS_TABSTOP, 79, 76, 72, 10
    CONTROL "Stretch B&utton", IDC_STRETCHBUTTON, "cstcheckbox",
            BS_AUTOCHECKBOX | WS_TABSTOP, 79, 86, 77, 10
    CONTROL "Basic Styles", -1, "BUTTON", BS_GROUPBOX | WS_GROUP, 6, 102, 158,
            34
    CONTROL "&Visible", IDC_VISIBLE, "cstcheckbox", BS_AUTOCHECKBOX |
            WS_GROUP | WS_TABSTOP, 10, 114, 34, 10
    CONTROL "&Disabled", IDC_DISABLED, "cstcheckbox", BS_AUTOCHECKBOX |
            WS_TABSTOP, 10, 124, 41, 10
    CONTROL "&Group", IDC_GROUP, "cstcheckbox", BS_AUTOCHECKBOX | WS_TABSTOP,
            79, 114, 34, 10
    CONTROL "&Tab Stop", IDC_TABSTOP, "cstcheckbox", BS_AUTOCHECKBOX |
            WS_TABSTOP, 79, 124, 44, 10
    CONTROL "OK", IDC_OK, "BUTTON", BS_DEFPUSHBUTTON | WS_GROUP | WS_TABSTOP,
            13, 142, 40, 14
    CONTROL "Cancel", IDC_CANCEL, "BUTTON", BS_PUSHBUTTON | WS_TABSTOP, 65,
            142, 40, 14
    CONTROL "Help", IDC_HELP, "BUTTON", BS_PUSHBUTTON | WS_TABSTOP,
            117, 142, 40, 14
END
/* End of DEI_PBTN.DLG */
```

Listing A.5

```
LIBRARY DEI_PBTN
DESCRIPTION 'Dialog Editor - CSTPUSHBTN DLL'
EXETYPE WINDOWS
CODE PRELOAD MOVEABLE SHARED DISCARDABLE
DATA PRELOAD MOVEABLE SINGLE
HEAPSIZE 1024
EXPORTS
        WEP                @1    RESIDENTNAME
        Dei_PBtnInfo       @2
        CstPushBtnStyle    @3
        CstPushBtnFlags    @4
        Dei_PBtnWndFn      @5
        CstPushBtnDlgFn    @6
```

Listing A.6

```
/****************************************************************
        File Name: DEI_RBTN.H
    Expanded Name: Dialog Editor Interface for CSTRADIOBTN
      Description: Include file for DEI_RBTN.C & DEI_RBTN.RC
      Portability: Microsoft Windows 3.X
****************************************************************/

#define IDC_AUTO         101
#define IDC_LEFTTEXT     103

#define IDC_VISIBLE      201
#define IDC_DISABLED     202
#define IDC_GROUP        203
#define IDC_TABSTOP      204

#define IDC_EDIT_ID      300
#define IDC_EDIT_TEXT    301

#define IDC_OK             1
#define IDC_CANCEL         2
#define IDC_HELP           8

/* End of DEI_RBTN.H */
```

Listing A.7

```
/***************************************************************************
            File Name: DEI_RBTN.C
        Expanded Name: Dialog Editor Interface for Custom Radio Button Control
          Description: Library of functions for interfacing the CSTRADIOBTN
                       control with the Dialog Editor.
         Program List: DEI_RBTN.C
                       DEI_RBTN.RC
                       DEI_RBTN.DEF
                       DEI_CTLS.C
                       CST_CTLS.LIB,DLL
  Global Function List: CstRadioBtnDlgFn
                       CstRadioBtnFlags
                       CstRadioBtnStyle
                       Dei_RBtnInfo
                       Dei_RBtnWndFn
                       LibMain
                       WEP
          Static Data: _hInstanceDLL
                       _szCstCtlName
          Portability: Microsoft Windows 3.X
***************************************************************************/

/* Microsoft Windows */
#include <windows.h>

/* Custom Control Interface */
#include <custcntl.h>

/* Standard C */
#include <stdlib.h>

/* Prototypes and Types */
#include <cst_rbtn.h>
#include <dei_ctls.h>

/* Own */
#include <dei_rbtn.h>

/* Library instance handle */
static HINSTANCE _hInstanceDLL = 0;

static char _szCstCtlName[] = "CstRadioBtn";

/* Prototypes of functions */
BOOL FAR PASCAL CstRadioBtnDlgFn( HWND hDlg, WORD wMessage, WORD wParam,
        LONG lParam );
WORD FAR PASCAL CstRadioBtnFlags( DWORD dwFlags, LPSTR szString,
        WORD wMaxString );
BOOL FAR PASCAL CstRadioBtnStyle( HWND hWnd, GLOBALHANDLE hCtlStyle,
        LPFNSTRTOID lpfnStrToId, LPFNIDTOSTR lpfnIdToStr );
GLOBALHANDLE FAR PASCAL Dei_RBtnInfo( void );
LONG FAR PASCAL Dei_RBtnWndFn( HWND hWnd, UINT wMessage, WPARAM wParam,
        LPARAM lParam );
```

Listing A.7 *continued*

```c
/******************************************************************************
        Name: CstRadioBtnDlgFn
 Description: Dialog box callback function for style selection.
******************************************************************************/
BOOL FAR PASCAL CstRadioBtnDlgFn( HWND hDlg, WORD wMsg, WORD wParam,
        LONG lParam )
    {

    switch ( wMsg )
        {
        case WM_INITDIALOG:
            {

            char szIdStr[CTLTITLE];

            /* Set the property */
            HCSTCTLSTYLE hCstCtlStyle = LOWORD( lParam );
            LPCSTCTLSTYLE lpCstCtlStyle =
                    (LPCSTCTLSTYLE)GlobalLock( hCstCtlStyle );
            LPCTLSTYLE lpCtlStyle =
                    (LPCTLSTYLE)GlobalLock( lpCstCtlStyle->hCtlStyle );
            DWORD dwStyle = lpCtlStyle->dwStyle;
            DWORD dwType = dwStyle & 0x0FL;

            SetProp( hDlg, _szCstCtlStyle, hCstCtlStyle );

            /* Center Dialog Box */
            CenterWindow( GetParent( hDlg ), hDlg, 0 );

            /* Text */
            SetDlgItemText( hDlg, IDC_EDIT_TEXT, lpCtlStyle->szTitle );

            /* Id */
            if ( !(*lpCstCtlStyle->lpfnIdToStr)( lpCtlStyle->wId, szIdStr,
                    CTLTITLE ) )
                {
                wsprintf( szIdStr, "%n", lpCtlStyle->wId );
                }
            SetDlgItemText( hDlg, IDC_EDIT_ID, szIdStr );
            GlobalUnlock( lpCstCtlStyle->hCtlStyle );
            GlobalUnlock( hCstCtlStyle );

            /* Radio Button styles */
            if ( dwType == BS_AUTORADIOBUTTON )
                {
                CheckDlgButton( hDlg, IDC_AUTO, TRUE );
                }
            if ( dwStyle & BS_LEFTTEXT )
                {
                CheckDlgButton( hDlg, IDC_LEFTTEXT, TRUE );
                }

            /* Basic styles */
            if ( dwStyle & WS_VISIBLE )
                {
                CheckDlgButton( hDlg, IDC_VISIBLE, TRUE );
                }
```

Listing A.7 *continued*

```c
            if ( dwStyle & WS_DISABLED )
                {
                CheckDlgButton( hDlg, IDC_DISABLED, TRUE );
                }
            if ( dwStyle & WS_GROUP )
                {
                CheckDlgButton( hDlg, IDC_GROUP, TRUE );
                }
            if ( dwStyle & WS_TABSTOP )
                {
                CheckDlgButton( hDlg, IDC_TABSTOP, TRUE );
                }

            break;
            }
        case WM_COMMAND:
            switch ( wParam )
                {
                case IDC_HELP:
                    WinHelp( hDlg, "CST_CTLS.HLP", HELP_KEY,
                            (DWORD)(LPSTR)"CstRadioBtn" );
                    break;
                case IDC_OK:
                    {

                    char szIdStr[32];
                    DWORD dwStyle, dwId;
                    HCSTCTLSTYLE hCstCtlStyle;
                    LPCSTCTLSTYLE lpCstCtlStyle;
                    LPCTLSTYLE lpCtlStyle;

                    hCstCtlStyle = GetProp( hDlg, szCstCtlStyle );
                    lpCstCtlStyle = (LPCSTCTLSTYLE)GlobalLock(
                            hCstCtlStyle );
                    lpCtlStyle = (LPCTLSTYLE)GlobalLock(
                            lpCstCtlStyle->hCtlStyle );
                    dwStyle = lpCtlStyle->dwStyle & 0xFFFF0000L;

                    /* Text */
                    GetDlgItemText( hDlg, IDC_EDIT_TEXT,
                            lpCtlStyle->szTitle, CTLTITLE );

                    /* Id */
                    GetDlgItemText( hDlg, IDC_EDIT_ID, szIdStr,
                            sizeof( szIdStr ) );
                    dwId = (*lpCstCtlStyle->lpfnStrToId)( szIdStr );
                    if ( LOWORD( dwId ) == 0 )
                        {
                        lpCtlStyle->wId = max( (WORD)atoi( szIdStr ),
                                lpCtlStyle->wId );
                        }
                    else
                        {
                        lpCtlStyle->wId = HIWORD( dwId );
                        }

                    /* Radio Button Styles */
                    if ( IsDlgButtonChecked( hDlg, IDC_AUTO ) )
                        {
```

Listing A.7 *continued*

```
                dwStyle |= BS_AUTORADIOBUTTON;
                }
        else
                {
                dwStyle |= BS_RADIOBUTTON;
                }
        if ( IsDlgButtonChecked( hDlg, IDC_LEFTTEXT ) )
                {
                dwStyle |= BS_LEFTTEXT;
                }
        else
                {
                dwStyle &= ~BS_LEFTTEXT;
                }

        /* Basic Styles */
        if ( IsDlgButtonChecked( hDlg, IDC_VISIBLE ) )
                {
                dwStyle |= WS_VISIBLE;
                }
        else
                {
                dwStyle &= ~WS_VISIBLE;
                }
        if ( IsDlgButtonChecked( hDlg, IDC_DISABLED ) )
                {
                dwStyle |= WS_DISABLED;
                }
        else
                {
                dwStyle &= ~WS_DISABLED;
                }
        if ( IsDlgButtonChecked( hDlg, IDC_GROUP ) )
                {
                dwStyle |= WS_GROUP;
                }
        else
                {
                dwStyle &= ~WS_GROUP;
                }
        if ( IsDlgButtonChecked( hDlg, IDC_TABSTOP ) )
                {
                dwStyle |= WS_TABSTOP;
                }
        else
                {
                dwStyle &= ~WS_TABSTOP;
                }

        lpCtlStyle->dwStyle = dwStyle;
        GlobalUnlock( lpCstCtlStyle->hCtlStyle );
        GlobalUnlock( hCstCtlStyle );
        EndDialog( hDlg, TRUE );
        break;
        }
    case IDC_CANCEL:
        EndDialog( hDlg, FALSE );
        break;
```

Listing A.7 continued

```
                    default:
                        return ( FALSE );
                }   /* switch wParam */
            break;
        case WM_DESTROY:
            WinHelp( hDlg, "CST_CTLS.HLP", HELP_QUIT, 0L );
            RemoveProp( hDlg, _szCstCtlStyle );
            break;
        default:
            return ( FALSE );
    }   /* switch wMsg */

    return ( TRUE );

}   /* function CstRadioBtnDlgFn */


/*******************************************************************************
        Name: CstRadioBtnFlags
  Parameters: dwFlags - current style of control
              lpstrStyle - buffer to store style string
              wMaxLen - maximum length of style string
      Return: length of style string
 Description: Converts a style into a string of style flags of all the
              class specific window styles for a control.  The basic, or
              class general styles are concatenated onto these by the dialog
              editor.
*******************************************************************************/
WORD FAR PASCAL CstRadioBtnFlags( DWORD dwFlags, LPSTR lpstrStyle,
        WORD wMaxLen )
{

    UINT uiType;
    char szBuf[32];
    int iBufLen = 32;

    wMaxLen = wMaxLen;

    /* Radio Button Type */
    uiType = (UINT)( dwFlags & 0x0FL );
    LoadString( _hInstanceDLL, uiType, szBuf, iBufLen );
    lstrcpy( lpstrStyle, szBuf );

    /* Radio Button Style */
    if ( dwFlags & BS_LEFTTEXT )
        {
        LoadString( _hInstanceDLL, (UINT)BS_LEFTTEXT, szBuf, iBufLen );
        lstrcat( lpstrStyle, " | " );
        lstrcat( lpstrStyle, szBuf );
        }

    return ( (WORD)lstrlen( lpstrStyle ) );

}   /* function CstRadioBtnFlags */
```

Listing A.7 *continued*

```
/****************************************************************************
        Name: CstRadioBtnStyle
  Parameters: hWnd - handle of dialog editor window
              hCtlStyle - global handle of CTLSTYLE structure
              lpfnStrToId - pointer to func to convert string to control id
              lpfnIdToStr - pointer to func to convert control id to string
      Return: TRUE if style has changed, FALSE if no change
 Description: Invokes the style dialog box for a custom control.
****************************************************************************/
BOOL FAR PASCAL CstRadioBtnStyle( HWND hWnd, GLOBALHANDLE hCtlStyle,
        LPFNSTRTOID lpfnStrToId, LPFNIDTOSTR lpfnIdToStr )
    {

    return ( CstCtlStyleDlg( _hInstanceDLL, _szCstCtlName,
             (FARPROC)CstRadioBtnDlgFn,
             hWnd, hCtlStyle, lpfnStrToId, lpfnIdToStr ) );

    }   /* function CstRadioBtnStyle */


/****************************************************************************
        Name: Dei_RBtnInfo
      Return: global handle to CTLINFO structure
 Description: Allocates a CTLINFO structure in the global heap.  Loads the
              structure with information about the custom control.
****************************************************************************/
GLOBALHANDLE FAR PASCAL Dei_RBtnInfo( void )
    {

    GLOBALHANDLE hCtlInfo = NULL;

    hCtlInfo = CtlInfoCreate( 100, _szCstCtlName, _szCstCtlName );
    if ( hCtlInfo )
        {

        LPCTLINFO lpCtlInfo = (LPCTLINFO)GlobalLock( hCtlInfo );
        if ( lpCtlInfo )
            {

            lpCtlInfo->Type[0].wType = 0;
            lpCtlInfo->Type[0].wWidth = 40;
            lpCtlInfo->Type[0].wHeight = 12;
            lpCtlInfo->Type[0].dwStyle = WS_CHILD | WS_VISIBLE |
                    BS_AUTORADIOBUTTON | WS_TABSTOP;
            lstrcpy( lpCtlInfo->Type[0].szDescr, _szCstCtlName );
            lpCtlInfo->wCtlTypes = 1;
            GlobalUnlock( hCtlInfo );

            }   /* if lpCtlInfo */
        }   /* if hCtlInfo */

    return ( hCtlInfo );

    }   /* function Dei_RBtnInfo */
```

Listing A.7 *continued*

```
/****************************************************************************
        Name: Dei_RBtnWndFn
      Return: Same as CstRadioBtnWndFn
 Description: Windows call back function for custom control.  This is a
              wrapper function for the existing function that resides in the
              CST_CTLS.DLL.
****************************************************************************/
LONG FAR PASCAL Dei_RBtnWndFn( HWND hWnd, UINT wMessage, WPARAM wParam,
        LPARAM lParam )
    {

    return ( CstRadioBtnWndFn( hWnd, wMessage, wParam, lParam ) );

    }   /* function Dei_RBtnWndFn */


/****************************************************************************
        Name: LibMain
      Return: TRUE
 Description: DLL main function
****************************************************************************/
int FAR PASCAL LibMain( HINSTANCE hInstance, WORD wDataSeg, WORD wHeapSize,
        LPSTR lpstrCmd )
    {

    lpstrCmd = lpstrCmd;

    if ( wHeapSize )
        {
        /* LibEntry called LocalInit - so unlock data segment */
        UnlockSegment( wDataSeg );
        }

    /* Set the external data value */
    _hInstanceDLL = hInstance;

    return ( TRUE );

    }   /* function LibMain */


/****************************************************************************
        Name: WEP
      Return: TRUE
 Description: DLL exit function
****************************************************************************/
int FAR PASCAL WEP( int nSystemExit )
    {

    nSystemExit = nSystemExit;

    return ( TRUE );

    }   /* function WEP */

/* End of DEI_RBTN.C */
```

Listing A.8

```
/***************************************************************************
         File Name: DEI_RBTN.RC
     Expanded Name: Dialog Editor Interface for CSTRADIOBTN
       Description: Resource file for DEI_RBTN.DLL
       Portability: Microsoft Windows 3.X
***************************************************************************/

#include <windows.h>
#include <cst_ctls.h>

#include <dei_rbtn.h>
#include <dei_rbtn.dlg>

STRINGTABLE
BEGIN
    BS_RADIOBUTTON,     "BS_RADIOBUTTON"
    BS_AUTORADIOBUTTON, "BS_AUTORADIOBUTTON"
    BS_LEFTTEXT,        "BS_LEFTTEXT"
END

/* End of DEI_RBTN.RC */
```

Listing A.9

```
/******************************************************************************
           File Name: DEI_RBTN.DLG
       Expanded Name: Dialog Editor Interface for CSTRADIOBTN
         Description: Style Dialog file for DEI_RBTN.DLL.
         Portability: Microsoft Windows 3.X
******************************************************************************/

CstRadioBtn DIALOG LOADONCALL MOVEABLE DISCARDABLE 16, 16, 140, 132
STYLE DS_MODALFRAME | WS_POPUP | WS_VISIBLE | WS_CAPTION | WS_SYSMENU
CAPTION "Custom Radio Button Styles"
FONT 8, "Helv"
BEGIN
    CONTROL "Id:" -1, "cststatic", CSS_TEXTLOWERED | WS_GROUP, 6, 6, 20, 10
    CONTROL "", IDC_EDIT_ID, "EDIT", ES_LEFT | ES_AUTOHSCROLL | WS_BORDER |
            WS_GROUP | WS_TABSTOP, 30, 4, 104, 12
    CONTROL "Text:", -1, "cststatic", CSS_TEXTLOWERED | WS_GROUP, 6, 20, 20, 10
    CONTROL "", IDC_EDIT_TEXT, "EDIT", ES_LEFT | ES_AUTOHSCROLL | WS_BORDER |
            WS_GROUP | WS_TABSTOP, 30, 18, 104, 12

    CONTROL "Custom Radio Button Styles", -1, "BUTTON", BS_GROUPBOX |
            WS_GROUP, 6, 34, 128, 34
    CONTROL "&Auto", IDC_AUTO, "cstcheckbox", BS_AUTOCHECKBOX | WS_GROUP |
            WS_TABSTOP, 10, 46, 28, 10
    CONTROL "&Left Text", IDC_LEFTTEXT, "cstcheckbox", BS_AUTOCHECKBOX |
            WS_TABSTOP, 10, 56, 43, 10

    CONTROL "Basic Styles", -1, "BUTTON", BS_GROUPBOX | WS_GROUP, 6, 72, 128,
            34
    CONTROL "&Visible", IDC_VISIBLE, "cstcheckbox", BS_AUTOCHECKBOX |
            WS_GROUP | WS_TABSTOP, 10, 84, 34, 10
    CONTROL "&Disabled", IDC_DISABLED, "cstcheckbox", BS_AUTOCHECKBOX |
            WS_TABSTOP, 10, 94, 41, 10
    CONTROL "&Group", IDC_GROUP, "cstcheckbox", BS_AUTOCHECKBOX | WS_TABSTOP,
            72, 84, 34, 10
    CONTROL "&Tab Stop", IDC_TABSTOP, "cstcheckbox", BS_AUTOCHECKBOX |
            WS_TABSTOP, 72, 94, 44, 10

    CONTROL "OK", IDC_OK, "BUTTON", BS_DEFPUSHBUTTON | WS_GROUP | WS_TABSTOP,
            6, 112, 40, 14
    CONTROL "Cancel", IDC_CANCEL, "BUTTON", BS_PUSHBUTTON | WS_GROUP |
            WS_TABSTOP, 50, 112, 40, 14
    CONTROL "Help", IDC_HELP, "BUTTON", BS_PUSHBUTTON | WS_TABSTOP,
            94, 112, 40, 14
END

/* End of DEI_RBTN.DLG */
```

Listing A.10

```
LIBRARY DEI_RBTN
DESCRIPTION 'Dialog Editor - CSTRADIOBTN DLL'
EXETYPE WINDOWS
CODE PRELOAD MOVEABLE SHARED DISCARDABLE
DATA PRELOAD MOVEABLE SINGLE
HEAPSIZE 1024
EXPORTS
        WEP                @1    RESIDENTNAME
        Dei_RBtnInfo       @2
        CstRadioBtnStyle   @3
        CstRadioBtnFlags   @4
        Dei_RBtnWndFn      @5
        CstRadioBtnDlgFn   @6
```

Listing A.11

```
/*****************************************************************************
            File Name: DEI_STTC.H
        Expanded Name: Dialog Editor Interface for CSTSTATIC
          Description: Include file for DEI_STTC.C & DEI_STTC.RC
          Portability: Microsoft Windows 3.X
*****************************************************************************/

#define IDC_TYPES            100
#define IDC_BITMAP           ( IDC_TYPES + CSS_BITMAP )
#define IDC_BITMAPSTRETCH    ( IDC_TYPES + CSS_BITMAPSTRETCH )
#define IDC_BITMAPWINDOW     ( IDC_TYPES + CSS_BITMAPWINDOW )
#define IDC_FRAME            ( IDC_TYPES + CSS_FRAME )
#define IDC_LINEHORZ         ( IDC_TYPES + CSS_LINEHORZ )
#define IDC_LINEVERT         ( IDC_TYPES + CSS_LINEVERT )
#define IDC_ICON             ( IDC_TYPES + CSS_ICON )
#define IDC_ICONWINDOW       ( IDC_TYPES + CSS_ICONWINDOW )
#define IDC_RECT             ( IDC_TYPES + CSS_RECT )
#define IDC_TEXT             ( IDC_TYPES + CSS_TEXT )
#define IDC_TEXTLOWERED      ( IDC_TYPES + CSS_TEXTLOWERED )
#define IDC_TEXTRAISED       ( IDC_TYPES + CSS_TEXTRAISED )
#define IDC_TEXTSHADOW       ( IDC_TYPES + CSS_TEXTSHADOW )

#define IDC_LEFT             114
#define IDC_HCENTER          115
#define IDC_RIGHT            116
#define IDC_TOP              117
#define IDC_VCENTER          118
#define IDC_BOTTOM           119
#define IDC_BORDER           120
#define IDC_LOWERED          121
#define IDC_RAISED           122
#define IDC_EXPANDTABS       123
#define IDC_LEFTNOWORDWRAP   124
#define IDC_NOPREFIX         125
#define IDC_SINGLELINE       126

#define IDC_VISIBLE          201
#define IDC_DISABLED         202
#define IDC_GROUP            203
#define IDC_TABSTOP          204

#define IDC_EDIT_ID          300
#define IDC_EDIT_TEXT        301

#define IDC_OK               1
#define IDC_CANCEL           2
#define IDC_HELP             8

/* End of DEI_STTC.H */
```

Listing A.12

```
/***************************************************************************
          File Name: DEI_STTC.C
      Expanded Name: Dialog Editor Interface for Custom Static Control
        Description: Library of functions for interfacing the CSTSTATIC
                     control with the Dialog Editor.
       Program List: DEI_STTC.C
                     DEI_STTC.RC
                     DEI_STTC.DEF
                     DEI_CTLS.C
                     CST_CTLS.LIB,DLL
Global Function List: CstStaticDlgFn
                     CstStaticFlags
                     CstStaticStyle
                     Dei_SttcInfo
                     Dei_SttcWndFn
                     LibMain
                     WEP
        Static Data: _hInstanceDLL
                     _szCstCtlName
        Portability: Microsoft Windows 3.X
***************************************************************************/

/* Microsoft Windows */
#include <windows.h>

/* Custom Control Interface */
#include <custcntl.h>

/* Standard C */
#include <stdlib.h>

/* Prototypes and Types */
#include <cst_sttc.h>
#include <dei_ctls.h>

/* Own */
#include <dei_sttc.h>

/* Library instance handle */
static HINSTANCE _hInstanceDLL = 0;

static char _szCstCtlName[] = "CstStatic";

/* Prototypes of functions */
BOOL FAR PASCAL CstStaticDlgFn( HWND hDlg, WORD wMessage, WORD wParam,
         LONG lParam );
WORD FAR PASCAL CstStaticFlags( DWORD dwFlags, LPSTR szString,
         WORD wMaxString );
BOOL FAR PASCAL CstStaticStyle( HWND hWnd, GLOBALHANDLE hCtlStyle,
         LPFNSTRTOID lpfnStrToId, LPFNIDTOSTR lpfnIdToStr );
GLOBALHANDLE FAR PASCAL Dei_SttcInfo( void );
LONG FAR PASCAL Dei_SttcWndFn( HWND hWnd, UINT wMessage, WPARAM wParam,
         LPARAM lParam );
```

Listing A.12 *continued*

```
/******************************************************************************
        Name: CstStaticDlgFn
 Description: Dialog box callback function for style selection.
******************************************************************************/
BOOL FAR PASCAL CstStaticDlgFn( HWND hDlg, WORD wMsg, WORD wParam,
        LONG lParam )
    {

    switch ( wMsg )
        {
        case WM_INITDIALOG:
            {

            char szIdStr[CTLTITLE];

            /* Set the property */
            HCSTCTLSTYLE hCstCtlStyle = LOWORD( lParam );
            LPCSTCTLSTYLE lpCstCtlStyle =
                    (LPCSTCTLSTYLE)GlobalLock( hCstCtlStyle );
            LPCTLSTYLE lpCtlStyle =
                    (LPCTLSTYLE)GlobalLock( lpCstCtlStyle->hCtlStyle );
            DWORD dwStyle = lpCtlStyle->dwStyle;
            DWORD dwType = dwStyle & 0x0FL;

            SetProp( hDlg, _szCstCtlStyle, hCstCtlStyle );

            /* Center Dialog Box */
            CenterWindow( GetParent( hDlg ), hDlg, 0 );

            /* Text */
            SetDlgItemText( hDlg, IDC_EDIT_TEXT, lpCtlStyle->szTitle );

            /* Id */
            if ( !(*lpCstCtlStyle->lpfnIdToStr)( lpCtlStyle->wId, szIdStr,
                    CTLTITLE ) )
                {
                wsprintf( szIdStr, "%n", lpCtlStyle->wId );
                }
            SetDlgItemText( hDlg, IDC_EDIT_ID, szIdStr );
            GlobalUnlock( lpCstCtlStyle->hCtlStyle );
            GlobalUnlock( hCstCtlStyle );

            /* Type */
            CheckDlgButton( hDlg, (UINT)( dwType + IDC_TYPES ), TRUE );

            /* Horizontal Alignment */
            if ( dwStyle & CSS_HCENTER )
                {
                CheckDlgButton( hDlg, IDC_HCENTER, TRUE );
                }
            else if ( dwStyle & CSS_RIGHT )
                {
                CheckDlgButton( hDlg, IDC_RIGHT, TRUE );
                }
            else
                {
                CheckDlgButton( hDlg, IDC_LEFT, TRUE );
                }
```

Listing A.12 *continued*

```
    /* Vertical Alignment */
    if ( dwStyle & CSS_VCENTER )
        {
        CheckDlgButton( hDlg, IDC_VCENTER, TRUE );
        }
    else if ( dwStyle & CSS_BOTTOM )
        {
        CheckDlgButton( hDlg, IDC_BOTTOM, TRUE );
        }
    else
        {
        CheckDlgButton( hDlg, IDC_TOP, TRUE );
        }

    /* 3D Appearance */
    if ( dwStyle & CSS_BORDER )
        {
        CheckDlgButton( hDlg, IDC_BORDER, TRUE );
        }
    if ( dwStyle & CSS_LOWERED )
        {
        CheckDlgButton( hDlg, IDC_LOWERED, TRUE );
        }
    if ( dwStyle & CSS_RAISED )
        {
        CheckDlgButton( hDlg, IDC_RAISED, TRUE );
        }

    /* Text styles */
    if ( dwStyle & CSS_EXPANDTABS )
        {
        CheckDlgButton( hDlg, IDC_EXPANDTABS, TRUE );
        }
    if ( dwStyle & CSS_LEFTNOWORDWRAP )
        {
        CheckDlgButton( hDlg, IDC_LEFTNOWORDWRAP, TRUE );
        }
    if ( dwStyle & CSS_NOPREFIX )
        {
        CheckDlgButton( hDlg, IDC_NOPREFIX, TRUE );
        }
    if ( dwStyle & CSS_SINGLELINE )
        {
        CheckDlgButton( hDlg, IDC_SINGLELINE, TRUE );
        }

    /* Basic styles */
    if ( dwStyle & WS_VISIBLE )
        {
        CheckDlgButton( hDlg, IDC_VISIBLE, TRUE );
        }
    if ( dwStyle & WS_DISABLED )
        {
        CheckDlgButton( hDlg, IDC_DISABLED, TRUE );
        }
    if ( dwStyle & WS_GROUP )
        {
```

Listing A.12 continued

```
                    CheckDlgButton( hDlg, IDC_GROUP, TRUE );
                    }
            if ( dwStyle & WS_TABSTOP )
                    {
                    CheckDlgButton( hDlg, IDC_TABSTOP, TRUE );
                    }

            break;
            }
        case WM_COMMAND:
            switch ( wParam )
                {
                case IDC_HELP:
                    WinHelp( hDlg, "CST_CTLS.HLP", HELP_KEY,
                            (DWORD)(LPSTR)"CstStatic" );
                    break;
                case IDC_OK:
                    {
                    char szIdStr[32];
                    DWORD dwStyle, dwId;
                    HCSTCTLSTYLE hCstCtlStyle;
                    int iTypeId;
                    LPCSTCTLSTYLE lpCstCtlStyle;
                    LPCTLSTYLE lpCtlStyle;

                    hCstCtlStyle = GetProp( hDlg, _szCstCtlStyle );
                    lpCstCtlStyle = (LPCSTCTLSTYLE)GlobalLock(
                            hCstCtlStyle );
                    lpCtlStyle = (LPCTLSTYLE)GlobalLock(
                            lpCstCtlStyle->hCtlStyle );
                    dwStyle = lpCtlStyle->dwStyle & 0xFFFF0000L;

                    /* Text */
                    GetDlgItemText( hDlg, IDC_EDIT_TEXT,
                            lpCtlStyle->szTitle, CTLTITLE );

                    /* Id */
                    GetDlgItemText( hDlg, IDC_EDIT_ID, szIdStr,
                            sizeof ( szIdStr ) );
                    dwId = (*lpCstCtlStyle->lpfnStrToId)( szIdStr );
                    if ( LOWORD( dwId ) == 0 )
                        {
                        lpCtlStyle->wId = max( (WORD)atoi( szIdStr ),
                                lpCtlStyle->wId );
                        }
                    else
                        {
                        lpCtlStyle->wId = HIWORD( dwId );
                        }

                    /* Type */
                    for ( iTypeId = ( IDC_TYPES + (int)CSS_BITMAP );
                            iTypeId <= ( IDC_TYPES + (int)CSS_TEXTSHADOW );
                            iTypeId++ )
                        {
                        if ( IsDlgButtonChecked( hDlg, iTypeId ) )
                            {
                            dwStyle |= (DWORD)( iTypeId - IDC_TYPES );
```

Listing A.12 *continued*

```
                    break;
                }
            }
        /* Horizontal Alignment */
        if ( IsDlgButtonChecked( hDlg, IDC_HCENTER ) )
            {
            dwStyle |= CSS_HCENTER;
            }
        else if ( IsDlgButtonChecked( hDlg, IDC_RIGHT ) )
            {
            dwStyle |= CSS_RIGHT;
            }
        else
            {
            dwStyle |= CSS_LEFT;
            }

        /* Vertical Alignment */
        if ( IsDlgButtonChecked( hDlg, IDC_VCENTER ) )
            {
            dwStyle |= CSS_VCENTER;
            }
        else if ( IsDlgButtonChecked( hDlg, IDC_BOTTOM ) )
            {
            dwStyle |= CSS_BOTTOM;
            }
        else
            {
            dwStyle |= CSS_TOP;
            }

        /* 3D Appearance */
        if ( IsDlgButtonChecked( hDlg, IDC_BORDER ) )
            {
            dwStyle |= CSS_BORDER;
            }
        else
            {
            dwStyle &= ~CSS_BORDER;
            }
        if ( IsDlgButtonChecked( hDlg, IDC_LOWERED ) )
            {
            dwStyle |= CSS_LOWERED;
            }
        else if ( IsDlgButtonChecked( hDlg, IDC_RAISED ) )
            {
            dwStyle |= CSS_RAISED;
            }
        else
            {
            dwStyle |= CSS_FLAT;
            }

        /* Text Styles */
        if ( IsDlgButtonChecked( hDlg, IDC_EXPANDTABS ) )
            {
            dwStyle |= CSS_EXPANDTABS;
```

Listing A.12 *continued*

```c
            }
        else
            {
            dwStyle &= ~CSS_EXPANDTABS;
            }
        if ( IsDlgButtonChecked( hDlg, IDC_LEFTNOWORDWRAP ) )
            {
            dwStyle |= CSS_LEFTNOWORDWRAP;
            }
        else
            {
            dwStyle &= ~CSS_LEFTNOWORDWRAP;
            }
        if ( IsDlgButtonChecked( hDlg, IDC_NOPREFIX ) )
            {
            dwStyle |= CSS_NOPREFIX;
            }
        else
            {
            dwStyle &= ~CSS_NOPREFIX;
            }
        if ( IsDlgButtonChecked( hDlg, IDC_SINGLELINE ) )
            {
            dwStyle |= CSS_SINGLELINE;
            }
        else
            {
            dwStyle &= ~CSS_SINGLELINE;
            }

        /* Basic Styles */
        if ( IsDlgButtonChecked( hDlg, IDC_VISIBLE ) )
            {
            dwStyle |= WS_VISIBLE;
            }
        else
            {
            dwStyle &= ~WS_VISIBLE;
            }
        if ( IsDlgButtonChecked( hDlg, IDC_DISABLED ) )
            {
            dwStyle |= WS_DISABLED;
            }
        else
            {
            dwStyle &= ~WS_DISABLED;
            }
        if ( IsDlgButtonChecked( hDlg, IDC_GROUP ) )
            {
            dwStyle |= WS_GROUP;
            }
        else
            {
            dwStyle &= ~WS_GROUP;
            }
        if ( IsDlgButtonChecked( hDlg, IDC_TABSTOP ) )
            {
            dwStyle |= WS_TABSTOP;
            }
```

Listing A.12 *continued*

```
                    else
                        {
                        dwStyle &= ~WS_TABSTOP;
                        }

                    lpCtlStyle->dwStyle = dwStyle;
                    GlobalUnlock( lpCstCtlStyle->hCtlStyle );
                    GlobalUnlock( hCstCtlStyle );
                    EndDialog( hDlg, TRUE );
                    break;
                    }
                case IDC_CANCEL:
                    EndDialog( hDlg, FALSE );
                    break;
                default:
                    return ( FALSE );
                }   /* switch wParam */
            break;
        case WM_DESTROY:
            WinHelp( hDlg, "CST_CTLS.HLP", HELP_QUIT, 0L );
            RemoveProp( hDlg, _szCstCtlStyle );
            break;
        default:
            return ( FALSE );
        }   /* switch wMsg */

    return ( TRUE );

    }   /* function CstStaticDlgFn */


/*******************************************************************************
        Name: CstStaticFlags
  Parameters: dwFlags - current style of control
              lpstrStyle - buffer to store style string
              wMaxLen - maximum length of style string
      Return: length of style string
 Description: Converts a style into a string of style flags of all the
              class specific window styles for a control.  The basic, or
              class general styles are concatenated onto these by the dialog
              editor.
*******************************************************************************/
WORD FAR PASCAL CstStaticFlags( DWORD dwFlags, LPSTR lpstrStyle,
        WORD wMaxLen )
    {

    UINT uiType;
    char szBuf[32];
    int iBufLen = 32;

    wMaxLen = wMaxLen;

    /* Type */
    uiType = (UINT)( dwFlags & 0x0FL );
    LoadString( _hInstanceDLL, uiType, szBuf, iBufLen );
    lstrcpy( lpstrStyle, szBuf );

    /* Horizontal Alignment */
```

Listing A.12 *continued*

```
        if ( dwFlags & CSS_HCENTER )
            {
            LoadString( _hInstanceDLL, (UINT)CSS_HCENTER, szBuf, iBufLen );
            lstrcat( lpstrStyle, " | " );
            lstrcat( lpstrStyle, szBuf );
            }
        else if ( dwFlags & CSS_RIGHT )
            {
            LoadString( _hInstanceDLL, (UINT)CSS_RIGHT, szBuf, iBufLen );
            lstrcat( lpstrStyle, " | " );
            lstrcat( lpstrStyle, szBuf );
            }

        /* Vertical Alignment */
        if ( dwFlags & CSS_VCENTER )
            {
            LoadString( _hInstanceDLL, (UINT)CSS_VCENTER, szBuf, iBufLen );
            lstrcat( lpstrStyle, " | " );
            lstrcat( lpstrStyle, szBuf );
            }
        else if ( dwFlags & CSS_BOTTOM )
            {
            LoadString( _hInstanceDLL, (UINT)CSS_BOTTOM, szBuf, iBufLen );
            lstrcat( lpstrStyle, " | " );
            lstrcat( lpstrStyle, szBuf );
            }

        /* 3D Appearance */
        if ( dwFlags & CSS_BORDER )
            {
            LoadString( _hInstanceDLL, (UINT)CSS_BORDER, szBuf, iBufLen );
            lstrcat( lpstrStyle, " | " );
            lstrcat( lpstrStyle, szBuf );
            }
        if ( dwFlags & CSS_LOWERED )
            {
            LoadString( _hInstanceDLL, (UINT)CSS_LOWERED, szBuf, iBufLen );
            lstrcat( lpstrStyle, " | " );
            lstrcat( lpstrStyle, szBuf );
            }
        else if ( dwFlags & CSS_RAISED )
            {
            LoadString( _hInstanceDLL, (UINT)CSS_RAISED, szBuf, iBufLen );
            lstrcat( lpstrStyle, " | " );
            lstrcat( lpstrStyle, szBuf );
            }

        /* Text Styles */
        if ( dwFlags & CSS_EXPANDTABS )
            {
            LoadString( _hInstanceDLL, (UINT)CSS_EXPANDTABS, szBuf, iBufLen );
            lstrcat( lpstrStyle, " | " );
            lstrcat( lpstrStyle, szBuf );
            }
        if ( dwFlags & CSS_LEFTNOWORDWRAP )
            {
            LoadString( _hInstanceDLL, (UINT)CSS_LEFTNOWORDWRAP, szBuf, iBufLen );
            lstrcat( lpstrStyle, " | " );
            lstrcat( lpstrStyle, szBuf );
```

Listing A.12 *continued*

```
        }
    if ( dwFlags & CSS_NOPREFIX )
        {
        LoadString( _hInstanceDLL, (UINT)CSS_NOPREFIX, szBuf, iBufLen );
        lstrcat( lpstrStyle, " | " );
        lstrcat( lpstrStyle, szBuf );
        }
    if ( dwFlags & CSS_SINGLELINE )
        {
        LoadString( _hInstanceDLL, (UINT)CSS_SINGLELINE, szBuf, iBufLen );
        lstrcat( lpstrStyle, " | " );
        lstrcat( lpstrStyle, szBuf );
        }

    return ( (WORD)lstrlen( lpstrStyle ) );

    }   /* function CstStaticFlags */


/*******************************************************************************
        Name: CstStaticStyle
  Parameters: hWnd - handle of dialog editor window
              hCtlStyle - global handle of CTLSTYLE structure
              lpfnStrToId - pointer to func to convert string to control id
              lpfnIdToStr - pointer to func to convert control id to string
      Return: TRUE if style has changed, FALSE if no change
 Description: Invokes the style dialog box for a custom control.
*******************************************************************************/
BOOL FAR PASCAL CstStaticStyle( HWND hWnd, GLOBALHANDLE hCtlStyle,
        LPFNSTRTOID lpfnStrToId, LPFNIDTOSTR lpfnIdToStr )
    {

    return ( CstCtlStyleDlg( _hInstanceDLL, _szCstCtlName,
            (FARPROC)CstStaticDlgFn,
            hWnd, hCtlStyle, lpfnStrToId, lpfnIdToStr ) );

    }   /* function CstStaticStyle */


/*******************************************************************************
        Name: Dei_SttcInfo
      Return: global handle to CTLINFO structure
 Description: Allocates a CTLINFO structure in the global heap.  Loads the
              structure with information about the custom control.
*******************************************************************************/
GLOBALHANDLE FAR PASCAL Dei_SttcInfo( void )
    {

    GLOBALHANDLE hCtlInfo = NULL;

    hCtlInfo = CtlInfoCreate( 100, _szCstCtlName, _szCstCtlName );
    if ( hCtlInfo )
        {
        LPCTLINFO lpCtlInfo = (LPCTLINFO)GlobalLock( hCtlInfo );
        if ( lpCtlInfo )
            {
```

Listing A.12 *continued*

```
        lpCtlInfo->Type[0].wType = 0;
        lpCtlInfo->Type[0].wWidth = 40;
        lpCtlInfo->Type[0].wHeight = 12;
        lpCtlInfo->Type[0].dwStyle = WS_CHILD | WS_VISIBLE | WS_TABSTOP |
              CSS_BITMAP | CSS_RAISED;
        lstrcpy( lpCtlInfo->Type[0].szDescr, _szCstCtlName );
        lstrcat( lpCtlInfo->Type[0].szDescr, " Bitmap" );

        lpCtlInfo->Type[1].wType = 0;
        lpCtlInfo->Type[1].wWidth = 40;
        lpCtlInfo->Type[1].wHeight = 12;
        lpCtlInfo->Type[1].dwStyle = WS_CHILD | WS_VISIBLE | WS_TABSTOP |
              CSS_FRAME | CSS_RAISED;
        lstrcpy( lpCtlInfo->Type[1].szDescr, _szCstCtlName );
        lstrcat( lpCtlInfo->Type[1].szDescr, " Frame" );

        lpCtlInfo->Type[2].wType = 0;
        lpCtlInfo->Type[2].wWidth = 24;
        lpCtlInfo->Type[2].wHeight = 24;
        lpCtlInfo->Type[2].dwStyle = WS_CHILD | WS_VISIBLE | WS_TABSTOP |
              CSS_ICON | CSS_RAISED;
        lstrcpy( lpCtlInfo->Type[2].szDescr, _szCstCtlName );
        lstrcat( lpCtlInfo->Type[2].szDescr, " Icon" );

        lpCtlInfo->Type[3].wType = 0;
        lpCtlInfo->Type[3].wWidth = 40;
        lpCtlInfo->Type[3].wHeight = 12;
        lpCtlInfo->Type[3].dwStyle = WS_CHILD | WS_VISIBLE | WS_TABSTOP |
              CSS_LINEHORZ | CSS_RAISED;
        lstrcpy( lpCtlInfo->Type[3].szDescr, _szCstCtlName );
        lstrcat( lpCtlInfo->Type[3].szDescr, " Line" );

        lpCtlInfo->Type[4].wType = 0;
        lpCtlInfo->Type[4].wWidth = 40;
        lpCtlInfo->Type[4].wHeight = 12;
        lpCtlInfo->Type[4].dwStyle = WS_CHILD | WS_VISIBLE | WS_TABSTOP |
              CSS_RECT | WS_CLIPSIBLINGS | CSS_RAISED;
        lstrcpy( lpCtlInfo->Type[4].szDescr, _szCstCtlName );
        lstrcat( lpCtlInfo->Type[4].szDescr, " Rect" );

        lpCtlInfo->Type[5].wType = 0;
        lpCtlInfo->Type[5].wWidth = 40;
        lpCtlInfo->Type[5].wHeight = 12;
        lpCtlInfo->Type[5].dwStyle = WS_CHILD | WS_VISIBLE | WS_TABSTOP |
              CSS_TEXT | CSS_RAISED;
        lstrcpy( lpCtlInfo->Type[5].szDescr, _szCstCtlName );
        lstrcat( lpCtlInfo->Type[5].szDescr, " Text" );

        lpCtlInfo->wCtlTypes = 6;
        GlobalUnlock( hCtlInfo );

        }  /* if lpCtlInfo */
    }  /* if hCtlInfo */

    return ( hCtlInfo );

}   /* function Dei_SttcInfo */
```

Listing A.12 *continued*

```c
/****************************************************************************
         Name: Dei_SttcWndFn
       Return: Same as CstStaticWndFn
  Description: Windows call back function for custom control.  This is a
               wrapper function for the existing function that resides in the
               CST_CTLS.DLL.
****************************************************************************/
LONG FAR PASCAL Dei_SttcWndFn( HWND hWnd, UINT wMessage, WPARAM wParam,
        LPARAM lParam )
    {

    return ( CstStaticWndFn( hWnd, wMessage, wParam, lParam ) );

    }   /* function Dei_SttcWndFn */


/****************************************************************************
         Name: LibMain
       Return: TRUE
  Description: DLL main function
****************************************************************************/
int FAR PASCAL LibMain( HINSTANCE hInstance, WORD wDataSeg, WORD wHeapSize,
        LPSTR lpstrCmd )
    {

    lpstrCmd = lpstrCmd;

    if ( wHeapSize )
        {
        /* LibEntry called LocalInit - so unlock data segment */
        UnlockSegment( wDataSeg );
        }

    /* Set the external data value */
    _hInstanceDLL = hInstance;

    return ( TRUE );

    }   /* function LibMain */


/****************************************************************************
         Name: WEP
       Return: TRUE
  Description: DLL exit function
****************************************************************************/
int FAR PASCAL WEP( int nSystemExit )
    {

    nSystemExit = nSystemExit;

    return ( TRUE );

    }   /* function WEP */

/* End of DEI_STTC.C */
```

Windows Custom Controls

Listing A.13

```
/*****************************************************************************
            File Name: DEI_STTC.RC
        Expanded Name: Dialog Editor Interface for CSTSTATIC
          Description: Resource file for DEI_STTC.DLL
          Portability: Microsoft Windows 3.X
*****************************************************************************/

#include <windows.h>
#include <cst_ctls.h>

#include <dei_sttc.h>
rcinclude dei_sttc.dlg

STRINGTABLE
BEGIN
    CSS_BITMAP,            "CSS_BITMAP"
    CSS_BITMAPSTRETCH,     "CSS_BITMAPSTRETCH"
    CSS_BITMAPWINDOW,      "CSS_BITMAPWINDOW"
    CSS_FRAME,             "CSS_FRAME"
    CSS_LINEHORZ,          "CSS_LINEHORZ"
    CSS_LINEVERT,          "CSS_LINEVERT"
    CSS_ICON,              "CSS_ICON"
    CSS_ICONWINDOW,        "CSS_ICONWINDOW"
    CSS_RECT,              "CSS_RECT"
    CSS_TEXT,              "CSS_TEXT"
    CSS_TEXTLOWERED,       "CSS_TEXTLOWERED"
    CSS_TEXTRAISED,        "CSS_TEXTRAISED"
    CSS_TEXTSHADOW,        "CSS_TEXTSHADOW"
    CSS_HCENTER,           "CSS_HCENTER"
    CSS_RIGHT,             "CSS_RIGHT"
    CSS_BOTTOM,            "CSS_BOTTOM"
    CSS_VCENTER,           "CSS_VCENTER"
    CSS_BORDER,            "CSS_BORDER"
    CSS_LOWERED,           "CSS_LOWERED"
    CSS_RAISED,            "CSS_RAISED"
    CSS_SINGLELINE,        "CSS_SINGLELINE"
    CSS_LEFTNOWORDWRAP,    "CSS_LEFTNOWORDWRAP"
    CSS_NOPREFIX,          "CSS_NOPREFIX"
    CSS_EXPANDTABS,        "CSS_EXPANDTABS"
END

/* End of DEI_STTC.RC */
```

Listing A.14

```
/******************************************************************
        File Name: DEI_STTC.DLG
    Expanded Name: Dialog Editor Interface for CSTSTATIC
      Description: Style Dialog file for DEI_STTC.DLL.
      Portability: Microsoft Windows 3.X
******************************************************************/

CstStatic DIALOG LOADONCALL MOVEABLE DISCARDABLE 16, 16, 186, 284
STYLE DS_MODALFRAME | WS_POPUP | WS_VISIBLE | WS_CAPTION | WS_SYSMENU
CAPTION "Custom Static Styles"
FONT 8, "Helv"
BEGIN
    CONTROL "Id:" -1, "cststatic", CSS_TEXTLOWERED | WS_GROUP, 6, 6, 20, 10
    CONTROL "", IDC_EDIT_ID, "EDIT", ES_LEFT | ES_AUTOHSCROLL | WS_BORDER |
            WS_GROUP | WS_TABSTOP, 30, 4, 106, 12
    CONTROL "Text:", -1, "cststatic", CSS_TEXTLOWERED | WS_GROUP, 6, 20, 20,
            10
    CONTROL "", IDC_EDIT_TEXT, "EDIT", ES_LEFT | ES_AUTOHSCROLL | WS_BORDER |
            WS_GROUP | WS_TABSTOP, 30, 18, 106, 12

    CONTROL "Custom Static Types", -1, "CstStatic", CSS_TEXTLOWERED,
            10, 36, 100, 10
    CONTROL "Custom Static Types", -1, "CstStatic", WS_GROUP |
            CSS_FRAME | CSS_BORDER | CSS_RAISED, 6, 34, 130, 84
    CONTROL "&Bitmap", IDC_BITMAP, "cstradiobtn", BS_AUTORADIOBUTTON |
            WS_GROUP | WS_TABSTOP, 10, 46, 50, 10
    CONTROL "Bitmap Stretch", IDC_BITMAPSTRETCH, "cstradiobtn",
            BS_AUTORADIOBUTTON | WS_TABSTOP, 10, 56, 62, 10
    CONTROL "Bitmap Win.", IDC_BITMAPWINDOW, "cstradiobtn",
            BS_AUTORADIOBUTTON | WS_TABSTOP, 10, 66, 58, 10
    CONTROL "Frame", IDC_FRAME, "cstradiobtn", BS_AUTORADIOBUTTON |
            WS_TABSTOP, 10, 76, 44, 10
    CONTROL "Line Horz.", IDC_LINEHORZ, "cstradiobtn", BS_AUTORADIOBUTTON |
            WS_TABSTOP, 10, 86, 58, 10
    CONTROL "Line Vert.", IDC_LINEVERT, "cstradiobtn", BS_AUTORADIOBUTTON |
            WS_TABSTOP, 10, 96, 57, 10
    CONTROL "Icon", IDC_ICON_, "cstradiobtn", BS_AUTORADIOBUTTON |
            WS_TABSTOP, 72, 46, 55, 10
    CONTROL "Icon Window", IDC_ICONWINDOW, "cstradiobtn", BS_AUTORADIOBUTTON |
            WS_TABSTOP, 72, 56, 58, 10
    CONTROL "Rectangle", IDC_RECT, "cstradiobtn", BS_AUTORADIOBUTTON |
            WS_TABSTOP, 72, 66, 58, 10
    CONTROL "Text", IDC_TEXT, "cstradiobtn", BS_AUTORADIOBUTTON | WS_TABSTOP,
            72, 76, 50, 10
    CONTROL "Text Lowered", IDC_TEXTLOWERED, "cstradiobtn",
            BS_AUTORADIOBUTTON | WS_TABSTOP, 72, 86, 58, 10
    CONTROL "Text Raised", IDC_TEXTRAISED, "cstradiobtn", BS_AUTORADIOBUTTON |
            WS_TABSTOP, 72, 96, 58, 10
    CONTROL "Text Shadow", IDC_TEXTSHADOW, "cstradiobtn", BS_AUTORADIOBUTTON |
            WS_TABSTOP, 72, 106, 58, 10

    CONTROL "Horizontal Alignment", -1, "CstStatic", CSS_TEXTLOWERED,
            10, 124, 100, 10
    CONTROL "Horizontal Alignment", -1, "CstStatic", WS_GROUP |
            CSS_FRAME | CSS_BORDER | CSS_RAISED, 6, 122, 130, 26
    CONTROL "&Left", IDC_LEFT, "cstradiobtn", BS_AUTORADIOBUTTON | WS_GROUP |
            WS_TABSTOP, 10, 134, 26, 10
```

Listing A.14 continued

```
CONTROL "&Center", IDC_HCENTER, "cstradiobtn", BS_AUTORADIOBUTTON |
        WS_TABSTOP, 54, 134, 36, 10
CONTROL "&Right", IDC_RIGHT, "cstradiobtn", BS_AUTORADIOBUTTON |
        WS_TABSTOP, 98, 134, 34, 10

CONTROL "Vertical Alignment", -1, "CstStatic", CSS_TEXTLOWERED,
        10, 152, 100, 10
CONTROL "Vertical Alignment", -1, "CstStatic", WS_GROUP |
        CSS_FRAME | CSS_BORDER | CSS_RAISED, 6, 148, 130, 26
CONTROL "&Top", IDC_TOP, "cstradiobtn", BS_AUTORADIOBUTTON | WS_GROUP |
        WS_TABSTOP, 10, 162, 26, 10
CONTROL "&Center", IDC_VCENTER, "cstradiobtn", BS_AUTORADIOBUTTON |
        WS_TABSTOP, 54, 162, 36, 10
CONTROL "&Bottom", IDC_BOTTOM, "cstradiobtn", BS_AUTORADIOBUTTON |
        WS_TABSTOP, 98, 162, 34, 10

CONTROL "3D Appearance", -1, "CstStatic", CSS_TEXTLOWERED,
        10, 180, 100, 10
CONTROL "3D Appearance", -1, "CstStatic", WS_GROUP |
        CSS_FRAME | CSS_BORDER | CSS_RAISED, 6, 178, 130, 26
CONTROL "&Border", IDC_BORDER, "cstcheckbox", BS_AUTOCHECKBOX | WS_GROUP |
        WS_TABSTOP, 10, 190, 44, 10
CONTROL "&Lowered", IDC_LOWERED, "cstcheckbox", BS_AUTOCHECKBOX |
        WS_TABSTOP, 54, 190, 44, 10
CONTROL "&Raised", IDC_RAISED, "cstcheckbox", BS_AUTOCHECKBOX |
        WS_TABSTOP, 98, 190, 34, 10

CONTROL "Text Styles", -1, "CstStatic", CSS_TEXTLOWERED,
        10, 208, 100, 10
CONTROL "Text Styles", -1, "CstStatic", WS_GROUP |
        CSS_FRAME | CSS_BORDER | CSS_RAISED, 6, 204, 130, 36
CONTROL "&Expand Tabs", IDC_EXPANDTABS, "cstcheckbox", BS_AUTOCHECKBOX |
        WS_GROUP | WS_TABSTOP, 10, 218, 58, 10
CONTROL "&Left No W.W.", IDC_LEFTNOWORDWRAP, "cstcheckbox",
        BS_AUTOCHECKBOX | WS_TABSTOP, 10, 228, 58, 10
CONTROL "&No Prefix", IDC_NOPREFIX, "cstcheckbox", BS_AUTOCHECKBOX |
        WS_TABSTOP, 72, 218, 58, 10
CONTROL "&Single Line", IDC_SINGLELINE, "cstcheckbox", BS_AUTOCHECKBOX |
        WS_TABSTOP, 72, 228, 58, 10

CONTROL "Basic Styles", -1, "CstStatic", CSS_TEXTLOWERED,
        10, 246, 100, 10
CONTROL "Basic Styles", -1, "CstStatic", WS_GROUP |
        CSS_FRAME | CSS_BORDER | CSS_RAISED, 6, 242, 130, 36
CONTROL "&Visible", IDC_VISIBLE, "cstcheckbox", BS_AUTOCHECKBOX |
        WS_GROUP | WS_TABSTOP, 10, 256, 36, 10
CONTROL "&Disabled", IDC_DISABLED, "cstcheckbox", BS_AUTOCHECKBOX |
        WS_TABSTOP, 10, 266, 42, 10
CONTROL "&Group", IDC_GROUP, "cstcheckbox", BS_AUTOCHECKBOX | WS_TABSTOP,
        72, 256, 34, 10
CONTROL "&Tab Stop", IDC_TABSTOP, "cstcheckbox", BS_AUTOCHECKBOX |
        WS_TABSTOP, 72, 266, 46, 10

CONTROL "", -1, "CstStatic", CSS_RECT | CSS_BORDER | CSS_RAISED,
        140, 64, 40, 176
CONTROL "DEI_STTC", -1, "CstStatic", CSS_ICON | CSS_BORDER | CSS_RAISED |
        CSS_HCENTER | CSS_VCENTER, 140, 242, 40, 36

CONTROL "OK", IDC_OK, "cstpushbtn", BS_DEFPUSHBUTTON | WS_TABSTOP, 140,
```

Listing A.14 *continued*

```
            4, 40, 14
    CONTROL "Cancel", IDC_CANCEL, "cstpushbtn", BS_PUSHBUTTON | WS_TABSTOP,
            140, 24, 40, 14
    CONTROL "Help", IDC_HELP, "cstpushbtn", BS_PUSHBUTTON | WS_TABSTOP,
            140, 44, 40, 14
END

ICON DEI_STTC ICON\DEM_STTC.ICO

/* End of DEI_STTC.DLG */
```

Listing A.15

```
LIBRARY DEI_STTC
DESCRIPTION 'Dialog Editor - CSTSTATIC DLL'
EXETYPE WINDOWS
CODE PRELOAD MOVEABLE SHARED DISCARDABLE
DATA PRELOAD MOVEABLE SINGLE
HEAPSIZE 1024
EXPORTS
        WEP                  @1      RESIDENTNAME
        Dei_SttcInfo         @2
        CstStaticStyle       @3
        CstStaticFlags       @4
        Dei_SttcWndFn        @5
        CstStaticDlgFn       @6
```

Listing A.16

```
/*****************************************************************************
        File Name: DEI_TABL.H
    Expanded Name: Dialog Editor Interface for CSTTABLE
      Description: Include file for DEI_TABL.C & DEI_TABL.RC
      Portability: Microsoft Windows 3.X
*****************************************************************************/

#define IDC_STANDARD           100
#define IDC_BORDER             101
#define IDC_SORT               102
#define IDC_NOTIFY             103
#define IDC_VERTSCROLLBAR      104
#define IDC_HORZSCROLLBAR      105
#define IDC_USETABSTOPS        106
#define IDC_NOREDRAW           107
#define IDC_DISABLENOSCROLL    108
#define IDC_NOINTEGRALHEIGHT   109
#define IDC_WANTKEYBOARDINPUT  110
#define IDC_MULTICOLUMN        111
#define IDC_MULTIPLESEL        112
#define IDC_EXTENDEDSEL        113
#define IDC_OWNERDRAWFIXED     114
#define IDC_OWNERDRAWVARIABLE  115
#define IDC_HASSTRINGS         116

#define IDC_VISIBLE            200
#define IDC_DISABLED           201
#define IDC_GROUP              202
#define IDC_TABSTOP            203

#define IDC_EDIT_ID            300
#define IDC_EDIT_TEXT          301

#define IDC_OK                   1
#define IDC_CANCEL               2
#define IDC_HELP                 8

/* End of DEI_TABL.H */
```

Listing A.17

```
/****************************************************************************
       File Name: DEI_TABL.C
    Expanded Name: Dialog Editor Interface for Custom Table Control
      Description: Library of functions for interfacing the CSTTABLE
                   control with the Dialog Editor.
     Program List: DEI_TABL.C
                   DEI_TABL.RC
                   DEI_TABL.DEF
                   DEI_CTLS.C
                   CST_CTLS.LIB,DLL
Global Function List: CstTableDlgFn
                   CstTableFlags
                   CstTableStyle
                   Dei_TablInfo
                   Dei_TablWndFn
                   LibMain
                   WEP
       Static Data: _hInstanceDLL
                   _szCstCtlName
       Portability: Microsoft Windows 3.X
****************************************************************************/

/* Microsoft Windows */
#include <windows.h>

/* Custom Control Interface */
#include <custcntl.h>

/* Standard C */
#include <stdlib.h>

/* Prototypes and Types */
#include <cst_tabl.h>
#include <dei_ctls.h>

/* Own */
#include <dei_tabl.h>

/* Library instance handle */
static HINSTANCE _hInstanceDLL = 0;

static char _szCstCtlName[] = "CstTable";

/* Prototypes of functions */
BOOL FAR PASCAL CstTableDlgFn( HWND hDlg, WORD wMessage, WORD wParam,
        LONG lParam );
WORD FAR PASCAL CstTableFlags( DWORD dwFlags, LPSTR szString,
        WORD wMaxString );
BOOL FAR PASCAL CstTableStyle( HWND hWnd, GLOBALHANDLE hCtlStyle,
        LPFNSTRTOID lpfnStrToId, LPFNIDTOSTR lpfnIdToStr );
GLOBALHANDLE FAR PASCAL Dei_TablInfo( void );
LONG FAR PASCAL Dei_TablWndFn( HWND hWnd, UINT wMessage, WPARAM wParam,
        LPARAM lParam );
```

Listing A.17 *continued*

```
/***************************************************************************
        Name: CstTableDlgFn
 Description: Dialog box callback function for style selection.
***************************************************************************/
BOOL FAR PASCAL CstTableDlgFn( HWND hDlg, WORD wMsg, WORD wParam,
        LONG lParam )
    {

    switch ( wMsg )
        {
        case WM_INITDIALOG:
            {

            char szIdStr[CTLTITLE];

            /* Set the property */
            HCSTCTLSTYLE hCstCtlStyle = LOWORD( lParam );
            LPCSTCTLSTYLE lpCstCtlStyle =
                    (LPCSTCTLSTYLE)GlobalLock( hCstCtlStyle );
            LPCTLSTYLE lpCtlStyle =
                    (LPCTLSTYLE)GlobalLock( lpCstCtlStyle->hCtlStyle );
            DWORD dwStyle = lpCtlStyle->dwStyle;

            SetProp( hDlg, _szCstCtlStyle, hCstCtlStyle );

            /* Center Dialog Box */
            CenterWindow( GetParent( hDlg ), hDlg, 0 );

            /* Text */
            SetDlgItemText( hDlg, IDC_EDIT_TEXT, lpCtlStyle->szTitle );

            /* Id */
            if ( !(*lpCstCtlStyle->lpfnIdToStr)( lpCtlStyle->wId, szIdStr,
                    CTLTITLE ) )
                {
                wsprintf( szIdStr, "%n", lpCtlStyle->wId );
                }
            SetDlgItemText( hDlg, IDC_EDIT_ID, szIdStr );
            GlobalUnlock( lpCstCtlStyle->hCtlStyle );
            GlobalUnlock( hCstCtlStyle );

            /* Custom Table Styles */
            if ( dwStyle & LBS_STANDARD )
                {
                CheckDlgButton( hDlg, IDC_STANDARD, TRUE );
                }
            if ( dwStyle & WS_BORDER )
                {
                CheckDlgButton( hDlg, IDC_BORDER, TRUE );
                }
            if ( dwStyle & LBS_SORT )
                {
                CheckDlgButton( hDlg, IDC_SORT, TRUE );
                }
            if ( dwStyle & LBS_NOTIFY )
                {
                CheckDlgButton( hDlg, IDC_NOTIFY, TRUE );
```

Listing A.17 *continued*

```
            }
        if ( dwStyle & WS_VSCROLL )
            {
            CheckDlgButton( hDlg, IDC_VERTSCROLLBAR, TRUE );
            }
        if ( dwStyle & WS_HSCROLL )
            {
            CheckDlgButton( hDlg, IDC_HORZSCROLLBAR, TRUE );
            }
        if ( dwStyle & LBS_USETABSTOPS )
            {
            CheckDlgButton( hDlg, IDC_USETABSTOPS, TRUE );
            }
        if ( dwStyle & LBS_NOREDRAW )
            {
            CheckDlgButton( hDlg, IDC_NOREDRAW, TRUE );
            }
#if defined ( LBS_DISABLENOSCROLL )
        if ( dwStyle & LBS_DISABLENOSCROLL )
            {
            CheckDlgButton( hDlg, IDC_DISABLENOSCROLL, TRUE );
            }
#endif
        if ( dwStyle & LBS_NOINTEGRALHEIGHT )
            {
            CheckDlgButton( hDlg, IDC_NOINTEGRALHEIGHT, TRUE );
            }
        if ( dwStyle & LBS_WANTKEYBOARDINPUT )
            {
            CheckDlgButton( hDlg, IDC_WANTKEYBOARDINPUT, TRUE );
            }
        if ( dwStyle & LBS_MULTICOLUMN )
            {
            CheckDlgButton( hDlg, IDC_MULTICOLUMN, TRUE );
            }
        if ( dwStyle & LBS_MULTIPLESEL )
            {
            CheckDlgButton( hDlg, IDC_MULTIPLESEL, TRUE );
            }
        if ( dwStyle & LBS_EXTENDEDSEL )
            {
            CheckDlgButton( hDlg, IDC_EXTENDEDSEL, TRUE );
            }
        if ( dwStyle & LBS_OWNERDRAWFIXED )
            {
            CheckDlgButton( hDlg, IDC_OWNERDRAWFIXED, TRUE );
            }
        if ( dwStyle & LBS_OWNERDRAWVARIABLE )
            {
            CheckDlgButton( hDlg, IDC_OWNERDRAWVARIABLE, TRUE );
            }
        if ( dwStyle & LBS_HASSTRINGS )
            {
            CheckDlgButton( hDlg, IDC_HASSTRINGS, TRUE );
            }

        /* Basic styles */
        if ( dwStyle & WS_VISIBLE )
            {
```

Listing A.17 *continued*

```
            CheckDlgButton( hDlg, IDC_VISIBLE, TRUE );
            }
    if ( dwStyle & WS_DISABLED )
            {
            CheckDlgButton( hDlg, IDC_DISABLED, TRUE );
            }
    if ( dwStyle & WS_GROUP )
            {
            CheckDlgButton( hDlg, IDC_GROUP, TRUE );
            }
    if ( dwStyle & WS_TABSTOP )
            {
            CheckDlgButton( hDlg, IDC_TABSTOP, TRUE );
            }

    break;
    }
case WM_COMMAND:
    switch ( wParam )
        {
        case IDC_HELP:
            WinHelp( hDlg, "CST_CTLS.HLP", HELP_KEY,
                    (DWORD)(LPSTR)"CstTable" );
            break;
        case IDC_OK:
            {

            char szIdStr[32];
            DWORD dwStyle, dwId;
            HCSTCTLSTYLE hCstCtlStyle;
            LPCSTCTLSTYLE lpCstCtlStyle;
            LPCTLSTYLE lpCtlStyle;

            hCstCtlStyle = GetProp( hDlg, _szCstCtlStyle );
            lpCstCtlStyle = (LPCSTCTLSTYLE)GlobalLock(
                    hCstCtlStyle );
            lpCtlStyle = (LPCTLSTYLE)GlobalLock(
                    lpCstCtlStyle->hCtlStyle );
            dwStyle = lpCtlStyle->dwStyle & 0xFFFF0000L;

            /* Text */
            GetDlgItemText( hDlg, IDC_EDIT_TEXT,
                    lpCtlStyle->szTitle, CTLTITLE );

            /* Id */
            GetDlgItemText( hDlg, IDC_EDIT_ID, szIdStr,
                    sizeof ( szIdStr ) );
            dwId = (*lpCstCtlStyle->lpfnStrToId)( szIdStr );
            if ( LOWORD( dwId ) == 0 )
                {
                lpCtlStyle->wId = max( (WORD)atoi( szIdStr ),
                        lpCtlStyle->wId );
                }
            else
                {
                lpCtlStyle->wId = HIWORD( dwId );
                }
```

Listing A.17 *continued*

```c
/* Custom Table Styles */
if ( IsDlgButtonChecked( hDlg, IDC_STANDARD ) )
    {
    dwStyle |= LBS_STANDARD;
    }
if ( IsDlgButtonChecked( hDlg, IDC_BORDER ) )
    {
    dwStyle |= WS_BORDER;
    }
if ( IsDlgButtonChecked( hDlg, IDC_SORT ) )
    {
    dwStyle |= LBS_SORT;
    }
if ( IsDlgButtonChecked( hDlg, IDC_NOTIFY ) )
    {
    dwStyle |= LBS_NOTIFY;
    }
if ( IsDlgButtonChecked( hDlg, IDC_VERTSCROLLBAR ) )
    {
    dwStyle |= WS_VSCROLL;
    }
if ( IsDlgButtonChecked( hDlg, IDC_HORZSCROLLBAR ) )
    {
    dwStyle |= WS_HSCROLL;
    }
if ( IsDlgButtonChecked( hDlg, IDC_USETABSTOPS ) )
    {
    dwStyle |= LBS_USETABSTOPS;
    }
if ( IsDlgButtonChecked( hDlg, IDC_NOREDRAW ) )
    {
    dwStyle |= LBS_NOREDRAW;
    }
#if defined ( LBS_DISABLENOSCROLL )
if ( IsDlgButtonChecked( hDlg, IDC_DISABLENOSCROLL ) )
    {
    dwStyle |= LBS_DISABLENOSCROLL;
    }
#endif
if ( IsDlgButtonChecked( hDlg, IDC_NOINTEGRALHEIGHT ) )
    {
    dwStyle |= LBS_NOINTEGRALHEIGHT;
    }
if ( IsDlgButtonChecked( hDlg, IDC_WANTKEYBOARDINPUT ) )
    {
    dwStyle |= LBS_WANTKEYBOARDINPUT;
    }
if ( IsDlgButtonChecked( hDlg, IDC_MULTICOLUMN ) )
    {
    dwStyle |= LBS_MULTICOLUMN;
    }
if ( IsDlgButtonChecked( hDlg, IDC_MULTIPLESEL ) )
    {
    dwStyle |= LBS_MULTIPLESEL;
    }
if ( IsDlgButtonChecked( hDlg, IDC_EXTENDEDSEL ) )
    {
    dwStyle |= LBS_EXTENDEDSEL;
    }
```

Listing A.17 *continued*

```
            if ( IsDlgButtonChecked( hDlg, IDC_OWNERDRAWFIXED ) )
                {
                dwStyle |= LBS_OWNERDRAWFIXED;
                }
            if ( IsDlgButtonChecked( hDlg, IDC_OWNERDRAWVARIABLE ) )
                {
                dwStyle |= LBS_OWNERDRAWVARIABLE;
                }
            if ( IsDlgButtonChecked( hDlg, IDC_HASSTRINGS ) )
                {
                dwStyle |= LBS_HASSTRINGS;
                }

        /* Basic Styles */
        if ( IsDlgButtonChecked( hDlg, IDC_VISIBLE ) )
            {
            dwStyle |= WS_VISIBLE;
            }
        else
            {
            dwStyle &= ~WS_VISIBLE;
            }
        if ( IsDlgButtonChecked( hDlg, IDC_DISABLED ) )
            {
            dwStyle |= WS_DISABLED;
            }
        else
            {
            dwStyle &= ~WS_DISABLED;
            }
        if ( IsDlgButtonChecked( hDlg, IDC_GROUP ) )
            {
            dwStyle |= WS_GROUP;
            }
        else
            {
            dwStyle &= ~WS_GROUP;
            }
        if ( IsDlgButtonChecked( hDlg, IDC_TABSTOP ) )
            {
            dwStyle |= WS_TABSTOP;
            }
        else
            {
            dwStyle &= ~WS_TABSTOP;
            }

        lpCtlStyle->dwStyle = dwStyle;
        GlobalUnlock( lpCstCtlStyle->hCtlStyle );
        GlobalUnlock( hCstCtlStyle );
        EndDialog( hDlg, TRUE );
        break;
        }
    case IDC_CANCEL:
        EndDialog( hDlg, FALSE );
        break;
    default:
        return ( FALSE );
```

Listing A.17 continued

```
                    }   /* switch wParam */
                break;
            case WM_DESTROY:
                WinHelp( hDlg, "CST_CTLS.HLP", HELP_QUIT, 0L );
                RemoveProp( hDlg, _szCstCtlStyle );
                break;
            default:
                return ( FALSE );
            }   /* switch wMsg */

        return ( TRUE );

        }   /* function CstTableDlgFn */


/*******************************************************************************
        Name: CstTableFlags
  Parameters: dwFlags - current style of control
              lpstrStyle - buffer to store style string
              wMaxLen - maximum length of style string
      Return: length of style string
 Description: Converts a style into a string of style flags of all the
              class specific window styles for a control.  The basic, or
              class general styles are concatenated onto these by the dialog
              editor.
*******************************************************************************/
WORD FAR PASCAL CstTableFlags( DWORD dwFlags, LPSTR lpstrStyle,
        WORD wMaxLen )
    {

    char szBuf[32];
    int iBufLen = 32;

    wMaxLen = wMaxLen;

    /* Custom Table Styles */
    if ( dwFlags & LBS_STANDARD )
        {
        LoadString( _hInstanceDLL, (UINT)LBS_SORT, szBuf, iBufLen );
        lstrcat( lpstrStyle, " | " );
        lstrcat( lpstrStyle, szBuf );
        }
    if ( ( dwFlags & LBS_SORT ) && !( dwFlags & LBS_STANDARD ) )
        {
        LoadString( _hInstanceDLL, (UINT)LBS_SORT, szBuf, iBufLen );
        lstrcat( lpstrStyle, " | " );
        lstrcat( lpstrStyle, szBuf );
        }
    if ( ( dwFlags & LBS_NOTIFY ) && !( dwFlags & LBS_STANDARD ) )
        {
        LoadString( _hInstanceDLL, (UINT)LBS_NOTIFY, szBuf, iBufLen );
        lstrcat( lpstrStyle, " | " );
        lstrcat( lpstrStyle, szBuf );
        }
    if ( dwFlags & LBS_USETABSTOPS )
        {
        LoadString( _hInstanceDLL, (UINT)LBS_USETABSTOPS, szBuf, iBufLen );
        lstrcat( lpstrStyle, " | " );
        lstrcat( lpstrStyle, szBuf );
```

Listing A.17 *continued*

```
        }
    if ( dwFlags & LBS_NOREDRAW )
        {
        LoadString( _hInstanceDLL, (UINT)LBS_NOREDRAW, szBuf, iBufLen );
        lstrcat( lpstrStyle, " | " );
        lstrcat( lpstrStyle, szBuf );
        }
#if defined ( LBS_DISABLENOSCROLL )
    if ( dwFlags & LBS_DISABLENOSCROLL )
        {
        LoadString( _hInstanceDLL, (UINT)LBS_DISABLENOSCROLL, szBuf, iBufLen );
        lstrcat( lpstrStyle, " | " );
        lstrcat( lpstrStyle, szBuf );
        }
#endif
    if ( dwFlags & LBS_NOINTEGRALHEIGHT )
        {
        LoadString( _hInstanceDLL, (UINT)LBS_NOINTEGRALHEIGHT, szBuf, iBufLen );
        lstrcat( lpstrStyle, " | " );
        lstrcat( lpstrStyle, szBuf );
        }
    if ( dwFlags & LBS_WANTKEYBOARDINPUT )
        {
        LoadString( _hInstanceDLL, (UINT)LBS_WANTKEYBOARDINPUT, szBuf, iBufLen );
        lstrcat( lpstrStyle, " | " );
        lstrcat( lpstrStyle, szBuf );
        }
    if ( dwFlags & LBS_MULTICOLUMN )
        {
        LoadString( _hInstanceDLL, (UINT)LBS_MULTICOLUMN, szBuf, iBufLen );
        lstrcat( lpstrStyle, " | " );
        lstrcat( lpstrStyle, szBuf );
        }
    if ( dwFlags & LBS_MULTIPLESEL )
        {
        LoadString( _hInstanceDLL, (UINT)LBS_MULTIPLESEL, szBuf, iBufLen );
        lstrcat( lpstrStyle, " | " );
        lstrcat( lpstrStyle, szBuf );
        }
    if ( dwFlags & LBS_EXTENDEDSEL )
        {
        LoadString( _hInstanceDLL, (UINT)LBS_EXTENDEDSEL, szBuf, iBufLen );
        lstrcat( lpstrStyle, " | " );
        lstrcat( lpstrStyle, szBuf );
        }
    if ( dwFlags & LBS_OWNERDRAWFIXED )
        {
        LoadString( _hInstanceDLL, (UINT)LBS_OWNERDRAWFIXED, szBuf, iBufLen );
        lstrcat( lpstrStyle, " | " );
        lstrcat( lpstrStyle, szBuf );
        }
    if ( dwFlags & LBS_OWNERDRAWVARIABLE )
        {
        LoadString( _hInstanceDLL, (UINT)LBS_OWNERDRAWVARIABLE, szBuf, iBufLen );
        lstrcat( lpstrStyle, " | " );
        lstrcat( lpstrStyle, szBuf );
        }
    if ( dwFlags & LBS_HASSTRINGS )
```

Listing A.17 continued

```
            {
            LoadString( _hInstanceDLL, (UINT)LBS_HASSTRINGS, szBuf, iBufLen );
            lstrcat( lpstrStyle, " | " );
            lstrcat( lpstrStyle, szBuf );
            }

    return ( (WORD)lstrlen( lpstrStyle ) );

    }   /* function CstTableFlags */


/****************************************************************************
        Name: CstTableStyle
  Parameters: hWnd - handle of dialog editor window
              hCtlStyle - global handle of CTLSTYLE structure
              lpfnStrToId - pointer to func to convert string to control id
              lpfnIdToStr - pointer to func to convert control id to string
      Return: TRUE if style has changed, FALSE if no change
 Description: Invokes the style dialog box for a custom control.
****************************************************************************/
BOOL FAR PASCAL CstTableStyle( HWND hWnd, GLOBALHANDLE hCtlStyle,
        LPFNSTRTOID lpfnStrToId, LPFNIDTOSTR lpfnIdToStr )
    {

    return ( CstCtlStyleDlg( _hInstanceDLL, _szCstCtlName,
            (FARPROC)CstTableDlgFn,
            hWnd, hCtlStyle, lpfnStrToId, lpfnIdToStr ) );

    }   /* function CstTableStyle */


/****************************************************************************
        Name: Dei_TablInfo
      Return: global handle to CTLINFO structure
 Description: Allocates a CTLINFO structure in the global heap.  Loads the
              structure with information about the custom control.
****************************************************************************/
GLOBALHANDLE FAR PASCAL Dei_TablInfo( void )
    {

    GLOBALHANDLE hCtlInfo = NULL;

    hCtlInfo = CtlInfoCreate( 100, _szCstCtlName, _szCstCtlName );
    if ( hCtlInfo )
        {
        LPCTLINFO lpCtlInfo = (LPCTLINFO)GlobalLock( hCtlInfo );
        if ( lpCtlInfo )
            {
            lpCtlInfo->Type[0].wType = 0;
            lpCtlInfo->Type[0].wWidth = 40;
            lpCtlInfo->Type[0].wHeight = 60;
            lpCtlInfo->Type[0].dwStyle = WS_CHILD | WS_VISIBLE |
                    LBS_STANDARD | WS_TABSTOP;
            lstrcpy( lpCtlInfo->Type[0].szDescr, _szCstCtlName );
            lpCtlInfo->wCtlTypes = 1;
            GlobalUnlock( hCtlInfo );
```

Listing A.17 *continued*

```
                    }   /* if lpCtlInfo */
            }   /* if hCtlInfo */

    return ( hCtlInfo );

    }   /* function Dei_TablInfo */


/*****************************************************************************
        Name: Dei_TablWndFn
      Return: Same as CstTableWndFn
 Description: Windows call back function for custom control.  This is a
              wrapper function for the existing function that resides in the
              CST_CTLS.DLL.
*****************************************************************************/
LONG FAR PASCAL Dei_TablWndFn( HWND hWnd, UINT wMessage, WPARAM wParam,
        LPARAM lParam )
    {

    return ( CstTableWndFn( hWnd, wMessage, wParam, lParam ) );

    }   /* function Dei_TablWndFn */


/*****************************************************************************
        Name: LibMain
      Return: TRUE
 Description: DLL main function
*****************************************************************************/
int FAR PASCAL LibMain( HINSTANCE hInstance, WORD wDataSeg, WORD wHeapSize,
        LPSTR lpstrCmd )
    {

    lpstrCmd = lpstrCmd;

    if ( wHeapSize )
        {
        /* LibEntry called LocalInit - so unlock data segment */
        UnlockSegment( wDataSeg );
        }

    /* Set the external data value */
    _hInstanceDLL = hInstance;

    return ( TRUE );

    }   /* function LibMain */
```

Listing A.17 *continued*

```
/*****************************************************************************
        Name: WEP
      Return: TRUE
 Description: DLL exit function
*****************************************************************************/
int FAR PASCAL WEP( int nSystemExit )
    {

    nSystemExit = nSystemExit;

    return ( TRUE );

    }   /* function WEP */

/* End of DEI_TABL.C */
```

Listing A.18

```
/****************************************************************************
        File Name: DEI_TABL.RC
    Expanded Name: Dialog Editor Interface for CSTTABLE
      Description: Resource file for DEI_TABL.DLL
      Portability: Microsoft Windows 3.X
****************************************************************************/

#include <windows.h>
#include <cst_ctls.h>

#include <dei_tabl.h>
#include <dei_tabl.dlg>

STRINGTABLE
BEGIN
    LBS_NOTIFY,            "LBS_NOTIFY"
    LBS_SORT,              "LBS_SORT"
    LBS_NOREDRAW,          "LBS_NOREDRAW"
    LBS_MULTIPLESEL,       "LBS_MULTIPLESEL"
    LBS_OWNERDRAWFIXED,    "LBS_OWNERDRAWFIXED"
    LBS_OWNERDRAWVARIABLE, "LBS_OWNERDRAWVARIABLE"
    LBS_HASSTRINGS,        "LBS_HASSTRINGS"
    LBS_USETABSTOPS,       "LBS_USETABSTOPS"
    LBS_NOINTEGRALHEIGHT,  "LBS_NOINTEGRALHEIGHT"
    LBS_MULTICOLUMN,       "LBS_MULTICOLUMN"
    LBS_WANTKEYBOARDINPUT, "LBS_WANTKEYBOARDINPUT"
    LBS_EXTENDEDSEL,       "LBS_EXTENDEDSEL"
#if defined ( LBS_DISABLEDNOSCROLL )
    LBS_DISABLENOSCROLL,   "LBS_DISABLENOSCROLL"
#endif
END

/* End of DEI_TABL.RC */
```

Listing A.19

```
/*****************************************************************************
        File Name: DEI_TABL.DLG
    Expanded Name: Dialog Editor Interface for CSTTABLE
      Description: Style Dialog file for DEI_TABL.DLL.
      Portability: Microsoft Windows 3.X
*****************************************************************************/

CstTable DIALOG 16, 16, 170, 202
STYLE DS_MODALFRAME | WS_POPUP | WS_VISIBLE | WS_CAPTION | WS_SYSMENU
CAPTION "Custom Table Styles"
FONT 8, "Helv"
BEGIN
    CONTROL "Id:" -1, "cststatic", CSS_TEXTLOWERED | WS_GROUP, 6, 6, 20, 10
    CONTROL "", IDC_EDIT_ID, "EDIT", ES_LEFT | ES_AUTOHSCROLL | WS_BORDER |
        WS_GROUP | WS_TABSTOP | WS_CHILD, 30, 4, 134, 12
    CONTROL "Text:", -1, "cststatic", CSS_TEXTLOWERED | WS_GROUP, 6, 20, 20, 10
    CONTROL "", IDC_EDIT_TEXT, "EDIT", ES_LEFT | ES_AUTOHSCROLL | WS_BORDER |
        WS_GROUP | WS_TABSTOP | WS_CHILD, 30, 18, 134, 12

    CONTROL "Custom Table Styles", -1, "Button", BS_GROUPBOX | WS_GROUP, 6,
        34, 158, 104
    CONTROL "&Standard", IDC_STANDARD, "cstcheckbox", BS_AUTOCHECKBOX |
        WS_GROUP | WS_TABSTOP, 10, 46, 42, 10
    CONTROL "&Border", IDC_BORDER, "cstcheckbox", BS_AUTOCHECKBOX |
        WS_TABSTOP, 10, 56, 34, 10
    CONTROL "S&ort", IDC_SORT, "cstcheckbox", BS_AUTOCHECKBOX | WS_TABSTOP,
        10, 66, 26, 10
    CONTROL "Notif&y", IDC_NOTIFY, "cstcheckbox", BS_AUTOCHECKBOX |
        WS_TABSTOP, 10, 76, 32, 10
    CONTROL "V&ert. Scroll Bar", IDC_VERTSCROLLBAR, "cstcheckbox",
        BS_AUTOCHECKBOX | WS_TABSTOP, 10, 86, 64, 10
    CONTROL "Hor&z. Scroll Bar", IDC_HORZSCROLLBAR, "cstcheckbox",
        BS_AUTOCHECKBOX | WS_TABSTOP, 10, 96, 66, 10
    CONTROL "&Use Tab Stops", IDC_USETABSTOPS, "cstcheckbox", BS_AUTOCHECKBOX |
        WS_TABSTOP, 10, 106, 63, 10
    CONTROL "No &Redraw", IDC_NOREDRAW, "cstcheckbox", BS_AUTOCHECKBOX |
        WS_TABSTOP, 10, 116, 50, 10
#if defined ( IDC_DISABLEDNOSCROLL )
    CONTROL "Disable No-Scroll", IDC_DISABLENOSCROLL, "cstcheckbox",
        BS_AUTOCHECKBOX | WS_TABSTOP, 10, 126, 70, 10
#endif
    CONTROL "No &Integral Height", IDC_NOINTEGRALHEIGHT, "cstcheckbox",
        BS_AUTOCHECKBOX | WS_TABSTOP, 79, 46, 75, 10
    CONTROL "&Want Keyboard Input", IDC_WANTKEYBOARDINPUT, "cstcheckbox",
        BS_AUTOCHECKBOX | WS_TABSTOP, 79, 56, 84, 10
    CONTROL "Multi-&Column", IDC_MULTICOLUMN, "cstcheckbox", BS_AUTOCHECKBOX |
        WS_TABSTOP, 79, 66, 54, 10
    CONTROL "&Multiple Selection", IDC_MULTIPLESEL, "cstcheckbox",
        BS_AUTOCHECKBOX | WS_DISABLED | WS_TABSTOP, 79, 76, 72, 10
    CONTROL "E&xtended Selection", IDC_EXTENDEDSEL, "cstcheckbox",
        BS_AUTOCHECKBOX | WS_DISABLED | WS_TABSTOP, 79, 86, 77, 10
    CONTROL "Owner-Draw &Fixed", IDC_OWNERDRAWFIXED, "cstcheckbox",
        BS_AUTOCHECKBOX | WS_DISABLED | WS_TABSTOP, 79, 96, 73, 10
    CONTROL "Owner-Draw V&ariable", IDC_OWNERDRAWVARIABLE, "cstcheckbox",
        BS_AUTOCHECKBOX | WS_DISABLED | WS_TABSTOP, 79, 106, 82, 10
    CONTROL "Has Stri&ngs", IDC_HASSTRINGS, "cstcheckbox", BS_AUTOCHECKBOX |
        WS_DISABLED | WS_TABSTOP, 79, 116, 51, 10

    CONTROL "Basic Styles", -1, "Button", BS_GROUPBOX | WS_GROUP, 6, 142,
```

Listing A.19 *continued*

```
            158, 34
    CONTROL "&Visible", IDC_VISIBLE, "cstcheckbox", BS_AUTOCHECKBOX |
            WS_GROUP | WS_TABSTOP, 10, 154, 34, 10
    CONTROL "&Disabled", IDC_DISABLED, "cstcheckbox", BS_AUTOCHECKBOX |
            WS_TABSTOP, 10, 164, 41, 10
    CONTROL "&Group", IDC_GROUP, "cstcheckbox", BS_AUTOCHECKBOX | WS_TABSTOP,
            79, 154, 34, 10
    CONTROL "&Tab Stop", IDC_TABSTOP, "cstcheckbox", BS_AUTOCHECKBOX |
            WS_TABSTOP, 79, 164, 44, 10

    CONTROL "OK", IDC_OK, "Button", BS_DEFPUSHBUTTON | WS_GROUP | WS_TABSTOP,
            13, 182, 40, 14
    CONTROL "Cancel", IDC_CANCEL, "Button", BS_PUSHBUTTON | WS_TABSTOP, 65,
            182, 40, 14
    CONTROL "Help", IDC_HELP, "Button", BS_PUSHBUTTON | WS_TABSTOP,
            117, 182, 40, 14
END

/* End of DEI_TABL.DLG */
```

Listing A.20

```
LIBRARY DEI_TABL
DESCRIPTION 'Dialog Editor - CSTTABLE DLL'
EXETYPE WINDOWS
CODE PRELOAD MOVEABLE SHARED DISCARDABLE
DATA PRELOAD MOVEABLE SINGLE
HEAPSIZE 1024
EXPORTS
        WEP                @1      RESIDENTNAME
        Dei_TablInfo       @2
        CstTableStyle      @3
        CstTableFlags      @4
        Dei_TablWndFn      @5
        CstTableDlgFn      @6
```

Listing A.21

```
/****************************************************************
        File Name: DEI_FLVW.H
    Expanded Name: Dialog Editor Interface for CSTFILEVIEW
      Description: Include file for DEI_FLVW.C & DEI_FLVW.RC
      Portability: Microsoft Windows 3.X
****************************************************************/

#define IDC_BORDER          101
#define IDC_CAPTION         102
#define IDC_DIALOGFRAME     103
#define IDC_MAXIMIZEBOX     104
#define IDC_MINIMIZEBOX     105
#define IDC_HORZSCROLL      106
#define IDC_SYSTEMMENU      107
#define IDC_THICKFRAME      108
#define IDC_VERTSCROLL      109

#define IDC_VISIBLE         201
#define IDC_DISABLED        202
#define IDC_GROUP           203
#define IDC_TABSTOP         204

#define IDC_EDIT_ID         301
#define IDC_EDIT_TEXT       302

#define IDC_OK                1
#define IDC_CANCEL            2
#define IDC_HELP              8

/* End of DEI_FLVW.H */
```

Listing A.22

```
/***************************************************************************
        File Name: DEI_FLVW.C
    Expanded Name: Dialog Editor Interface for Custom Static Control
      Description: Library of functions for interfacing the CSTFILEVIEW
                   control with the Dialog Editor.
     Program List: DEI_FLVW.C
                   DEI_FLVW.RC
                   DEI_FLVW.DEF
                   DEI_CTLS.C
                   CST_CTLS.LIB,DLL
Global Function List: CstFileViewDlgFn
                   CstFileViewFlags
                   CstFileViewStyle
                   Dei_FlVwInfo
                   Dei_FlVwWndFn
                   LibMain
                   WEP
      Static Data: _hInstanceDLL
                   _szCstCtlName
      Portability: Microsoft Windows 3.X
***************************************************************************/

/* Microsoft Windows */
#include <windows.h>

/* Custom Control Interface */
#include <custcntl.h>

/* Standard C */
#include <stdlib.h>

/* Prototypes and Types */
#include <cst_flvw.h>
#include <dei_ctls.h>

/* Own */
#include <dei_flvw.h>

/* Library instance handle */
static HINSTANCE _hInstanceDLL = 0;

static char _szCstCtlName[] = "CstFileView";

/* Prototypes of functions */
BOOL FAR PASCAL CstFileViewDlgFn( HWND hDlg, WORD wMessage, WORD wParam,
        LONG lParam );
WORD FAR PASCAL CstFileViewFlags( DWORD dwFlags, LPSTR szString,
        WORD wMaxString );
BOOL FAR PASCAL CstFileViewStyle( HWND hWnd, GLOBALHANDLE hCtlStyle,
        LPFNSTRTOID lpfnStrToId, LPFNIDTOSTR lpfnIdToStr );
GLOBALHANDLE FAR PASCAL Dei_FlVwInfo( void );
LONG FAR PASCAL Dei_FlVwWndFn( HWND hWnd, UINT wMessage, WPARAM wParam,
        LPARAM lParam );
```

Listing A.22 *continued*

```c
/******************************************************************************
        Name: CstFileViewDlgFn
  Description: Dialog box callback function for style selection.
******************************************************************************/
BOOL FAR PASCAL CstFileViewDlgFn( HWND hDlg, WORD wMsg, WORD wParam,
        LONG lParam )
    {

    switch ( wMsg )
        {
        case WM_INITDIALOG:
            {

            char szIdStr[CTLTITLE];

            /* Set the property */
            HCSTCTLSTYLE hCstCtlStyle = LOWORD( lParam );
            LPCSTCTLSTYLE lpCstCtlStyle =
                    (LPCSTCTLSTYLE)GlobalLock( hCstCtlStyle );
            LPCTLSTYLE lpCtlStyle =
                    (LPCTLSTYLE)GlobalLock( lpCstCtlStyle->hCtlStyle );
            DWORD dwStyle = lpCtlStyle->dwStyle;

            SetProp( hDlg, _szCstCtlStyle, hCstCtlStyle );

            /* Center Dialog Box */
            CenterWindow( GetParent( hDlg ), hDlg, 0 );

            /* Text */
            SetDlgItemText( hDlg, IDC_EDIT_TEXT, lpCtlStyle->szTitle );

            /* Id */
            if ( !(*lpCstCtlStyle->lpfnIdToStr)( lpCtlStyle->wId, szIdStr,
                    CTLTITLE ) )
                {
                wsprintf( szIdStr, "%n", lpCtlStyle->wId );
                }
            SetDlgItemText( hDlg, IDC_EDIT_ID, szIdStr );
            GlobalUnlock( lpCstCtlStyle->hCtlStyle );
            GlobalUnlock( hCstCtlStyle );

            /* Custom File View Styles */
            if ( dwStyle & WS_BORDER )
                {
                CheckDlgButton( hDlg, IDC_BORDER, TRUE );
                }
            if ( dwStyle & WS_CAPTION )
                {
                CheckDlgButton( hDlg, IDC_CAPTION, TRUE );
                }
            if ( dwStyle & WS_DLGFRAME )
                {
                CheckDlgButton( hDlg, IDC_DIALOGFRAME, TRUE );
                }
            /*
            if ( dwStyle & WS_MAXIMIZEBOX )
                {
```

Listing A.22 continued

```
                CheckDlgButton( hDlg, IDC_MAXIMIZEBOX, TRUE );
                }
            if ( dwStyle & WS_MINIMIZEBOX )
                {
                CheckDlgButton( hDlg, IDC_MINIMIZEBOX, TRUE );
                }
            */
            if ( dwStyle & WS_HSCROLL )
                {
                CheckDlgButton( hDlg, IDC_HORZSCROLL, TRUE );
                }
            if ( dwStyle & WS_SYSMENU )
                {
                CheckDlgButton( hDlg, IDC_SYSTEMMENU, TRUE );
                }
            if ( dwStyle & WS_THICKFRAME )
                {
                CheckDlgButton( hDlg, IDC_THICKFRAME, TRUE );
                }
            if ( dwStyle & WS_VSCROLL )
                {
                CheckDlgButton( hDlg, IDC_VERTSCROLL, TRUE );
                }

            /* Basic styles */
            if ( dwStyle & WS_VISIBLE )
                {
                CheckDlgButton( hDlg, IDC_VISIBLE, TRUE );
                }
            if ( dwStyle & WS_DISABLED )
                {
                CheckDlgButton( hDlg, IDC_DISABLED, TRUE );
                }
            if ( dwStyle & WS_GROUP )
                {
                CheckDlgButton( hDlg, IDC_GROUP, TRUE );
                }
            if ( dwStyle & WS_TABSTOP )
                {
                CheckDlgButton( hDlg, IDC_TABSTOP, TRUE );
                }

            break;
            }
        case WM_COMMAND:
            switch ( wParam )
                {
                case IDC_HELP:
                    WinHelp( hDlg, "CST_CTLS.HLP", HELP_KEY,
                            (DWORD)(LPSTR)"CstFileView" );
                    break;
                case IDC_OK:
                    {

                    char szIdStr[32];
                    DWORD dwStyle, dwId;
                    HCSTCTLSTYLE hCstCtlStyle;
                    LPCSTCTLSTYLE lpCstCtlStyle;
                    LPCTLSTYLE lpCtlStyle;
```

Listing A.22 *continued*

```c
    hCstCtlStyle = GetProp( hDlg, _szCstCtlStyle );
    lpCstCtlStyle = (LPCSTCTLSTYLE)GlobalLock(
            hCstCtlStyle );
    lpCtlStyle = (LPCTLSTYLE)GlobalLock(
            lpCstCtlStyle->hCtlStyle );
    dwStyle = lpCtlStyle->dwStyle & 0xFFFF0000L;

    /* Text */
    GetDlgItemText( hDlg, IDC_EDIT_TEXT,
            lpCtlStyle->szTitle, CTLTITLE );

    /* Id */
    GetDlgItemText( hDlg, IDC_EDIT_ID, szIdStr,
            sizeof ( szIdStr ) );
    dwId = (*lpCstCtlStyle->lpfnStrToId)( szIdStr );
    if ( LOWORD( dwId ) == 0 )
        {
        lpCtlStyle->wId = max( (WORD)atoi( szIdStr ),
                lpCtlStyle->wId );
        }
    else
        {
        lpCtlStyle->wId = HIWORD( dwId );
        }

    /* Custom File View Styles */
    if ( IsDlgButtonChecked( hDlg, IDC_BORDER ) )
        {
        dwStyle |= WS_BORDER;
        }
    if ( IsDlgButtonChecked( hDlg, IDC_CAPTION ) )
        {
        dwStyle |= WS_CAPTION;
        }
    if ( IsDlgButtonChecked( hDlg, IDC_DIALOGFRAME ) )
        {
        dwStyle |= WS_DLGFRAME;
        }
    if ( IsDlgButtonChecked( hDlg, IDC_HORZSCROLL ) )
        {
        dwStyle |= WS_HSCROLL;
        }
/*
    if ( IsDlgButtonChecked( hDlg, IDC_MAXIMIZEBOX ) )
        {
        dwStyle |= WS_MAXIMIZEBOX;
        }
    if ( IsDlgButtonChecked( hDlg, IDC_MINIMIZEBOX ) )
        {
        dwStyle |= WS_MINIMIZEBOX;
        }
*/
    if ( IsDlgButtonChecked( hDlg, IDC_SYSTEMMENU ) )
        {
        dwStyle |= WS_SYSMENU;
        }
    if ( IsDlgButtonChecked( hDlg, IDC_THICKFRAME ) )
```

Listing A.22 *continued*

```
                        {
                        dwStyle |= WS_THICKFRAME;
                        }
                    if ( IsDlgButtonChecked( hDlg, IDC_VERTSCROLL ) )
                        {
                        dwStyle |= WS_VSCROLL;
                        }

                    /* Basic Styles */
                    if ( IsDlgButtonChecked( hDlg, IDC_VISIBLE ) )
                        {
                        dwStyle |= WS_VISIBLE;
                        }
                    else
                        {
                        dwStyle &= ~WS_VISIBLE;
                        }
                    if ( IsDlgButtonChecked( hDlg, IDC_DISABLED ) )
                        {
                        dwStyle |= WS_DISABLED;
                        }
                    else
                        {
                        dwStyle &= ~WS_DISABLED;
                        }
                    if ( IsDlgButtonChecked( hDlg, IDC_GROUP ) )
                        {
                        dwStyle |= WS_GROUP;
                        }
                    else
                        {
                        dwStyle &= ~WS_GROUP;
                        }
                    if ( IsDlgButtonChecked( hDlg, IDC_TABSTOP ) )
                        {
                        dwStyle |= WS_TABSTOP;
                        }
                    else
                        {
                        dwStyle &= ~WS_TABSTOP;
                        }

                    lpCtlStyle->dwStyle = dwStyle;
                    GlobalUnlock( lpCstCtlStyle->hCtlStyle );
                    GlobalUnlock( hCstCtlStyle );
                    EndDialog( hDlg, TRUE );
                    break;
                    }
                case IDC_CANCEL:
                    EndDialog( hDlg, FALSE );
                    break;
                default:
                    return ( FALSE );
                } /* switch wParam */
            break;
        case WM_DESTROY:
            WinHelp( hDlg, "CST_CTLS.HLP", HELP_QUIT, 0L );
            RemoveProp( hDlg, _szCstCtlStyle );
            break;
```

Listing A.22 *continued*

```
        default:
            return ( FALSE );
    }   /* switch wMsg */

    return ( TRUE );

}   /* function CstFileViewDlgFn */


/*****************************************************************************
       Name: CstFileViewFlags
 Parameters: dwFlags - current style of control
             lpstrStyle - buffer to store style string
             wMaxLen - maximum length of style string
     Return: length of style string
Description: Converts a style into a string of style flags of all the
             class specific window styles for a control.  The basic, or
             class general styles are concatenated onto these by the dialog
             editor.
*****************************************************************************/
WORD FAR PASCAL CstFileViewFlags( DWORD dwFlags, LPSTR lpstrStyle,
        WORD wMaxLen )
    {

    dwFlags = dwFlags;
    wMaxLen = wMaxLen;

    lstrcpy( lpstrStyle, "" );

    return ( (WORD)lstrlen( lpstrStyle ) );

    }   /* function CstFileViewFlags */


/*****************************************************************************
       Name: CstFileViewStyle
 Parameters: hWnd - handle of dialog editor window
             hCtlStyle - global handle of CTLSTYLE structure
             lpfnStrToId - pointer to func to convert string to control id
             lpfnIdToStr - pointer to func to convert control id to string
     Return: TRUE if style has changed, FALSE if no change
Description: Invokes the style dialog box for a custom control.
*****************************************************************************/
BOOL FAR PASCAL CstFileViewStyle( HWND hWnd, GLOBALHANDLE hCtlStyle,
        LPFNSTRTOID lpfnStrToId, LPFNIDTOSTR lpfnIdToStr )
    {

    return ( CstCtlStyleDlg( _hInstanceDLL, _szCstCtlName,
            (FARPROC)CstFileViewDlgFn,
            hWnd, hCtlStyle, lpfnStrToId, lpfnIdToStr ) );

    }   /* function CstFileViewStyle */
```

Listing A.22 continued

```
/*****************************************************************************
        Name: Dei_FlVwInfo
      Return: global handle to CTLINFO structure
 Description: Allocates a CTLINFO structure in the global heap.  Loads the
              structure with information about the custom control.
*****************************************************************************/
GLOBALHANDLE FAR PASCAL Dei_FlVwInfo( void )
    {

    GLOBALHANDLE hCtlInfo = NULL;

    hCtlInfo = CtlInfoCreate( 100, _szCstCtlName, _szCstCtlName );
    if ( hCtlInfo )
        {

        LPCTLINFO lpCtlInfo = (LPCTLINFO)GlobalLock( hCtlInfo );
        if ( lpCtlInfo )
            {

            lpCtlInfo->Type[0].wType = 0;
            lpCtlInfo->Type[0].wWidth = 60;
            lpCtlInfo->Type[0].wHeight = 80;
            lpCtlInfo->Type[0].dwStyle = WS_CHILD | WS_VISIBLE |
                    WS_BORDER | WS_HSCROLL | WS_VSCROLL | WS_TABSTOP;
            lstrcpy( lpCtlInfo->Type[0].szDescr, _szCstCtlName );
            lpCtlInfo->wCtlTypes = 1;
            GlobalUnlock( hCtlInfo );

            }   /* if lpCtlInfo */
        }   /* if hCtlInfo */

    return ( hCtlInfo );

    }   /* function Dei_FlVwInfo */


/*****************************************************************************
        Name: Dei_FlVwWndFn
      Return: Same as CstFileViewWndFn
 Description: Windows call back function for custom control.  This is a
              wrapper function for the existing function that resides in the
              CST_CTLS.DLL.
*****************************************************************************/
LONG FAR PASCAL Dei_FlVwWndFn( HWND hWnd, UINT wMessage, WPARAM wParam,
        LPARAM lParam )
    {

    return ( CstFileViewWndFn( hWnd, wMessage, wParam, lParam ) );

    }   /* function Dei_FlVwWndFn */
```

Listing A.22 *continued*

```c
/***************************************************************************
        Name: LibMain
      Return: TRUE
 Description: DLL main function
***************************************************************************/
int FAR PASCAL LibMain( HINSTANCE hInstance, WORD wDataSeg, WORD wHeapSize,
        LPSTR lpstrCmd )
    {

    lpstrCmd = lpstrCmd;

    if ( wHeapSize )
        {
        /* LibEntry called LocalInit - so unlock data segment */
        UnlockSegment( wDataSeg );
        }

    /* Set the external data value */
    _hInstanceDLL = hInstance;

    return ( TRUE );

    }   /* function LibMain */


/***************************************************************************
        Name: WEP
      Return: TRUE
 Description: DLL exit function
***************************************************************************/
int FAR PASCAL WEP( int nSystemExit )
    {

    nSystemExit = nSystemExit;

    return ( TRUE );

    }   /* function WEP */

/* End of DEI_FLVW.C */
```

Listing A.23

```
/*****************************************************************************
            File Name: DEI_FLVW.RC
         Expanded Name: Dialog Editor Interface for CSTFILEVIEW
           Description: Resource file for DEI_FLVW.DLL
           Portability: Microsoft Windows 3.X
*****************************************************************************/

#include <windows.h>
#include <cst_ctls.h>

#include <dei_flvw.h>
#include <dei_flvw.dlg>

/* End of DEI_FLVW.RC */
```

Listing A.24

```
/***************************************************************
          File Name: DEI_FLVW.DLG
      Expanded Name: Dialog Editor Interface for CSTFILEVIEW
        Description: Style Dialog file for DEI_FLVW.DLL.
        Portability: Microsoft Windows 3.X
****************************************************************/

CstFileView DIALOG 16, 16, 170, 162
STYLE DS_MODALFRAME | WS_POPUP | WS_VISIBLE | WS_CAPTION | WS_SYSMENU
CAPTION "Custom File View Styles"
FONT 8, "Helv"
BEGIN
    CONTROL "Id:" -1, "cststatic", CSS_TEXTLOWERED | WS_GROUP, 6, 6, 20, 10
    CONTROL "", IDC_EDIT_ID, "EDIT", ES_LEFT | ES_AUTOHSCROLL | WS_BORDER |
            WS_GROUP | WS_TABSTOP, 30, 4, 134, 12
    CONTROL "File:", -1, "cststatic", CSS_TEXTLOWERED | WS_GROUP, 6, 20, 20, 10
    CONTROL "", IDC_EDIT_TEXT, "EDIT", ES_LEFT | ES_AUTOHSCROLL | WS_BORDER |
            WS_GROUP | WS_TABSTOP, 30, 18, 134, 12
    CONTROL "Custom File View Styles", -1, "BUTTON", BS_GROUPBOX | WS_GROUP,
            6, 34, 158, 64
    CONTROL "&Border", IDC_BORDER, "cstcheckbox", BS_AUTOCHECKBOX |
            WS_GROUP | WS_TABSTOP, 10, 46, 42, 10
    CONTROL "&Caption", IDC_CAPTION, "cstcheckbox", BS_AUTOCHECKBOX |
            WS_TABSTOP, 10, 56, 64, 10
    CONTROL "&Dialog Frame", IDC_DIALOGFRAME, "cstcheckbox", BS_AUTOCHECKBOX |
            WS_TABSTOP, 10, 66, 64, 10
    CONTROL "M&aximize Box", IDC_MAXIMIZEBOX, "cstcheckbox", BS_AUTOCHECKBOX |
            WS_TABSTOP | WS_DISABLED, 10, 76, 64, 10
    CONTROL "M&inimize Box", IDC_MINIMIZEBOX, "cstcheckbox", BS_AUTOCHECKBOX |
            WS_TABSTOP | WS_DISABLED, 10, 86, 64, 10
    CONTROL "&Horz Scroll", IDC_HORZSCROLL, "cstcheckbox", BS_AUTOCHECKBOX |
            WS_TABSTOP, 79, 46, 75, 10
    CONTROL "&System Menu", IDC_SYSTEMMENU, "cstcheckbox", BS_AUTOCHECKBOX |
            WS_TABSTOP, 79, 56, 84, 10
    CONTROL "&Thick Frame", IDC_THICKFRAME, "cstcheckbox", BS_AUTOCHECKBOX |
            WS_TABSTOP, 79, 66, 54, 10
    CONTROL "&Vert Scroll", IDC_VERTSCROLL, "cstcheckbox",
            BS_AUTOCHECKBOX | WS_TABSTOP, 79, 76, 72, 10

    CONTROL "Basic Styles", -1, "BUTTON", BS_GROUPBOX | WS_GROUP, 6, 102, 158,
            34
    CONTROL "&Visible", IDC_VISIBLE, "cstcheckbox", BS_AUTOCHECKBOX |
            WS_GROUP | WS_TABSTOP, 10, 114, 34, 10
    CONTROL "&Disabled", IDC_DISABLED, "cstcheckbox", BS_AUTOCHECKBOX |
            WS_TABSTOP, 10, 124, 41, 10
    CONTROL "&Group", IDC_GROUP, "cstcheckbox", BS_AUTOCHECKBOX | WS_TABSTOP,
            79, 114, 34, 10
    CONTROL "&Tab Stop", IDC_TABSTOP, "cstcheckbox", BS_AUTOCHECKBOX |
            WS_TABSTOP, 79, 124, 44, 10

    CONTROL "OK", IDC_OK, "BUTTON", BS_DEFPUSHBUTTON | WS_GROUP | WS_TABSTOP,
            13, 142, 40, 14
    CONTROL "Cancel", IDC_CANCEL, "BUTTON", BS_PUSHBUTTON | WS_TABSTOP, 65,
            142, 40, 14
    CONTROL "Help", IDC_HELP, "BUTTON", BS_PUSHBUTTON | WS_TABSTOP,
            117, 142, 40, 14
END
```

Listing A.25

```
LIBRARY DEI_FLVW
DESCRIPTION 'Dialog Editor - CSTFILEVIEW DLL'
EXETYPE WINDOWS
CODE PRELOAD MOVEABLE SHARED DISCARDABLE
DATA PRELOAD MOVEABLE SINGLE
HEAPSIZE 1024
EXPORTS
        WEP                 @1      RESIDENTNAME
        Dei_FlVwInfo        @2
        CstFileViewStyle    @3
        CstFileViewFlags    @4
        Dei_FlVwWndFn       @5
        CstFileViewDlgFn    @6
```

Listing A.26

```
ORIGIN   = QCWIN
ORIGIN_VER   = 1.00

PROJ =DEI_FLVW
DEBUG    =0
PROGTYPE =2
CALLER   =
ARGS =
DLLS =
CVPACK   =1
CC   =cl -qc
RC   =rc
CFLAGS_G_WEXE =/AS /W4 /Ze /D_WINDOWS /G2w /Zp  /Aw
CFLAGS_D_WEXE =/Zi /Od
CFLAGS_R_WEXE =/O /Os /Gs /DNDEBUG
CFLAGS_G_WDLL =/AS /W4 /Ze /D_WINDOWS /D_WINDLL /G2w /Zp /Aw
CFLAGS_D_WDLL =/Zi /Od
CFLAGS_R_WDLL =/O /Os /Gs /DNDEBUG
CFLAGS_G_WTTY =/AS /G2w /W3 /D_WINDOWS
CFLAGS_D_WTTY =/Gi /Od /Zi
CFLAGS_R_WTTY =/O /Os /DNDEBUG
CFLAGS_G_DEXE =/AS /W2
CFLAGS_D_DEXE =/Gi /Od /Zi
CFLAGS_R_DEXE =/O /Ot /DNDEBUG
CFLAGS   =$(CFLAGS_G_WDLL) $(CFLAGS_R_WDLL)
LFLAGS_G_WEXE =/NOE/A:16/ST:10240
LFLAGS_D_WEXE =/CO
LFLAGS_R_WEXE =
LFLAGS_G_WDLL =/NOE/A:16/ST:5120
LFLAGS_D_WDLL =/CO
LFLAGS_R_WDLL =
LFLAGS_G_WTTY =/ST:5120 /A:16
LFLAGS_D_WTTY =/CO
LFLAGS_R_WTTY =
LFLAGS_G_DEXE =/NOI /ST:2048
LFLAGS_D_DEXE =/CO
LFLAGS_R_DEXE =
LFLAGS   =$(LFLAGS_G_WDLL) $(LFLAGS_R_WDLL)
RCFLAGS  =
RESFLAGS =
RUNFLAGS =
DEFFILE =      DEI_FLVW.DEF
OBJS_EXT =
LIBS_EXT =     CST_CTLS.LIB

.rc.res: ; $(RC) $(RCFLAGS) -r $*.rc

all: $(PROJ).DLL

DEI_CTLS.OBJ: DEI_CTLS.C $(H)

DEI_FLVW.OBJ: DEI_FLVW.C $(H)

DEI_FLVW.RES: DEI_FLVW.RC $(RESFILES) $(H)

$(PROJ).DLL:  DEI_CTLS.OBJ DEI_FLVW.OBJ $(OBJS_EXT) $(DEFFILE)
    echo >NUL @<<$(PROJ).CRF
```

Listing A.26 *continued*

```
DEI_CTLS.OBJ +
DEI_FLVW.OBJ +
$(OBJS_EXT)
$(PROJ).DLL

F:\PRGLNG\QCWIN\LIB\+
/NOD sdllcew oldnames  libw+
CST_CTLS.LIB
$(DEFFILE);
<<
    link $(LFLAGS) @$(PROJ).CRF
    rc $(RESFLAGS) DEI_FLVW.RES $(PROJ).DLL

$(PROJ).DLL:  DEI_FLVW.RES
    rc $(RESFLAGS) DEI_FLVW.RES $(PROJ).DLL

run: $(PROJ).DLL
    $(PROJ) $(RUNFLAGS)
```

Listing A.27

```
ORIGIN    = QCWIN
ORIGIN_VER   = 1.00

PROJ =DEI_PBTN
DEBUG    =0
PROGTYPE =2
CALLER   =
ARGS =
DLLS =
CVPACK   =1
CC   =cl -qc
RC   =rc
CFLAGS_G_WEXE =/AS /W4 /Ze /D_WINDOWS /G2w /Zp  /Aw
CFLAGS_D_WEXE =/Zi /Od
CFLAGS_R_WEXE =/O /Os /Gs /DNDEBUG
CFLAGS_G_WDLL =/AS /W4 /Ze /D_WINDOWS /D_WINDLL /G2w /Zp /Aw
CFLAGS_D_WDLL =/Zi /Od
CFLAGS_R_WDLL =/O /Os /Gs /DNDEBUG
CFLAGS_G_WTTY =/AS /G2w /W3 /D_WINDOWS
CFLAGS_D_WTTY =/Gi /Od /Zi
CFLAGS_R_WTTY =/O /Os /DNDEBUG
CFLAGS_G_DEXE =/AS /W2
CFLAGS_D_DEXE =/Gi /Od /Zi
CFLAGS_R_DEXE =/O /Ot /DNDEBUG
CFLAGS    =$(CFLAGS_G_WDLL) $(CFLAGS_R_WDLL)
LFLAGS_G_WEXE =/NOE/A:16/ST:10240
LFLAGS_D_WEXE =/CO
LFLAGS_R_WEXE =
LFLAGS_G_WDLL =/NOE/A:16/ST:5120
LFLAGS_D_WDLL =/CO
LFLAGS_R_WDLL =
LFLAGS_G_WTTY =/ST:5120 /A:16
LFLAGS_D_WTTY =/CO
LFLAGS_R_WTTY =
LFLAGS_G_DEXE =/NOI /ST:2048
LFLAGS_D_DEXE =/CO
LFLAGS_R_DEXE =
LFLAGS    =$(LFLAGS_G_WDLL) $(LFLAGS_R_WDLL)
RCFLAGS  =
RESFLAGS =
RUNFLAGS =
DEFFILE =    DEI_PBTN.DEF
OBJS_EXT =
LIBS_EXT =    CST_CTLS.LIB

.rc.res: ; $(RC) $(RCFLAGS) -r $*.rc

all: $(PROJ).DLL

DEI_PBTN.OBJ: DEI_PBTN.C $(H)

DEI_PBTN.RES: DEI_PBTN.RC $(RESFILES) $(H)

DEI_CTLS.OBJ: DEI_CTLS.C $(H)

$(PROJ).DLL:  DEI_PBTN.OBJ DEI_CTLS.OBJ $(OBJS_EXT) $(DEFFILE)
    echo >NUL @<<$(PROJ).CRF
DEI_PBTN.OBJ +
```

Listing A.27 continued

```
DEI_CTLS.OBJ +

$(OBJS_EXT)
$(PROJ).DLL

C:\PRGLNG\QCW\LIB\+
/NOD sdllcew oldnames  libw+
CST_CTLS.LIB
$(DEFFILE);
<<
    link $(LFLAGS) @$(PROJ).CRF
    rc $(RESFLAGS) DEI_PBTN.RES $(PROJ).DLL

$(PROJ).DLL: DEI_PBTN.RES
    rc $(RESFLAGS) DEI_PBTN.RES $(PROJ).DLL

run: $(PROJ).DLL
    $(PROJ) $(RUNFLAGS)
```

Listing A.28

```
ORIGIN    = QCWIN
ORIGIN_VER    = 1.00

PROJ =DEI_RBTN
DEBUG    =0
PROGTYPE =2
CALLER    =
ARGS =
DLLS =
CVPACK    =1
CC    =cl -qc
RC    =rc
CFLAGS_G_WEXE =/AS /W4 /Ze /D_WINDOWS /G2w /Zp  /Aw
CFLAGS_D_WEXE =/Zi /Od
CFLAGS_R_WEXE =/O /Os /Gs /DNDEBUG
CFLAGS_G_WDLL =/AS /W4 /Ze /D_WINDOWS /D_WINDLL /G2w /Zp /Aw
CFLAGS_D_WDLL =/Zi /Od
CFLAGS_R_WDLL =/O /Os /Gs /DNDEBUG
CFLAGS_G_WTTY =/AS /G2w /W3 /D_WINDOWS
CFLAGS_D_WTTY =/Gi /Od /Zi
CFLAGS_R_WTTY =/O /Os /DNDEBUG
CFLAGS_G_DEXE =/AS /W2
CFLAGS_D_DEXE =/Gi /Od /Zi
CFLAGS_R_DEXE =/O /Ot /DNDEBUG
CFLAGS    =$(CFLAGS_G_WDLL) $(CFLAGS_R_WDLL)
LFLAGS_G_WEXE =/NOE/A:16/ST:10240
LFLAGS_D_WEXE =/CO
LFLAGS_R_WEXE =
LFLAGS_G_WDLL =/NOE/A:16/ST:5120
LFLAGS_D_WDLL =/CO
LFLAGS_R_WDLL =
LFLAGS_G_WTTY =/ST:5120 /A:16
LFLAGS_D_WTTY =/CO
LFLAGS_R_WTTY =
LFLAGS_G_DEXE =/NOI /ST:2048
LFLAGS_D_DEXE =/CO
LFLAGS_R_DEXE =
LFLAGS    =$(LFLAGS_G_WDLL) $(LFLAGS_R_WDLL)
RCFLAGS    =
RESFLAGS =
RUNFLAGS =
DEFFILE =     DEI_RBTN.DEF
OBJS_EXT =
LIBS_EXT =    CST_CTLS.LIB

.rc.res: ; $(RC) $(RCFLAGS) -r $*.rc

all: $(PROJ).DLL

DEI_RBTN.OBJ: DEI_RBTN.C $(H)

DEI_RBTN.RES: DEI_RBTN.RC $(RESFILES) $(H)

DEI_CTLS.OBJ: DEI_CTLS.C $(H)

$(PROJ).DLL: DEI_RBTN.OBJ DEI_CTLS.OBJ $(OBJS_EXT) $(DEFFILE)
    echo >NUL @<<$(PROJ).CRF
```

Listing A.28 *continued*

```
DEI_RBTN.OBJ +
DEI_CTLS.OBJ +
$(OBJS_EXT)
$(PROJ).DLL

C:\PRGLNG\QCW\LIB\+
/NOD sdllcew oldnames  libw+
CST_CTLS.LIB
$(DEFFILE);
<<
    link $(LFLAGS) @$(PROJ).CRF
    rc $(RESFLAGS) DEI_RBTN.RES $(PROJ).DLL

$(PROJ).DLL:  DEI_RBTN.RES
    rc $(RESFLAGS) DEI_RBTN.RES $(PROJ).DLL

run: $(PROJ).DLL
    $(PROJ) $(RUNFLAGS)
```

Listing A.29

```
ORIGIN   = QCWIN
ORIGIN_VER   = 1.00

PROJ =DEI_STTC
DEBUG    =0
PROGTYPE =2
CALLER   =
ARGS =
DLLS =
CVPACK   =1
CC   =cl -qc
RC   =rc
CFLAGS_G_WEXE =/AS /W4 /Ze /D_WINDOWS /G2w /Zp  /Aw
CFLAGS_D_WEXE =/Zi /Od
CFLAGS_R_WEXE =/O /Os /Gs /DNDEBUG
CFLAGS_G_WDLL =/AS /W4 /Ze /D_WINDOWS /D_WINDLL /G2w /Zp /Aw
CFLAGS_D_WDLL =/Zi /Od
CFLAGS_R_WDLL =/O /Os /Gs /DNDEBUG
CFLAGS_G_WTTY =/AS /G2w /W3 /D_WINDOWS
CFLAGS_D_WTTY =/Gi /Od /Zi
CFLAGS_R_WTTY =/O /Os /DNDEBUG
CFLAGS_G_DEXE =/AS /W2
CFLAGS_D_DEXE =/Gi /Od /Zi
CFLAGS_R_DEXE =/O /Ot /DNDEBUG
CFLAGS   =$(CFLAGS_G_WDLL) $(CFLAGS_R_WDLL)
LFLAGS_G_WEXE =/NOE/A:16/ST:10240
LFLAGS_D_WEXE =/CO
LFLAGS_R_WEXE =
LFLAGS_G_WDLL =/NOE/A:16/ST:5120
LFLAGS_D_WDLL =/CO
LFLAGS_R_WDLL =
LFLAGS_G_WTTY =/ST:5120 /A:16
LFLAGS_D_WTTY =/CO
LFLAGS_R_WTTY =
LFLAGS_G_DEXE =/NOI /ST:2048
LFLAGS_D_DEXE =/CO
LFLAGS_R_DEXE =
LFLAGS   =$(LFLAGS_G_WDLL) $(LFLAGS_R_WDLL)
RCFLAGS  =
RESFLAGS =
RUNFLAGS =
DEFFILE =        DEI_STTC.DEF
OBJS_EXT =
LIBS_EXT =       CST_CTLS.LIB

.rc.res: ; $(RC) $(RCFLAGS) -r $*.rc

all: $(PROJ).DLL

DEI_STTC.OBJ: DEI_STTC.C $(H)

DEI_STTC.RES: DEI_STTC.RC $(RESFILES) $(H)

DEI_CTLS.OBJ: DEI_CTLS.C $(H)

$(PROJ).DLL: DEI_STTC.OBJ DEI_CTLS.OBJ $(OBJS_EXT) $(DEFFILE)
    echo >NUL @<<$(PROJ).CRF
```

Listing A.29 continued

```
DEI_STTC.OBJ +
DEI_CTLS.OBJ +
$(OBJS_EXT)
$(PROJ).DLL

C:\PRGLNG\QCW\LIB\+
/NOD sdllcew oldnames  libw+
CST_CTLS.LIB
$(DEFFILE);
<<
    link $(LFLAGS) @$(PROJ).CRF
    rc $(RESFLAGS) DEI_STTC.RES $(PROJ).DLL

$(PROJ).DLL:  DEI_STTC.RES
    rc $(RESFLAGS) DEI_STTC.RES $(PROJ).DLL

run: $(PROJ).DLL
    $(PROJ) $(RUNFLAGS)
```

Listing A.30

```
ORIGIN   = QCWIN
ORIGIN_VER  = 1.00

PROJ =DEI_TABL
DEBUG   =0
PROGTYPE =2
CALLER  =
ARGS =
DLLS =
CVPACK  =1
CC   =cl -qc
RC   =rc
CFLAGS_G_WEXE =/AS /W4 /Ze /D_WINDOWS /G2w /Zp  /Aw
CFLAGS_D_WEXE =/Zi /Od
CFLAGS_R_WEXE =/O /Os /Gs /DNDEBUG
CFLAGS_G_WDLL =/AS /W4 /Ze /D_WINDOWS /D_WINDLL /G2w /Zp /Aw
CFLAGS_D_WDLL =/Zi /Od
CFLAGS_R_WDLL =/O /Os /Gs /DNDEBUG
CFLAGS_G_WTTY =/AS /G2w /W3 /D_WINDOWS
CFLAGS_D_WTTY =/Gi /Od /Zi
CFLAGS_R_WTTY =/O /Os /DNDEBUG
CFLAGS_G_DEXE =/AS /W2
CFLAGS_D_DEXE =/Gi /Od /Zi
CFLAGS_R_DEXE =/O /Ot /DNDEBUG
CFLAGS    =$(CFLAGS_G_WDLL) $(CFLAGS_R_WDLL)
LFLAGS_G_WEXE =/NOE/A:16/ST:10240
LFLAGS_D_WEXE =/CO
LFLAGS_R_WEXE =
LFLAGS_G_WDLL =/NOE/A:16/ST:5120
LFLAGS_D_WDLL =/CO
LFLAGS_R_WDLL =
LFLAGS_G_WTTY =/ST:5120 /A:16
LFLAGS_D_WTTY =/CO
LFLAGS_R_WTTY =
LFLAGS_G_DEXE =/NOI /ST:2048
LFLAGS_D_DEXE =/CO
LFLAGS_R_DEXE =
LFLAGS    =$(LFLAGS_G_WDLL) $(LFLAGS_R_WDLL)
RCFLAGS  =
RESFLAGS =
RUNFLAGS =
DEFFILE =    DEI_TABL.DEF
OBJS_EXT =
LIBS_EXT =    CST_CTLS.LIB

.rc.res: ; $(RC) $(RCFLAGS) -r $*.rc

all: $(PROJ).DLL

DEI_TABL.OBJ: DEI_TABL.C $(H)

DEI_TABL.RES: DEI_TABL.RC $(RESFILES) $(H)

DEI_CTLS.OBJ: DEI_CTLS.C $(H)

$(PROJ).DLL:  DEI_TABL.OBJ DEI_CTLS.OBJ $(OBJS_EXT) $(DEFFILE)
    echo >NUL @<<$(PROJ).CRF
```

Listing A.30 *continued*

```
DEI_TABL.OBJ +
DEI_CTLS.OBJ +
$(OBJS_EXT)
$(PROJ).DLL

C:\PRGLNG\QCW\LIB\+
/NOD sdllcew oldnames  libw+
CST_CTLS.LIB
$(DEFFILE);
<<
    link $(LFLAGS) @$(PROJ).CRF
    rc $(RESFLAGS) DEI_TABL.RES $(PROJ).DLL

$(PROJ).DLL:  DEI_TABL.RES
    rc $(RESFLAGS) DEI_TABL.RES $(PROJ).DLL

run: $(PROJ).DLL
    $(PROJ) $(RUNFLAGS)
```

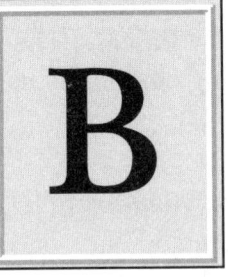# Annotated Bibliography

Bonneau, Paul. "Windows Questions and Answers." *Windows/DOS Developer's Journal*, January, 1992, Vol. 3, No. 1., pp. 5-6.

> This article answers a question about customizing the background of a dialog box. The author covers the `WM_CTLCOLOR` message and painting a dialog box background with `PatBlt()` or `ExtTextOut()`.

Bonneau, Paul. "Windows Questions and Answers." *Windows/DOS Developer's Journal*, February, 1992, Vol. 3, No. 2., pp. 43-44.

> This article answers a question about custom edit controls. The author describes the `WM_GETDLGCODE` message and responses.

Bonneau, Paul. "Windows Questions and Answers." *Windows/DOS Developer's Journal*, September, 1992, Vol. 3, No. 9., pp. 59-60.

> This article answers a question about custom button controls. The author describes the important messages for button controls and presents a subclass filter routine for drawing an icon on a button.

Brockschmidt, Kraig. "A Primer on Designing Custom Controls." *Microsoft Systems Journal*, May/April 1992, Vol. 7, No. 2., pp. 87-101.

> This article creates a spin button custom control called microscroll. In the process, it describes the general design process for custom controls.

Burk, Ron. "Creating Masked Edit Controls." *TECH Specialist*, November, 1991, Vol. 2, No. 11., pp. 31-37.

> This article presents a subclassed edit control in Pascal. The custom control provides for embedding formatting characters in the edit control.

Burk, Ron. "Custom Control Dialog Editor Interfaces." *Windows/DOS Developer's Journal*, January, 1993, Vol. 4, No. 1, pp. 23-34.

> This article explains how the Borland interface differs from the Microsoft interface, suggests mechanisms for specifying custom control data in the resource script, and offers a code template that can generate interfaces compatible with both products.

Dieterle, Rex. "Make Your Text and Data Bloom." *Windows Tech Journal*, August, 1992, Vol. 1, No. 7., pp. 36-42.

> In exhaustive detail, this article covers how to use the `WM_CTLCOLOR` message to customize control appearance.

Klein, Mike. "Subclassing Applications." *Dr. Dobbs Journal*, December, 1991, No. 183 Supplement., pp. 19-27.

> This article shows how to subclass applications and controls.

Klein, Mike. *Windows Programmer's Guide To DLLs and Memory Management.* Carmel, IN. Sams. 1992.

> This book is difficult to characterize. While it includes a great deal of information on memory management and DLLs, it also covers a wide variety of other topics, including subclassing and custom controls.

Levaro, Richard. "A Perfect Fit." *Windows Tech Journal*, January, 1992, Vol. 1, No. 1., pp. 52-63.

> This is a comprehensive article on custom controls. In a side note, It also discusses subclassing and the `WM_CTLCOLOR` message. It creates a custom static control and a toolbar control.

Ng, Kanhom. "Windows and Objects: A Three-Dimensional Custom Control Object." *C Gazette*, October/November, 1991, Vol. 5, NO. 6., pp. 43-56.

> This article presents a bitmap button and toolbar control. It contains a discussion of properties and extra bytes for storing instance data. It also covers some concepts about window hierarchy and relationships between popup and child windows.

Overmyer, Doug. "Colorizing Windows." *Windows/DOS Developer's Journal*, August, 1992, Vol. 3, No. 8., pp. 25-33.

> This article creates a toolbar control in Pascal.

Petzold, Charles. "Bitmaps and Buttons: Creating Customized Dialog Boxes." *PC Magazine*, October 15, 1991, Vol. 10, No. 17., pp. 411-416.

> This articles presents information on using owner-draw buttons and bitmaps to create customized effects.

Richter, Jeffery. *Windows 3: A Developer's Guide*. Redwood City, CA. M&T Publishing, Inc. 1991. pp. 209-300.

> This book devotes an entire chapter to custom controls. Richter develops both a spin button and a meter control and interfaces them to the dialog editor.

Swan, Tom. "Here's Pie in Your Eye." *PC Techniques*, February/March, 1992, Vol. 2, No. 6., pp. 71-79.

> This article creates a pie style meter control using Pascal.

Swan, Tom. "Toolbars for Turbo Pascal." *PC Techniques*, August/September, 1992, Vol. 3, No. 3., pp. 17-22.

> This article creates a toolbar custom control using Pascal.

Volkman, Victor. "Fading-In Custom Controls for Windows 3: Part 1." *Windows/DOS Developer's Journal*, February, 1992, Vol. 3, No. 2., pp. 15-26.

Volkman, Victor. "Fading-In Custom Controls for Windows 3: Part 2." *Windows/DOS Developer's Journal*, March, 1992, Vol. 3, No. 3., pp. 5-16.

> This is a comprehensive treatment of a fader (multiple position button) custom control. This is an example of a custom control with a class specific message interface. The second article explains how to interface the control with the dialog editor.

Welch, Kevin. "Extending the Windows 3.0 Interface with Installable Custom Controls." *Microsoft Systems Journal*, July 1990, Vol. 5, No. 4., pp. 29-51.

> This article develops a page custom control. In the process it covers messages that are important to custom controls and how to interface custom controls with the Dialog Editor.

Wilton, Richard. *Windows 3: Developer's Workshop*. Redmond, WA. Microsoft Press. 1991. pp. 83-131.

> This book devotes an entire chapter to custom controls. The material is instructional. The custom controls are for demonstration only and do not offer any practical functionality.

Wyld, Brian. "Making CUA-Compliant MLEs." *TECH Specialist*, September, 1991, Vol. 2, No. 9., pp. 5-14.

> This article subclasses the standard *EDIT* control. It traps the return key so multiline edit controls behave more naturally inside dialog boxes.

Index

.mak *109*
3-D Effects *94-95, 102*
3-D Shading *149*
3-D Styles *100, 104, 106, 108*
Access Functions *26, 38-39*
AlignBrush *46, 48, 90*
Alignment Styles *18*
Application Context *383*
Background *31*
Background Brush *107*
Base Class Extra Bytes *228, 230*
Base Class Instance Data *233*
Base Class Procedure *228*
Base Class Structure *229-230*
BaseClassWndFn *232-233*
BeginPaint *107-108*
Bibliography *519*
BitBlt *155*
Bitmap Background *11*
Bitmap Style *94, 107*
Bitmap, Determining Size of *325*
Bitmaps *31, 108*
Bitmaps & Owner Draw Compared *149*

Bitmaps, Device Dependence *148*
BM_GETCHECK *152, 157*
BM_GETSTATE *152, 157*
BM_GETSTYLE *152, 163*
BM_SETCHECK *152, 156-157, 163*
BM_SETSTATE *152, 158*
BM_SETSTYLE *152, 163*
BM_CLICKED *163*
Bonneau, Paul *519*
Border Styles *100*
Borland's Resource Workshop *399-400, 403, 405*
Bounding Rectangle *26*
Brockschmidt, Kraig *520*
Browsing Utility *269*
Brush Alignment *46*
Brushes *31, 43-44, 46, 107-108, 361*
BS_3STATE *149*
BS_AUTO3STATE *156*
BS_AUTOCHECKBOX *149, 156*
BS_AUTORADIOBUTTON *163*
BS_CHECKBOX *149*
BS_DEFPUSHBUTTON *160*
BS_LEFTTEXT *146, 149*

BS_OWNERDRAW *146*
BS_PUSHBUTTON *160*
Buffer Descriptors *271*
Buffering *267, 271*
Burk, Ron *520*
BUTTON Control *1, 12, 145, 146*
BUTTON Control, Class Specific Style *146-147*
Byte Alignment *8*
Call Back Function *34, 353, 356*
cbClsExtra *234, 28*
cbWndExtra *26, 234*
CCB_STATE_INSIDE *160*
CenterWindow *412, 414, 432*
CenterWindowRect *433*
CFVM_LOADFILE *276*
Character Height & Width *278*
Check Box *(See CSTCHECKBOX)*
Class Data *25*
Class Extra Bytes *28-29*
Class General Styles *8, 22, 24, 104*
Class Registration *35-36*
Class Specific Messages *39, 267, 326*
Class Specific Styles *7, 8, 96, 102*

ClassNameDlgFn *407, 409, 413*
ClassNameFlags *408*
ClassNameInfo *404*
ClassNameStyle *406-407, 409, 413*
ClassNameWndFn *408, 416*
ClassNameStyle Parameters *406*
Cleanup Procedures 36, *105, 152*
Client Area 10, *26, 358*
Clipping Region *10*
Close Option *9*
Coding Schemes, Style Interface 17, 24, *96*
Coding Techniques *14*
Color Information *46*
Color Message, Code for *71*
Color Styles *18*
Colors 31, *43, 277*
Combinable Styles 14, *97*
COMBOBOX *1*
Common Data Interface *228*
Common Data Structure 30, *32*
Components, Nonclient *12*
Control Group *13*
Control Statement *13*
Controlling Appearance *238*
Conventions, Design *30*
CPBS_NOFRAME *166*
CPBS_NOSHADOW *166*
CPBS_TEXTLEFT *163*
CPBS_TEXTRIGHT *163*
Create Handler *152*
CreatePatternBrush *107*
CREATESTRUCT 13, *276*
CreateWindow 13, 35, *276, 384-385*
Creating a Subclass *231*
CSS_BITMAP *98*
CSS_BITMAPSTRETCH *98*
CSS_BITMAPWINDOW *98*
CSS_BORDER *100*
CSS_BOTTOM *101*
CSS_EXPANDTABS *102*
CSS_FLAT *100*
CSS_FRAME *98*

CSS_HCENTER *100*
CSS_ICON *99*
CSS_ICONWINDOW *99*
CSS_LEFT *101*
CSS_LEFTNOWORDWRAP *101*
CSS_LINEHORZ 98, *107*
CSS_LINEVERT 98, *107*
CSS_LOWERED *100*
CSS_NOBORDER *100*
CSS_NOPREFIX *102*
CSS_RAISED 100, *102*
CSS_RECT 99, *107-108*
CSS_RIGHT *101*
CSS_SINGLELINE *101*
CSS_TEXT *99*
CSS_TEXTLOWERED *99*
CSS_TEXTRAISED *99*
CSS_TEXTSHADOW *99*
CSS_TOP *101*
CSS_VCENTER *101*
CSTCHECKBOX *(See Chapter 6)*
    Bitmaps *151*
    Code For *169-182*
    Class Specific Styles *151*
    CstCheckBoxBitmapIndex 154, *170*
    CstCheckBoxDefDataCreate *152, 171*
    CstCheckBoxDefDataDelete *172*
    CstCheckBoxDlgFn *420*
    CstCheckBoxDraw *154-155, 173*
    CstCheckBoxFlags *423*
    CstCheckBoxRegister 150, *175*
    CstCheckBoxStyle *411*
    CstCheckBoxUnregister *176*
    CstCheckBoxWndFn *152-154, 156, 159-160, 176*
    Draw Code *173*
    State Flags *155*
    Styles *145, 409*
    Registration *150*
    Window Call Back Function *176*
CstCtlColorMsg 44, *71, 107*
CSTCTLDATA *29-31, 39, 104-105*

CstCtlData 43, *71*
    CstCtlDataCreate 38, 75, *105, 152*
    CstCtlDataDelete 38, 75, *107, 276*
    CstCtlDefDataCreate 38, *76, 152*
    CstCtlDefDataDelete *38*
    CstCtlDefGet* *77*
    CstCtlDefSet* *79*
    CstCtlGet* *81*
    CstCtlSet* *83*
    CstCtlSetBitmap *107*
    CstCtlSetBrush *107*
    CstCtlSetRects 85, *154*
    CstCtlSetShadow *106*
    CstCtlSetStyle *106*
    CstCtlState 87, *155*
CstCtlDlg *411-413*
CSTCTLSTYLE *409, 411*
CstCtlStyleDlg *434*
CSTDIALOG *(See Chapter 10)*
    Code for 363-369
    CstDialogDefDataCreate *364*
    CstDialogDefDataDelete *365*
    CstDialogRegister *357, 366*
    CstDialogUnregister *357, 366*
    CstDialogWndFn *357-358, 361, 366*
    Demonstration Program *361, 369-378*
    Enhancements *362*
    Message Process *353*
    Window Function *358*
CstDraw3DFrame 46, *48, 60*
CstDraw3DLine 46, *48, 62*
CstDraw3DRect 46, 48, *63, 361*
CstDrawBitmap 48, *59*
CSTFILEVIEW *(See Chapter 8)*
    Class Specific Messages *273, 275*
    Code for *282-310*
    Data Interface *272*
    Demo Program *311-320*
    Instantiation and Cleanup *276*
    Keyboard Interface *268*
    CstFileViewAppendLine *285*
    CstFileViewClearFile *276, 287*

Index

CSTFILEVIEW, Continued
   CstFileViewCreateData *276, 288*
   CstFileViewCreateWindow *276, 289*
   CstFileViewDefDataCreate *290*
   CstFileViewDlgFn *499*
   CstFileViewDraw *276, 291*
   CstFileViewFlags *503*
   CstFileViewGetLine *276, 281, 293*
   CstFileViewInitScrl *278, 294*
   CstFileViewLoadBuf *276, 295*
   CstFileViewLoadFile *276, 281, 298*
   CstFileViewParseBuf *276, 296*
   CstFileViewRegister *299*
   CstFileViewStyle *503*
   CstFileViewUnregister *300*
   CstFileViewWndFn *276, 278-279, 300*
   Design Overview *269*
   Possible Enhancements *281*
   Scrolling *278*
CSTGETCLASSLONG *231*
CSTINFO Structure Members *403*
CSTPUSHBTN *(See Chapter 6)*
   Styles *145, 161, 411*
   Code for *183-200*
   CstPushBtnBitmapIndex *184*
   CstPushBtnDefDataCreate *185*
   CstPushBtnDefDataDelete *186*
   CstPushBtnDlgFn *442*
   CstPushBtnDraw *186*
   CstPushBtnDrawFocus *163, 189*
   CstPushBtnDrawText *163, 190*
   CstPushBtnFlags *446*
   CstPushBtnRegister *194*
   CstPushBtnStyle *447*
   CstPushBtnUnregister *194*
   CstPushBtnWndFn *194*
   Demo Program 214-224
   State Flags *161, 162*
CSTRADIOBTN *(See Chapter 6)*
   Styles *145, 163, 410*
   Code for *201-214*
   CstRadioBtnBitmapIndex *202*
   CstRadioBtnDefDataCreate *203*
   CstRadioBtnDefDataDelete *204*
   CstRadioBtnDlgFn *455*
   CstRadioBtnDraw *204*
   CstRadioBtnFlags *458*
   CstRadioBtnRegister *207*
   CstRadioBtnStyle *459*
   CstRadioBtnUnregister *208*
   CstRadioBtnWndFn *163, 208*
   Demo Program *214-224*
   State Flags *163*
CSTSETWINDOWWORD *231*
CSTSTATIC *(See Chapter 5)*
   Code for *115-132*
   CstStaticDefDataCreate *105, 117*
   CstStaticDefDataDelete *107, 118*
   CstStaticDlgFn *466*
   CstStaticDraw *105, 107-108, 118*
   CstStaticFlags *471*
   CstStaticRegister *105, 125*
   CstStaticStyle *473*
   CstStaticUnregister *105, 126*
   CstStaticWndFn *104-107, 109, 126*
   Demo Program *132-144*
CSTTABLE *(See Chapter 7)*
   Code for *242-256*
   CstTableDefDataCreate *243*
   CstTableDefDataDelete *244*
   CstTableDlgFn *483*
   CstTableFlags *488*
   CstTableRegister *237, 252*
   CstTableStyle *490*
   CstTableUnregister *252*
   CstTableWndFn *237, 240, 253*
   Demo Program *242-256*
   Edit Mode Keyboard Interface *226-227*
   Possible Enhancements *240*
   Styles *413*
CSTTABLEEDIT *225, 227, 235-237*
   CstTableEditOff *239, 245*
   CstTableEditOn *239, 246*
   CstTableEditRegister *237, 248*
   CstTableEditUnregister *248*
   CstTableEditWndFn *237, 239, 249*
CSTTOOLBOX *(See Chapter 9)*
   Code for *330-343*
   CstToolBoxCreateWindow *323-325, 332*
   CstToolBoxDefDataCreate *333*
   CstToolBoxDefDataDelete *334*
   CstToolBoxDraw *334*
   CSTTOOLBOXGETCOLS *324*
   CSTTOOLBOXGETROWS *324*
   CstToolBoxRect *335*
   CstToolBoxRegister *336*
   CstToolBoxSelect *327, 336*
   CstToolBoxState *337*
   CstToolBoxUnregister *338*
   CstToolBoxWndFn *338*
   Class Specific Messages *327*
   Class Specific Window Styles *324*
   Demo Program *344-352*
CST_CKBX.C *170*
CST_CKBX.H *150*
CST_CKBX.RC *150, 182*
CST_CTLS *382*
CST_CTLS.C *385, 390*
CST_CTLS.DLL *399, 410, 416*
CST_CTLS.H *387, 390*
CST_CTLS.LIB *387*
CST_CTLS.RC *393*
CST_DATA.C *38-39, 42, 70, 155*
CST_DATA.H *42, 65, 105*
CST_DILG.C *357, 364*
CST_DILG.RC *361, 369*
CST_DRAW.C *46, 59, 108, 149*
CST_DRAW.H *58*
CST_EXTRA.C *231*
CST_FLVW.C *268, 283*
CST_FLVW.H *268, 282*
CST_FLVW.RC *268-269, 310*
CST_PBTN.C *163, 184*
CST_PBTN.H *163, 183*
CST_RBTN.C *202*
CST_RBTN.H *201*
CST_RBTN.RC *214*
CST_STTC.C *104, 117*
CST_STTC.H *102, 115*

CST_STTC.RC *132*
CST_TABL.C *237, 243*
CST_TABL.H *242*
CST_TLBX.C *331*
CST_TLBX.H *330*
CST_UTIL.C *46, 90*
CST_UTIL.H *89*
CST_UTILS.C *29, 48*
CST_XTRA.C *39, 56*
CST_XTRA.H *55, 231*
CS_BYTEALIGNCLIENT *8*
CS_BYTEALIGNWINDOW *8*
CS_CLASSDC *8*
CS_DBLCLKS *9, 104, 150, 407*
CS_GLOBALCLASS *9, 104, 150, 234, 387*
CS_HREDRAW *9, 104, 150, 276*
CS_NOCLOSE *9, 269*
CS_OWNDC *9*
CS_PARENTDC *10, 150*
CS_SAVEBITS *10*
CS_VREDRAW *10, 104, 150, 276*
CTBM_CLICKED *327*
CTBM_GETBITMAP *327*
CTBM_GETCHECK *327*
CTBM_SETBITMAP *327*
CTBS_CHECK *324*
CTBS_RADIO *324*
CTLCOLOR_BTN *49*
CTLCOLOR_CSTSTATIC *45*
CTLCOLOR_DLG *49*
CTLCOLOR_EDIT *49*
CTLCOLOR_LISTBOX *49*
CTLCOLOR_MSGBOX *49*
CTLCOLOR_SCROLLBAR *49*
CTLCOLOR_STATIC *49*
CTLINFO *402, 404*
CtlInfoCreate *410, 435*
CTLSTYLE *402, 404, 405, 411, 413*
CtlStyleLock *436*
CtlStyleUnlock *436*
CTLTYPE *403-405*
CUSTCNTL.H *402, 404*
Custom Check Box *(See CSTCHECKBOX)*

Custom Dialog *(See CSTDIALOG)*
Custom File View *(See CSTFFILEVIEW)*
Custom Push Button *(See CSTPUSHBTN)*
Custom Radio Button *(See CSTRADIOBTN)*
Custom Table *(See CSTTABLE)*
Custom Toolbox *(See CSTTOOLBOX)*
Data Entry Table *225, 243*
Data Interface *4, 25, 33, 65, 70, 71*
Data Storage *38*
Deallocate Window Structure *27*
Decoding Masks *18*
Default Button *163*
Default Instance Data *28, 35-36, 44, 152*
  Accessing *38*
  Create *117*
  Delete *118*
  Function Interface *40*
  Storage *30*
  Structure *105*
Default Message Processing *225, 354*
Default Style *20, 163*
Defaults *22, 28*
Defaults And Synonyms *20*
DefDlgProc *355-356, 358, 361-362*
DefWndProc *43-44, 108-109, 326, 354, 356, 362*
DEI_CKBX.C *419*
DEI_CKBX.DLG *427*
DEI_CKBX.H *418*
DEI_CKBX.RC *416, 426*
Dei_CkBxInfo *424*
Dei_CkBxWndFn *425*
DEI_CTLS.C *432*
DEI_CTLS.H *409, 431*
DEI_FLVW.C *498*
DEI_FLVW.DLG *507*
DEI_FLVW.H *497*
DEI_FLVW.QCW *509*
DEI_FLVW.RC *506*
Dei_FlVwInfo *504*
Dei_FlVwWndFn *504*
DEI_NAME.DLL *416*
DEI_PBTN.C *441*
DEI_PBTN.DLG *451*

DEI_PBTN.H *440*
DEI_PBTN.QCW *511*
DEI_PBTN.RC *450*
Dei_PBtnInfo *447*
Dei_PBtnWndFn *448*
DEI_RBTN.C *454*
DEI_RBTN.DLG *462*
DEI_RBTN.H *453*
DEI_RBTN.QCW *513*
DEI_RBTN.RC *461*
Dei_RBtnInfo *459*
Dei_RBtnWndFn *460*
DEI_STTC.C *465*
DEI_STTC.DG. *477*
DEI_STTC.H *464*
DEI_STTC.QCW *515*
DEI_STTC.RC *476*
Dei_SttcInfo *473*
Dei_SttcWndFn *475*
DEI_TABL.C *482*
DEI_TABL.DLG *494*
DEI_TABL.H *481*
DEI_TABL.QCW *517*
DEI_TABL.RC *493*
Dei_TablInfo *490*
Dei_TablWndFn *491*
Demo Programs 109
  Check Box, Pushbutton, Radio Button *214-224*
  Dialog Window *134 259, 316, 37*
  File Viewer *311-320*
  Static Control *132-137*
  Table *240, 257-262*
  Toolbox *344-352*
DEM_BTTN *167*
DEM_BTTN.C *215*
DEM_BTTN.H *214*
DEM_DILG *361*
DEM_DILG.C *370*
DEM_DILG.H *369*
DEM_DILG.RC *374*
DEM_FLVW.C *280, 312*
DEM_FLVW.H *311*
DEM_FLVW.RC *317*

Index 527

DEM_STTC *109*
DEM_STTC.C *133*
DEM_STTC.H *132*
DEM_STTC.RC *137*
DEM_TABL.C *240, 258*
DEM_TABL.H *240, 257*
DEM_TABL.RC *240, 262*
DEM_TLBX.C *328, 345*
DEM_TLBX.H *344*
DEM_TLBX.RC *350*
Design Conventions *13, 30*
Design Goals *2*
Design Issues *228*
Design Tradeoffs *163*
Device Context & Coordinates *8-10*
Device Dependence, Bitmaps *148*
Dialog Boxes *11, 399*
Dialog Class
    Callback Functions *260, 354, 356*
    Data Interface *357*
    Extra Bytes *357*
    Specific Styles *358*
    Function Interface *357*
    Message Process *353*
Dialog Coordinates *10*
Dialog Editor *399-409, 416*
Dialog Editor Interface DLLs *401-402*
    CSTCHECKBOX *418-430*
    CSTFILEVIEW *497-510*
    CSTPUSHBTN *440-452*
    CSTRADIOBTN *453-463*
    CSTSTATIC *464-480*
    CSTTABLE *481-496*
    Importance of *34-35*
    Requirements *399*
    Support Functions *432-438*
Dialog Function *412*
DialogBoxParam *412*
DialogDemoDialogProc *372*
Dieterle, Rex *520*
Disabling System Close *269*
Display Capabilities *148*
Display Font *269*
Display Sizing *278*

DLGC_BUTTON *51*
DLGC_DEFPUSHBUTTON *51, 163*
DLGC_HASSETSEL *51*
DLGC_PUSHBUTTON *163*
DLGC_RADIOBUTTON *51*
DLGC_STATIC *51, 108*
DLGC_UNDEFPUSHBUTTON *51*
DLGC_WANTALLKEYS *50*
DLGC_WANTARROWS *50*
DLGC_WANTCHARS *51*
DLGC_WANTMESSAGE *50*
DLGC_WANTTAB *50*
DlgFn *35, 407, 412-413*
DlgFn Function *407*
DLLs *4, 35, 379, 381-387, 389, 399, 402, 405, 408, 410, 416-417*
    Data References *380*
    Interface to Dialog Editor *402*
    Linkage *385-386*
    Main Function *448*
    Required Library Functions *382*
    Requirements *379*
    Steps Required *389*
    Support in Code *388*
    Building a *113*
    Loading *384, 387*
    And Code Sharing *387*
Double-Click Messages *9*
Draw 3-D Box Frame, Code For *60*
Draw 3-D Filled Rectangle, Code For *63*
Draw 3-D Line, Code For *62*
Draw Bitmap, Code For *59*
Draw Button Controls *148*
Draw, Code For *58-59*
Drawing *46, 48, 94, 148-149, 154, 361*
Drawing Attributes *9-10, 45*
DrawText *105*
DS_LOCALEDIT *358*
DS_MODALFRAME *358*
DS_NOIDLEMSG *358*
DS_SYSMODAL *358*
Dummy Window *35*
Dynamic Controls *2, 145*

Dynamic Linking *113, 379-380*
Dynamic Loading DLL *387*
Dynamic Memory *26-28*
EDIT *1, 225, 231, 235-236, 267, 269, 271*
EndDialog *361, 407*
Entry Points *35*
EnumProp *27*
Epilogues, Function *386*
_export *381*
Exported Functions *385*
Extra Bytes *26-28, 357*
    Code For *55-56*
    Complications *227*
    Offset *228*
    Region *231*
FAR *380-382*
File Browser *(See CSTFILEVIEW)*
FileViewDemoDialogProc *316*
Flags *35*
Flags Function *408, 415*
Floating Menu Custom Control *11*
Focus *160, 327, 357*
Focus Rectangle *155, 163*
Font *31*
Fonts, Changing *269*
Frames *108*
Freeing Resources *154*
_fsprintf *381*
_fstrcpy *381*
Function for Invoking Dialog Boxes *134*
Function Interface *4, 38-40, 155*
Function, Exported *385*
Function, Prologues and Epilogues *386*
Fundamental Styles *14-15*
FVBUF *271-272*
FVLINE *271-272, 276*
GCL_MENUNAME *231*
GCL_WNDPROCPARENT *235*
General Purpose Interface *32*
Get Check Box Bitmap Index *170*
Get Push Button Bitmap Index *184*
Get Radio Button Bitmap Index *202*
GetClassInfo *231, 233, 235, 237*

GetClassLong *231*
GetClassWord *29, 231*
GetClientRect *26*
GetDialogBaseUnits *404*
GetDrawTextStyle *105, 131*
GetIdString *439*
GetKeyState *279*
GetParent *326*
GetProcAddress *386*
GetProp *27*
GetSystemMetrics *149*
GetTextMetrics *278*
GetWindowLong *26, 106*
GetWindowRect *26*
GetWindowWord *26*
Global Heap *26, 28*
Global* *28*
GlobalAlloc *28, 381*
GMEM_SHARE *28, 380*
Granularity *28*
Grayed Text *163*
Group Box *147*
Group Boxes *146*
Heap, Global *26*
Heap, Local *26*
hFont *31*
Hit Detection *154*
Horizontal Position *100*
Horizontal Position Controls *97*
Horizontal Size Changes *9*
HTTRANSPARENT *108*
HWnd *227*
Hybrid Control *226, 235*
Hybrid Controls, Registering *237*
iBkMode *31, 324*
Icons *108*
IDC_OK *407*
iFrame *31*
Implementation Strategy *146, 408*
IMPLIB.EXE *387*
Implicit Linkage *386*
Import Library *387*
Import Linkage *386*
Info Function *35, 404-405, 410-411*

Information Hiding *38*
Initialization *36*
Input Focus *156, 166, 357*
Instance Data *25, 28-29, 31, 42, 106, 150, 152, 228, 358*
 Accessing *38*
 Data Structure *39, 46*
 Default *44*
 Function Interface *40*
 Message Interface *38-39*
 Storage *29-30, 33*
Instance Uniqueness *26*
Instantiation and Cleanup *105, 152*
iNumTabPos *273, 276*
Invalid Rectangle *155*
Invoking Dialog Boxes, Code for *259*
iShadow *31, 324*
iTabPos *276*
Keyboard Event Messages *150*
Keyboard Input *155*
Keyboard Interface *156, 268*
Keystrokes, Control-shifted *280*
Klien, Mike *520*
Large Memory Model Issues *381-383*
LBS_MULTIPLESEL *226, 237*
Levaro, Richard *521*
LibEntry *382-383, 404*
LibMain *35-36, 382-386, 404, 410, 425, 448, 460, 475, 491, 505*
Line Descriptors *271*
Line Style *94*
Line Width Styles *18*
Lines *108*
Linkage *385*
List Box, Capacity Limits *240*
LISTBOX Class *1, 12, 225-226, 235*
Loading, DLL *384, 387*
LoadLibrary *384-385*
Local Heap *26-28*
Local* *28*
Lock, Data *105*
Lock, Handle *105*
Lock, Memory *105*
lParam *105, 274, 329, 412, 46, 109*

lpCreateParams *276*
LPTBCREATE *324*
lstrcpy *381*
lValue *31*
Macros *42*
Main Window Function *133*
Main Window Function, Code for *215, 258*
MainWindowProc *135, 220, 260, 372*
Make Files *109*
MakeProcInstance *416*
Manipulating States *155*
Memory Management *28*
Memory Models *380*
Memory Overhead *10*
Message Handling *150*
Message Interface *4, 33, 42, 38-39, 106, 155,*
Message Numbering *39*
Message Processing Hierarchy *354, 356*
Message Responses *46*
Messages *49, 156*
Messages Status *157*
Messaging, Safe *34*
Microsoft Dialog Editor *400*
Microsoft PWB *109*
MINIMIZE /MAXIMIZE *12*
Minimum Size Window *327*
Modal Styles *17-18*
Module Definition File *386*
Mouse Capture *160*
Mouse Cursor *159-160*
Mouse Input & Messages *150, 155*
Mouse Interface *152, 156*
MoveWindow *9*
Mutually Exclusive Styles *14*
Naming Conventions *13, 30, 35, 150*
Navigation Key *166*
Ng, Kanhom *521*
NMAKE *109*
Nonclient Components *12*
Nontasked Functions *383*
NOTEPAD *267*
Notification Messages *166*
Offset, Extra Bytes *228*

OFSTRUCT *272*
Ordinal Value *386*
Overlapped Window *11*
Overlapping Siblings *11*
Overmyer, Doug *521*
Overriding Defaults *152*
Owner Draw & Bitmaps Compared *149*
Owner-Draw Style *146*
Painting *43*
Painting the Control *107*
Painting, Unwanted *239*
Parent Window *107*
Persistence *25-26*
Petzold, Charles *521*
Predefined Controls *1*
Predefined Styles *13*
Prioritized Styles *97*
Programmer's Interface *93*
Programming Interface *4*
Prologues, Function *386*
Property Lists *26-28*
Property Ownership *27*
PtInWnd *48, 90*
Push Button *(See CSTPUSHBTN)*
PushBtnDemoDialogProc *218*
PWB *109*
Radio Button *(See CSTRADIOBTN)*
RadioBtnDemoDialogProc *217*
RECT *155*
Rectangle In Rectangle *200*
Rectangle Style *107*
Rectangles *108*
RectBitmap *31*
RectInRect *200*
RectText *31*
Redrawing *9-10, 155*
Reentrancy *33, 380*
RegisterClass *234*
Registering Hybrid Controls *237*
Registration *150*
Registration counter *36*
ReleaseCapture *160*
RemoveProp *27*
Repainting, Flags *156*

ResetBrushFix *48, 91*
RESIDENTNAME *386*
Resize A Window *9*
Resource Script *11, 13, 399*
Resource Scripting Tool *5*
Richter, Jeffery *521*
SafeDeleteObject *48, 91*
Save Display Area *10*
SCRL *272*
Scroll Messages to Itself *278*
SCROLLBAR *1, 271, 278*
Scrolling *267, 278*
Secondary Window *11*
Segment Selectors *28*
SendMessage *34*
SetCapture *159*
SetFocus *160*
SetIdValue *439*
SetProp *27*
SetWindowLong *26*
SetWindowWord *231*
Sibling Controls *164*
Siblings, Overlapping *11*
Sizing, Minimum Window *327*
Speed Drawing *8*
Spreadsheet Control *240*
Stack, Caller's *386*
Stack, Kernal Supplied *384*
Standard BUTTON Control *145, 147*
Standard Control Default Sizes *405*
Standard Controls *1-2*
State Control Messages *150*
State Function, Mode Flags *156*
State Information *150*
State Interface Messages *157*
State Value *155*
STATIC *1, 93-94*
Static Control *(See CSTSTATIC)*
Static Draw *118*
Static Linking Versus Dynamic Linking *379*
STATIC Styles *96*
Static Window Function *126*
Statically Linked Applications *113*
StaticDemoDialogProc *135*

Storage Requirements *25*
String Table *416*
Styles (See Chapter 3)
   Bitmap *107*
   Rectangle *107*
   3-D Appearance *100*
   Combinable *97*
   Fundamental *98*
   Horizontal Position *100*
   Mutually Exclusive *96*
   Prioritized *97*
   Style Dialog Box *407*
   Style Function *406-407, 411*
   Style Interface *4, 7, 95*
   Style Interface Design *14*
   Style Statement *13*
   Supplemental *100*
   Text Format *101*
   Vertical Position *101*
Subclassed Controls *(See Chapter 7) 39, 148*
Extra Bytes *228-230*
Implementation *235*
Instance Data *232*
Window Procedure *227-228*
SubClassWndFn *232*
Subsegment Manager *28*
Supplemental Styles *15, 100*
Swan, Tom *521*
Synonyms *22*
System Menu *9*
szClass *403*
szDescr *403*
szTitle *402*
Tab Stops *269*
TableDemoDialogProc *260*
TBCREATE *325-326*
TBDATA *324, 326*
Text Format Styles *101*
Text Placement *102*
Text Positioning Styles *163*
TextOut *276*
Tool Bar *323*
Tool Icon Bitmaps *323*

Toolbox Class *(See CSTTOOLBOX)*
Top Level Windows *12*
Untasked Process *35*
User Defined Messages *39*
User Input Messages *159*
User Interaction *148, 156, 238*
User Interface *3, 7, 93*
Utilities, Code for *89-90*
Utility Functions *33, 46, 48*
Vertical Position Controls *97*
Vertical Position Styles *101*
Vertical Size Changes *10*
VGA *148*
Virtual Key Codes *278*
Virtual Memory Controls *267*
Virtual Memory, Style Interface *268*
Volkman, Victor *522*
wCtlColorMsg *31, 44*
wCtlTypes *403*
Welch, Kevin *522*
WEP *35, 382-386, 392, 404, 425, 449, 460, 475, 491, 505*
wHeight *403*
Wilton, Richard *522*
WINDLL *388*
Window Call Back Function *260, 354*
Window Class Styles *8*
Window Counter *36, 152*
Window Extra Bytes *26*
Window Handle *26, 46*
Window Maintenance & Data Interface *160*
Window Management Messages *158*
Window Procedure for Main Window, Code for *220*
Window Struct *228*
Window Style Word *8*
Window Styles *11*
WinMain *36, 133, 215, 258, 312, 370, 410*
WM_ (Window Messages)
　WM_?SCROLL Messages *279*
　WM_CANCELMODE *49*
　WM_COMMAND *49, 407, 413*
　WM_CREATE *36-38, 49, 105, 152, 238, 276, 324-326, 358, 384*
　WM_CSTCTLGETDATA *39, 71*
　WM_CSTCTLGETDEFDATA *39, 72*
　WM_CSTCTLSETDATA *39, 73*
　WM_CSTCTLSETDEFDATA *39, 74*
　WM_CTLCOLOR *31, 43-46, 49, 105, 107, 238, 276, 361*
　WM_DESTROY *36-37, 50, 105, 107, 153, 238, 276, 326, 358, 384, 407, 414*
　WM_ENABLE *50, 152, 158, 163*
　WM_ERASEBKGND *50, 105, 108, 358, 361*
　WM_GETDLGCODE *50, 105, 108, 163, 166, 239*
　WM_GETFONT *51*
　WM_GETMINMAXINFO *326-327*
　WM_INITDIALOG *361, 407, 412*
　WM_KEYDOWN *53, 152, 156, 278-279*
　WM_KEYUP *53, 152, 156*
　WM_KILLFOCUS *53, 152, 158, 163*
　WM_LBUTTONDBLCLK *53*
　WM_LBUTTONDOWN *53, 152, 156, 159-160, 327*
　WM_LBUTTONUP *53, 152, 156, 160*
　WM_MOUSEMOVE *54, 152, 156, 159-160*
　WM_MOVE *51*
　WM_NCACTIVATE *52, 326-327*
　WM_NCCREATE *52*
　WM_NCDESTROY *52*
　WM_NCHITTEST *52, 105, 108*
　WM_NCPAINT *240*
　WM_PAINT *10, 51, 105, 107, 109, 154, 238*
　WM_PARENTNOTIFY *9, 36, 38, 52, 105, 107, 152-154, 361*
　WM_SETFOCUS *54, 152, 158, 163*
　WM_SETFONT *54, 105, 109, 278*
　WM_SETTEXT *54, 105, 109*
　WM_SIZE *54, 278*
　WM_SYSCOLORCHANGE *54*
　WM_USER *39, 274*
WND *30*
WNDCLASS *26, 28, 231, 233-234*
WNDCLASS Structure *7*
WndFn Function *35, 407, 416*
wParam *36, 105, 274, 278*
Wrapper Function *416*
wsprintf *323, 381*
wState *31, 227*
wStyle *358, 31*
WS_BORDER *12*
WS_CAPTION *12, 269, 323*
WS_CHILD *11, 104, 269*
WS_CLIPCHILDREN *10-11*
WS_CLIPSIBLINGS *11, 104*
WS_DISABLED *12*
WS_DLGFRAME *12*
WS_GROUP *13, 24*
WS_HSCROLL *12*
WS_MAXIMIZE *13, 24*
WS_MAXIMIZEBOX *12, 269*
WS_MINIMIZE *12, 24*
WS_MINIMIZEBOX *12, 269*
WS_OVERLAPPED *11, 24, 104*
WS_OVERLAPPEDWINDOW *11*
WS_POPUP *11, 24, 269*
WS_SYSMENU *12, 269, 323*
WS_TABSTOP *13, 24*
WS_THICKFRAME *12, 269*
WS_VISIBLE *12, 104, 325*
WS_VSCROLL *12*
WVersion *402*
wWidth *403*
Wyld, Brian *522*